AGAINST THE PEACE AND DIGNITY OF THE STATE

North Carolina Laws
Regarding Slaves,
Free Persons of Color,
and Indians

William L. Byrd, III

HERITAGE BOOKS
2007

HERITAGE BOOKS
AN IMPRINT OF HERITAGE BOOKS, INC.

Books, CDs, and more—Worldwide

For our listing of thousands of titles see our website at
www.HeritageBooks.com

Published 2007 by
HERITAGE BOOKS, INC.
Publishing Division
65 East Main Street
Westminster, Maryland 21157-5026

Copyright © 2003 William L. Byrd, III

All rights reserved. No part of this book may be reproduced or transmitted in any form or by any means, electronic or mechanical, including photocopying, recording or by any information storage and retrieval system without written permission from the author, except for the inclusion of brief quotations in a review.

International Standard Book Number: 978-0-7884-2480-9

Even then the thought came to me that someone should tell about this as it really happened, from the very beginning, omitting nothing and inventing nothing -- Anatoly Kuznetsov

Contents

Introduction _____ *vii*
Acknowledgements _____ *ix*
NORTH CAROLINA LAW _____ *1*
Chronology of Laws _____ *435*
Index _____ *467*

Introduction

"*Against the Peace and Dignity of the State*" was six years in the making. The idea was to locate and find every law pertaining to Slaves, Free Persons of Color, and Indians. It turned out to be a formidable task. The only way to ferret out that specific group of laws demanded that one had to read, page by page, the entire collection of North Carolina Statutes from 1669 to the year 1862.

The evolution of North Carolina's Slave Codes begins in 1669, and for the most part, ends in 1862. Nestled within those years, was an ever growing number of new laws enacted by the North Carolina General Assembly; the purpose of which was to control the great numbers of Slaves in the Colony of North Carolina, and later, the State of North Carolina.

The Sheer size of the Slave Codes are mind boggling. The drain on society had to be great, just to support the laws and to control the Slave population who were not always docile. There were insurrections, uprisings, and runaways; all of which were crushed in the end. Some Slaves were treated fairly, and others were treated brutally. Some Slaves did escape to freedom, and others were caught.

Slavery in the South was a perfect example of man's inhumanity to man. We've all seen the movies, and we've all heard the stories. Since that time, we've come a long way to understanding, but we still have a long way to go.

The North Carolina Slaves Codes speak for themselves. There is no reason for them to be extrapolated. Read this book and weep.

Acknowledgements

Acknowledgements for this book belong to the staff of the North Carolina State Archives. Without their help it would never have been published. They copied large groups of the Acts of the General Assembly of North Carolina pertaining to the title of this book. They also ran down law books that were not on the shelves. I always appreciate their patience and courteousness.

North Carolina Law

NORTH CAROLINA LAW

THE STATE RECORDS OF NORTH CAROLINA
VOLUME XXV., SUPPLEMENT, 1669-1771
EDITED BY: WALTER CLARK
NASH BROTHERS BOOK AND JOB PRINTERS
GOLDSBORO, N.C., 1906

LAWS OF NORTH CAROLINA - 1669
1669. An Act Prohibiting Strangers Tradeing With Indians. (Page 121).

    Forasmuch as there is often recourse of Strangers from other parts into this County to truck and trade with the Indians which is conceived may prove very prejudiciall Wherefore be it enacted by the Pallatine and Lords Proprietors by and with the advice and consent of the Grand Assembly and the authority thereof that if any person or persons of what quallity or condition so ever they shall be presume to come into this County to truck or trade with any of our neighboring Indians belonging to the County or that shall be found to have any Indian trade purchased from them or being found or appearing that they come to trade with any Indians as aforesaid Whether in their Townes or elsewhere within the County which is hereby left for the Magistrate to judge it shall bee lawfull for any person or persons to apprehend any such persons or Forreigners that shall be found amongst the Indians or elsewhere within the limitts of the County and him or them bring before the Governor or any one of the Councell who shall hereby have power to comitt them to prison there to abide till they have paid tenn thousand pounds of tobacco and caske otherwise to stand to the censure of the Vice Pallatine and Councell And it is further declared that whatsoever Trade is found with the person apprehended One halfe thereof and one halfe of the fine shall belong to the Apprehendor and the other halfe to the Lords Proprietors.

THE COLONIAL RECORDS OF NORTH CAROLINA
VOLUME II., 1713-1728
EDITED BY:WILLIAM L. SAUNDERS
RALEIGH, P.M. HALE, PRINTER TO THE STATE, 1886
[B.P.R.O. COLONIAL ENTRY BOOK. NO. 22.]

COPY OF THE FUNDAMENTAL CONSTITUTIONS OF CAROLINA AGREED ON BY ALL YE LORD PROPRIETORS AND SIGN'D AND SEAL'D BY THEM (THE ORIGINAL BEING SENT TO CAROLINA BY MAJOR DANIEL) APRIL 11TH 1698.

40. Every Freeman of Carolina shall have Absolute power & authority over his Negro slaves of what Opinion or Religion soever.

****

THE STATE RECORDS OF NORTH CAROLINA
VOLUME XXIII., 1715-1776
EDITED BY: WALTER CLARK
NASH BROTHERS BOOK AND JOB PRINTERS
GOLDSBORO, NORTH CAROLINA, 1904

CHAPTER IV.
1715. An Act prohibiting Trading with the Indians. (Page 2).
   I.   Forasmuch as there is often recourse of strangers from other parts into this Country to truck & trade with the Indians which is conceived may prove prejudicial, wherefore.
   II.   Be it Enacted by the Palatin & Lords Proprietors by & with the advice & consent of the present Grand Assembly & the Authority thereof, that if any person or persons of what Quality or Condition soever they be, shall presume to come into this Country to Truck & Trade with any of our Neighbour Indians belonging to the Country, or shall be found to have any Indian Trade purchased from them, or being found or appearing that they come to trade with any Indians as aforesaid whether in their Town or Elsewhere within the Country, which is hereby left for the Majistrate to judge, It shall be lawful for any person or persons to apprehend any such person or Foreigner that shall be found amongst the Indians or elsewhere

North Carolina Law

within the limits of the Country and him or them bring before the Governor or any one of the Council, who shall hereby have power to commit them to prison there to abide until they have paid Ten thousand pounds of Tobacco & Cask; otherwise to stand to the censure of the Governor.

  III. And it is further declared that whatsoever Trade is found with the person apprehended one half thereof & one half of the Fine shall belong to the Apprehender & the other half to the Lords Proprietors. **Obsolete in 1791. [See Iredell's Laws, 1791, p. 9.]**

CHAPTER XLVI.
1715. An Act Concerning Servants & Slaves. (Repealed by Act 4 April, 1741, ch. 24.). (Pages 62-66)
  VII. And Be It Further Enacted by the Authority afors'd that if any person or persons shall entertain or Harbour any Runaway Servant or Slave above one Night he or they so offending shall for every Four & Twenty hours afterwards forfeit & pay the sum of Tenn Shillings to the Master or Mistress of such servant or Slave together with all Costs, Losses & damages which the Master or Mistress shall sustain by means of such entertainment or Concealment to be recovered in any Court of Record within this Government wherein no Essoign, Protection, Injunction or Wager of Law shall be allowed or admitted of.
  VIII. And Be It Further Enacted by the Authority afors'd that no Master or Mistress Nor Overseer shall give leave to any Negro, Mulatto or Indyan Slave (except such as wait upon their persons or wear Liverys) to go out of their Plantations without a Ticket or White servant along with them which Ticket at least the name of either the Master, Mistress or Overseer shall be subscribed & therein shall be inserted the place from whence he came & whither going under the Penalty of Five Shillings besides the charge of paying for the taking up of such slave or runaway.
  IX. And Be It Further Enacted that all persons shall use their utmost endeavours to apprehend all such Servants & Slaves as they conceive to be Runaways or Travell without Tickett as afors'd or that shall be seen off his Master's ground Arm'd with any Gun, Sword or any other Weapon of defence or offence altho' provided with a Tickett unless particularly mentioned and him, her or them having Apprehended shall carry & convey before the next Magistrate which Magistrate is hereby impowered to order and adjudge such Corporal Punishment to the said suspected Runaway as he shall think fitt and after correction shall order &

North Carolina Law

command the Apprehender or Apprehenders to carry such slave immediately to the proper Owner if known & if not known then to the Provost Marshall for all which service the said Apprehender or Apprehenders shall be allowed the sum of Five Shillings over & above the sum of one Shilling per Mile for any distance not exceeding Ten Miles & for every Mile above Ten at the rate of Three pence per Mile According to Computation to be paid by the Master of such Slave or Servant. But in case where the Master or Owner is not known then the Provost Marshall shall pay & satisfy the Apprehender or Apprehenders the several Premiums or Rewards before mentioned & the said Marshall before he delivers such servant or slave to the Owner or Order is hereby Authorized & Impowered to demand, receive & take of & from the said Owner not only the afors'd premiums or Rewards but also the sum of Six Pence per day during the time of the Servant or Slaves Imprisonment. Provided there be a necessity of Confinement otherwise the Labour of such Servant or Slave shall satisfy for his Imprisonment And the said Marshall is hereby Required & Commanded to Proclaim such Servant or Slave in every Precinct at the three next Courts after the Receipt of such servant or Slave And if it shall happen in the mean time that such Servant or Slave shall make his Escape, the Marshall shall not be oblidged to make satisfaction unless there be sufficient Prisons provided for the security of such or that it can be made appear that he has connived at the escape or doth anyways concele such Servant or Slave from the Owner. And if any person or persons shall kill any Runaway Slave that hath lyen out two months such person or persons shall not be called to answer for the same if he give Oath that he could not apprehend such Slave but was constrained to kill him.

    X.   And Be It Further Enacted by the Authority afors'd that whosoever shall buy, sell, Trade, Truck, Borrow or Lend to or with any Servant or Servants or Slave or Slaves without the License or Consent in Writing under the Hand of his or her or their Master or Owners for any Condition whatsoever such person or persons so offending contrary to the true Intent & Meaning of this Act shall forfeit treble the Value of the thing Bought, sold, Traded or Trucked or Borrowed or lent. And also the sum of Ten pounds to be recovered by the Master or Mistress of such Servant or Slave in such manner as is before in this Act directed, Provided that if the said Master or Mistress of such servant or slave shall neglect or refuse to prosecute such Offender within Six months next after notice or knowledge thereof that then it shall & may be Lawful for any other person to Prosecute the same & to have & receive the same benefit thereby as should have accrued to the said Master or Mistress had they done the same.

XI. And Be It Further Enacted by the Authority afors'd that where any slave shall be guilty of any Crime or Offence whatsoever the same shall be heard & determined by any three Justices of the Precinct Court where such Offence or Crime shall be Committed & three Freeholders such as have Slaves in that Precinct or the Major part of them shall have full power & authority & they are hereby required & commanded to Trye the same according to their best Judgment & Discretion at such time & place as the first in Commission in the said precinct shall appoint & to pass Judgment for life or Member or any other Corporal Punishment on such Offender & cause Execution of the same Judgment to be made & done. And if any Slave shall be killed in apprehending or that shall by Judgment of the said Justices & Freeholders shall give a Certificate of Value of such Slave under their hands to the Master or Owner of such Slave who shall be thereby Entitulled to a Poll-Tax on all Slaves in the Government to make up that sum to the Owner of such Slave so publickly Executed or killed in Apprehending.

XIV. And Be It Further Enacted by the Authority afors'd that where any White woman whether Bond or Free shall have a Bastard child by a Negro, Mulatto or Indyan over & above the Two years service to her Master or Owner she shall immediately upon the Expiration of her time to her present Master or Owner pay down to the Church Wardens of the Parish wherein such shall be born for the use of the said Parish the sum of Six pounds Current Money of this Province or be by them sold for two years to the use aforesaid.

XV. And Be It Further Enacted that in the case last aforementioned the Church Wardens aforesaid are hereby Impowered to bind out the said children to be servants untill they arrive at & be of the full age of Thirty One Years. And if any Proffits shall accrue or may be made by the Binding out of such Children the same shall be accounted for by the Church Wardens to the Vestry or applied for & toward the use of the Parish.

XVI. And Be It Further Enacted By the Authority aforesaid that no White man or Woman shall Intermarry with any Negro, Mulatto or Indyan Man or Woman under the Penalty of Fifty Pounds for each White man or Woman.

XVII. And Be It Further Enacted that no Clergyman, Justice of the Peace or other person licensed to marry shall hereafter presume to celebrate such marriage under the like Penalty of Fifty Pounds for every such marriage one half to the Informer & the other half to be lodged in the hands of the Governor or Commander in Chief for the time being to be applied for & towards the building of any Publick Church, Court-House or Bridges as the Governor shall think fit, and in case no such building shall require it then to the Lords Proprs. to be recovered as is hereafter in this Act appointed.

 XVIII. And Be It Further Enacted by the Authority aforesaid that no person within this Government shall make any contract with his or their Negro or Negroes for his or their freedom or Liberty that are Runaways or Refractory Negroes. Provided that this Act shall not hinder any man from setting his Negro free as a Reward for his, or their honest & Faithful service. And Provided that such Negro depart the Government within Six Months after his Freedom But if any Negro set free as aforesaid shall not within the time Limitted & according to the true Intent & Meaning of this Act depart the Government then such Negro or Negroes shall by the precinct Court be sold for Five Years to such person or Persons as shall give security for their Transportation & the Moneys arising by such sale shall be paid into the Publick Treasury.

 XIX. And Be It Further Enacted that if any Master or Owner of Negroes or Slaves or any other person or persons whatsoever in this Government shall permitt or suffer any Negro or Negroes to build on their or either of their land or any part thereof any house under pretence of a Meeting House upon the Acct. of Worship or upon any pretence whatsoever & shall not suppress & hinder the same he, she or they so offending shall for every default forfeit & pay Fifty Pounds One half towards defraying the contingent charge of the Government the other halfe to him or them that shall sue for the same to be recovered by Action of Debt, Plaint or Information in any Court of Record in this Government wherein no Essoign, Wager of Law, or Injunction shall be allowed or admitted of.

CHAPTER LXIX.
1715. An Act for Restraining the Indyans from molesting or Injureing the Inhabitants of this Government and for Secureing to the Indyans the right and property of their own lands. (Pages 87-88).

 I. Whereas (before ye late war) dayly and grievous Complaints of Depredations & Insults of ye Indyans were Exhibited against them by

North Carolina Law

Divers persons bordering upon and residing near to ye Inhabitants of ye said Indyans for ye prevention of ye like Disorder for ye time to come and for Cultivating a better Understanding with ye said Indyans the want of which has been so Injurious to the Government.

II. Be It Enacted by his Excellency the Pallatine, &c. And It Is Hereby Enacted that whoever shall Discover or find any Indyan or Indyans Killing, Hunting or in pursuit of any horses, Cattle or hogs the right and property whereof is in any white man Inhabitting within this Government every such person or persons on Discovery or Sight thereof may & he is hereby Impowered to apprehend every such Indyan or Indyans & him or them so apprehended & taken to Convey before Some one of the Commissioners to be appointed for Indyan affairs (& for want of such before ye nearest Magistrate) which said Commissioners or Magistrate together with the ruler or head man of the Town to which such Indyan Delinquent may belong is and are hereby Impowered to punish every such Delinquent in such manner as the nature of the offence may require and to award satisfaction to the party injured for all Damages by him Sustained (saving always the right of appeal to the Governor & Council) if either party shall think themselves agrieved or wronged thereby.

III. And Be It Further Enacted by the Authority aforesaid that if any difference shall for the future Arise between any whyte man and Indyan concerning trade or otherwise howsoever, Every such Difference shall be heard, Tryed and Determined by such Commissioners as the Governor or Commander in Chief for the time being shall appoint together with the ruler or head man of the town to which the Indyan belongs (Saving only the right of appeal as is herein before Saved & Excepted).

IV. And whereas we have too great reason to believe that disputes concerning land have already been of fatall Consequence to the peace and wellfare of this Collony.

V. Be It Further Enacted by the Authority Aforesaid that no whyte man shall for any Consideration whatsoever Purchase or buy any tract or Parcell of Land claimed or actually in possession of any Indyan without special liberty for so Doing from the Governor and Councill first had and obtained under the penalty of Twenty pounds for every hundred acres of Land so bargained for and purchased one halfe to the Informer & the other halfe to him or them which shall sue for the same to be recovered by Bill, Plaint or Information in any Court of Record within this Government wherein no Essoign, protection, Injunction nor Wager of Law shall be allowed or admitted of.

VI. And Be It Further Enacted by the Authority aforesaid that whatever whyte man shall Defraud or take from any of the Indyans his goods or shall beat or abuse or Injure his person each and every person so offending shall make full satisfaction to the party Injured and shall suffer such other punishment as he should or ought to have done had the offence been Committed to any Englishmen.

Edw'd Moseley, Speaker   Chas. Eden, N. Chevin, C. Gale, Fran. Foster, T. Knight

The acts below refer to the Meherrin and Tuscarora land claims.
See acts, Nov. 1729, ch. 2; Oct. 1748, ch. 3; April 1778, ch. 16; Aug. 1778, ch. 5; April 1780, ch. 23, ch. 25, s. 9; April 1783, ch. 21. [See Iredell's Laws, 1791, p. 31.]

****

THE STATE RECORDS OF NORTH CAROLINA
VOLUME XXV., SUPPLEMENT, 1669-1771
EDITED BY: WALTER L. CLARK
NASH BROTHERS BOOK AND JOB PRINTERS
GOLDSBORO, N.C., 1906

CHAPTER I.
1720. An Act for the Lessening the Pole and Lands Tax and Preventing of Concealments. (Pages 162-163).

III. Be it Enacted, that every Constable in each District in every precinct (under penalty of twenty pounds, to be levied by a Warr't of Distress from any Justice, on the Complaint of the Treasurer or Clerk of the precinct) shall go to the Dwelling House of each House Keeper in his District on or before the 30th of Decemb'r next after the Ratification of this Act, and demand of Such House keeper a true List of Tythables, which List every House Keeper is required to give in writing the Number, Name and Condition of every Tythable person he or they ought to pay Tax for, and in the Said List shall mention whether the same Tythable or Tythables be free Servant or Slave, Negro, Indian or Mulatto, Men or Women, and on Neglect or Refusal of Such House keeper giving Such List to the Several Constables He or they shall be lyable to the forfeiture of five pounds, to be recovered by a Warr't from any Justice of the Precinct, upon Complaint of Such Constable, over and above besides the Concealment as by the Act for raising the Sum of two Thousand pounds, And each and every Constable for the performance of which according to the true Intent of this Act shall receive over and above the Allowance of the Act ascertaining Tythables how to be taken the sum of tenn shillings, and which List so taken is by Such Constables to be returned to the Several Clerks of the precinct Courts where Such Tythables are given in on or before the first Day of January next, under the penalty afores'd.

CHAPTER IV.
1720. An Act in Explanation of an Act Concerning Servants and Slaves. (Pages 169-170).

Whereas, the Special Court appointed by the Said Act for the Tryall of Slaves have power thereby Granted them against Slaves convict before them to pass Judgm't for Life Member or other Corporal punishments, and it hath been ascerted that power is thereby granted to the Said Court if they see Cause to give Judgm't for the imprisoning any Slave, deemed it a Corporal punishment, and inasmuch as the imprisoning a Slave is an apparant Damage and Loss to the Master,

I. Be it therefore Enacted by his Excellency, the palatin and the rest of the true and absolute Lords Prop'ts of Carolina, by and with the Advice and Consent of the Rest of the Members of the General Assembly not met at the General Court House at Queen Anne's Creek in Chowan precinct for the N'o. East Part of the Said Province, and it is hereby Enacted, That Corporal punishments in that Case shall not be Construed to extend or include Imprisonment of the Offender, nor shall any such Judgment of the said Court hereafter to be passed, be good or Execution thereof be done.

Rep. By act, April 4, 1741, ch. 24. [See Iredell's Laws, 1791, p. 35.]

****

THE STATE RECORDS OF NORTH CAROLINA
VOLUME XXIII., 1715-1776
EDITED BY: WALTER L. CLARK
NASH BROTHERS BOOK AND JOB PRINTERS
GOLDSBORO, N.C., 1904

CHAPTER V.

North Carolina Law

1723. An Act for an additional Tax on all free Negroes, Mulattoes, Mustees, and such Persons, Male and Female, as now are, or hereafter shall be, intermarried with any such Persons, resident in this Government. (Pages 106-107).

    I. Whereas Complaints have been made by divers Freeholders and other Inhabitants of this government, of great Numbers of Free Negroes, Mulattoes, and other Persons of mixt Blood, that have lately removed themselves into this Government, and that several of them have intermarried with the white Inhabitants of this Province; in Contempt of the Acts and Laws in those Cases made and provided:

    II. Be it therefore Enacted, by his Excellency the Palatine, and the rest of the true and absolute Lords Proprs. of Carolina, by and with the Advice and Consent of the rest of the Members of the present General Assembly, now met at Edenton, for the North East Part of the said Province, and it is hereby Enacted, by the Authority of the same, That all free Negroes, Mulattoes, and other Persons of that kind, being mixed Blood, including the Third Generation, who are, or hereafter shall be, Inhabitants or Residents in this Government, both Male and Female, who are of the age of Twelve years and upwards, shall, from the Ratification of this Act, be deemed and taken for Tithables, and as such each and every of them shall, Yearly, pay the same Levies and Taxes as the other Tithables Inhabitants do, and shall, and are hereby made liable to pay the same Yearly to such Person or Persons, in such Manner, and at such Times and Places, and to be subject to such Fines and Penalties, as in and by an Act, intituled, An Act for making the sum of Twelve Thousand Pounds Public Bills of Credit, for exchanging such of the Public Bills of Credit as are now current, thereby to render them the more useful to the Government; and for regulating the Taxes; which the other Inhabitants of this Province, being Tithables, are obliged and subject to.

    III. And be it further Enacted, by the Authority aforesaid, That from and after the Ratification of this Act, any White Person whatsoever, Male or Female, Inhabitant of this Government, or that may or shall remove themselves hither from other Parts, that now is, or hereafter shall be, married with any Negro, Mulatto, Mustee, or other Person being of mixed Blood, as aforesaid, shall be, and are hereby made liable to the same Levies and Taxes, as the Negroes, Mulattoes, or other mixed Blood, as herein above is expressed; and it is the true Intent and Meaning of this Act, that all and every of the aforesaid Tithables removing themselves into this

North Carolina Law

Government, shall pay the Levy and Taxes asessed for the Year they come hither, provided they come before the Tenth Day of June in that Year.

IV. And forasmuch as divers of the Inhabitants of this Government, for Causes them thereunto moving, have set free Slaves of Sundry kinds, who are, all by Law, obliged to depart the Government in Six Months after their being so freed, otherwise they are liable to be sold to such Person or Persons as shall give security for transporting them out of this Government; notwithstanding the said Law, and contrary to the true Intent and Meaning thereof, many of such freed Negroes, and Slaves of other Kinds, after having departed this Government for a Little Time, Have returned again, deeming themselves Inhabitants of this Government by such Departure and Return: For the Prevention whereof for the future;

V. Be it therefore Enacted, by the Authority of the aforesaid, That all Slaves, of what kind soever, which shall hereafter be set free, that shall be obliged to depart this Government within Six Months after being so freed, according to the Direction of the aforesaid Act, and shall not return into this Government, under the Penalties and Pains hereafter expressed: And if any Slave or Slaves being so freed and set at Liberty, having departed as before directed, shall presume to return back into this Province, it shall and may be lawful for any Person or Persons whatsoever to apprehend and take up such Slave or Slaves so offending, and carry him or them before some Magistrate, who is hereby authorized and empowered, upon due proof made, to commit such Person or Persons so offending, to the Provost Marshall of the County where such offender or offenders shall be apprehended, till the next General Court, to be held for this Government, and shall then sell him or them for Seven Years, at Public Vendue, to the highest Bidder; and the Money arising by the said Sale, after Charges paid, shall be applied, the one Half to the Apprehender, and the other Half towards defraying the contingent charges of the Government; and at the End and Expiration of the said Seven Years, the said Slave or Slaves so set free, shall, and are hereby compelled to depart this Government, within Six Months after being so freed: And if any such Person or Persons so departing shall presume to return a Second Time, they are hereby made liable to be apprehended, taken up, and sold, as aforesaid.

VI. And be it further Enacted, by the Authority aforesaid, That after such Sale is made as aforesaid, if any Person or Persons, Inhabitants of this Government, shall presume to harbour, conceal, or detain any such Negroe or Slave set free, upon pretence of Debt, or otherwise, such Person or Persons so offending shall forfeit and pay One Hundred Pounds Current

Money; shall sue for the same: to be recovered by Bill, Plaint, or Information, in any Court of record within this Government; wherein no Injunction, or Wager of Law, shall be allowed or admitted of.
Rep. as to that part relating to taxables, by act, Nov. 30, 1760, ch. 2. As to the remainder, by act, April 4, 1741, ch. 24. [See Iredell's Laws, 1791, p. 43.]

****

THE STATE RECORDS OF NORTH CAROLINA
VOLUME XXV., SUPPLEMENT, 1669-1771
EDITED BY: WALTER L. CLARK
NASH BROTHERS BOOK AND JOB PRINTERS
GOLDSBORO, N.C., 1906

CHAPTER V.
1729. An additional Act to an Act, for appointing Toll Books, and for preventing People from driving Horses, Cattle, or Hogs, to other Persons' Lands. (Page 114).

VII. And whereas great damages are frequently done, by Slaves being permitted to hunt or range with Dogs or Guns: For prevention whereof, Be it Enacted, by the Authority aforesaid, That it shall not be lawful for any Slave, on any pretence whatsoever, to go, range, or hunt on any Person's Land other than his Master's, with Dogs or Gun, or any Weapon, unless there be a white Man in his Company; under the Penalty of Twenty Shillings, to be paid by his Master, for every Offence, unto the Owner of the Land whereon such Slaves shall range or hunt, and that no Slave shall travel from his Master's Land by himself to any other Place, unless he shall keep the most usual and accustomed Road: And if any Slave shall offend contrary hereto, it shall be lawful for the Owner of the Land whereon such Slave shall be found, to give him a severe Whipping, not exceeding Forty Lashes; and if any Loose, disorderly or suspected Person, be found eating or drinking, or keeping with Slaves in the Night Time, such Person shall be apprehended and carried before a Justice of the Peace; and if he cannot give a good and satisfactory account of his Behaviour, such Person shall be Whipped, at the discretion of the Justice, not exceeding Forty Lashes.

VIII. And for the better suppressing of Negroes travelling and Associating themselves together in great Numbers, to the Terror and

Damage of the white People; Be it Enacted, by the Authority aforesaid, That if any Negro or Negroes shall presume to travel in the Night, or be found in the Quarters or Kitchens among other Persons' Negroes, such Negroes so found shall receive Correction, not exceeding Forty Lashes, as aforesaid; and such Negroes in whose Company they shall be found, shall receive Correction, not exceeding Twenty Lashes.

IX. Provided always, That nothing in this Act shall be construed to prevent any Person from sending his Slaves on his lawful Business, with a pass, in Writing; nor to hinder Neighbors' Negroes intermarrying together, so that a License being first had and obtained of their several Masters.

CHAPTER II.
1729. An Act for the More quiet settling the bounds of the Meherrin Indian Lands. (Page 211).

I. Whereas complaint is made by the Meherrin Indians, that the English people disturb them in their settlements, by coming to inhabit and send corn among them; and also, that their bounds allowed by order of council dated October the twenty sixth, one thousand seven hundred and twenty six did not extend high enough up from the fork of Meherrin neck: for remedy whereof,

II. Be it Enacted, by his Excellency the Palatine, and the rest of the true and absolute Lords Proprietors of Carolina, by and with the advice and consent of the rest of the members of the General Assembly now met at Edenton, for the North East Part of the said Province, and by the authority of the same, that the said order of council be vacated, and that the Indian bounds and limits shall be extended as followeth, viz. beginning at the mouth of Meherrin river, and so up the river to the mouth of Horse Pasture Creek formerly called Indian creek; then by the said creek up to the fork of it; then by the North East branch thereof to the head of the same; then by a straight line across to Chowan river, by the upper line of Mulberry old field survey, to Samuel Power's lands; then along the various courses of the river, to the first station.

III. And be it also enacted, by the authority aforesaid, that all English people, or any other, living in the said bounds, shall move off, and that no persons but the said Indians shall inhabit or cultivate any lands within the limits aforesaid, while the said Indians remain a nation, and live thereon: And if any person shall offend against this act, on complaint made to Mr. John Boude, who is hereby appointed a commissioner for the said Indians, he shall grant his warrant to the constable, requiring him with aid (if need be) to remove such person, at or before the twenty fifth of December next ensuing; and any person refusing to move, shall be brought before the said Commissioners, and upon his conviction of the same, shall forfeit for the first offence, five pounds: and if he still persist, and refuse to go off from the said lands, after warning from the commissioner, or by his order, for the second offence shall forfeit the sum of ten pounds, and for the third time of his so offending shall forfeit Twenty Pounds, and Two months Imprisonment, and give security for his or their good behaviour: to be recovered by bill, plaint or information, in any court of record in this government; wherein no essoin, protection, or wager of law, shall be allowed or admitted of.

     IV. And be it further Enacted, by the authority aforesaid, that the said commissioner is hereby impowered and ordered to reinstate and settle the said Indians, in giving them peaceable possession of the said lands, and to turn off any other person or persons inhabiting within the said bounds, unless such person have special leave from the Governor and Council, for continuing thereon; provided that this act shall not invest the fee simple of the said lands in the Indians, but such as have patents for the same, or any part thereof, their title shall be good and valid; neither shall the said Indians have liberty or leave to rent, sell, or in anyways dispose of the said lands.
Considered as a Private Law in 1791. [See Iredell's Laws, 1791, p. 49.]

****

NORTH CAROLINA STATE ARCHIVES
GENERAL ASSEMBLY SESSIONS RECORDS
COLONIAL (UPPER AND LOWER HOUSES
1709 - JANUARY 1760, BOX 1

JULY, 1733, JOINT COMMITTEE PAPERS - COMMITTEE OF JOINT
PROPOSITIONS & GRIEVANCES TO THE UPPER HOUSE, JULY 12, 1733

Reported from the Committee of Propositions & Grievances that the Committee has had several complaints laid before them & Sundry Petitions from divers Inhabitants setting forth that divers free people Negros &

Mollattos residing in this Province were taken up by the Directions of Thomas Bryant James Tompson Benjamen Hill John Edwards Thomas Kerney & William Lattimore of Bertie precinct Benjamen Payton & Robert Peyton of Bath County Justices of the Peace and others & by these Justices bound out untill they come to 31 years of age Contrary to the Consent of the parties bound out. The said Committee further report that these practices are well known to divers of the said Committee & that they fear that divers persons will desert the Settlement of those parts fearing to be also in like manner so unlawfully. It is therefore humbly recommended by the said Committee that a law pass this House declaring the illegality of such a practice and that all such persons so taken from their parents or Guardians be returned to their respective parents or to those under whose Care they were, and that those Magistrates who have bound out such persons & those to whom they have been bound do attend the next Biennial Assembly to answer for such their Doings; with which Report ye House Concurred and Ordered ye same to be sent to the Upper House for Concurrence.

Sent to Upper House   By Order Moseley Vail JP CLK

Mr. John Leahy Mr. William Handcock

****

THE STATE RECORDS OF NORTH CAROLINA
VOLUME XXIII., 1715-1776
EDITED BY: WALTER L. CLARK
NASH BROTHERS BOOK AND JOB PRINTERS
GOLDSBORO, N.C., 1904

CHAPTER I.
1741. An Act Concerning Marriages. (Page 160).

    XIII. And for Prevention of that abominable Mixture and spurious issue, which hereafter may increase in this Government, by white Men and women intermarrying with Indians, Negroes, Mustees, or Mulattoes, Be it Enacted, by the Authority aforesaid, That if any white Man or Woman, being free, shall intermarry with an Indian, Negro, Mustee, or Mulatto Man or Woman, or any Person of Mixed Blood, to the Third Generation, bond or free, he shall, by Judgement of the County Court, forfeit and pay the sum of Fifty Pounds, Proclamation Money, to the Use of the Parish.

XIV. And be it further Enacted, by the Authority aforesaid, That no Minister of the Church of England, or other Minister, or Justice of the Peace, or other Person whatsoever within this Government, shall hereafter presume to marry a white Man with an Indian, Negro, Mustee, or Mulatto Woman, or any Person of Mixed Blood, as aforesaid, knowing them to be so, upon Pain of Forfeiture and paying, for every such Offence, the Sum of Fifty Pounds, Proclamation Money, to be applied as aforesaid.

CHAPTER XIII.
1741. An Act to prevent the taking away Boats, Canoes, or Pettiaguas, from Landings, or elsewhere, without Leave. (Page 172-173).

IV. And be it further Enacted, by the Authority aforesaid, That if any White Servant, Negroe or Slave, shall Offend against this Act, and be thereof convicted, and the Master, Mistress or Owner of such White Slave, Negroe, or Slave, shall refuse to pay the said Sum of Twenty Shillings, Proclamation Money, such Servant or Slave shall suffer Correction by whipping, at the Discretion of the Magistrate, not exceeding Thirty Nine Lashes.

V. Provided always, and be it Enacted, That neither this Act, nor the Penalties thereof, shall be construed to extend to any Person who shall press any Boat, Canoe or Pettiagua, by Public Authority, to any Person who shall seize his own proper Boat, Canoe or Pettiagua, or any other Person or Persons, being lawfully impowered so to do by the Owner, from any Place or Landing, or from any Person in whose Custody he shall find the same, or to any Servant or Slave taking any Boat, Canoe or Pettiagua, from any Landing or other Place, by Order of his or her Master, Mistress or Overseer.

VI. And be it further Enacted, That if any Master, Mistress or Overseer, shall order any Servant or Slave, belonging to them or under the Care of any of them, to take from any Landing or other Place, any Boat, Canoe or Pettiagua, contrary to the Intent and Meaning of this Act, such Master, Mistress or Overseer of such Servant or Slave so offending shall be liable to the Forfeitures and Penalties of this Act, as if they, in their proper Person, had done the same; anything herein before contained, to the contrary, notwithstanding.

North Carolina Law

CHAPTER XXIV.
1741. An Act Concerning Servants and Slaves. (Pages 191-204).
   I.   Be it Enacted, by his Excellency Gabriel Johnston, Esq., Governor, by and with the Advice and Consent of his Majesty's Council, and General Assembly of this Province, and it is hereby Enacted, by the Authority of the same, That no Person whatsoever, being a Christian, or of Christian Parentage, who, from and after the Ratification of this Act, shall be imported or brought into this Province, shall be deemed a Servant for any Term of Years, unless the Person importing him or her shall produce an Indenture, or some Specialty or Agreement, signifying that the Person so imported did contract to serve such Importer, or his Assigns, any Number of Years, in Consideration of his or her Passage, or some other Consideration therein expressed; and upon any Contest arising between the Master of any Vessel, or other Person importing any Servant or Servants, without Indenture, upon any Bargain or Specialty as aforesaid, the same shall be determined at the next County Court to be held for the County where the said Servant or Servants shall be imported, the Justices of which Court are hereby Impowered to hear and determine the same, in a summary way; and such Determination or Judgment shall be conclusive and binding on the Importer of Servant or Servants, either for the Discharge of the said Servant or Servants, or to oblige him, her, or them, to serve the Importer, or his Assigns, as the Matter shall appear.
   II.   And be it further Enacted, by the Authority aforesaid, That if any Christian Servant, whether he or she be a Servant by Importation or otherwise, shall at any Time or Times absent him or herself from the service of his or her Master or Mistress, without License first had, he or she shall satisfy and make good such Loss of Time of Service by Indenture or otherwise is expired, double the Time of Service lost or neglected by such Absence; and also such longer Time as the County Court shall think fit to adjudge, in Consideration of any further Charge or Damage the Master or Mistress of such Servant may have sustained, by Reason of his or her Absence as aforesaid.
   III.   And be it further Enacted, by the Authority aforesaid, That if any Christian Servant shall lay Violent Hands on his or her Master or Mistress, or Overseer, or shall obstinately refuse to obey the lawful Commands of any of them, upon Proof thereof by one or more Evidences before any Justice of the Peace, he or she shall, for every such Offence,

North Carolina Law

suffer such Corporal Punishment as the said Judge shall think fit to adjudge, not exceeding Twenty One Lashes.

IV. And as an Encouragement for Christian Servants to perform their Service with Fidelity and Cheerfulness; Be it further Enacted, by the Authority aforesaid, That all Masters and Owners of any Servant or Servants shall find and provide for their Servant or Servants wholesome and competent Diet, Clothing and Lodging, at the Discretion of the County Court, and shall not, at any Time, give immoderate Correction, neither shall at any Time whip a Christian Servant naked, without an Order from the Justice of the Peace: And if any Person shall presume to whip a Christian Servant naked, without such Order, the Person so offending shall forfeit and pay the Sum of Forty Shillings, Proclamation Money, to the Party injured; to be recovered, with Costs, upon Petition to the County Court (without the formal Process of an Action), as in and by this Act is provided for Servants' complaints to be heard and determined; provided Complaint be made Six Months after such whipping.

V. And be it further Enacted, by the Authority aforesaid, That all Servants by Indenture or otherwise as aforesaid, shall have their Complaints received by a Justice of the Peace, who, if he find Cause, shall bind the Master, Mistress, or Overseer over, to answer the Complaint at the next County Court; and it shall be there determined: And all Complaints of any Servant or Servants shall and may, either immediately or as aforesaid by Virtue hereof, be received at any Time, upon Petition or Information in the Court of the County wherein they reside, without the formal Process of an Action; and also, full Power and Authority is hereby given to the said Court, at their Discretion (having first summoned the Master, Mistress or Overseer, to justify themselves, if they think fit), to adjudge, order and appoint what shall be necessary as to Diet, Lodging, Clothing, or Correction, and if any Master, Mistress or Overseer shall not thereupon comply with the Order of the said Court, the said Court is hereby authorized and impowered, upon a second just Complaint, to order such Servant or Servants to be immediately sold, at Public Vandue, by the Sheriff; and after the Charges are deducted the remainder of what the said Servant or Servants shall be sold for, to be paid to the Owner.

VI. Provided always, That if such Servant or Servants shall be sick or lame, or otherwise rendered so incapable that he, she, or they cannot be sold for such Value at least as shall satisfy the Fees, and other incident Charges accrued, the said Court shall then order such Servant or Servants into the Care of the Church Wardens of the Parish; and the Master,

North Carolina Law

Mistress or Owner shall provide the said Servant or Servants with such convenient Necessaries as they shall direct and judge sufficient for his, her or their Support, until the Time due by Law from such Servant or Servants to their Master, Mistress or Owner, shall be expired, or until such Servant or Servants shall be recovered so as to be sold, for defraying the said Fees and Charges.

VII. And be it further Enacted, That the said Court, from Time to Time, shall order the Charges of keeping such Servant or Servants, to be levied upon the Goods and Chattels of the Master or Owner of such Servant or Servants in Case they should neglect or refuse to provide for the same.

VIII. And be it further Enacted, by the Authority aforesaid, That all Servants aforesaid, whether by Indenture or otherwise, as well as Femme Coverts as others, shall in the like manner (as is provided upon Complaints of Misusage) have their Petitions received in the said County Court for their Wages, Freedom and Freedom Dues (in this Act hereafter expressed), without the formal Process of an Action; and Proceedings and Judgment shall, in like manner, be had thereupon.

IX. And be it further Enacted, by the Authority aforesaid, That no Master or Mistress of any Servant or Servants, who shall happen to be sick or diseased during the Time of their Servitude, and unable to perform their daily labour, shall, upon ant Pretext whatsoever, remit to such Servant or Servants, any Part of his, her or their Time, to be cleared of them, whereby the said Servant or Servants may perish, or become a Charge to the Parish: And whosoever shall hereafter offend herein, or shall not use and endeavour all Lawful Means for Recovery of such their Servant or Servants as shall happen to be sick or diseased, during the Time of his, her or their Servitude, shall forfeit, for each and every Servant so turned off or neglected, Five Pounds, Proclamation Money, to be levied by an Order from the County Court before whom the Fact shall be proved, by the Oath of one or more Witness or Witnesses, and to be paid into the Hands of the Church Wardens of that Parish where the offence shall be committed, and disposed of towards the Support and Maintenance of each Servant or Servants so turned off or neglected, for the recovery of his, her or their Health and Strength; and such Servant or Servants shall be, by the County Court or any Two Justices, during the Time of their Infirmity, ordered into the Hands and Care of the Church Wardens of the Parish in which his, her or their Master or Owner shall dwell, but in case such sick or diseased Servant or Servants respectively shall not live to the expending the said whole Sum of Five Pounds, Proclamation Money, then the Remainder to be disposed of to the Use of that Parish; or in Case the said Sum of Five Pounds should not be sufficient to support each Servant during his Servitude, or until his Recovery, in such Case the County Court is hereby authorized and impowered to order a Sufficiency to be levied (from Time to Time, as the same shall become due) upon the Goods and Chattels of the Master or Owner of such Servant or Servants, if they shall neglect or refuse to provide the same, agreeable to the Orders of the said Court; and such Servant or Servants so neglected or turned off, shall, upon their Recovery, be set free from their Master or Owner.

X. Provided always, and be it further Enacted, That if any Servant or Servants in this Government shall, thro' his, her or their own wilful Misbehaviour, happen to have any Disease or any broken Bones, Bruises or other Impediments whereby they may be disabled to perform their Labour as they ought to do, and become Chargeable to their Master or Owner, such Servant or Servants shall serve his, her or their Master or Owner, after the Time of his, her or their Service by Indenture or otherwise is expired, such Time as shall by the County Court be adjudged sufficient to satisfy the Charges expended on him, her or them for his, her or their Recovery; and shall also serve over so much Time as he, she or they by any such Means were disabled to serve: Anything herein contained to the contrary notwithstanding.

XI. And be it further Enacted, by the Authority aforesaid, That if any Servant or Servants shall unjustly vex and trouble his, her or their Master or Owner with Groundless Complaints against them to the County Court, or any Justice or Justices of the Peace, such Servant or Servants shall, by the County Court, be ordered to serve his, her or their Master or Owner so injured by such unjust and groundless Vexation, after the Expiration of the Time he, she or they have then to serve, the double Term and Space of that Time he, she or they neglected and lost in Prosecution of such Complaints.

XII. And be it further Enacted, by the Authority aforesaid, That every Servant who shall be in Gaol for his, her or their own Offence, shall serve his, her or their Master or Owner double the Time he, she or they shall there remain, after the Expiration of the Time he, she or they have to serve by Indenture or otherwise; and further, serve his, her or their said Master or Owner such Time as shall be ordered by the County Court as a satisfaction for the Fees and other Charges his, her or their Master or Owner hat expended for such Servant or Servants.

XIII. And be it further Enacted, by the Authority aforesaid, That in all Cases of Penal Laws, whereby Persons free are punishable by Fine, Servants shall be punished by whipping, at the Discretion of any Court or Justice or Justices before whom such Fine or Fines are recoverable, not exceeding Thirty Nine Lashes; unless the Servant so culpable can and will procure some Person or Persons to pay the Fine.

XIV. And be it further Enacted, by the Authority aforesaid, That no free Man or Trader whatsoever, shall buy, sell, trade, barter or borrow any Commodities whatsoever, with, to or from any Apprentice or Servant, whether so by Indenture or otherwise, or with any Slave within this Government, without the Consent of the Master, Mistress or Owner of such Apprentice, Servant or Slave, upon Pain of forfeiting treble the Value of the Commodity or Commodities so traded for, bartered or sold, and also shall pay the Sum of Six Pounds, Proclamation Money, to the Use of the said Master, Mistress or Owner; to be recovered, in the Court of the County where the Offence shall be committed, by Action of Debt, Bill, Plaint or Information, wherein no Essoign, Protection, Injunction or Wager of Law shall be allowed or admitted of: And if it shall so happen that the Person so offending shall not be able to pay treble the Value of the Commodities so traded for, sold or bartered, and the Sum of Six Pounds, such Person shall then be adjudged by the County Court to be sold as a Servant for the same.

XV. Provided always, That if the Master, Mistress or Owner of such Apprentice, Servant or Slave shall not, within Six Months after he or she shall have Information or Knowledge of such Offence, Prosecute the Offender or Offenders for the same, that then it shall and may be lawful for any other Person so to do, and to have and receive every Advantage and Benefit arising from such Prosecution.

XVI. And be it further Enacted, by the Authority aforesaid, That every Servant, by Indenture or otherwise, who shall embezzel, purloin, wilfully waste or shall trade, sell or barter, or otherwise make away any of his or her Master or Mistress' Corn, Cattle, Sheep, Hogs, Stock, or other Goods or Provisions, or Commodities whatsoever, shall, upon Conviction of every such Offence, by one or more Testimonies, upon Oath, or Confession of the Party, before any County Court within this Government, be adjudged by the said Court, to serve his or her said Master or Mistress such Time as the said Court shall think reasonable, for the said Offence, after the said Time by Indenture or otherwise, as aforesaid, is expired.

XVII. And whereas many Women Servants are begotten with Child by free Men, or Servants, to the great Prejudice of their Master or

Mistress, whom they serve, Be it therefore further Enacted, by the Authority aforesaid, That if any Woman Servant shall hereafter be with Child, and bring forth the same during the Time of her Servitude, she shall for such Offence be adjudged by the County Court to serve her Master or Mistress one Year after her Term of Service by Indenture or otherwise is expired.

XVIII. And be it further Enacted, by the Authority aforesaid, That if any Woman Servant shall hereafter be delivered of a Child, begotten by her Master, such Servant shall immediately after Delivery be sold by the Church Wardens of the Parish where the Offence is committed for One Year, after the Time of Service by Indenture or otherwise is expired, and the Money arising by such Sale shall be for the use of the Parish: And if any White Servant Woman shall, during the Time of her Servitude, be delivered of a Child begotten by any Negro, Mulatto or Indian, such Servant, over and above the Time she is by this Act to serve her Master or Owner for such Offence, shall be sold by the Church Wardens of the Parish, for Two Years, after the Time by Indenture or otherwise is Expired: and the Money arising thereby applied to the Use of the said Parish; and such Mulatto Child or Children of such Servant, to be bound by the County Court until he or she arrive at the age of Thirty One Years.

XIX. And whereas many abuses have and may be committed by Persons who, under Pretence of understanding several Trades and Misteries, have procured, and may hereafter procure, large Sums of Money to be advanced to them, and have entered, and may hereafter enter, into Covenants with Merchants and others in Great Brittain, or elsewhere, for the Payment of large Wages, Yearly, though they were, or may be, totally ignorant of and unable to perform such Trade and Mistery: For Remedy whereof,

XX. Be it Enacted, by the Authority aforesaid, That all and every Person or Persons already imported, or who shall be hereafter imported, into this Government as a Tradesman or Workman on Wages, and shall be found not to understand such Trade or Employment, the Master or Owner of such Servant may bring him or her to any County Court of this Government; which Court, upon Complaint made to them of such Deceit, are hereby impowered and directed to enquire into the same, and upon finding any such Fraud, may judge and direct such Satisfaction to be made to the Master or Owner of such Servant, either by Defalcation of the Wages or Part thereof, as to them shall seem just.

North Carolina Law

XXI. And be it further Enacted, by the Authority aforesaid, That if any Person, who is or shall hereafter be imported or brought into this Government, as a Tradesman or other Workman on Wages, shall refuse or neglect to perform his Duty, or shall absent himself from his Master or Owner's Service without Leave, in every such Case it shall an may be lawful for the Justices of the County Court wherein such Master or Owner resides, upon Complaint and Proof to them made, to order such Satisfaction and Reparation to the Master or Owner of such Servant for the Damages sustained by him for such Refusal or Neglect, as to them shall seem just; and for every Day such Servant shall absent himself from his Master or Owner's Service as aforesaid, to order and direct such Servant to serve his or her said Master or Owner, two days for every Day's Absence, after this Time by Indenture or otherwise is expired, and that without any Wages to be paid for such Service.

XXII. And be it further Enacted, by the Authority aforesaid, That there shall be allowed to every Servant, whether by Indenture or Otherwise, not having Yearly Wages, at the Expiration of his or her Service, Three Pounds, Proclamation Money, besides one sufficient Suit of wearing Clothes for such Servant or Servants.

XXIII. And be it further Enacted, by the Authority aforesaid, That if any Person or Persons already have, or shall hereafter, import into this Government, and here sell or retain for his own Use as a Slave, any Person or Persons that shall have been free in any Christian Country, Island or Plantation, or Turk or Moor, in Amity with his Majesty, such Importer or Seller as aforesaid shall forfeit and pay to the party, from whom the said free Person shall recover his or her Freedom double the Sum for which such free Person was sold; to be recovered in any Court of Record within this Government, according to the Course of Common Law, wherein the Defendant shall not be admitted to plead in Bar any Act or Statute for Limitations of Actions: And moreover, such Importer or Seller of any such free Person as aforesaid shall be committed until he enter into Bond before the said Court, with Two good and sufficient Sureties, in the Sum of Five Hundred Pounds, Sterling Money of Great Brittain, payable to our Sovereign Lord the King, his Heirs and Successors with Condition, That he shall and do, within One Year next ensuing, transport and Land (Dangers of the Seas and Life only excepted) such free Person sold by him as a Slave as aforesaid (if he or she shall so require), in the Country, Island or Plantation from whence he or she was directly brought as aforesaid; and shall produce an authentic Certificate of his Performance thereof to the said Court.

XXIV. And be it further Enacted, by the Authority aforesaid, That each and every Justice of the Peace for the several Counties within this Government, are hereby impowered and directed, upon the Complaint of any Person who now is, or hereafter shall be, imported into this Government, and who was free in any Christian Country, Island or Plantation before his or her transportation hither, who is kept or sold as a Slave, to cause the pretended Owner of such Person Complaining, to appear before him, together with such Evidence or Evidences as shall be material; and after Examination taken in Writing, shall bind them over to appear at the next County Court of which he is a Member, where the said Complaint shall be heard and determined without any formal Process of Law.

XXV. And be it further Enacted, by the Authority aforesaid, That if any Person or Persons whatsoever, shall, directly or indirectly, at any Time after the Ratification of this Act, tempt or persuade any Apprentice or other Servant, during the Time of his or her Service due by Indenture or Otherwise, or any Negro or other Slave, to leave their Master or Mistress' Service to whom he or they are Apprenticed Servant, or Slave, or shall knowingly give Encouragement to relieve, assist, harbour or entertain any such, or shall knowingly encourage, relieve, assist, harbour, entertain, for any Space of Time whatsoever, any Apprentice, Servant or Slave, who shall wilfully absent him or herself from the Service of his or her Master or Mistress, such Person or Persons so Offending shall forfeit and pay for each and every such Apprentice or other Servant, and for each and every Negro or other Slave, the Sum of Forty Shillings, Proclamation Money, and for each Twelve Hours such Apprentice or other Servant, Negro or Slave be afterwards absent from his Master or Mistress' Service, the Sum of Five Shillings, Proclamation Money; to be recovered by the Master or Owner of such Apprentice, Servant or Slave, by Action of Debt, Bill, Plaint or Information, in the General County Court, wherein no Essoign, Protection or Injunction shall be allowed or admitted of; And if it should so happen that any Person or Persons, convicted Offenders herein, should not be able or refuse to pay the Fines by this Act inflicted, in such Case the Offender shall be, by Order of the General or County Court, sold as a Servant for such Time as the said Court shall think sufficient to pay the same; and shall be, during such Servitude, liable to the Penalties and Forfeitures inflicted for Breaches of this Act.

XXVI. And be it further Enacted, by the Authority aforesaid, That if any Person shall hire or contract himself to serve as an Overseer, either upon Wages or Share of the Produce, with any Person or Planter whatsoever within this Government, and shall absent himself or depart from the service of his Master or Mistress before the Time mentioned in his Agreement or Contract be expired he shall for such Offence forfeit his Right and Title to his Wages, or share of the Produce.

XXVII. And be it further Enacted, by the Authority aforesaid, That if any Person or Persons whatsoever shall directly or indirectly, at any Time after the Ratification of this Act, tempt or persuade any Negro or Negroes, or other Slave or Slaves, to leave his, her or their Master or Mistress' Service, out of an Intent and Design to carry or convey away him, her or them out of this Government, or shall harbour or conceal him, her or them for that Intent and Purpose, and be thereof Convicted by his, her or their own Confession, or the Oath of One credible Witness, such Person or Persons shall, by the Two next Justices of the Peace, be committed to Gaol or bound over to the next Court to be held for the County where the Offence shall be committed, and shall be prosecuted by Indictment for the said Offence; and being thereof lawfully convicted, shall, by the said Court, be adjudged to pay to the Master or Mistress for each Negro or other Slave so enticed or persuaded for the Purpose aforesaid, the Sum of Twenty Five Pounds, Proclamation Money, or the Value thereof; to be levied by order of the said Court: But in Case the Party offending shall not be found worth Lands, Goods or Chattels to the value aforesaid, then the said Court shall adjudge him, her or them to serve the Owner of such Slave or Slaves, or his Assigns, Five Years; and so deliver him, her or them over to the Master, Mistress or Owner of such Slave or Slaves, so tempted or persuaded as aforesaid, and make Record thereof: But if any Person or Persons shall so tempt and practice with any Negro or Negroes, or other Slave or Slaves, and him, her or them so tempted shall actually convey away, or send out of this Government, and be afterwards be apprehended and convicted thereof, he, she or they shall, by the said Court, be severally adjudged and condemned as guilty of Felony, and shall suffer accordingly.

XXVIII. And for Encouragement of all Persons to take up Runaways, Be it Enacted, by the Authority aforesaid, That for the taking up Servants or Slaves, if Ten Miles or under from the House or Quarter where such Servant or Slave was kept there shall be allowed by the Master, if known and residing in the County; if not, by the Public, as a Reward to the Taker-up, Seven Shillings and Six Pence, Proclamation Money, and for every Mile above Ten, Three Pence over and above the said Sum; which said several Rewards shall be paid by the Church Wardens of the Parish where such Taker-up shall reside, or where he shall bring such Runaway before a Justice of the Peace; and shall be levied again by the Church Wardens of the Parish, upon the said Master or Owner of such Runaway, for Reimbursement of the same to the Parish; and for the greater Certainty in paying the said Rewards and reimbursing the Parish, every Justice of the Peace before whom such Runaway shall be brought, upon the taking up, shall grant a Certificate thereof, in which he shall mention the proper Name and Surname of the Taker-up, and the County of his or her Residence, together with the Time and Place of taking up said Runaway, and shall also mention the Name of the said Runaway, and the proper Name and Surname of the Master or Owner of such Runaway, and the County of his or her Residence, together with the Distance of Miles, in the said Justice's judgment, from the Place of taking up the said Runaway to the House or Quarter where such Runaway was kept; upon producing which Certificate to the Church Wardens of the Parish where the same was granted, they shall pay to the Taker-up of such Runaway, or his Assigns, the Reward aforesaid; and shall levy the same again as aforesaid: But if it should happen That the Master or Owner of such Runaway should not reside or have Effects in the County where the Certificate shall be granted by the Justice as aforesaid, the Church Wardens shall transmit the said Certificate to the Sheriff of the County where the Owner of such Runaway resides, or hath Effects, who shall, upon Receipt thereof, immediately levy the same upon the Goods and Chattels of the Master or Owner of such Runaway, and return the same to the Church Wardens aforesaid, or their Order; any Law, Usage or Custom to the contrary notwithstanding.

XXIX. And be it further Enacted, by the Authority aforesaid, That if any Negro or other Person, who shall be taken up as a Runaway and brought before any Justice of the Peace, and cannot speak English, or through Obstinacy, will not declare the name of his or her Owner, such Justice shall in such Case, and he is hereby required, by Warrant under his Hand, to commit the said Negro, Slave or Runaway to the Gaol of the County wherein he or she shall be taken up; and the Sheriff or Under Sheriff of the County into whose Custody the said Runaway shall be committed, shall forthwith cause Notice, in Writing, of such Commitment to be set up on the Court-House Door of the said County, and there continued during the Space of Two Months; in which Notice a full description of the said Runaway and his Clothing shall be particularly set down; and shall cause a Copy of such Notice to be sent to the Clerk or Reader of each Church or Chappel within this County, who are hereby

North Carolina Law

required to make Publication thereof, by setting up the same in some open and convenient Place, near the said Church or Chappel, on every Lord's Day for the Space of Two Months from the date thereof: And every Sheriff failing to give such Notice as is herein directed shall forfeit and pay Five Pounds, Proclamation Money; which said Forfeiture shall and may be recovered with costs in any Court of Record in this Government by Action of Debt, Bill, Plaint or Information, wherein no Essoign, Privilege, Protection, Injunction or Wager of Law shall be allowed: The One Moiety whereof shall be to the Church Wardens, for the Use of the Parish, as well as towards the defraying of the Charges that shall arise and become due by Virtue of this Act, and the other Moiety to the Person who shall sue for the same.

XXX. And be it further Enacted, by the Authority aforesaid, That if within the Space of Two Months the Owner of any such Negro, Slave or Runaway cannot be known, or doth not claim the same, that the Sheriff of the said County to whose Custody such Runaway shall be committed, shall cause the said Runaway to be delivered to the next Constable, to be by him delivered to the next Constable, and so from Constable to Constable, to the Public Gaol of this Government, after such Manner and to receive such Punishment as in this Act is mentioned and directed

XXXI. And be it further Enacted, by the Authority aforesaid, That when any Negro or Runaway, as aforesaid, shall be delivered to the Keeper of the Public Gaol of this Government by Virtue of this Act, and his or her Master or Owner cannot be known, it shall and may be lawful for the Keeper of the said Gaol, upon his application to the General Court, or the nearest County Court to the said Gaol, or to any Two Justices, as aforesaid, to let the said Negro or Runaway to Hire, to any Person or Persons whom they shall approve of, for such Sum or Sums of Money, or Quantity of Commodities, and for such Term of Time, as they shall direct; and that out of the money or Commodities arising by such Hire, all Fees relating to the taking up, Imprisonment and conveying to Gaol and Charges of maintaining such Negro or Runaway, shall be first paid and discharged, and the Overplus, if any, disposed of as such Court who shall order the said Negro or Runaway to let out to Hire shall direct.

XXXII. Provided always, That when the Owner of such Negro or Runaway shall demand the same, the Person to whom such Negro or Runaway shall be let out to Hire shall forthwith deliver him or her into the Custody of the Keeper of the Public Gaol, and shall then also pay the Hire, in Proportion to the Time the said Runaway hath served; and the Keeper of

North Carolina Law

the said Gaol shall deliver the said Runaway to his Master or Owner, he or she paying down all Fees and Charges of taking up, Imprisonment, conveying to Gaol, and maintaining such Runaway, in Case the Hire of the said Runaway be not sufficient to satisfy the same.

XXXIII. And be it further Enacted, by the Authority aforesaid, That when the Keeper of the said Public Gaol shall, by Direction of such Court as aforesaid, let out any Negro or Runaway to Hire to any Person or Persons whomsoever, the said Keeper shall, at the Time of his Delivery, cause an iron Collar to be put on the Neck of such Negro or Runaway with the Letters P.G. stamped thereon; and that thereafter the said Keeper shall not be answerable for the Escape of the said Negro or Runaway.

XXXIV. And be it Enacted, by the Authority aforesaid, That when any Runaway Servant or Slave shall be brought before any Justice of the Peace within this Government such Justice shall, by his Warrant, Commit the said Runaway to the next Constable, and therein also order him to give the said Runaway so many lashes as the said Justice shall think fit, not exceeding the Number of Thirty Nine, well laid on, on the Bare back of such Runaway; and then to be conveyed from Constable to Constable, until the said Runaway shall be carried home, or to the Public Gaol, as aforesaid.

XXXV. And be it further Enacted, That every Constable shall, on his receipt of such Runaway, give a receipt for him or her; that every Constable failing to execute such Warrant, according to the Tenor thereof or refusing to give such Receipt, shall forfeit and pay Twenty Shillings, Proclamation Money, or the Value thereof in Bills, to the Church Wardens, for the Use of the Parish wherein such Failure shall be; to be recovered by a Warrant under the Hands of any Two Justices within the County where such Constable shall reside: And such Corporal Punishment shall not deprive the Master or Owner of any Runaway Servant of the other Satisfaction herein by this Act appointed to be had of such Servant, for his or her running away.

XXXVI. And be it further Enacted, by the Authority aforesaid, That if any Sheriff, or under-Sheriff, or Constable shall set to work, employ or let out to Hire, without Order of Court as aforesaid, any Runaway Servant or Slave committed to the Custody of any of them, or shall detain such Runaway longer in his or their Custody than by this Act is directed, he or they so offending shall forfeit and pay Five Pounds, Proclamation Money; to be recovered in any Court of Record in this Government by Action of Debt, Bill, Plaint or Information, wherein no Essoign, Protection, Privilege, or Wager of Law shall be allowed: One Moiety whereof, to be

North Carolina Law

paid to the Church Wardens, for the Use of the Parish where the Offence shall be committed, and the other to him or them who shall sue for the same: And if any Sheriff, or his Under-Sheriff, or any Constable into whose Hands any Runaway Servant or Slave shall be committed by Virtue of this Act, shall negligently or wilfully suffer such Runaway to escape the said Sheriff, Under-Sheriff, or Constable, he or they shall be liable to the Action of the Party grieved for Recovery of his Damages at the Common Law with Costs.

XXXVII. And be it further Enacted, by the Authority aforesaid, That all and every the Constables within this Government, for their Encouragement to perform their Duty be, and they are hereby, for the future, exempted from the Payment of all Public, County and Parish Levies, for their own Persons, during their Continuance in Office; and that the Keepers of Ferries within this Government shall give immediate Passage to all Constables and their Assistants charged with conducting any Runaway or Runaways, either to the Public Gaol or to such Runaway or Runaways' Master or Owner, without charging such Constable or their Assistants for the Ferriage, either going or returning: But all such Ferriages of Constables or their Assistants shall be paid by the Church Wardens of the Parish where such Ferry-keepers respectively live, and levied, as aforesaid, upon the respective Masters or Owners of such Runaways.

XXXVIII. And be it Enacted, by the Authority aforesaid, That from and after the Publication of this Act, the Fees and Allowances of the said Sheriffs and Gaolers be as followeth; That is to say, For the Commitment of every such Negro or Runaway to any County Gaol, the Sheriff shall be paid, for his Fee, the Sum of Two Shillings and Six Pence, Proclamation Money, and for the keeping and maintaining him or her in Gaol for every Twenty Four Hours, the Sum of Six Pence, and for his or her Releasment, the Sum of Two Shillings and Six Pence; and that the Keeper of the Public Gaol of this Government, for the Commitment of every such Negro or Runaway, shall be paid the Sum of Two Shillings and Six Pence, Proclamation Money, and for his or her keeping in Gaol, every Twenty Four Hours, the Sum of Six Pence, Proclamation Money, and for his or her Releasment, the Sum of Two Shillings and Six Pence, Proclamation Money, and no more. And if any Sheriff, in any County in this Government, or Keeper of the Public Gaol, shall demand or take any greater Fee or Allowance than is hereby before appointed and allowed for the Service and Maintenance aforesaid, or any of them, he or they so offending shall, for every Offence, forfeit and pay to the Party grieved, the

North Carolina Law

Sum of Twenty Shillings, Proclamation Money, and shall also refund and pay back to the Parties, such Sum of Money which such Sheriff or Gaoler shall receive and take, over and above the Fees and Allowances hereinbefore appointed; which aforesaid Forfeiture of Twenty Shillings shall and may be recovered by a Warrant from any Justice of the Peace of the County where such Offence shall be committed.

XXXIX. And be it further Enacted, by the Authority aforesaid, That when any Negro or other Runaway whose Owner is supposed to be a resident in any other Province, shall be committed to any Public Gaol of This Government, the Keeper of the said Gaol shall, by the first Opportunity after such Commitment, send such Description of such Negro or Runaway, together with the Account of the Time of the Commitment and the County where such Runaway is committed, to the Press, to be advertised in the Virginia or South Carolina Gazette; for which he shall be reimbursed by the Owner of the said Slave or Runaway.

XL. And be it further Enacted, by the Authority aforesaid, That no Slave shall go armed with Gun, Sword, Club or other Weapon, or shall keep any such Weapon, or shall Hunt or Range in the Woods, upon any pretence whatsoever (except such Slave or Slaves who shall have a Certificate, as is herein provided), and if any Slave shall be found offending herein, it shall and may be lawful for any Person or Persons to seize and take, to his own Use, such Gun, Sword or other Weapon, and to apprehend and to deliver such Slave to the next Constable, who is enjoined and required, without further Order or Warrant, to give such Slave Twenty Lashes on his or her bare Back, and to send him or her home, and the Master or Owner of such Slave shall pay the taker up of such armed Slave the same Reward as by this Act is allowed for taking up of Runaways.

XLI. Provided always, That nothing in this Act shall be construed or extended, to prohibit or debar any Master or Owner of any Slave or Slaves within this Government from employing any one Slave in each and every district Plantation, from hunting in the Woods on their Master's Lands with a Gun, to preserve his or her Stock, or to kill Game for his or her Family.

XLII. Provided also, That such Master or Owner shall first deliver into the County Court an Account in Writing of the name of any such Slave to be employed as aforesaid, and the Chairman of the Court shall sign a Certificate that such Slave is allowed to carry a Gun, and hunt in the woods on his Master's or Mistress Lands: And the Master, Mistress or Overseer of such Slave shall give him the said Certificate, which such

North Carolina Law

Slave shall always carry about him, on Pain of being apprehended and punished as aforesaid: Anything herein before contained to the contrary notwithstanding.

XLIII. And be it further Enacted, by the Authority aforesaid, That no Slave shall go from off the Plantation or Seat of Land where such Slave shall be appointed to live, without Certificate of leave, in Writing for so doing, from his or her Master or Overseer (negroes wearing Liveries always excepted).

XLIV. And be it further Enacted, by the Authority aforesaid, That no slave shall be permitted, on any Pretence whatsoever, to raise any Horses, Cattle or Hogs; and all Horses, Cattle and Hogs that Six Months from the Date thereof, shall belong to any Slave, or of any Slave's Mark in this Government, shall be seized and sold by the Church Wardens of the Parish where such Horses, Cattle or Hogs shall be, and the Profit thereof applied, One Half thereof to the Use of the said Parish, and the other Half to the Informer.

XLV. And whereas many Times Slaves run away and lie out hid and lurking in the Swamps, Woods and other Obscure Places, killing Cattle and Hogs, and committing other Injuries to the Inhabitants in this Government: Be it therefore Enacted, by the Authority aforesaid, That in all such Cases, upon Intelligence of any Slave or Slaves lying out as aforesaid, any Two Justices of the Peace for the County wherein such Slave or Slaves is or are supposed to lurk to do Mischief, shall, and they are hereby impowered and required, to issue Proclamation against such Slave or Slaves (reciting his or their Name or Names, and the Name or Names of their Owner or Owners, if known), thereby requiring him or them, and every of them, forthwith to surrender him or themselves; and also, to impower and require the Sheriff of the said County to take such Power with him as he shall think fit and necessary for going in search and pursuit of and effectual apprehending such outlying Slave or Slaves; which Proclamation shall be published on a Sabbath Day, at the Door of every Church or Chappel, or for want of such, at the Place where Divine Service shall be performed in the said County, by the Parish Clerk or Reader, immediately after Divine Service: And if any Slave or Slaves against whom Proclamation hath been thus issued, stay out and do not immediately return home, it shall be lawful for any Person or Persons whatsoever to kill and destroy such Slave or Slaves by such Ways and Means as he or she shall think fit, without Accusation or Impeachment of any Crime for the same.

North Carolina Law

XLVI. Provided always, and it is further Enacted, that for every Slave killed in Pursuance of this Act, or put to Death by Law, the Master or Owner of such Slave shall be paid by the Public; and all Tryals of Slaves for Capital or other Crimes, shall be in the Manner and according as hereinafter is directed.

XLVII. And be it further Enacted, by the Authority aforesaid, That if any Number of Negroes or other Slaves, that is to say, Three or more, shall at any Time hereafter, consult, advise or conspire to rebell, or make insurrection, or shall plot or conspire the Murther of any Person or Persons whatsoever, every such consulting, plotting, or conspiring, shall be adjudged and deemed Felony; And the Slave or Slaves convicted thereof, in Manner hereafter directed, shall suffer Death.

XLVIII. And be further Enacted, by the Authority aforesaid, That every Slave committing such Offence, or any other Crime or Misdemeanor, shall forthwith be committed, by any Justice of the Peace, to the Common Gaol of the County within which the said Offence shall be committed, there to be safely kept; and that the Sheriff of such County, upon such Commitment, shall forthwith Certify the same to any Justice in the Commission for the said Court, for the Time being, resident in the County, who is thereupon required and directed to issue a Summons for Two or more Justices of the said Court, and Four reeholders, such as shall have Slaves in the said County; which said Three Justices, and Four Freeholder Owners of Slaves, are hereby impowered and required, upon Oath, to try all Manner of Crimes and Offences that shall be committed by any Slave or Slaves, at the Court House of the County, and to take for Evidence the Confession of the Offender, the Oath of one or more credible Witnesses, or such Testimony of Negroes, Mulattoes or Indians, bond or free, with pregnant Circumstances, as to them shall seem convincing without the Solemnity of a Jury; and the Offender being then found guilty, to pass such Judgment upon such Offender, according to their Discretion, as the Nature of the Crime or Offence shall require; and on such Judgment, to award Execution.

XLIX. Provided always, and be it Enacted, That it shall and may be lawful for each and every Justice, being in the Commission of the Peace for the County where any Slave or Slaves shall be tried, by Virtue of this Act (who is Owner of Slaves), to set up such Tryal, and act as a Member of such Court, tho' he or they be not summoned thereto: Anything before herein contained to the Contrary, in any wise, notwithstanding.

North Carolina Law

L. And to the End such Negro, Mulatto or Indian, bond or free, not being Christians, as shall hereafter be produced as an Evidence on the Tryal of any Slave or Slaves for Capital or other Crimes, may be under the greater Obligation to declare the Truth; Be it further Enacted, That where any such Negro, Mulatto or Indian, bond or free, shall, upon due Proof made, or pregnant Circumstances, appearing before any County Court within this Government, be found to have given False Testimony, every such Offender shall, without further Tryal, be ordered by the said Court to have one Ear nailed to the Pillory, and there stand for the Space of One Hour, and the said Ear to be cut off, and thereafter the other Ear nailed in like manner, and cut off, at the Expiration of one other Hour; and moreover, to order every such Offender Thirty Nine Lashes well laid on, on his or her bare Back, at the common whipping Post.

LI. And be it further Enacted, by the Authority aforesaid, That at every such Tryal of Slaves committing Capital or other Offences, the first Person in Commission setting on such Tryal shall, before the Examination of every Negro, mulatto or Indian, not being a Christian, charge such to declare the Truth.

LII. Provided Always, and it is hereby intended, That the Master, Owner or Overseer of any Slave, to be arraigned and tryed by Virtue of this Act, may appear at the Tryal and make what just Defence he can for such Slave or Slaves; so that such Defence do not relate to any Formality in the Proceeding on the Tryal.

LIII. And be it further Enacted, by the Authority aforesaid, That when any Slave shall be convicted Capitally by Virtue of this Act, the Justices and Freeholders that shall sit on such Tryals, shall put a Valuation, in Proclamation Money, upon such Slave so convicted, and Certify under their Hands and Seals, such Valuation to the next Assembly; that the said Assembly may make suitable Allowance thereupon, to the Master or Owner of such Slave.

LIV. And be it further Enacted, by the Authority aforesaid, That if in the dispersing any unlawful Assemblies of rebel Slaves or Conspirators, or seizing the Arms and Ammunition of such as are prohibited by this Act to keep the same, or in apprehending Runaways, or in Correction by Order of the County Court, any Slave shall happen to be killed or destroyed, the Court of the County where such Slave shall be killed, upon Application of the Owner of such Slave, and due Proof thereof made, shall put a Valuation, in Proclamation Money, upon such Slave so killed, and certify such Valuation to the next Session of Assembly; that the said Assembly may make suitable Allowance thereupon, to the Master or Owner of such Slave.

LV. Provided always, and be it further Enacted, That nothing herein contained, shall be construed, deemed or taken, to defeat or bar the Action of any Person or Persons, whose Slave or Slaves shall happen to be killed by any other Person whosoever, contrary to the Directions and true Intent and Meaning of this Act; but that all and every Owner or Owners of such Slave or Slaves, shall and may bring his, her or their Action for Recovery of Damages for such Slave or Slaves so killed.

LVI. And be it further Enacted, by the Authority aforesaid, That no Negro or Mulatto Slaves shall be set free, upon any pretence whatsoever, except for meritorious Services, to be adjudged and allowed of by the County Court, and Licence thereupon first had and obtained; And that where any Slave shall be set free by his or her Master or Owner, otherwise than is herein before directed, it shall and may be lawful for the Church Wardens of the Parish wherein such Negro, Mulatto or Indian shall be found, at the Expiration of Six Months, next after his or her being set free, and they are hereby authorized and required, to take up and sell the said Negro, Mulatto or Indian as a Slave, at the next Court to be held for the said County at Public Vendue; and the Monies arising by such Sale, shall be applied to the Use of the Parish, by the Vestry thereof: And if any Negro, Mulatto or Indian Slave, set free otherwise than is herein directed, shall depart this Province within Six Months next after his or her Freedom, and shall afterwards return into this Government, it shall and may be lawful for the Church Wardens of the Parish where such Negro or Mulatto shall be found, at the Expiration of one Month, next after his or her return into this Government, to take up such Negro or Mulatto, and sell him or them, as Slaves at the next Court to be held for the County, at Public Vendue; and the Monies arising thereby, to be applied, by the Vestry, to the Use of the Parish, as aforesaid.

LVII. And be it further Enacted, by the Authority aforesaid, That until this Act shall be printed, it shall be publicly read, Yearly, and every Year, Two several Times in the year, in every County within this Government, by the Clerk of each County, in open Court, that is to say, at the Courts in or next to the Months of April and September; under the Penalty of Twenty Shillings, Proclamation Money, for every such Omission and Neglect; to be levied by a Warrant from any Justice of the Peace, and applied to the Use of the Parish where the Offence shall be committed: and

North Carolina Law

the Church Wardens of every Parish are hereby required to provide a Copy of this Act, at the Charge of the Parish.

LVIII. And be it further Enacted, by the Authority aforesaid, That all and every other Act and Acts, and every Clause and Article thereof heretofore made, so far as relates to Servants and Slaves, or to any other Matter or Thing whatsoever, within the Purview of this Act, is and are hereby repealed and made void, to all Intents and Purposes, as if the same had never been made.

CHAPTER II.
1746. An Act to fix a Place for the Seat of Government, and for keeping Public Offices; for appointing Circuit Courts and defraying the Expence thereof; and also for establishing the Courts of Justice and regulating the Proceedings therein. (Page 262).

XLIX. And be it further Enacted, That if any Persons whatsoever, be summoned as a Witness, and upon his or her appearance in the General or County Court, or before the Person appointed to take Depositions as aforesaid, shall refuse to give Evidence, upon Oath, such Person so refusing, shall immediately be thereupon committed to the Common Gaol, there to remain without Bail or Mainprize, until he or she shall be willing to give Evidence, upon Oath, in such a Manner as the Law now doth, or at any Time hereafter, shall direct.

L. Provided always, that the People called Quakers, shall have the same Liberty of giving their Evidence, by way of Solemn Affirmation or Declaration, as by an Act of Parliament, made in the Eighth Year of the reign of the late King George, intituled An Act, for granting to the People called Quakers, such Forms or Affirmation or Declaration, as may remove the Difficulties which many of them lie under; and that all Negroes, Mulattoes, bond and free, to the Third Generation, and Indian Servants or Slaves, shall be deemed and taken to be Persons incapable in Law to be Witnesses in any Cause whatsoever, except against each other.

CHAPTER III.
1748. An Act for ascertaining the Bounds of a certain Tract of Land formerly laid out by Treaty to the use of the Tuskerora Indians, so long as they, or any of them, shall occupy and live upon the same; and to prevent any Person or Persons taking up Lands, or settling within

the said Bounds, by Pretence of any Purchase or Purchases made, or that shall be made, from the said Indians. (Pages 299-301).

I. Whereas Complaints are made by the Tuskerora Indians, of diverse Incroachments made by the English on their Lands, and being but just that the ancient Inhabitants of this Province shall have and enjoy a quiet and convenient Dwelling-place in this their native County; Wherefore,

II. We pray it may be Enacted, And be it Enacted, by his Excellency Gabriel Johnston, Esq., Governor, by and with the advice and Consent of his Majesty's Council, and the General Assembly of this Province, and it is hereby Enacted, by the Authority of the same, That the Lands formerly allotted the Tuskerora Indians, by solemn Treaty, lying on the Morattock River, in Bertie County, being the same whereon they now dwell, butted and bounded as follows, viz., Beginning at the Mouth of Quitsnoy Swamp, running up the said Swamp Four Hundred and Thirty Poles, to a Scrubby Oak, near the head of the said Swamp, by a Great Spring; then North Ten Degrees East, Eight Hundred and Fifty Poles, to a Persimmon Tree on the Raquis Swamp; then along the Swamp and Pocoson main Course, North Fifty Seven Degrees West, Two Thousand Six Hundred and Forty Poles to a Hickory on the East Side of the Falling Run, or Deep Creek, and down the various Courses of the said Run to Morattock River; then down the River to the first Station; shall be confirmed and assured, and by Virtue of this Act, is confirmed and assured, unto James Blount, Chief of the Tuskerora Nation, and the People under his Charge, their Heirs and Successors, forever; any Law, Usage, or Grant, to the contrary, notwithstanding.

III. Provided always, That it shall and may be lawful for any Person or Persons, that have formerly obtained any Grant or Grants, under the late Lords Proprietors, for any Tracts or Parcels of Land within the aforesaid Boundaries, upon the said Indians deserting or leaving the said Lands, to enter, occupy, and enjoy the same, according to the Tenor or their several Grants; any Thing herein to the contrary notwithstanding.

IV. And be it further Enacted, by the Authority aforesaid, That it shall not nor may be lawful, for the Lord Granville's Receiver to ask, have, or demand, any Quit Rents for any of the said Tracts or Parcels of Land, taken up within the said Indian Boundaries, as aforesaid, until such Time the Indians have deserted the same, and the Patentee be in Possession thereof, and then only for such Rents as shall from thence arise and become due; any Law, Usage, or Custom, to the contrary, notwithstanding.

North Carolina Law

V. And be it further Enacted, by the Authority aforesaid, That no Person, for any Consideration whatsoever, shall purchase or buy any Tract or Parcel of Land, claimed or in Possession of any Indian or Indians, but all such Bargains and Sales shall be, and are hereby declared to be null and void, and of none Effect; and the Person so purchasing or buying any Land of any Indian or Indians, shall further forfeit the Sum of Ten Pounds, Proclamation Money for every Hundred Acres by him purchased and bought; one Half to the Use of the Public, the other Half to him or them that will sue for the same; to be recovered, by Action of Debt, Bill, Plaint, or Information, in any Court of Record within this Government, wherein no Essoign, Protection, Injunction, or Wager of Law shall be allowed or admitted of.

VI. And be it further Enacted, by the Authority aforesaid, That all and every Person or Persons, other than the said Indians who are now dwelling on any of the Land within the Bounds above mentioned, to have been allotted, laid out, and prescribed to the said Tuskerora Indians, shall, on or before the Twenty Fifth Day of March, next ensuing the Ratification of this Act, remove him or herself and Family off the said Land, under the Penalty of Twenty Pounds, Proclamation Money; And if any Person or Persons, other than the said Indians, shall neglect or refuse to move him or herself and Family off the said Lands, on or before the Twenty Fifth Day of March next; and if any Person or Persons, other than the said Indians, shall hereafter presume to settle, inhabit, or occupy any of the said Lands hereby allotted and assigned for the said Tuskerora Indians; such Person or Persons shall forfeit the further Penalty of Twenty Shillings, Proclamation Money, for each and every Day he, or she, or they shall inhabit or occupy any Lands within the said Indian Bounds, after the said Twenty Fifth Day of March next; and the said Penalties to be recovered and applied in the same Manner as the Penalty in this Act first above mentioned.

VII. And whereas the said Lands belonging to the Tuskerora Indians, have been lately laid out and new Marked, by George Gould, Esq., Surveyor General, at the Request of the said Indians; Therefore be it Enacted, That the said George Gould, Esq., have and receive, for the Trouble and Expence he hath been at in laying out and marking the Indians' Land aforesaid, the Sum of Twenty Five Pounds, Proclamation Money; to be paid by the Public out of the Monies in the Public Treasury.

VIII. And whereas the Indians complain of Injuries received from People driving Stocks of Horses, Cattle, and Hogs, to range on their Lands; for Remedy whereof, Be it Enacted, That Persons driving Stocks to range, or Stocks Actually ranging on the Indians' Lands, shall, and are hereby declared, to be liable and subject to the like Penalties and Forfeitures, and may be proceeded against in the same Manner, and subject to the same Recoveries, as by the Law of this Province Stocks driven or ranging upon any White People's Land are liable and subject to; and the said Indians shall and may enjoy the Benefit of the Laws in that Case made and provided, in the same Manner as the white People do or can; any Law, Usage, or Custom, to the contrary notwithstanding.

Chapter II.
Page 332
1749. "An Act to confirm the several Acts of Assembly of this Province therein mentioned ... "

Page 333
1749. "An Act for restraining the Indians from molesting or injuring the Inhabitants of this Government: and for securing to the Indians the Right and Property of their own Lands."

Page 334
1749. "An Act for an additional Tax on all free Negroes, Mulattoes, Mustees, and such persons, male and female, as now, or hereafter shall be intermarried with any such Persons resident in this Government."

Page 340
1749. "An Act for ascertaining the Bounds of a certain Tract of Land, formerly laid out by a Treaty, to the Use of the Tuskerora Indians, so long as they, or any of them, shall occupy and live upon the same; and to prevent any Person or Persons taking up Lands or settling within the said Bounds, by Pretence of any Purchase or Purchases made, or that shall be made, from the said Indians."

Chapter III.
1749. An additional Act to an Act for obtaining an exact List of Taxables; and for the effectual Collecting as well as all Arrears of Taxes, as all other Taxes, for the future due and payable. (Page 345).
    II. "Be it Enacted, by his Excellency Gabriel Johnston, Esq., Governor, by and with the Advice and Consent of his Majesty's Council,

North Carolina Law

and General Assembly of this Province, and by the Authority of the same, That all and every White Person, Male, of the Age of Sixteen Years, and upwards, all Negroes, Mulattoes, Mustees Male or Female, and all Persons of Mixt Blood, to the Fourth Generation, of the Age of Twelve Years, and upwards, and all Persons of Mixt Blood, while to intermarry with no other Person or Persons whatsoever, shall be deemed Taxables: Any Law, Usage, or Custom, to the Contrary, notwithstanding."

III. And whereas it sometimes happens, that through Death or Removal of the several Constables out of their respective Counties, the several Masters, Mistresses, or Overseers, are not duly summoned to appear, and give in, upon Oath, their respective Lists, whereby Deficiencies have happened and Disputes arisen: For Remedy whereof;

IV. Be it Enacted, by the Authority aforesaid, That every Master or Mistress of a Family, or Overseer of a Plantation, of which there is no Master or Mistress, within the County, although not summoned, is hereby required to appear before one of his Majesty's Justices of the Peace for the County, on or before the Second Court to be held for the County, after the First Day of May, Yearly, and to give in his or her List of Taxables, setting forth in such List, the Name and Sex of each Taxable Person, whether white or black, bond or free, and distinguishing such Male Slaves as are Sixteen Years of Age, and upwards; under the Penalty of Forty Shillings, Proclamation Money, over and above Twenty Shillings, like Money, for each and every Month he or she shall neglect giving in such List, after the said Second Court to be held for the said County, after the said First Day of May: To be recovered in any Court, or before two Justices of the Peace, according as the same may be cognizable, by Action of Debt, Bill, Plaint, or Information; wherein no Essoign, Protection, Injunction, or Wager of Law, shall be allowed or admitted of: One Half to the Informer, and the other Half to be paid to the Justices, for the Use of the County where the same shall be recovered.

CHAPTER VI.
1753. An additional Act to an Act concerning servants and slaves. (Pages 388-390).

I. Whereas by an Act, intitled An Act concerning Servants and Slaves, among other Things, it is provided, that no Slave shall go armed with Gun, Sword, Club, or any other Weapon, or shall keep any such Weapon, or shall hunt or range in the Woods with Gun, upon any pretence

North Carolina Law

whatever, except such Slave or Slaves who shall have a Certificate, as is in the said Act provided: and whereas the Remedy in the said Act provided has proved ineffectual to restrain many Slaves in divers Parts of this Province from going armed, which may prove of dangerous Consequence: for Remedy whereof,

II. We pray it may be Enacted, And be it Enacted, by the Honorable Matthew Rowan, Esq., President, by and with the advice and consent of his Majesty's Council, and the General Assembly of this Province, That from and after the passing of this Act, no Certificate shall be signed by any Chairman of any County Court in this Province, allowing any slave to carry a Gun and hunt in the Woods, unless the Master, Mistress, or Manager of such Slave, shall first enter into Bond, with sufficient security, to the County Court, either before, or at the time such Certificate shall be given, for the good and honest Behaviour of such Slave; which Bond may be assigned over to any Person or Persons who shall be injured by such Slave; which Assignee shall and may maintain an Action thereon, and recover such damages as he or she shall or may sustain by such Slave, in any Court of Record in this Province, by Action of Debt, Bill, Plaint, or Information; wherein no Essoign, Injunction, Protection, or Wager of Law, shall be allowed or admitted of.

III. And be it further Enacted, That no slave shall have or carry a Gun in any Plantation where a Crop is not tended, nor more than one in any Plantation where there is Crop tended, nor after Crop is Housed: And the Master, Mistress or overseer of any Slave, with whom shall be found any Gun, Sword, or other Weapon, contrary to the true intent and meaning of this and the before recited Act, shall forfeit and pay, to the person finding the same, the Sum of Twenty Shillings, Proclamation Money; to be recovered by a Warrant before any Justice of the Peace for the County where the Offence shall be committed, any punishment inflicted on the Slave, forfeiture of the Gun, Sword, or other Weapon notwithstanding; unless such Master, Mistress, or Overseer shall by their own Oath, or other Proof, make appear that such Slave carrying a Gun, Sword, or other Weapon, was without their Consent or Knowledge.

IV. And be it further Enacted, That the Justices of each County Court, when and where they judge it necessary, shall divide their respective Counties into Districts, and yearly, at the first Court to be held for their Counties respectively after the first day of May, shall appoint three Freeholders in each District as Searchers, who shall take the following Oath, viz:

North Carolina Law

I, A.B., do swear that I will, as Searcher for Guns, Swords, and other Weapons, among the Slaves in my District faithfully, and as privately as I can, discharge the Trust reposed in me, as the Law directs, to the best of my power. So help me God.

Which Searchers shall four Times in a Year or oftener if they think necessary, search and examine the Quarters and the other Places where Negroes resort in their District, for any Gun, Sword, or other Weapon, and upon finding any of the said Weapons, are hereby required to seize the same, and convert them to their own use, as by the afore-recited Act is directed.

V. And be it further Enacted, That any Person appointed Searcher as aforesaid, who shall neglect or refuse to act, shall forfeit and pay the Sum of Forty Shillings, Proclamation Money, , to such Person, who shall next succeed him; to be recovered as other Fines in this Act mentioned.

VI. And for the Encouragement of such Searchers faithfully to execute their Office, Be it further Enacted, by the authority aforesaid, That each and every Searcher shall, as to his own Person, be, during the Time of his Continuance in his Office, exempted from serving as a Constable, or upon the Roads, or in the Militia, or as a Juror, and shall not be obliged to pay any Provincial, County, or Parish Tax, of what Kind or Nature soever.

VII. Provided always, That no Person but such as are liable to be appointed Constables, shall be obliged to serve as Searchers; any Thing in this Act to the contrary, notwithstanding.

VIII. And be it Enacted, by the authority aforesaid, That no Slave shall hunt or range in the Woods with a Dog or Dogs, except such as shall have a Certificate for hunting, obtained as in this Act directed: And if any Slave shall be found offending herein, it shall and may be lawful for any Person or Persons to kill and destroy the said Dog or Dogs, and to bring the said Slave before the next Magistrate, who shall on due Proof of his Offence, order the said Slave such Correction as he shall judge reasonable, not exceeding thirty lashes.

IX. And be it further Enacted, by the authority aforesaid, That if any Slave or Slaves shall be killed on outlawry, or shall commit any Crime or Misdemeanor for which, he, she, or they, shall be capitally convicted, the Owner of such Slave or Slaves so outlawed or executed, shall be debarred all claim on the Public for the Value of such Slave or Slaves, and the Justices of the County Court and Freeholders, who shall value the Slave or Slaves so killed, or sit on the Trial of such Slave or Slaves so capitally convicted, shall not make any certificate of the value of the same, unless it shall be made appear, on Motion for such Certificate, by the Owner, or some other Person, that such Slave or Slaves, killed on outlawry, or capitally convicted, shall have been sufficiently cloathed, and shall likewise have constantly received, for the preceeding Year, an Allowance not less than a Quart of Corn per Diem.

X. And be it Enacted, by the authority aforesaid, That in case any Slave or Slaves, who shall not appear to have been cloathed and fed according to the Intent and Meaning of this Act, shall be convicted of stealing any Corn, Cattle, Hogs, or other Goods whatsoever, from any Person not the owner of such Slave or Slaves, such injured Person shall and may maintain an Action of Trespass against the Master, Owner, or Possessor of such Slave, in the General or County Court, and shall recover his or her Damages, with Costs of Suit; any Law, Usage, or Custom, to the contrary notwithstanding.

****

THE STATE RECORDS OF NORTH CAROLINA
VOLUME XXV., SUPPLEMENT, 1669-1771
EDITED BY: WALTER L. CLARK
NASH BROTHERS BOOK AND JOB PRINTERS
GOLDSBORO, N.C., 1906

CHAPTER I.
1754. An Act, for Establishing the Supreme Courts of Justice, Oyer and Terminer, and General Gaol Delivery of North Carolina. (Page 283).

XXXIII. And be it further Enacted, That if any Person who shall be summoned as a Witness, and upon his or her Appearance in either of the Supreme Courts, or any County Court, or before any Person appointed to take Depositions as aforesaid, shall refuse to give Evidence, upon Oath, such Person so refusing, shall immediately be thereupon committed to the Common Gaol, there to remain without Bail or mainprize, until he or she shall be willing to give Evidence, in such Manner as the Law now doth, or hereafter at any Time, shall direct.

XXXIV. Provided always, That the People called Quakers, shall have the same Liberty of giving their Evidence by way of solemn Affirmation or Declaration as by an Act of Parliament, made in the Eighth of the Reign of the late King George, intituled, An Act, for granting to the People called Quakers, such Terms of Affirmation or Declaration, as may remove the Difficulties which many of them lie under; and that all Negroes and Mulattoes, bond or free, to the Third Generation, and Indian Servants and Slaves, shall be deemed and taken to be incapable in Law to be Witnesses, in any Cause whatsoever, except against each other.

CHAPTER VI.
1754. An Act for securing the payment of Quit Rents due to His Majesty, and Earl Granville, for quieting the Freeholders in the Possession of their lands, and for other Purposes. (Page 308).
XVI. And be it further Enacted by the Authority aforesaid, That where any person or persons shall hold Lands under his Majesty or the Earl Granville and and shall fail to pay the Quit Rents due for the same it shall be Lawful for the Sheriff or such other person as shall be Lawfully authorized by Warrant of Distress to Distrain any Slaves, Goods and Chattels, which shall be found on the Land or in the possession of the person so indebted or failing to pay notwithstanding such Slaves, Goods and Chattels shall be comprized in any Deed of Mortgage, and if the Quit Rents shall not be paid nor the said Slaves, Goods or Chattles replevyed within five days after such Distress such Sheriff, or other person so authorized as aforesaid shall & may Lawfully sell by auction ye Slaves, Goods and Chattels distrained or so much thereof as shall be sufficient to satisfy the said Quit Rents and the Charges of Distress & Sale But shall give Notice by Advertisement of the Day and Place of sale at the Court House of the County where such Distress shall be made and also at the Church Door or most publick place of worship in the Parish where the same distress shall be made and by publishing the same among the people immediately after Divine Service on the next Sunday after the expiration of the said five days which sale shall not be in less than three nor more than six Days after notice so given and shall be good and effectual in Law. Provided, That no sheriff or other Person, authorized as herein before mentioned shall at any time make or take unreasonable Distress, or seize or Distrain the Slave or Slaves of any Person for Quit Rents if other sufficient Distress can be had upon penalty of being liable to the action of the party grieved grounded on this Act wherein the plaintiff shall recover his full Costs although the Damages do not exceed twenty five shillings.

North Carolina Law

****

THE COLONIAL RECORDS OF NORTH CAROLINA
VOLUME V., 1752-1759
EDITED BY: WILLIAM SAUNDERS
JOSEPHUS DANIELS, PRINTER TO THE STATE

8 JANUARY 1755
(Page 295).
The petition of sundry Inhabitants of the Counties of Northampton, Edgecombe, and Granville was read setting forth that by the laws now in force free negroes and Mulattoes Intermarrying with white women are obliged to pay taxes for their wives and Families Praying Relief and on which the House Resolved that the Matters in the said petition contained are reasonable and that the Committee appointed to Revise the Laws receive a Clause or Clauses to be inserted in the said Laws for their Relief.

****

THE STATE RECORDS OF NORTH CAROLINA
VOLUME XXIII., 1715-1776
EDITED BY: WALTER CLARK
NASH BROTHERS BOOK AND JOB PRINTERS
GOLDSBORO, NORTH CAROLINA, 1904

CHAPTER XIII.
1756. An Act for the Regulation of the Town of Wilmington. (Page 458).

XI. And be it further Enacted, by the authority aforesaid, That the Commissioners of the said Town for the Time being, or the Majority of them, are hereby impowered to pass such Orders as they may judge proper for the bringing to Justice, or prosecute those who shall deal or traffick with Negroes, without proper Tickets from their Masters, mistresses, or Overseers; and for preventing all Mobs or Cabals of Negroes, or others; for the more effectually bringing to Justice all Criminals and Offenders against the Laws of this Province; and also for preserving the Peace and Safety of the said Town; to appoint proper Guards or Watches in the said Town, as often as Occasion may Require; to be ready on all Occasions of Riot and Disturbance, or to prevent Malefactors breaking the Prison or Gaol.

Provided that one of the Commissioners be of the Number of the said Watch, to give necessary Orders.

****

THE STATE RECORDS OF NORTH CAROLINA
VOLUME XXV., SUPPLEMENT, 1669-1771
EDITED BY: WALTER L. CLARK
NASH BROTHERS BOOK AND JOB PRINTERS
GOLDSBORO, N.C., 1906

CHAPTER VIII.
1757. An Act for Preserving Peace and continuing a good Correspondence with the Indians in Alliance with his Majesty's Subjects. (Pages 356-358).

I. Whereas, nothing can contribute more to the welfare and security of the British Colonies in North America than the preserving a sincere Peace and friendly Correspondence with the several Nations or Tribes of Indians bordering thereon, And it hath been represented that many flagrant Frauds and Abuses have been too frequently committed in the commercial dealings of his Majesty's Subjects with the said Indians, which cannot but tend to alienate their Affections, and give the French the greater opportunity of insinuating themselves and carrying on their destructive Schemes against the British Colonies, and Whereas, his Majesty hath been pleased to appoint the Honorable Edmund Atkins, Esquire, to be Agent for and Superintendent of the Affairs of several Nations or Tribes of Indians inhabiting the Frontiers of Virginia, North and South Carolina, and Georgia, and their Confederates, in order therefore to render the Execution of a Commission of so great importance to the welfare and security of his Majesty's Colonies the more Effectual to the good purposes for which it is intended, Be it Enacted by the Governor, Council and Assembly, and by the Authority of the same, That from and after the first day of May next no Person whatsoever shall presume to deal or Traffic with either the Catawbas or Cherokees or other Western Indians within the limits of this Province without having first obtained a License or Permission for such purpose from The Honorable Edmund Atkins, Esq., his Majesty's Agent for an Superintendent of Indian Affairs in Virginia, North and South Carolina and Georgia and given Bond with two sufficient Sureties in the Sum of two hundred Pounds Proclamation Money Payable to the said

Edmund Atkins, or his Successor in Office, with Condition that he and those he shall employ shall demean themselves honestly and innoffensively to the Indians with whom he shall have License to deal and duly observe such Instructions and Orders in Writing as shall for the purposes aforesaid and for the better regulation of Trade be given to him from time to time by the said Edmund Atkins, or his Successor in Office.

II. And be it further Enacted by the Authority aforesaid, That if any Person whatever shall after the said first day of May next, Trade or Traffick with any of the said Indian Nations within the limits of this Province without having obtained a License or permission agreeable to the direction of this Act he shall forfeit the sum of two hundred Pounds to be recovered by such person as will sue for the same in any Court of Record, one half to his own use and the other half to the use of his Majesty towards defraying the Contingent charges of Government. And it shall and may be lawful for the said Edmund Atkins, or his Successor in Office, to cause the Person so offending to be Arrested and to seize his Goods and to cause the Goods so seized after Ten days notice by advertisement to be sold at Public Auction and the Money arising by such Sale to lay out for presents to be distributed among the said Indians in such manner as the said Edmund Atkins, or his Successor in Office, shall think most likely to fix and confirm the said Indians in Friendship and Amity with his Majesty's subjects. And to cause the Person so arrested to enter into Bond to the said Edmund Atkins, or his Successor in Office in the Sum of Two Hundred Pounds Proclamation Money with Conditions that he shall not thereafter deal with any of the said Indians contrary to the form and Effect of this Act. And in Case the person so offending shall fail or refuse to give Bond and Security as aforesaid, The said Edmund Atkins, or his Successor in Office, shall and may cause such Offender to be sent to the Public Gaol of the district wherein such Offence is committed till he shall before the Supreme Court or the Chief Justice, or one other of the Justices of the said Supreme Court enter into recognizance with two sufficient Sureties in the Sum of Five Hundred Pounds Proclamation Money, for his good behaviour for one Year.

III. And be it further Enacted by the Authority aforesaid, That if the said Edmund Atkins, or any other Person or Persons, shall be sued for by reason of any Act or thing by him or them done agreeable to the directions of this Act, he or they may plead the general Issue and give this Act in Evidence. And the Plaintiff, if he shall be cast on the Trial, shall pay double Costs.

North Carolina Law

IV. And be it further Enacted, That this Act shall continue and be in force Two Years from the said first Day of May next and no longer. **This Act repealed by Act of 1758, chapter XIX., p. 501.**

****

THE STATE RECORDS OF NORTH CAROLINA
VOLUME XXIII., 1715-1776
EDITED BY: WALTER L. CLARK
NASH BROTHERS BOOK AND JOB PRINTERS
GOLDSBORO, N.C., 1904

CHAPTER VII.
1758. An additional Act, intituled, An Act concerning Servants and Slaves. (Pages 488-489).

    I. Whereas many great Charges have arisen to the Province by Punishment of Slaves, who having Liberty from their Owners to hire themselves out, and having committed Robberies; by the Importation of Slaves from Foreign Parts for Crimes by them committed; by the condemnation of Slaves to Death for capital Crimes, for want of a punishment adequate to the Crimes they have been guilty of; and by the high Valuation of Slaves condemned to Death, or killed by Virtue of an Outlawry;

    II. Be it Enacted, by the Governor, Council, and Assembly, and by the authority of the same, That no Person who shall Permit any Slave to hire himself or herself out, shall be intitled to receive any Pay from the Public, should they be punished for any Crimes by them committed during the Time of such permission; any Usage or Custom, to the contrary, notwithstanding.

    III. And be it further Enacted, by the Authority aforesaid, That no Person hereafter purchasing any Slave, transported for Crimes from foreign Parts, into this Province, shall be intitled to receive any Payment from the Public, should such Slave afterwards be convicted and punished for any Crimes committed within this Province; unless he first make Oath, in the Court appointed for trying such Slave, that he did not at the Time of his purchasing, know that such Slave had been transported here for any Crimes committed in Foreign Parts.

    IV. And be it further Enacted, by the Authority aforesaid, That no male Slave shall for the First Offence, be condemned to death, unless

North Carolina Law

for Murder or Rape; but for every other Capital Crime, shall for the First Offence, suffer castration, which punishment every Court trying such Slave, shall be empowered, and are hereby directed to cause to, be inflicted; and the Sheriff shall cause such Judgment to be duly Executed; for which he shall have and receive, from the Public, Twenty Shillings, Proclamation Money, and no more; any Usage or Custom to the contrary, notwithstanding.

V. Provided always, That such Slave be valued by the Court Trying him, in the Usual Manner, that in case Death should ensue the Owner might be paid by the Public; and that the Sum of Three Pounds, Proclamation Money, shall be allowed and paid by the Public, to defray the expence of the Cure, of each Slave Castrated.

VI. And be it further Enacted, by the Authority aforesaid, That there shall not be allowed by the Public to the owner of any Slave which shall hereafter happen to be convicted of any Capital Offence, killed on outlawry, or in being apprehended when run away, more than the Sum of Sixty Pounds, Proclamation Money; any Law or Custom to the contrary, notwithstanding.

The 3 last sections of this act repealed by act of Oct. 25, 1764, ch. 8. The remainder repealed by act Nov. 18, 1786, ch. 17. [See Iredell's Laws, 1791, p. 184.]

CHAPTER XIX.
1758. An Act for repealing an Act therein mentioned. (Page 501).

I. Whereas an Act of Assembly, entitled, An Act for preserving Peace, and continuing a good Correspondence with the Indians in Alliance with his Majesty's Subjects, has not procured the good Effects hoped for; but, on the contrary, is likely to alienate the Affections of the said Indians from the Inhabitants of this Province:

II. Be it therefore enacted by the Governor, Council, and Assembly, and the Authority of the same, That the said recited Act, and every Clause and Article thereof, shall be from henceforth repealed, and made null and void.

****

THE STATE RECORDS OF NORTH CAROLINA
VOLUME XXV., SUPPLEMENT, 1669-1771

North Carolina Law

EDITED BY: WALTER L. CLARK
NASH BROTHERS BOOK AND JOB PRINTERS
GOLDSBORO, N.C., 1906

CHAPTER I.
1759. An Act to Amend and Continue an Act, Intituled, an Act for the better Regulation of the Militia, and for other Purposes. (Page 393).

I. Whereas, an Act Intitluled an Act for the better Regulation of the Militia, and other Purposes, is near expiring and the Power by the said Act for raising Militia and Marching them agains the Enemy, is limited to the Opposing Invasions and Supporting Expeditions within this Province only,

II. And Whereas, it is absolutely necessary on this present Immergency that part of the Militia should march to joyn the Troops of South Carolina, now near our Frontier, and upon an Expedition to Obtain Satisfaction of the Cherokee Indians, for divers Murders and Depredations committed by them on our back Settlements, for remedy whereof,

III. Be it Enacted by the Governor, Council and Assembly, and by the Authority of the same, That the Governor or Commander in Chief for the time being, by, and with the Advice and Consent of His Majesty's Council, may during the Continuance of this Act, Order to be raised and Marched out of this Province so many of the Militia as shall be judged expedient to joyn the Forces of our Neighboring Provinces of South Carolina and Virginia in Opposing any Invasions or Supporting any Expedition against the Common Enemy, And the Several Officers and Soldiers so raised shall be under the same rules and regulations and lyable to the same pains and Punishments as are Provided in the before recited Act in case of Invasions within this Province.

CHAPTER II.
1759. An Act for Granting an Aid to His Majesty for paying and Subsisting the Forces and Militia now in the pay of this Province, and for other Purposes. (Pages 394-395).

I. Whereas, the Cherokee Indians contrary to their Allegiance have lately committed several horrid Murders and Depredations on his Majesty's Subjects in this and the Neighbouring Provinces, and the present Assembly out of a desire of Satisfaction for the same, as well as to prevent future Injuries of the like kind, have by one Act of Assembly, Intituled, An

Act to amend and continue an Act, Intituled, "An Act for the better Regulation of the Militia, and for other Purposes," Impowered his Excellency the Governor to March the Troops now in the Pay of this Province and so many of the Militia thereof, as he shall think necessary to Join the Forces of South Carolina in an Expedition intended against the said Cherokees.

II. Be it therefore Enacted by the Governor, Council and Assembly, and it is hereby Enacted by the Authority of the same, That his Excellency the Governor, may and he is hereby Authorized and Impowered to Order the Troops now in the Pay of this Province, and so many of the Militia thereof as he shall think necessary to March and Join the Forces of South Carolina in an Expedition as aforesaid, and to continue on the said Duty until the tenth day of February next, if His Majesty's Service shall so long require it, and no longer.

CHAPTER II.
1760. An Act for the better Care of Orphans, ,and Security and Management of their Estates. (Pages 418-419).

XIII. And be it further Enacted by the Authority aforesaid, That it shall and may be lawful for every Guardian to charge in his Account all reasonable disbursements and expences, and if upon rendering such Account it shall appear to the Court that such Guardian hath really and bona fide disbursed more in one Year than the profits in the Orphan's Estate do amount unto for the education and maintenance of the Orphan, such Guardian shall be allowed and paid for the same out of the Profits of such Orphan's Estate in any other Year.

Provided always, That such disbursements be in the Opinion of such Court suitable to the degree and circumstances of the Estate of such Orphan, and that where such Estate shall be of so small value that no person will educate and maintain him or her for the profit thereof, such Orphan shall by direction of the Court be Bound apprentice, every male to some Tradesman, Merchant, Mariner or other person approved by the Court, until he shall attain to the Age of Twenty one Years, and every Female to some Suitable Employment 'til her age of eighteen years, and also such Court may in like manner bind apprentice all free base born children, and every such Female Child being a Mulatto or Mustee, until she shall attain the Age of Twenty one Years, and the Master or Mistress of every such apprentice shall find and provide for him or her diet, cloaths, lodging and Accommodation, fit and necessary and shall teach, or cause him or her to be taught, to Read and Write and at the Expiration of his or her apprenticeship, shall pay every such apprentice the like allowance as is by Law appointed for servants by indenture or Custom, and on refusal shall be Compelled thereto in like manner, and if upon Complaint made to the Inferior Court of Pleas and Quarter Sessions it shall appear that any such apprentice is ill used, or not taught the trade, profession, or Employment, to which he or she was bound, it shall be Lawful for such Court to remove and bind him or her to such other person or persons as they shall think fit.

CHAPTER I.
1760. An Act, for establishing Superior Courts of Pleas and Grand Sessions, and Regulating the Proceedings therein. (Page 445).
      XLV. Provided always, That the party praying such Commission as aforesaid, shall make known to the adverse Party, the Time and Place when and where such Commission is to be executed, at least Ten days before the Execution thereof; and the adverse Party shall have Liberty to cross examine any Witness or Witnesses whose Deposition otherwise taken than is herein directed, unless by Consent of Parties, shall be void, to all Intents and Purposes; And if any Person who shall be summoned as a Witness in either of the Superior Courts, or before any Person appointed to take Depositions as aforesaid, shall refuse to give Evidence, on Oath, such Person so refusing, shall be committed to the common Gaol, there to remain without Bail or Mainprize, until he or she shall be willing to give Testimony in such Manner as the Law now doth, or hereafter shall direct: Provided, That the People called Quakers, shall have the same Liberty of giving their Evidence, by Way of solemn Affirmation, as by Act of Parliament made in the Eighth Year of the Reign of his Majesty King George the First, intituled, An Act, for granting to the People called Quakers, such Terms of Affirmation or Declaration as may remove the Difficulty which many of them lie under; and that all Negroes, Indians, Mulattoes, and all of mixed Blood, descended from Negro or Indian Ancestors to the Third Generation, Bond or Free, shall be deemed and taken to be incapable in Law to be Witnesses in any Cause whatsoever, except against each other.

****

North Carolina Law

THE STATE RECORDS OF NORTH CAROLINA
VOLUME XXIII., 1715-1776
EDITED BY: WALTER L. CLARK
NASH BROTHERS BOOK AND JOB PRINTERS
GOLDSBORO, N.C., 1904

CHAPTER I.
1760. An Act for granting an aid to his Majesty. (Pages 516-518).

XIII. And for the greater Encouragement of Persons as shall enlist voluntarily to serve in the said Companies, and other Inhabitants of this Province who shall undertake any Expedition against the Cherokees, and other Indians in Alliance with the French; Be it further Enacted, by the Authority aforesaid, That each of the said Indians who shall be taken a Captive during the present War by any Person as aforesaid, shall, and is hereby declared to be a Slave, and the Absolute Right and Property of who shall be the Captor of such Indian; and shall and may be possessed, pass, go and remain to such Captor, his Executors, Administrators, and Assigns, as a Chattel personal; And if any Person or Persons, inhabitant or Inhabitants of this province, not in actual Pay, shall kill an Enemy Indian or Indians, he or they, shall have and receive Ten Pounds for each and every Indian he or they shall so kill; and any Person or Persons who shall be in the actual Pay of this Province, shall have and receive Five Pounds for every Enemy, Indian or Indians he or they shall so kill, to be paid out of the Treasury; any Law, Usage or Custom, to the contrary, notwithstanding.

XIV. Provided always, That any Person claiming the said Reward, before he be allowed or paid the same, shall produce to the Assembly the Scalp of every Indian so killed, and make Oath, or otherwise prove that he was the Person who killed, or was present at the killing the Indian whose Scalp shall be so produced; and that he hath not before had or received any allowance from the Public for the same; And as a further Encouragement, shall also have, and keep to his or their own Use or Uses, all Plunder taken out of the Possession of any Enemy Indian or Indians, or within Twenty Miles of any of the Cherokee Towns, or any Indian Town at War with any of his Majesty's Subjects.

XV. And be it further Enacted, by the Authority aforesaid, That Two Thousand Pounds of the Remainder of the aforesaid Twelve Thousand Pounds, shall be, and is hereby appropriated, to and for the Payment of the aforesaid Rewards to such Person and Persons as, by killing any of the aforesaid Indians, shall be intitled to receive the same; but if a less Sum

North Carolina Law

shall be found sufficient for the said Purpose, the Surplus shall be applied towards paying the several Creditors of the Public such Claims as already have been, or shall be allowed by the General Assembly, and to any other Purpose: And the Residue of the said Twelve Thousand Pounds is hereby appropriation to and for the Payment of the Debts of the Public, chargeable on the Contingent Fund, and shall not be otherwise applied.

CHAPTER II.
1760. An Act for obtaining an exact List of Taxables, and for the effectual collecting all Taxes for the Future due and payable, and other Purposes therein mentioned. (Pages 526-527).
    I. Whereas it appears, by the List of Taxables delivered in by the Magistrates at the several and respective Counties of this Province, that a full and compleat List has never yet been obtained by any Law now in Force; and whereas the equal Payment of Taxes is of great Consequence; therefore;
    II. Be it Enacted by the Governor, Council, and Assembly, and by the Authority of the same, That all and every white Person, Male, of the Age of Sixteen Years and upwards, all Negroes, Mulattoes, Mustees, Male and Female, and all Persons of Mixt Blood to the Fourth Generation, of the age of Twelve Years and upwards, and all white Persons intermarrying with any Negro, Mulatto, Mustee, or other Person of Mixt Blood, while so intermarried, and no other Person or Persons whatsoever, shall be deemed Taxables; any Law, Usage, or Custom, to the contrary notwithstanding.
    III. And be it further Enacted, by the Authority aforesaid, That from the passing of this Act, the Method for obtaining an exact List of Taxables shall be in the following Manner, any Law, Usage, or Custom, to the contrary notwithstanding; that is to say, the Justices of each County shall, at the next Court to be held for their respective Counties after the First Day of May next, and so yearly, issue their Warrant, signed by the Chairman, directed to the Constable in each and every District in the respective Counties, Authorizing and commanding him to go from House to House in his District, and summon the Master or Mistress of every Family, and the Overseer of every Plantation of which there is no Master or Mistress within his District to appear, and they are hereby required to appear, before the Magistrate that shall be appointed by the Court to receive the List of Taxables in such District preceeding the Time of holding the then next Court to be held for such County, and there to give in, upon

North Carolina Law

Oath, a List in Writing of all the Taxables in his or her Family, setting forth in such List the Name and Sex of each Taxable Person, whether white or black, bond or free, and distinguishing such Male Slaves as are Sixteen Years of Age or upwards and the Constable of each and every District shall likewise give in to the Magistrates of his District a List, upon Oath, of all such Persons so warned, which List shall contain the Names of all the Masters and Mistresses of Families, and Overseers of Plantations, within his District; And in Case any Constable shall die, remove, or be anywise rendered incapable of serving in his Office, the Magistrate of such District is hereby required to appoint and Qualify another Person to act as a Constable to serve in such District, until the Time appointed by Law for appointing a Constable, which Constable so appointed, shall be under the like Rules and Penalties as the former Constable.

    IV. And be it further Enacted, by the Authority aforesaid, That each Constable neglecting to summon the Master, Mistress, or Overseer, as aforesaid, or neglecting to return such List as is herein before directed, shall forfeit and pay the Sum of Five Pounds, Proclamation Money, for each and every Neglect; to be recovered and applied as is by this Act Directed.

    V. And be it further Enacted, by the Authority aforesaid, That the Court of each and every respective County shall, at the same Court they appoint Constables, appoint one Magistrate for each District to take and receive the List of Taxables for such District; which Justice so appointed is hereby required and directed to receive, upon Oath, from all Persons that are liable that offer to enlist, being Inhabitants of such District, and shall make a List of all such, and shall compare the same with the Constable's List returned to Him, and if it shall appear that any Person or Persons within his District that ought inlist him or herself according to the Directions of this Act, hath failed to do so, or that the Constable hath failed to summon any such Person or Persons, such Justice shall report the same to the second Court to be held for such County after the First Day of May, and also shall return to the said Court the Constable's List, and the List of Taxables by him so taken, that all such Person or Persons as have failed in their Duty may be prosecuted; and such Justice shall set forth in his List the Names of every Master or Mistress of Families, and Overseers of Plantations of which there is no Master or Mistress in the County, the Name and sex of each Taxable Person, whether white or black, bond or free, and distinguishing such Male Slaves as are sixteen Years old and upwards.

CHAPTER VIII.
1760. An Act for raising Money by a Lottery, towards finishing the Churches at Wilmington and Brunswick; and for applying the Produce of the Slaves, and other Effects taken from the Spaniards at Cape Fear, in the Year of our Lord One Thousand Seven Hundred and Forty Eight, to the same Purposes. (Pages 536-537).

VII. And whereas the finishing the building of the said Two Churches will be greatly expedited, provided the Money arising by the Sale of the Slaves, and other effects saved out of the Wreck of the Spanish Privateer that blew up before Brunswick, in the Year One Thousand Seven Hundred and Forty Eight, and is now in Private Hands, unapplied to any Public use, might be appropriated to the compleating the said Two Churches: Be it Enacted by the Authority aforesaid, That the Slaves and other Effects, saved out of the Spanish Wreck as aforesaid, or taken from the Spaniards at the Time of their Invasion, not already sold; as also the money arising by the Sale of those which have been sold, after deducting the Expences of such Sales, shall be applied towards the compleating the building the said Two Churches, in Manner following; that is to say, Two Third Parts of the Net Proceeds towards finishing the Church at Brunswick; and the other Third Part towards finishing the Church at Wilmington, and to no other use or purpose whatsoever.

VIII. And be it further Enacted, by the Authority aforesaid, That the Commissioners, by Law appointed, for building and finishing the said Churches, shall have full Power and Authority to ask for, demand, and receive, of and from each and every Person or Persons in whose Possession any of the Slaves, Money, or other Effects, saved or arising by the Sale of the Effects taken as aforesaid, and from their Heirs, Executors, and Administrators; and upon refusal, to sue for and recover the same, by Action upon the Case, in any Court of Record in this Province, Respect being had to their Jurisdiction; wherein no plea of the Act of Limitation of Actions, shall be allowed or admitted of.

CHAPTER XVII.
1762. An Act to establish a public Road from the Court House, in Currituck County, across the great Swamp, to the Bridge on North River, near the Indian Town.

North Carolina Law

See Iredell's Laws, 1791, p. 210. [This is considered a Private Law]

****

NORTH CAROLINA STATE ARCHIVES
GENERAL ASSEMBLY SESSIONS RECORDS
COLONIAL (UPPER AND LOWER HOUSE) BOX 2
FILE MARKED (LOWER HOUSE PAPERS)
9 NOVEMBER 1762

To the Worshipful the Speaker and Gentleman of the Assembly:
The petition of Sundry of the Inhabitants of the Counties of Northampton Edgecombe and Granville.
Humbly sheweth,
  That by an Act of Assembly passed in the Year 1723 Intitled "An Act for an Additional Tax on all free Negroes, Mulattoes, Mustees and such Persons Male and Female, as now are or hereafter shall be intermarried with any such Persons resident in this Government." Amongst other Things it was enacted That all free Negroes &C that were or shou'd thereafter be Inhabitants of this Province Male & Female & being of the Age of twelve Years & upwards shou'd be deemed Tythables and as such should Yearly pay the same Levies and Taxes as other Tythable Inhabitants. That many Inhabitants of the sd. Counties who are Free Negroes & Mulattoes and Persons of Probity & good Demeanor and cheerfully contribute towards the Discharge of every Public Duty injoined them by Law. But by reason of being obliged by the sd. Act of Assembly to pay Levies for their Wives and Daughters as therein mentioned and greatly Impoverished and many of them rendered unable to support themselves and Families with the common Necessaries of Life. Wherefore your Petitioners would humbly pray in behalf of the sd. Free Negroes &C. That so much of the said recited Act as compels such of them as Intermarry with those of their own complection to pay Taxes for their Wives and Daughters may be repealed Or that they may be otherwise relieved as to your Worships in Your great Wisdom soon.
  And your Petitioners as in Duty bound shall pray &C

Granville County   **Edgecombe**
Willm. Eaton   Jno Sallis   Jos. Jno.
Alston

North Carolina Law

Phil Hawkins Anderson
Thos. Lowe
Patrick Lashley
Fras. King
Aaron Fussel
Tho. Dulaney
Zack Bullock
John Williams
John Gibbs
Thos. Hampton
Moses Coppock
Wm. Johnson
Jona. Parker
Richd. Harris
Amus Newsum
Shurley Whately
John Martin
George Jordan
Northampton ?
John McCand
Benj. Nevill
James Brown
Joseph Strickland
Jacob Strickland
Ebenezer Folsom
William Richerson

Phil Pryor

Jno. Bowie
John Wade
George Buttler
William Falkner
John [?]
Thomas Woodliff
Marton Dickson
Amanuel Falkner
Ezekiel Fuller
James Smith
Wm. Smith
Jos. Brantly
James Brantly
Edwd. Young
Jno. Glover
John Hawkins

John Cheves
John Fish
Wm. Irby
Benjn. Sherrod
Nathan Joyner
Wm: Adams
Richd. McKinne

Willm.

Thos. Wood
John Jones

[The rest of this page is torn off. (WLB)]

****

THE STATE RECORDS OF NORTH CAROLINA
VOLUME XXIII., 1715-1776
EDITED BY: WALTER CLARK
NASH BROTHERS BOOK AND JOB PRINTERS
GOLDSBORO, NORTH CAROLINA, 1904

CHAPTER I.
1764. An Act for appointing a Militia. (Page 601).

XXIV. And be it further Enacted, by the Authority aforesaid, For the Encouragement for any Person or Persons who shall range and reconnoitre the Frontiers of this Province as Volunteers at his or their Own Expence; it shall and may be lawful for such Ranger or Rangers, in Case of an Indian War, or an Invasion of this Province by Indians, to kill or take Prisoner any Enemy Indian of what Nation soever; and on producing such Indian or Indians, his, her, or their Scalp or Scalps before any two Justices of the Peace of this Province, that are most convenient to the Place where the said Indian or Indians shall be taken or Killed, and due Proof made thereof on Oath, of such Indian or Indians being taken or killed in this Province, and producing a Certificate thereof from the said two Justices, together with the Indian or Indians' Scalps to the Assembly; such Person or Persons shall be intitled to Thirty Pounds, Proclamation Money, for each and every Captive or Scalp so taken and produced as aforesaid; to be paid out of the Public Treasury of this Province.

XXV. Provided nevertheless, That it shall not be lawful for any Party of Volunteers as aforesaid, to range or Reconnoitre the Frontiers of this Province, without leave first had from the Colonel or Commanding Officer of the Regiment to which they belong, and under the Command of an Officer appointed by Warrant from such Colonel or Commanding Officer.

XXVI. And be it further Enacted, by the Authority aforesaid, That this Act shall be and continue in Force for and during Three Years, and no longer.

CHAPTER IV.
1764. An Act concerning Vestries. (Page 602).

IV. And to prevent Disputes concerning who shall be understood to be a Freeholder capable of voting for Vestryman, Be it further Enacted, by the Authority aforesaid, That every Person in Actual Possession of an Estate real, for his own life, or the life of some other Person, or an Estate of greater Dignity, of Fifty Acres of Land, or a Lot in some Town, saved according to Law, in the Parish of which such Election shall be made, and no other Person whatsoever, shall be deemed a Freeholder within the meaning of this Act; And any one of the Candidates may, in Case he suspects any Person going to give his Vote hath not a Freehold within the Meaning of this Act, object such Person giving his vote, and require the Sheriff to tender him an Oath of Affirmation, concerning his Qualification; Which Oath or Affirmation the Sheriff is hereby impowered and directed to administer, in the following Words, to-wit:

You shall swear (or affirm) that you are in actual Possession of a Freehold of Fifty Acres of Land, in your Own Right, or the Right of some other Person; or a Lot in the Town of ------- saved according to Law, in the Parish of ------- and that you have not given your Vote before in this Election. So Help You God.

Chapter VIII.
1764. An Act to amend An Act therein mentioned, concerning Servants and Slaves. (Page 656).

I. Whereas by the Fourth, Fifth, and Sixth Sections of an Act of Assembly of this Province, passed in the Year of our Lord One Thousand Seven Hundred and Fifty Eight, intituled, an Additional Act to an Act Intituled, An Act concerning Servants and Slaves, it is Enacted, That no male Slave Shall, for the First Offence, be condemned to Death, unless for Murder or Rape; but for every other Capital Crime, shall, for the First Offence, suffer Castration; and that the Court trying such Slave shall value the same:

II. Be it Enacted, by the Governor, Council, and Assembly, and it is hereby Enacted, by the Authority of the same, That the Fourth, Fifth, and Sixth Sections of the aforesaid Act be, and are hereby, repealed and made void.

III. And be it further Enacted, by the Authority aforesaid, That there shall not be allowed by the Public to the Owner of any Slave who shall hereafter be executed in Virtue of the Judgment of the Court who shall try such Slave, any larger Sum than Eighty Pounds, Proclamation Money; any Law, Usage, or Custom to the Contrary notwithstanding.

Repealed by act, Nov. 18, 1786, ch. 7. [See Iredell's Laws, 1791, p. 219.]

****

THE STATE RECORDS OF NORTH CAROLINA
VOLUME XXV., SUPPLEMENT, 1669-1771
EDITED BY: WALTER L. CLARK
NASH BROTHERS BOOK AND JOB PRINTERS

North Carolina Law

GOLDSBORO, N.C., 1906

CHAPTER VII.
1766. An Act to amend an Act intitled, an Act for rendering more effectual the laws making Lands and other real Estates liable to the payment of debts. (Pages 496-498).

I. Whereas, an Act of Assembly passed at Wilmington the twenty fifth day of October, in the Year of our Lord One Thousand Seven hundred and Sixty four, Intitled an Act for rendering more effectual the laws making Lands and other real Estates liable for the payment of debts, hath by Experience been found Injurious and of pernicious Tendency, for remedy whereof,

II. Be it Enacted by the Governor, Council and Assembly, and it is hereby Enacted by the Authority of the same, That from and after the passing of this Act, every Sheriff or other Officer within this Province, who by Virtue of an Execution does expose to sale any Lands or negroes shall first Summons two Justices of the Peace and one Freeholder of the County wherein such lands are situated, to appear at a particular day by him directed diligently to inspect and true valuation of the same to render in writing under their hands and Seals, which said Instrument shall by them be produced before any other Justice of the said County wherein such lands are situated or Negroes taken in Execution, which Justices is hereby required to administer the following Oath, and make a Certificate thereof on the back of such Instrument, to wit: You and each of you shall swear that this Instrument of writing by you produced contains a true valuation of one (or more as the Case may be) tract or Tracts of Land Situate in the County of _____ on _____ (or Negroes as the Case may be) and taken by virtue of an Execution at the Instance of _____ and that you have proceeded in such Valuation without favor or dislike to either Party upon a careful view and according to the best of your knowledge and Information, So help you God; which said Instrument of writing with the certificate as aforesaid shall by them be delivered to the said Sheriffs who upon exposing such lands or Negroes to Sale, shall not dispose of them to any person or persons whatsoever for a less Sum than two thirds of such Valuation, under the Penalty of One Thousand Pounds Proclamation Money, to be recovered by an action of Debt in any Court of Record within this Province, by and for the use of the party Grieved. Provided always, if any Land or Lands, Negroe or Negroes, set up for sale as aforesaid, shall not be disposed of agreeable to the true intent and meaning of this Act, the

Plaintiff may, if he chooses, take the said Land or Negroes at two thirds the Valuation thereof, and the Sheriff is hereby Impowered and directed to give such Plaintiff a deed or bill of Sale for the same in the same manner as he might have done had the land or Negroes been sold at Public Vendue. Provided, also, that if the Plaintiff doth not take the Land at two thirds of the valuation the Sheriff or other officer shall again advertise them till they are Sold, and in Case the Justices and Freeholders when summoned by the Sheriff or other officer to value any lands or Negroes as aforesaid, shall neglect or refuse to attend, unless prevented by sickness or some very sufficient Cause, he or they so neglecting, shall forfeit and pay the Sum of Forty Shillings for such Neglect or refusal, to be recovered by a Warrant from any Justice of the peace in the County and to be applied to the use of the party injured.

III. And be it Further Enacted by the Authority aforesaid, that the said Sheriff or other Officer for summoning the Justices and Freeholders as aforesaid, shall be and is hereby Intitled to receive the Sum of two Shillings and Eight pence for each person so summoned.

IV. Provided always, That in Case any person at whose Suit any Execution against Lands or Negroes has or may issue as aforesaid, shall conceive himself aggrieved or injured by any such Valuation made as aforesaid, he may appeal to the Inferior Court of the County wherein such Lands or Negroes may be, who on examining into the matter (in a summary way) may appoint two other Justices and one other Freeholder to proceed in a second valuation of the said Lands or Negroes--under the aforesaid Oath and regulations, upon which valuation returned to the next Court, the Justices shall judge upon the same and determine without Appeal on the Valuation to be fixed on such Land or Negroes upon which valuation the Sheriff and parties shall proceed as aforesaid.

V. Provided always, That nothing in this Act contained shall be deemed or construed to extend to any Execution or Executions for any debt or debts payable to Merchants in Great Britain; or to any Executions already levied.

VI. And be it further Enacted by the Authority aforesaid, That this Act shall continue and be in force for and during the term of One Year, and from thence to the end of the next Session of Assembly, and no longer.

CHAPTER XXIX.

1766. An Act for confirming a lease made by the Tuscarora Indians to Robert Jones, Jun., William Williams and Thomas Pugh, Esquires. (Pages 507-509).

I. Whereas, a number of the Tuscarora Indians, being desirous of moving themselves from their lands on Roanoke river, in Bertie county, in this province, and settling and incorporating themselves with the nations of Indians on the River Susquehannah; and whereas, the said Tuscarora Indians, in order to defray the expence of removing themselves and their effects from this province to the settlements on the river Susquehannah, did, on the twelfth day of July, in the year one thousand seven hundred and fifty six, for the consideration of fifteen hundred pounds, proclamation money, before that time paid and advanced to them, the said Tuscarora Indians, by the said Robert Jones, William Williams and Thomas Pugh, by an indenture under the hands and seals of James Allen, John Wiggins, Billy George, Snip Nose George, Billy Cain, Charles Cornelius, Thomas Blount, John Rogers, George Blount, Wineoak Charles, Billy Basket, Billy Owen, Lewis Tuffdick, Isaac Miller, Harry, Samuel Bridgers, Thomas Seneca, Thomas Howit, Billy Socket, Billy Cornelius, John Seneca, Thomas Basket, John Cain, Billy Dennis, William Taylor, Owens, John Walker, Billy Mitchell, Billy Netop, Billy Blount, Tom Jack, John Lightwood, Billy Roberts, James Mitchell, Captain Joe, and William Pugh, chieftains and headmen of the said nation of Tuscarora Indians, for and on behalf of themselves and the rest of the Indians of the said Tuscarora nation, on the one part, and the said Robert Jones, William Williams and Thomas Pugh, of the other part, did demise, grant and to farm let, a certain dividend of land, situate and lying on Roanoke river, in the county aforesaid, containing about eight thousand acres, be the same more or less, and bounded as follows, towit: Beginning at the mouth of Deep creek, otherwise called Falling run, thence running up the said creek to the Indian head line; hence by the said line south fifty seven degrees east one thousand two hundred and eighty poles; thence a course parallell with the general current of the said creek to Roanoke river aforesaid, and up the river to the beginning; together with all trees, timber trees, woods, underwoods, ways, waters and appurtenances whatsoever, to the said dividend, tract or parcel of land belonging or in any wise appertaining; to have and to hold the said dividend, tract or parcel of land, with all and singular the appurtenances unto the said Robert Jones, William Williams and Thomas Pugh, their executors, administrators or assigns, without impeachment of waste, to be by the said Robert Jones, William Williams and Thomas Pugh, respectively, their executors, administrators and assigns, held and enjoyed in severalty; that is to say, one third part of the said dividend, tract or parcel of land, into three equal parts to be divided, unto the said Robert Jones, his executors, administrators and assigns; one other third part thereof, the same into three equal parts to be divided, unto the said William Williams, his executors, administrators and assigns; the remaining third part thereof, the same into three equal parts to be divided, unto the said Thomas Pugh, his executors, administrators and assigns; from the said twelfth day of July, in the year aforesaid, for and during the term of one hundred and fifty years from thence next ensuing, and fully to be compleated and ended, the said Robert Jones, William Williams and Thomas Pugh, their executors, administrators and assigns, yielding and paying therefor yearly, and every year during the said term, to the said Tuscarora Indians and their assigns one pepper corn, if demanded, at or upon feast of St. Michael the archangel.

II. And whereas, the said nation of Tuscarora Indians are desirous that the indenture of the lease made between the said James Allen, John Wiggins, Billy George, Snip Nose George, Billy Cain, Charles Cornelius, Thomas Blount, John Rogers, George Blount, Wineoak Charles, Billy Basket, Billy Owen, Lewis Tuffdick, Isaac Miller, Harry, Samuel Bridgers, Thomas Seneca, Thomas Howit, Billy Socket, Billy Cornelius, John Seneca, Thomas Basket, John Cain, Billy Dennis, William Taylor, Owens, John Walker, Billy Mitchell, Billy Netop, Billy Blount, Tom Jack, John Lightwood, Billy Roberts, James Mitchell, Captain Joe and William Pugh, Chieftains and headmen of the said nation of Tuscarora Indians, and the said Robert Jones, William Williams and Thomas Pugh, should have the force and validity of the Assembly; and that it shall be lawful for the said Robert Jones, William Williams and Thomas Pugh, their executors, administrators and assigns, to enter upon, occupy, possess and enjoy the said dividend, tract or parcel of land, demised as aforesaid, without let, hindrance or molestation of any person or persons whatsoever, and without incurring any penalties whatsoever by reason of their so entering upon, occupying, possessing and enjoying the said tract or parcel of land, without impeachment for waste.

III. And whereas, the said Robert Jones, since the said twelfth day of July, in the year aforesaid, hath departed this life, having first made his last will and testament, and therein and thereby bequeathed his proportion and share of the said tract or parcel of land, demised as before said, unto his sons Allen Jones and Willie Jones, their executors, administrators, and assigns;

IV. Be it therefore Enacted by the Governor, Council and Assembly, and by the Authority of the same, and it is hereby Enacted, That the said indenture of the demise is hereby ratified and confirmed; and it shall and may be lawful for the said Allen Jones and Willie Jones, in right of the said Robert Jones, the said William Williams, and Thomas Pugh, their executors, administrators, and assigns, to enter upon, occupy, possess, and enjoy the said dividend, tract or parcel of land, according to the form and effect of the said indenture of the demise; that is to say, that it shall and may be lawful for the said Allen and Willie Jones, their executors, administrators, and assigns, to enter upon, occupy, possess, and enjoy, one third part of the said dividend, tract or parcel of land, the same to be divided into three equal parts, for, and during the term aforesaid; the said William Williams, his executors, administrators and assigns, to enter upon, occupy, possess, and enjoy, one third part thereof, the same into three equal parts to be divided, for and during the term aforesaid; and the said Thomas Pugh, their executors, administrators, and assigns, to occupy, possess, the said dividend, tract or parcel of land demised as aforesaid, during the term aforesaid, without impeachment of waste, and without the let, molestation, or hindrance, of any person or persons whatsoever.

VI. Provided always, and be it Enacted, by the Authority aforesaid, That nothing herein contained shall be construed as to invalidate the title or titles of any person or persons who have obtained in a grant or grants for any tract or parcel of land within the limits or boundaries of the lands of the said Tuscarora Indians, before the fifteenth day of October, one thousand seven hundred and forty eight.

VII. Provided also, and it is hereby Enacted, by the authority aforesaid; That the said Allen Jones, Willie Jones, William Williams, and Thomas Pugh, their executors, administrators, and assigns, shall yearly and each year, during the term aforesaid, on the twenty first day of March pay the right honourable Earl of Granville, his heirs and assigns, a quit rent of four shillings, Proclamation Money, for every hundred acres of land contained within the limits or boundaries of the lands demised as aforesaid: and in case the said quit rents shall be in arrear at any time within the term aforesaid, that then it shall and may be lawful for the Earl of Granville, his heirs and assigns, to sue for and recover all such arrearages of rent, of and from the said Allen Jones, Willie Jones, William Williams, and Thomas

Pugh, their executors, administrators and assigns, by all lawful ways and means whatsoever.

****

THE STATE RECORDS OF NORTH CAROLINA
VOLUME XXIII., 1715-1776
EDITED BY: WALTER L. CLARK
NASH BROTHERS BOOK AND JOB PRINTERS
GOLDSBORO, N.C., 1904

CHAPTER XI.
1771. An Act to amend an Act, entitled, An Act for the Regulation of the Town of Wilmington. (Page 868).

XI. And be it further Enacted, by the Authority aforesaid, That the Commissioners or the Majority of them, shall, and they are hereby impowered, to pass such Orders as they may judge necessary to prevent Slaves from keeping Houses in the said Town, or any Person or Persons dealing with Slaves not having Tickets from their Masters, Mistresses, or overseers; to prevent or remove all Kinds of Nuisances whatsoever; to oblige the Inhabitants to keep a Sufficient Number of Leather Buckets, in their Houses, with their Names thereon, to be ready in Case of Fire; to erect a Fire Company, under such Regulations as they may think necessary; to prevent any Persons making Fires upon the Wharves, in the Night Time; and every other Matter and Thing, for the good Government and Safety of the said Town, consistent with the Laws of this Province; and to inforce such Orders, by laying Fines on all Persons neglecting or refusing to comply therewith; to be recovered and applied in the same Manner, and under the same Limitations, as is prescribed by the before recited Act.

XII. Provided always, That if the Offender be a Slave, then and in such Case the said Slave shall be whipped by one of the Constables of the said Town, at the discretion of the said Commissioners, or the Majority of them, not exceeding Forty Lashes, unless the Master or Mistress of such Slave shall pay the Fine.

CHAPTER XXXI.
1774. An Act to Prevent the wilful and malicious killing of Slaves. (Pages 975-976).

North Carolina Law

Whereas some Doubts have arisen with Respect to the Punishment proper to be inflicted upon such as have been guilty of willfully and maliciously killing Slaves:

I. Be it therefore Enacted by the Governor, Council, and Assembly, and by the Authority of the same, That from and after the first day of May next, if any Person shall be guilty of wilfully and maliciously killing a Slave, so that, if he had in the same Manner killed a Freeman, he would by the Laws of the Realm be held and deemed guilty of Murder, that then and in that Case such Offender shall, upon due and legal Conviction thereof, in the Superior Court of the District where such offence shall happen, or have been committed, suffer Twelve Months Imprisonment: And upon a second Conviction thereof, shall be judged guilty of Murder, and shall suffer Death, without benefit of Clergy.

II. And be it further Enacted by the Authority aforesaid, That if the Slave so wilfully and maliciously killed, shall be the property of another, and not of the Offender, he shall on the first Conviction thereof, pay the Owner thereof such sum as shall be the Value of the said Slave, to be assessed by the Inferior Court of the County where such Slave was killed, and shall stand committed to the Gaol of the District where such conviction shall happen, until he shall satisfy and pay the said Sum so assessed.

III. Provided always, That this Act shall not extend to any Person killing any Slave outlawed by virtue of any Act of Assembly in this Province, or to any Slave in the Act of Resistance to his lawful Owner or Master, or to any Slave dying under moderate Correction.

****

**NORTH CAROLINA STATE ARCHIVES
GENERAL ASSEMBLY SESSIONS RECORDS
NOV., - DEC., 1777
HOUSE BILLS, BOX 2**

FILE MARKED: Nov. - Dec., 1777 House Bills
Bill for establishing Courts of Law and for regulating the proceedings therein.

Page 17, Section 55

And be it further enacted by the authority aforesaid, that if any person who shall be summoned as a witness in any of the said Courts, or before any persons appointed to take depositions as aforesaid, shall refuse to give testimony on oath, such person so refusing, shall, by the Court, or by the Commissioner before whom he shall be summoned, be committed to the common prison, there to remain without bail or main prise, until he shall be willing to give testimony in such manner as the law doth or may direct: Provided that the people called Quakers shall have the liberty of giving their testimony by way of solemn affirmation, in all causes whatsoever, criminal as well as civil: And provided also, that all negroes, Indians, Mulattoes, and all persons of mixed blood, descended from Negroe and Indian ancestors to the fourth generation inclusive (though one ancestor of each generation may have been a white person) whether bond or free, shall be deemed and taken to be incapable in law to be witnesses in any case whatsoever, except against each other.

****

THE STATE RECORDS OF NORTH CAROLINA VOLUME XXIV., 1777-1788
EDITED BY: WALTER L. CLARK
NASH BROTHERS BOOK AND JOB PRINTERS
GOLDSBORO, N.C., 1906

CHAPTER VI.
1777. An Act to prevent domestic Insurrections, and for other Purposes. (Pages 14-15).

I. Whereas the evil and pernicious Practice of freeing Slaves in this State, ought at this alarming and critical Time to be guarded against by every friend and Wellwisher to his Country:

II. Be it therefore enacted by the General Assembly of the State of North Carolina, and by the authority of the same, That no Negro or Mulatto Slave shall hereafter be set free, except for meritorious Services, to be adjudged of and allowed by the County Court, and License first had and obtained thereupon. And when any Slave is or shall be set free by his or her Master or Owner otherwise than is herein before directed, it shall and may be lawful for any Free holder in this State, to apprehend and take up such Slave, and deliver him or her to the Sheriff of the County, who, on receiving such Slave, shall give such Freeholder a Receipt for the same;

and the Sheriff shall committ all such Slaves to the Gaol of the County, there to remain untill the next Court to be held for such County; and the Court of the County shall order all such confined Slaves to be sold during the Term to the highest Bidder.

 III. Provided always, That the Sheriff, upon committing any such Slave or Slaves, shall at least five Days before such Sale, give Notice in Writing to the last Owner or Owners, or the reputed Owner or Owners of such Slave or Slaves, of the Time and Place of Sale, and of the Name and Names of such Slaves, to the End that such Owner or Owners may, if he or they think proper, make his or their Claim to the same; but if such Owner or Owners shall neglect or refuse to appear on the Day of Sale (due Proof of the Service of such Notice being made to the Satisfaction of the Court) such Owner or owners, so neglecting or refusing, shall be forever barred from making any Claim to such Slaves.

 IV. And be it further enacted by the Authority aforesaid, That the net Proceeds of the Money arising by such Sale shall be disposed of in the following Manner, that is to say, That one-fifth Part thereof shall be paid to the Takers up of such Negroes or Mulattoes, and that the remaining Part of such Money be paid into the Hands of the Public Treasurers, to defray the contingent Charges of Government, and to no other Intent, Use or Purpose, whatsoever.

 V. And be it enacted by the Authority aforesaid, That if any Slave or Slaves shall hereafter be allowed by his or her Master, Mistress, or Overseer, or other Person having the Care of such Slave or Slaves, to hire out him or herself, such Slave may be taken up by any Magistrate or Freeholder, and kept to hard Labour, for the Use of the Poor of the County, for any Time not exceeding Twenty Days; any Law, Usage, or Custom, to the contrary notwithstanding.

CHAPTER VII.
1777. An Act for the Encouragement of the Militia and Volunteers employed in prosecuting the present Indian War. (Page 15).
 I. Whereas the vigorous prosecution of the present Indian War may much sooner put an end to the same; On order therefore to encourage and stir up an enterprising spirit among the Militia and Volunteers employed in the said War.

 II. Be it Enacted by the General Assembly of the State of North Carolina, and by the authority of the same, that from and after the first day of June next, if peace shall not be made with the Cherokees before that time, and until peace shall be made, a Premium of fifteen Pounds for each Prisoner, and a premium of ten pounds for each scalp, shall be paid out of the Treasury to the Captor being in the service of the State, on producing a prisoner or scalp, and making oath that the prisoner was taken by him after the said first day of June, or that the scalp was taken and fleeced off the Head of an Indian Man slain by himself, after the said first day of June.

III. And be it further enacted by the authority aforesaid, That a premium or reward of forty pounds for each scalp of an Indian Man, and a premium, or reward of Fifty Pounds, for producing an Indian Man Prisoner, be paid to any person in this State, not in the pay thereof who shall voluntarily undertake to make war upon the said Indians after the time aforesaid; Provided peace shall not before that time be made with the same Indians, and until peace shall be made, the Captors making oath as aforesaid, that such scalp or prisoner was taken by him after the said first day of June, and that the Indian so killed or taken was of the Nation of Indians commonly known by the name of Cherokees; and that the scalp produced was actually taken from an Indian killed by the person claiming the same.

CHAPTER XV.
1777. An Act to amend an Act, Intituled, An Act to establish a Militia in this State. (Page 118).
XXIII. Whereas the Penalties incurred by some of the Militia, who refused to march on the late Expedition against the Cherokee Indians, and other Enemies, for the necessary Defence of this State, have been imposed agreeable to Act of Assembly, and the Resolves of Congress; and whereas some of the said Penalties Incurred and imposed as aforesaid have not been collected, Be it therefore Enacted, by the Authority aforesaid, That the Colonel or Commanding Officer of every Regiment of Militia in this State shall, and he is hereby empowered and authorized to issue his Precept under his Hand and Seal, directed to the Sheriff of the County where the offender resides, to levy the said Fines by Distress and Sale of the Offenders Goods and Chattels, and the said Fines shall be applied in the same Manner as other Fines imposed by this Act; and the Sheriffs for this Service, shall out of the said Fines receive the Fees allowed by Law for levying Executions, and for every Neglect or Refusal shall forfeit and pay the Sum of Ten Pounds.

XXVI. And be it also Enacted, by the Authority aforesaid, That where any Invasion or Insurrection shall happen within this State, the nearest Militia Officer shall give immediate Notice thereof to his next superior Officer, who shall communicate the same to the next Superior, and so on to the Brigadier General, who shall convey the same to the Governor or Commander in Chief, and in the mean Time every such Officer shall use his utmost Endeavours to collect a Force sufficient to repel the Enemy, or suppress the Insurrection; and every Officer failing herein, shall be subject to such Punishment as shall be adjudged by a Court Martial.

CHAPTER XXIV.
1777. An Act to encourage the destroying Vermin in the Several Counties of this State. (Pages 133-134).
   I. Whereas the Counties of this State are much infested with Wolves, and other Vermin, to the great Prejudice of the Inhabitants thereof:
   II. Be it Enacted by the General Assembly of the State of North Carolina, and it is hereby Enacted by the Authority of the same, That every Person who shall kill any of the Vermin herein after mentioned within Ten Miles of any settled Plantation, shall be entitled to a Claim on the County where such Vermin shall be killed to the several Rewards as follows: For every grown Wolf, Twenty Shillings; every young one, Ten Shillings; for every Wild Cat, Five Shillings; and for every Panther, Twenty Shillings; to be paid as herein after directed.
   III. And be it further Enacted, by the Authority aforesaid, That any Person who shall have a Claim for killing any of the aforesaid Vermin, are hereby directed to produce the Scalp of the aforesaid Vermin, with both Ears, before a Magistrate, who is to administer an Oath to such Person claiming the same, that it was taken and killed within the Bounds of such County where the Claim shall be made; and if any Slave or Indian that kill any Vermin, of which the Head or Scalp shall be produced as aforesaid, the Master or Owner of such Slave or Indian, or he that makes Claim for such Scalp or Scalps in Behalf of any Slave or Indian, shall make Oath before such Magistrate, that he verily believes the same was taken and killed within the Counties wherein the same was claimed; which Oath being administered, the Magistrate is hereby directed to give a Certificate for the same, and immediately cause such Scalp to be destroyed.
   IV. And be it further Enacted, by the Authority aforesaid, That any Person having a Certificate from any such Justice of the Peace shall,

upon producing the same to the Person who shall be appointed to collect and account for the Taxes of the County where such Certificate was obtained, be intitled to receive the Reward by this Act given for such Scalp or Scalps, or to have the same discounted in the Settlement of his County Tax; and every such Certificate shall be deemed a sufficient Voucher for the Collector of the County Tax, on his Settlement for the same.

V. And be it further Enacted, by the Authority aforesaid, That this Act shall be and continue in Force for and during the Term of Three Years, and from thence to the End of the next Session of Assembly, and no longer.

CHAPTER XXV.
1777. An Act to Prevent burning the Woods. (Page 134).

III. And be it further Enacted, by the Authority aforesaid, That every Person offending against this Act shall forfeit and pay the sum of Ten Pounds, to be recovered by Action of Debt, Bill, Plaint or Information, to the Use of the Person who shall sue or prosecute for the same; and shall also be further liable to the Party injured by such unlawful firing of the Woods, for all Damages that may accrue therefrom.

IV. And be it further Enacted, by the Authority aforesaid, That if any Slave, Free Negro or Mulatto, or vagrant Person, unable to pay the Fine aforesaid, shall be convicted of setting fire to any Woods, contrary to the true Meaning of this Act, such Person, upon Conviction thereof, shall have and receive on his bare back Thirty Nine Lashes, well laid on, at the Public Whipping Post.

CHAPTER XXI.
1777. An Act to prevent hunting with a gun, by Fire Light in the Night. (Page).

I. Whereas, many persons under pretence of hunting for deer in the night by Fire Light, kill Horses and Cattle to the prejudice of the owners thereof.

II. Be it therefore Enacted by the General Assembly of the State of North Carolina, and by the authority of the same, that if any person or persons shall be discovered hunting in the woods with a gun in the night time by Fire Light, such person or persons so offending shall upon conviction thereof, by the proof of one credible witness, before any justice of the peace in the County where the offence was committed, be compelled to go into the service of the United States, and there serve as a Continental soldier for the space of three years, subject to the same rules, regulations and restrictions as are prescribed by the Continental Congress for the government of the Army, and shall be turned over to the army in the same manner as is directed by an act passed this Session, for the encouragement of recruiting service.

III. Provided, nevertheless that in case the said offender shall immediately procure an able bodied an effective man to serve in the Continental Army for the aforesaid term of three years, then the said convicted person shall be excused, and stand acquitted of the judgment passed upon him.

IV. And be it further enacted by the authority aforesaid, that if any slave or slaves shall be discovered hunting in the manner herein before mentioned, such slave or slaves shall upon due conviction thereof before any justice of the peace for the County in which the offence was committed, by the oath of a credible witness, be sentenced to receive thirty nine lashes on his bare back; and the gun or guns found in the possession of any slave so hunting in the night as aforesaid, shall be forfeited to and become the property of the person or persons that shall discover and prosecute any slave or slaves in manner aforesaid; and the owner of the slave convicted shall be fined in the sum of Five Pounds, to be recovered by warrant before any justice of the peace for the County in which the offence was committed; to be applied towards defraying the contingent charges of the said County.

V. And be it further enacted by the authority aforesaid, that this Act shall be and continue for the term of five months, and from thence to the end of the next Session of Assembly and no longer.

CHAPTER II.
1777. An Act for Establishing Courts of Law, and for Regulating the Proceedings therein.

XLII. And be it further Enacted, by the Authority aforesaid, That if any Person who shall be summoned as a Witness in any of the said Courts, or before any persons appointed to take depositions as aforesaid, shall refuse to give Testimony on Oath, such Person so refusing shall by the Court, or by the Commissioner before whom he shall be summoned, be committed to the common Prison, there to remain, without Bail or Mainprize, until he shall be willing to give Testimony, in such a Manner as the Law doth or may direct. Provided, the People called Quakers shall have the Liberty of giving their Testimony by way of Solemn Affirmation, in all Causes whatsoever, criminal as well as civil. And provided also, That all Negroes, Indians, Mulattoes, and all Persons of mixed Blood, descended from Negro and Indian Ancestors, to the fourth Generation inclusive (though one Ancestor in each Generation may have been a white Person) whether Bond or free, shall be deemed and taken to be incapable in Law to be Witnesses in any Case whatsoever, except against each other.

CHAPTER XVI. 1ST SESSION
1778. An Act for quieting and securing the Tuscarora Indians, and others claiming under the Tuscaroras, in the Possession of their Lands. (Pages 171-173).

 I. Be it Enacted, by the General Assembly, and it is hereby Enacted by the Authority of the same, That Whitmell Tuffdick, Chief or Headman of the Tuscarora Nation, and the Tuscarora Indians, now living in the County of Bertie, shall have, hold, occupy, possess and enjoy, all the Lands lying in the County of Bertie aforesaid, whereof they are now seized and possessed (being Part of the Lands heretofore allotted to the Indians aforesaid by solemn Treaty, and confirmed to them and their Successors by Act of Assembly, in the Year One Thousand Seven Hundred and Forty Eight) without Let, Molestation, or Hindrance, clear of all Quitrents, or any Public Demand by Way of Tax whatever, to them the said Tuscarora Indians, and their Heirs and Successors; and that they the said Tuscaroras, and their Heirs and Successors, shall for ever be clear and exempt from every Kind of Poll Tax.

 II. And whereas the said Tuscarora Indians, by Nature ignorant, and strongly addicted to drinking, may be easily imposed on by designing Persons, and unwarily deprived of their said Lands; Be it Enacted by the Authority aforesaid, That no Person, for any Consideration whatever, shall hereafter purchase, buy or lease, any Tract or Parcel of Land now claimed by, or in Possession of the said Tuscarora Indians, or any of them; nor shall any Person settle on or cultivate the said Lands, or any Part thereof, in his own Right, or under Pretence as acting as Overseer for the Indians, all such Purchases, Sales, Leases and Agreements, shall be, and they are hereby declared null and void; and the Person so purchasing, buying or leasing, settling on, or cultivating the said Lands, or any Part thereof, shall forfeit and pay the Sum of Three Hundred Pounds current Money for every

Hundred Acres by him so purchased, bought or leased, settled on or cultivated as aforesaid, one Half to the Use of the said Tuscarora Indians, the other to the Use of him or her who shall sue for the same; to be recovered by Action of Debt, Bill, Plaint, or Information, in any Court having Cognizance thereof. Provided, That the said Tuscarora Indians may sell or dispose of their Lands, or any Part thereof, with Consent of the General Assembly first had and obtained.

III. And whereas the Chieftains and Headmen of the Tuscarora Nation living in the County, did on the Twelfth Day of July, in the Year One Thousand Seven Hundred and Sixty Six, for the Consideration of Fifteen Hundred Pounds to them paid by Robert Jones, Jun., William Williams, and Thomas Pugh, by Indenture under their Hands and Seals, demise, grant, and to Farm let, unto the said Robert Jones, William Williams, and Thomas Pugh, a certain Tract of Land lying in the County aforesaid, containing about Eight Thousand Acres, more or less, bounded as follows, to-wit, Beginning at the Mouth of Deep Creek, otherwise called Falling Run; thence running up the said Creek, to the Indian Head Line; thence by the said Line South, Seventeen Degrees East, Twelve Hundred and Eighty Poles; thence a Course parallel with the general Current of the said Creek, to Roanoke River; and then up the River to the Beginning; together with the Appurtenances thereto belonging, to be held and enjoyed by the said Robert Jones, William Williams, and Thomas Pugh, their Executors, Administrators, and Assigns, in Severalty, for and during the Term of One Hundred and Fifty Years, as may more fully appear by the said Indenture, registered in the County Court of Bertie aforesaid, and ratified by Act of Assembly, passed at New Bern in the Year One Thousand Seven Hundred and Sixty-Six; Be it Enacted by the Authority aforesaid, That each and every of the Persons intitled to claim under the Demise afore mentioned, or by Grants from the Persons claiming under the same, or either of them, and their Heirs and Assigns, shall and may have, hold, occupy, possess and enjoy, the several Shares, Dividends, or Parcels of the said Land to them belonging, in as full, free, and absolute Manner, and with the same legal privileges and Advantages, in every Respect, and subject to the same Taxes, as if the said Land had been originally granted to the said Robert Jones, William Williams, and Thomas Pugh, by Lord Granville, or by this State.

IV. And whereas the said Tuscarora Indians, for good and sufficient Reasons, and for valuable Considerations, have since the Twelfth Day of July, One Thousand Seven Hundred and Sixty Six, and previous to

North Carolina Law

the First Day of December last, demised, granted, and to Farm let, sundry Tracts or Parcels of Land lying in said County of Bertie, to sundry Persons, as by Indentures duly executed may more fully appear; Be it Enacted by the Authority aforesaid, That all the Lands contained in the last mentioned Demises, if the said Demises were fairly, bona fide, and without Fraud, made by, and obtained from the said Tuscarora Indians, since the Year One Thousand Seven Hundred and Sixty Six, and previous to the First Day of December last past, shall not be deemed vacant Lands, or be liable to be entered as such in the Land Office, unless the General Assembly shall hereafter so direct, but nevertheless shall be subjected to the same Taxes as other Lands in this State are liable to.

V. And whereas it is suggested by the said Tuscarora Indians that unfair Dealing has been used in obtaining one or more of the Demises afore mentioned, and they the said Indians have at present no Mode for obtaining Redress in such Cases: Be it therefore Enacted by the Authority aforesaid, That the Commissioners herein after mentioned, or a Majority of them, shall and may, upon Complaint of the said Tuscarora Indians, in Court or Meeting assembled, that any Person or Persons has or have unfairly or fraudulently obtained any Grant or Demise for Lands to them belonging since the Year One Thousand Seven Hundred Sixty Six, and previous to the First Day of December last, summon the Person or Persons so complained against, or cause him or them to be summoned, to appear before them on a certain Day on the Land in Dispute (giving at least Ten Days Notice previous to the Day in such Summons appointed) then and there to answer the Complaints of the Indians for having fraudulently or unfairly obtained a Grant or Demise of the Land in Question; and shall also summon, or cause to be summoned, a Jury of Twelve Men, being Freeholders in the said County of Bertie, and not resident on, or Owners of any Lands purchased of the said Tuscarora Indians: And the said Commissioners, or a Majority of them, shall attend at the time and Place appointed, with the Jury aforesaid, and having first sworn the Jury to try and determine fairly between the said Indians and the Person or Persons complained against, shall and may cause Witnesses to be examined on both Sides, and receive the Verdict of the Jury, and return the same, with the Pannel, to the next County Court of the said County of Bertie, to be entered upon Record, and such Verdict shall be as good and effectual as if obtained in any Court of Record; and if the same be general, the said Commissioners, or a Majority of them, shall and may appoint one or more Person or Persons to carry the same into Execution; but if special, then the Court shall decide thereon, and cause the Sheriff of the County to carry such Decision into Execution.

VI. And whereas the said Indians are often injured by Horses, Cattle and Hogs, driven on their Lands by the white People, the said Horses, Cattle and Hogs, breaking into their Inclosures, and destroying their Corn and other Effects, and are also frequently deprived of their Property, and abused by ill disposed Persons: For Remedy whereof, and also for Recovery of Rents or Demands now due, or which may hereafter become due and owing to the said Tuscarora Indians; Be it Enacted by the Authority aforesaid, That William Williams, Thomas Pugh, Willie Jones, Simon Turner, and Zedekiah Stone, be and they are hereby appointed Commissioners for the said Indians; and they, or any Three of them, shall and may inquire into Complaints made by the said Indians, summon the persons complained against before them, and award such Restitution and Redress as to them shall seem just an necessary; and may appoint an Officer or Officers to serve Subpoenas, and to execute such Awards and Determinations as they shall or may make in Regard of the Premises: And the Court of the said County of Bertie is hereby authorized and required to fill up, from Time to Time, by new Appointments, any Vacancies which may happen among the Commissioners, by Death or Resignation; and upon Complaint of the Chief or Headman of the Nation, and the Rest of the Indians, in Court of Meeting properly assembled, against any one of the Commissioners for Misbehaviour, may inquire into the Conduct of the Persons or Persons complained against, remove him or them, if necessary, and appoint another or others in his or their Stead.

VII. And be it further Enacted by the Authority aforesaid, That the Lands leased by the said Tuscarora Indians to Robert Jones, Jun., William Williams, and Thomas Pugh, and to other Persons, shall revert to, and become the Property of the State, at the Expiration of the Terms the several Leases mentioned, if the said Nation be then extinct: And the Lands now belonging to, and possessed by the said Tuscaroras, shall revert to, and become the Property of the State, whenever the said Nation shall become extinct, or shall entirely abandon or remove themselves of the said Lands, and every Part thereof. Provided, That no Person shall have any Preference of Entry to any of the said Lands by Virtue of any Lease or Occupancy whatsoever since December, One Thousand Seven Hundred and Seventy-Six, whenever the General Assembly shall declare the said Lands to be vacant.

North Carolina Law

CHAPTER V. 2ND SESSION
1778. An Act to prevent trading with the Cherokee Indians without license first had and obtained; and also to prevent Trespasses upon the Indian Hunting Grounds. (Pages 188-189).

I. Whereas, divers Avaricious and ill-disposed persons, have by Frauds in Traffick, or by Trespassing upon the Hunting Grounds of the Cherokee Indians, and divers other abuses, excited their Jealousies and Suspicions, which if not seasonably quieted, and such abuses in future prevented, may involve this and other of the United States in a bloody and expensive Indian War,

II. Be it therefore enacted by the Assembly of this State, and by the authority of the same, that no Person or Inhabitant of this State, shall trade, traffick, or barter with the Cherokee Indians within the Indian Country, unless he shall first obtain a License for so doing, from the Judges of the Superior Courts; and if any person shall trade, traffick, or barter contrary to the true Spirit and Intention of this Act, such person or persons so offending, shall, upon conviction thereof, duly had and obtained in the Superior Court of the District nearest the place where such offence shall have been committed, forfeit and pay the sum of Five Hundred Pounds Current Money of this State, one half thereof to the use of the Informer, the other to the Governor of this State, to applied to defray the Contingent Charges of Government; to be recovered by action of Debt, Bill, Plaint or Indictment, wherein no Essoign, Excuse, or Plea in Abatement shall be admitted to the Jurisdiction of the said Court, nor shall Process be discontinued for or by reason of any Omission or Errors not substantially material; and in case such Offender or Offenders shall not within twenty four hours after conviction pay into the hands of the Sheriff of the County in which such District Court shall be held, the said sum of Five Hundred Pounds, and all Costs arising upon such prosecution, he shall stand in the Pillory two hours, and receive thirty nine lashes upon his bare back, and shall stand Committed to the Gaol of the District until such sums shall be compleatly discharged and paid.

III. And be it further enacted by the authority aforesaid, That if any person shall hereafter be guilty of trespassing upon the Indian Hunting Grounds, knowing them to be such, he shall suffer the same Penalties, Fines, and forfeitures, to be prosecuted, sued for and recovered, and inflicted, as are by this act heretofore directed, with respect to Persons trafficking with the Cherokee Indians, and under the same Rules,

Regulations, Latitude and Restrictions, prescribed to be had against the offenders specified in this Act heretofore, and all Fines and Forfeitures shall be applied in Manner as before directed.

          Allen Jones, S.S.
          Thomas Benbury, S.C.

CHAPTER III. 3RD SESSION
1778. An Act for Ascertaining what Property in this State shall be deemed Taxable Property, the Method of Assessing the same, and Collecting the Public Taxes and other purposes. (Pages 200-201).

    II. Be it therefore Enacted by the General Assembly of the State of North Carolina, and it is hereby enacted by the authority of the same, that all Lotts and Lands with their improvements, Slaves under the age of Sixty Years, Horses, all Cattle from one year old and upward, Money, Money at Interest, and Stocks in Trade of every kind wherever the same may be, all Bonds, Notes and other obligations, which bear or include Interest, shall be held and deemed taxable property liable to be assessed and the Taxes laid thereon by law collected agreeable to the Directions of this Act.

    VIII. Provided nevertheless, that all cattle from one year old and upwards, shall be, and they are hereby rated at ten pounds per head, that all slaves under five years of age and all who are between the ages of fifty and sixty shall be rated at one hundred and fifty pounds each, all slaves of five years old and under ten years, and all between the age of forty and fifty shall be rated at four hundred pounds each, and all slaves of ten years old and upwards not exceeding the age of forty years shall be rated at seven hundred pounds each; Provided nevertheless, that slaves disabled by bodily infirmities or void of reason, such incapacity to be adjudged and certified by the County Court, shall not be considered as taxable property, nor given in as such by the respective proprietors.

CHAPTER XI. 3RD SESSION
1778. An Act to Prevent the Stealing of Slaves or by Violation, Seduction or any other Means, taking or conveying away any slave or slaves, the property of another; and for other purposes therein mentioned. (Pages 220-221).

North Carolina Law

I. Whereas, it is necessary that the promiscuous practice of stealing or other ways carrying away slaves the property of others, as also of stealing and carrying off free negroes and mulattoes with an intention to sell and appropriate the same, should be discouraged by a law with additional penalties.

II. Be it enacted by the General Assembly and by the authority of the same, that any person or persons who shall hereafter steal or shall by violence, seduction or any other means, take or convey away any slave or slaves, the property of another, with an intention to sell or dispose of to another or appropriate to their own use such slave or slaves, or who shall hereafter by violence or any other means, take or convey any free negro or free negroes or persons of mixed blood, out of this State to another, with an intention to sell or dispose of such free Negro or free negroes or persons of mixed blood, and being thereof legally convicted or shall upon his arraignment peremptorily challenge more than thirty five jurors or shall stand mute, shall be judged guilty of Felony and shall suffer death without benefit of Clergy.

III. And whereas, many evil disposed and dishonest persons make it a practice to deal and traffick with slaves to the very great injury of the owners of such slaves.

IV. Be it therefore further enacted by the authority aforesaid, That any person or persons who shall hereafter purchase any articles or commodity of or shall have any kind of dealing whatsoever with any slave or slaves, without permission first had and obtained from the master or mistress of such slave or slaves either personally or in writing being thereof legally convicted in the Superior Court of the County where such offence shall be committed, shall forfeit the sum of One Hundred Pounds Current money to be applied by the said Court for the use of the poor of the County and shall stand imprisoned ten days without bail or mainprize.

V. And whereas, many evil disposed persons frequently entice or persuade slaves, without any intention to steal them, and servants to absent themselves from their master or mistress and oftentimes harbour and maintain runaway servants and slaves.

VI. Be it therefore further enacted by the authority aforesaid, That any person or persons who shall hereafter entice or persuade any servant or slave to absent him or herself, from his or her master or mistress, or who shall harbour or maintain any run away servant or slave shall for every such offence forfeit and pay to the master or mistress of such servant or slave, the sum of one hundred pounds Current money, to be recovered by action of debt in any jurisdiction having cognizance thereof, and be further liable to the said Master or Mistress, in an action for damages wherein no Essoign, injunction, protection, or wager of Law shall be allowed or admitted; notwithstanding any Law, Usage, or Custom to the contrary.

VII. And be it further enacted by the authority aforesaid, That the Clerk of every County Court of this State, shall on the third day of every Court, read this Act in the presence and hearing of the County Court, under penalty of five pounds for every neglect.

VIII. And be it further enacted by the authority aforesaid, That this Law shall take effect and be binding upon the subjects of this State on the first day of April next, and afterwards, and not sooner.

IX. And be it further enacted by the authority aforesaid, That so much of an Act of Assembly of this State, entitled An Act concerning Servants and Slaves, as comes within the purview of this Act, is hereby repealed and declared to void and of no effect to all intents and purposes whatsoever.

CHAPTER XII. 3RD SESSION.
1778. An Act for Apprehending and selling certain Slaves set free contrary to Law and for Confirming the Sales of Others, and for other purposes. (Page 221).

I. Whereas, by an Act entitled an Act to prevent Domestick Insurrections & for other purposes, it is provided, that no person shall liberate his or her slave except for meritorious Services, to be judged of and allowed by the County Court, and by the said Act, it is Directed in what Manner and for what purposes such liberated slaves shall be apprehended and sold; and whereas, before the passing of the said Act, and since the sixteenth day of April, one thousand seven hundred and seventy five, divers evil minded persons, intending to disturb the public peace, did liberate and set free their slaves, notwithstanding the same was especially contrary to the Laws ofthis State and the County Courts of Perquimans and Pasquotank, conceiving they had power to proceed against all such liberated slaves, did order them to be sold to the highest bidder, and whereas, doubts have now arisen whether the purchasers of such slaves have good and legal title thereto, for remedy whereof,

II. Be it Enacted by the General Assembly of the State of North Carolina, and it is hereby Enacted by the Authority of the same, that all such sales made bona fide and for valuable consideration shall be deemed good and valid to all intents and purposes, and as many negroes are now going at large to the terror of the good People of this State, who were liberated in manner aforesaid previous to the passing of the said recited Act,

III. Be it further enacted by the Authority aforesaid, That the same Proceeding shall and may be had against all such illegally liberated slaves as is directed in the said recited Act intituled, An Act to prevent domestic insurrections, and for other purposes, in the same manner as if such negro slaves had been set free after the passing of the same; Provided, that nothing herein contained shall deprive of Liberty any Slave who having been liberated & not sold by order of any Court has inlisted in the service of this or the United States previous to the passing of this Act.

CHAPTER V. 2ND SESSION.
1779. An Act for amending an Act for making provision for the poor, and for other purposes. (Page 260).

VI. And whereas, by an Act, intituled, an act concerning servants and slaves, it is enacted,That no slave shall be permitted, on any pretence whatsoever, to raise any horses, cattle, hogs or sheep; Be it therefore enacted by the authority aforesaid, That all horses, cattle, hogs or sheep, that, one month after the passing this act, shall belong to any slave, or be of any slave's mark, in this State, shall be seized and sold by the county wardens, and by them applied, the one half to the support of the poor of the county, and the other half to the informer.

CHAPTER III. 2ND SESSION.
1779. An Act to prevent hunting in the night time with gun and fire light, and other purposes therein mentioned. (Pages 268-269).

I. Be it enacted by the General Assembly of the State of North Carolina, and it is hereby enacted by the authority of the same, that from and after the passing of this Act, if any free person or persons shall be found hunting in the night, except on his own plantations, with gun and firelight, upon conviction of such offence on sufficient testimony, shall be turned over into the Continental service for the term of eighteen months, or during the war; and the person so informing shall be exempt from any kind of military duty or draft for the space of twelve months, provided the offender be found guilty agreeable to this law.

II. And be it further enacted by the authority aforesaid, that if any soldier belonging to the Continental army, or servant (otherwise than slaves) should be found hunting as aforesaid, such soldier or servant, on due conviction as by this Act directed, shall receive twenty-nine lashes on his or their bare back.

III. And be it further enacted by the authority aforesaid, That if any slave be found transgressing this law, on conviction before any one justice of the peace, shall receive thirty nine lashes on his or their bare back, and the owner or master of such slave or slaves, shall forfeit and pay the sum of one hundred pounds, to be applied one half to the use of the informer, and the other to the use of the poor of the county; and wardens of said county are hereby directed to sue for the same, to be recovered in any court of record having cognizance thereof. Provided, nevertheless that the master or owner of such slave or slaves shall not be liable to any fine by this law directed, if it shall appear by his own oath, or other sufficient testimony, that the offence was committed without his or her approbation or knowledge.

CHAPTER VII. 2ND SESSION.
1779. An Act to amend an Act, entitled, An Additional Act concerning Servants and Slaves, passed at New Bern in the year One Thousand Seven Hundred and fifty three, and other purposes therein mentioned. (Pages 276-277).

I. Whereas by the before recited act, the encouragement given to searchers or patrollers, the penalty inflicted on them in case of a non compliance of their duty, and the times appointed for searching, are insufficient;

II. Be it therefore enacted by the General Assembly of the State of North Carolina, and it is hereby enacted by the authority of the same, that each and every searcher or patroller appointed in pursuance of the aforesaid act shall, as to his own person, during the time of his continuance in office, be exempted from serving as a constable, or working upon the roads, attending private musters, or as a juror, and shall be entitled to such further allowance out of the county tax as the court shall think necessary.

III. And be it further enacted by the authority aforesaid, that such searchers in their respective districts shall search once in every month for guns and other weapons, as the before recited act directs, and shall make return on oath of all such guns, or other weapons, which they shall so find, to the succeeding county court, to be applied to the use of the county, or returned to the owner, as the court may direct; and in case they find any slave or slaves on the Sabbath, or other unseasonable time, off his master or mistress's plantation, without a pass, or in company with some white person who will vouch for his or their honest intention, it shall be lawful for them to apprehend such slave or slaves, and convey, or cause to be conveyed, to the master, mistress, or overseer, who shall pay to the said searchers or patrollers in like manner as for apprehending and conveying runaways, as a compensation for their trouble.

IV. And be it enacted, by the authority aforesaid, that every searcher or patroller who shall refuse to serve, or neglect to do his duty, shall forfeit and pay the sum of one hundred pounds, to be recovered in any jurisdiction having cognizance thereof.

V. And be it further enacted by the authority aforesaid, that so much of the before recited act, intituled, An additional Act to an Act concerning servants and slaves, passed at New Bern the twenty-seventh day of March, one thousand seven hundred and fifty three, as comes within the purview of this act, be, and is hereby repealed and made void.

CHAPTER XII. 2ND SESSION.
1779. An Act to amend an Act, intituled, An Act concerning servants and slaves. (Pages 282-283).

I. Whereas from the present very small and inadequate allowance by the public to the owners of executed slaves, crimes and thefts by them committed go frequently unpunished, such slaves being screened from public justice often by their owners;

II. Be it therefore enacted by the General Assembly of the State of North Carolina, and it is hereby enacted by the authority of the same, that there shall not be allowed by the public to the owner of any slave who shall hereafter be executed in virtue of the judgment of the court who shall try such slave, any larger sum than seven hundred pounds current money for a prime slave, and so in proportion for slaves of a less value; any law, usage or custom, to the contrary, notwithstanding.

III. And be it further enacted by the authority aforesaid, that so much of the before recited act as comes within the purview and meaning of this act, shall be, and the same is hereby repealed and made void.

Repealed by Act Nov. 1786, c. 17. [See Iredell's Laws, 1791, p. 393.]

CHAPTER XXIII. 1ST SESSION.
1780. An Act to amend an Act, intituled "An Act for quieting and securing the Tuscarora Indians, and others claiming under the Tuscaroras, in the possession of their lands. (Page 335).

I. Whereas by the said Act there is no penalty imposed on jurors or witnesses, duly summoned, and failing to attend;

II. Be it enacted by the General Assembly of the State of North Carolina, and it is hereby enacted by the authority of the same, that the commissioners by the said Act appointed, or any three of them, assembled for the purpose of holding a court, shall and may inflict fines on jurors or witnesses so failing to attend, not exceeding one hundred pounds, at their discretion; and unless sufficient excuse be to them afterwards shewn, cause the same to be levied and applied towards defraying the county charges of Bertie: And the witnesses and jurors who shall attend on the trial of any disputes between the Tuscaroras and others, shall have and receive ten dollars per day for their attendance, to be paid by the party cast, with all other costs; and such trial may hereafter be had on any part of the lands belonging to said Tuscaroras in Bertie County, which the commissioners shall direct.

CHAPTER XXIV. 1ST SESSION.
1780. An Act to amend an Act, intituled, "An Act to regulate and establish a Militia in this State." (Pages 335-336).

VIII. And be it further enacted by the authority aforesaid, that no Frenchman, Spaniard, British deserter, Hessian deserter, Indian or slave, shall in the future be received by any militia officer as a substitute for any militia soldier or officer, under any pretence whatsoever.

CHAPTER IV. 2ND SESSION.
1780. An Act for securing the quiet and inoffensive inhabitants of this State from being injured, for preventing such property as hath or may be confiscated from being wasted or destroyed, and for other purposes. (Pages 350-351).

North Carolina Law

I. Whereas, great and frequent complaints have been made, that many acts of violence and barbarity have lately been committed in divers counties of this State, under the pretence of seizing the property of disaffected persons, and of those who have joined, or are supposed to have joined the enemy, and under various other pretences and it is suggested that these unwarrantable depredations have been carried so far as to deprive many poor people of their kitchen utensils, and even some part of their wearing apparel, and whereas persons have unlawfully seized upon, and carried away negro slaves, and other valuable effects, which fall within the description of confiscated property, with intention as it is suggested, of applying the same to their own particular use, and many slaves are said to be conveyed to distant parts, and others have been publicly sold, in violation of law and justice. That the public may not therefore be defrauded, and that the quiet and inoffensive inhabitants may be protected and redressed;

II. Be it enacted by the General Assembly of the State of North Carolina, and it is hereby enacted by the authority of the same, that the commissioners of confiscated estates in every county of this State, and where there no lawful commissioners, the sheriff or coroner of the county, shall seize and take into his or their respective counties, not claimed by any other person, and shall secure the same, to be hereafter applied as the General Assembly shall direct; and it is hereby declared, that the property of all persons, who may at any time have joined, or shall hereafter join or attach themselves to the enemy, shall be comprehended within the meaning of this act.

III. And be it further enacted, by the authority aforesaid, that no person or persons whatsoever but the commissioners of confiscated estates in each county, or for want of lawful commissioners, the sheriff or coroner, shall have any authority to take possession of any confiscated property, and every person offending, or who hath already offended, in the premises on their refusal to deliver the same, shall forfeit and pay treble the value of the property so illegally seized as aforesaid; to be recovered by action of the debt, in the name of the Governor, and shall moreover be compelled to make restitution of all property so illegally taken as aforesaid and in default thereof, shall suffer imprisonment at the discretion of the court.

IV. And be it enacted, by the authority aforesaid, that the Governor or commander in chief for the time being, or the board of war, shall take such measures as to them shall appear necessary for inforcing the execution of this act, and shall cause all offenders therein directed to be prosecuted and punished agreeable to the directions thereof.

V. And whereas no provision has been made in the several counties of this State for the hiring out for the benefit of the State, negroes seized under the confiscation law; Be it therefore enacted by the General Assembly of the State, and the authority of the same, that where no provision has been made adequate to this purpose, or such provision not carried into execution, that the sheriff, or coroner, if there is no sheriff, shall be impowered to hire out until the first day of February, such negroes to the highest bidder, at public auction, at the court house, after giving ten days notice.

VI. And whereas divers evil disposed persons, taking advantage of the present unsettled state of public affairs, and under the pretence of distressing the enemies of the United States, make a practice of going into the State of South Carolina, plundering and committing depredations upon all persons indiscriminately, and bringing the plundered property into this State, whereby many faithful citizens of that State are reduced to most distressing circumstances: In order to prevent such unlawful and cruel proceedings, Be it enacted by the authority aforesaid, that all property heretofore brought, or that may hereafter be brought, from South Carolina by any person or persons residing in this State, shall be seized by the sheriff of the county to which the same shall be brought and the commanding officer of the county shall, if required, assist the sheriff with such aid as may be necessary for that purpose; and all such property shall be safely kept and secured, and returned to the owner, if it shall appear that such owner is a faithful citizen of any of the United States, but if otherwise, shall remain in the hands of such sheriff, to be applied to the use of the State, in such manner as the General Assembly may hereafter direct: And every person or persons who shall offend against this act, by plundering as aforesaid, shall upon conviction thereof, for the first offence receive thirty nine lashes upon his bare back, and for the second offence shall be deemed guilty of felony, and shall suffer death as a felon, without benefit of clergy.

VII. And be it further enacted, by the authority aforesaid, that any person or persons, formerly inhabitants of the State of Georgia, who have taken refuge in this State, shall be, and they are hereby exempted from the payment of any taxes whatever to this State for the present year, any law to the contrary notwithstanding.

North Carolina Law

CHAPTER X. 3RD SESSIONS.
1781. An additional Act to an Act, intitled, An Act concerning Servants and Slaves. (Pages 382-383).

I. Forasmuch as by the laws of this State in all cases whatsoever where a slave has been guilty of a criminal offence which inflicts the punishment of death, and is tried and convicted thereof, many poor widows, orphan children, and other good citizens of this State, may be deprived of their chief, and perhaps only support, as the allowances heretofore made by law can in no case exceed the sum of seven hundred pounds: For remedy whereof:

II. Be it enacted by the General Assembly of the State of North Carolina, and it is hereby enacted by the authority of the same, that when a slave shall hereafter be guilty of a criminal offence, for which such slave shall be condemned to suffer death, the court before whom the trial shall happen are hereby required to certify in writing under their hands, the value of the slave in the currency of the State at the time of the trial; and the owner of the slave so condemned and executed shall be intitled to the one half of such valuation, to be paid out of the public treasury of this State, any custom or law to the contrary notwithstanding.

CHAPTER I. 1ST SESSION.
1781. An Act for raising Troops out of the Militia of this State for the defence thereof, and for other purposes. (Page 386).

XIV. And be it further enacted, that no British deserter, Hessian deserter, apprentice, Indian, sailor, or negro slave, shall be received as a substitute for any volunteer or person drafted in consequence of this act; nor shall any such persons (apprentices excepted) be classed or admitted into the service, in order to exempt any of the said classed from a draft.

CHAPTER XVI. 1ST SESSION.
1781. An Act for securing all articles left by the British troops in this State, taken from the citizens as well as others, and for other purposes. (Pages 410-411).

I. Whereas the British troops in marching through this State have left a number of horses, waggons, negroes and other articles, which have been chiefly taken from the citizens thereof; In order that the same may be secured, so that the proper owners secure them again.

II. Be it enacted, by the General Assembly of the State of North Carolina, and it is hereby enacted by the authority of the same, that the sheriff of each respective county is hereby strictly required and impowered to take into his care all such waggons, horses, negroes and arms so left, he first entering all such horses on the stray book in the county where he resides; which horses when entered and appraised, and the waggons and arms, shall be delivered to the most convenient quartermaster, who is hereby required to give a receipt for the same, which receipt the sheriff shall keep in his hands until called for; And all negroes and other articles which he may find in his county as before described, the negroes he is hereby impowered to hire out for any term not exceeding twelve months (to be delivered however to the owner at any time before the expiration of the said term, in which case the hire shall be proportionately discounted) and shall make return of the waggons, horses and arms to the next General Assembly, and also make return of the sum arising from the hire of such negroes, and the sale of the horses.

CHAPTER I. 1ST SESSION.
1782. An Act for Raising troops to compleat the Continental Battallions of this State, and other purposes. (Page 414).
  IV. Provided always, That no British or Hessian deserter who hath not been a resident of this State twelve months, or orphan or apprentice under eighteen years of age, Indian, sailor or negro slave, shall be received as a substitute for any class volunteer or draft whatever: And provided further, That no militia officer shall take or receive any person offered as a substitute for any person, then being himself a substitute for any person or class under this Act, on pain of forfeiting for every such offence, the sum of fifty pounds specie, to be recovered by action of debt in any court of record in this State, by any person who will sue for the same, and applied one half to his own use, the other half to the use of the State, and becoming moreover liable to be removed from office.

CHAPTER XIV. 1ST SESSION.
1783. An Act to amend an Act passed in the year of our Lord, one thousand seven hundred and forty one, intituled, An Act concerning Servants and Slaves. (Pages 496-497).

North Carolina Law

I. Whereas the mode directed in the said Act for thr trial of slaves where the offence may be of a small and trivial nature is found to be attended with delay, great loss of time, and expence to the owner; For remedy whereof,

II. Be it therefore enacted by the General Assembly of the State of North Carolina, and it is hereby enacted by the authority of the same, That where any slave or slaves shall hereafter committ any misdemeanor or offence which is not by law declared capital, and which in the opinion of the justice or justices before whom such offending slave may be carried for examination, shall appear to be of so trivial a nature as not to deserve a greater punishment than a single justice of the peace is by this Act impowered to inflict, such justice shall, and he is hereby authorised and impowered forthwith to issue subpoenas if necessary, to compell the attendance of witnesses, and proceed immediately upon the trial of such slave in a summary way, and to pass sentence and award execution; provided the punishment extends no further than by ordering the offender to be publicly whipped not exceeding forty lashes: And where the offence for which any slave shall be apprehended shall appear to the justice or justices to be of such nature as to deserve any other or greater punishment, such offending slave shall be committed to gaol, and stand his or her trial by a court in the way prescribed by the afore recited Act.

III. Provided, That upon all trials of slaves before any justice of the peace, for any misdemeanor under this Act, any other of the justices of the county where such slave may be upon trial, may, if they think proper, sit upon and assist in the examination and trial.

IV. And whereas the laws now in force in this State are not sufficient to prevent the bainful practice of free persons trading or trafficking with slaves; Be it therefore enacted by the authority aforesaid, That if any free person whatsoever shall hereafter presume to buy, or receive from any negro or other slave any commodity whatsoever, without leave of the owner or overseer of such slave in writing, the person or persons so offending shall for every offence forfeit and pay the sum of forty shillings specie, over and above the value of the article purchased or received by them, to be recovered by the owner or overseer of such slave, before any jurisdiction having cognizance thereof.

V. Provided nevertheless, That on the failure or neglect of the person owning or overlooking such slave, any other person may sue for and recover such fine, and apply the same to his own use, after giving the owner or overseer aforesaid one months notice.

CHAPTER XXI. 1ST SESSION.
1783. An Act for appointing an agent and holding a treaty with the Cherokee Indians, and for other purposes. (Pages 509-510).

    I. Whereas, holding treaties and appointing one or more agents to keep up a continual friendly correspondence with the said Indians, may prevent future wars, and save expence of blood and treasure;

    II. Be it therefore enacted by the General Assembly of the State of North Carolina, and it is hereby Enacted by the authority of the same, That his Excellency, the Governor, as soon as may be shall hold, or by such persons as he shall commissionate for that purpose, cause to be held a treaty with the Chickamawga and Over-Hill Cherokees, and also with the Cherokees of the Middle and Valley settlements, at the Long Island on Holston River; and his Excellency the Governor is hereby impowered to cause the musket powder belonging to this State, or so much thereof as he shall think necessary, not exceeding one thousand weight, to be removed to the frontiers convenient to the place where the said treaty shall be held, and to give the said powder, or cause the same to be given in presents to the said Indians; and his Excellency the Governor is hereby impowered to issue warrants on the treasury for any sum not exceeding two thousand five hundred pounds specie, and cause the same to be laid out in the purchase of goods suitable for the said Indians, and the same goods to give or cause to be given in consideration of the lands by the said Indians to be ceded to the State, and also to issue warrants on the treasury for the sum of one thousand pounds specie, to defray the expences of removing the said powder and goods, and the purchase of necessary provisions for the support of the said Indians, attending the treaty, and other expences thereof: And a full and accurate account of all expenditures, articles, stipulations, cessions, agreements and proceedings of the said treaty, wherein this State is or may be interested, shall be laid before the next General Assembly.

    III. And be it further Enacted by the authority aforesaid, That Joseph Martin be, and he is hereby appointed agent in behalf of this State for the Chickamawga and Over-Hill Cherokees, and for the Cherokees of the Middle settlements and Valley towns; and the said agent shall visit the Indians under his agency in their own country once in six months, shall deliver to them messages from the Governor, receive their talks, record them in his journal, record in the like manner such public talks as he without order may deliver them, and send copies of both to the Governor.

North Carolina Law

IV. And in order that all the dealings and intercourses with the said Indians may be carried on in the most friendly and upright manner, and every fraud and imposition as far as possible prevented, Be it therefore Enacted by the authority aforesaid, That no person whatsoever shall deal or traffic with the said Indians within the limits of this State, without license first had and obtained from the Governor for the same, and that these licenses shall be granted only to men of the most upright and unexceptional honest characters, and shall not authorize any person obtaining them to trade with the said Indians for any longer time than one year, and those be annually received and obtained.

V. And be it further Enacted by the authority aforesaid, That every person obtaining such licence, shall pay for the same to the Governor the sum of five pounds specie: And if any person shall without such licence presume to deal with the said Indians within the limits of this State, he shall forfeit and pay fifty pounds specie for the first offence, and one hundred pounds specie for every subsequent offence, one half to the use of the public, the other half to him or them that shall prosecute for the same, to be recovered by action of debt, bill, plaint, or information, in any court of record.

VI. And be it Enacted by the authority aforesaid, That the said agent shall be allowed one hundred pounds specie per annum for all services.

CHAPTER LXX.
1784. An Act for Enfranchising Ned Griffin, Late the Property of William Kitchen. (Page 639).

I. Whereas, Ned Griffin, late the property of William Kitchen, of Edgecombe county, was promised the full enjoyments of hie liberty, on condition that he, the said Ned Griffin, should faithfully serve as a soldier in the continental line of this State for and during the term of twelve months; and whereas the said Ned Griffin did faithfully on his part perform the condition, and whereas it is just and reasonable that the said Ned Griffin should receive the reward promised for the services which he performed;

II. Be it therefore Enacted by the General Assembly of the State of North Carolina, and it is hereby Enacted by the authority of the same, That the said Ned Griffin, late the property of William Kitchen, shall forever hereafter be in every respect declared to be a freeman; and he shall be, and he is hereby enfranchised and forever delivered and discharged from the yoke of slavery; any law, usage or custom to the contrary thereof in anywise notwithstanding.

CHAPTER II. 1ST SESSION.
1784. An Act to ascertain the number of White and Black Inhabitants, and the Citizens of every Age and Condition in the State. (Pages 650-651).

    I. Whereas it is recommended by the United States in Congress assembled, that the number of white and black inhabitants, and free citizens of every age, sex and condition, including those bound to servitude for a term of years, and three fifths of all other persons not comprehended in the forgoing description shall be taken in each State; and in order to comply with the above recommendation,

    II. Be it Enacted by the General Assembly of the State of North Carolina, and it is hereby Enacted by the authority of the same, That the several county courts in this State, shall within six months after the passing of this Act, appoint a proper person in each captain's district to take a list of the number of white and black inhabitants and the free citizens of every age, sex and condition in each district, which lists shall distinguish the number of blacks from the whites and other free inhabitants in the following manner:

White males from twenty one years old to sixty.
White males under twenty one years old and above sixty.
White females of every age.
Blacks of each sex from twelve to fifty.
Blacks upwards fifty and under twelve years old.

CHAPTER XLII. 1ST SESSION.
1784. An Act for Clearing and Opening the Navigation of Tar River and Fishing Creek, in the Counties of Pitt, Edgecombe and Halifax. (Pages 702-703).

    III. And in order to keep the navigation of the said river and creek open, Be it Enacted, That in case any person shall fall any tree, or make any hedge in or across the said river or creek, or otherwise obstruct the navigation thereof, shall for every such offence, being thereof convicted before any justice of the peace of the county wherein the offence shall be committed, forfeit and pay the sum of five pounds current money, and be obliged to remove the obstruction at their own expence, and shall be further liable to the action of any person or persons injured thereby; and if any negro slave found guilty of any of the above mentioned offences and convicted thereof, he, she or they, by order of a justice of the peace shall receive thirty nine lashes well laid on his or her bare back for each and every such offence.

CHAPTER VI. 1ST SESSION.
1785. An Additional Act to Amend the Several Acts for Regulating the Town of Wilmington, and to Regulate and Restrain the Conduct of Slaves and Others in the said Town, and in the Towns of Washington, Edenton and Fayetteville. (Pages 725-730).

    V. And be it Enacted by the authority aforesaid, That it shall and may be lawful for the commissioners of the said town, and they are hereby required as soon as their funds will permit, to build cellars under their market places or other public buildings in the said town, where the elevation of the ground will permit such cellars to be sunk of a proper depth; and such cellars to rent out from time to time for the benefit of the said town.

    And whereas it is customary for many persons, as well in the country as in the several towns in this State, to permit their slaves to hire themselves out from day to day, by which great profits are acquired, and it is reasonable that those persons who derive such advantages from the labour of their slaves in the towns should contribute more than the ordinary taxes towards its support, and at the same time that a distinction should be made between such slaves as may be returned as taxable property in the said towns respectively, and such whose owners reside in the country, and return their taxable property there, although part of their slaves generally work in the towns. And whereas permitting slaves to hire themselves under proper restrictions and regulations, may be rendered convenient for such persons as may occasionally want daily labourers:

    VI. Be it therefore Enacted by the authority aforesaid, That from and after the first day of May next, it shall not be lawful for any slave in the towns of Wilmington, Edenton or Fayetteville, to hire her or himself out, without first producing a permission in writing from the owner, or other persons having the care or management of such slave, directed to the commissioners, trustees or directors of the town where such slave shall be;

who thereupon shall cause the said permission to be entered by the town clerk in their books and filed, for which the owner of the slave shall pay a fee of one shilling; and the commissioners shall cause a leaden or pewter badge to be affixed to some conspicuous part of the outer garment of such slave with a device, which may be altered from time to time, expressive of the intention of such badge; and every slave having a badge in manner by this Act directed, may hire him or herself out, and may lawfully be hired by any person or persons whatever.

  VII. And be it Enacted by the authority aforesaid, That for all slaves who shall have badges as above directed, and who shall be town taxables, there shall be paid as follows, to wit, For every male slave being a tradesman there shall be paid yearly to the commissioners, trustees or directors the sum of sixteen shillings; for every male slave not being a tradesman the sum of ten shillings, and for every female slave the sum of eight shillings; but if any slaves having such badges shall not be returned as town taxables, then there shall be paid for every male slave being a tradesman twenty four shillings; for every male slave not being a tradesman the sum of fifteen shillings, and for every female slave twelve shillings, to be applied as other taxes assessed and collected in the said towns.

  And that the taxes upon slaves having badges may be more easily collected and all fraud and evasion prevented:

  VIII. Be it Enacted by the authority aforesaid, That the taxes imposed by this Act on slaves who shall be returned as town taxables, shall be paid and collected in the same manner as other town taxes; and that the taxes imposed on such slaves as may not be returned as town taxables, shall be paid or secured to be paid, to the satisfaction of the commissioners, trustees or directors, on or before the first day of July in every year, before any badge shall be by them granted as aforesaid. And whereas there are many slaves in the said towns, who contrary to law have houses of their own, or are permitted to reside in the outhouses or kitchens of divers of the inhabitants, or in the houses of the free negroes, mulattoes, persons of mixed blood and others, and work and labour for themselves in several trades and occupations, stipulating to pay their owners such daily, weekly or monthly wages as shall be demanded of them; by reason of which robberies and frauds frequently happen, servants are corrupted, and the poor white inhabitants are deprived of the means of earning their subsistence by labour: For remedy whereof,

  IX. Be it Enacted by the authority aforesaid, That no slave shall be permitted to exercise any trade or occupation in the said towns respectively without a certificate from the owner, or other persons having the care or management thereof, directed as aforesaid, or without such badge as shall be given to slaves permitted to hire themselves; and all slaves permitted to exercise any trade or occupation as aforesaid, shall be subject to pay the same tax as slaves who are not returnable as taxable property in the towns aforesaid, and to be paid or secured in manner as before directed. Provided always, That nothing herein contained, shall extend or be construed to extend to prohibit any person or persons residing in the said towns respectively, from hiring out their slaves, or in employing such slaves in exercising any trade or occupation under the immediate direction of their owners residing in the said town, so that such slave or slaves be not permitted to receive the wages contracted for, nor the value of any article manufactured or made, or the work and labour done, but in all such cases the owner or other person having the care of slaves, shall make the contract and receive the monies arising therefrom.

And in order to discriminate between free negroes, mulattoes and other persons of mixed blood, and slaves:

X. Be it Enacted by the authority aforesaid, That all persons of the above mentioned description, who are or shall be free, shall on or before the said first day of May next, apply to the commissioners, trustees or directors of the respective towns aforesaid, in order to have their names registered; and every such person coming into the said towns respectively to reside, shall within three days after their arrival make the like application; and the commissioners, trustees or directors are hereby authorised and required to give every such free person a badge of cloth, of such colour or colours as they shall respectively direct, to be fixed on the left shoulder, and to have thereon wrought in legible capital letters the word FREE: For registration of each of which names the town clerk shall receive two shillings, and the commissioners, trustees and directors respectively shall receive the sum of eight shillings for the use of their respective towns; which registration and badge shall continue in force during the time that such free person shall remain an inhabitant of the town in which he or she shall reside; and if any free negro, mulatto or other person of mixed blood, shall neglect or refuse to apply to the commissioners, trustees or directors as aforesaid, or shall refuse to receive a badge in manner by this Act directed, every such person so neglecting or refusing shall be subject to pay the same tax that is hereby imposed on slaves who are not returned as town taxables, and who shall have badges to enable them to hire themselves; and that such free persons may be the better known, the justices of the peace who shall receive the returns of taxable property in said towns, shall in their yearly returns describe all such persons as are free, and are negroes, mulattoes or otherwise of mixed blood as aforesaid; and all such persons as aforesaid not paying their fines, fees and taxes shall be hired out for so long a time as will pay the same respectively.

XI. And be it further Enacted by the authority aforesaid, That the commissioners of the said town, shall and may from time to time, make such ordinances and regulations, and under such fines, forfeitures and penalties as to them shall seem reasonable, for the better carrying the intentions of this Act, and other Acts for the better regulation of the said towns into execution, but so as that such ordinances and regulations do not contravene the fundamental constitution and laws of the State, and so that the party thinking himself aggrieved thereby may appeal to the county court.

XII. And be it Enacted by the authority aforesaid, That if any slave permitted to hire him or herself out in a manner by this Act directed should happen to be capitally convicted for any crime committed during the time that he or she shall have such permission, the owner of such slave shall not be allowed any compensation from the public or otherwise for the value thereof when executed.

XIII. And be it also Enacted by the authority aforesaid, That if any free person of mixed blood, or any free negro, residing within any of the said towns, shall be convicted of any felonious crimes with slaves in the town where he or she shall so reside, or shall receive any goods from any slave or slaves without a ticket from his, her or their owner or other person having the care and management of such slave or slaves, or shall receive or harbour in his or her house or otherwise, any runaway or absconding slave or slaves, every such person being a free negro or of mixed blood as aforesaid, shall upon conviction, forfeit and pay to the commissioners, trustees or directors of the town in which he or she shall reside the sum of ten pounds, to be levied of his or her property real or personal and applied to the stock of the town. Provided always, That if any such free person so convicted as aforesaid, shall upon conviction signify his or her consent to remove from such town, and shall give security for such removal within ten days thereafter; and also that he or she will not reside in such town or within ten miles thereof, for the space of seven years, then it shall and may be lawful for the commissioners, trustees or directors as the case may be to take such security payable to themselves and their successors in office, and upon breach of the condition to put the same in suit and recover the penalty for the use of their town; and upon such bond being taken with security as aforesaid, the penalty inflicted upon conviction as before directed, shall be remitted to the offender, any thing herein contained to the contrary notwithstanding.

And whereas the laws and regulations made to prevent dealing and trafficing with slaves, have been found insufficient to prevent that dangerous and pernicious practice:

XIV. Be it therefor Enacted by the authority aforesaid, That if any free person shall either buy from or sell to any slave or slaves, or shall barter with any slave or slaves, any kind of goods or commodities whatsoever, or other thing, without a permission in writing from the master, mistress or other person having the management of such slave or slaves, every such free person shall on conviction forfeit and pay the sum of ten pounds, to be levied of his or her property as other recoveries by law; and if the offender shall not have sufficient property to satisfy the judgment, then such offender shall be committed to close custody, and shall remain in prison without bail or mainprize for any time not exceeding three months.

XV. And it is hereby further Enacted by the authority aforesaid, That if any person or persons shall be convicted of entertaining any slave or slaves in his, her or their house or houses, or other place or places, in any manner whatsoever, for any money or otherwise, every person convicted thereof shall forfeit and pay to the commissioners, trustees or directors of the town where such offence shall be committed, for the first offence ten pounds, for the second offence twenty pounds, and for the third offence shall be whipped publicly not exceeding thirty nine lashes, and shall be thereby rendered infamous. Provided always, That when the offender shall be unable to pay the forfeiture, he or she may be whipt for the first or second offence or either of them.

And in order that persons dealing with slaves without permission as aforesaid, may the more easily be convicted:

XVI. Be it Enacted by the authority aforesaid, That if any slave shall be seen going into any store or other house, and such slave shall carry into such store or house, any article or articles which may be supposed for sale, or any bottle, jug or other thing in which liquor may be conveyed, or shall bring out of such house or store anything which may be supposed to have been purchased therein, and such slave shall not have a badge as herein before directed for slaves who may be permitted to follow some trade or occupation, and proof shall be made of the facts, the same shall be deemed sufficient to convict the offender, unless he or she can produce a permission as aforesaid in writing from the master, mistress or person having the management of such slave. Provided always, That nothing herein contained shall be construed to prevent any slave or slaves from delivering to any person or persons residing in any of the said towns, any article of provision or other thing which may be sent to any such person from their friends in the country or elsewhere, provided such slave has a written permission for so doing.

 XVII. And be it further Enacted by the authority aforesaid, That commissioners, trustees and directors of the said towns respectively, are hereby empowered and required to make such additions to and explanations of the several clauses of this Act, relative to slaves, free negroes, and free persons of mixed blood, as may tend to carry the same more effectually into execution against all persons who come within the purview thereof. Provided always, That all appeals from the commissioners, trustees or directors of the said towns respectively shall be tried by a jury.

(Passed December 29, 1785.)

CHAPTER V. 1ST SESSION.
1786. An Act to Impose a Duty on all Slaves Brought Into This State by Land or Water. (Pages 792-794).
 Whereas the importation of slaves into this State is productive of evil consequences, and highly impolitic:
 I. Be it therefore Enacted by the General Assembly of the State of North Carolina, and it is hereby Enacted by the authority of the same, That from and after the passing of this Act, a duty of fifty shillings per head on all slaves under seven and over forty years of age, and a duty of five pounds per head on all slaves between the ages of seven and twelve years, and between the ages of thirty and forty years, and a duty of ten pounds per head on all slaves of twelve years and upwards to the age of thirty years, shall be collected by the collectors of the different ports in this State, on all slaves brought into any of the said ports; which duty shall be collected and accounted for in the same manner, and under the same regulations as are prescribed for collecting and accounting for the duties on goods, wares and merchandise, &c. imported into this State.

 II. And be it further Enacted by the authority aforesaid, That if any slave or slaves shall be brought into this State by land, except as herein after excepted, the person or persons who shall have the care of the same or

North Carolina Law

claim thereto, shall within ten days after his or their arrival within the State, make faithful return of the number of slaves so brought into the State, to the clerk of court of the county where he may be, and shall swear to and subscribe the said return or list, as just and true, and shall pay into the hands of the clerk the aforesaid duties for each and every slave, for the use of the State, or give bond and sufficient security for the payment of the said sum in three months after such return is made; and upon failing to perform the condition of the said bond, the clerk is hereby directed at the first court which may be held after the said bond is due, to enter up final judgment thereon, and the court is hereby directed to award execution.

III. And be it further Enacted, That the clerks of each court respectively, shall annually account with the treasurer on oath, for all the duties they may receive in virtue of this Act, under the same pains and penalties as they are liable to for failing to account for other public monies.

IV. And be it further Enacted by the authority aforesaid, That if any person or persons who may bring slaves hereafter into this State by land, shall fail or neglect to comply with the directions of this Act, in making return of the same on oath as is by this Act directed, he shall forfeit and pay the sum of one hundred pounds for each slave so brought in and not accounted for, to be recovered in any court of record within this State, one half to the person who shall sue for the same, and the other half to the use of the State; and shall be moreover liable to pay the aforementioned duty on each slave, in manner as is before prescribed: Provided nevertheless, That nothing in this Act shall be construed to compel any person or persons who may remove to this State with their families and property, in order to become citizens thereof, to pay the aforesaid duty on any slave or slaves belonging to them; but in such case the person or persons bringing such slave or slaves into this State, shall, before some justice of the peace of the county in which he or she may be, take the following oath: "I, A.B. do swear that the slaves brought by me into this State are for my own service, and that I have not brought them into this State with intention to sell or dispose of them, or to evade the payment of the duties imposed on slaves brought into this State by land or water. So help me God." And provided also, That this duty shall not be imposed or collected on any slaves which may become the property of any of the citizens of this State by gift, devise, marriage, or descent, or any which are now the property of any of the said citizens, and taken by the British in the late war, and which may be within any of the United States or elsewhere.

V. Be it Enacted, That a tax of five pounds per head shall be levied and collected by the collectors of the different ports within this State, upon all slaves imported therein from the coast of Africa, and which have not been more than one month in any other port or place after leaving the said coast; provided, That no slave born on the passage shall be subject to this tax.

VI. And be it further Enacted, That every person who shall introduce into this State any slave or slaves after the passing hereof, from any of the United States which have passed laws for the liberation of slaves, shall on complaint thereof before any justice of the peace, be compelled by such justice to enter into bond with sufficient surety in the sum of fifty pounds current money for each slave, for the removing of such slave or slaves to the State from whence such slave or slaves were brought, within three months thereafter, the penalty whereof shall be recovered, one half for the use of the State, the other for the use of the prosecutor, on failure of a compliance therewith; and the person introducing such slaves shall also in case of such failure, forfeit and pay the sum of one hundred pounds, to be recovered by any person suing for the same, and applied to his own use.

VII. And be it Enacted by the authority aforesaid, That all slaves brought into this State, unless in vessels which enter with the collectors of duties in some of the ports in this State, shall be considered as having been brought in by land, and liable to the same fines, penalties and duties, as is directed by this Act; provided, That nothing herein contained shall be construed so as to impose the aforesaid duty or forfeiture on any slave or slaves who may pass through this State to any other State, under the direction of their owners.

VIII. And be it further Enacted by the authority aforesaid, That this Act shall not be in force or take effect, before the first day of February next.

IX. And be it further Enacted, That all laws and clauses of laws which come within the meaning of this Act, as far forth as they respect a duty or imposition on slaves imported or brought into this State by land or water, are hereby repealed and made void. **(Passed Jan. 6, 1787.)**

CHAPTER XV. 1ST SESSION.
1786. An Act to Amend an Act, Entitled, "An Act to Amend an Act, Entitled, 'An Act for Ascertaining What Property in This State Shall

Be Deemed Taxable Property, The Method of Assessing the Same, and Collecting Public Taxes.'" (Page 807).

I. Be it Enacted by the General Assembly of the State of North Carolina, and it is hereby Enacted by the authority of the same, That all land held by deed or entry, where there is no caveat, or by lease, or in right of dower, all town lots with certain improvements, all free males and servants between the ages of twenty one and sixty years, all slaves male and female between the ages of twelve and sixty years within this State, shall be subject to the payment of public taxes; and the public taxes on such property and persons shall be assessed and proportioned in the manner directed by this Act, that is to say, all lands shall be taxed by the hundred acres, and so in proportion for a greater or less quantity.

CHAPTER XVII. 1ST SESSION.
1786. An Act to Repeal the Several Acts of Assembly Respecting Slaves Within This State, as far as the Same Relates to Making an Allowance to the Owner or Owners for any Executed or Outlawed Slave or Slaves. (Page 809).

Whereas many persons by cruel treatment to their slaves, cause them to commit crimes for which many of the said slaves are executed, whereby a very burdensome debt is unjustly imposed on the good citizens of this State: For remedy whereof,

I. Be it Enacted by the General Assembly of the State of North Carolina, and it is Enacted by the authority of the same, That from and after the passing of this Act, the several Acts of Assembly of this State, as far as relates to making an allowance for any outlawed or executed slave or slaves, shall be, and the same is hereby repealed and made utterly void. (Passed Jan. 6, 1787.)

CHAPTER XLVIII. 1ST SESSION.
1786. An Act to emancipate Caesar, formerly a Servant of Samuel Yeargen, Deceased. (Page 850).

Whereas by the last will and testament of Samuel Yeargen, deceased, late of the county of Warren, he did desire in his said will that a certain negro man of his property, should after the death of his daughter Anne Alston, wife to William Alston, of Chatham county, be set free, for and during the full term of fifty five years: And whereas the said Anne being now dead, it is thought just and right the said last will and testament should be adhered to:

I. Be it therefore Enacted by the General Assembly, That from and after the passing of this Act, that the aforesaid Caesar shall and may be at his own liberty, for and during the term mentioned in his master's will, upon the same footing, and under the same restrictions as other free negroes are intitled to in this State, and shall be known and called by the name of Caesar Henry; any law to the contrary notwithstanding. **(Passed Jan. 6, 1787).**

CHAPTER LVIII. 1ST SESSION.
1786. An Act to Emancipate Hannah Bowers, a Person of Mixed Blood, Belonging to the Estate of the Late Alexander Gaston Deceased. (Page 859).

Whereas it appears to this General Assembly, That the late Alexander Gaston, of the town of New Bern, did in his lifetime frequently express a desire that the said girl Hannah should be set free, and did certify the same in his own handwriting, which certificate has been since found among the papers of the deceased: And whereas the widow of the said Alexander Gaston has also signified her desire that the said girl should in her compliance with her husbands wishes in his lifetime be set free:

I. Be it therefore Enacted by the General Assembly of the State of North Carolina, and it is hereby Enacted by the authority of the same, That the said Molatto girl called Hannah, alias Hannah Bowers, shall be, and is hereby declared to be emancipated and made free to all intents and purposes, and shall be entitled to all privileges and benefits of a free person in as full and absolute manner, as if she the said Hannah had been born of a free woman. **(Passed Jan. 6, 1787.)**

CHAPTER VI. 1ST SESSION.
1787. An Act to Prevent Thefts and Robberies by Slaves, Free Negroes and Mulattoes. (Pages 890-891).

Whereas it is represented that slaves and free negroes are encouraged to rob or steal from the inhabitants all kinds of produce, by the facility with which they may conceal and dispose of such produce to the masters of trading vessels in the several bays, harbours, creeks and rivers within this State:

North Carolina Law

I. Be it therefore Enacted by the General Assembly of the State of North Carolina, and it is hereby Enacted by the authority of the same, That from and after the passing of this Act, it shall not be permitted for the master or commander of any vessel to entertain any slave, negro or mulatto on board such vessel at any time between sun set and sun rise, nor during the Sabbath day, unless such slave, negro or mulatto as shall belong to the vessel, or shall have a pass from his, her or their master or mistress, or from some justice of the peace, expressing the time when and the business for which they go on board: And if any slave, negro or mulatto who has not such a pass, or is not statedly employed on board the vessel as one of the hands, shall be found on board any vessel in any bay, harbour, creek or river within this State, on the Sabbath day, or in the night between sun set and sun rise, he shall presumed to have been disposing of stolen goods; and the master or commander of such vessel on complaint and conviction before any two justices of the peace, shall be subject to a fine for the entertainment of such slave, negro or mulatto of five pounds for the first offence, and ten pounds for every succeeding offence, to be applied to the use of the poor of the county in which such conviction shall be had: But any person dissatisfied with the judgment of the said two justices, shall have the right of appealing to the court of the county, the determination whereof shall be final; the person appealing to be subject to the same regulations as in the cases of other persons appealing from the judgment of a justice.

And whereas the property of many of the citizens of this State may be greatly affected by permitting a private intercourse between slaves and free negroes and mulattoes:

II. Be it Enacted by the authority aforesaid, That if any free negro or mulatto shall entertain any slave in his or her house during the Sabbath, or in the night between sun set and sun rise, he or she shall for entertaining such slave be subject to a fine of twenty shillings for the first offence, and forty shillings for every subsequent offence, to be recovered on conviction before any one justice of the peace, and applied to the use of the poor of the county in which the offence shall be committed, saving to the party the same right of appealing as aforesaid. And in case the said free negro or mulatto shall not be able to pay the fine aforesaid, the constable who shall have attended at such conviction shall hire out said free negro or mulatto to the person who shall take him or her for the shortest space of time in payment of the said fine with costs, the said constable having previously advertised at least ten days at the door of the court house and other public places of the said county, that such negro or mulatto would be hired out for the purpose aforesaid; and the person who shall hire such free negro or mulatto, shall be bound to pay at the time and place of such hiring the amount of the fine with costs as aforesaid.

III. And be it further Enacted by the authority aforesaid, That in case any free negro or mulatto shall from and after the passing of this Act, intermarry or cohabit with any slave, without the consent of his or her master had in writing, and attested by two justices of the peace, such free negro or mulatto shall be liable and held to pay to the master or mistress of such slave the sum of ten pounds; and on failing to pay such sum, shall be held to service to the master or mistress of such slave for and during the term of one year.

CHAPTER XXVIII. 1ST SESSION.
1787. An Act for the Better Regulation of the Town of Edenton. (Pages 920-921).

XXIII. And be it further Enacted by the authority aforesaid, That no person shall under any pretence whatsoever make any fires, or cause any to be made, on the wharfs or in the streets in the night time, and any person offending against this regulation shall forfeit and pay the sum of five pounds for every such offence, to be recovered before any justice of the peace of the county and for the use of the said town; and if the offender should be a slave, he or she shall on conviction receive thirty nine lashes on his or her bare back; provided said slave did not act by order of his owner or the person having the care of such slave, in which case such owner or person shall be subject to the above fine: Provided, That no person shall be subject to these penalties until the commissioners have made publication of the regulations last mentioned for the space of three months at least at the door of the court house of Chowan county.

And whereas the regulations heretofore made to prevent dealing and trafficking with slaves, have been found insufficient to prevent that dangerous and pernicious practice:

XXIV. Be it Enacted by the authority aforesaid, That if any free person shall buy from or sell to any slave or slaves within the limits of the said town, or shall barter with any slave or slaves any kind of goods or commodities whatsoever or other thing, without a permission in writing from the master or mistress, or any other person having the management of such slave or slaves, every such person shall on conviction before any justice of the peace of the said county of Chowan, forfeit and pay the sum of five pounds, to be levied of his or her property as other recoveries by law for the use of the said town, subject nevertheless to the appeal of the party grieved; and if the offender shall not have sufficient property to satisfy the judgment, then such offender shall be committed to close custody and shall remain in prison without bail or mainprise for any time not exceeding three months.

XXV. And be it further Enacted by the authority aforesaid, That if any person or persons shall be convicted of entertaining any slave or slaves in his, her or their house or houses, or other place or places, in any manner whatsoever, for money or otherwise, every person convicted in the above recited manner, shall forfeit and pay the sum of ten pounds for the first offence, and the sum of twenty pounds for every other offence, to be levied of his or her property as other recoveries by law, and for the use of the said town; and if the offender shall be unable to pay the forfeiture, then such offender shall be committed to close custody, and shall remain in prison without bail or mainprise for any time not exceeding six months.

XXVI. And be it further Enacted by the authority aforesaid, That after the passing of this Act it shall not be lawful for any slave in the town to hire her or himself out or exercise any trade or occupation without first producing a permission in writing from the owner, or other person having the management of such slave, directed to the commissioners of the said town, who shall thereupon (if there is no just cause to the contrary) cause the said permission to be entered by the town clerk in their book and filed, for which the owner of the said slave shall pay to the clerk a fee of four shillings; and the commissioners or a majority of them shall grant a license under their hand and seal to such slave to hire her or himself out, for any time not exceeding twelve months, and any slave having a license as directed by this Act may hire him or herself out, and may lawfully be hired to any person or persons whatsoever; and if any person after the passing of this Act hires any slave or slaves in the said town, without such license from the commissioners as directed by this Act, he or she shall forfeit and pay the sum of five pounds for every such offence to be recovered before any justice of the peace of the county, and for the use of the said town. Provided always, That nothing herein contained shall extend or be construed to prohibit any person or persons residing in the said town from hiring out their slaves, or in employing such slaves in exercising any trade or occupation under the immediate direction of their owners, so that such slave or slaves be not permitted to receive the wages contracted for, but in all such cases the owner or the person having the care of such slave, shall make the contract and receive the monies arising therefrom.

CHAPTER XXIX. 1ST SESSION.
1787. An Act for the Better Regulation of the Town of Fayatteville. (Page 925).
  XI. And be it further Enacted, That the said Commissioners are hereby fully authorized and particularly required and directed to make such laws and regulations as they may deem necessary, to prevent hogs running at large in the said town, slaves from keeping houses without a license from the Commissioners, and to prevent all persons from dealing with slaves not having tickets from their masters, mistresses or overseers, and to make such other and further laws and regulations respecting the same as they may think expedient. Provided nevertheless, That regulations respecting hogs or other stock, shall not be considered to extend beyond the present limits of the town: And provided also, That the powers hereby committed to the said Commissioners, shall not be construed to extend to the imprisonment of any slave as a punishment, or in any instance to exceed the punishment of thirty nine lashes. Provided that in all cases where any person shall be dissatisfied with the judgment of the said Commissioners, he shall have the liberty of appealing therefrom to the court of pleas and quarter sessions for the county of Cumberland.

CHAPTER XXXV. 1ST SESSION.
1787. An Act to Emancipate Certain Persons therein mentioned. (Pages 929-930).
  Whereas Agerton Willis, late of Bladen county, was in his lifetime possessed of a certain slave called Joseph, and in consideration of the services of him the said Joseph, and the particular obligations he conceived himself under to the said Joseph for his fidelity and attention, did by his last will and testament devise to the said Joseph his freedom and emancipation, and did also give unto the said Joseph a considerable property, both real and personal: And whereas the executor and next of kin to the said Joseph did in pursuance of the said will take counsel thereon, and were well advised that the same could not by any means take effect, but would be of prejudice to the said slave and subject him still as property of the said Agerton Willis; whereupon the said executor and next of kin, together with

the heirs of the said Agerton Willis, deceased, did cause a fair and equal distribution of the said estate, as well to do equity and justice in the said case to the said Joseph, as in pursuance of their natural love and affection to the said Agerton, and did resolve on the freedom of the said Joseph and to give an equal proportion of the said estate: Wherefore,

I. Be it Enacted by the General Assembly of the State of North Carolina, and it is hereby Enacted by the authority of the same, That from and after the passing of this Act, the said Joseph shall and is hereby declared to be emancipated and set free; and from hence forward he be called and known by the name of Joseph Willis, by which name he may take, hold, occupy, possess and enjoy to him and his heirs forever, all and singular the property both real and personal so given him by the said distribution of the said executor, heirs and next of kin, and by the said name of Joseph Willis shall hence forward be entitled to all the rights and privileges of a free person of mixed blood: Provided nevertheless, That this act shall not extend to enable the said Joseph by himself or attorney, or any other person in trust for him, in any manner to commence or prosecute any suit or suits for any other property but such as may be given him by this act or such as he may have acquired by his own industry, but this act may in all such cases be plead in bar, and the property therein given be considered as a full and ample consideration for the final accommodation and settlement of all doubts concerning the freedom and property either real, personal or mixed belonging or in any manner appertaining to the said Joseph.

And whereas it hath been made appear to the satisfaction of the General Assembly that Richard Dobbs Spaight, of Craven county, Esquire, hath consented and is desirous to liberate and set free a certain mulatto girl now his property, called or known by the name of Mary Long:

II. Be it therefore Enacted by the authority aforesaid, That from and after the passing of this act the before mentioned mulatto girl called Mary Long, now the property of Richard Dobbs Spaight, Esquire, shall be and continue liberated and set free, and shall thenceforward be entitled to all the rights and privileges of a free person of mixed blood in this State, and by the said name of Mary Long shall and may receive and hold, possess and enjoy any real and personal estate or property which she may hereafter acquire or become possessed of, in the same manner as any other person of mixed blood might or could acquire, and possess the same to all intents and purposes as if she had been born free.

Whereas it hath been represented to this General Assembly by the memorial of John Allen, a free man of mixed blood, that he hath purchased a mulatto woman named Betty and her child named Mary, which woman he has long lived with and considered as his wife, and praying that the General Assembly would be pleased to emancipate and set free the said mulatto woman and her child:

III. Be it therefore Enacted by the authority aforesaid, That the said mulatto woman named Betty and her child named Mary, shall be and they and each of them are hereby emancipated and made free, and they and each of them may hereafter take and use the surname of Allen, and are hereby declared to be able and capable in law to possess and enjoy every right, privilege and immunity in as full and ample manner as they could or might have done if they had been born free.

Chapter III. 1ST SESSION.
1788. An Act to confirm the Rights and Titles of several Citizens of this State in certain Negroes therein described, and preventingUnjust and Vexatious Law Suits. (Page 954).

Whereas in the year one thousand seven hundred and eighty one, sundry of the citizens of this State did enlist in the service of the State of South Carolina, in the brigade commonly called the state troops, commanded by Brigadier General Sumpter, and several of them agreeable to their enlistment and service did draw negroes, one for each private soldier, and officers in proportion to their rank, which negroes were at that time taken from the disaffected citizens of said State by order of General Sumpter for that purpose; and the General Assembly of the State of South Carolina did since, to wit, on the twenty first day of March, one thousand seven hundred and eighty four, pass an ordinance to indemnify Brigadier General Sumpter and the officers acting under his command during the British invasion, in the second section of which ordinance it is ordained, that in all cases where any property hath been taken from any person resident in said State, and appropriated to public use by order of the said Brigadier General Thomas Sumpter, such person or persons shall apply for redress to the Legislature and not elsewhere, yet the disaffected citizens of that state, from whom those negroes were taken, have since instituted sundry suits against the citizens aforesaid of this state for the recovery of said negroes. For remedy whereof,

I. Be it Enacted by the General Assembly of the State of North Carolina, and it is hereby Enacted by the authority of the same, That where any citizen of this state shall have actually served in the aforesaid brigade, and drawn a negro or negroes for said service, if there is or hereafter shall be any suit or suits for said negroes commenced against them, or any of them, or any person or persons claiming by, from or under them or any of them, on the fact being proved to the satisfaction of the court and jury trying the cause, that such negro or negroes were regularly drawn in consequence of said service, a verdict and judgment shall be given for the defendants; any law, usage or custom to the contrary notwithstanding. Provided nevertheless, That nothing herein contained shall be construed to vest the property of any negro or negroes taken by any person or persons of the aforesaid brigade, and not specially delivered to the said troops for their pay in the manner aforesaid for said service. And provided also, That nothing herein contained shall preclude citizens of other states, except those of South Carolina, from recovering their negroes, if any may have been taken for the purposes aforesaid who have not applied to the State of South Carolina agreeable to the directions of the aforesaid ordinance for satisfaction and received the same.

CHAPTER VII. 1ST SESSION.
1788. An Act to amend the several Acts of Assembly to prevent dealing or Trafficking with Slaves. (Page 956).

Whereas the laws and regulations made to prevent dealing and trafficking with slaves, have been found insufficient to prevent that pernicious practice:

I. Be it therefore Enacted by the General Assembly of the State of North Carolina, and it is hereby Enacted by the authority of the same, That if any free person shall either buy from or sell to any slave or slaves, any kind of goods or commodities whatsoever, or any other thing, without permission in writing, setting forth the identical article or articles such slave or slaves may have for sale from the master, mistress or other person having the management of such slave or slaves, every such free person shall on conviction forfeit and pay the sum of ten pounds, and be further liable to pay all damages that may accrue in consequence of such trading or trafficking; one half thereof to the person informing, the other half to the person injured, to be levied of his or her property as other recoveries by law; and if the offender shall not have sufficient property to satisfy judgment, then such offender shall be committed to close custody, and shall remain in prison without bail or mainprize for any time not exceeding three months.

II. And be it further Enacted, That if any slave or slaves shall hereafter offer any article whatever for sale, without permission from his or her owner, master or overseer, it shall or may be lawful for any person knowing the same, to apprehend such slave or slaves, and on due proof of the offence being made on oath before a Justice of the Peace of the county, he may order the said slave or slaves to receive any number of lashes, not exceeding thirty nine, on his, her or their bare back. Provided nevertheless, That this Act shall not have effect or be in force until after the first day of March next.

CHAPTER XVIII. 1ST SESSION.
1788. An Act to Emancipate a certain Negro Slave named Phillis, late the Property of George Jacobs, of the Town of Wilmington, Deceased. (Page 963).

Whereas it is represented to the General Assembly that the aforesaid George Jacobs, deceased, in his last illness, did earnestly request that his negro slave named Phillis should be liberated for her great attention to her said master during her continuance with him, and more especially for her care and assiduity in his last illness: In order therefore to carry into effect the dying request of the said George Jacobs, deceased:

I. Be it Enacted by the General Assembly of the State of North Carolina, and it is hereby Enacted by the authority of the same, That from and after the passing of this Act, the aforesaid negro woman named Phillis, shall be emancipated and forever discharged from her bondage, in as full and ample manner as if she had been born free; any law, usage or custom to the contrary notwithstanding: And the said negro woman shall forever hereafter be known by the name of Phillis Freeman.

CHAPTER XX. 1ST SESSION.
1788. An Act to Amend an Act Entitled "An Act to Prevent Domestic Insurrections." (Page 964).

Whereas by the before recited Act it is Enacted, that no person shall liberate or set free his or her slave except for meritorious services to be adjudged and allowed of by the county court, and by the said Act it is directed in what manner and for what purpose slaves illegally liberated shall be apprehended and sold: And whereas divers persons from religious motives, in violation of the said law, continue to liberate their slaves, who are now going at large to the terror of the people of this State: And whereas the mode prescribed for apprehending such slave or slaves is found by experience not to answer the good purposes by the said Act intended, the power of apprehending liberated slaves being confined to freeholders only, and optional in them whether they will exercise the authority or not; and it appearing the said law is not fully adequate to the good purposes intended: Therefore,

 I. Be it Enacted by the General Assembly of the State of North Carolina, and it is hereby Enacted by the authority of the same, That from and after the passing of this Act, if any slave hath been liberated contrary to the before recited Act, should be still be within the limits of this State, and all slaves liberated after the passing of this Act should be known or suspected to be lurking in any of the uninhabited parts thereof, then and in such case, on information made to any justice of the peace by any freeman of such liberated slave or slaves going at large or lurking about, contrary to the true intent and meaning of the said Act, then and in such case the justice to whom such information is made, is hereby impowered and required immediately to issue his warrant, directed to the sheriff of the county, commanding him to make diligent search and to apprehend all such slave or slaves, and to commit him, her or them to the gaol of the county, there to remain until the next succeeding court of the county, on which warrant all proceedings shall be regulated in the same manner as is directed by the before recited Act; and that the person or persons apprehending any such slave or slaves by virtue of any such warrant, shall be entitled to the emoluments as is allowed to freeholders by the before recited Act. Provided nevertheless, That nothing in this Act shall be construed to debar any freeholder or freeholders from stepping forward in the execution of said law in the usual manner, or to divest them of the emoluments given by the said Act.

****

THE STATE RECORDS OF NORTH CAROLINA
VOLUME XXV., SUPPLEMENT, 1669-1771
EDITED BY: WALTER CLARK
NASH BROTHERS BOOK AND JOB PRINTERS

GOLDSBORO, N.C., 1906

CHAPTER XXXV
1789. An Act to Emancipate Certain Negroes Therein Mentioned. (Page 37).

Whereas, it hath been represented to this General Assembly, that Robert Shaw, in his life-time, did receive a valuable consideration for the further services of a certain negro woman named Amelia, and has certified the same and declared her to be free: And by petition of Thomas Lovick, it appears to be his desire that a certain negro woman by the name of Betty, belonging to him, should be set free; also a petition of Monsieur Chaponel, desiring to have set free a mulatto slave belonging to him, by the name of Lucy, of three and half years old: And whereas, it appears by the petition of Ephraim Knight, of Halifax County, that he is desirous to emancipate two young mulatto men, called Richard and Alexander, the property of said Ephraim: And it hath also been represented to this Assembly by John Alderson, of Hyde County, that it is his desire to set free a mulatto boy belonging to him, called Sam: And whereas, it hath been made appear to this Assembly by the petition of Thomas Newman, of Fayetteville, that he hath a mulatto boy belonging to him, which he is desirous to emancipate, and known by the name of Thomas:

I. Be it enacted by the General Assembly of the State of North Carolina, and it is hereby enacted by the authority of the same, That the said negro women called Amelia and Betty, and the mulatto girl called Lucy, and the said mulatto men Richard and Alexander, and the mulatto boy called Sam, and the negro boy named Thomas Clinch, shall be, and each of them are hereby emancipated and declared free; and the said Richard and Alexander shall take and use the surname of Day, and the mulatto boy Sam shall be known and called by the name of Samuel Johnson; and the said slaves so liberated, and each of them, are hereby declared to be able and capable in law to posses and enjoy every right, privelege and immunity, in as full and ample manner as they could or might have done if they had been born free.

CHAPTER LXIII.
1789. An Act for the Relief of Such Persons Who May Bee Wounded by the Indians Within the District of Mero, and for Other Purposes. (Pages 58-59).

North Carolina Law

Whereas, it hath been represented to the General Assembly, that several persons within the district of Mero being wounded by the Indians, had it not in their power to employ physicians, surgeons, nurser, or to provide themselves with the necessary medicines and attendance, by which means their lives have been much endangered: And whereas, it is probable that several persons under the said circumstances have died for want of proper care: For remedy thereof,

I. Be it therefor enacted by the General Assembly of the State of North Carolina, and it is hereby enacted by the authority of the same, That from and after the passing of this Act, the county courts of Davidson, Sumner, and Tennessee shall be and they are hereby empowered and authorised, whenever it may appear to their satisfaction that the person wounded by the Indians is not able to defray the expences of his treatment and cure, to pass the accounts of physicians, surgeons and nurses, and those for the necessary medicines, provisions and attendance, the same being properly attested and proven on oath; which accounts thus passed by the said courts shall be received in payment of all public taxes by the collectors, sheriff or other officers in said district; any law or custom to the contrary notwithstanding.

And whereas, it is good policy to keep up a friendly intercourse with the Indian tribes in amity with the good people of this State:

II. Be it therefore enacted by the authority aforesaid, That all accounts of provisions furnished to Indians within the district of Mero by any of the inhabitants thereof, being duly proven upon oath, and the same being exhibited in the court of the county wherein such persons reside, the said court shall be and is hereby empowered to pass all such accounts, and to fix the price of such provisions furnished to the Indians; which accounts thus passed by the court as aforesaid, shall be received in payment of any of the public taxes in said district; any law or custom to the contrary notwithstanding.

III. Be it further enacted, That on account of the scarcity of physicians and surgeons within the district of Mero, that all practising physicians and surgeons within the said district shall be exempt from all militia duty, except in the case of actual invasion or insurrection.

IV. Be it further enacted, That all Acts of Assembly, or parts of Acts, which come within the purview of this Act, are hereby repealed and made null and void, to all intents and purposes, as if the same had never been made.

North Carolina Law

CHAPTER LXV.
1789. An Act to Repeal Part of an Act, Entitled, "An Act for Appointing an Agent, and Holding a Treaty With the Cherokee Indians, and for Other Purposes." (Page 59).
I. Be it enacted by the General Assembly of the State of North Carolina, and it is hereby enacted by the authority of the same, That so much of the before recited Act as relates to the Appointment of an Indian Agent, his duty and pay, be and the same is hereby repealed and made void.

CHAPTER LXXI.
1789. An Act to Prescribe the Mode of Paying the Militia Officers and Soldiers for Their Services on an Expedition Carried on Against the Chicamoga Indians by Brigadier General Joseph Martin, in the Year One Thousand Seven Hundred and Eighty-Eight. (Pages 62-63).
Whereas, the militia of Washington district were called out on actual service by order and under command of Brigadier General Joseph Martin, against the Chicamoga Indians, who at that time were plundering and killing the inhabitants of said district:
I. Be it therefore enacted by the General Assembly of the State of North Carolina, and it is hereby enacted by the authority of the same, That the commanding officer of the said expedition shall, any time after the passing of this Act, exhibit into the comptroller's office of this State, attested pay-rolls on oath for the service of the said militia, stating therein the true number and names of the officers and soldiers in each company, proportioning the officers to the number of soldiers so called out; also a roll with the names of the field and staff officers who served on the said expedition, reporting in each roll the exact time of service of the said militia respectively, on the exhibiting whereof, the comptroller is hereby directed and required to examine the same, and pursuant thereto make out and issue according to the law unto and in the name of each officer and soldier respectively, who were ordered out as aforesaid, certificates of such service; which certificates shall be received by the several sheriffs of the said district, and by the treasurer of this State from the said sheriffs, in payment of the public money tax that is or may become due within the said district of Washington, and no other until all such certificates be paid. Provided, That those who have no such certificates shall pay their taxes as otherwise provided by law.

North Carolina Law

And for the intent and purpose that the above specified certificates shall and may be received for taxes as above mentioned, due or which may become due in the district of Washington:

II. Be it enacted by the authority aforesaid, That the collectors of public money tax in the said district in their respective counties, are hereby required to delay the collection of taxes due in said district for the term of three months after the passing of this Act.

III. And be it further enacted by the authority aforesaid, That so much of an Act passed at Fayetteville, in the year one thousand seven hundred and eighty-eight, as relates to raising men for the purpose of fixing a garrison on the north side of Tennessee river, be and the same is hereby repealed and made void; and the men raised by virtue thereof, shall be and they are hereby discharged from service.

IV. And be it enacted by the authority aforesaid, That the comptroller shall liquidate and adjust, on exhibiting the same to him, the commissary's accounts of the expedition, and issue certificates for the same; which shall be received and paid as above mentioned, such accounts being supported by proper vouchers and the oath of the said commissary.

Read three times and ratified in General Assembly, the 22d day of December, 1789, except Chap. I., which was ratified the 18th of December, and Chap. XXXVIII. which was ratified the 18th of November, 1789.

      Charles Johnson,
      Speaker of the Senate.
      Stephen Cabarrus,
      Speaker of the House of Commons
      (Copy Test.) J. Glasgow, Secretary.

CHAPTER XXXIV.
1790. An Act for Vesting the Property of Certain Negroes in the heirs of Mark Newby. (Page 100).

Whereas, it is the earnest request of Ezekiel Arrington, who intermarried with one of the heirs of Mark Newby, late of Perquimans county, that the property of certain negroes emancipated by the said Mark Newby, in his lifetime, may by an Act of Assembly be vested in the heirs of the said Mark Newby:

I. Be it enacted by the General Assembly of the State of North Carolina, and it is hereby enacted by the authority of the same, That the heirs of the said Mark Newby shall have full power and authority to hold and possess, sell and dispose of, sue for and recover the said negroes, in the same manner as they may any other part or parcel of their property; and finally, that the right to the said negroes shall vest and continue in the heirs of the said Mark Newby, as fully and completely, as if no such emancipation had ever taken place; any law, usage or custom to the contrary notwithstanding.

****

THE ACTS OF THE GENERAL ASSEMBLY OF THE STATE OF NORTH CAROLINA PASSED DURING THE SESSIONS HELD IN THE YEARS 1791, 1792, 1793 AND 1794 BY: FRANCOIS XAVIER MARTIN NEWBERN: FRANCOIS XAVIER MARTIN, 1795

CHAPTER XLVI.
1791. An Act to emancipate certain persons therein mentioned. (Page 27)

Whereas sundry petitions have been presented to this General Assembly, praying that Austin Curtis, a mulatto slave belonging to Willie Jones; Grace, and her children, to wit, Richard, Harriot, Samuel, Rebecca and Elizabeth, formerly the property of John Davis, deceased; Absalom Spicer, formerly the property of Benjamin Rush; and Rachel, formerly the property of Sarah Rush, deceased; Richard, Dolly, and her son Nathan, the property of George Merrick; and Linney, the property of John Spencer; and Richard and William, the property of the estate of Thomas Prichard, deceased, be liberated and set free:

I. Be it therefore enacted by the General Assembly of the State of North Carolina, and it is hereby enacted by the authority of the same, That the aforesaid Austin Curtis by and under the name of Austin Curtis Jones; and the aforesaid Grace, Richard, Harriot, Samuel, Rebecca and Elizabeth, by and under the names of Grace Davis, Richard Davis, Harriot Davis, Samuel Davis, Rebecca Davis and Elizabeth Davis; and the aforesaid Absalom Spicer and Rachel Spicer, by and under the names of Absalom Spicer and Rachel Spicer; and the aforesaid Richard, Dolly and Nathan, by and under the names of Richard Green, Dolly Green, and Nathan Green; and aforesaid Linney, under the name of Linney Charlton; and Richard and

North Carolina Law

William above mentioned, under the name of Richard Prichard Morris, and William Prichard Morris, shall be, and they, and each and every of them, are hereby declared to be free, by and under the names aforesaid; and they, and each and every of them, shall from henceforward enjoy the protection of the laws and the benefits of the constitution of this state, in the same manner as others of their colour who were born free. Provided, nevertheless, That nothing herein contained shall be construed so as to affect the title or claime of any person or persons, other than the persons named in this act.

****

LAWS OF THE STATE OF NORTH CAROLINA REVISED, UNDER THE AUTHORITY OF THE GENERAL ASSEMBLY VOLUME I.
HENRY POTTER
RALEIGH: PRINTED AND SOLD BY J. GALES, 1821

CHAP. 335.
1791. An act to amend an act, entitled, "An act to prevent thefts and robberies by slaves, free negroes and mulattoes," passed at Tarborough, in the year one thousand seven hundred and eighty seven; and to amend an act, passed in the year one thousand seven hundred and seventy four, entitled, "An act to prevent the wilful and malicious killing of slaves." (Pages 653-655).
Whereas by the before recited act it shall not be permitted for any master or commander of a vessel to entertain any slave, free negro, or mulatto on board such vessel at any time between sun-set and sun-rise, or during the Sabbath-day, unless such slave, free negro, or mulatto shall belong to the vessel, or shall have a pass from his, her, or their master, mistress, or from some justice of the peace, expressing the time when, and the business for which they go on board. And whereas it appears to this General Assembly that the number of persons from other states and foreign parts, bring goods in vessels into this state, land and store them, and harbour slaves, free negroes and mulattoes in their stores during the night and on the Sabbath-days, to the great prejudice of the citizens and the honest trader: For remedy whereof,

North Carolina Law

1. Be it enacted, &c. That from and after the passing of this act, it shall not be lawful for any merchant or trader within this state to harbour or trade with any slave, free negro or mulatto, in their storehouses, shops or tenements, wherein they keep goods and merchandize, at any time between sun-set and sun-rise, or on the Sabbath-day, without a pass from his, her or their master, mistress or overseer, or from some justice of the peace, expressing the time when and the business for which they go. Any person so offending shall be subject to the same fines and penalties, to be recovered and applied in the same manner as the fines and penalties on owners and masters of vessels in the before recited act, **(See 1787, c. 267.)** any law, usage or customs to the contrary notwithstanding.

2. And whereas it is also represented to this General Assembly, that the numbers of slaves, belonging to citizens of this state, pass from county to county, and to other states, and when apprehended produce a free pass or certificate signed with the name of some citizen of the place where they are owned, which it is represented are often forged, and frequently even by some other servant or slave, and is there is no law now in force in this state to prevent such pernicious practices: Be it further enacted by the authority aforesaid, That from and after the passing of this act, if any slave shall be guilty of producing such forged free pass or certificate, he or she so offending, shall on conviction, suffer such corporal punishment as a court shall inflict (death excepted) to be tried in the same manner as slaves are tried for other capital offences.

3. And whereas by another act of Assembly passed in the year 1774, the killing of a slave, however wanton, cruel and deliberate, is only punishable in the first instance by imprisonment and paying the value thereof to the owner; which distinction of criminality between the murder of a white person and of one who is equally a human creature, but merely of different complexion, is disgraceful to humanity and degrading in the highest degree to the laws and principles of a free, christian and enlightened country: Be it enacted by the authority aforesaid, That if any person shall hereafter be guilty of wilfully and maliciously killing a slave, such offender shall upon the first conviction thereof be adjudged guilty of murder, and shall suffer the same punishment as if he had killed a free man; **(Benefit of clergy taken away - see 1801, c. 585. Modified - see 1817, c. 949.)** any law, usage or custom to the contrary notwithstanding. Provided always, That this act shall not extend to any person killing a slave outlawed by virtue of any act of Assembly of this state, or to any slave in the act of

resistance to his lawful owner or master, or to any slave dying under moderate correction.

4. And whereas the present penalty for harbouring slaves is in depreciated money, and altogether insufficient to prevent or punish the offence: Be it enacted by the authority aforesaid, That any person who shall hereafter entice or persuade any servant or slave to absent him or herself from his or her owner's service, or who shall harbour or maintain under any pretence whatever, any runaway servant or slave, shall for every such offence, forfeit and pay to the owner of such servant or slave the sum of fifty pounds, to be recovered by action of debt before any jurisdiction having cognizance thereof, and be further liable to the said owner in an action for damages.

5. And be it further enacted, That all acts and clauses of acts coming within the meaning of this act and contrary thereto, be and the same are hereby repealed and made void.

CHAP. 348.
1791. An act for giving a further time for probate and registration of bills of sale for slaves and marriage settlements. (Pages 669-670).

Whereas it appears to the General Assembly that many of the good citizens of this state, through inattention or neglect, failed to have their bills of sale for slaves proved and registered within the time limited by law, and may thereby be much injured unless a longer time is given for that purpose: and the Legislature ever being ready to give a just and equitable relief; Therefore, (See **1789, c. 315, and 1802, c. 622.**)

1. Be it enacted, &c. That all bills of sale for slaves, not already recorded in manner required by law, shall have a further time of twelve months allowed for probate and registration; and shall when thus authenticated and perpetuated, be held and deemed as valid in law to all intents and purposes, as if they had been proved and registered within the time required by law; any law, usage or custom to the contrary notwithstanding.

2. And whereas in the first section of an act, entitled, "An act directing that marriage settlements and other marriage contracts shall be registered, and for preventing injury to creditors," passed at Newbern in the year one thousand seven hundred and eighty-five, it is directed that all marriage settlements and other marriage contracts shall be proved in the same manner as other deeds, and shall be registered: and whereas it appears to this General Assembly, that a number of good citizens, for want of sufficient information, have neglected to avail themselves of the benefit of the said act: For remedy whereof, Be it enacted, That all marriage contracts which were made, formed and entered into previous to the passing of the above recited act, shall have a further time of twelve months allowed for probate and registration; **(See 1785, c. 238, s. 1, and 1799, c. 540, s. 1)** and shall when thus authenticated and perpetrated, be held and deemed as valid in law, to all interests and purposes, as if they had been proved and registered within the time required by the above recited act; any law, usage or custom to the contrary notwithstanding.

****

THE ACTS OF THE GENERAL ASSEMBLY OF THE STATE OF NORTH CAROLINA PASSED DURING THE SESSIONS HELD IN THE YEARS 1791, 1792, 1793 AND 1794
BY: FRANCOIS XAVIER MARTIN
NEWBERN: FRANCOIS XAVIER MARTIN, 1795

CHAPTER XXXVIII.
1792. An Act to emancipate the persons therein named. (Page 61).
Whereas it hath been made appear to this General Assembly that Andrew, Peter and Juno, the illegitimate children of John Moore, of Craven County; Charlotte Green, the property of John Waite, of the town of Newbern, merchant; John Marshall, the property of Peter Thomeguex, of the same place, merchant; Rose, the property of Mary Clear, of the said place; Jack the property of Caleb White, of the County of Currituck; Peggy Handy, daughter of Nancy Handy, the property of Miss Betsy Vail, of the town of Newbern; Betsey and Jim, the property of Thomas Neale, of Brunswick County, should be liberated and set free:

I. Be it therefore enacted by the General Assembly of the State of North Carolina, and it is hereby enacted by the authority of the same, That the said Andrew, Peter, and Juno, under the names of Andrew Moore, Peter Moore and Juno Moore; Charlotte Green, under the name of Elizabeth Johnston; John Marshall, under the name of John Marshall; Rose, under the name of Rose Mary Clear; Jack, under the name of John Jasper White; Peggy Handy, under the name of Peggy Handy; Betsey and Jim, under the names of Elizabeth Phillips and James Phillips, shall be, and they and each

North Carolina Law

and every of them, are hereby declared to be free by and under the names aforesaid; and they and each and every of them, shall from henceforward, enjoy the protection of the laws and the benefits of the constitution of this State, in the same manner as others of their colour who were born free.

CHAPTER LXII.
1792. An Act to confirm the rights and privileges of a certain mulatto man called Frank, formerly the property of Thomas Lytle, late of Randolph County, and to confirm on him the name of Frank Lytle. (Page 160).
      Whereas the court of the County of Randolph, at their session held in the month of November last, on the petition of Catherine Lytle, William Bell, John Beard and Samuel Millikin, the executors and legatees of the last will and testament of the said Thomas Lytle, deceased, did order that the said Frank should be at liberty, agreeable to an act of the General Assembly in such cases made and provided, for meritorious services done by him for the said Thomas Lytle in his lifetime: And whereas the said Catherine, William, John and Samuel have mentioned this this Assembly to pass an act to entitle the said Frank to be called and known by the name of Frank Lytle:
      I. Be it therefore enacted by the General Assembly of the State of North Carolina, and it is hereby enacted by the authority of the same, That the said order of the court of Randolph County aforesaid, liberating the said Frank, be and is hereby ratified and confirmed; and by virtue thereof the said Frank, by and under the name of Frank Lytle, shall be and is hereby declared to be free, and shall henceforth enjoy the protection of the laws, and the benefit of the Constitution of this State, in the same manner as others of his colour who were born free, to every intent and purpose.

CHAPTER LXXVI.
1792. An Act to emancipate Jack, alias Jack Small, a person of colour. (Page 168).
      Whereas Jemima Barrs, a free woman of mixed blood, hath represented to this General Assembly, that she hath purchased a certain Jack Small, for a valuable consideration, and since hath become his legal wife: And whereas the said Jemima Barrs hath petitioned this General

Assembly to emancipate and set free her said husband, Jack Small aforesaid:

I. Be it therefore enacted by the General Assembly of the State of North Carolina, and it is hereby enacted by the authority of the same, That the aforesaid person of colour Jack Small, shall henceforth be emancipated and absolutely set free, by the name of Jack Small; and be entitled to all the privileges and immunities which free people of colour enjoy and possess in this state, any law to the contrary notwithstanding.

****

LAWS OF THE STATE OF NORTH CAROLINA REVISED, UNDER THE AUTHORITY OF THE GENERAL ASSEMBLY
VOLUME I.
HENRY POTTER
RALEIGH: PRINTED AND SOLD BY J. GALES, 1821

CHAP. 362.
1792. An act to amend an act, entitled, "An act to prevent the stealing of slaves, or by violence, seduction or any other means taking or carrying away any slave or slaves the property of another, and for other purposes therein mentioned". (1799, c. 142.) (Pages 684-685).

Whereas the above recited act hath been found insufficient to prevent the iniquitous practice of carrying and conveying slaves out of this state:

1. Be it enacted, &c. That from and after the passing of this act, if any master or commander of any ship or vessel trading within this state, shall carry and convey out of the same on board any such ship or vessel any negro or mulatto slave or slaves, the property of any citizen or citizens of this state, without the consent in writing of the owner or owners, his, her or their guardian or guardians, of such slave or slaves previously obtained; or shall take and receive on board of any such vessel or ship, any such slave or slaves, or permit or suffer the same to be done with the intent and for the purpose of carrying and conveying such slave or slaves out of this state, or shall wickedly and willingly conceal or permit to be concealed on board of any such ship or vessel any negro or mulatto slave or slaves, who shall or may hereafter abscond from his, her or their master or mistress, being citizens of this state, with the intent and for the purpose of enabling such

slave or slaves to effect his, her or their escape out of this state, every such master or commander of any such ship or vessel so carrying or conveying, or so taking or receiving or concealing, or causing or permitting the same to be done with an intent as aforesaid, shall be deemed and taken to be guilty of felony, and shall suffer death as a felon without benefit of clergy.

CHAP. 363.
1792. An act to amend the seventh section of an act, entitled, "An act to explain, amend and supply the deficiencies of an act, passed last Assembly at Hillsborough, entitled, An act to regulate the descent of real estates, to do away with entails, to make provision for widows, to prevent frauds in the execution of last wills and testaments, and for directing how deeds of gifts and bills of sale of slaves shall be executed, authenticated and perpetuated," passed at Newbern, in October, in the year one thousand seven hundred and eighty-four. (1784, c. 225, s. 7. See 1806, c. 701.) (Pages 685-686).

    1. Be it enacted, &c. That all sales of slaves bona fide made, and accompanied with the actual delivery of the slave or slaves to the purchaser, and which would have been held good and valid before the passing of the said recited act, shall be and the same are hereby declared good and valid without any bill of sale. **(Must be in writing, see 1819, c. 1016.).**

    2. Be it further enacted, That when any transfer or conveyance of any slave or slaves shall be in writing, such writing, after being legally proved, shall be registered in the county where the purchaser (he being in actual possession of the slave or slaves so transferred or conveyed) shall reside; but if under any special agreement at the time of the sale, the seller shall remain in possession of the slave or slaves sold, then the writing transferring or conveying the same slave or slaves, shall be registered in the county where the vendor lives.

    3. Be it further enacted, That on all trials at law, where a written transfer or conveyance of a slave or slaves shall be introduced to support the title of either party, the due and fair execution of such writing shall be proved by a witness subscribing and attesting the execution of such writing; but if such witness shall be dead or removed out of the state, then the probate and registration of such writing may be given in evidence.

CHAP. 381.
1793. An act to extend the right of trial by jury to slaves. (Pages 706-707).

1. Be it enacted, &c. That in all cases hereafter happening, where any slave shall be accused of an offence, the punishment whereof shall extend to life, (See 1816, c. 912, and 1818, c. 972.) limb, or member, such slave shall be entitled to trial by jury, (See 1794, c. 412, and 1796, c. 467.) on oath, consisting of twelve good and lawful men, owners of slaves, in a summary way, and in open court of the county wherein such offence was committed. Provided nevertheless, That if the court of the county shall not meet within fifteen days from the time of commitment, the sherif of the county shall and may summon three justices of the peace of the said county, and a jury of good and lawful men owners of slaves, who shall have as full and ample power and authority to try and pass sentence on any slave accused and brought to trial before them, as the county court might or could have by virtue of this act. And provided always, That the said jury and three justices shall not be connected with the owner of such slave, or the prosecutor, either by affinity or consanguinity.

2. And be it further enacted, That when a slave shall be apprehended for any offence, the punishment whereof may effect life, member, or limb, it shall be the duty of the sheriff, and he is hereby required to serve the owner of such slave, if known, with notice of trial ten days previous thereto (which notice shall be proved to the court) in order that the owner may have an opportunity of defending the said slave; and the costs of the said notice, and all other costs attending the said trial of any slave so apprehended, where the owner or owners shall be known, shall be paid by the said owner or owners, provided the said slave, if a freeman, would be liable to the payment thereof. And in case of refusal to pay the same, process may issue from the clerk of the court to compel payment, in the same manner as for other costs.

3. And be it further enacted, That when the owner of any slave to be tried by virtue of this act, shall not be known, or cannot be discovered or ascertained, or shall reside out of this state, it shall and may be lawful for the court, and they are hereby authorised and required, to appoint counsel to appear for and in behalf of the prisoner, who shall be allowed the same fees as the attorney for the state is allowed for criminal prosecutions. After which they may proceed to trial in the same manner as if the owner had been notified agreeable to the directions of this act, in which case the fees

for the counsel, clerk and sheriff, shall be paid by the county in which the court is held in the same manner as other county charges.

CHAP. 406.
1794. An act to prevent the owners of slaves from hiring to them their time, to make compensation to patrols, and to restrain the abuses committed by free negroes and mulattoes. (Pages 740-742).
Whereas great mischiefs have arisen from slaves being permitted to hire their own time:
1. Be it enacted, &c. That it shall not be lawful, under any pretence whatever, for any person or persons to allow his, her or their slave, or any slave under his, her or their command or direction, to hire his, her or their time, under the penalty of forfeiting the sum of twenty pounds for each and every offence; to be recovered before any justice of the peace, to the sole benefit of the part prosecuting: And it shall be part of the duty and charge of the grand jury both in the county and superior courts, to make presentment of any slave who shall be permitted by his or her master or mistress to go at large, having hired his or her time, and on such presentment being made, the court shall issue an order to the sheriff of the county where such negro may be, to take up such negro, and him or her safely secure, so that he can have such negro before the next county court: And it shall be the duty of the sheriff to give the owners notice thereof (if residing within the the district) at least ten days before the sitting of the court; and the said court shall empannel a jury to enquire and try the truth of such presentment, on which trial or enquiry the owner may produce evidence as in other cases; and if the jury shall find that the said presentment is true, such negro shall then be hired out by the sheriff of the county, at public vendue, for the space of one year, taking bond with security for the same, payable to the wardens of the poor, for the use of the poor of said county, subject to the payment of any charges respecting said negro. Provided always, That when the owner resides out of the district, the sheriff shall give notice by advertisement in the nearest Gazette, for at least two weeks, where a gazette shall be published in the district in which the sheriff shall live, but in other cases the sheriff shall advertise the same at the district court-house and the court-house of the county in which the said slave shall be presented or shall be taken up. Provided always, That when any person who shall hire the negroes of an orphan, shall hire to such slave his or her time, the slave shall only be hired out under this act, for

such time or the remainder of the time as said slave may have been hired to such person.

2. And be it further enacted, That no person shall grant permission for any meeting or meetings of the negroes of others, or people of colour, at his, her or their houses, or on his, her or their plantation, for the purpose of drinking or dancing, under the penalty of forfeiting ten pounds on conviction of such offence, in any court having jurisdiction thereof, unless such slave shall have a special permit in writing or otherwise from his or her owner for that purpose.

3. And be it further enacted, That the justices of the courts of pleas and quarter-sessions, if they deem it necessary, shall, at the first or second court which shall be held after the first day of January, in the year one thousand seven hundred and ninety-five; and the first court which shall be held after the first day of January in each year afterwards, appoint in each captains district or company, any number, not exceeding six discreet and proper persons, to act as patrollers for the space of one year; and as a compensation for the services required of them as such, shall be exempted from serving on juries, working on roads, and from the payment of all county and parish taxes to the amount of forty shillings, and in addition to the fees hitherto allowed by law, the patrollers so appointed shall be entitled to receive the one-half of the penalties recovered under this act in the district in which such patrollers may respectively act and reside, except such penalties as may be incurred by hiring to negroes their own time.

4. And be it further enacted, That it shall be the duty of the patrollers, or two of them at least, appointed as aforesaid, to patrol their respective districts once at least in two weeks, for the purpose of carrying this act into effect; and on failure or neglect to perform such services, every person so failing or neglecting shall forfeit and pay the sum of ten pounds, recoverable before any jurisdiction having cognizance thereof, one half to the use of the informer, and the other half to the use of the county where the same is recoverable.

5. And be it further enacted, That the patrollers in each district, or a majority of those present, shall have power to inflict a punishment, not exceeding fifteen lashes, on all slaves they may find off their owner's plantation, or traveling on the sabbath, or other unseasonable time, without a proper permit or pass.

6. And be it further enacted, That the fines and penalties heretofore recoverable for the use of the poor of the county, under an act, entitled "An act to prevent thefts and robberies by slaves, free negroes and

mulattoes," passed in the year 1787, **(C. 726)** shall hereafter be recovered by and for the use of the person who may sue or may prosecute for the same, subject however to the claim of the patrollers, agreeably to the third section of this act.

****

THE ACTS OF THE GENERAL ASSEMBLY OF THE STATE OF NORTH CAROLINA
PASSED DURING THE SESSIONS HELD IN THE YEARS 1791, 1792, 1793 AND 1794
BY: FRANCOIS XAVIER MARTIN
NEWBERN: FRANCOIS XAVIER MARTIN, 1795

CHAPTER XCIII.
1794. An Act to emancipate a mulatto girl named Mary, the property of Michael Beam, deceased, should be emancipated. (Page 177).
    Whereas by the last will and testament of Michael Beam, deceased, late of Rowan County, it is devised that a mulatto girl, named Mary, the property of the said deceased, should be emancipated.
    I. Be it therefore enacted by the General Assembly of the State of North Carolina, and it is hereby enacted by the authority of the same, That from and after the passing of this act, that the said mulatto girl named Mary, the property of the said deceased, be liberated and set free, and henceforward called and known by the name of Mary German; under which name she shall also henceforward be entitled to all the privileges of a free person of mixed blood in this state; and shall and may receive, hold, enjoy and possess all the real and personal property which she has or may hereafter acquire by the last will and testament of the said deceased, or which she may hereafter lawfully acquire, in as full and ample a matter as if she had been born free, any thing to the contrary notwithstanding.

****

STATE OF NORTH CAROLINA
LAWS OF THE STATE OF NORTH CAROLINA
1790-1802

CHAPTER XXXVIII.

1795. An Act to emancipate a mulatto boy by the name of Gustavus Adolphus Johnston, in the county of Chowan, and also a mulatto girl by the name of Amy Phillips, in the County of Brunswick. (Page 22).

I. Be it enacted by the General Assembly of the State of North Carolina, and it is hereby enacted by the authority of the same, That from and after the passing of this act that the said mulatto boy, now aged about four years, by the name of Gustavus Adolphus Johnston, in the county of Chowan, shall be liberated and set free, and henceforward called and known by the said name; under which he shall henceforward be entitled to all the privileges of a free person of mixed blood in this state, and shall and may receive, hold, enjoy and possess any real or personal property which he may hereafter acquire by purchase or descent, in as full and ample manner as if he had been born free.

II. And be it further enacted, That Amy a mulatto girl, the property of Drury Allen, in the county of Brunswick, be also liberated and forever set free, and henceforward called and known by the name of Amy Phillips, under which name she shall henceforward be entitled to all the privileges of a free person of mixed blood in this state, and shall and may receive, hold and enjoy any real or personal estate which she may hereafter acquire by purchase or by descent, in as full and ample a manner as if she had been born free, any thing to the contrary notwithstanding.

CHAPTER XLI.
1795. An Act to emancipate Frank, a person of colour. (Page 23).

Whereas Milly Anderson, a free woman of colour, hath represented to this General Assembly that she hath purchased a certain negro man Frank, for a valuable consideration, and is his legal wife: And whereas the said Milly hath petitioned this General Assembly to emancipate and set free her said husband:

Be it therefore enacted by the General assembly of the State of North Carolina, and it is hereby enacted by the authority of the same, That the aforesaid person of colour, Frank, shall hereafter be emancipated and absolutely set free, by and under the name of Frank Anderson, and be entitled to all the privileges and immunities which free people of colour enjoy in this state.

CHAPTER XLVI.

North Carolina Law

1795. An Act to emancipate James, a mulatto man, the property of John Cunningham, of Gates County. (Page 24).

Whereas it is the request of John Cunningham, of Gates County, that a mulatto man called James, should be liberated and set free, for certain meritorious services:

I. Be it therefore enacted by the General Assembly of the State of North Carolina, and it is hereby enacted by the authority of the same, That from and after the passing of this act, the said mulatto man called James, the property of John Cunningham, be liberated and set free, and henceforward called and known by the name of James Cunningham, under which name he shall also henceforward be entitled to all the privileges of a free person of mixed blood in this state, and shall and may receive, hold, enjoy and possess all real and personal estate which he has now, or may hereafter lawfully acquire, either by purchase or by descent, in as full and ample manner, as if he had been born free, any thing to the contrary notwithstanding.

CHAPTER XLVII.
1795. An Act to emancipate a certain mulatto girl therein named. (Page 24).

I. Be it enacted by the General Assembly of the State of North Carolina, and it is hereby enacted by the authority of the same, That Sally, a mulatto girl, the property of William Person, by the name of Sally Pamilia, be and she is hereby declared to be free, by and under the name aforesaid: and she shall from henceforward enjoy the protection of the laws, and the benefits of the constitution of this state, in the same manners as others of her colour who were born free.

CHAPTER LXII.
1795. An Act to emancipate certain persons therein mentioned. (Page 28).

Whereas Lemuel Hall, a free man of mixed blood, hath represented to this General Assembly, that he hath purchased a certain woman slave, called Jenny, for a valuable consideration, who hath since become his legal wife; and he hath had by his said wife Jenny three children, called Seth, Milley and Tabitha: And whereas the said Lemuel

Hall hath petitioned the General Assembly to emancipate and set free his said wife and children aforesaid:

I. Be it therefore enacted by the General Assembly of the State of North Carolina, and it is hereby enacted by the authority of the same, That the aforesaid persons, Jenny, Seth, Milley and Tabitha, shall henceforth be emancipated and absolutely set free, by the name of Jenny Hall, Seth Hall, Milley Hall and Tabitha Hall; and the said persons of colour so liberated, and each of them, are hereby declared to be entitled to all the privileges and immunities which free people of colour enjoy and possess in this state, any law to the contrary notwithstanding, That nothing contained in this act shall be so construed as to deprive any person or persons of his or their lawful claim, other than the said Lemuel Hall.

****

LAWS OF THE STATE OF NORTH CAROLINA REVISED, UNDER THE AUTHORITY OF THE GENERAL ASSEMBLY
VOLUME I.
HENRY POTTER
RALEIGH: PRINTED AND SOLD BY J. GALES, 1821

CHAP. 444.

1795. An act to prevent any person who may emigrate from any of the West India or Bahama islands, or the French, Dutch, or Spanish settlements on the southern coast of America, from bringing slaves into this state, an also for imposing certain restrictions on free persons of colour who may hereafter come into this state. (See act of Congress, 20th April, 1818, c. 86.). (Pages 786-788).

1. Be it enacted, &c. That from and after the first day of April next, it shall not be lawful for any person coming into this state, with an intent to settle or otherwise, from any of the West India or Bahama islands, or the settlements on the southern coasts of America, to land any negro or negroes, or people of colour, over the age of fifteen years, under the penalty of one hundred pounds for each and every such slave or persons of colour, to be recovered before any jurisdiction having cognizance of the same, one fifth to the use of the informer, and the other four fifths to the use of the state.

2. And be it further enacted, That it shall be the duty of such person or persons bringing in any such negro or negroes, or people of colour, under the age of fifteen years, to prove the age of the same by his own oath, or the oath of some other person, before some justice of the peace, if the same be required.

3. And be it further enacted, That if any free person of colour shall come into this state, by land or water, or any slave shall hereafter be emancipated, **(See 1788, c. 289, and the acts there referred to.)** he, she or they shall be compelled to give bond and security to the sheriff, payable to the governor for the use of the state, in the sum of two hundred pounds, for his, her or their good behaviour, during the time he, she or they may remain in this state; and it is hereby declared to be the duty of the sheriff to apply to the above described persons, and take from them a bond as aforesaid; and if any person so applied to should refuse to give such bond, the sheriff of the county where the person so applied to for the time being resides, shall be and is hereby authorised and directed, to take him, her or them into custody, and confine them and every of them in the gaol of the county, until the ensuing court, when it shall be the duty of the said court to empannel a jury to enquire whether the person so confined comes within the meaning and purview of this act; and if the said jury shall find that such person does come within the meaning of this act, then and in that case the court shall compel such person to give bond as aforesaid for his, her or their good behaviour, and upon failing so to do, the court shall order such person to be sold, for the benefit of the state, at public auction.

4. And be it further enacted, That it shall be the duty of the severall county courts in the state, to charge the grand juries of the respective counties to make presentments of all such free persons of colour as conduct themselves so as to become dangerous to the peace and good order of the state and county, upon which the said presentments, it shall be the duty of the court to whom the same is made, to issue an order to the sheriff to take into custody the person so presented, and him safely keep until the next county court, when a jury shall be empannelled, as before directed in this act, and a trial agreeably thereto had; and if any person shall be found guilty on such trial, he shall be compelled to give bond and security, as in cases of persons coming into this state contrary to this act; and in case of failure of the person so found guilty to give bond, he, she or they shall be sold for the use and in the manner aforementioned.

5. And be it further enacted, That when any number of negroes, or other slaves, or free people of colour, shall collect together in arms, and

be going about the country, committing thefts, and alarming the inhabitants of any county, it shall be the duty of the commanding officer of such county, or captain of a troop of horse, upon three or more justices of the peace requiring the same, (See 1802, c. 618, s. 7, 8.) immediately to call out a sufficient number to suppress such depredations or insurrections; which detachment of militia shall be under the same rules and regulations, as in cases of invasion and Insurrection, and shall be entitled to receive the same pay and rations as the troops of the United States, when in actual service; and if any person shall be wounded or disabled in suppressing such insurrection, he shall be provided for at the public expense, in the same manner as heretofore practised in this state. Provided nevertheless, That if the officer above mentioned shall fail or neglect to order out a detachment of the militia in the above directed cases, his superior officer may, upon sufficient proof being made of the necessity of such a measure, order him or any other officer under his command, to suppress such depredation or insurrection, and if the person so ordered shall fail to obey the same, they shall suffer as in cases of insurrection or invasion.

****

LAWS OF THE STATE OF NORTH CAROLINA REVISED, UNDER THE AUTHORITY OF THE GENERAL ASSEMBLY VOLUME II HENRY POTTER RALEIGH: PRINTED AND SOLD BY J. GALES, 1821

CHAP. 453.
1796. An act to amend, strengthen and confirm the several acts of Assembly of this State against the emancipation of slaves. (Page 801). (See 1777, c. 109, s. 1.).
Whereas doubts have arisen in the construction of the said acts, as to the extent of the liberation powers vested in the county courts, by an act passed in the year one thousand seven hundred and seventy-seven, chapter sixth, entitled, "An act to prevent domestic insurrection," and another act passed in the year one thousand seven hundred and forty-one, chapter twenty-nine:
    1. Be it further enacted, &c. That no slave shall be set free in any case, or under any pretence whatever, except for meritorious services,

to adjudged of and allowed by the county court, and license first had and obtained therefor; and that such liberation when entered of record, shall vest in the said slave, so as aforesaid liberated, all the right and privilege of a free born negro, any thing in the said act to the contrary notwithstanding.

CHAP. 454.
1796. An act to prevent people from impeding the free passage of fish up the rivers and creeks in this state. (Page 801).
  1. Be it enacted, &c. That from and after the passing of this act, it shall not be lawful for any person in this state to set or cause to be set, any net of any description, across the main channel of any navigable river or creek in this state, under the penalty of twenty pounds, to be recovered by any person suing for the same, to his or her own use, before any jurisdiction having cognizance thereof.
  2. Be it further enacted, That if any servant or slave shall be guilty of the aforesaid offence, without the knowledge or consent of his or her master or mistress, he or she so offending shall have and receive thirty-nine lashes on his or her bare back.
  3. And be it further enacted, That nothing in this act contained, shall prevent or be construed to prevent any person or persons from working and hauling their seines across any of the rivers or creeks in the same manner as heretofore in use.

CHAP. 467.
1796. An act making compensation to the owners of outlawed and executed slaves, for the counties of Bladen, Halifax, Granville, Cumberland, Perquimans, Beaufort and Pitt. (Pages 828-829).
(Extended to other counties. See 1797, c. 480, s. 1.).
  1. Be it enacted, &c. That when a slave shall be tried in any of the counties aforesaid, and shall be found guilty by the jury of any crime, the punishment whereof shall extend to life, the said jury shall fix and ascertain the value of the said slave, and shall give the said valuation in at the time they return their verdict; which said evaluation shall be certified by the chairman of the court and given to the owner of the said slave, who shall be entitled to receive two thirds of such valuation from the sheriff of any of the said counties in which such slave may have been executed.

2. Be it further enacted, That when any slave shall be legally outlawed in any of the counties within mentioned, the owner of which shall reside in one of the said counties, and the said slave shall be killed in consequence of such outlawry, the value of such slave shall be ascertained by a jury which shall be empannelled at the succeeding court of the county where the said slave was killed, and a certificate of such valuation shall be given by the clerk of the court to the owner of said slave, who shall be entitled to receive two thirds of such valuation from the sheriff of the county wherein the slave was killed.

3. Be it further enacted, That the jury who shall try and return the valuation of any negro by them convicted and valued, shall previously enquire whether the owner of the said slave did or did not feed, clothe and treat him or her with the humanity consistent with his or her situation, except such slave was the property of orphans or minors, which if not proven to their satisfaction, that the owner or owners of said slave did feed, clothe or treat him or her in manner aforesaid, then and in that case the owner or owners shall not be entitled to the benefit of this act.

4. And be it further enacted, That the courts of the several counties aforesaid respectively, shall be, and they are hereby authorised and required when necessary, to lay a tax on all black polls, in any of the said counties where the owner or owners of any slaves shall be entitled to receive pay for the same under this act, sufficient to defray the charge of any of the said counties which shall be made by the owner or owners of any slave under this act; and the sheriff of the said counties respectively, shall collect such tax under the same rules and regulations as are prescribed for the collection of county taxes, and shall pay to the owner or owners of the slave or slaves valued under this act, when collected, two thirds of the valuation, which shall be certified by the chairman of the court where the same was valued; which certificate together with the owner's receipt shall be a sufficient voucher for him in the settlement of his account with the court; and the said sheriff shall account with the court of his county for any surplus money which shall remain in his hands after paying the certificate or certificates, which shall be obtained and paid under this act; which said surplus shall be received by the said court for the purpose of discharging any similar claim that shall be made for the value of any slave under this act. Provided nevertheless, That this act and no part thereof shall have effect or be construed to extend to any county in this state not herein particularly mentioned and expressly named, or to negroes belonging to persons living out of this state.

North Carolina Law

****

STATE OF NORTH CAROLINA
LAWS OF THE STATE OF NORTH CAROLINA
1790-1802

CHAPTER LIII.
1797. An Act to emancipate a mulatto girl Sally, formerly the property of John Ingram. (Page 19).
Whereas the said John Ingram by his last will and testament, has requested that the said girl Sally should be emancipated:
    I. Be it enacted by the General Assembly of the State of North Carolina, and it is hereby enacted by the authority of the same, That the said girl Sally be, and she is hereby emancipated and declared free by the name of Sally Robinson; and hereby declared able and capable in law to possess and enjoy every right, privilege and immunity, in as full and able manner as she could or might have done had she been born free.

****

LAWS OF THE STATE OF NORTH CAROLINA
REVISED, UNDER THE AUTHORITY OF THE GENERAL ASSEMBLY
VOLUME II
HENRY POTTER
RALEIGH: PRINTED AND SOLD BY J. GALES, 1821

CHAP. 480.
1797. An act to amend an act passed in the year one thousand seven hundred and ninety-six, entitled, "An act making compensation to the owners of outlawed and executed slaves for the counties of Bladen, Halifax, Granville, Cumberland, Perquimans, Beaufort and Pitt." (Pages 841-842). (See 1796, c. 467, s. 1.).
    1. Be it enacted, &c. That from and after the passing of this act, the force, meaning and intent of an act passed in the year one thousand seven hundred and ninety-six, entitled, "An act making compensation to the owners of outlawed and executed slaves for the counties of Bladen, Halifax, Granville, Cumberland, Perquimans, Beaufort and Pitt," shall be

extended to the counties of Warren, Onslow and Chatham, under the same rules, regulations and restrictions in every respect whatsoever, as fully as if they had been mentioned in the said act; and the courts respectively of the counties of Warren, Onslow and Chatham, shall take notice and be bound by the same accordingly; any thing to the contrary notwithstanding.

CHAP. 494.
1798. An act to amend the fifth section of an act, chapter sixteenth, passed at Raleigh, on the second of November, one thousand seven hundred and ninety five, providing among other things for the suppression of insurrections. (Pages 859-860). (See 1795, c. 444, s. 5.).

1. Be it enacted, &c. That when any two justices of the peace shall know, or have any reason to believe that any conspiracy hath taken place to promote insurrection among the slaves or people of colour, or that there may be danger of such measures taking place, it shall be their duty to issue an order to the sheriff of the county, or his deputy, to summon the magistrates of the county to meet at the court house on some day fixed by said order, which it shall be the duty of the sheriffs to obey; and if a majority of magistrates present, shall be of opinion that any such combination exists, or that there may be danger of an insurrection, they shall immediately, by express, make a representation thereof to the governor of the state for the time being; and the governor shall by warrant, order the expense of said express to be paid out of the treasury.

2. And be it further enacted, That when the governor shall receive such representation made as aforesaid, he shall be and he is hereby authorised to issue orders for a patrol of the militia, with the instructions to the commanding officer or other officer of the county, as the exigency of the case may require.

3. And be it further enacted, That when application shall be made to the commanding officer of the county, or other officer of the militia, under the said act, passed in the year one thousand seven hundred and ninety-five, it shall be the duty of such officer to report the same immediately to the governor for the time being, who shall thereon take the necessary measures, by ordering out a sufficient body of militia to preserve and ensure the public safety, who shall when ordered out as aforesaid, be governed by the before recited act, passed in the year one thousand seven hundred and ninety-five.

North Carolina Law

CHAP. 498.

1798. **An act to compel the owners of slaves to provide proper maintenance for such of their slaves as may be rendered incapable of service by reason of advancement in years or otherwise. (Pages 863-864).**

Whereas it is represented to this General Assembly that slaves rendered incapable of serving their owners from advancement in years and other disability, are often neglected by such owners, and by them permitted to go at large and become a common nuisance:

1. Be it therefore enacted, &c. That the owner of every slave who shall be rendered incapable of service from advancement in years or other disability, shall provide and furnish such slave with the usual allowance of food, raimant and lodging furnished to slaves in the neighborhood where such slave may be; and if any such slave shall be unprovided for by his or her owner as aforesaid, it shall and may be lawful for the wardens of the poor of the county where such slave may be, (if the owner of such slaves lives in such county) and they are hereby required to furnish such slave with the food, raimant and lodging aforesaid, and make a charge of the same to the owner of such slave; which sum so expended the said wardens shall and may recover by warrant against such owner before any justice of the peace, if the sum so expended exceeds no the sum cognizable before a justice by law; if so, then before any jurisdiction having cognizance of the same. Provided always, That the said wardens shall not at the expense of the owner provide such slave as aforesaid, until they or one of them shall first have given the owner of such slave notice to provide for and furnish such slave as is herein required, which notice shall be served upon such owner ten days previous to the wardens' providing for such slave, and shall and may be issued by any one of the said wardens, upon information being given to him, and by him directed to the sheriff or any constable of the county, who are hereby required forthwith to execute the same, and make return of the same to the warden who issued such notice, or to any one of them.

2. And be it further enacted, That if the owner of any such slave shall be dead, the executors or administrators of such deceased owner, shall provide for such slave in manner aforesaid, out of the estate of such deceased owner, and upon failure so to do the wardens aforesaid shall provide for such slave as aforesaid, and proceed against such executors or administrators in every respect as herein directed against the owner; or if

any such slave shall be liable to the direction of any guardian, such guardian shall make the provision aforesaid for such slave out of the estate of his ward; and upon failure, the wardens aforesaid shall provide for such slave as aforesaid, and proceed against such guardian in manner aforesaid; and such executors, administrators and guardians shall be allowed the expense of making such provision for such slave in their settlements.

3. And be it further enacted, That when any such slave shall be in a county other than the county where the owner of such slave, or the executors or administrators of a deceased owner, or guardian reside, the wardens aforesaid may remove such slave to the owner, or to the executors or administrators of a deceased owner, or to any guardian, at the expense of such owner, and at the expense of the executors, administrators and guardians in such cases.

4. And be it further enacted, That any two of the wardens of the poor, shall have power and authority to carry the forgoing provisions into effect.

****

STATE OF NORTH CAROLINA
LAWS OF THE STATE OF NORTH CAROLINA
1790-1802

CHAPTER CXII.
1798. An Act to emancipate certain persons therein named. (Page 49).

Whereas Alexander Stewart and Lydia his wife, have by deed under their hands and seals, given, granted and confirmed unto John Caruthers Stanly, a person of mixed blood, heretofore their slave, his freedom, as a reward for his meritorious services: And whereas the said John Caruthers Stanly is desirous of having his emancipation confirmed law. And whereas Amelia Green, a free woman of colour, has petitioned this General Assembly, to emancipate her daughter Princess Green;

I. Be it therefore enacted by the General Assembly of the State of North Carolina, and it is hereby enacted by the authority of the same, That the said John Caruthers Stanly and Princess Green, by the said names, are hereby emancipated and set free: and the said persons hereby liberated, and each of them are hereby declared to be able and capable in law, to possess and enjoy every right, privilege and immunity, in as full and ample manner as they could or might have done if they had been born free.

Chapter CXIII.
1798. An Act to emancipate certain persons therein mentioned. (Page 49).

I. Be it enacted by the General Assembly of the State of North Carolina, and it is hereby enacted by the authority of the same, That from and after the passing of this act, Rose the wife of Lemuel Overton, and her two sons John, Burdock, a negro woman named Grace, and her son Harry, the property of Thomas Amis, deceased; a negro girl named Bett, and a negro boy named John, the property of Moses Parker; a mulatto girl named Nancy, and her child Eliza, the property of General Thomas Person, of Granville County; a negro woman named Crease; a negro fellow named Tom, and his wife Pris and her five children, to wit, Allen, Charity, Breny, Willie and Crease, the property of Samuel Williams, deceased, of the county of Warren, also the increase of the said Pris and her female children, since the date of the last Will of the said Williams; also one negro man Daniel, formerly the property of James Allen; and a negro man named Ginger, formerly the property of Mark Allen, of Montgomery County, be and they are hereby emancipated and set free, and hereafter shall be called and known by the following names, to wit: Rose Overton, John Overton, Burdock Overton, Grace Webb, Harry Webb, Betty Black, John Black, Nancy Hart, Eliza Hart, Crease Green, Tom Green, Pris Green, Allen Green, Charity Green, Breny Green, Willie Green, and Crease Green, and in increase of the said Priss and her female children as aforesaid, by their respective names, with the addition of Green, Daniel Shad and Ginger Pepper; and by the names aforesaid, they and each of them shall have, enjoy and possess all the rights, privileges and immunities which they would have been entitled to, had they been born free; any law to the contrary notwithstanding.

II. And be it further enacted, That a negro man the property of Ozborne Jeffries, named Sam, and a negro woman the property of Dixon Bogye, named Chelsea, shall be and they are hereby emancipated and set free, the said Sam by the name of Buffalo Sam, and the said Chelsea by the name of Chelsea Reed, and they shall be entitled to the same privileges, which persons of colour born free are entitled to.

CHAPTER LIII.

North Carolina Law

1799. An Act to emancipate certain persons therein named. (Page 23).
Whereas Joseph R. Gautier, of Elizabeth Town, in the County of Bladen, has by his petition represented to this General Assembly, that he is desirous of procuring the emancipation of two mulatto boys belonging to him; and that as their childhood would render fruitless a recourse to the county court, he prays the aid at the Legislature to establish by a law the freedom of the said boys:

I. Be it therefore enacted by the General Assembly of the State of North Carolina, and it is hereby enacted by the authority of the same, That the said mullato boys be emancipated and set free from slavery, and henceforward be called and known by the names of Thomas Sheridan and Louis Sheridan; under which names respectively they shall be, and are hereby invested with, and henceforward entitled to, every right and privilege they would have had they been severally born free; any law or usage to the contrary notwithstanding.

****

LAWS OF THE STATE OF NORTH CAROLINA REVISED, UNDER THE AUTHORITY OF THE GENERAL ASSEMBLY
VOLUME II
HENRY POTTER
RALEIGH: PRINTED AND SOLD BY J. GALES, 1821

CHAP. 540.
1799. An act to amend an act, for giving further time for probate and registration of bills of sale for slaves and marriage settlements. (Pages 908-909).

Whereas in the first section of an act, entitled "An act directing that marriage settlements and other marriage contracts shall be registered, and for preventing injury to creditors," passed at Newbern in the year one thousand seven hundred and eighty-five, **(See 1785, c. 238, and 1814, c. 875, s. 2.)** it is directed that all marriage settlements and other marriage contracts shall be proved in the same manner as other deeds, and shall be registered: and whereas it appears to this General Assembly that a number of good citizens, for want of sufficient information, have neglected to avail themselves of said act: for remedy whereof,

North Carolina Law

1. Be it enacted, &c. That all marriage contracts which were made, formed and entered into previous to the passing of the above recited act, shall have a further time of twelve months allowed for probate and registration; and shall when thus authenticated and perpetuated, be held and deemed as valid in law, to all intents and purposes, as if they had been proved and registered within the time required by the above recited act; any law, usage or custom to the contrary notwithstanding.

2. And whereas the time allowed for registering bills of sale is expired: Be it enacted, That a further time of two years be allowed for proving and registering bills of sale for slaves, which, when registered in the time aforesaid, shall be good and valid to all intents and purposes as if proved and registered within the time required by an act, passed in the year one thousand seven hundred and ninety-seven, entitled "An act granting a further time for proving and registering bills of sale and deeds of gift." (See 1797, c. 481, s. 1., 1802, c. 622.).

****

STATE OF NORTH CAROLINA
LAWS OF THE STATE OF NORTH CAROLINA
1790-1802

CHAPTER XCVI.
1800. An Act to emancipate certain persons therein named. (Page 45).
Whereas by the last will and testament of Ephraim Knight, of the County of Halifax, he appeared to be desirous to emancipate two Mulatto girls belonging to him by the name of Sabina and Polly; and as the said Ephraim Knight died without making application to the General Assembly to pass a law to that effect,

Be it therefore enacted by the General Assembly of the State of North Carolina, and it is hereby enacted by the authority of the same, That the said Mulatto girls Sabina and Polly be emancipated and set free from slavery, and henceforward be called and known by the names of Sabina Curtis and Polly Curtis; under which names respectively they shall be, and are hereby invested with, and henceforward entitled to every right and privilege they would have, had they been severally born free, any law or usage to the contrary notwithstanding.

And whereas James Cunningham of Chowan, has, by his petition for that purpose, represented to this General Assembly, that he is desirous of procuring the emancipation of a mulatto woman slave named Betsey, belonging to him,

Be it therefore enacted by the authority aforesaid, That the said mulatto woman named Betsey, be emancipated and set free from slavery, and that she be henceforth called and known by the name of Elizabeth Cunningham, under which name she shall be and is hereby invested and henceforward shall be entitled to every right and privilege that she would have been entitled to, had she been born free, any law, usage or custom to the contrary notwithstanding.

CHAPTER XCIX.
1800. An Act to liberate and set free the persons therein named. (Page 46).

Whereas Daniel Shad is desirous of setting free a certain woman slave named Betty, his property, and her child Winny,

Be it therefore enacted by the General Assembly of the State of North Carolina, and it is hereby enacted by the authority of the same, that from and after the passing of this act, that Betty, a woman slave, the property and wife of Daniel Shad, and her child Winny, be and they are hereby liberated and set free, and shall be entitled to the same privileges of other free persons of colour in this State.

II. And be it further enacted, That hereafter the said Betty shall be called and known by the name of Winny Shad; and by those names respectively shall be entitled and enjoy all the privileges that they would or could have done, had they borne the said names from their nativity.

Read three times and ratified in the General Assembly, the 20th day of December Anno Domini 1800.
William White, Secretary
    Joseph Riddick, S.S.

    Stephen Cabarrus, S.H.C.

****

LAWS OF THE STATE OF NORTH CAROLINA
REVISED, UNDER THE AUTHORITY OF THE GENERAL
ASSEMBLY
VOLUME II

North Carolina Law

HENRY POTTER
RALEIGH: PRINTED AND SOLD BY J. GALES, 1821

CHAP. 562.
1800 An act to amend an act, entitled "An act to prevent the stealing of slaves, or by violence, seduction, or any other means, taking or conveying away any slave or slaves, the property of another, and for other purposes therein mentioned," passed at Halifax, in the year 1779. (Page 927). (See 1779, c. 142, s. 2.).

Whereas by the above recited act, no penalty is annexed to the stealing, carrying off and selling free negroes and mulattoes within the limits of this state: For remedy whereof,

Be it enacted, &c. That any person or persons who shall hereafter steal or sell any free negro, or free negroes, or persons of mixed blood, knowing the same to be free or stolen; or shall by violence, seduction, or any other means, take or conveyany free negro or free negroes, or persons of mixed blood, from any part of this state to another, with an intention to sell or dispose of such free negro, or free negroes, or persons of mixed blood, or appropriate the same to his, her, or their own use, and being thereof legally convicted, shall for every such offence be fined not less than fifty pounds, nor more than five hundred pounds, and imprisoned not less than three months, nor more than eighteen months, any thing in the before recited act notwithstanding.

CHAP. 583.
1801. An act to amend the nineteenth section of an act, entitled "An act for the better care of orphans, and security and management of their estates." (Pages 946-947). (See 1762, c. 69, & 1796, c. 468.).

Whereas great abuses frequently happen to children of colour who are bound by the county courts, by the master or mistress removing from the county where such children are bound, or by taking them to some distant place, and there selling them to some person to serve the remainder of their time, or as slaves; and such child or children having no friend to apply to in their behalf for justice to be done them, they are often held or disposed of as slaves: To prevent such evil and pernicious practices in future, therefore,

    1. Be it enacted, &c. That when any county court in this state shall bind any orphan, or base born child of colour, they shall be authorised

and directed to take bond, with sufficient security, in the sum of two hundred and fifty pounds, from the master or mistress, that they shall not remove such child out of the county where he or she was bound, and to produce him or her before such court, at any time when the said court may require it, and also to produce such person at the expiration of the time of his or her service; and on failure thereof, the chairman of the court shall and he is hereby required to bring suit against such persons on said bond, for the benefit and use of the person bound to serve as aforesaid.

2. And be it further enacted, That the several county courts in this state are hereby authorised and required to call on all masters and mistresses to whom any persons of colour hath heretofore been bound by the said court, whose time of service is not expired, to give sufficient security, in the sum of two hundred and fifty pounds, to produce such person or apprentice before them, and not to remove him or her out of said county; and on failure thereof, the chairman of the said court is hereby required and directed to commence suit for the recovery thereof, for the use and benefit of the person so bound to service.

3. And be it further enacted, That if any person to whom any child of colour hath heretofore been bound, and whose time of service is not expired, shall fail, refuse or neglect, on notice from the court to appear and give security as aforesaid, it shall be the duty of the court, and they are hereby required to bind such person of colour to some proper person until he or she shall arrive to full age; any law, usage or custom to the contrary notwithstanding: Provided nevertheless, That nothing in this act contained shall subject any seafaring person to the penalties herein mentioned to whom any person shall be bound in pursuance of this act, if he can make it appear that the person so bound to him died on a voyage, without the limits of the county, or deserted from his service, so that he could not again procure him for the purpose of complying with the condition of the bond.

CHAP. 584.

1801. An act to compel persons who are permitted to have their slaves liberated, to give bond and security for keeping such slaves from becoming a public or county charge, and other purposes. (Pages 947-948). (See 1777, c. 109, s. 2, & 1796, c. 453.).

Whereas it has been represented to this General Assembly, it frequently happens that slaves or negroes emancipated by their owners, become a county charge: For remedy whereof, Be it enacted, &c. That from and after the passing of this act, all persons who are permitted to liberate their slaves or negroes, either by an act of the General Assembly, or by the county courts within this state, it shall be their express duty to enter into bond in the sum of one hundred pounds for each slave so liberated, with approved security; which bond shall be made payable to the chairman of the court and his successors, for the use of the poor of the county in which the slave or negro may reside, that such slave or negro shall not become chargeable on the parish or county, previous to his having the same effected; and every person or persons who shall fail for six months after the said slave or slaves shall be so set free, to enter into bond and security as above directed, shall forfeit and pay the sum of three hundred pounds to the wardens of the poor of the county, for the benefit of the poor of the county in which such slave or slaves shall be so liberated, to be recovered by an action of debt in any court having cognizance of the same.

2. And be it further enacted, That the wardens of the poor in the several counties in this state, or any one of them, shall have power and authority, on application to them made, that any person or persons are about to remove themselves out of the county, and have any slave or slaves that are likely to become a county charge, to issue their or his warrant to bring such person or persons before him or them, and take such security by bond as may be deemed sufficient to indemnify the parish or county; which bond shall be made payable to the chairman of the county court and his successors. And in case such person or persons shall refuse to give bond as is herein directed, he shall have power and authority to commit the said person or persons, and keep him or them committed until he or they shall enter into such bonds, or remove the slave or slaves so about to be left, usage or custom to the contrary notwithstanding.

CHAP. 585.
1801. An act to amend an act, entitled, "An act to amend an act, entitled, An act to prevent thefts and robberies by slaves, free negroes or mulattoes, and to amend an act, entitled An act to prevent the wilful and malicious killing of slaves." (Pages 948-949). (See 1791, c. 335, s. 3 & 1817, c. 949).

Whereas doubts have arisen under the construction of the third section of the above recited act, whether persons can be convicted and properly punished: For remedy whereof,

Be it enacted, &c. That if any person shall hereafter be guilty of feloniously, wilfully and maliciously killing any slave, such offender, upon conviction thereof, on being arraigned stands mute, or challenge peremptorily mor than thirty five jurors, shall suffer death without benefit of clergy.

****

LAWS OF NORTH CAROLINA
1802--1816

CHAPTER LXII.
1802. An Act authorising the county courts therein mentioned, to lay a tax for defraying the expence incurred in suppressing the late insurrection of negroes in said counties. Currituck, Cambden, Pasquotank, Tyrell, Martin and Perquimans. (Page 32).

CHAPTER CXIII.
1802. An Act to emancipate Charles, the property of Matthew Davis, senior, of the county of Surry. (Page 48).

Whereas it is the request of Matthew Davis, senior, of the county of Surry, that his negro man Charles should be emancipated and set free.

Be it enacted by the General Assembly of the State of North Carolina, and it is hereby enacted by the authority of the same, That from and after the passing of this act, the said negro man Charles be emancipated and set free from slavery, and that he be henceforth be called and known by the name of Charles Peters, under which name he shall be invested, and henceforward be entitled to possess and enjoy all the rights, privileges and immunities of what kind or nature soever, and to all intents and purposes in as full and ample a manner, as any free person of colour; any thing to the contrary notwithstanding.

LAWS OF THE STATE OF NORTH CAROLINA
REVISED, UNDER THE AUTHORITY OF THE GENERAL ASSEMBLY
VOLUME II
HENRY POTTER
RALEIGH: PRINTED AND SOLD BY J. GALES, 1821

North Carolina Law

CHAP. 607.
1802. An act for the relief of the Tuscarora nation of Indians. (Pages 965-967).

Whereas the Indians composing the Tuscarora nation, have by their Chief Sacarusa, and others, regularly deputed and authorised, requested the concurrence of the General Assembly of this state to enable them to lease or demise, for a number of years, the residue of their lands situate in the county of Bertie, in such a manner that the whole of the leases on said land shall terminate at the same period;

1. Be it enacted, &c. That the said Chief Sacarusa, Longboard and Samuel Smith, or a majority of them, be, and they are hereby authorised to lease and to farm let, the undemised residue of the lands allotted to the Tuscarora nation in Bertie county, for a term of years that shall expire and end when the lease made by the Tuscarora nation to Robert Jones and others, in the year one thousand seven hundred and sixty six, shall end and expire, and also extend the term or terms of the leases already made or granted for a shorter term, to a term or terms which shall expire at the same time with the said lease made in the year one thousand seven hundred and sixty six, in such parcels and on such rents and conditions as may be approved by the commissioners appointed in pursuance of this act, and which may best promote the interest and convenience of the said Indian nation.

And whereas some difficulties have arisen respecting the receipt and payment of the rents on some of the present leases,

2. Be it further enacted, That the said Chiefs, or a majority of them, be, and they are hereby authorised to make such alterations, by covenant or agreement, respecting the payment and receipt of any of the rents due, or that may become due on any of the existing leases, as the commissioners appointed in pursuance of this act, or a majority of them, shall approve.

Whereas the said Indian Chiefs are ignorant of the usual forms of business, and may want advice and assistance in transacting the business respecting their lands, for remedy whereof, and to prevent their being injured,

3. Be it further enacted, That the governor shall appoint three commissioners for the purposes of carrying the provisions of this act into effect; and no lease, grant, demise, covenant or agreement made by said Indian Chiefs as aforesaid respecting their lands, or the rents thereof, shall

be good or valid in law, unless the same shall be approved by said commissioners, or a majority of them, and such approbation shall be expressed in writing, and annexed or endorsed on such lease, covenant or agreement, and registered in the register's office of the county of Bertie, together with said lease or agreement; and the said commissioners shall receive the sum of twenty five shillings per day for their compensation, and expenses, to be paid out of the monies received by the said Chiefs on leasing said lands.

4. And be it further enacted, That the occupancy and possession of the tenants under the said leases, heretofore confirmed by act or acts of the General Assembly, and such leases as may be made under this act, shall be held and deemed, in all cases whatsoever, the occupancy and possession of the said Tuscarora nation, to all intents and purposes as if the said nation, or the Indians thereof, or any of them, actually resided on said lands.

Whereas the said Chiefs Sacarusa, Longboard and Samuel Smith, being duly and fully authorised and empowered by the said Tuscarora nation, have consented that the Indian claim to the use, possession and occupancy of said lands, shall cease and be extinguished, when the said lease made in the year one thousand seven hundred and sixty six, to Robert Jones and others, shall expire.

5. Be it enacted, That from and after the twelfth day of July, which shall be in the year one thousand nine hundred and sixteen, the whole of the lands allotted to the said Tuscarora Indians, by an act of the General Assembly passed at Newbern, on the fifteenth day of October, in the year of our Lord one thousand seven hundred and forty eight, (**C. 43.**) shall revert to, and become the property of the state, and the Indian claim thereto, shall, from that time, be held and deemed forever extinguished.

6. And be it further enacted, That after the said lands shall revert to the state, if the same, or any part thereof, shall be vacant, the same shall not be liable to the entry or entries of any person or persons, without an express act of the legislature to that effect: Provided always, That it shall not be lawful for any person or persons to make any entry or entries on the said land, after the passing of this act: Provided always, That nothing in this act contained shall be construed so as to effect the title of any individual: Provided nevertheless, That no lot or parcel of lands laid off under the direction of said commissioners, shall exceed two hundred acres: And provided further, That no lease shall be made but by public auction, of which due notice shall be given in the Halifax and Edenton newspapers.

CHAP. 618.
1802. An act to prevent conspiracies among the slaves. (Pages 977-979).

    1. Be it enacted, &c. That if any number of negroes or other slaves, shall, at any time hereafter, consult, advise or conspire to rebel or make insurrection, or shall plot or conspire the murder of any person or persons whatsoever, every such consulting, plotting or conspiring, shall be adjudged and deemed felony, and the slave or slaves convicted thereof in the manner prescribed by law, shall suffer death, or be transported, as hereinafter provided.

    2. Be it further enacted, That if any negro or other slave shall be found in a state of rebellion or insurrection, or shall agree to join any conspiracy or insurrection, or shall procure or persuade others to join or enlist for that purpose, or shall knowingly and wilfully aid or assist any slave or slaves in a state of rebellion, or engaged in a conspiracy to make insurrection, as by furnishing, or agreeing to promise to furnish, such person with arms, ammunition, or any other article for their aid and support, every slave so offending, and being thereof legally convicted, shall be adjudged guilty of felony, and shall suffer death, or be transported, as hereinafter provided.

    3. And be it further enacted, That if any free person shall join in any conspiracy, rebellion or insurrection of the slaves, or shall agree to join in any such conspiracy, rebellion or insurrection, or shall procure or persuade others to join or enlist for that purpose, or shall knowingly and wilfully aid or assist any slave or slaves in a state of rebellion, or engaged in a conspiracy to make insurrection, as by furnishing, or agreeing or promising to furnish, such slave with arms, ammunition, or any other articles for their aid and support, every free person so offending, and being thereof legally convicted, shall be adjudged guilty of felony, and shall suffer death without benefit of clergy.

    4. And be it further enacted, That in all cases wherein a slave shall hereafter be prosecuted for the offences described in this act, the court may take for evidence, the oath of one or more creditable witnesses, the confession of the offender, freely given without any undue influence, either by terror or persuasion, or the testimony of a negro or other person of colour, bond or free; but in all cases where the testimony of one negro or person of colour shall be admitted, the same shall not be deemed conclusive and sufficient to convict the person charged, unless the same shall be supported by such pregnant circumstances as to the jury on said trial, shall appear convincing proof, when taken together with the testimony of such negro or person of colour.

5. Be it enacted, That in all cases of conspiracy, rebellion or insurrection by the slaves, when a sufficient example has been made, by the conviction and execution of any number concerned in such rebellion or insurrection, the court before whom the slave or slaves shall be convicted, shall have full power to commute the punishment of death for transportation out of the state, and beyond the limits of the United States, under such restrictions and upon such conditions as good policy and the public safety at the time shall require.

6. Be it further enacted, That whenever a slave shall be transported in consequence of the provisions of this act, either by the owner or the state, and such slave, shall ever thereafter voluntarily return to, and be found in the state, such slave shall suffer death in pursuance of the original sentence passed against him, on proof of his identity in the usual form of law; and if such slave shall be brought into any county in this state by his or her master or mistress, or by any other person, such slave shall be forfeited, (on proof thereof) to the county into which the same may be brought, which slave shall be again transported by order of the county court, and sold for the use of the county.

And whereas the civil authority may be found insufficient for the suppression and detection of a conspiracy or insurrection among the slaves in this state:

7. Be it therefore enacted, That it shall be the duty of any commissioned officer of the militia of this state, on application or order of any two or more justices of his county, to order out the militia under his command, or such part thereof as may be necessary to detect and suppress such conspiracy, rebellion or insurrection of the negroes or other slaves; and the militia so raised shall perform such duty and services as they shall be required to do by their commanding officer, and shall appear furnished with arms, ammunition and accoutrements, and shall receive the same pay and rations as is directed by the laws now in force. **(See 1798, c. 494 & 1795, c. 444, s. 5.)**

8. And be it further enacted, That the governor be, and he is hereby authorised and required, in all cases of conspiracy or insurrection, to take such measures for the detection or suppression of the same as the public safety at the time may require.

North Carolina Law

****

LAWS OF NORTH CAROLINA
1802--1816

CHAPTER LXV.
1803. An Act to repeal part of an act, entitled "An Act to empower the County Courts therein mentioned to lay a tax to defray the expences incurred by the late Insurrection of the Negroes, passed at Raleigh in the year one thousand eight hundred and two. (Page 40).
Be it enacted by the General Assembly of the State of North Carolina, and it is hereby enacted by the authority f the same, That so much of the above recited act as relates to the county of Martin, shall be, and the same is hereby repealed.

CHAPTER LXIV.
1803. An Act to authorise the County of Hertford to lay a tax for defraying the expenses incurred in suppressing the late Insurrection of the Negroes in said County. (Page 39).

CHAPTER LXVI.
1803. An Act authorising the County Court of Washington to lay a tax in said county, for the purpose of defraying the expenses of the late Insurrection of Negroes in said county. (Page 40).

CHAPTER CIX.
1805. An Act to emancipate Isaac Jones and others, therein mentioned, of the County of Anson. (Page 45).
Be it enacted by the General Assembly of the State of North Carolina, and it is hereby enacted by the authority of the same, That Isaac Jones, Jacob Jones, John Jones, Thomas Jones, Abraham Jones, Lewis Jones, Sukey Jones, John Jones and Sally Jones, of the county of Anson, be, and they are hereby emancipated and set free, in as full as ample a manner, to all intents and purposes, as if they had been free from their nativity; any law, usage or custom to the contrary notwithstanding.

North Carolina Law

****

LAWS OF NORTH CAROLINA
1803--1816

CHAPTER CVI.
1805. An Act for the relief of Lauchlin M'Keller. (Page 45).

Whereas Lauchlin M'Keller hath made known to this General Assembly, that by means of the death of his Uncle Peter M'Donald, of Kingston, in the islands of Jamaica, he hath become entitled to the negro slaves of his said uncle, which he is desirous to remove to Cumberland county, in this State, to the place of his usual residence there:

Be it therefore enacted by the General assembly of the State of North Carolina, and it is hereby enacted by the authority of the same, That it shall and may be lawful for the said Lauchlin M'Keller to bring the negro slaves which have so become his property, into this State, not exceeding the number of twenty; any law, usage or custom to the contrary notwithstanding.

****

LAWS OF THE STATE OF NORTH CAROLINA
REVISED, UNDER THE AUTHORITY OF THE GENERAL
ASSEMBLY
VOLUME II
HENRY POTTER
RALEIGH: PRINTED AND SOLD BY J. GALES, 1821

CHAP. 690.
1805. An act to prevent the masters and owners of vessels and boats, and other persons from trading with slaves. (Page 1048) (1788, c. 285.).

Be it enacted, &c. That if, after the passing of this act, any master or owner of any vessel or boat, or any other person belonging to, or on board of any vessel or boat, lying or being within any river, bay, harbour or creek, within the state, shall buy, sell, or carry on any kind of trade or merchandize to and with any slave or slaves, without permission from the master, mistress or owner of such slave or slaves, such master or owner, or other person, so buying, selling, or carrying on trade or merchandize, shall, for every such offence, forfeit and pay the sum of thirty pounds, to be recovered before any jurisdiction having cognizance of the same; any law, usage or custom to the contrary notwithstanding.

****

NORTH CAROLINA STATE ARCHIVES
LAWS OF NORTH CAROLINA, 1806
Raleigh: PRINTED BY J. GALES, PRINTER TO THE STATE

CHAPTER XCV.
1806. An Act to authorise Francis Briols of the Island of Guadaloupe, to bring into this State certain Negroes therein mentioned. (Page 50).
 Be it enacted by the General Assembly of the State of North Carolina, and it is hereby enacted by the authority of the same, That Francis Briols (late resident and planter of the county of Chowan) now of the island of Guadaloupe, be, and he is hereby empowered and authorized to bring into this State, the following negroes belonging to the said Francis, viz. Lubin, Matthias, Moses, Morris, Charles, Hector, Alice, Dada and her child, Bagett and two other children; any law, usage or custom to the contrary notwithstanding.

CHAPTER XCVI.
1806. An Act to authorise Richard Boyd, of the County of Mecklenburg and State of Virginia, to bring into this State a certain number of Negroes. (Page 50).
 Whereas it is represented to this General Assembly, that Richard Boyd, of the county of Mecklenburg and State of Virginia, is possessed of some valuable land in this State, and that he will be able to derive but little profit therefrom unless he shall be permitted by law to remove some of his negroes from the State of Virginia into this State, to settle and cultivate said land:
 Be it enacted by the General Assembly of the State of North Carolina, and it is hereby enacted by the authority of the same, That Richard Boyd, of the county of Mecklenburg and State of Virginia, is hereby authorised to bring into this State any number of negroes not exceeding fifteen: Provided, that the said Boyd, previous thereto, shall

make oath before some justice of the peace for the county where the said negroes are intended to be brought, that he designs them for his own use, and not for the purpose of sale or speculation.

****

LAWS OF THE STATE OF NORTH CAROLINA REVISED, UNDER THE AUTHORITY OF THE GENERAL ASSEMBLY VOLUME II BY: HENRY POTTER RALEIGH: PRINTED AND SOLD BY J. GALES, 1821

CHAP. 701.
1806. An act declaring what gifts of slaves shall be valid. (Pages 1068-1069). (See 1819, c. 1016.).
For the prevention of frauds:
    1. Be it enacted, &c. That no gift hereafter to be made of any slave or slaves, shall be good or available, either in law or equity, unless the same shall be made in writing, signed by the donor, and attested by at least one credible subscribing witness; neither shall such gift be valid, unless the writing by which the title by which any slave or slaves is transferred shall be proven or acknowledged, as conveyances of land, and registered in the office of the public register of the county where the donee resides, within one year after the execution thereof, if the donee be in actual possession of the slave or slaves so given and transferred; but if, under any special agreement made at the time of the gift, the donor shall remain in possession of the slave or slaves so given, then the writing transferring or conveying the same slave or slaves, shall be proven or acknowledged as aforesaid, and registered within the same time, in the county where the donor resides.
    2. And be it further enacted, That on all trials, where any such writing shall be introduced to support the title of either party, the due and fair execution of such writing shall be proved by a witness subscribing and attesting the execution of such writing; but if such witness shall be dead or removed out of the state, the probate or acknowledgment and registration of such writing, may be given in evidence.
    3. And be it further enacted, That every person claiming title to any slave or slaves, by virtue of any parole gift heretofore made, shall

commence and prosecute his or her suit for the same within three years from the passing of this act, otherwise the same shall be forever barred: Provided however, That if any such person or persons be, at the time of passing this act, within the age of twenty one years, non compos mentis, feme covert, imprisoned, or beyond seas, such person or persons shall, within three years next after full age, coming of sound mind, discoverture, enlargement out of prison, or return from beyond the seas, commence and prosecute his or her suit for any such slave or slaves, claimed by force of such parole gift, and not afterwards. Provided, That when any person shall have put into the actual possession of his or her child or children, any slave or slaves, and the said slave or slaves shall remain in the possession of such child or children, at the time of the death of such person, he or she dying intestate, such slave or slaves shall be considered as an advancement to such child or children, and be regulated by the laws now in force relating to advancements made to children by a parent in his life time.

  4. And be it further enacted, That this act shall commence and be in force from and after the first day of April next.

****

LAWS OF NORTH CAROLINA
1802--1816

CHAPTER LXXV.
1807. An Act to authorise Barnet Beasely, of the County of Warren, and John Rutherford, to bring into this State certain slaves therein mentioned. (Page 31).

CHAPTER LXXVI.
1807. An Act to authorise Samuel Morgan, of Nottoway County, and Commonwealth of Virginia, to bring certain slaves into this State. (Page 31).

****

LAWS OF THE STATE OF NORTH CAROLINA
REVISED, UNDER THE AUTHORITY OF THE GENERAL
ASSEMBLY

North Carolina Law

VOLUME II
BY: HENRY POTTER
RALEIGH: PRINTED AND SOLD BY J. GALES, 1821

CHAP. 719.
1807. An act to amend the penal laws, so far as respects the trial of slaves charged with capital offences. (Page 1113).

1. Be it enacted, &c. That from and after the passing of this act, all slaves charged with criminal offences, the punishment of which is capital, shall be tried at the regular terms of the county courts **(By superior court. See 1816, c. 912.)** of the county in which such offences are alleged to have been committed, and under the same rules, regulations and restrictions as by law now directed.

2. Be it further enacted, That so much of the laws now in force as authorises courts to be specially convened for the trial of slaves charged with capital offences, be, and the same is hereby repealed and made void. (See 1793, c. 381.).

****

LAWS OF NORTH CAROLINA
1802--1816

CHAPTER CXIX.
1808. An Act to emancipate Joseph Blackwell of the County of Brunswick. (Page 40).

Whereas it is represented to this General Assembly, that Blackwell M'Alister, of Brunswick County, was manumitted and set free for meritorious services by him rendered; and that he has purchased and paid for his grandson, Joseph Blackwell, and that he is desirous that the said Joseph should be emancipated by an act of this Legislature.

Be it therefore enacted by the General Assembly of the State of North Carolina, and it is hereby enacted by the authority of the same, That Joseph Blackwell, of the County of Brunswick, and he is hereby emancipated and set free, and declared to possess all the rights, privileges and advantages, in as full and ample manner as if he the said Joseph had been born free, any law to the contrary notwithstanding.

North Carolina Law

CHAPTER CXX.
1808. An Act to emancipate Charlotte Green of Chowan County. (Page 40).

Whereas it is represented to this General Assembly, that Rose, a free woman of colour, late the property of Angus Cabarrus, of Chowan County, was emancipated by the court of said county; and that the said Angus Cabarrus has since made, to the said Rose, a deed of gift of her two children Charlotte and Leon,

Be it enacted by the General Assembly of the State of North Carolina, and it is hereby enacted by the authority of the same, That the negro slaves Charlotte and Leon, be, and each of them is hereby emancipated and set free; and they and each of them may hereafter take and use the surname of Green, and are hereby declared to be able and capable in law to possess and enjoy all the rights and privileges of free persons of mixed blood in this State, in as full and ample manner as the several laws heretofore enacted will permit.

****

LAWS OF THE STATE OF NORTH CAROLINA
REVISED, UNDER THE AUTHORITY OF THE GENERAL
ASSEMBLY
VOLUME II
BY: HENRY POTTER
RALEIGH: PRINTED AND SOLD BY J. GALES, 1821

CHAP. 774.
1809. An act to prevent speculations in obtaining lands which may hereafter accrue to this state, by purchase from the Indians. (Page 1161).

Whereas, from the several acts of Assembly establishing a boundary between this state and the Cherokee Indians, **(See 1783, c. 185, s. 5.)** and the several treaties between the said Indians and the United States, and the several lines run pursuant thereto, it is rendered doubtful where the present boundary extends, and whether the penalties for entering or surveying lands beyond the same, are in full force: And whereas speculators, regardless of the friendship and good faith which ought to be supported with the said Indians, are making entries on their lands; and it is suspected a great speculation is on foot to appropriate most of the valuable lands of the said Indians which lie within this state, so soon as their title shall have been extinguished by treaty, and thereby deprive the honest citizens, who regard the laws of their country, from appropriating lands when permitted by law, without much litigation and expense:

    1. Be it therefore enacted, &c. That the land lying west of the line run by Meigs and Freeman, within the bounds of this state, shall not be subject to be entered under the entry laws of this state; but that the same, when the Indian title shall be extinct, shall remain and insure to the sole use and benefit of the state; any law to the contrary notwithstanding. (See 1817, c. 950.).

    2. And be it further enacted, That all entries made, or grants obtained, or which may hereafter be made or obtained, shall be null and void.

****

LAWS OF NORTH CAROLINA
1802--1816

CHAPTER CXXI.
1810. An Act to alter the Names of the persons therein mentioned, and to legitimate a part thereof. (Page 48).
.... the name of Ned (a man of colour) of Richmond County, to that of Edward Gauntlett.

****

LAWS OF THE STATE OF NORTH CAROLINA
REVISED, UNDER THE AUTHORITY OF THE GENERAL ASSEMBLY
VOLUME II
BY: HENRY POTTER
RALEIGH: PRINTED AND SOLD BY J. GALES, 1821

CHAP. 802.
1810. An act extending the law respecting insolvent debtors to free persons of colour. (Pages 1196-1197).

    Whereas doubts have arisen whether free persons of colour are entitled to the benefits arising to the citizens of this state under the act

North Carolina Law

respecting insolvent debtors: **(See 1773, c. 100.)** For remedy whereof, Be it enacted, &c. That the laws now in force in this state granting any privilege to insolvent debtors, are hereby extended to all free persons of colour, under the same rules, regulations and restrictions, to all intents and purposes, as the acts now are to insolvent debtors; any thing to the contrary notwithstanding.

****

LAWS OF NORTH CAROLINA
1802--1816

CHAPTER XCIV.
1811. An Act to emancipate certain persons therein mentioned. (Page 37).

Be it enacted by the General Assembly f the State of North Carolina, and it is hereby enacted by the authority of the same, That Prince, a negro man, formerly the property of James Baird, late of the county of Lincoln, and Rose, the wife of the said Prince, be, and the said slaves are hereby emancipated and made capable of exercising, holding and enjoying all such rights as if they and each of them had been born free, Provided always, That the property which any person or persons, other than such person or persons as claim by, from or through the said James Baird, shall not be impaired by this act, nor shall this act extend to defeat the creditors of the said James Baird of their just debts, but the said Prince shall remain liable to satisfy the same.

II. And be it further enacted, That this act shall not take effect, or be considered in force, until the heirs or representatives of the said James Baird shall enter into bond with security, payable to the Chairman of the county court of Lincoln, in such sum of money as may be by the said court required, to be void on condition that the negroes intended to be emancipated by this act, do never become a public charge; and that they shall also stand bound by the said bond for their good behaviour.

CHAPTER XCV.
1811. An Act to emancipate certain persons therein mentioned. (Page 37-38).

Be it enacted by the General Assembly of the State of North Carolina, and it is hereby enacted by the authority of the same, That the following Negroes, the property of William Williams, Esquire, of Martin County, to wit, Boson, Penny, and Freeman Hill, are hereby emancipated and made free, and shall be entitled to all the privileges of free persons of colour within the State, in the same manner and to all intents and purposes as if they had been born free: Provided, That the emancipation of the said Negroes shall not injure or prejudice the claim or claims which any person or persons, except William Williams of Martin, may have to the said Negroes.

II. And be it further enacted, That the said Boson and Penny be hereafter known by the name of Boson Hill and Penny Hill.

III. And be it further enacted, That this act shall not be in force until the said William Williams shall have entered into bond with sufficient security, to the Chairman of Bertie county court, in the sum of two hundred and fifty pounds, conditioned that the said Negroes nor either of them, shall become chargeable to the county of Bertie, or any county in the state.

CHAPTER XCVI.
1811. An Act to emancipate James, a man of colour of the county of Lenoir. (Page 38).

Be it enacted by the General Assembly of the State of North Carolina, and it is hereby enacted by the authority of the same, That James, a man of colour of the county of Lenoir, and the property of Richard W. Caswell, late of this State and now of the State of Tennessee, and the said James is hereby emancipated and set free, and made capable of taking, holding and disposing of property, and of enjoying all such privileges as persons of colour born free in this State, do enjoy; and that the said James shall hereafter be known by the name of James Charlton, Provided, always, That this act shall not operate so as to defeat the rights of any person or persons to the property in said James, except the right of the said Richard W. Caswell, and such persons as may claim by, through, from or under him.

II. And be it further enacted, That nothing in this act contained, shall be so construed as to authorise the emancipation of the said negro man James, until Francis Kilpatrick and James Bright, or one of them, shall have entered into bond in the sum of two hundred and fifty pounds, with good and sufficient security, made payable to the Chairman of the County

Court of Lenoir and his successors in office, that the said James shall never become a charge to any of the counties in this State, and making themselves responsible for his good behaviour.

CHAPTER XCVIII.
1811. An Act to emancipate a Negro called Silvia. (Page 38).

Be it enacted by the General Assembly of the State of North Carolina, and it is hereby enacted by the authority of the same, That a certain Negro girl named Silvia, belonging to the estate of Abraham Bass, late of the county of Nash, be, and she is hereby emancipated and made capable of taking, holding and possessing property of every kind, and of enjoying all such privileges as all other free persons of color.

II. And be it further enacted, That the above named girl shall be known and called by the name of Silvia Spears: Provided always, That this act shall not affect the right which any person or persons may have to the service of and property in said girl Silvia, except such person or persons as may claim by, from or through the said Abraham Bass.

III. And be it further enacted, That nothing in this act contained shall be construed so to authorise the emancipation of the said girl Silvia, until Thomas Hamilton shall have entered into bond with sufficient security, in the sum of two hundred and fifty pounds, made payable to the Chairman of the County Court of Nash and his successors in office, to be void on condition that the said Silvia will never become a charge or burthen to any of the counties of this State.

CHAPTER LXI.
1812. An Act to emancipate a Negro girl named Violet. (Page 24).

Be it enacted by the General assembly of the State of North Carolina, and it is hereby enacted by the authority of the same, That a certain Negro Girl named Violet, late the property of Abraham Bass, late of the County of Nash, daughter of Silvia, who was emancipated by an act of the Legislature at its last session, be, and she is hereby emancipated and made capable of taking, holding and possessing property of every kind, and enjoying all such privileges as all other free persons of colour.

II. And be it further enacted, That this act shall not Affect the right of which any person or persons may have to the service of, and property in said Girl Violet, except such person or persons as may claim by, from, and through the said Abraham Bass, deceased.

III. And be it further enacted, That nothing in this act contained shall be so construed as to authorise the emancipation of the said Violet, until Thomas Hamilton shall have entered into bond with sufficient security in the sum of two hundred and fifty pounds, made payable to the Chairman of the County Court of Nash, and his successors in office, to be void on condition, that the said Violet never become a charge or burthen to any of the Counties in this State.

IV. And be it further enacted, That the above named Negro Girl called Violet, shall be known and called by the name of Violet Spears.

CHAPTER LXII.
1812. An Act to emancipate Isabella and Jane, two negro slaves belonging to the estate of James Allen, deceased. (Pages 24-25).

Be it enacted by the General Assembly of the State of North Carolina, and it is hereby enacted by the authority of the same, That Isabella and Jane, two female slaves belonging to the estate of the late James Allen of the town of Wilmington, be, and they are hereby emancipated and made free, by the names of Isabella Allen and Jane Allen; and they are hereby made able and capable in law to possess and enjoy all the rights and privileges which free persons of colour in this state are capable of possessing and enjoying: Provided always, That this act shall not be construed to effect the claim of any creditor of the said James Allen, if the personal estate of said Allen should be insufficient to discharge the demands which are against it; and Provided further, that this act shall not take effect until bond with good and sufficient security to be judged of, and approved by the Justices of the Court of Pleas and Quarter Sessions of the County of New Hanover, and payable to the Chairman thereof, be entered into, conditioned that neither of the persons liberated by this act shall ever become burdensome to the Parish in any County in this State; which bond may be put in suit without assignment by any Parish damnified by the breach thereof.

CHAPTER LXII.
1812. An Act to emancipate certain persons therein mentioned. (Page 25).

North Carolina Law

Be it enacted by the General Assembly of the State of North Carolina, and it is hereby enacted by the authority of the same, That three negro slaves by the names of Hannah, Peggy and Sally, the property of Jacob Spelman of the County of Currituck, be, and they are hereby emancipated and set free, by the names of Hannah Spelman, Peggy Spelman, and Sally Spelman; and the said persons are hereby invested with all the rights which free persons of colour are capable of enjoying by law; Provided, That before this act shall be of any force or effect, bond shall be entered into, in such sum and with such security as shall be approved by the Justices of the County Court of Currituck, and payable to the Chairman thereof, and his successors, conditioned, that neither of the persons hereby emancipated, shall ever become burdensome to the Parish in any County of this State; which bond may be put in suit without assignment, as often as any County in this State may be damnified by breach of the condition thereof.

CHAPTER CXXXI.
1816. An Act to emancipate Hannah Howe, Balaam Howe, John Howe and Sally Howe children of Balaam and Lucy Howe of the County of Brunswick. (Page 53).

Be it enacted by the General assembly of the State of North Carolina, and it is hereby enacted by the authority of the same, That Hannah Howe, John Howe, Balaam Howe and Sally Howe children of Balaam and Lucy his wife, of the County of Brunswick, be, and they are hereby emancipated and set free, and shall be entitled to all the rights and privileges of free persons of color within this state in as full and ample manner as if they had been born free.

****

LAWS OF THE STATE OF NORTH CAROLINA
REVISED, UNDER THE AUTHORITY OF THE GENERAL
ASSEMBLY
VOLUME II
BY: HENRY POTTER
RALEIGH: PRINTED AND SOLD BY J. GALES, 1821

CHAP. 910.

1816. An act to direct the disposal of negroes, mulattoes and persons of colour, imported into this state, contrary to the provisions of an act of the Congress of the United States, entitled "an act to prohibit the importation of slaves into any port or place, within the jurisdiction of the United States, from and after the first day of January, in the year of our Lord one thousand eight hundred and eight." (Pages 1350-1353).

    1. Be it enacted, &c. That each and every negro, mulatto, or person of colour, imported into this state, from any foreign port or place for a slave, or to be held to service or labour, since the first day of January, in the year one thousand eight hundred and eight, contrary to the provisions of an act of Congress, entitled "an act to prohibit the importation of slaves into any port or place within the jurisdiction of the United States, from and after the first day of January, in the year of our Lord one thousand eight hundred and eight," approved the second day of March, 1807, **(See act of Congress 1807, N.E. U.S. Laws, c. 77. p. 94, 4th vol.)** (except as hereinafter provided) shall be sold and disposed of for the use of the state.

    2. Be it further enacted, That the sheriff of each county of this state shall, and he is hereby authorised and required, to seize and take into his possession, every negro, mulatto and person of colour, of the description aforesaid, as well as those which have been, as those which shall be imported as aforesaid, found or which shall be found, in the county of which he is sheriff, and such negro, mulatto or person of colour, so taken in his possession, to sell and dispose of at public sale (giving previous notice of fifteen days of the time of such sale, by advertisement in one of the newspapers published in this state,) to the highest and best bidder, at a credit of six months, the purchaser entering into bond with security, to be approved by said sheriff, for the payment of the purchase money, which money when received, the sheriff so receiving shall account for and pay to the treasurer of this state, after deducting from the gross amount thereof, the several sums hereinafter authorised by him to be retained: the monies collected by virtue of this act shall be paid and accounted for at the treasury, by the several sheriffs, at the same time, and under the regulations and penalties as prescribed in accounting for and paying the public taxes.

    3. Be it further enacted, That were any such negro, mulatto or person of colour, as is above mentioned, shall abscond, or so conceal himself or herself, that he or she cannot be taken by the sheriff, said sheriff may offer a reward not exceeding one fifth part of the value of such negro, mulatto or person of colour, to any person or persons who shall apprehend and deliver him or her to the sheriff or his deputy, and shall then sell said negro, mulatto or person of colour, as above directed; or such sheriff may in his discretion proceed to advertise and sell such negro, mulatto or person of colour, as directed in the forgoing section, without offering a reward, although such negro, mulatto or person of colour, may not be in the custody or possession of said sheriff, at the time of said sale.

  4. Be it further enacted, That whenever any person shall discover any negro of the description aforesaid, in any county of this state, and give such notice thereof to the sheriff of the county, that he shall, in consequence of such information, obtain the said negro, mulatto or person of colour, the person or persons giving such information shall be entitled to receive from the said sheriff, one fifth part of the sum for which said negro, mulatto or person of colour shall afterwards sell, to be retained as well as the reward offered as directed in the preceeding section, out of the proceeds of the sale, and paid to the person entitled to the same by the sheriff.

  5. Be it further enacted, That all sales by virtue of this act shall be made at the court house of each respective county, and the sheriff selling, or his successor, in case of his death, resignation or removal from office, shall execute and deliver to the purchaser, his executors, administrators or assigns, a bill of sale for such negro, mulatto or person of colour so sold, which shall vest in the purchaser the absolute property in the same, and the title so acquired shall not be affected by the want of advertisement, or by any other irregularity in such sale or proceedings, on the part of the sheriff.

  6. Be it further enacted, That every sheriff selling as aforesaid, may retain out of the purchase money of such negro, mulatto or person of colour, so sold, besides the rewards above directed to be paid, and besides the reasonable charges at which the said sheriff shall be, in keeping such negro, mulatto or person of colour till the day of sale, and in advertising as aforesaid, the further sum of six per centum on the gross proceeds of such sale, which shall be in full compensation of his services.

  7. Be it further enacted, That where any person or persons shall have purchased before the 18th of November, 1816, for a fair and valuable consideration, any such negro, mulatto or person of colour so imported into this state contrary to the provisions of the said act of Congress, of and from any person or persons originally importing such negro, mulatto or person of colour, or the master, agent or attorney of such importer or importers, and such sale or purchase shall not be merely colorable to defeat or evade the provisions of this act, in that case the sheriff in whose county such negro,

mulatto or person of colour is found, and the sheriff of the county where such purchaser resides, shall not proceed to sell such negro, mulatto or person of colour, but upon due proof being made of such sale and purchase before the chief or other justice of the supreme or superior courts, such chief or other justice shall give to such purchaser, a certificate under his hand, directed to the sheriff of the county where such negro, mulatto or person of colour is or the purchaser resides, specifying the negro, mulatto or person of colour, with respect to which such proof shall have been exhibited, and on receipt of such certificate, , such sheriff shall execute and deliver to such purchaser or his representative, a bill of sale for such negro, mulatto or person of colour, and the benefit of this section shall extend to the assignee or assignees of such purchaser, as well as to such purchaser and his representatives.

 8. And be it further enacted, That the several provisions of this act shall extend and apply to every negro, mulatto or person of colour, the issue of any negro, mulatto or person of colour so imported as aforesaid.

CHAP. 912.
1816. An act to amend the laws (See 1741, c. 35, 1793, c. 381, 1807, c.719.) in force respecting the trial of slaves in capital cases. (Page 1354).

 1. Be it enacted, &c. That in all cases in which a slave or slaves shall be charged with the commission of an offence, the punishment whereof may extend to life, the superior courts of law shall have exclusive jurisdiction within their respective counties, the trial shall be conducted in the same manner, and under the same rules, regulations and restrictions, as trials of freemen for a like offence are now conducted, except as is hereinafter provided, and notice of trial shall be given to the owner or owners of such slave or slaves, in the manner now directed in the case of the trial of slaves in the county courts.

 2. Be it further enacted, That such cases may be removed for trial to an adjoining county, upon affidavit from the owner, or in his absence, of the counsel of such slave or slaves, in the same manner as causes may now be removed by freemen.

 3. Be it further enacted, That a slave shall not be tried for a capital offence, but on presentment or indictment of the grand jury, and on his trial shall be entitled to the right of challenge for cause only, which challenge he shall make by and with the advice and assistance of his owner, or in his absence, of his counsel.

4. Be it further enacted, That a slave convicted of a clergiable offence, shall be entitled to the benefit of clergy, in like manner with a free man.

5. Be it further enacted, That in all cases of conspiracy, insurrection, or rebellion of slaves, upon the information, and at the request of any five justices of the peace of the county in which such conspiracy, insurrection, or rebellion shall happen, it shall be the duty of the governor for the time being, to issue a commission of oyer and terminer, to any of the judges of the superior courts of law, for the trial of such slaves, in the manner prescribed in the **act of 1777, chapter 2, (C. 115.) and of 1779, chapter 6. (C. 157.).**

6. Be it further enacted, That all laws and clauses of laws, which come within the meaning and purview of this act, be and the same are hereby repealed.

****

THE LAWS OF THE STATE OF NORTH CAROLINA ENACTED IN THE YEAR, 1817 RALEIGH: PRINTED BY THOMAS HENDERSON, STATE PRINTER 1818

CHAP. I.
1817. On Negro Traders of 5$ for each slave. (Page 10).

XXI. And be it further enacted, That all persons who shall bring negro slaves from another state into this state for sale, or shall take negroes through any part of this state for any other state for sale, shall pay the sheriff of some one of the counties, the sum of five dollars upon each negro slave so brought; and it shall be the duty of the respective sheriffs in this state and their deputies to collect the tax hereby imposed; but if the said person or persons shall produce to the sheriff of any one county, the certificate of the sheriff of any other county, duly authenticated under the seal of the clerk of the county in which such sheriff resides, that he has paid the tax hereby imposed, he or they shall be permitted to proceed without the payment of any other tax; and it shall be the duty of the sheriff and his deputy of each county into which any such negro slave shall be carried by any person or persons whatsoever, to seize every such negro or slave until the tax hereby imposed is paid, or until the person or persons in whose possession said negro slaves may be, shall produce to said sheriff or his deputy the receipt of the sheriff of some other county duly certified as above in the state, that the tax hereby imposed has been paid , or until he shall produce to said sheriff or his deputy, a certificate from the clerk of some court of record of the state from which said negro slaves may have been removed, duly certified according to law, that said negro slaves are not removed for sale, which certificate shall contain the name or names of each and every negro or slave so removed.

CHAP. LXXXV.
1817. An act to regulate slaves navigating decked boats in Craven county. (Pages 66-67).

WHEREAS the privilege afforded to slaves of navigating decked boats without the presence of a white man is frequently abused by the reception and speedy removal of property stolen from the shores, for remedy whereof.

BE it enacted by the General Assembly of the State of North-Carolina, and it is hereby enacted by the authority of the same, That every owner, hirer or person employing a decked boat upon any of the waters of Craven county, no white man forming a part of the crew thereof, shall give a bond in the sum of fifty pounds, with at least one sufficient security, payable to the Chairman of the county court of Craven and his successors in office, with condition to be void if no stolen property shall be received on board such boat, while the same shall continue under the management of slaves, for the use of the person giving such bond which bond shall be sued for and recovered upon breach of the condition thereof, and the money recovered shall be applied one half to the use of the county, the other half to the use of the person suing therefor.

II. And be it further enacted, That if any person shall employ a decked boat upon the waters of Craven county, no white man forming a part of the crew thereof, without first giving such bond required by this act, such person shall forfeit twenty pounds, to be recovered by any person suing for the same, in the name of such person, one half to the use of the County, the other half to theuse of the person suing.

III. And be it further enacted by the authority aforesaid, That the court of said counties, and if upon hearing evidence for and against the parties they of Craven county whenever such bond is given, shall annually require such bond to be renewed with other or better security at the first term after notice of such order of renewal, the said boat shall be thenceforth considered as navigated in violation of this act, and the person so employing her shall be liable to the penalties of this act.

****

THE LAWS OF THE STATE OF NORTH CAROLINA ENACTED IN THE YEAR, 1819.
RALEIGH: PRINTED BY THOMAS HENDERSON, STATE PRINTER 1820.

CHAPTER I.
1819. Negro traders. (Pages 6-7)

IX. Be it further enacted, That all persons who shall bring negro slaves from another state into this state for sale, or shall take any negro slaves through any part of this state for sale, shall pay to the sheriff of some one county, the sum of ten dollars, upon each negro slave so brought; and it shall be the duty of the respective sheriffs in this state and their deputies to collect the tax hereby imposed; but if the said person or persons shall produce to the sheriff of any one county, the certificate of the sheriff of any other county duly authenticated under the seal of the clerk of the county in which such sheriff resides, that he has paid the tax hereby imposed, he or they shall be permitted to proceed without the payment of any further tax; And it shall be the duty of the sheriff and his deputy , of each county into which any such negro slave shall be carried by any person or persons whatsoever, to seize such negro slave until the tax hereby imposed is paid, or until the person or persons in whose possession such negro slave may be, shall produce to the said sheriff or his deputy, the certificate of the clerk of some court of record of the state from which the negro slaves may have been removed, duly certified according to law, that said negro slaves are not removed for sale, which certificate shall contain the name or names of each and every negro slave so removed; and the owners or possessors of all such slsves so seized, shall pay to the sheriff or his deputy all expences that may accrue in consequence of seizing, keeping and feeding such slaves.

X. And be it further enacted, That all free males between the ages of of twenty-one and forty-five years, and slaves between the ages of twelve and fifty years, shall pay a poll tax; and all slaves shall be listed in the county wherein they reside.

CHAPTER II.
1819. An act to create a fund for Internal Improvements, and to establish a Board for the management thereof. (Page 7).

I. Be it enacted by the General Assembly of the State of North Carolina, and it is hereby enacted by the authority of the same, That a fund shall be, and the same is hereby created, to be denominated "the Fund for Internal Improvements," and to be applied exclusively to the internal improvement of this state, unless the necessities of this state shall render it necessary for some future legislature to apply the said fund or part thereof to some other purposes of state.

II. Be it further enacted, That the said fund shall consist of the nett proceeds of the sales of the lands lately acquired by treaty from the Cherokee Indians.

CHAPTER XIV.
1819. An act to prevent fraudulent trading with slaves. (Pages 23-24).

Be it enacted by the General Assembly of the State of North Carolina, and it is hereby enacted by the authority of the same, That if any person or persons shall deal, trade or traffic with any negro slave, the property of another, for any cotton, tobacco, flax, corn, wheat, rice, rye, oats, barley, bacon, pork, spiritous liquors or beef, at any time, or for any kind of goods or commodities, or anything in the night time, or between the setting of the sun and the rising thereof, or on the sabbath day, without a permission in writing from the master, mistress or other person having the management of such slave or slaves, setting forth the specific article or articles such slave or slaves may have for sale, every such person or persons, on conviction before any justice of the peace in the county where such offence was committed, shall pay the sum of fifty dollars, the one half thereof to the use of the person suing for the same, and the other half to the wardens of the poor of said county.

II. Be it further enacted, That the said offence shall moreover be indictable in the County or Superior Court; and the defendant on conviction, shall be fined or imprisoned at the discretion of the Court, Provided, the fine shall not exceed fifty dollars, or the imprisonment three months.

III. Be it further enacted, That if it shall appear on the trial that the defendant is a licenced retailer of spiritous liquors by the small measure, he or she shall also forfeit his or her retailing licence for the space of two years from and after the date of his or her conviction.

IV. Be it further enacted, That either of the parties being dissatisfied with the judgment of the justice, or verdict of the jury, may appeal therefrom as in other cases.

CHAPTER XXII.
1819. An Act to ammend an act passed in the year one thousand eight hundred and two, entitled "An act to prevent conspiracies and insurrections among slaves." (Page 28).

Be it enacted by the General Assembly of the State of North Carolina, and it is hereby enacted by the authority of the same, That when any slave or slaves shall hereafter be convicted of either of the felonies created and recited in the first or second section of said recited act, he, she or they shall suffer death without benefit of clergy; or be transported according to the provisions of said recited act.

CHAPTER XXVII.
1819. An Act relative to the apprehension of runaway slaves. (Page 30).

Be it enacted by the General assembly of the State of North Carolina, and it is hereby enacted by the authority of the same, That all persons hereafter, who may apprehend and confine in jail any runaway slave agreeably to the existing laws, for whom a reward shall not have been offered, shall be entitled to recover and receive from the owner of such slave, the sum of five dollars, to be taxed by the jailor against the owner, and collected with his prison fees, Provided however, That this act shall not be construed to extend to cases where a slave is apprehended in the county in which their master, mistress or overseer resides.

CHAPTER XXIX.
1819. An Act to make void parol contracts for the sale of Lands and Slaves. (Page 30).

North Carolina Law

Be it enacted by the General Assembly of the State of North Carolina, and it is hereby enacted by the authority of the same, That all contracts to sell or convey any lands, tenements or hereditaments, or any interest in or concerning them, or any slave or slaves, shall be void and of no effect, unless such contract or memorandum or note thereof, shall be put in writing and signed by the party to be charged therewith, or some other person thereto by him lawfully authorized: except nevertheless contracts for leases not exceeding in duration the term of three years.

II. And be it further enacted, by the authority aforesaid, That this act shall be in force, from and after the first day of January, one thousand eight hundred and twenty one, and not before that time.

CHAPTER CI.
1819. An act for the relief of Mary Ann Sansum. (Pages 69-70).

Whereas it appears from the memorial of Mary Ann Sansum, and the documents accopanying the same, that the six negroes or mullattoe slaves mentioned in said memorial were imported into this State, without any intention to violate the laws of the the United States or North Carolina.

Be it enacted by the General Assembly of the State of North Carolina, and it is hereby enacted by the authority of the same, That the Sheriff of New Hanover county, be and he is hereby authorised and required to surrender and deliver over to the said Mary Ann Sansum the six negroes or mulattoe Slaves imported into the port of Wilmington in August last, in the brig Sally, whereof Anthony S. Delisle was master; provided the said Mary Ann Sansum enter into bond with approved security payable to the Sheriff of New-Hanover county, in an amount of double the value of said negro or mulattoe slaves to carry the same beyond the limits of the State of North Carolina within four months from the date of said delivery.

II. And be it further enacted by the authority aforesaid, That in case the Sheriff of New-Hanover shall have sold said negro or mulattoe slaves, or any part of them agreeable to an act of Assembly in such case provided and passed in the year one thousand eight hundred and sixteen, previous to obtaining notice of this act, then and in that case, the Sheriff of New-Hanover county is hereby authorised and required to assign and deliver to the said Mary Ann Sansum, all bonds which may have been taken for the payment of the purchase money arising from the sale of said negro or mulattoe slaves, on her paying to the Sheriff all expences and charges which may have arisen from the seizure of the said slaves.

III. And be it further enacted, That this act shall be in full force, from and after the ratification thereof.

CHAPTER CIII.
1819. An Act to prevent obstructions to the passage of fish up Neuse River, Contentnea Creek and Little River. (Pages 70-71).
(Editors Note: Section III. of this act applies to punishment administered to free persons. Section IV. applies to slaves.)

III. And be it further enacted, That every person offending against the provisions of this act shall be further subject to indictment in any court of the county, and upon conviction shall be fined in a sum of not less than twenty dollars and not more than one hundred dollars and be imprisoned at the discretion of the court, not exceeding two months.

IV. And be it further enacted, That if any slave or slaves shall offend against the provisions of this act and shall be thereof convicted before any Justice of the Peace for the county in which such offence shall have been committed, he, she, or they so convicted, shall receive thirty nine lashes upon his or her bare back, and the owner of such slave shall pay the costs of prosecution.

V. And be it further enacted, That an act to prevent any person or persons from working seins or skiming with nets in Neuse River on Sundays, and Sunday nights, from the 15th day of January to the 25th day of April in each and every year, passed in 1809 be and the same is hereby repealed.

CHAPTER CXVIII.
1819. An act to repeal certain parts of three acts concerning patrollers, one passed in the year 1794, one other in the year 1802 and the other in the year 1816, so far as relates to the county of Edgecombe. (Page 77).

Be it enacted by the General Assembly of the State Of North Carolina, and it is hereby enacted by authority of the same, That so much of the above recited acts as exempts patrollers from serving on juries, working on roads, from the payment of all parish and county taxes to the amount of forty shillings, and that authorises the court of pleas and quarter sessions to lay a tax on the black poll, for the purpose of paying patrollers by them appointed, be, and the same is hereby repealed so far as relates to the county of Edgecombe: Provided however, That none other than owner or overseers of slave or slaves shall be compelled to serve as patrollers.

****

THE LAWS OF THE STATE OF NORTH CAROLINA ENACTED IN THE YEAR, 1820
RALEIGH:PRINTED BY THOMAS HENDERSON JR. PRINTER TO THE STATE 1821

CHAP. 6.
1820. On negro traders. (Pages 9-10).

9. And be it further enacted, That all persons who shall bring Negro Slaves from another state into this state, for sale, shall pay the Sheriff of some one county the sum of ten dollars upon each Negro Slave so brought; and it shall be the duty of the respective Sheriffs in this state, and their deputies, to collect the tax hereby imposed; but if the said person or persons shall produce to the Sheriff of any other county, duly authenticated, under the seal of the clerk of the county in which such Sheriff resides, that he has paid the tax hereby imposed, he or they shall be permitted to proceed without the payment of any further tax. And it shall be the duty of the Sheriff, and his deputy, of each county in which any Negro Slave shall be taken by any person or persons whatsoever to seize such Negro Slave until the tax hereby imposed be paid, or until the person in whose possession such Negro Slave may be, shall produce to said Sheriff, or his deputy, the receipt of the Sheriff of some other county, duly authenticated as above, that the tax hereby imposed has been paid, or until he shall produce to the Sheriff, or his deputy the certificate of the clerk of some court of record of the state from which the said Negro Slaves may have been removed, duly certified according to law, that said Negro Slaves are not removed for sale, which certificate shall contain the name or names of each and every Negro Slave so removed, and the owners or possessors of all such Slaves so seized shall pay to the Sheriff or his deputy, all expences that may accrue in consequence of seizing, keeping, and feeding such Slaves.

10. And be it further enacted, That for the year one thousand eight hundred and twenty one, a tax of twenty cents on each and every free poll, and a tax of twenty cents on each and every black poll, shall be levied, collected and accounted for, under the same rules, regulations and restrictions as poll taxes heretofore have been collected and accounted for.

11. And be it further enacted. That all free males between the ages of twenty one and forty five years, and slaves between the ages of twelve an fifty years, shall pay a poll tax, and all slaves shall be listed in the county wherein they reside.

CHAP. 21.
1820. An Act to quiet the title of persons in possession of Slaves. (Page 24).

1. Be it enacted by the General Assembly of the State of North Carolina, and it is hereby enacted by the authority of the same, That whenever any person or persons shall remain in the possession of a slave or slaves until such possession is protected by the Statute of Limitations; the person or persons so in possession and those claiming under them, shall be deemed and held to have a good and absolute title to such slave or slaves against all persons whose claim is barred by the Statute of Limitations: Provided, That nothing herein contained shall in any way affect the Law now in force, that requires all gifts of slaves to be by deeds of gift.

CHAP. 32.
1820. An Act directing the manner in which property levied on by Sheriffs and Constables shall be sold hereafter. (Page 33).

1. Be it enacted by the General Assembly of the State of North Carolina, and it is hereby enacted by the authority of the same, That from and after the passing of this act it shall be the duties of the several Sheriffs and Constables in this state, when they or any of them do levy an execution on land or slaves, to sell the same at the Court House of their respective counties, on the last Thursday in each and every month in each year, which shall happen after the first day of February next, and the last Thursday in each and every month in each year, is hereby set apart for that purpose, and shall be considered as a sale day in every county in this state; and if on any sale day as aforesaid, the whole of the property taken by virtue of an execution cannot be sold on the same day, the Constables or Sheriff shall be authorised to continue the same from day to day until the whole shall be sold, on giving notice at the Court House that such sale will be continued on the ensuing day: Provided nevertheless, That the same notice shall be

North Carolina Law

given at least forty days previous thereto, of the sale of real estate, and twenty days notice of the sale of slaves; and the sale shall be conducted under the same rules and restrictions as heretofore prescribed in such cases, and the said sale shall be made between the hours of ten and four o'clock.

2. And be it further enacted, That any Sheriff or Constable who shall sell any land or slaves, taken by virtue of an execution at any other time or place than as above prescribed, shall forfeit and pay the sum of two hundred dollars, to be recovered in the name of any person who shall sue for the same.

3. And be it further enacted, That sales in the county of Currituck shall be held at the usual places of holding petit musters in said county in which the defendant may reside.

4. And be it further enacted, That all laws and clauses of laws, coming within the purview and meaning of this act, be and the same is hereby repealed and made void.

CHAPTER 39
1820. An Act to provide for the payment of costs when a Slave is convicted of a Capital Crime. (Page 38).

1. Be it enacted by the General Assembly of the State of North Carolina, and it is hereby enacted by the authority of the same, That hereafter, when any slave shall be convicted of a capital crime, and executed in consequence of such conviction, the costs of prosecution shall be paid by the county in which such prosecution shall have commenced.Read three times and ratified in General Assembly,

the 25th day of December, A.D. 1820
R.M. Sanders,
S.H.C.
B. Yancey S.S.
A true Copy   W.M. Hill, Sec'y.

CHAPTER 58
1820. An act to prevent the fishing with nett, or netts, at the mouth of Great Contentea Creek. (Pages 49-50).
[Editors Note: Punishment for whites and free persons was $25.00]

2. And be it further enacted, That if any slave or slaves shall be convicted of the offence of fishing contrary to the provisions of this act, that he, she or they, shall receive twenty-five lashes on his, her, or their bare backs; and the owner of such slave or slaves shall be liable for the costs of prosecution.

RESOLUTIONS - NORTH CAROLINA - IN GENERAL ASSEMBLY IN HOUSE OF COMMONS
December 19, 1820

Resolved, That Jeremiah Slade, Simmons J. Baker and Thomas Brickell be, and are hereby appointed Commissioners to enquire into the business relating to the claim for lands in Bertie County of the Tuskarora nation of Indians; and also into the expediency of the state of North Carolina to make sale of the reversionary interests in said lands; and further to enquire into the claims of the several occupants of the lands to a preference in purchase; and to report to the General Assembly of 1821 the result of their enquiries.

****

THE LAWS OF NORTH CAROLINA ENACTED IN THE YEAR 1821 RALEIGH: PRINTED BY THOMAS HENDERSON, PRINTER TO THE STATE 1822

CHAPTER I.
1821. Slaves bro't into this state, for sale, taxed 10 dollars. (Pages 6-7).

VIII. Be it further enacted, That all persons who shall bring negro slaves from another state into this state, for sale, shall pay pay the sheriff of some one county, the sum of ten dollars upon each negro slave so brought; and it shall be the duty of the respective sheriffs in this state, and their deputies, to collect the tax hereby imposed; but if the said person or persons, shall produce to the sheriff of any one county the certificate of the sheriff of any other county, duly authenticated, under the seal of the clerk of the county in which such sheriff resides, that he has paid the tax hereby imposed, he or they shall be permitted to proceed without the payment of any further tax. And it shall be the duty of the sheriff and his deputy, of each county in which any negro slave shall be taken by any person or persons whatsoever, to seize such negro slave, until the tax hereby imposed, be paid, or until he or they shall produce to the sheriff an affidavit, subscribed by him or them, before some Justice of the Peace, within this state, duly authenticated by the certificate of the clerk, and seal of the court of the county, setting forth that the sl or slaves so seized, were not by him or them or any other person with his or their privity and consent, bought in evasion or elusion of the revenue laws of this state; and every person guilty of making any false affidavit for such person, shall, on conviction, be deemed guilty of wilful and corrupt perjury: and the owners or possessors of all such slaves so seized, shall pay to the sheriff, or his deputy, all expense that may accrue in consequence of seizing, keeping and feeding such slaves; and the slaves so seized, may be detained by the sheriff until such payment; and in default thereof, the said sheriff may sell the same at public auction, at the Court-House of the county, upon twenty days previous notice; which sale shall convey an absolute title to the purchaser.

  IX. Be it further enacted, That for the year one thousand eight hundred and twenty-two, a tax of twenty cents on each and every free poll, and a tax of twenty cents on each and every black poll, shall be levied, collected and accounted for under the same rules, regulations, and restrictions, as poll taxes heretofore have been collected and accounted for.

  XI. Be it further enacted, That all free males, between the ages of twenty one and forty five years, and slaves between the ages of twelve and fifty years, shall pay a poll tax, and all slaves shall be listed in the county wherein they reside.

CHAP. XIX.
1821. An act directing the time and place of sale of lands and slaves under execution. (Pages 20-21).
  Be it enacted by the General Assembly of the State of North Carolina, and it is hereby enacted authority of the same, That hereafter all sales of slaves or slaves or land made by any sheriff, coroner, constable, or by any clerk and master in equity, under any execution or decree, shall be made at the court house of their respective counties; and such sales may commence and be made on any Monday, in any week, and if the property levied on under execution, for want of time, shall not be all sold on the Monday, or if properly levied on under other executions cannot be offered by reason that the sale first commenced is not completed for want of time,

all such sales may be adjourned to the next day, and the property remaining unsold on the Tuesday, may, under the same circumstances, be sold on the next day, and all sales not the completed, may be adjourned to the Monday of the ensuing week; and all such sales shall commence between the hours of ten and four o'clock on each sale day; Provided nevertheless, That nothing herein contained shall be construed to alter in any manner the rules and restrictions under which sales are by law directed to be conducted, and executions required to be returned.

II. And be it further enacted, That hereafter it shall be lawful for a sheriff, coroner or constable to sell slaves, under any process to him or them directed, by giving ten days' previous notice of the time and place of such sale.

III. And be it further enacted, That any sheriff, coroner, constable or clerk and master in equity, who shall make any sale contrary to this act, shall forfeit and pay the sum of two hundred dollars, to be recovered by any person suing for the same, one half to his own use, and one half to the use of the county in which the offence is committed.

IV. And be it further enacted, That the provisions of this act, and the provisions of the act of one thousand eight hundred and twenty entitled "An act directing the manner in which property levied on by sheriffs and constables shall be sold hereafter," shall not apply to the counties of Currituck, Carteret and Tyrell, and that so far as regards the counties aforesaid, the before recited act is hereby repealed.

V. And be it further enacted, That the land and slaves lying and being in the third or Haw river regiment, in Orange county, shall be sold under the directions of this act at the place of the usual regimental musters of the said regiment; and all lands and slaves, owned by persons not residing in said regiment, shall be sold at the court-house.

CHAP. XLIII.
1821. An act providing further punishment for harboring or maintaining runaways. (Page 40).

Be it enacted by the General Assembly of the State of North Carolina, and it is hereby enacted by the authority of the same, That in addition to the penalty already imposed by law, any person who shall entice or persuade any slave to absent him or herself from the service of his or her owner, or from the service of any other person legally entitled to the service of such slave, or who shall harbor or maintain any runaway slave, shall be subject to indictment for such offence, and, being thereof convicted shall be fined at the discretion of the Court, not exceeding one hundred dollars, and be imprisoned not exceeding six months.

CHAP. XLVI.
1821. An act to amend and explain the forty-second section of an act, passed in the year one thousand seven hundred and seventy-seven, entitled "an act for establishing Courts of Law, and for regulating the proceedings therein." (Pages 41-42).

Whereas doubts have arisen as to the proper construction of that part of the forty-second section of the act of the General Assembly, passed in the year one thousand seven hundred and seventy seven, entitled "an act for establishing Courts of Law, and for regulating the proceedings therein," which provides that all negroes, Indians, mulattoes, and all persons of mixed blood, descended from negro or Indian ancestors, to the fourth generation inclusive, (though one ancestor of each generation may have been a white person,) whether bond or free, shall be deemed and taken to be incapable in law to be witnesses in any case whatsoever, except against each other; and whereas the decisions of the Courts upon the said provision, have been various and contradictory.

Be it therefore enacted by the General Assembly of the State of North Carolina, and it is hereby enacted by the authority of the same, That in all pleas of the state, where the defendants may be a negro, Indian or mulatto or person of mixed blood, descended from negro or Indian ancestors, to the fourth generation inclusive, (though one ancestor of each generation may have been a white person,) whether such defendant be bond or free, the evidence of a negro or negroes, Indian or Indians, mulatto or mulattoes, and of all persons of mixed blood, descended from negro and Indian ancestors to the fourth generation inclusive, (though one ancestor of each generation may have been a white person,) whether the person or persons whose evidence is offered, be bond or free, shall be admissible and the witness competent, subject nevertheless to be excluded upon any other grounds of incompetency which may exist.
(Editors Note: a note in the margin reads, "Evidence of negroes, &c. admitted in certain cases.")

II. And be it further enacted, That this act shall be in force from and after its ratification.

North Carolina Law

****

THE LAWS OF NORTH CAROLINA ENACTED IN THE YEAR 1822 RALEIGH: PRINTED BY BELL & LAWRENCE 1823

CHAPTER I.
1822. Slaves bro't into this state for sale taxed 10 dollars. (Pages 6-7).

VIII. Be it further enacted, That all persons who shall bring negro slaves from another state into this state for sale, shall pay to the sheriff of some one county the sum of ten dollars upon each negro slave so brought; and it shall be the duty of the respective sheriffs in this state, and their deputies, to collect the tax hereby imposed. But if the said person or persons shall produce to the sheriff of any one county the certificate of the the sheriff of any other county, duly authenticated, under the seal of the clerk of the county in which such sheriff resides, that he has paid the tax hereby imposed, he or they shall be permitted to proceed without the payment of any further tax. And it shall be the duty of the sheriff and his deputy, of each county in which any negro slave shall be taken, by any person or persons whatsoever, to seize such such negro slave, until the tax, hereby imposed, be paid; or until he or they shall produce to the sheriff an affidavit, subscribed by him or them, before some justice of the peace, within this state, duly authenticated by the certificate of the clerk, and seal of the court, of the county, setting forth that the slave or slaves so seized, were not by him or them, or any other person, with his or their privity and consent, bought in evasion or elusion of the revenue laws of this state. And every person guilty of making any false affidavit for such person, shall, on conviction, be deemed guilty of wilful and corrupt perjury; and the owners or possessors of all such slaves, so seized, shall pay to the sheriff or his deputy, all expense that may accrue in consequence of seizing, keeping, and feeding such slaves; and the slaves, so seized, may be detained by the sheriff until such payment; and, in default thereof, the said sheriff may sell the same, at public auction, at the court house of the county, upon twenty days previous notice; which sale shall convey an absolute title to the purchaser.

IX. Be it further enacted, That an annual tax of twenty cents on each and every free poll, and a tax of twenty cents on each and every black poll shall be levied, collected and accounted for under the same rules, regulations and restrictions, as poll taxes heretofore have been collected and accounted for.

X. Be it further enacted, That all free males, between the ages of twenty-one and forty-five years, and all slaves between the ages of twelve and fifty, shall pay a poll tax, and all slaves shall be listed in the county wherein they reside.

CHAPTER II.
1822. An act to amend an act, passed in 1821, entitled "an act to promote the administration of justice." (Page 8).

Be it enacted by the General Assembly of the State of North Carolina, and it is hereby enacted by the authority of the same, That when any application shall be made to remove any cause, whether civil or criminal, to an adjacent county for trial, which cause shall have been before removed, it shall be the duty of the person so applying, to set forth, on affidavit, particularly and in detail, the grounds of such application; and the presiding judge may, in his discretion, remove the same to any adjacent county for trial: Provided, That no cause, under any circumstances, shall be removed more than twice.

II. And be it further enacted, That hereafter, on the trial of any slave or slaves for capital offences, if it shall appear to the presiding judge, by affidavit or otherwise, that such slave or slaves cannot have a fair trial in the county wherein the offence is charged to have been committed, it shall, and may be lawful for such judge to order the removal of such cause to an adjacent county for trial, notwithstanding the master or owner of such slave or slaves may neglect or refuse to make an application to the court for that purpose.

CHAPTER XIV.
1822. An Act to repeal the fifth section of an act, passed in the year 1821, entitled "an act directing the time and place of sale of lands and slaves under execution." (Page 17).

Be it enacted by the General Assembly of the State of North-Carolina, and it is hereby enacted by the authority of the same, That from and after the passing of this act, the fifth section of all the before recited act, be, and the same is hereby repealed.

CHAPTER XXV.
1822. An act directing the time and place of selling lands and slaves under execution. (Page 24).

Be it enacted by the General Assembly of the State of North-Carolina, and it is hereby enacted by the authority of the same, That hereafter all sales of land or slaves made by any Sheriff, Coroner, Constable or by any Clerk and Master in Equity, under any execution or decree, shall be made at the court house of their respective counties; and such sales shall be made on the same Monday, in each and every month, on which the several Courts of Pleas and Quarter Sessions are generally held, for their respective counties, always making the Monday of each County Court the only sale day in that month; and if, on any sale day, as aforesaid, the whole of the property taken by virtue of an execution, cannot be sold on the same day, the Sheriff, Constable, or other public officer shall be authorised to postpone the same from day to day until the whole shall be sold, on giving public notice at the court house, that such sale will be continued on the ensuing day; and all such sales shall commence between the hours of eleven and four o'clock on such sale day: Provided, nevertheless, That nothing herein contained shall be construed to alter, in any manner, the rules and restrictions under which sales are, by law, directed to be conducted, and executions required to be returned.

II. And be further enacted, That hereafter it shall not be lawful for any Sheriff, Coroner or Constable to sell slaves, under any process to him or them directed, without giving ten days' previous notice of the time of such sale.

III. And be it further enacted, That any Sheriff, Coroner, Constable or Clerk and Master in Equity, who shall make any sale contrary to this act, shall forfeit and pay the sum of two hundred dollars, to be recovered by any person suing for the same, one half to his own use, and the other half to the use of the county in which the offence is committed.

IV. And be it further enacted, That the provisions of this act shall not apply to the counties of Warren, Currituck, Carteret and Tyrell.

V. And be it further enacted, That all laws and clauses of laws coming within the purview and meaning of this act be, and the same are hereby repealed.

CHAPTER XXXVI.

1822. An act to encourage the apprehension of runaway slaves in the Great Dismal Swamp. (Pages 28-29).

Whereas, it being dangerous and difficult to apprehend runaway slaves who have secreted themselves in the Great Dismal Swamp, from whence they commit depredations, to the great injury of the citizens of the neighboring counties; for remedy whereof,

Be it enacted by the General Assembly of the State of North-Carolina, and it is hereby enacted by the authority of the same, That from and after the first day of April next, whenever any runaway slave shall be apprehended in that part of the Great Dismal Swamp which lies within the limits of this State, and committed to the jail of any county, the magistrate committing said slave on satisfactory evidence that the said slave was captured within the limits of the Great Dismal Swamp, shall direct three freeholders, owners of slaves, to be summoned, who shall appraise such slave, on oath, and return the appraisement to the clerk of the County Court, who shall file the same in his office.

II. Be it further enacted, by the authority aforesaid, That when the owner or owners of said slave, captured as aforesaid, shall apply to the Jailor for such slave, he shall, previous to the delivery of said slave, pay into the office of the Clerk of the County Court one fourth part of the appraised value of such slave to the only use of the captor or captors: Provided, always, That any person whose slave may be apprehended and committed according to the provisions of this act, shall have the election of appealing to the County Court, where the value of said slave shall be assessed by persons appointed by the County Court, or to direct the Sheriff to sell such slave at public auction, after twenty days' notice, and pay to the captors one fourth part of the price at which said slave shall be sold.

III. Be it further enacted, That whenever any slave, captured as aforesaid, shall remain in jail more than one year, the Sheriff of the county in which such jail is situated shall proceed to advertise and sell said slave in manner now, by law, directed; and, after paying all prison charges and advertisements, shall pay one fourth part to the captor or captors, and the remaining three fourths to the county Trustee for the use of the county.

IV. And be it further enacted, That the provisions of this act shall not apply to any negro who has not been absent as a runaway from his or her master or owner's service for three months, nor to negroes the property of orphans, who have not been so absent for twelve months.

V. And be it further enacted, That it shall be the duty of the Jailor to whom any runaway slave may be delivered, apprehended within the aforesaid limits of said Great Dismal Swamp, and liable to appraisement as herein provided, to advertise the same, not only as is now by law required, but also for three months next immediately after his or her apprehension and delivery as aforesaid, in some public Gazette published in or near said county, within this State, and also some paper published in Norfolk, Virginia, and in the Gazette of this State.

VI. And be it further enacted, That no person apprehending any slave, within the limits of the said Swamp, shall be entitled to claim any other reward than that which is secured by this act.

****

ACTS PASSED BY THE GENERAL ASSEMBLY OF THE STATE OF NORTH CAROLINA AT ITS SESSION COMMENCING ON THE THE 17TH OF NOVEMBER, 1823 RALEIGH: PRINTED BY J. GALES & SON - STATE PRINTERS. 1824

CHAPTER XXXIII.
1823. An Act authorising certain limitations of Slaves by deed or writing. (Pages 34-35).

Be it enacted by the General Assembly of the State of North Carolina, and it is hereby enacted by the authority of the same, That every limitation, by deed or writing, of a slave or slaves, hereafter made, which limitation if contained in a last will and testament would be good and effectual as an executory devise or bequest, shall be, and is hereby declared to be a good and effectual limitation in remainder of such slave or slaves.

II. And be it further enacted by the authority aforesaid, That any limitation made or reserved to the grantor, vendor or donor, in any such deed or writing of a slave or slaves, shall be good and effectual in law: Provided, such limitation, had it been made to another person, would be good and effectual, according to the first section of this act.

III. Be it further enacted, That all such deeds or writings shall be witnessed, proved and registered, as other written conveyances of slaves are or may be by law required to be witnessed, proved and registered.

CHAPTER XLIX.

1823. An Act to amend an Act, passed in the year one thousand eight hundred and nineteen, entitled "An Act relative to the apprehension of runaway slaves." (Page 42).

Be it enacted by the General Assembly of the State of North Carolina, and it is hereby enacted by the authority of the same, That all persons hereafter, who may apprehend any runaway slave or slaves, within the county in which the owner or owners of such slave or slaves reside, and for whom a reward greater than three dollars shall not have been offered, shall be entitled to recover and receive from the owner of such slave, the sum of three dollars, for each and every slave so apprehended and delivered to the owner, or confined in jail.

II. And be it further enacted, That where any runaway slave or slaves thus apprehended, shall be lodged in jail, it shall be the duty of the jailer to tax the reward of three dollars on each slave, against such owner, and collect the same with his prison fee.

CHAPTER L.
1823. An Act to repeal the forty-fourth section of an Act passed in the year one thousand seven and forty-one, entitled "An Act concerning Servants And Slaves." (Page 42).

Whereas the forty-fourth section of the act of one thousand seven hundred and forty-one, entitled "An act concerning Servants and Slaves," is contrary to good policy and public expediency: therefore,

Be it enacted by the General Assembly of the State of North Carolina, and it is hereby enacted by the authority of the same., That the forty-fourth section of the above mentioned act, be, and the same is hereby repealed.

CHAPTER LI.
1823. An Act declaring the punishment of persons of colour, in certain cases. (Page 42).

Be it enacted by the General Assembly of the State of North Carolina, and it is hereby enacted by the authority of the same, That any person of colour, convicted by due course of law, of an assault with intent to commit rape upon the body of a white female, shall suffer death without the benefit of clergy.

North Carolina Law

CHAPTER LII.
1823. An Act to repeal an Act, passed in the year 1822, entitled "An Act to encourage the apprehension of runaway slaves in the Great Dismal Swamp." (Page 43).

Be it enacted by the General Assembly of the State of North Carolina, and it is hereby enacted by the authority of the same, That the before recited act, be, and the same is hereby repealed, and made void.
Read three and ratified in General Assembly, this 8th day of Dec. 1823.
                A. Moore, S.H.C.
                B. Yancy S.S.
A true Copy,
Wm. Hill, Secretary

CHAPTER LXXIII.
1823. An Act to repeal an act passed in the year one thousand eight hundred and twenty two, entitled "An Act directing the time and place of selling lands and slaves under execution," so far as relates to certain counties therein named. (Page 58).

Be it enacted by the General assembly of the State of North Carolina, and it is hereby enacted by the authority of the same, That the above recited act, be, and the same is hereby repealed and made void, so far as respects the counties of Perquimons, Pasquotank, Randolph, Brunswick, Sampson and Camden: Provided, That this repeal shall not affect the cases, where either of the parties in the executions are not residents of the county so exempted from the act aforesaid: And provided further, that nothing in this act shall be so construed as to revive either of the acts of 1820 or 1821, authorising the sale of lands and slaves at the court-house of the said counties above named.

CHAPTER LXXIV.
1823. An Act to repeal an act passed in the year one thousand eight hundred and twenty two, entitled "An Act directing the time and place of selling lands and slaves under execution," so far as respects the counties of Washington and New Hanover. (Page 58).

Be it enacted by the General Assembly Of the State Of North Carolina, and it is hereby enacted by the authority of the same, That the above recited act be, and the same is hereby repealed and made void, so far as respects the counties of Washington and New Hanover: Provided, that this repeal shall not affect the cases where either of the parties in the execution are not residents of the aforesaid counties: And provided further, that nothing in this act shall be so construed as to revive either of the acts of 1820 or 1821, authorising the sale of land and slaves, at the court-house of the said counties above named.

CHAPTER LXXV.
1823. An Act to amend an act, entitled "An Act directing the time and place of sales of land and slaves under execution." (Page 58).

Be it enacted by the General Assembly of the State of North Carolina, and it is hereby enacted by the authority of the same, That from and after the ratification of this act, all sales of land situated in that part of Rowan county, called the Forks of the Yadkin, shall be made at Mocksville, on the Fridays preceding the Mondays prescribed by the before recited act, as the days of sale in Rowan county: Provided, that the Sheriff, if he believes that the price of the property will thereby be enhanced, may postpone the sale to the court house, to be made on the days now prescribed by law.

CHAPTER LXXXI.
1823. An Act to repeal an act, passed at the last General Assembly, entitled "An act to regulate the patrol of Richmond county," and for other purposes. (Page 62).

III. And be it further enacted, That it shall be the duty of the patroll so appointed, to patrol their respective districts at least once every two weeks, and may inflict punishment, not exceeding fifteen lashes, on all slaves by them found, who may going at large, unless they be on the land or plantation of their Master or mistress, or have a written permission to pass from under the hand of their master, mistress or overseer, specifying the place or places to which such slave or slaves have permission to pass, or unless the said patrol shall have good reason to believe that such slave or slaves are going to or returning from some place of public worship; and each and every patrol failing to discharge his duty as enjoined by this act, shall forfeit and pay the sum of five dollars for every offence, to be recovered and applied in the same manner as prescribed in the second section of this act.

CHAPTER CLXVI.
1823. An Act to emancipate Sally Zimmerman, a slave belonging to the estate of Andrew Caldcleugh, deceased, late of Rowan County. (Page 96).

Whereas the said Andrew Caldcluegh, in and by his last will, did devise that a female slave, called and known by the name of Sally Zimmerman, a child of tender years, should be emancipated and set free; and whereas the executors of the said Andrew Caldcleugh, by and with consent of the heirs at law, and residuary legatee of the said Andrew Caldcleugh, have petitioned this General Assembly to carry the will of the said Andrew into effect as it relates to the said slave:

Therefore be it enacted by the General Assembly of the State of North Carolina, and it is hereby enacted by the authority of the same, That from and after the ratification of this act, the said Sally shall be, and hereby is emancipated, and set free from slavery, fully and absolutely, and shall be called and known by the name of Sally Zimmerman.

Read three times and ratified in General Assembly, this 31st day of Dec. 1823
A. Moore, S.H.C.
B. Yancy, S.S.   A true Copy   Wm. Hill, Secretary

****

ACTS PASSED BY THE GENERAL ASSEMBLY
OF THE STATE OF NORTH CAROLINA AT ITS SESSION
COMMENCING ON THE 15TH OF NOVEMBER, 1824
RALEIGH: PRINTED BY J. GALES & SON - STATE PRINTERS.
1825

CHAPTER XIII.
1824. An Act concerning the Lands held under leases from the Tuscarora Tribe Indians. (Page 13).

Whereas it is represented to this General Assembly, in behalf of persons holding lands under leases for a long term of years from the Tuscarora tribe of Indians, that they are subject to great inconveniences from their estates being mere chattel interest: For remedy whereof,

Be it enacted by the General Assembly of The State Of North Carolina, and it is hereby enacted by the authority of the same, That the estates in land now held by certain individuals, under leases for a term of years from the Tuscarora tribe of Indians, made in pursuance of certain acts of the General Assembly of this State, shall be hereafter considered real estate; shall descend to, and be divided among the heirs of any intestate, subject to dower and tenancy by curtesy, and other incidents to real estate, and its liability to execution, and its conveyance and devise, shall be governed by the same rules as are now prescribed in the case of real estate held in fee simple: Provided, that nothing herein contained, shall be so construed as to give to the individuals holding the said terms for years, a right to enjoy the same for a longer period than is designated in the leases executed by the said Tuscarora Indians, in pursuance of acts of the General Assembly of this State, nor so as to give to said individuals any right which, by the constitution of this State, is exclusively confined to freeholders.

CHAPTER LXXVI.
1824. An Act to repeal in part, the first section of an Act passed in the year 1823, entitled "An Act to regulate the patrol of Richmond County, and for other purposes." (Pages 63-64)

Be it enacted by the General Assembly of the State of North Carolina, and it is hereby enacted by the authority of the same, That from and after the passing of this act, it shall be the duty of each Captain of the several militia companies in the counties of Richmond, Cabarrus, and New Hanover, at the first muster which they may hold after the 1st day of January next, and every three months thereafter to appoint not less than five fit and proper persons of the age of twenty one years, who shall be known as men of good character and free from habits of intoxication, to act as patrols for three months, whose duty it shall be to patrol their respective districts at least twice a month , and oftener, if necessary, and such patrol so appointed, or any one of them, shall inflict not more than fifteen lashes on the bare back of any negro slave, whom they find beyond his or her master's or mistress's premises, without a permit in writing, from the master, mistress or overseer of such slave or slaves, designating the place or places, to which such slave is permitted to go, an further should it so happen that one or more of said patrol, after being duly appointed should have just cause, to beat, wound or ill treat any negro slave or slaves, for their insolence or improper conduct, or on refusal of shewing their pass, or being taken by said patrol, in this case it shall be the duty of such patrol to bring such slave or slaves immediately to his or her master or mistress or overseer, and make a statement of the fact.

II. Be it further enacted, It shall be the duty of the patrol to keep good order and decorum among negroes at public places, and such patrol so appointed shall be exempt from working on roads, serving as Jurors and performing military duty, except battalion and regimental musters, Provided, that no person shall be compelled to serve more than six months in every year.

CHAPTER LXXVII.
1824. An Act to regulate the patrol of the counties of Ashe and New Hanover. (Pages 64-65).

Be it enacted by the General Assembly of the State Of North Carolina, and it is hereby enacted by the authority of the same, That from and after the passage of this act, it shall be the duty of each Captain of the Militia companies in the counties of Ashe an New Hanover, at the first muster, which they may hold after the first day of January next, and every three months thereafter, to appoint not less than three fit and suitable persons of the age of twenty one years, who shall be known as men of good character and free from habits of intoxication, to act as patrols for three months, whose duty it shall be to patrol their respective districts at least twice a month, and oftener if necessary, and such patrol so appointed, or any one of them, shall inflict not more than fifteen lashes on the bare back of any negro slave, whom they may find beyond his or her master or mistresses premises, without a permit in writing from the master, mistress or overseer of such slave or slaves, designating the place or places to which such slave is permitted to go, or other reasonable excuse.

II. And be it further enacted, That it shall be the duty of the patrol to keep good order and decorum among negroes at public places, and such patrol so appointed, shall be exempt from serving on Juries, and performing military duty; except battalion and regimental musters: Provided, That no person shall be compelled to serve more than six months in any one year.

****

North Carolina Law

ACTS PASSED BY THE GENERAL ASSEMBLY
OF THE STATE OF NORTH CAROLINA AT ITS SESSION
COMMENCING ON THE 21ST OF NOVEMBER 1825
RALEIGH: PRINTED BY BELL & LAWRENCE, PRINTERS TO
THE STATE, 1826.

CHAPTER XXII.
1825. An act to amend an act, entitled "an act to prevent the stealing of Slaves , or by violence, seduction, or any other means, taking or carrying away any Slave or Slaves, the property of another, and for other purposes therein mentioned," passed in the year one thousand seven hundred and ninety-two. (Pages 13-14).

Be it enacted by the General Assembly of the State of North Carolina, and it is hereby enacted by the authority of the same, That from and after the passing of this act, if any master of any ship or vessel, mariner, or any other person or persons, trading or being within this state, shall carry, convey, or conceal on board of any ship or vessel, any negro, or mulatto slave or slaves, the property of any citizen or citizens of this State, without the consent in writing of the owner or owners, his, her or their Guardian or Guardians, of such slave or slaves previously obtained; or shall take and receive on board of any such vessel or ship, any such slave or slaves, or permit or suffer the same to be done, with the intent and for the purpose of carrying and conveying such slave or slaves out of this State, or shall wickedly and willingly conceal, or permit to be concealed on board of any such ship or vessel, any negro or mulatto slave or slaves, who shall, or may hereafter abscond from his, her, or their master or mistress, being citizens of this State, with the intent and for the purpose of enabling such slave or slaves to effect his, her or their escape out of this State, every such master, mariner, or other person or persons, on board of any such ship or vessel, so carrying or conveying, or so taking, receiving, or concealing, or causing or permitting the same to be done, with the intent as aforesaid, shall be taken and deemed guilty of felony, and shall suffer death as a felon, without benefit of clergy.

II. And be it further enacted, That if any negro or mulatto slave or slaves, shall be found concealed on board any ship or vessel, trading in this State, without the consent or knowledge of the master or mistress, his, her or their Guardian or Guardians, of such slave or slaves, after the vessel shall have weighed anchor, or hoisted sail for leaving the port, the master of such ship or vessel shall forfeit and pay to the owner or owners of said slave or slaves, the sum of five hundred dollars, to be recovered by action of debt in any of the Courts of this State, having jurisdiction of the same.

CHAPTER XXIV.
1825. An act to amend an act, passed in the year one thousand eight hundred and sixteen, entitled "an act to amend the laws in force respecting the trial of Slaves in capital cases," and to extend the provisions thereof to the trial of Slaves in certain other cases. (Pages 14-15).

Be it enacted by the General Assembly of the State of North Carolina, and it is hereby enacted by the authority of the same, That the Superior Courts of Law within the several counties of this State, shall hereafter have original exclusive jurisdiction of all felonies within clergy, when committed, or alleged to have been committed by any slave or slaves, and the trial of such slave or slaves shall be conducted and prosecuted under the same rules, regulations and restrictions as the trial of a free man, when charged with a like offence: Provided, That when any slave shall be convicted of any clergiable felony, and shall pray for and obtain the benefits of the fourth section of the before mentioned act, the Court shall have power to direct and adjudge such corporal punishment short of death or dismemberment as to the Court shall seem right, under all the circumstances of the case; and the entry of such judgment shall have the same legal effects and consequences, as if the slave or slaves were burned in the hand, as in case of a free man convicted of a similar offence.

CHAPTER XXIX.
1825. An act to amend and explain the eighth section of an act, passed in the year one thousand seven hundred and eighty four, entitled "an act to empower the County Courts of Pleas and Quarter Sessions of the several counties within this State to order the laying out of Public Roads." (Page 17).

Whereas difficulties have arisen in some parts of this State, and sometimes litigation, in consequence of the before recited section of said act not being more plain and explicit; for remedy whereof,

Be it enacted by the General Assembly of the State of North Carolina, and it is hereby enacted by the authority of the same, That from and after the passing of this act, no white person under the age of eighteen, and over the age of forty-five and no male slave under sixteen, nor over fifty years of age, shall be held bound or made liable to work on the public roads of this State.

II. And be it further enacted, That all free persons of colour shall be liable to work on the public roads of this State, under the same rules, restrictions and regulations as male slaves are.

III. And be it further enacted, That all laws and clauses of laws coming within the meaning and purview of this act, be, and the same are hereby repealed.

CHAPTER XXXVI.
1825. An act to repeal in part the several acts of the General Assembly, respecting the sales of land and slaves under execution, so far as regards the county of Gates. (Page 25).

Be it enacted by the General Assembly of the State of North Carolina, and it is hereby enacted by the authority of the same, That so much of the acts of one thousand eight hundred and twenty, one thousand eight hundred twenty-one, and one thousand eight hundred and twenty-two, directing the manner in which property levied on by Sheriffs and Constables shall be sold, be, and the same is hereby repealed, so far as relates to the county of Gates, excepting only such executions as may issue from any other county; which executions shall be collected in manner as heretofore prescribed.

CHAPTER XLVIII.
1825. An act for the better Regulation of the town of Beaufort. (Page 35).

XXII. And be it further enacted, That if any free white person or free negro shall be guilty of destroying or stopping up any drain made by the commissioners as aforesaid, he or she shall, on conviction before the attendant of police or any justice of the peace of the county of Carteret, forfeit and pay a fine of ten dollars; or such offender may be indicted for such offence in the County or Superior Court, and, on conviction, shall be fined or imprisoned at the discretion of the court; and if a slave shall be guilty of the like offence, he or she shall, on conviction, be punished not exceeding thirty-nine lashes on his or her bare back at the public whipping post.

CHAPTER LVII.
1825. An act to regulate the patrol of Lenoir county. (Page 40).

Be it enacted by the General Assembly of the State of North Carolina, and it is hereby enacted by the authority of the same, That it shall be the duty of the Court of Pleas and Quarter Sessions of the county of Lenoir, at the first term of said court which shall happen after the first day of January next, and at every subsequent term, to appoint not less than four fit and suitable persons in each captain's district, whose duty it shall be to patrol their respective districts, and any other district within the limits of said county, if they think proper, at least twice a month, and oftener if necessary, and should the said patrol find any negro or negroes from his, her or their master or mistress's plantation on the Sabbath day, or at any other unseasonable time, without a permit in writing from the master, mistress, or overseer of such slave or slaves, designating the places to which they are permitted to go, it shall be the duty of said patrol, or any of them, to inflict a punishment, not exceeding fifteen lashes on the bare back of such slave or slaves.

II. Be it further enacted, That it shall be the duty of the patrol to keep good order and decorum among slaves at all public places in said county; and in consideration of the duties above prescribed, the said patrol shall receive, each, the sum of one dollar and fifty cents for the time they are compelled by this act to serve, and for that period shall be exempt from serving on juries, working on roads, and performing military duty.

CHAPTER LXV.
1825. An act concerning the appointment and power of patrols in the county of Robeson. (Page 46).

Be it enacted by the General Assembly of the State of North Carolina, and it is hereby enacted by the authority of the same, That each captain of militia in the county of Robeson shall appoint twice a year any number of discreet persons, not exceeding six, to act as patrols for the space of not more than six months; and, as a compensation for their services, they shall be exempt from working on the public highways and from mustering during their time of their appointment; and the captain shall cause the patrols to be notified of their appointment in writing, subscribed with his proper signature, which service shall empower the patrols to perform the duties herein required.

  II. Be it further enacted, That it shall be their duty to go on patrols in their respective districts, at least once a fortnight; and the patrols in each district, or a majority of them, shall have power to inflict a punishment, not exceeding fifteen lashes, on all slaves they may find off their owners' plantation, either on the Sabbath or other unseasonable time, without proper permit or pass.

  III. Be it further enacted, That if the captain shall neglect to make the appointment as by this act directed, he shall forfeit and pay the sum of ten dollars, to be recovered by warrant before any justice of the peace, in the name of the county trustee, for the use of the county, by any person suing for the same; and if any one of the patrols shall neglect to perform the duty required in the second section of this act, he shall forfeit and pay the sum of five dollars, to be recovered and appropriated in like manner; and the said patrols are further required to perform all other duties not herein already specified, which are required of patrols under the general laws of the State.

CHAPTER XCVI.
1825. An act to amend an act, entitled "an act directing the time and place of sales of land and slaves under execution in Rowan county." (Pages 70-71).

  Be it enacted by the General Assembly of the State of North Carolina, and it is hereby enacted by the authority of the same, That from and after the ratification of this act, all sales of slaves, the owners of which live in that part of Rowan, called the Forks of the Yadkin, may be had and made on the Friday preceding the Monday prescribed by the before recited act, as the days of sale for Rowan county, at Mocksville: Provided, that the sheriff shall have power and authority to postpone the sale to be had and made, at the court house of said county, on the days now prescribed by law, if in his opinion it will enhance the price of the property.

****

ACTS PASSED BY THE GENERAL ASSEMBLY OF THE STATE OF NORTH CAROLINA AT ITS SESSION,

North Carolina Law

COMMENCING ON THE 25TH OF DECEMBER, 1826
RALEIGH: PRINTED BY LAWRENCE & LEMAY
PRINTERS TO THE STATE, 1827

CHAPTER XIII.
1826. An act to prohibit the trading with Slaves, except in the manner therein prescribed. (Pages 7-8).

Be it enacted by the General Assembly of the State of North Carolina, and it is hereby enacted by the authority of the same, That from and after, the first day of May next, if any person or persons shall buy of, traffic with, or receive from any slave or slaves, any cotton, tobacco, wheat, rice, oats, corn, rye, pork, bacon, beef, leather, rawhides, iron, castings, farming utensils, nails, meal, flour, spiritous liqour or wine, peas, saltfish, flax, flaxseed, hogs, cattle, sheep, wool, lumber, staves, tar, pitch, turpentine, fodder, shingles, hoops, white oak heading, and potatoes; or if any person or persons shall sell, barter with, or deliver to any slave or slaves, any goods, wares, and merchandize, or other article of personal property, every person so offending, shall for each offence, forfeit and pay the sum of one hundred dollars, to be recovered by warrant, before any Justice of the Peace, and applied one half to the use of the party suing for the same; the other half to the wardens of the poor of the county: Provided, however, that it shall and may be lawful for any person or persons, in the day time only, Sundays excepted, viz. between the rising of the sun and the setting thereof, to buy of, traffic with, or receive from any slave or slaves any such article or articles as aforesaid, for which he, she, or they may have a permission in writing, from his, her, or their owner or manager, to dispose of the same: and further, it shall and may be lawful for any person or persons, in the day time as aforesaid, to sell and deliver to any slave or slaves, any goods, wares, or merchandize, or other thing (spirituous liquors always excepted) in exchange for, or payment of the money, or article, or articles, which the said slave or slaves may have been, by the written permission aforesaid, authorised to sell.

II. Be it further enacted, That the foregoing offences shall moreover be indictable in the County or Superior Courts of Law, and the defendant, on conviction, shall be fined, or imprisoned at the discretion of the Court; the fine, however, not to exceed fifty dollars, or the imprisonment, three months; and if it shall appear on the trial, that the defendant is a licensed retailer of spirituous liquor, by the small measure, he or she shall also forfeit his or her retailing license, for the space of two years, from and after the date of his or her conviction.

III. Be it further enacted, That if any person shall fraudulently give, or cause to be giveth to any slave, the property of another, a permission in writing to sell, trade, or traffic in any article of personal property, without the consent or authority of the master, owner, or the person having the management of such slave, he, she, or they so offending, shall, upon conviction before any Justice of the Peace in the county where such offence is committed, forfeit and pay the sum of one hundred dollars; on half to the use of the person suing for the same, and the other half to the use of the wardens of the poor of said county.

IV. Be it further enacted, That if any slave or slaves shall buy or receive any of the aforesaid prohibited property from any slave or slaves, or shall or deliver any of the same to a slave or slaves, contrary to the true meaning of this act, he, she or they, on conviction thereof before any justice of the peace, shall receive on his, her or their bare backs, not exceeding thirty nine lashes, to be well laid on, by any constable of the said county, or other person appointed for that purpose.

V. Be it further enacted, That if any free negro or mulatto shall trade with any slave or slaves, either buying from, or selling to him, her or them, any article or articles of property contrary to the true meaning of this act, he or she may be prosecuted by indictment in the County or Superior Court, and, on conviction, shall receive not exceeding thirty nine lashes on his or her bare back.

VI. Be it further enacted, That if any slave or slaves shall be found in any store house, ware house, tippling shop, or other place fitted up for trading, unless sent by his, her or their owner, overseer or employer, after the hour of nine o'clock at night, or before daybreak in the morning, or on the Sabbath day; or if any slave or slaves shall be found, at any time, in any of the aforementioned places, unless sent as aforesaid, where he, she or they shall have been permitted to remain for the space of fifteen minutes, with the door of the aforementioned places closed; or if any slave or slaves shall be seen to carry into any of the aforementioned places any article or articles supposed for sale, and not bring the same out; or if he, she or they shall bring out of the said places any article or articles, which may have been purchased therein, shall be taken and received as presumptive evidence against the person or persons owning or keeping the store house, ware house, tippling shop, or other place fitted up for trading, of a violation of this act, to be rebutted, however, like other presumptions, by other circumstances in favor of the accused.

VII. And be it further enacted, That either of the parties or master of the slave, being dissatisfied with the judgment of the justice or the verdict of the jury, may pray an appeal therefrom as in other cases: Provided, that no suit or indictment shall be prosecuted for any violation of this act, unless such suit or indictment be commenced within twelve months after such violation.

VIII. And be it further enacted, That the act, passed in the year one thousand eight hundred and nineteen, entitled "An act to prevent fraudulent trading with slaves," be, and the same is hereby repealed, saving the rights of the wardens of the poor, and of individuals, which may have accrued under said act.

CHAPTER XXI.
1826. An act to prevent free persons of colour from migrating into this State, for the good government of such persons resident in the State, and for other purposes. (Pages 13-16).

Be it enacted by the General Assembly of the State of North Carolina, and it is hereby enacted by the authority of the same, That it shall not be lawful hereafter for any free negro or mulatto to migrate into this State: and if he or she shall do so contrary to the provisions of this act, and being therefore informed, shall not, within twenty days thereafter, remove out of the State, he or she, being thereof convicted in manner hereinafter directed, shall be liable to a penalty of five hundred dollars: and upon failure to pay the same, within the time prescribed in the judgment awarded against such person or persons, he or she shall be liable to be held in servitude, and at labor for a term of time not exceeding ten years, in such manner, and upon such terms as may be prescribed by the court awarding such sentence; and the proceeds arising therefrom, shall be paid over to the county trustee for county purposes: Provided also, that in case any free negro or mulatto shall pay the penalty of five hundred dollars according to the provisions of this act, it shall be the duty of such free negro or mulatto to remove him or herself out of this State within twenty days thereafter, and for every such failure, shall be subject to the like penalty, as is prescribed for failure to remove in the first instance.

II. And be further enacted, That if any free negro or mulatto shall come into this State as aforesaid, he or she may be arrested upon a warrant from any justice of the peace, and carried before any justice of the peace of the county in which he or she may be arrested; who is hereby authorised and required to examine into the case, and if upon such examination it shall appear to him, that the said free negro or mulatto has come into this State contrary to the provisions of this act, he shall bind him or her over to the next County Court of said county which shall happen thereafter, taking such security for his or her appearance as may be reasonable; and upon refusing or neglecting to give such security, the said justice shall commit such free negro or mulatto to the jail of the county, there to be confined until the next County Court, unless, in the mean time, he or she shall give security as aforesaid: and at the said court, it shall be the duty of the said justices thereof to inquire into the case, and if it shall appear to them that the said free negro or mulatto has migrated into this State, contrary to the provisions of this act, they shall enter judgment against him or her for the aforesaid penalty, and may award execution thereon; and if in case he or she shall have no property, or not sufficient to satisfy the said debt, the said court shall adjudge, that the said free negro or mulatto shall be hired out for a term of time, not exceeding that prescribed in the first section of this act, in such manner and upon such terms as may seem expedient to the said court.

III. Be it further enacted, That if after the expiration of the term of service for which free negro or mulatto shall have been held in servitude, he or she shall remain in this State for thirty days, such free negro or mulatto shall be liable to the same penalties and punishment as are prescribed in the first and second sections of this act.

IV. Be it further enacted, That any person, who shall bring into this State by water or land, any free negro or mulatto, he or she shall forfeit and pay for every such person, so brought into the State, the sum of five hundred dollars, to be recovered by action of debt in the name of the chairman of the County Court for the time being, and his successors in office, where such offence shall be committed, for the use of the county: Provided, that this act shall not extend to masters of vessels, bringing into this State any free negro or mulatto employed on board, and belonging to said vessel, and who shall therewith depart, not to any person travelling in or through this State, having any free negro or mulatto as a servant, and who shall, with such person, depart out of the State.

V. Be it further enacted, That if any free negro or mulatto in any county of this State, who is able to labor, shall be found spending his or her time in idleness and dissipation, or who has no regular or honest employment or occupation, which he or she is accustomed to follow, it shall and may be lawful for any citizen to apply to a justice of the peace of said county, and upon affidavit obtain a warrant to arrest such person and bring him or her before some justice of said county; and if, upon examination of the cause, it shall appear to the said justice that the said free negro or mulatto comes within the provisions of this act, the said justice shall bind him or her with reasonable security to appear at the next County Court of said county: and in case he or she shall fail to give security, such free negro or mulatto shall be committed to the jail of the county until the next County Court thereafter: and it shall be the duty of the said court, if, upon examination of the case, he or she shall come within the meaning of this act, to require such free negro or mulatto to enter into bond, with sufficient security, in such sum as may be considered by the court reasonable, payable to the chairman of the County Court for the time being and his successors in office, conditioned for his or her good behaviour and industrious, peaceable deportment for one year: and in case he or she shall fail to give such security, or shall not pay the cost and charges of the prosecution, it shall be lawful for the said court, and they are hereby required to hire out such free negro or mulatto for a term of time to service and labor, which to them may seem reasonable and just, and calculated to reform him or her to habits of industry and morality, not exceeding three years for any one offence.

  VI. Be it further enacted, That all sums of money, which may arise under the provisions of this act from the hire of free negroes or mulattoes, shall be paid to the county trustee for county uses.

  VII. And be it further enacted, That the justices of the Courts of Pleas and Quarter Sessions, in each of the counties of this State, shall have power, in cases where it may appear expedient, to bind out the children of free negroes and mulattoes, where the parent, with whom such children may live, does or shall not habitually employ his or her time in some honest industrious occupation.

  VIII. Be it further enacted, That all persons with whom any free negro or mulatto may be held to service under this act, shall, and they are hereby required to provide him or her with good and sufficient clothing and food, treat him or her with humanity, and teach him or her some mechanical trade, or some useful or industrious employment during the term for which such free negro or mulatto may be compelled to serve: he or she shall not be removed from the county by such master or any other person, and shall be produced to the County Court at the expiration of the term of service as aforesaid, or whenever thereto required by them: and if any such master or mistress shall violate this act, he or she may be indicted for such offence in any court of the county, where such offence may be committed, and, on conviction thereof, may be fined or imprisoned at the discretion of the court: and in case such free negro or mulatto shall run away before the expiration of his or her term of service, he or she shall be compelled to serve after the said expiration such a length of time as he or she shall have absented him or herself.

IX. Be it further enacted, That in all cases arising under this act, the free negro or mulatto, who is charged with an offence, upon application to the court for that purpose, shall have a right to have the facts of his or her case tried by a jury upon an issue or issues made up under the direction of the court for that purpose.

X. Be it further enacted, That all free mulattoes descended from negro ancestors to the fourth generation inclusive, though one ancestor of each generation may been a white person, shall come within the provisions of this act.

XI. And be it further enacted, That it shall be the duty of the several county attornies in this State to give in charge this act to the grand jurors, and it is hereby made their duty to present all cases in their county arising under this act within the knowledge of either of them: and the said attornies are hereby required in all cases arising under the provisions of this act, to prosecute for and on behalf of the State: and it shall be the duty of the several courts of this State before whom any proceedings may be had under this act , so to construe the same as to prohibit the evils intended to be remedied, and they are hereby authorised and required to make all necessary rules and regulations, according to the usual course of justice, which may be required for the purposes and objects of this act.

CHAPTER XXII.
1826. An act to amend the laws regulating the sale of lands and slaves, so far as respects the counties of Anson, Onslow, Wake, Craven, Mecklenburg, Orange, Cumberland, Nash, Stokes, Guilford, Rowan, Davidson, Columbus, Beaufort, Person, Caswell, Rutherford, Brunswick, Pitt, Hyde, Halifax, Randolph, Wayne, Greene, Robeson, Chatham, Franklin, Warren, Bladen, Duplin and Edgecombe. (Page 16).

Be it enacted by the General Assembly of the State of North Carolina, and it is hereby enacted by the authority of the same, That the sheriff and other returning officers of said counties, be, and they are hereby authorised to make sale of lands and slaves on the first day of the Superior Courts of Law and Equity for said counties: any law or usage to the contrary notwithstanding.

****

ACTS PASSED BY THE GENERAL ASSEMBLY OF THE STATE OF NORTH CAROLINA AT THE SESSION OF 1827-1828
RALEIGH: PRINTED BY LAWRENCE & LEMAY PRINTERS TO THE STATE. 1828

CHAPTER CXXVIII.
1827-1828. An act to regulate the sale of lands and slaves so far as respects the county of Northampton. (Page 83).
Be it enacted by the General Assembly of the State of North Carolina, and it is hereby enacted by the authority of the same, That the sheriff and other returning officers of said county be, and they are hereby authorised to make sale of land and slaves on the first day of each Superior Court of Law and Equity for said county, and continue the same under the same rules and regulations as other sales are held; any law, usage or custom to the contrary notwithstanding.

****

ACTS PASSED BY THE GENERAL ASSEMBLY OF THE STATE OF NORTH CAROLINA AT THE SESSION OF 1828-1829
RALEIGH: PRINTED BY LAWRENCE & LEMAY PRINTERS TO THE STATE. 1829

CHAPTER XIX.
1828-1829. An act concerning the lands formerly occupied by the Tuskarora tribe of Indians, lying in Bertie county, on the north side of Roanoke river. (Pages 11-13).

North Carolina Law

Whereas the Tuskarora Indians have for more than a century been the firm and undeviating friends of the white people of this country, insomuch that the State of North Carolina is disposed not only to render to them full and complete justice, but also to exercise towards them that spirit of generosity which their conduct has merited: Therefore,

Be it enacted by the General Assembly of the State of North Carolina, and it is hereby enacted by the authority of the same, That William R. Smith, of Halifax; Simmons J. Baker, of Martin; and William Brittain, of Bertie,be, and they are hereby appointed commissioners for the purpose of advertising and selling, in manner hereinafter directed, the above named tract of land, lying in Bertie county, butted and bounded as follows, to wit: Beginning at the mouth of Quoitsney Swamp; running up the swamp 480 poles to a scrubby oak, near the head of said swamp by a great spring; thence north 10 degrees east 850 poles, to a persimmon tree, on Raquis Swamp; thence along the swamp and pocosin, main course north 57 degrees west 2640 poles, to a hickory on the east side of Falling Run or Deep Creek, and down the various courses of said run to Roanoke River; then down the river to the first station.

II. And be it further enacted, That the title so to be sold by said commissioners shall be understood to extend only to the reversion of the State in said lands after the expiration of the leases from the Indians under which they are now held; and that immediately after the ratification of this act, and notice thereof to the commissioners, it shall be their duty to proceed forthwith to advertise in the newspaper most convenient to the premises, and also at five of the most public places in the counties of Bertie, Halifax and Martin, including the court houses in said court houses in said counties, that a sale of land, according to the provisions of this act, will take place on Tuesday of the ensuing March term of the Superior Court of Bertie county, that is, on the 17th day of March next; and it shall be the duty of the said commissioners to attend at the aforesaid time and place, and offer, in the court house yard, at public sale, to the highest bidder, the said lands according to advertisement, subject however to the leases as aforesaid; and the commissioners shall have power to continue or postpone the sale from day to day until the end of that week; and should they, by unavoidable accident or otherwise, be prevented from selling all or any part of said lands during the said week, it shall be their duty to advertise in like manner for two months next preceding the following September term of Bertie Court and to sell at said term as is heretofore directed, at March term; and said commissioners shall be empowered to put up said lands in such parcels as they may deem most advantageous for selling; and that they shall give the purchasers a credit of twelve months on one half of the purchase money, and a credit of twenty-four months on the other half: Provided always that the purchaser shall deliver to the commissioners bonds with good and sufficient security for the same, payable to the Governor of the State.

III. And be it further enacted, That should the commissioners upon offering said lands as aforesaid, perceive that they were likely to be sacrificed, or to sell for an amount greatly below the real value, it shall be their duty forthwith to discontinue the sale; and that it shall be the duty of the commissioners, after making sale, or if no sale be made, immediately after September next, to make report to the Public Treasurer of the State of all such proceedings as they may have had under this act, and also to hand over to him all such bonds as they may have taken from purchasers; and it shall be the duty of the Secretary of State, upon certificate from the Treasurer of payment of the purchase money and a certificate from the commissioners of the boundaries of the land so purchased, to grant a title of release from the State of North Carolina to such persons as may be reported as purchasers by said commissioners under this act of Assembly.

IV. And be it further enacted, That it shall be the duty of the Public Treasurer to collect the money on said bonds when they shall become due, and to hold the same subject to the order of the Tuskarora tribe of Indians; and whenever such order shall be presented properly and duly authenticated, by the said tribe or nation of Indians, it shall be his duty to pay the same over accordingly: Provided always, that upon paying over such monies, the Public Treasurer shall take from the Indians, or their properly authorised agent or agents, a full and complete release of all such claim or pretence of title, as they now make, or ever may have to the aforesaid tract of land.

V. And be it further enacted, That the commissioners shall be allowed each the sum of three dollars for every day they shall necessarily be employed in examining said lands, or in attending to the sale of the same, to be paid out of the funds arising from the sales.

VI. Be it further enacted, That if it should appear at any time hereafter that the said Indians have parted with their claims, or contracted for the same, so that in fact the benefit of the sale would go to some stranger, then the benefit of the sale shall, agreeable to the provisions of this act, tenure to the State.

CHAPTER XXII.
1828-1829. An act to alter and amend the act of one thousand eight hundred and nineteen, entitled an act prescribing the mode of surveying and selling the lands lately acquired by treaty from the Cherokee Indians. (Pages 13-14).

Whereas by the said act it is directed, that upon proof of the payment of the purchase money made to the Secretary of State by the Treasurer's receipts, it is made the duty of the Secretary of State to issue a grant to the purchaser; and in many instances, from the lapse of the time between the first and last payment, the receipts that are given by the Treasurer have been lost, or mislaid: for remedy whereof,

Be it enacted by the General Assembly of the State of North Carolina, and it is hereby enacted by the authority of the same, That whenever any of the purchasers of the Cherokee lands shall have lost or mislaid the receipt or receipts that shall have been given by the Treasurer, if it shall appear from the books of the Treasury Office that the whole amount due from any purchaser has been paid, the Treasurer shall make out a certificate of such payment, and upon the same being filed with the Secretary of State, together with the other certificates, as prescribed by the said act, the Secretary of State shall issue a grant to such purchaser, in the same manner as directed by said act.

CHAPTER XXVIII.
1828-1829. An act concerning the action of replevin. (Pages 15-17).

Whereas slaves are frequently seduced from the possession of their owners, under a pretence of right by persons who are insolvent, and intend to convey the same beyond the jurisdiction of the Courts of this State, whereby great injury is produced to the bona fide holder of slaves; and whereas the writ of sequestration issuing from Courts of Equity in such cases, is a tedious, expensive, and frequently ineffectual remedy:

Be it therefore enacted by the General assembly of the State of North Carolina, and it is hereby enacted by the authority of the same, That from and after the passage of this act, writs of replevin for slaves, shall be held and deemed to be sustainable, against persons in possession of such slave in all cases, where actions of detinue or trover are now proper: Provided, that the plaintiff his or her agent or attorney, in such action of replevin, shall make oath before the clerk issuing such writ, that he or she has been in the lawful possession of such slave within two years next preceding the issuing of said writ, and that he or she has been deprived of such possession, without his or her permission or consent.

    II. Be it further enacted, That whenever person shall hereafter apply to the Clerk of any Court in this State to obtain a writ of replevin for any slave, it shall be the duty of such Clerk before he issues the same, to take an affidavit from the plaintiff in such writ, or from his or her agent or attorney of the value of such slave; and also to take a bond with approved security, in double the alleged value of such slave, payable to the defendant and conditioned to perform the final judgment on such writ.

    III. Be it further enacted, That in issuing writs of replevin the clerk shall, as nearly as may be convenient, describe every slave therein demanded, and shall annex to such description a value which shall be equal to double the sworn value of such slave.

    IV. Be it further enacted, That the Sheriff, to whose hands any writ of replevin for any slave or slaves shall hereafter come shall forthwith take into his custody all such slaves, and deliver them to the plaintiff in such writ, or his or her agent or attorney: Provided always that if the defendant in such writ shall execute and deliver to the Sheriff a bond with approved security, in double the amount of the sworn value of the slave or slaves described in said writ, payable to the plaintiffs therein, with a condition to perform the final judgment, which shall rendered thereon, it shall not be lawful for said sheriff to take such slaves from his or her possession; but he shall return the bond so given, with the writ, to the Court from which it issued.

    V. Be it further enacted, That if upon the trial of such action, the plaintiff or plaintiffs, shall recover, final judgment shall be rendered against the defendant and his security, in case he shall have given bond as required by the fourth section of this act, for such value as shall be assessed by the jury upon such slave or slaves, with a condition to be discharged by the surrender of such slave or slaves demanded by the writ, and the payment of such damages, as may have been assessed by the jury, for the taking and detention of such slaves, which damages for the taking and detention of such slave or slaves, shall be assessed by the jury, as double the real value.

    VI. Be it further enacted, That in case the slave demanded in any writ of replevin, shall have been taken by the sheriff and delivered to the plaintiff in such writ, agreeably to the fourth section of this act, then if the plaintiff recovers in such action, he shall recover judgment for his costs, and double the real damage sustained by the taking and detention of such slave or slaves; but if the plaintiff in such action shall fail to recover, and a verdict be rendered, establishing the property to be in the defendant, it shall be the duty of the court, rendering judgment thereon, forthwith to direct an issue to be tried, in which the damages the defendant has sustained from being deprived of his property shall be ascertained, and judgment shall be rendered against the plaintiff and his securities for the amount of the bond given by them, agreeably to the second section of this act, with a condition to be discharged upon payment of the amount of damages thus assessed, and all costs, for which the defendant is entitled to judgment.

CHAPTER XXXII.

1828-1829. An act to amend an act entitled "an act to prohibit trading with slaves, except in the manner therein prescribed," passed in the year one thousand eight hundred and twenty-six. (Page 19).

Be it enacted by the Generally Assembly of the State of North Carolina, and it is hereby enacted by the authority of the same, That if any white person or persons shall hereafter sell, barter with, or deliver to any slave or slaves, any fire arms, powder or shot, or lead, except it be for the owner or employer of such slave or slaves, or by the order of the owner or person having the management of the same, every person so offending, shall, for each offence, forfeit and pay the sum of one hundred dollars to be recovered by warrant, before any justice of the peace, by the party suing for the same; and shall moreover be liable to indictment, for each offence, in the County or Superior Courts of Law, and, on conviction, shall be fined or imprisoned at the discretion of the Court, the fine not to exceed fifty dollars, and the imprisonment three months.

II. And be it further enacted, That if any free negro or mulatto shall hereafter sell, barter with or deliver to any slave or slaves, any fire arms, powder or shot, or lead, except by order of the owner or manager of such slave, he or she may be prosecuted by indictment in the County or Superior Court, and, on conviction, shall receive not exceeding thirty-nine lashes on his or her bare back.

III. And be it further enacted, That if either of the parties being dissatisfied with the judgment of the justice, or verdict of the jury, may pray an appeal therefrom as in other cases: Provided, that no suit or indictment shall be prosecuted for any violation of this act, unless such suit or indictment be commenced within twelve months after such violation.

IV. And be it further enacted, That this act shall not take effect until after the first day of May next.

CHAPTER XXXIV.
1828-1829. An act to enforce the payment of taxes from free negroes and mulattoes in certain cases. (Pages 21-22).

Whereas many free negroes and mulattoes living on other persons' land frequently neglect to pay their taxes, and from the small value of their chattles, and from other causes, it has been found impractical to enforce the collection thereof; for remedy whereof,

Be it enacted by the General Assembly of the State of North Carolina, and it is hereby enacted by the authority of the same, That; hereafter, when any free negro or mulatto, liable to pay a public tax shall reside on the land of another person, with his or her consent, the person on whose such land free negro or mulatto shall reside, shall include each and every such free negro or mulatto, as a free poll, in his or her list of taxable property, and be liable to pay all public, and county and parish taxes on every such free negro or mulatto.

II. And be it further enacted, That if any person, on whose land any such free negro or mulatto may reside, shall neglect or refuse to give in every such free negro or mulatto in his or her list of taxable property as aforesaid, he or she so neglecting or refusing, shall be liable to all the penalties to which by law he or she would be liable for neglecting or refusing to give in a list of his or her taxable property; and it shall be the duty of the sheriff or other officer to collect from every such person so neglecting or refusing, the full amount of taxes due for every such free negro or mulatto, including the full amount of the penalties aforesaid: Provided, that nothing herein contained shall be so construed as to prevent the person, on whose land such free negro or mulatto may reside, from recovering from such free negro or mulatto the amount of taxes so paid for such free negro or mulatto.

CHAPTER LXXXIX.
1828-1829. An act to legitimate Joseph Smith and Mary Bently, illegitimate children of John Smith and Susanna Berry, of Burke county. (Page 53).

Be it enacted by the General Assembly of the State of North Carolina, and it is hereby enacted by the authority of the same, That Joseph Smith and Mary Bently, wife of Hugh Bently, illegitimate children of John Smith and Susanna Berry, be, and they are hereby declared legitimate; shall inherit property by descent and distribution; and shall in all respects be legal heirs to the said John Smith in as full and ample manner as if they had been born in lawful wedlock; and any laws to the contrary notwithstanding.

****

ACTS PASSED BY THE GENERAL ASSEMBLY OF THE STATE OF NORTH CAROLINA AT THE SESSION OF 1829-1830
RALEIGH: PRINTED BY LAWRENCE & LEMAY PRINTERS TO THE STATE. 1830

CHAPTER XI.
1829-1830. An act directing the removal of certain papers from the office of the Treasurer to that of the Secretary of State. (Pages 16-17).

Be it enacted by the General Assembly of the State of North Carolina, and it is hereby enacted by the authority of the same, That the descriptive list accompanying the report made to the Public Treasurer by the commissioners under the act of one thousand eight hundred and twenty-eight, entitled an act concerning the lands formerly occupied by the Tuscarora tribe of Indians, lying in Bertie County, on the north side of Roanoke river, authorising them to sell the reversion of certain lands therein named, containing the boundaries of the several tracts of land by them sold, be, and the said descriptive list is hereby directed to be transferred by the Treasurer from his office to that of the Secretary of State; and that the Secretary of State, upon the payment of the purchase money, grant titles according to the boundaries therein contained, and agreeably to the provisions of the before recited act.

CHAPTER XV.
1829-1830. An act concerning the bonds in the office of the Public Treasurer for the purchase of the Cherokee and Tuscarora lands. (Pages 20-21).

North Carolina Law

Whereas, according to the provisions of the several acts of Assembly prescribing the mode of surveying and selling the lands lately acquired from the Cherokee Indians, the Comptroller is directed to raise an account against the several obligors for their respective purchases; and the bonds given by them were deposited with the Treasurer by the commissioners who took the same, without any statement or receipt therefor being filed with the Comptroller, so as to enable him to perform his duty: and whereas the check intended to be preserved upon the Treasurer in the discharge of his duty in this respect, as required by the several laws passed for that purpose, does not exist: Therefor,

Be it enacted by the General Assembly of the State of North Carolina, and it is hereby enacted by the authority of the same, That it shall be the duty of the Public Treasurer to prepare a full and particular statement of the bonds in his office given for the purchase of the lands lately acquired by treaty from the Cherokee Indians, as they were at the time he received the same from the committee of investigation of the Treasury Department in one thousand eight hundred and twenty-seven, which shall be certified by him to be and contain a true and correct statement thereof as aforesaid; and it shall be his duty to deliver the same to the Comptroller, to be by him filed in his office, who shall raise an account against the Public Treasurer for the same, and debit his bond account with the interest that has or may hereafter accrue on said bonds, as the same shall have been or may hereafter be paid, and credit his said account with such sums of principal or interest as may have been by the Public Treasurer heretofore paid according to receipts on file in the Comptroller's office, and for all sums that may hereafter be paid agreeably to law, for and on account of said bonds.

II. And be it further enacted, That it shall be the duty of the Comptroller to make out and complete the books in his office, on which the accounts of the obligors in the bonds for the purchase of the lands acquired as aforesaid are opened and kept up to the end of each fiscal year, in the same manner as the same are now kept in the office of the Public Treasurer, so as to exhibit the different amounts of principal and of interest to the time of the payments heretofore made, or which may hereafter be made, and the true and actual amount of each debt, and the balance due the State on account thereof.

III. And be it further enacted, That a statement and certificate of the bonds in the office of the Public Treasurer for the purchase of the Tuscarora lands, shall be made out by him and filed with the Comptroller;

and that the same accounts shall be raised and general course pursued in regard to them as is required in the first and second section of this bill as to those therein referred to.

****

ACTS PASSED BY THE GENERAL ASSEMBLY OF THE STATE OF NORTH CAROLINA AT THE SESSION OF 1830-1831
RALEIGH: PRINTED BY LAWRENCE & LEMAY PRINTERS TO THE STATE. 1831

CHAPTER IV.
1830-1831. An act more effectually to prevent intermarriages between free negroes or free persons of colour and white persons and slaves, and for other purposes. (Pages 9-10).

Be it enacted by the General Assembly of the State of North Carolina, and it is hereby enacted by the authority of the same, That hereafter it shall not be lawful for any free negro or free person of colour to marry a white person; and any marriage hereafter solemnized or celebrated between any free negro or free person of colour and a white person shall be null and void.

II. Be it further enacted, That if hereafter any clerk of the Court of Pleas and Quarter Sessions shall knowingly issue any license for a marriage between any free negro or free person of colour and a white person, he shall be guilty of a misdemeanor, and upon conviction before any court having jurisdiction, shall be fined and imprisoned at the discretion of the court; and any clergyman, minister of the Gospel or justice of the peace, who shall knowingly marry any free negro or free person of colour to a white person, shall be guilty of a misdemeanor, and upon conviction in any court having jurisdiction, shall be fined and imprisoned at the discretion of the court.

III. Be it further enacted, That hereafter it shall not be lawful for any free negro or free person of colour to intermarry or cohabit and live together as man and wife with any slave; and any free negro or person of colour so intermarrying or cohabiting and living as man and wife with a slave, shall be subject to indictment, and upon conviction shall be fined and imprisoned or whipt at the discretion of the court; the whipping not exceed thirty-nine lashes: Provided, that this section shall not extend to any case where an intermarriage or cohabiting or living together took place before the passing of this act.

CHAPTER VI.
1830-1831. An act to prevent from teaching slaves to read or write, the use of figures excepted. (Page 11).

Whereas the teaching of slaves to read and write, has a tendency to excite dissatisfaction in their minds, and to produce insurrection and rebellion, to the manifest injury of the citizens of this State: Therefore,

Be it enacted by the General Assembly of the State of North Carolina, and it is hereby enacted by the authority of the same, That if any free person, who shall hereafter teach, or attempt to teach, , any slave within this State to read or write, the use of figures excepted, or shall give or sell to such slave or slaves any books or pamphlets, shall be liable to indictment in any court of record in this State having jurisdiction thereof; and upon conviction, shall, at the discretion of the court, if a white man or woman, be fined not less than one hundred dollars, nor more than two hundred dollars, or imprisoned; and if a free person of colour, shall be fined, imprisoned, or whipped, at the discretion of the court, not exceeding thirty-nine lashes, nor less than twenty lashes.

II. Be it further enacted, That if any slave shall hereafter teach, or attempt to teach, any other slave to read or write, the use of figures excepted, he or she may be carried before any justice of the peace, and on conviction thereof, shall be sentenced to receive thirty nine lashes on his or her bare back.

III. Be it further enacted, That the judges of the Superior Courts and the Justices of the County Courts shall give this act in charge to grand jurors of their respective counties.

CHAPTER VIII.
1830-1831. An act providing further punishment for harbouring or maintaining runaway slaves. (Page 12).

Be it enacted by the General Assembly of the State of North Carolina, and it is hereby enacted by the authority of the same, That any person who shall entice or persuade any slave to absent him or herself from the service of his or her owner, or from the service of any other person or persons legally entitled to the service of the same, or who shall harbour or maintain any runaway slave, shall be subject to a penalty of one hundred dollars, to be recovered before any justice of the peace, by any person suing for the same, the one half to the use of the informer, and the other half to the use of the wardens of the poor of the county where suit is brought; any law to the contrary notwithstanding.

CHAPTER IX.
1830-1831. An act to regulate the emancipation of slaves in this State. (Pages 12-14).
Be it enacted by the General Assembly of the State of North Carolina, and it is hereby enacted by the authority of the same, That hereafter any inhabitant of this State, desirous to emancipate a slave or slaves, shall file a petition in writing in some one of the Superior Courts of this State, setting forth, as near as may be, the name, sex and age of each slave intended to be emancipated, and praying permission to emancipate the same; and the court before whom such petition shall be filed, shall grant the prayer thereof on the following conditions, and not otherwise, That the petitioner shall show that he has given public notice of his intention to file such petition at the court house of the county and in the State Gazette for at least six weeks before the hearing of such petition; and that the petitioner shall enter into bond, with two securities, each to be good and sufficient, payable to the Governor of the State and his successors in office, in the sum of one thousand dollars for each slave named in the petition, conditioned that the said slave or slaves shall honestly and correctly demean him, her, or themselves, while he, she or they shall remain within the State of North Carolina; and that he, she or they will, within ninety days after granting the prayer of the petitioner to emancipate him, her or them, leave the State of North Carolina, and never afterwards come within the same: Provided, nevertheless, that no such emancipation shall in any manner whatever invalidate the or affect the rights or claims of any creditor of such petitioner.

II. And be it further enacted, That any emancipation hereafter granted to any slave or slaves, as herein directed, shall be upon the express condition that he, she or they will leave the State within ninety days from the granting thereof, and will never return within the State afterwards.

III. And be it further enacted, That it shall hereafter be lawful for any person, by his or her last will and testament, to direct and authorise his or her executor or executors to cause to be emancipated any slave or slaves, pursuant to this act; and such bequest or authority shall be good and available in law and equity, and shall justify said executor or executors in emancipating such slave or slaves at any time thereafter, provided he, she or they file his, her or their petition, and pursue the directions of this act in the same manner as if he, she or they were the absolute owners of such slave or slaves: and provided further, that nothing herein contained shall be taken or held to interfere with the claims of creditors, or exempt any slave directed to be emancipated from liability to the claims of creditors: and provided further, that any slave, emancipated by an executor, pursuant to the directors of the testator, shall be emancipated on the same conditions, and under the same liabilities, as herein before set forth: Provided further, that no permission shall be granted to any executor or executors to emancipate any slave or slaves under the directions of the last will and testament of his or their testator, before the expiration of two years from and after the probate of said last will and testament, unless the said executor or executors shall enter into bond, with approved security, to the Governor of the State for the time being, in double the value of the slave or slaves proposed to be emancipated, conditioned to be answerable to the creditors of his, her or their testator for the value of the said slave or slaves.

IV. And be it further enacted, That it may be lawful at any time hereafter to emancipate, upon petition filed and under the order of any Superior Court of Law in this State, any slave over the age of fifty years, provided his or her owner shall prove by their own oath or otherwise to the satisfaction of the court and jury that said slave has performed meritorious services, (which meritorious services must consist in more than mere general performance of duty:) Provided, nevertheless, that the petitioner shall swear that he or she has not received in money or otherwise the price or value, or any part thereof, of said slave, or been induced to petition for his or her emancipation in consideration for any price paid therefore or to be paid: And provided further, that before such slave shall be emancipated, the petitioner shall give bond and good security in the sum of five hundred dollars, payable to the Governor and his successors in office, that said slave shall honestly and correctly demean him or herself so long as she or he shall remain in the State, and shall not become a parish charge; which bond may be sued upon in the name of the Governor for the time being, to the use of the parish or of any person injured by the mal conduct of such slave.

V. And be it further enacted, That if any slave shall refuse or neglect to leave the State within ninety days after permission to emancipate him or her has been granted as aforesaid by any Superior Court, or shall ever come within the State after having left it, it shall be the duty of any justice of the peace of any county wherein said slave may be found, to issue a warrant to arrest said slave, and shall, upon proper proof being made of his or her having violated the provisions of this act, commit him or her to the jail of the county, there to remain until the next ensuing term of the Court of Pleas and Quarter Sessions where an issue shall be made up and immediately tried, whether the accused has violated the provisions of this act; and upon the finding of the jury that said accused has violated the provisions of this act, he, she or they shall by the said Court of Pleas and Quarter Sessions be ordered to be sold; which sale shall vest an absolute right of property in the purchaser in and to the accused, and the proceeds thereof be equally divided between the informer and the wardens of the poor of the county.

VI. And be it further enacted, That if any slave shall refuse or neglect to leave the State as aforesaid, or shall ever come within the same after having left it, it shall and may be lawful for any person to bring suit in the name of the Governor, for the joint use of himself and the wardens of the poor of the county, and to be applied by them to the support of the poor of said county, upon the bond which may have been given in pursuance of the provisions of this act.

VII. Be it further enacted, That it shall be the duty of all grand juries within the State to make presentment of all slaves who may hereafter be emancipated, who may violate the provisions of this act of Assembly; and upon such presentment it shall be the duty of the prosecuting officer of the county wherein the presentment may be made, to prosecute such slave as herein before provided.

VIII. Be it further enacted, That all laws and clauses of laws heretofore passed relative to the emancipation of slaves, be, and the same are hereby replaced.

CHAPTER X.
1830-1831. An act to prevent the gaming of slaves, and to prevent free persons from gaming with them or suffering them to game in their houses. (Pages 14-15).

Be it enacted by the General Assembly of the State of North Carolina, and it is hereby enacted by the authority of the same, That it shall not be lawful for any slave or slaves to play any game of cards, dice, nine pins, or any game of hazard or chance, for any money, liquor or any kind of property, whether the same be staked or not; and any slave so offending shall, upon conviction of a justice of the peace, receive a whipping on his or her bare back, not exceeding thirty nine lashes.

II. Be it further enacted, That it shall not be lawful for any white person or free negro, mulatto or person of mixed blood, descended from negro ancestors to the fourth generation inclusive, (though one ancestor in each generation may have been a white person,) to play at any game of cards, dice, nine pins or any game of chance or hazard, whether for money, liquor, or any kind of property, or not, with any slave or slaves; and any white person so offending shall be deemed guilty of a misdemeanor, and upon conviction shall be fined or imprisoned at the discretion of the court: Provided said imprisonment shall not exceed six months; and any free negro, mullato or person of mixed blood as aforesaid, so offending, shall, upon conviction before any court having jurisdiction, receive a whipping, not to exceed thirty nine lashes on his or her bare back.

III. Be it further enacted, That if any white person, free negro, mulatto, or person of mixed blood as aforesaid, shall knowingly suffer any slave or slaves to play at any game of cards, dice, nine pins, or any game of chance or hazard, whether for money, liquor, or any kind of property or not, in his or her house, or in the yard, field or garden attached or belonging to his or her house, he or she shall be liable to indictment in any court having jurisdiction, and upon conviction the white person so offending shall be fined or imprisoned at the discretion of the court, not exceeding six months; and the free negro, mulatto or person of mixed blood as aforesaid shall receive a whipping on his or her bare back, not to exceed thirty nine lashes; and if the persons convicted be a retailer of spiritous liquors by the small measure, he or she shall forfeit his or her license, and be forever incapable of receiving a license to retail spiritous liquors by the small measure.

IV. Be it further enacted, That it shall be the duty of the patrol, whenever they shall see or receive information of the gaming of slaves within their district, to proceed to disperse them; and the patrol shall have power to apprehend any slave so gaming and inflict upon him or her a whipping, not to exceed fifteen lashes. And nothing in this section shall prevent any such slave from being punished as prescribed in the first section of this act.

V. And be it further enacted, That the above recited act shall not go into operation till the tenth day of May next.

CHAPTER XIV.
1830-1831. An act to amend an act, passed in the year one thousand eight hundred and twenty six, entitled "an act to prevent free persons of colour from emigrating into this State, for the good government of such persons resident in the State, and for other purposes." (Page 16).

Be it enacted by the General Assembly of the State of North Carolina, and it is hereby enacted by the authority of the same, That if at any time hereafter, any free negro or person of colour, who may be a resident of this State, shall migrate from this State and go into any other State, and shall be absent for the space of ninety days or more, it shall not be lawful for such free negro or person of colour to return to this State; and if any free negro or person of colour shall violate this law, he shall be liable to the same penalties as are prescribed by the above recited act, for the punishment of free negroes and persons of colour who migrate to this State: Provided, That no person shall incur the penalties or disabilities prescribed in this act, if he or she shall have been prevented from so returning to this State by sickness or other unavoidable occurrence.

CHAPTER XV.
1830-1831. An act to amend an act, passed in the year one thousand eight hundred and twenty six, entitle " an act to prohibit trading with slaves, except in manner therein prescribed." (Pages 16-17).

Be it enacted by the General Assembly of the State of North Carolina, and it is hereby enacted by the authority of the same, That the word "and" immediately following the words white oak heading, in the first section of said act, shall be construed "or".

Chapter XVI.
1830-1831. An act for regulation of the patrol. (Pages 17-18).

Be it enacted by the General Assembly of the State of North Carolina, and it is hereby enacted by the authority of the same, That from and after the passage of this act, it shall be the duty of the County Court of each county in this State, should the court deem it necessary, at the first court that shall happen after the first day of January in each and every year, or any subsequent court, to appoint a patrol committee, of three persons in each captain's district in said county, whose duty it shall be to employ a patrol, of such number of persons as they may think necessary, to patrol their district.

II. And be it further enacted, That it shall be the duty of the said County Courts, at the same term, to lay a tax of not more ten cents on each taxable slave in said county; which tax shall be levied and collected by the sheriffs of the several counties in the same manner as other taxes, and be applied under the direction of the County Courts to defray the expenses of the patrol.

III. And be it further enacted, That it shall be the duty of the patrol to visit the negro houses in their respective districts as often as may be necessary, to inflict a punishment not exceeding fifteen lashes on all slaves they may find off their owner's plantation without a proper permit or pass. It shall also be the duty of the patrollers to visit all suspected places, and suppress all collections of slaves; it shall also be their duty to be diligent in apprehending all runaway negroes in their respective districts; to be vigilant and endeavor to detect all thefts, and bring the perpetrators to justice, and also all persons guilty of trading with slaves. The patrol committee shall here all complaints lodged against the patrollers for abuse or neglect of duty, and shall full power and authority to discharge any one or more of the patrollers, and employ others, at any time when they may think it expedient. The patrols thus employed shall have as full powers as those heretofore appointed by the County Courts; and if, upon taking up a negro and chastising him as now directed by law, he shall behave insolently, they may inflict further punishment for his conduct, not exceeding thirty nine lashes.

IV. Be it further enacted, That nothing herein contained shall be construed to prevent the County Courts from appointing such patrols as they may deem proper.

V. Be it further enacted, That it shall be the duty of the several County Courts of this State to adopt rules and regulations for the government of the patrols of their county, pursuant to the authority given them by the act passed in the year one thousand eight hundred and two, chapter fifteen.

VI. Be it further enacted, That any person who shall be appointed a patrol under this act, and who shall refuse or neglect to serve, shall be subject to a penalty of twenty dollars, to be sued for by the patrol committee of his particular district, and when recovered, shall be paid over by them to the county trustee, to form a fund in aid of the tax for the support of the patrol.

CHAPTER XVII.

1830-1831. An act to amend an act, entitled an act to authorise the County Courts in this State to direct the sheriff to sell any slave that may be taken up and confined in any jail as a runaway after certain length of imprisonment and public notice, passed in the year one thousand eight hundred and eighteen. (Page 18).

Be it enacted by the General Assembly of the State of North Carolina, and it is hereby enacted by the authority of the same, That if any runaway slave, confined in any jail of this State under the provisions of the aforesaid act, and his or her owner be unknown, and the said slave should die, or by the regular process of law be removed from said jail before a sale of said runaway slave is effected according to the directions of said act, then and in either of said cases it shall be the duty of the Court of Pleas and Quarter Sessions of the county where said slave was confined to direct the county trustee to pay all the expenses of his or her imprisonment out of the county funds: Provided, that the Jailor shows to the court that he has complied with the law requiring advertisement of runaways.

II. Be it further enacted, That in case the trustee of any county, by order of the Court of Pleas and Quarter Sessions therein, should pay the expenses of the confinement of any runaway slave in pursuance of the provisions of the first section of this act, and the owner thereafter become known, it shall be the duty of the said trustee to recover for the use of the county, from the owner or his representative, the amount he may have previously paid on account of said runaway slave.

CHAPTER XXX.

1830-1831. An act to amend the several laws now in force in this State regulating quarantine (Page 29-30).

III. And be it further enacted, That if any free negro or person of colour on board any ship or vessel coming into any port in this State from any other State or country shall before the expiration of thirty days from the arrival of the vessel on board which he or she may be, shall go on shore, or if any slave or free negro or person of colour residing in this State shall have any communication by words or writing with such free person of colour while on board such ship or vessel, the captain, commander or chief officer of such ship or vessel shall forfeit and pay the sum of five hundred dollars, to be recovered by and in the name of any person suing for the same.

IV. And be it further enacted, That if any free negro or person of colour so coming in such ship or vessel, shall come on shore or have any communication with any person of colour residing in this State while the said ship or vessel shall be riding quarantine as aforesaid, such negro or person of colour shall be immediately apprehended and committed to the common jail of the county where he, she or they may be apprehended; and the magistrate or intendant of police of any city or town within this State or any judge or justice of any Superior or inferior Court of this State is hereby authorised to issue a warrant to any sheriff or constable within this State for the apprehension of such free negro or person of colour, and to commit him, her or them to any common jail within this State as aforesaid, there to remain until the said ship or vessel shall be actually departing from the waters of this State, or shall hauled off from the wharf and ready to proceed to sea, or until he, she or they shall be otherwise discharged by law.

V. And be it further enacted, That if any negro or person of colour shall communicate with any free negro or person of colour so coming into this State, while the said ship or vessel is riding quarantine as aforesaid, such negro or person of colour so offending shall be forthwith arrested by a warrant to be issued by the authorities, and in manner herein before provided and directed; and if a slave, on conviction thereof before any intendant, judge or justice as aforesaid, before whom the said warrant shall be made returnable, shall be sentenced to be whipped not exceeding thirty nine lashes; and if a free negro or person of colour, shall be indicted in any court having cognizance thereof, and on conviction shall be punished by thirty nine lashes on his or her bare back.

VI. And be it further enacted, That when said vessel is ready to sail, the captain of the said vessel shall be bound to carry away the said free negro or person of colour, and to pay the expenses of his detention; and in case such captain shall refuse or neglect to pay the said expenses, and carry away the said free negro or person of colour, he shall be liable to indictment, and on conviction shall be fined five hundred dollars.

VII. And be it further enacted, That every free negro or person of colour coming into this State as aforesaid, and who shall not depart the State, in case the captain refusing or neglecting to carry him away within ten days after the vessel in which he came has departed, shall be liable to indictment, and on conviction before any court having cognizance thereof shall be whipped not exceeding thirty nine lashes, and be further liable to the penalties now by law in force against free persons of colour coming into this State.

CHAPTER LXXXI.
1830-1831. An act to authorise Aquilla Day, otherwise called Aquilla Wilson, a free person of colour, to reside in this State.(Page 79).
Whereas it is represented to this General Assembly, that Thomas Day, a free person of colour of good behaviour, residing in this State, hath intermarried with Aquilla Wilson, a free woman of colour, and an inhabitant of the State of Virginia; and whereas the said Thomas Day is desirous to remove his said wife into this State; and whereas further, it is represented to this General Assembly that the said Thomas and Aquilla are of good and exemplary reputation and behaviour:

Be it enacted by the General Assembly of the State of North Carolina, and it is hereby enacted by the authority of the same, That Aquilla Day otherwise called Aquilla Wilson, be, and she is hereby authorised to come into, and reside in this State.

II. And be it further enacted, That the said Aquilla Day, otherwise called Aquilla Wilson, shall not, by coming into and residing in this State, incur or be subject to any of the pains, penalties or liabilities of an act passed in the year one thousand eight hundred and twenty six, entitled an act to prevent free persons of colour from migrating into this State, and for other purposes.

CHAPTER CXXXIX.
1830-1831. An act to compel owners of slaves to keep white persons on their plantations in certain cases, in the counties of Brunswick and New Hanover. (Page 119).
Be it enacted by the General Assembly of the State of North Carolina, and it is hereby enacted by the authority of the same, That hereafter it shall be the duty of all farmers and planters in the counties aforesaid, who have as many as fifteen slaves of the age of twelve years or upwards employed on any one plantation, to employ some white person to superintend and control said slaves, and remain on such plantation in the absence of the owner, whenever such absences shall exceed forty days.

II. Be it further enacted, That any person failing to employ some white person to remain on his or her plantation as above specified, shall be liable to the penalty of one hundred dollars, to be recovered by and in the name of any person suing for the same, one half to the use of the wardens of the poor, the other half for his own benefit: Provided nevertheless, that whenever such absence shall proceed from sickness or other unavoidable accident, no such penalty shall be incurred.

CHAPTER CLIII.
1830-1831. An act more effectually to prevent the depredations of runaway slaves, and to promote their apprehension in the counties of Onslow, Jones, Craven, Lenoir, New Hanover, Brunswick and Carteret. (Page 128).

Be it enacted by the General Assembly of the State of North Carolina, and it is hereby enacted by the authority of the same, That the County Courts of the several counties aforesaid, not less than ten justices being present, shall have full power and authority, whenever satisfactory information is lodged before them that runaway slaves have collected together in their county, and are committing depredations on the citizens of the county, to direct the colonel or commanding officer of the county, to order out as many men as said court may deem expedient for apprehending such runaways; and it shall be the duty of such commanding officer immediately to draft from the militia, or receive volunteers, in such number as the court may direct, and order them into service; and it shall be the duty of the officers and men thus ordered out to search diligently throughout the county, or any adjoining county if deemed necessary, for such runaways, until they are taken: Provided, that no one company shall be compelled to remain on duty longer than twenty days at any one time.

II. Be it further enacted, That each person who may be ordered out as aforesaid, shall furnish his own provisions, gun and ammunition, and shall be paid for his service at the following rates, viz., each captain of a company one dollar per day, each lieutenant seventy five per day, and each private or inferior officer fifty cents per day, to be paid as hereafter specified.

III. Be it further enacted, That any officer or private who shall be ordered to perform duty as aforesaid, and shall fail to perform the same, and to obey all reasonable commands of the superior officer, shall be liable to indictment in any court having cognizance thereof, and on conviction shall be fined or imprisoned at the discretion of the court not exceeding a fine of one hundred dollars, or imprisonment for three months.

IV. Be it further enacted, That it shall be the duty of the County Court of the several counties aforesaid, at the same time to lay a tax not exceeding twenty five cents on each black poll in their county for the purpose of defraying the expenses thereof; which tax the sheriff of the county shall forthwith collect and pay into the Treasury of the county for the purposes aforesaid.

V. Be it further enacted, That any person who shall hereafter apprehend any runaway slave over fifteen years of age in either of the aforesaid counties, and shall deliver him or her to the owner, or the jailor of the county at the jail, shall be entitled to receive and recover from the owner of such slave the sum of ten dollars, to be recovered before any jurisdiction having cognizance thereof.

VI. Be it further enacted, That whenever any runaway slave shall be found in any of the aforesaid counties, it shall be lawful for any person to apprehend such runaway slave, and in so doing to use all the powers and force which a sheriff may lawfully use in apprehending a felon against whom he has legal process, without incurring any liability to any civil suit, and without impeachment of any crime whatever.

****

ACTS PASSED BY THE GENERAL ASSEMBLY OF THE STATE OF NORTH CAROLINA AT THE SESSION OF 1831-1832 RALEIGH: PRINTED BY LAWRENCE & LEMAY PRINTERS TO THE STATE. 1832

CHAPTER IV.
1831-1832. An act for the better regulation of the conduct of negroes, slaves and free persons of color. (Page 9).

Be it enacted by the General Assembly of the State of North Carolina, and it is hereby enacted by the authority of the same, That it shall not be lawful under any pretence for any free negro, slave or free person of color to preach or exhort in public, or in any manner to officiate as a preacher or teacher in any prayer meeting or other association for worship where slaves of different families are collected together; and if any free negro or free person of color shall be thereof duly convicted on indictment before any court having jurisdiction thereof, he shall for each offence receive not exceeding thirty nine lashes on his bare back; and where any slave shall be guilty of a violation of this act, he shall on conviction before a single magistrate receive not exceeding thirty nine lashes on his bare back.

II. And be it further enacted by the authority aforesaid, That it shall not be lawful for any slave to go at large as a freeman, exercising his or her own discretion in the employment of his or her time; nor shall it be lawful for any slave to keep house to him or herself as a free person, exercising the like discretion in the employment of his or her time; and in case the owner of any slave shall consent or connive at the commission of such offence, he or she so offending shall be subject to indictment, and on conviction be fined in the discretion of the court not exceeding one hundred dollars: Provided, that nothing herein shall be construed to prevent any person permitting his or her slave or slaves to live or keep house upon his or her land for the purpose of attending to the business of his or her master or mistress.

CHAPTER XIII.
1831-1832. An act to provide for the collection of fines imposed upon free negroes or free persons of colour. (Pages 12-13).

Be it enacted by the General Assembly of the State of North Carolina, and it is hereby enacted by the authority of the same, That when any free negro or free person of colour shall be hereafter convicted of an offence against the criminal laws of this State, and sentenced to pay a fine, and it shall appear to the satisfaction of the court that the free negro or free person of colour so convicted is unable to pay the fine imposed, the court shall direct the sheriff of the county, where such fine is imposed to hire out the free negro or free person of colour so convicted to any person who will pay the fine for his services for the shortest space of time.

II. Be it further enacted, That it shall be the duty of the sheriff, during the week of court, , or as soon thereafter as convenient, publicly at the door of the court house, to hire out such free negro or free person of colour to any person who will pay the fine so imposed for his services for the shortest space of time, and to take from the person so hiring bond and security in double the amount of the fine so paid, payable in the same manner, and with the same conditions for the proper treatment of the free negro or free person of colour during the time for which he is so hired, as are now contained in apprentice bonds, except to learn them to read and write.

III. Be it further enacted, That the person to whom the sheriff shall so hire any free negro or free person of colour, shall, during the time for which the hiring is so made, have the same authority over, and the same right to control and require the services of such free negro or free person of colour, and shall be liable in all respects to the same obligations and duties as masters now have, and are liable to in cases of apprentice bonds.

IV. Be it further enacted, That if no person can be found who will pay the fine so imposed for the services of the free negro or free person of colour so fined, for a space of time not exceeding five years, then it shall be the duty of the sheriff to hire the free negro or free person of colour to any person who will pay the highest sum for his services for five years; which sum shall discharge the fine; and it shall be the duty of the sheriff, after deducting five per cent commissions, to account for and pay over the money collected by virtue of this act as other fines: Provided always, that if any free negro or free person of colour hired out under the provisions of this act, shall abscond or leave the services of his master before the expiration of his or her time, he or she shall be liable and bound to make up such time so elapsed by serving double the time thereof: And provided further, that the fine imposed shall in all cases be at least equal to the amount of the costs of such prosecution.

V. And be it further enacted, That this act shall be in force from and after the ratification thereof.

CHAPTER XXVIII.
1831-1832. An act to amend the first section of an act, passed in the year one thousand eight hundred and thirty, which authorises free persons of colour to hawk and peddle out of the limits of the county in which they reside. (Page 24).

Be it enacted by the General Assembly of the State of North Carolina, and it is hereby enacted by the authority of the same, That hereafter it shall not be lawful for any free negro, mulatto or free person of colour to hawk or peddle within the limits of any county in this State without first obtaining a license from the Court of Pleas and Quarter Sessions of the county in which they propose to hawk or peddle; which license shall be granted only when seven or more justices are present, and annually thereafter, and upon satisfactory evidence of good character of the applicant, to be approved by said court; and for issuing such license the clerk shall be entitled to demand and receive from such applicant the sum

North Carolina Law

of eighty cents: Provided, nevertheless, that nothing in this act shall be construed so as to allow such persons coming from another State to peddle in this State.

II. And be it further enacted, That if any free negro or free person of colour shall offend against this act, he or she shall be subject to indictment.

III. And be it further enacted, That this act shall not be in force until the first day of March, one thousand eight hundred and thirty two.

Chapter XXX.
1831-1832. An act to amend the fifth section of an act, passed in the year of our Lord one thousand eight hundred and sixteen, chapter nine hundred and twelve, entitled an act for the more speedy trial of slaves in capital cases. (Pages 25-26).

Be it enacted by the General Assembly of the State of North Carolina, and it is hereby enacted by the authority of the same, That in all cases of insurrection or rebellion, or of conspiracy to make insurrection or to murder or rebel or any such contemplated conspiracy, insurrection or rebellion, of any slave or slaves, upon the information and at the request of any five justices of the peace of the county in whuch conspiracy, insurrection or rebellion shall happen or may be contemplated, the Governor for the time being shall be authorised and have power to issue a commission of Oyer and Terminer to any one of the judges of the Superior Courts of Law; and in case the said judges are necessarily engaged on their circuits, the Governor shall be authorised and have power to issue a commission to one of the judges of the Supreme Court, whose duty it shall be to hold said court forthwith, and shall be clothed with all the powers necessary for the trial of all such slave or slaves that may be charged with any of the before mentioned offences.

II. And be it further enacted, That every judge holding a court of Oyer and Terminer, and the prosecuting officer in behalf of the State attending the said court, shall be entitled to receive the same compensation as may be allowed by the law generally for holding and attending a term of a Superior Court.

III. Be it further enacted, That the prisoner or prisoners who shall be tried before any court of Oyer and Terminer in this State, shall have the right of appeal to the Supreme Court under the rules and regulations now prescribed by law for appeals.

IV. Be it further enacted, That when the prisoner who shall be indicted before a court of Oyer and Terminer in this State, shall, upon upon affidavit of himself or any other person, shew such circumstances and facts to the court as would induce the judge in the regular courts of this State to remove the trial of said indictment out the county, the judge holding such court of Oyer and terminer may in his discretion continue the said indictment and commit or bind over the prisoner as the case may require for trial at the next Superior Court for said county, when the same shall be disposed of according to the rules and regulations in force for the trial of such offences.

V. Be it further enacted, That in all trials of slaves hereafter for capital offences, the defendant Shall be entitled to be tried by a jury composed of the owners of slaves.

CHAPTER XXXII.
1831-1832. An act pointing out the mode whereby the militia of this State shall hereafter be called into service in cases of insurrection or invasion, and outlawed and runaway negroes. (Pages 28-29).

Be it enacted by the General Assembly of the State of North Carolina, and it is hereby enacted by the authority of the same, That in all cases of insurrection among slaves or free persons of colour, either in the county, an adjoining county, or in a distant county of the State, or in an adjoining State, seven justices of the peace deeming the emergency requiring it, may, at their discretion, require in writing of the commanding officer or officers of their county to call out the militia to repress or repel such an invasion or insurrection, or to protect the inhabitants of their county from the danger apprehended; and may again require of the said officer to dismiss his men when they think the danger is over, and the commanding officer may dismiss in like manner.

III. Be it further enacted, That the commanding officer of any regiment, as soon as he has called out the militia under the provisions of this act, shall immediately send out an express to the Brigadier or Major General of his brigade or division, informing him of that fact, and any other official facts he may be in possession of, and continue to do so from time to time; and the Brigadier or Major General shall immediately apprise the Governor, either by express mail, as he judge the emergency requires, of all the circumstances; in the mean time said general officer shall pursue the most effective measures for repelling such invasion or suppressing such

North Carolina Law

insurrection; and the militia thus called out shall be armed according to law.

IV. Be it further enacted, That when there may be outlawed or runaway negroes committing depredations, or in any way alarming the citizens of any county, or when the guarding of a jail is necessary, three justices of the peace when certifying the same in writing, and requesting of the officer in command in their county, he is hereby required to effect the object set forth in said request of the justices; and the expenses of said militia so called out shall be paid by the court of the county, who are hereby authorised to lay a sufficient tax to pay said militia at the same rates as the regular troops of the United States are by law now entitled to when in actual service.

V. Be it further enacted, That all acts and clauses of acts coming within the meaning and purview of this act, and the same are hereby repealed.

CHAPTER CLII.
1831-1832. An act to appoint lay days for fishing with seines, nets, &c. at New Inlet, in the counties of Currituck and Hyde. (Page 129).

Be it enacted by the General Assembly of the State of North Carolina, and it is hereby enacted by the authority of the same, That in future it shall not be lawful for any person whatsoever to haul a seine, set a net, or cause any other obstruction to the free passage of fish through New Inlet, or any of the slues or channels leading through the shoals or marshes into Pamlico Sound, or within three miles of said inlet, from Saturday sun down until Monday twelve o'clock of each and every week, between the first day of February and the first day of June, inclusive, in every year.

II. And be it further enacted, That if any person or persons shall directly or indirectly offend against any of the provisions contained in the foregoing section, he or they shall, upon conviction before any justice of the peace for the counties of Currituck or Hyde, be fined the sum of one hundred dollars; for which judgement may be entered up by the said justice for each and every time a seine is so hauled,, a net set, or other obstructions made; one half of the penalty hereby imposed to be given to him, her or them that will first inform of the offence, and the other half to the poor of the county in which the conviction may be had.

III. And be it further enacted, That any slave or slaves offending against any of the provisions of this act, unless he or they appear to have acted under the express directions of their owners or employers, shall be sentenced to receive thirty nine lashes, and all cost paid by the owner or owners of said slaves.

CHAPTER CLIII.
1831-1832. An act to prevent obstructions to the passage of fish up Neuse and Trent rivers. (Pages 129-130).

Be it enacted by the General Assembly of the State of North Carolina, and it is hereby enacted by the authority of the same, That no person or persons shall work any seine, set net, fish trap or slide in the channel of the Neuse river below Newbern, or in the Neuse or Trent rivers above Newbern to the Wayne county line, from the fifteenth of January to the twenty fifth of April, in the time hereinafter specified, viz. from sun set on Saturday until sun set on Monday, in each and every week, in each and every year hereafter, under the following penalty, that is to say, that every person who shall work a seine, set net, skimming net, fish trap or slide in the time above specified contrary to the true intent and meaning of this act, shall for each and every offence, upon conviction, forfeit and pay the sum of one hundred dollars, one half to the use of the informer, and the other half to the use of the poor of the county in which the offence may be committed.

II. Be it further enacted, That any slave or slaves who shall be convicted before any justice of the peace for having violated this act, shall receive thirty nine lashes on his or her bare back, and the master or owner shall be subject to pay the cost of such prosecution and whipping.

III. Be it further enacted, That so much of an act, passed in the year one thousand eight hundred and thirty , entitled "an act to prevent obstructions in the passage of fish up Neuse river, Brices creek and Trent river," as comes within the meaning and purview of this act, be, and the same is hereby repealed.

CHAPTER CLXIII.
1831-1832. An act to prevent obstructions to the passage of fish up Tar or Pamptico river. (Page 135).

Be it enacted by the General Assembly of the State of North Carolina, and it is hereby enacted by the authority of the same, That no person shall work any seine, set net, skimming net, fish trap, slide or weir in Tar or Pamptico river, from the fifteenth of January to the twenty fifth of April, in the time herein specified, to wit: from sunrise on Saturday till sunrise on Monday in each and every week, under the following penalty, that is to say, every person who shall offend against the true intent of this act, shall, for each and every offence, upon conviction, forfeit and pay the sum of one hundred dollars, one half to the use of the county, the other half to the informer.

II. Be it further enacted, That any slave who shall be convicted before any magistrate of having offended this act, shall receive thirty lashes, and the owner of said slave shall pay the costs of prosecution and whipping.

III. Be it further enacted, That all laws and clauses of laws coming within the meaning and purview of this act, be, and the same are hereby repealed: Provided, however, that nothing in this act shall be so construed as to prevent any person from fishing in any manner in Tar river above the upper line of Pitt county, or below Wade's Point in said river.

RESOLUTIONS.
1831-1832.

Whereas it appears that much confusion exists in the accounts of the purchasers of Cherokee lands, on the books of the Public Treasurer, and that many discrepancies exist between the bonds given for the purchases of Cherokee lands and the entries made on those books; and it also appears that some errors occurred in making out the lists of those bonds in December, 1830, for the purpose of transferring them to the present Public Treasurer: Therefore,

Be it resolved, That the Public Treasurer be, and he is hereby directed to have a new set of books opened in his office, in which he shall cause to be entered a true and accurate statement, and account of all the bonds for the purchase of Cherokee lands which came to his possession on the twenty ninth December, eighteen hundred and thirty, so that it may clearly appear what was the total amount due, and what was due on each bond on that day; and that he enter on these books all sums which may have been since paid to him, or which may hereafter be paid, so as to exhibit at all times the true amount due on these bonds.

Resolved further, That the Public Treasurer make out and sign a correct list of these bonds, as they existed at the time he came into office, and deposit the same in the office of the Comptroller, for the examination and action of the committee of Finance at the next session of the General Assembly; and it shall be the duty of the Comptroller to receive and preserve said list; but he shall not be required to open accounts with the several purchasers of Cherokee lands as heretofore required.

Resolved lastly, That the Public Treasurer pay out of the Treasury the sum necessary to carry the object of the foregoing resolutions into effect: Provided, the same should not exceed one hundred dollars.

****

ACTS PASSED BY THE GENERAL ASSEMBLY OF THE STATE OF NORTH CAROLINA AT THE SESSION OF 1833-1834 RALEIGH: PRINTED BY LAWRENCE & LEMAY PRINTERS TO THE STATE 1834

CHAPTER XVIII.
1833-1834. An act to prevent the conveying of slaves out of this State and to prevent injuries being done to live stock upon rail roads. (Pages 36-37).

Whereas from attempts made there is reason to apprehend facilities may be given to slaves, by rail road conveyance, to leave the State, and their owners be thereby deprived of their services for a time or altogether: For remedy whereof,

Be it enacted by the General Assembly of the State of North Carolina, and it is hereby enacted by the authority of the same, That from and after the passage of this act, if any agent or manager of any rail road engine or car, or any other person, shall convey or conceal on or about any rail road engine or car any negro or mulatto slave or slaves, the property of any citizen or citizens of this State, without the consent, in writing, of the owner or manager of such slave or slaves previously obtained; or shall take and receive on any such rail road engine or car any such slave or slaves, or permit or suffer the same to be done, with the intent and for the purpose of carrying such slave or slaves out of this State; or shall wickedly and willingly conceal or permit to be concealed in or about any rail road engine or car, any negro or mulatto slave or slaves, who shall or may hereafter abscond from his or their master or mistress, being citizens of this State, with the intent and for the purpose of enabling such slave or slaves to effect his, her or their escape out of this State, every such agent or manager or other person or persons so taking, receiving or concealing such slave or slaves, or causing or permitting the same to be done, with the intent as aforesaid, shall be deemed to be guilty of felony, and shall suffer death without benefit of clergy.

II. Be it further enacted, That if any negro or mulatto slave or slaves shall be found concealed on or about any rail road engine or car in this State, without the consent or knowledge of the master or mistress or other person having the management of such slave or slaves, after the engine or car shall have left any depot or point, the agent or manager of rail road engine or car shall forfeit and pay to the owner or owners of such slaves the sum of five hundred dollars, to be recovered by action of debt in any of the courts of this State having jurisdiction of the same.

CHAPTER XIX.
1833-1834. An act more effectually to prohibit the trading with slaves. (Page 38).
Be it enacted by the General Assembly of the State of North Carolina, and it is hereby enacted by the authority of the same, That no person or persons shall hereafter buy of, traffic with or receive from any slave or slaves, any mutton, cloth, cotton or woollen yarn, wearing apparel, gold or silver bullion, under the same rules, regulations, restrictions, prohibitions and penalties as are contained in the act of one thousand eight hundred and twenty six, entitled an act to prohibit the trading with slaves except in the manner herein prescribed.

II. Be it further enacted, That the provisions of the before recited act shall be extended and made applicable to the articles mentioned in this act, in the same manner and to the same extent as if the said articles had been contained in the said recited act of one thousand eight hundred and twenty six.

[Editors note: The following laws were included in the appendix of the 1833-1834 laws.]

Pamphlet Acts 1822, Chap. 1.
XXIII. All free males between the ages of twenty one and forty five, and all slaves between the ages of twelve and fifty years, shall pay a poll tax; and all slaves shall be listed in the county wherein they reside.

Pamphlet Acts 1828, Chap. 34.
XXIV. Where any free negro or mulatto, liable to pay a public tax, shall reside on the land of another person, with his or her consent, the person on whose land such free negro or mulatto may reside shall include each and every such free negro or mulatto as a free poll in his or her list of taxable property, and be liable to pay all public, county and parish taxes on every such free negro or mulatto.

XXV. And any person, for refusing or neglecting to give in such free negro or mulatto as aforesaid, shall be liable to all the penalties for refusing or neglecting to give in a list of his or her own taxable property.

****

ACTS PASSED BY THE GENERAL ASSEMBLY
OF THE STATE OF NORTH CAROLINA, AT THE SESSION OF
1833-34
RALEIGH: PRINTED BY LAWRENCE & LEMAY
PRINTERS TO THE STATE, 1834

CHAPTER XIII.
1833-34. An act directing the sale of the lands remaining unsold, acquired by treaty from the Cherokee Indians. (Pages 34-35).
Be it enacted by the General Assembly of the State of North Carolina, and it is hereby enacted by the authority of the same, That the Governor be, and he is hereby authorised to direct the sale of so much of the lands lately acquired by treaty from the Cherokee Indians as have been surveyed and remain unsold, at such time and place as he may deem proper, under the direction of a commissioner to be by him appointed for that purpose, after having advertised the same for at least three months in the public newspapers of this city, the Western Carolinian of Salisbury, and such other papers as he may think proper; which sale shall be kept open one week, and no longer.

II. Be it further enacted, That if, during the sale, any section of land noticed to be of the first quality, shall not command in the market one dollar and fifty cents per acre, and in like manner, lands of the second quality not commanding seventy five cents per acre, and the lands of a third quality not commanding twenty five cents per acre, the commissioner shall postpone the sale of such lands; and when the commissioner discovers that any section of land is likely to bring less than its value, either for want of competition or from combination among the bidders, he shall bid off the same for the State.

III. Be it further enacted, That the provisions of the second section of an act, passed in the year one thousand eight hundred and twenty one, entitled "an act concerning the lands lately acquired by treaty from the Cherokee Indians;" and the provisions of the seventh, twelfth, thirteenth, sixteenth and eighteenth sections of an act, passed in the year one thousand eight hundred and nineteen, entitled "an act prescribing the mode of surveying and selling the lands lately acquired by treaty from the Cherokee Indians," be, and the same are hereby continued in force.

IV. Be it further enacted, That the Governor be, and he is hereby authorised to cause twelve additional lots to be surveyed in the town of Franklin, out of the four hundred acres reserved for the State, which may, together with those already surveyed, be exposed to sale under like rules and regulations as is prescribed in the before recited acts: Provided always, that the said commissioner be authorised, if in his opinion the interest of the State require it, to purchase in the same for the State.

V. Be it further enacted, That nothing in this act shall be so construed as to authorise the sale of any lands, the title of the State to which may be regarded as doubtful.

VI. Be it further enacted, That in case the said lands should be sold, that nothing in this act shall be so construed as to prevent persons who may have crops growing on the said lands, from gathering the same.

CHAPTER XVIII.
1833-34. An Act to prevent the conveying of slaves out of this State and to prevent injuries being done to live stock upon rail roads. (Pages 36-37).

Whereas from attempts made there is reason to apprehend facilities may be given to slaves, by rail road conveyance, to leave the State, and their owners be thereby deprived of their services for a time altogether: For remedy whereof,

Be it enacted by the General Assembly of the State of North Carolina, and it is hereby enacted by the authority of the same, That from and after the passage of this act, if any agent or manager of any rail road engine or car, or any other person, shall convey or conceal on or about any rail road engine or car any negro or mulatto slave or slaves, the property of any citizen or citizens of this State, without the consent, in writing, the owner or manager of such slave or slaves previously obtained; or shall take and receive on any such rail road engine or car any such slave or slaves, or permit or suffer the same to be done, with the intent and for the purpose of carrying such slave or slaves out of this State; or shall wickedly and willingly conceal or permit to be concealed in or about any rail road engine or car, any negro or mulatto slave or slaves, who shall or may hereafter abscond from his or their master or mistress, being citizens of this State, with the intent and for the purpose of enabling such slave or slaves to effect his, her or their escape out of this State, every such agent or manager or other person or persons so taking, receiving or concealing such slave or slaves, or causing or permitting the same to be done, with the intent as aforesaid, shall be deemed guilty of felony, and shall suffer death without benefit of clergy.

  II. Be it further enacted, That if any negro or mulatto slave or slaves shall be found concealed on or about any rail road engine or car in this State, without the consent or knowledge of the master or mistress or other person having the management of such slave or slaves, after the engine or car shall have left any depot or point, the agent or manager of such rail road engine or car shall forfeit and pay to the owner or owners of such slaves the sum of five hundred dollars, to be recovered by action of debt in any of the courts of this State having jurisdiction of the same.

CHAPTER XIX.
1833-1834. An act more effectually to prohibit the trading with slaves. (Page 38).
  Be it enacted by the General Assembly of the State of North Carolina, and be it enacted by the authority of the same, That no person or persons shall hereafter buy of, traffick with or receive from any slave or slaves, any mutton, cloth, cotton or woolen yarn, wearing apparel, gold or silver bullion, under the same rules, regulations, restrictions, prohibitions and penalties as are contained in the act of one thousand eight hundred and twenty six, entitled an act to prohibit the trading with slaves except in the manner herein prescribed.

  II. Be it further enacted, That the provisions of the before recited act shall be extended and made applicable to the articles mentioned in this act, in the same manner and to the same extent as if the said articles had been contained in the said recited act of one thousand eight hundred and twenty six.

CHAPTER XXI.
An act for revising and digesting the public statute laws of this State.
(Pages 38-39).

Be it enacted by the General Assembly of the State of North Carolina, and it is hereby enacted by the authority of the same, That three commissioners be appointed by the Governor of the State to collate, digest and revise all the public statute laws of this State, commencing with the earliest English statutes now in force and including those which may be enacted during the present session of this General Assembly; that in the performance of this duty they shall carefully collect and reduce into one act the different acts and parts of acts which, from similarity of subject, ought in their judgment to be so arranged and consolidated, distributing the same under such titles, divisions and sections as they shall think proper, omitting all such acts and parts of acts before passed as shall have either expired by their own limitation, become obsolete or been repealed; that in every other respect they shall complete the said revision in such manner as to them shall seem most useful and proper to render the said acts more plain and easy to be understood; and that, from time to time, they shall lay before the Legislature the acts so arranged and revised by them, to be re-enacted if the Legislature shall so determine: Provided, that no change shall be made by the said commissioners in the phraseology or distribution of the sections of any statute which has been the subject of judicial decision, by which the construction thereof established by such decision shall or can be affected, and in all such cases marginal references shall be made to the decision fixing the construction.

II. And be it further enacted, That when the said acts shall be so presented to the Legislature for re-enactment, the said commissioners shall also suggest to the Legislature such contradictions, omissions or imperfections as may appear in the acts so to be revised, and the mode in which the same may be reconciled, supplied or reformed; may also designate such acts or parts of acts, if any, as in their judgment ought to be repealed, with reasons for advising such repeal; and may also recommend the passage of such new acts or parts of acts as such repeal may in their judgment render necessary.

III. And be it further enacted, That after the laws so revised as aforesaid shall have been submitted to and approved of by the Legislature, the said commissioners shall prepare the same for the press, with such marginal notes and references as shall appear best calculated for the public information. They shall also prepare for publication with the said laws the constitution of the United States, the constitution of this State, the articles of confederation and perpetual union proposed by the Congress of the United States on the seventeenth day of November, one thousand seven hundred and seventy seven, the second charter granted by Charles the second to the proprietors of Carolina, the great deed of grant from the lords proprietors, the grant from George the second to John Lord Granville, and the other matters not herein before mentioned, embraced in the last revisal. And the said commissioners shall make an index of the matters contained in the said work, and also a separate index of the public acts in force and omitted, together with a reference to the years when they were severally passed. And when the work shall be so prepared for the press and approved by the Legislature, they shall secure the copy right thereof for the benefit of the State.

IV. And be it further enacted, That the said commissioners shall be allowed the term of two years to complete the duties assigned to them in and by this act; and that in the execution of those duties they shall have free access to any public records or papers of this State, and be permitted to examine the same without fee or reward.

V. And be it further enacted, That the said commissioners shall be, and they are hereby allowed the sum of three thousand dollars for the services hereby required of them, and the Legislature shall by law make provision for further payment if they shall be deemed entitled thereto.

VI. And be it further enacted, That the persons appointed under the provisions of this act, shall, before entering on the discharge of their duties, take the following oath, to be administered by the Governor for the time being: I do solemnly and sincerely swear that I will faithfully and truly digest, revise and consolidate the laws and statutes of this State, and the laws of England applicable to this State, in the manner and form required by law, to the best of my knowledge and ability; so help me God.

CHAPTER CVIII.
1833-1834. An act to emancipate Joe, a slave. (Page 156).

Be it enacted by the General assembly of the State of North Carolina, and it is hereby enacted by the authority of the same, That Joe, a slave belonging to Sophia L. Smith, executrix of David Smith, deceased, late of Cumberland county, is hereby, with the consent and at the request of his said owner, emancipated and set free; and by the name of Joseph Hostler shall hereafter possess and exercise all the rights and privileges which are enjoyed by other free persons of color within this State: Provided, nevertheless, that before such slave shall be emancipated, the petitioner shall give bond and good security to the Governor and his successors in office, in the County Court of Cumberland county, that the said slave shall honestly and correctly demean himself as long as he shall remain in the State, and shall not become a parish charge; which bond may be sued upon in the name of the Governor for the time being, to the use of the parish and of any person injured by the malconduct of such slave.

CHAPTER CIX.
1833-1834. An act to emancipate Ned Hyman, a slave. (Page 156-157).

Be it enacted by the General Assembly of the State of North Carolina, and it is hereby enacted by the authority of the same, That Ned Hyman, a slave belonging to Elizabeth Hagans, of Martin County, is hereby, with the consent and at the request of his said owner, emancipated and set free; and by the name of Ned Hyman, shall hereafter possess and exercise all the rights and privileges which are enjoyed by other free persons of color within this State: Provided, nevertheless, that before such slave shall be emancipated, the petitioner shall give bond and good security to the Governor and his Successors in office, in the County Court of Martin county, that the said slave shall honestly and correctly demean himself as long as he shall remain in the State, and shall not become a parish charge; which bond may be sued upon in the name of the Governor for the time being, to the use of the parish and of any person injured by the malconduct of such slave.

CHAPTER CXLVIII.
1833-1834. An act to prevent the hauling of seines or obstructing passage of fish on certain days in Upper Broad creek, in Craven county. (Page 176).

Be it enacted by the General Assembly of the State of North Carolina, and it is hereby enacted by the authority of the same, That hereafter it shall not be lawful for any person, between the fifteenth day of February and the fifteenth day of May in each and every year, to haul or put in the water so as to obstruct the passage of fish any seine in Upper Broad creek, in Craven county, from Saturday evening at sunset to Monday evening sunset.

II. Be it further enacted, That any person offending against the provisions of the first section of this act, if a free person, shall forfeit and pay to any person suing for the same the sum of one hundred dollars for each and every offence, to be recovered before any tribunal having jurisdiction of the same; and be furthermore liable to indictment, and upon conviction be fined or imprisoned at the discretion of the court, the fine not to be less than twenty five dollars or more than fifty dollars, or imprisoned more than thirty days; if a slave, to receive a whipping on his or her bare back, upon conviction before any justice of the peace of Craven county, not to exceed thirty nine lashes.

****

ACTS PASSED BY THE GENERAL ASSEMBLY OF THE STATE OF NORTH CAROLINA AT THE SESSION OF 1834-1835
RALEIGH: PHILO WHITE, PRINTER TO THE STATE, 1835

CHAPTER CXV.
1834-1835. An Act to amend an act, entitled "an act to prevent the felling of timber in the run of Hogan's Creek in Caswell county," passed in the year eighteen hundred and thirty three. (Page 66).

Be it enacted by the General Assembly of the State of North Carolina, and it is hereby enacted by the authority of the same, That if any person or persons shall fell timber into, or shall otherwise obstruct the channel of Hogan's Creek in the county of Caswell, or cause it to be done, he, she or they shall be, and they are hereby declared to be guilty of a misdemeanor, by each and every such offence for which he, she or they may be indicted in the county or superior court of said county, and upon conviction shall be fined at the discretion of the court, not exceeding however, twenty dollars for each and every offence against the provisions of this act: Provided, that nothing herein contained shall be so construed as to prevent owners of land on said creek, from erecting water fences, or from building mill dams thereon; nor shall any person incur the penalty herein prescribed, who shall fell timber in, or otherwise obstruct the channel of said water course in clearing his, her or their lands, if he, she or they remove the same in ten days.

North Carolina Law

II. Be it further enacted, That if any slave or slaves shall be guilty of obstructing the channel of said creek, without the order of his or her owner or manager, he, she or they shall upon conviction thereof, before two justices of the peace in said county, be sentenced to receive a public whipping not exceeding thirty nine lashes; and the owner of such slave or slaves, shall be liable for the cost of the prosecution.

CHAPTER CXLI.
1834-1835. An Act to authorize the Commissioners of Wilmington to assess and cause to be collected, a tax on all slaves whose owners reside out of town; but permit the slaves to work in town. (Page 82).
Be it enacted by the General Assembly of the State of North Carolina, and it is hereby enacted by the authority of the same, That the commissioners of the town of Wilmington be, and they are hereby authorized and empowered to assess and cause to be levied and collected, a tax on all slaves, not exceeding four dollars each per annum, whenever the owners reside beyond the limits of said town, and permit their slaves to hire their own time, or work out in said town; under such rules, regulations and penalties, as the said commissioners may deem proper and necessary to adopt; due regard being had to the work, occupation, usefulness and character of said slaves: Provided, that said tax shall not be assessed on the slaves of persons residing in the county New Hanover, to a greater amount than are now paid by persons on the same species of property who live in town.

CHAPTER CLXVI.
1834-1835. An Act to emancipate Daniel, a slave. (Page 91).
Be it enacted by the General Assembly of the State of North Carolina, and it is hereby enacted by the authority of the same, That Daniel, a slave, the property of William Macay of Rowan County, be, and he is hereby, with the consent and at the request of his said owner, emancipated and set free; and by the name of Daniel Macay shall hereafter possess and exercise all the rights and privileges which are enjoyed by other free persons of color in this State: Provided, nevertheless, that before such slave shall be emancipated, the petitioner shall give bond and good security to the Governor and his successors in office in the county court of Rowan county, that the said slave shall honestly and correctly demean himself as

long as he shall remain in the State, and shall not become a parish charge; which bond may be sued upon in the name of the Governor, for the time being to the use of the parish, and of any person injured by the malconduct of such slave.

RESOLUTIONS
Passed by the General Assembly of 1834-35. (Pages 94-95).

The joint select committee to whom was referred that part of the Governor's message, which relates to the outrage committed on American citizens at Nassau: Report,

From a memorial addressed to the General Assembly, by John Waddell, Esq. of Wilmington, and from other papers in possession of the committee, they derive the following facts:

On the second day of February last, the Brig Ecomium, an American vessel, commanded by an American, and engaged in lawful trade between Charleston and New Orleans, sailed from the latter bound to the former place. Among other American citizens on board that vessel, was your memorialist John Waddell, Esq. who represents that he there had with him twenty two slaves, which he was removing from North Carolina to locate on a plantation on Red River, in the State of Louisiana. That about fifty six hours after the departure of said brig from Charleston, she was wrecked at midnight on the reefs of Abaco. That after having been confined for many hours to the wreck, the passengers were extricated from their perilous condition by the kind assistance of the inhabitants of Abaco. That they there procured a vessel which conveyed them and the crew of the wrecked brig to Nassau, in the British Island of New Providence. That arrived in the harbour of Nassau, they sent to the authorities of the Island for permission to land for the purpose of procuring means of subsistence, of which they were destitute. That to their astonishment such permission was denied, and they were informed that they should hold no intercourse with the shore, not even for the purpose of procuring food, and if they presumed to hold such intercourse, their vessel should be fired into by a British Sloop of War, lying in the harbour. That after having been kept for some hours in that situation, they were ordered up under the guns of the Sloop of War, where they remained for some hours as prisoners of War. That by the interposition of one of the passengers who was a British subject, they were at length permitted to land at eight o'clock at night. That early on the succeeding morning, the negroes belonging to the memorialist, and twenty

North Carolina Law

three belonging to other passengers, were taken on shore by order of the Lieutenant Governor of the Island, carried before the officer of the Customs, where they were immediately declared free, and directed to repair to the quarters of a black regiment in town, where they would be accommodated until they could obtain suitable conditions. That some days after this, when there were vessels about to sail to New Orleans, the memorialist, John Waddell, addressed a note to the Governor through the American Consul, respectfully inquiring whether there were any obstacles to his proceeding on his voyage with his property, to which the Governor replied, that if he, the memorialist, presumed to interfere with the manumitted slaves, it would be his (the Governor's) duty to hang him and all accessories.

The foregoing is a brief and simple statement of the circumstances of the outrage perpetrated upon your memorialist, and for the redress of which he prays the interposition of this General Assembly. Although it is not competent for North Carolina, consistently with her federal relations, to take into her own hands, a matter of this kind; yet the committee deem it the duty of the General Assembly, as the immediate guardians of the rights of our citizens, to take such measures for the vindication of those rights as may comport with the dignity of North Carolina, and with her relations to the General Government and her sister States.

A leading object of the States in confederating, was mutual defence against foreign aggression; and whenever the humblest is aggrieved by a power beyond the reach of the civil tribunals of the country, he has a right to appeal to the General Government, and it is the duty of that government to extend over him its protecting or avenging arm.

The committee believe that the case referred to their consideration, is one that imperiously demands the interposition of North Carolina, in the manner adverted to, and the decisive action of the General Government.

Were it not for the peculiar condition of North Carolina, in common with all the Southern States, in one particular momentous consideration, the General Assembly might be content with barely communicating with the General Government the facts herein recited, in full confidence that the justice and energy of that government, would be speedily and duly exerted in behalf of the injured memorialist.

But, under those peculiar circumstances it should not be concealed, that she feels much anxiety, and cannot but anticipate the direst calamities to herself, to the whole South, and indeed to the whole confederacy, if the Federal Government should permit so flagrant an outrage upon the peculiar rights of Southern citizens to pass unheeded.

Not many months have elapsed since events occurred in a portion of our own country, well calculated to excite, as they did, the most serious apprehensions. Happily for our common country, and her free institutions, the justice, prudence and patriotism of the great mass of society where those events transpired, triumphed over the wild fanaticism of the misguided few, and inspired the southern people with fresh confidence in the good feelings and good faith of their northern brethren. But the recent manumission of the slaves in the British West Indies, the vicinity of those islands to our coast, our frequent intercourse with them, and the outrage from that quarter which is the subject of this report, all concur in admonishing us that the situation of the southern States is perilous; that they cannot rely with security upon the imbecile or corrupt functionaries of a foreign power, but that they must look for protection to that government whose duty it is to afford it, even at the hazard of the last resort of nations. For although peace, not war, is the favorite element of this confederacy, history teaches us that peace obtained at the sacrifice of honor, or a tame submission to injury, is never permanent, unless it terminates in entire subserviency to the nation perpetrating the wrong. As much, therefore, as North Carolina would deprecate a war, especially with that nation whence are derived so many valuable principles of our free institutions, she would not hesitate to choose it, in preference to peace preserved at the expense of private rights and the national honor. But it is confidently believed that both alternatives may be avoided by prudent, yet firm and energetic conduct, on the part of the General Government, in demanding indemnity to our citizens for injuries committed by the authorities of the British Crown, and the adoption of such measures as may tend to prevent a recurrence of such injuries.after a mature consideration of all the circumstances connected with this unfortunate affair, and the consequences that may result from it, the committee recommend to the Legislature the adoptions of the following resolutions, viz:

Resolved, That the forcible detention by the authorities of the British Island of New Providence, of the property of American citizens thrown upon that island by shipwreck, was a breach of the rights of hospitality, and an infraction of the laws of nations.

Resolved, That the General Assembly of North Carolina will not recognize any distinction in principle between property in persons (as known to the Constitution of the United States) and property in things.

North Carolina Law

Resolved, That the General Assembly of North Carolina has full confidence in the good faith of the respective members of the Union, in regard to all those rights guarantied to each by the federal compact, and doubts not that the General Government, as the common agents of the States, will take such measures at the present juncture, as may be wise and expedient.

Resolved, that his Excellency the Governor be requested to transmit a copy of this report and these resolutions to the President of the United States, to the Executive of each of the States, and to the Senators and Representatives of North Carolina in the Congress of the United States.

****

PROCEEDINGS AND DEBATES OF THE CONVENTION OF NORTH CAROLINA CALLED TO AMEND THE CONSTITUTION OF THE STATE WHICH ASSEMBLED AT RALEIGH, JUNE 4, 1835 TO WHICH ARE SUBJOINED THE CONVENTION ACT AND THE AMENDMENTS TO THE CONSTITUTION TOGETHER WITH THE VOTES OF THE PEOPLE RALEIGH: PRINTED BY JOSEPH GALES & SON, 1836 PAGES 403-425

APPENDIX

AN ACT

Concerning a convention to amend *the Constitution of the State*

Whereas the General Assembly of North Carolina have reason to believe that a large portion, if not a majority, of the free men of the State, are anxious to amend the Constitution thereof, in certain particulars, hereinafter specified; and whereas the General Assembly disclaim all right and power in themselves to alter the fundamental law, they consider it their duty to adopt measures for ascertaining the will of their constituents, and to provide the means for carrying that will into effect, when ascertained; therefore

Be it enacted by the General Assembly of the State of North Carolina, and it is hereby enacted by the authority of the same, That the Court of Pleas and Quarter Sessions of each and every county in the State, at the first term that shall be held after the first day of January, 1835, shall appoint two inspectors to superintend the polls to be opened at each and every election precinct in said counties, for ascertaining by ballot, the will of the freemen of North Carolina relative to the meeting of a State Convention. And if any Court or Courts should fail to make such appointments, or if any inspector so appointed shall fail to act, it shall be the duty of the Sheriff, or the person acting as his deputy on such occasion, with the advice of one justice of the peace, or, if none be present, with the advice of three freeholders, to appoint an inspector or inspectors in the place of him or them who failed to act, which inspectors, when duly sworn by some justice of the peace, or freeholder, to perform the duties of the place with fidelity, shall have the same authority as if appointed by the Court.

II. *Be it further enacted,* That it shall be the duty of the Sheriffs of the respective counties in this State, to open polls at the several election precincts in said counties, on Wednesday and Thursday the first and second of April next, when and where all persons qualified by the Constitution to vote for members of the House of Commons, may vote for, or against a State Convention; those who wish a Convention, voting with a printed or written ticket, "Convention," and those who do not want a Convention, voting in the same way, "No Convention," or "Against Convention."

III. *Be it further enacted,* That it shall be the duty of the Sheriffs to make out duplicate statements of their polls in their respective counties, sworn to before the clerk of the county court, one copy of which shall be deposited in the said clerk's office, and the other copy transmitted to the Governor of the State, at Raleigh, immediately after the election.

IV. *Be it further enacted,* That it shall be the duty of the Governor, as soon as he shall have received the returns of the Sheriffs, in the presence of the Secretary of State, Public Treasurer and Comptroller, to compare the number of votes for and against a Convention; and if it shall appear that a majority of the votes polled are in favor of it, he shall forthwith publish a proclamation of the fact in such of the newspapers as he may think proper; and shall issue a writ of election to every Sheriff of the State, requiring him to open polls for the election of delegates in the Convention, at the same places, and under the same rules, as are prescribed for holding other State elections, and at such time as the Governor may designate.

V. *Be it further enacted,* That the same persons who were appointed to hold the polls in taking the vote on Convention, shall hold them for the election of delegates; provided, that if any of such inspectors shall fail to attend or act, the Sheriffs and their deputies shall supply their places in the manner herein before pointed out.

VI. *Be it further enacted,* That the several county courts shall allow the Sheriffs the same compensation for holding said elections, that they usually allow for holding other State elections. And if any Sheriff or other officer appointed to hold said elections, shall fail to comply with the requisitions of this act, he shall be liable to a fine of one thousand dollars, recoverable before any competent jurisdiction, to the use of the county whose officer he is; and it shall be the duty of the county solicitors to prosecute such suits.

VII. *Be it further enacted,* That all persons qualified to vote for members of the House of Commons, under the present Constitution, shall be entitled to vote for members to said Convention; and all free white men, of the age of twenty one years, who shall have been resident in the State one year previous to, and shall continue to be so resident at the time of election, shall be eligible to a seat in said Convention: Provided, he possess the freehold required of a member of the House of Commons under the present Constitution.

VIII. *Be it further enacted,* That each county in this State shall be entitled to elect two delegates to said Convention, and no more.

IX. *Be it further enacted,* That if any vacancy shall occur in any county delegation, by death or otherwise, the Governor shall forthwith issue a writ to supply the vacancy. And the delegates shall convene in or near the City of Raleigh, on the first Thursday in June next; and provided that a quorum does not attend on that day, the delegates may adjourn from day to day until a quorum is present; and a majority of delegates elected shall constitute a quorum to do business.

X. *Be it further enacted,* That no delegate elect shall be permitted to take his seat in Convention, until he shall have taken and subscribed the following oath or affirmation: "I, A.B. do solemnly swear, (or affirm, as the case may be,) that I will not, either directly or indirectly, evade or disregard the duties enjoined, or the limits fixed to this Convention by the people of North Carolina, as set forth in the Act of the General Assembly, passed in 1834, entitled "An Act concerning a Convention to amend the Constitution of the State of North Carolina," which Act was ratified by the people. So help me God!"

XI. *Be it further enacted*, That the public Treasurer be, and he is hereby authorized to pay, upon the warrant of the Governor, such sums of money as may be necessary for the contingent charges of the Convention, one dollar and fifty cents per day, during his attendance thereon, and five cents for every mile he may travel to and from the Convention.

XII. *Be it further enacted*, That it shall be the duty of the Governor, immediately after the ratification of this Act, to transmit a copy to each county court clerk in the State, and cause it to be published until the meeting of the Convention, in the newspapers of the State.

XIII. *Be it further enacted*, That the following propositions shall be submitted to the people for their assent or dissent to the same; the former of which shall be understood as expressed by the votes for "Convention," and the latter by the votes "No Convention," or "Against Convention," at the time and in the mode herein before provided, to wit: That the said Convention, when a quorum of the delegates who shall have been elected and assembled, shall frame and devise amendments to the Constitution of this State, so as to reduce the number of members in the Senate to not less than thirty four, nor more than fifty, to be elected by districts; which districts shall, be laid off at convenient and prescribed periods by counties, in proportion to the public taxes paid into the Treasury of the State by the citizens thereof: *Provided*, that no county shall be divided in the formation of a Senatorial district. And when there are one or more counties having an excess of taxation, above the ratio required to form a Senatorial district, adjoining a county or counties deficient in such ratio, the excess or excesses aforesaid shall be added to the taxation of the county or counties deficient; and if, with such addition, the county or counties receiving it shall have the requisite ratio, such county and counties each shall constitute a Senatorial district. **2.** That the said Convention shall frame and devise a further amendment to the said Constitution, whereby to reduce the number of members in the House of Commons to not less than ninety, nor more than one hundred and twenty, exclusive of borough members, which the Convention shall have the discretion to exclude in whole or in part, and the residue to be elected by counties or districts, or both, according to their federal population; i.e. according to their respective numbers, which shall be determined by adding to the whole number of free persons, including those bound to serve for a term of years, and excluding Indians not taxed, three fifths of all other persons, and the enumeration to be made at convenient and prescribed periods; but each county shall have at least one member in the House of Commons, although it may not contain the requisite ratio of population. 3. That the said Convention shall also frame and devise amendments to said Constitution, whereby it shall be made necessary for persons voting for a Senator, and persons eligible to the Senate, to possess the same residence and freehold qualification respectively in the Senatorial district, as is now required in the county: *Provided*, that they shall not in any manner disqualify any of the free white men of this State from voting for members in the House of Commons who are qualified to vote under the existing Constitution of this State. 4. That said Convention may also consider of, and in their discretion propose the following other amendments to the said Constitution, or any of them to wit: So as,

    1st. To abrogate or restrict the right of free negroes or mulattoes to vote for members of the Senate or House of Commons. 2nd. To disqualify members of the Assembly and officers of the State, or those who hold places of trust under the authority of this State, from being or continuing such, while they hold any other office or appointment under the Government of this State or of the United States, or any other Government whatsoever. **3d. To provide that capitation tax on slaves and free white polls shall be equal throughout the State. 4th.** To provide for some mode of appointing and removing from office militia officers and justices of the peace, different from that which is now practised. **5th.** To compel the members of the General Assembly to vote viva voce in the election of officers whose appointment is conferred on that body. **6th.** To amend the thirty second article of the Constitution of the State. **7th.** To provide for supplying vacancies in the General Assembly of this State, when such vacancies occur by resignation or death, or otherwise, before the meeting of the General Assembly. **8th.** To provide for biennial meetings, instead of annual meetings of the General Assembly; and if they shall determine on biennial sessions, then they may alter the Constitution in such parts of it as require the annual election of members of Assembly and officers of State, and the triennial election of Secretary of State, and provide for their election every two years. **9th.** To provide for the election of Governor of the State by the qualified voters for the members of the House of Commons, and to prescribe the term for which the Governor shall be elected, and the number of terms during which he shall be eligible. And the said Convention shall adopt ordinances for carrying into effect the amendments which shall be made, and shall submit such amendments to the determination of all the qualified voters of the State; but they shall not alter any other Article of the Constitution or Bill of Rights, nor propose any amendments to the same, except those which are herein before enumerated.

XIV. *Be it further enacted,* That if a majority of voters at the election first directed to be held by this Act, shall be found "for Convention," it shall be considered and understood that the people, by their vote as aforesaid, have conferred on the delegates to said Convention the power and authority to make alterations and amendments in the existing Constitution of the State, in the particulars herein enumerated, or any of them, but in no others.

XV. *Be it further enacted,* That the said Convention, after having adopted amendments to the Constitution, in any or all of said particulars, shall prescribe some mode for the ratification of the same by the people or their representatives; and shall rescribe all necessary ordinances and regulations for the purpose of giving full operation and effect to the Constitution as altered and amended.

XVI. *Be it further enacted,* That the Convention shall provide in what manner amendments shall in future be made to the Constitution of the State.

AN ACT

Supplemental to an Act, passed at the present Session, entitled "An Act concerning a Convention to amend the Constitution of the State of North Carolina.

Be it enacted by the General Assembly of the State of North Carolina, and it is hereby enacted by the authority of the same, That the following propositions shall be submitted to the people for their assent or dissent, in the same manner, and under the same forms, regulations and restrictions as were prescribed and adopted in an Act, passed at the present Session, entitled "An Act concerning a Convention to amend the Constitution of the State of North Carolina," that the said Convention may, in their discretion, devise and propose the following Amendments to the said Constitution, or any of them, so as -- **1.** To provide that the Attorney General shall be elected for a term of years. **2.** To provide a tribunal whereby the Judges of the Supreme and Superior Courts, and other Officers of the State, may be impeached and tried for corruption and mal-practices in office. **3.** To provide, that upon conviction of any Justice of the Peace of any infamous crime, or of corruption and mal-practice in office, his commission shall be vacated, and said Justice rendered forever disqualified from holding such appointment. **4.** To provide for the removal of any of the Judges of the Supreme or Superior Courts in consequence of mental or physical inability, upon a concurrent resolution of two thirds of both branches of the Legislature. **5.** To provide that the salaries of the Judges shall not be diminished during their continuance in office. **6.** And to provide against unnecessary private legislation. **7.** To provide that no Judge of the Supreme or Superior Courts shall, whilst retaining their Judicial office, be eligible to any other, except to the Supreme Court Bench.

II. *And be it further enacted*, That should the people decide in favor of a call of a Convention, as is provided for in the before referred to Act, the said Convention is hereby authorised and empowered to consider of, and, in their discretion, propose the above additional amendments to the said Constitution, or any of them.

CONSTITUTION OF NORTH CAROLINA

ADOPTED DECEMBER 17, 1776:

And the Amendments made thereto by the Convention which assembled at Raleigh, June 4, 1835

DECLARATION OF RIGHTS

MADE BY THE

Representatives of the Freemen of the State of North Carolina

Section 1. That all political power is vested in, and derived from the people only.

Sec. 2. That the people of this State ought to have the sole and exclusive right of regulating the internal government and police thereof.

Sec. 3. That no man, or set of men, are entitled to exclusive or separate emoluments or privileges from the community, but in consideration of public services.

Sec. 4. That the Legislative, Executive, and Supreme Judicial powers of Government, ought to be forever separate and distinct from each other.

Sec. 5. That all power of suspending laws, or the execution of laws, by any authority, without consent of the representatives of the people, is injurious to their rights, and ought not to be exercised.

Sec. 6. That elections of Members to serve as Representatives in General Assembly, ought to be free.

Sec. 7. That in all criminal prosecutions, every man has a right to be informed of the accusation against him, and to confront the accusers and witnesses with other testimony, and shall not be compelled to give evidence against himself.

Sec. 8. That no freeman shall be put to answer any criminal charge, but by indictment, presentment, or impeachment.

Sec. 9. That no freeman shall be convicted of any crime, but by the unanimous verdict of a jury, of good and lawful men, in open court, as heretofore used.

Sec. 10. That excessive bail should not be required, nor excessive fines imposed, nor cruel or unusual punishments inflicted.

Sec. 11. That general warrants, whereby any officer or messenger may be commanded to search suspected places, without evidence of the fact committed, or to seize any person or persons not named, whose offence is not particularly described and supported by evidence, are dangerous to liberty, and ought not to be granted.

Sec. 12. That no freeman ought to be taken, imprisoned or disseized of his freehold, liberties, or privileges, or outlawed or exiled, or in any manner destroyed or deprived of his life, liberty or property, but by the law of the land.

Sec. 13. That every freeman restrained of his liberty, is entitled to a remedy to enquire into the lawfulness thereof, and to remove the same if unlawful, and that such remedy ought not to be denied or delayed.

Sec. 14. That in all controversies at law respecting property, the ancient mode of trial by jury, is one of the best securities of the rights of the people, and ought to remain sacred and inviolable.

Sec. 15. That the freedom of the Press is one of the great bulwarks of liberty, and therefore, ought never to be restrained.

Sec. 16. That the people of this State ought not to be taxed or made subject to the payment of any impost or duty without the consent of themselves or their Representatives in General Assembly, freely given.

Sec. 17. That the people have a right to bear arms for the defence of the State; and, as standing armies in time of peace, are dangerous to liberty, they ought not to be kept up; and that the Military should be kept under strict subordination to, and governed by, the Civil power.

Sec. 18. That the people have a right to assemble together, to consult for their common good, to instruct their Representatives, and to apply to the Legislature, for the redress of grievances.

Sec. 19. That all men have a natural and inalienable right to worship Almighty God according to the dictates of their own consciences.

Sec. 20. That for redress of grievances, and for amending and strengthening the laws, elections ought to be often held.

Sec. 21. That a frequent recurrence to fundamental principles is absolutely necessary to preserve the blessings of liberty.

Sec. 22. That no hereditary emoluments, privileges or honors, ought to be granted or conferred in this State.

Sec. 23. That the perpetuities and monopolies are contrary to the genius of a free State, and ought not to be allowed.

Sec. 24. That retrospective laws, punishing facts committed before the existence of such laws, and by them only declared criminal, are oppressive, unjust and incompatible with liberty, wherefore, no *ex post facto* law ought to be made.

Sec. 25. The property of the soil in a free government, being one of the essential rights of the collective body of the people, it is necessary, in order to avoid future disputes, that the limits of the State should be ascertained with precision; and as the former temporary line between *North* and *South Carolina* was confirmed and extended by Commissioners appointed by the Legislatures of the two States, agreeable to the order of the late King *George* the Second, in Council, that line, and that only, should be esteemed the Southern boundary of this State, as follows: *that is to say*, beginning on the sea side, at a Cedar stake, at or near the mouth of *Little River*, being the southern extremity of *Brunswick* county, and running from thence, a north west course through the boundary house, which stands in thirty three degrees fifty six minutes, to thirty five degrees north latitude; and from thence a west course, so far as is mentioned in the Charter of King *Charles* the Second, to the late proprietors of *Carolina*. Therefore, all the territories, seas, waters and harbors, with their appurtenances, lying between the line above described, and the southern line of the State of *Virginia*, which begins on the sea shore in thirty six degrees thirty minutes north latitude, and from thence runs west, agreeable to the said Charter of King *Charles*, are the right and property of the people of this State, to be held by them in sovereignty, any partial line without the consent of the Legislature of this State, at any time thereafter directed or laid out, in any wise notwithstanding. *Provided always*, That this declaration of right shall not prejudge any nation or nations of *Indians* from enjoying such hunting grounds, as may have been, or hereafter shall be secured to them by any former or future Legislature of this State. *And provided also*, That it shall not be construed so as to prevent the establishment of one or more Governments westward of this State, by consent of the Legislature. *And provided further*, That nothing herein contained, shall affect the titles or possessions of individuals, holding or claiming under the laws heretofore in force, or grants heretofore made by the late King *George* the Third, or his predecessors, or the late Lords Proprietors or any of them.

December the seventeenth day Anno}
Dom. one thousand, seven hundred } R. CASWELL, *Pres.*
and seventy-six, read the third time }
and ratified in open Congress }

James Green, Jun. *Secretary.*

CONSTITUTION OF NORTH CAROLINA

Those Sections to which material Amendments are made, are printed in *Italics*.

The Constitution or Form of Government, agreed to and resolved upon, by the Representatives of the Freemen of the State of North Carolina, elected and chosen for that particular purpose, in Congress assembled, at Halifax, the eighteenth day of December, in the year of our Lord, one thousand seven hundred and seventy six.

Whereas allegiance and protection are in their nature reciprocal, and the one should of right be refused when the other is withdrawn: And whereas *George* the Third, King of *Great Brittain*, and late Sovereign of the *British American* Colonies, hath not only withdrawn from them his protection, but by an Act of the *British* Legislature, declared the inhabitants of these States out of the protection of the *British* Crown, and all their property found upon the high seas liable to be seized and confiscated to the uses mentioned in the said Act. And the said *George* the Third has also sent fleets and armies to prosecute a cruel war against them, for the purpose of reducing the inhabitants of the said Colonies to a state of abject slavery. In consequence whereof, all Government under the said King within the said Colonies, hath ceased, and a total dissolution of Government in many of them hath taken place. And whereas the Continental Congress having considered the premises, and other previous violations of the rights of the good People of *America*, have therefore declared that the Thirteen United Colonies are, of right, wholly absolved from all allegiance to the *British* Crown, or any other foreign jurisdiction whatsoever, and that the said Colonies now are and forever shall be, free and independent States: Wherefore, in our present state, in order to prevent anarchy and confusion, it becomes necessary that a Government should be established in this State: Therefore, we, the Representatives of the Freemen of *North Carolina*, chosen and assembled in Congress for the express purpose of framing a Constitution, under the authority of the People, most conducive to their happiness and prosperity, do declare that a Government for this State shall be established in manner and form following, to wit:

    Section the first. -- That the Legislative authority shall be vested in two distinct branches, both dependent on the People, to wit: a Senate and House of Commons.

    Sec. 2. That the Senate shall be composed of Representatives *annually* chosen by ballot, one from each *County* in this State.

    Sec. 3. That the House of Commons shall be composed of Representatives *annually chosen by ballot, two for each County, and one for each of the Towns of Edenton, Newbern, Wilmington, Salisbury, Hillsborough and Halifax.*

    Sec. 4. That the Senate and House of Commons, assembled for the purpose of Legislation, shall be dominated the General Assembly.

Sec. 5. That each member of the Senate shall have usually resided in the *County* in which he is chosen, for one year immediately preceding his election; and for the same time shall have possessed, and continue to possess, in the *County* which he represents, not less than three hundred acres of land in fee.

Sec. 6. That each member of the House of Commons shall have usually resided in the county in which he is chosen, for one year immediately preceding his election, and for six months shall have possessed, and continue to possess, in the County which he represents, not less than one hundred acres of land in fee, or for the term of his own life.

Sec. 7. That all *freemen* of the age of twenty one years, who have been inhabitants of any one *County* within the State twelve months immediately preceding the day of any election, and possessed of a freehold within the same *County*, of fifty acres of land for six months next before and at the day of election, shall be entitled to vote for a member of the Senate.

Sec. 8. That all *freemen* of the age of twenty one years, who have been inhabitants of any *County* within this State twelve months immediately preceding the day of any election, and shall have paid public taxes, shall be entitled to vote for members of the House of Commons for the county in which he resides.

Sec. 9. That all persons possessed of a freehold in any Town in this State, having a right of representation, and also all freemen who have been inhabitants of any such town twelve months next before and at the day of election, and shall have paid public taxes, shall be entitled to vote for a member to represent such Town in the House of Commons. Provided always, That this section shall not entitle any inhabitant of such Town to vote for members of the House of Commons for the county in which he may reside, nor any freeholder in such county, who resides without or beyond the limits of such town, to vote for a member for said Town.

Sec. 10. That the Senate and House of Commons, when met, shall each have power to choose a Speaker and other their officers, be judges of the qualifications and elections of their members, sit upon their own adjournment from day to day, and prepare bills to be passed into laws. The two Houses shall direct writs of elections for supplying intermediate vacancies, and shall also jointly, by ballot, adjourn themselves to any future day and place.

Sec. 11. That all bills shall be read three times in each House before they pass into laws, and be signed by the Speaker of both Houses.

Sec. **12.** That every person that shall be chosen a member of the Senate or House of Commons, or appointed to any office or place of trust, before taking his seat, or entering upon the execution of his office, shall take an oath to the State; and all officers shall also take an oath of office.

Sec. **13.** That the General Assembly shall, by joint ballot of both Houses, appoint Judges of the Supreme Courts of Law and Equity, Judges of Admiralty, and *Attorney General*, who shall be commissioned by the Governor, and hold their offices during good behaviour.

Sec. **14.** *That the Senate and House of Commons shall have power to appoint the Generals and Field Officers of the Militia, and all Officers of the Regular Army of this State.*

Sec. **15.** *That the Senate and House of Commons jointly, at their first meeting after each annual election, shall by ballot elect a Governor for one year, who shall not be eligible to that office longer than three years in six successive years*: That no person under thirty years of age, and who has not been a resident in this State above five years, and having in the State a freehold in lands and tenements above the value of one thousand pounds, shall be eligible as Governor.

Sec. **16.** That the Senate and House of Commons jointly, at their first meeting after each *annual* election, shall by ballot elect seven persons to be a Council of State for *one year*, who shall advise the Governor in the execution of his office; and that four members shall be a quorum; their advice and proceedings shall be entered in a Journal to be kept for that purpose only, and signed by the members present; to any part of which any member present may enter his dissent; and such Journal shall be laid before the General Assembly when called for by them.

Sec. **17.** That there shall be a Seal of this State, which shall be kept by the Governor, and used by him as occasion may require, and shall be called the Great Seal of the State of North Carolina, and be affixed to all Grants and Commissions.

Sec. **18.** That the Governor for the time being, shall be Captain General and Commander in Chief of the Militia; and in the recess of the General Assembly, shall have power, by and with the advice of the Council of State, to embody the Militia for the public safety.

Sec. **19.** That the Governor for the time being, shall have power to draw for and supply such sums of money as shall be voted by the General Assembly for the contingencies of Government, and be accountable to them for the same; he also may, by and with the advice of the Council of State, lay embargoes, or prohibit the exportation of any commodity, for any term not exceeding thirty days at any one time, in the recess of the General Assembly, and shall have the power of granting pardons and reprieves, except where the prosecution shall be carried on by the General Assembly, or the law shall otherwise direct; in which case, he may, in the recess, grant a reprieve until the next sitting of the General Assembly; and may exercise all the other Executive powers of Government, limited and restrained as by this Constitution is mentioned, and according to the laws of the State; and on his death, inability, or absence from the State, the Speaker of the Senate for the time being, and in case of his death, inability, or absence from the State, the Speaker of the House of Commons shall exercise the powers of the Governor, after such death, or during such absence or inability of the Governor or Speaker of the Senate, *or until a new nomination is made by the General Assembly.*

Sec. **20.** That in every case where any officer, the right of whose appointment is, by this Constitution vested in the General Assembly, shall, during their recess, die, or his office by other means become vacant, the Governor shall have power, with the advice of the Council of State, to fill up such vacancy by granting a temporary commission, which shall expire at the end of the next session of the General Assembly.

Sec. **21.** That the Governor, Judges of the Supreme Courts of Law and Equity, Judges of Admiralty and Attorney General, shall have adequate salaries during their continuance in office.

Sec. **22.** That the General Assembly shall, by joint ballot of both Houses, *annually* appoint a Treasurer or Treasurers for this State.

Sec. **23.** That the Governor and other officers offending against the State, by violating any part of this Constitution, mal-administration or corruption, may be prosecuted on the impeachment of the General Assembly, presentment of the Grand Jury of any Court of Supreme jurisdiction in this State.

Sec. **24.** That the General Assembly shall, by joint ballot of both Houses, *triennially* appoint a Secretary for this State.

Sec. **25.** That no persons who heretofore have been or hereafter may be, receivers of public monies, shall have a seat in either House of General Assembly, or be eligible to any office in this State, until such person shall have fully accounted for and paid into the Treasury, all sums for which they may be accountable and liable.

Sec. **26.** That no Treasurer shall have a seat in either the Senate, House of Commons, or Council of State, during his continuance in that office, or before he shall have finally settled his accounts with the public, for all monies which may be in his hands, at the expiration of his office, belonging to the State, and hath paid the same into the hands of the succeeding Treasurer.

Sec. **27.** That no Officer in the Regular Army or Navy, in the service and pay of the United States, of this or any other State, or any contractor or agent for supplying such Army or Navy with clothing or provisions, shall have a seat in either the Senate, House of Commons, or Council of State, or be eligible thereto; and any member of the Senate, House of Commons, or Council of State, being appointed to and accepting of such office, shall thereby vacate his seat.

Sec. **28.** That no member of the Council of State shall have a seat either in the Senate or House of Commons.

Sec. **29.** That no Judge of the Supreme Court of Law or Equity, or Judge of Admiralty, shall have a seat in the Senate, House of Commons, or Council of State.

Sec. **30.** That no Secretary of this State, Attorney General or Clerk of any Court of Record, shall have a seat in the Senate, House of Commons, or Council of State.

Sec. **31.** That no Clergyman, or Preacher of the Gospel, of any denomination, shall be capable of being a member of either the Senate, House of Commons, or Council of State, while he continues in the exercise of the Pastoral function.

Sec. **32.** That no person who shall deny the being of God, or the truth of the *Protestant* Religion, or the divine authority either of the Old or New Testament, or who shall hold Religious principles incompatible with the freedom and safety of the State, shall be capable of holding any office or place of trust or profit in the Civil department within this State.

Sec. **33.** That the Justices of the Peace, within the respective counties in this State, shall in future be recommended to the Governor for the time being by the Representatives in General Assembly, and the Governor shall commission them accordingly: And the Justices, when so commissioned, shall hold their offices during good behaviour, and shall not be removed from office by the General Assembly, unless for misbehaviour, absence or inability.

Sec. **34.** That there shall be no establishment of any one Religious Church or denomination in this State in preference to any other; neither shall any person, on any pretence whatsoever, be compelled to attend any place of worship, contrary to his own faith or judgment; nor be obliged to pay for the purchase of any glebe, or the building of any house of worship, or for the maintenance of any minister or ministry, contrary to what he believes right, or has voluntarily and personally engaged to perform; but all persons shall be at liberty to exercise their own mode of worship: *Provided*, that nothing herein contained shall be construed to exempt preachers of treasonable or seditious discourses from legal trial and punishment.

Sec. 35. That no person in the State shall hold more than one lucrative office at any one time. *Provided*, That no appointment in the Militia or to the office of a Justice of the Peace, shall be considered as a lucrative office.

Sec. 36. That all Commissions and Grants shall run in the name of the State of North Carolina and bear test and be signed by the Governor. All writs shall run in the same manner, and bear test and be signed by the Clerks of the respective Courts. Indictments shall conclude, against the peace and dignity of the State.

Sec. 37. That the Delegates for this State to the Continental Congress, while necessary, shall be chosen annually by the General Assembly, by ballot, but may be superseded in the mean time, in the same manner: and no person shall be elected to serve in that capacity for more than three years successively.

Sec. 38. That there shall be a Sheriff, Coroner or Coroners, and Constables, in each county within this State.

Sec. 39. That the person of a debtor, where there is not a strong presumption of fraud, shall not be continued in prison after delivering up, *bona fide*, all his estate, real and personal, for the use of his creditors, in such manner as shall be hereafter regulated by law. All prisoners shall be bailable by sufficient sureties, unless for capital offences, when proof is evident, or presumption great.

Sec. 40. That every foreigner, who comes to settle in this State, having first taken an oath of allegiance to the same, may purchase, or by other just means acquire, hold and transfer land or other real estate; and after one year's residence, shall be deemed a free citizen.

Sec. 41. That a school or schools shall be established by the Legislature for the convenient instruction of youth, with such salaries to the masters, paid by the public, as may enable them to instruct at low prices; and all useful learning shall be duly encouraged and promoted in one or more Universities.

Sec. 42. That no purchase of lands shall be made of the **Indian Natives**, but on behalf of the public, by authority of the General Assembly.

Sec. **43.** That the future Legislature of this State shall regulate entails in such a manner as to prevent perpetuities.

Sec. **44.** That the declaration of rights is hereby declared to be part of the Constitution of this State, and ought never to be violated on any pretence whatever.

Sec. **45.** That any member of either house of the General assembly shall have liberty to dissent from and protest against any act or resolve which he may think injurious to the public, or any individual, and have the reasons of his dissent entered on the Journals.

Sec. **46.** That neither House of the General Assembly shall proceed upon public business, unless a majority of all the members of such House are actually present; and that upon a motion made and seconded, the Yeas and Nays upon any question shall be taken and entered on the Journals; and that the Journals of the Proceedings of both Houses of the General Assembly, shall be printed and made public, immediately after their adjournment.

This Constitution is not intended to preclude the present Congress from making a temporary provision for the well ordering of this State, until the General Assembly shall establish Government agreeable to the mode herein before prescribed.

December the eighteenth, one thousand seven hundred and seventy-six, read the third time and ratified in open Congress   } R. CASWELL, *President*

James Green, Jun. *Secretary*

AMENDMENTS TO THE CONSTITUTION, AS RATIFIED BY THE PEOPLE

Whereas the General Assembly of North Carolina, by an Act passed the sixth day of January, one thousand eight hundred and thirty five, entitled "An Act concerning a Convention to Amend the Constitution of the State," and by an Act, supplemental thereto, passed on the eighth day of January, one thousand eight hundred and thirty five, did direct that the polls should be opened in every election precinct throughout the State, for the purpose of ascertaining whether it was the will of the freemen of North

Carolina that there should be a Convention of Delegates, to consider of certain Amendments proposed to be made in the Constitution of said State; and did further direct, that if a majority of all the votes polled by the freemen of North Carolina should be in favor of holding such Convention, the Governor should, by Proclamation, announce the fact, and thereupon the freemen aforesaid should elect Delegates to meet in Convention at the City of Raleigh, on the first Thursday in June, one thousand eight hundred and thirty five, to consider of the said Amendments:

And whereas a majority of the freemen of North Carolina did, by their votes at the polls so opened, declare their will that a Convention should be had to consider of the Amendments proposed, and the Governor did, by Proclamation, announce the fact that their will had been so declared, and an election for Delegates to meet in Convention as aforesaid, was accordingly had. Now, therefore, we, The Delegates of the good People of North Carolina, having assembled in Convention, at the City of Raleigh, on the first Thursday in June, one thousand eight hundred and thirty five, and having continued in session from day to day, until the eleventh of July, one thousand eight hundred and thirty five, for the more deliberate consideration of said Amendments, do now submit to the determination of all the qualified voters of the State, the following amendments in the Constitution thereof, that is to say:

ARTICLE I.
SECTION 1.

1. The Senate of this State shall consist of fifty Representatives, biennially chosen by ballot, and to be elected by districts; which districts shall be laid off by the General Assembly, at its first session after the year one thousand eight hundred and forty one; and afterwards, at its first session after the year one thousand eight hundred and fifty one; and then every twenty years thereafter, in proportion to the public taxes paid into the Treasury of the State by the citizens thereof; and the average of the public taxes paid by each county into the Treasury of the State, for the five years preceding the laying off of the districts, shall be considered as its proportion of the public taxes, and constitute the basis of apportionment: *Provided*, that no county shall be divided in the formation of a Senatorial district. And when there are one or more counties, having an excess of taxation above the ratio to form a Senatorial district, adjoining a county or counties deficient in such ratio, the excess or excesses aforesaid shall be added to the taxation of the county or counties deficient; and if, with such

addition, the county or counties receiving it shall have the requisite ratio, such county and counties each shall constitute a Senatorial district.

2. The House of Commons shall be composed of one hundred and twenty Representatives, biennially chosen by ballot, to be elected by counties according to their federal population, that is, according to their respective numbers, which shall be determined by adding to the whole number of free persons, including to those bound to service for a term of years, and excluding Indians not taxed, three fifths of all other persons; and each county shall have at least one member in the House of Commons, although it may not contain the requisite ratio of population.

3. This apportionment shall be made by the General Assembly, at the respective times and periods when the districts for the Senate are herein before directed to be laid off; and the said apportionment shall be made according to an enumeration to be ordered by the General Assembly, or according to the Census which may be taken by order of Congress, next preceding the period of making such apportionment.

4. In making the apportionment in the House of Commons, the ratio of representation shall be ascertained by dividing the amount of Federal population of the State, after deducting that comprehended within those counties which do not severally contain the one hundred and twentieth part of the entire Federal population aforesaid, by the number of Representatives less than the number assigned to the said counties. To each county containing the said ratio, and not twice the said ratio, there shall be assigned one Representative; to each county containing twice, but not three times the said ratio, there shall be assigned two Representatives, and so on progressively, and then the remaining Representatives shall be assigned severally to the counties having the largest fractions.

SECTION 2.

1. Until the first Session of the General Assembly which shall be had after the year eighteen hundred and forty one, the Senate shall be composed of members to be elected from the several districts herein after named, that is to say: the 1st district shall consist of the counties of Perquimons and Pasquotank; the 2nd district, of Camden and Currituck; the 3d. district, of Gates and Chowan; the 4th district, Washington and Tyrell; the 5th district, Northampton; the 6th district, Hertford; the 7th district, Bertie; the 8th district, Martin; the 9th district, Halifax; the 10th district, Nash; the 11th district, Wake; the 12th district, Franklin; the 13th district, Johnston; the 14th district, Warren; the 15th district, Edgecomb; the 16th

district, Wayne; the 17th district, Greene and Lenoir; the 18th district, Pitt; the 19th district, Beaufort and Hyde; the 20th district, Carteret and Jones; the 21st district, Craven; the 22d district, Chatham; the 23d district, Granville; the 24th district, Person; the 25th district, Cumberland; the 26th district, Sampson; The 27th district, New Hanover; the 28th district, Duplin; the 29th district, Onslow; the 30th district, Brunswick, Bladen and Columbus; the 31st district, Robeson and Richmond; the 32d district, Anson; the 33d district, Cabarrus; the 34th district, Moore and Montgomery; the 35th district, Caswell; the 36th district, Rockingham; the 37th district, Orange; the 38th district, Randolph; the 39th district, Guilford; the 40th district, Stokes; the 41st district, Rowan; the 42d district, Davidson; the 43d district, Surry; the 44th district, Wilkes and Ashe; the 45th district, Burke and Yancy; the 46th district, Lincoln; the 47th district, Iredell; the 48th district, Rutherford; the 49th district, Buncombe, Haywood and Macon; and the 50th district, Mecklenburg; each district to be entitled to one Senator.

2.   Until the first Session of the General Assembly after the year eighteen hundred and forty one, the House of Commons shall be composed of members elected from the counties in the following manner, viz: The counties of Lincoln and Orange shall elect four members each. The counties of Burke, Chatham, Granville, Guilford, Halifax, Iredell, Mecklenburg, Rowan, Rutherford, Surry, Stokes, and Wake, shall elect three members each. The counties of Anson, Beaufort, Bertie, Buncombe, Cumberland, Craven, Caswell, Davidson, Duplin, Edgecomb, Franklin, Johnson, Montgomery, New Hanover, Northampton, Person, Pitt, Randolph, Robeson, Richmond, Rockingham, Sampson, Warren, Wayne and Wilkes, shall elect two members each. The counties of Ashe, Bladen, Brunswick, Camden, Columbus, Chowan, Currituck, Carteret, Cabarrus, Gates, Greene, Haywood, Hertford, Hyde, Jones, Lenoir, Macon, Moore, Martin, Nash, Onslow, Pasquotank, Perquimons, Tyrell, Washington and Yancy, shall elect one member each.

SECTION 3.

1.   Each member of the Senate shall have usually resided in the district for which he is chosen for one year immediately preceding his election, and for the same time shall have possessed and continue to possess in the district which he represents not less than three hundred acres of land in fee.

North Carolina Law

2. All free men of the age of twenty one years, (except as hereinafter declared) who have been inhabitants of any one district within the State twelve months immediately preceding the day of any election, and possessed of a freehold within the same district of fifty acres of land for six months next before and at the day of election, shall be entitled to vote for a member of the Senate.

3. **No free negro, free mulatto, or free person of mixed blood, descended from negro ancestors to the fourth generation inclusive (Though one ancestor of each generation may have been a white person,) shall vote for members of the Senate or House of Commons.**

SECTION 4.

1. In the election of all officers whose appointment is conferred on the General Assembly by the Constitution, the vote shall be *viva voce*.

2. The General Assembly shall have power to pass laws regulating the mode of appointing and removing Militia officers.

3. The General Assembly shall have power to pass general laws regulating divorce and alimony, but shall not have power to grant a divorce or secure alimony in any individual case.

4. The General Assembly shall not have power to pass any private law, to alter the name of any person, or to legitimate any persons not born in lawful wedlock, or to restore the rights of citizenship any person convicted of an infamous crime; but shall have power to pass general laws regulating the same.

5. The General Assembly shall not pass any private law, unless it be made to appear that thirty days notice of application to pass such a law shall have been given, under such directions and in such manner as shall be provided by law.

6. If vacancies shall occur by death, resignation or otherwise, before the meeting of the General Assembly, writs may be issued by the Governor, under such regulations as may be prescribed by law.

7. The General Assembly shall meet biennially, and at each biennial session shall elect, by joint vote of the two Houses, a Secretary of State, Treasurer and Council of State, who shall continue in office for the term of two years.

ARTICLE II.

1. The Governor shall be chosen by the qualified voters for the members of the House of Commons, at such time and places as members of the General Assembly are elected.

2. He shall hold his office for the term of two years from the time of his installation, and until another shall be elected and qualified; but he shall not be eligible more than four years in any term of six years.

3. The returns of every election for Governor shall be sealed up and transmitted to the seat of Government, by the returning officers, directed to the Speaker of the Senate, who shall open and publish them in the presence of a majority of the members of both Houses of the General Assembly. The person having the highest number of votes, shall be Governor; but if two or more shall be equal and the highest in votes, one of them shall be chosen Governor by a joint vote of both Houses of the General Assembly.

4. Contested elections for Governor shall be determined by both Houses of the General Assembly, in such a manner as shall be prescribed by law.

5. The Governor elect shall enter on the duties of the office on the first day of January next after his election, having previously taken the oaths of office in presence of the members of both branches of the General Assembly, or before the Chief Justice of the Supreme Court, who, in case the Governor elect should be prevented from attendance before the General Assembly, by sickness or other unavoidable cause, is authorised to administer the same.

ARTICLE III.
SECTION 1.

1. The Governor, Judges of the Supreme Court, and Judges of the Superior Courts, and all other officers of this State, (except Justices of the Peace and Militia officers,) may be impeached for wilfully violating any Article of the Constitution, mal-administration or corruption.

2. Judgment, in case of Impeachment, shall not extend further than to removal from office and disqualification to hold and enjoy any office of honor, trust or profit under this State; but the party convicted, may, nevertheless, be liable to indictment, trial, judgment and punishment according to law.

3. The House of Commons shall have the sole power of impeachment. The Senate shall have the sole power to try all

impeachments; no person shall be convicted upon any impeachment, unless two thirds of the Senators present shall concur in such conviction; and before the trial of any impeachment, the members of the Senate shall take an oath or affirmation truly and impartially to try and determine the charge in question according to evidence.

SECTION 2.

1. Any Judge of the Supreme Court, or of the Superior Courts, may be removed from office for mental or physical inability, upon a concurrent resolution of two thirds of both branches of the General Assembly. The Judge, against whom the Legislature may be about to proceed, shall receive notice thereof, accompanied by a copy of the causes alleged for his removal, at least twenty days before the day on which either branch of the General Assembly shall act thereon.

2. The salaries of the Judges of the Supreme Court, or of the Superior Courts, shall not be diminished during their continuance in office.

SECTION 3.

Upon the conviction of any Justice of the Peace, of any infamous crime, or of corruption and malpractice in office, the commission of such Justice shall be thereby vacated, and he shall be forever disqualified from holding such appointment.

SECTION 4.

The General Assembly, at its first session after the year one thousand eight hundred and thirty nine, and from time to time thereafter, shall appoint an Attorney General, who shall be commissioned by the Governor, and shall hold his office for the term of four years; but if the General Assembly should hereafter extend the term during which Solicitors of the State shall hold their offices, then they shall have power to extend the term of office of the Attorney General to the same period.

ARTICLE IV.
SECTION 1.

1. No Convention of the People shall be called by the General Assembly, unless by the concurrence of two thirds of all the members of each House of the General Assembly.

2. No part of the Constitution of this State shall be altered, unless a Bill to alter the same shall have been read three times in each

North Carolina Law

House of the General Assembly, and agreed to by three fifths of the whole number of members of each House respectively; nor shall any alteration take place until the Bill so agreed to shall have been published six months previous to a new election of members to the General Assembly. If, after such publication, the alteration proposed by the preceding General Assembly, shall be agreed to in the first session thereafter by two third of the whole representation in each House of the General Assembly, after the same shall have been read three times on three several days in each House, then the said General Assembly shall prescribe a mode by which the Amendment or Amendments may be submitted to the qualified voters of the House of Commons throughout the State; and if, upon comparing the votes given in the whole State, it shall appear that a majority of the voters have approved thereof, then, and not otherwise, the same shall become a part of the Constitution.

SECTION 2.

The thirty second section of the Constitution shall be amended to read as follows: No person who shall deny the being of God, or the truth of the Christian Religion, or the divine authority of the Old or New Testament, or who shall hold religious principles incompatible with the freedom or safety of the State, shall be capable of holding any office or place of trust or profit in the civil department within this State.

SECTION 3.

1. Capitation tax shall be equal throughout the State upon all individuals subject to the same.
2. All free males over the age of twenty one years, and under the age of forty five years, and **all slaves over the age of twelve years**, and under the age of fifty years, shall be subject to Capitation tax, and no other person shall be subject to such tax; provided that nothing herein contained shall prevent exemptions of taxable polls as heretofore prescribed by law in cases of bodily infirmity.

SECTION 4.

No person who shall hold any office or place of trust or profit under the United States, or any department thereof, or under this State, or any other State or Government, shall hold or exercise any other office or place of trust or profit under the authority of this State, or be eligible to a seat in either House of the General Assembly: *Provided*, that nothing herein contained shall extend to officers in the Militia, or Justices of the Peace.

Ratified in Convention, this }
eleventh day of July, in the year } NATH'L MACON, *Prest.*
of our Lord, one thousand eight }
hundred and thirty five }
Edmund B. Freeman,
    Secretary of the Convention.
Joseph D. Ward, *Assistant Secretary.*

****

LAWS OF THE STATE OF NORTH CAROLINA
PASSED BY THE GENERAL ASSEMBLY
AT THE SESSION OF 1836-1837
RALEIGH: THOMAS J. LEMAY, PRINTER, 1837.

CHAP. VII. CHEROKEE LANDS.
1836-1837. An Act to amend an Act, entitled "an act authorising the entering of the unsurveyed lands acquired by treaty from the Cherokee Indians, A.D. 1817 and 1819, in the counties of Haywood and Macon." (Page 29).

Be it enacted by the General Assembly of the State of North Carolina, and it is hereby enacted by the authority of the same, That nothing in the aforesaid act contained shall be so construed as to authorize or allow the entry of any portion of the said lands, which were reserved or allotted to any Indian or Indians under said treaties, which the State has since acquired by purchase; and that the Secretary of State be, and he is hereby directed to issue no grant for any portion of the lands of the latter description, until the General Assembly shall otherwise order and direct.
[Ratified 10th January, 1837.].

CHAP. VIII.
1836-1837. An Act to prevent frauds on Cherokee Indians, residing in this State. (Page 30).

Be it enacted by the General Assembly of the State of North Carolina, and it is hereby enacted by the authority of the same, That all contracts and agreements of every description, made after the eighteenth

day of May one thousand eight hundred and thirty eight, with any Cherokee Indian, or any person of Cherokee Indian Blood, within the second degree, for an amount equall to ten dollars or more, shall be null and void, unless some note or memorandum thereof be made in writing and signed by such Indian or person of Indian blood, or some other person by him authorised, in the presence of two creditable witnesses, who shall also subscribe the same.
[Ratified 21st January, 1837.]

CHAP. XXXV. [Revised Statute]. Miscellaneous.
1836-1837. An Act to Reduce into one, the several acts concerning Pilots and Commissioners of Navigation. (Page 166).

Sec. 45. If any slave or slaves shall, with the consent of his or her owner, and not accompanied by a pilot, go off to any ship or vessel for the purpose of bringing such ship or vessel over any bar or inlet of this State, or shall pilot any such ship or vessel out and over any bar or inlet, the owner of such slave or slaves shall forfeit the value of such slave or slaves, to be recovered in any court having cognizance thereof, one half to the person suing for the same, the other half to the use of the county where the owner resides.

NO. IV. [Revised Statute]. Militia.
1836-1837. An Act concerning the Militia of this State. (Page 171).

Sec. 5. It shall not be lawful for any captain or other militia officer in this State, to enroll any free person of colour, except for musicians.

NO. XVIII. [Revised Statute]. Revenue.
1836-1837. An Act to provide for the collection and management of a Revenue for this State. (Page 265).

Sec. 6. An annual tax of twenty cents on each and every free male poll between the age of twenty one and forty five years, and a tax of twenty cents on each and every slave poll, of both sexes, between the ages of twelve and fifty years, shall be levied, collected, and accounted for as hereinafter provided: Provided always, that the several County Courts shall be authorised to exempt from the payment of a poll tax; such infirm free persons as they may think proper objects, and also the slaves disabled by bodily infirmities or void of reason; such incapacity to be judged of and certified by the County Court, shall not be deemed taxable property, nor given in as such by their respective owners.

Sec. 16. All persons who shall bring negro slaves from another State into this State, for sale, shall pay to the sheriff of some one county the sum of ten dollars upon each negro slave so brought; and it shall be the duty of the respective sherrifs in this State to collect the tax hereby imposed; but if the said person or persons shall produce to the sheriff of any one county the certificate of the sheriff of any other county, duly authenticated, under the seal of the clerk of the county in which such sheriff resides, that he has paid the tax hereby imposed, he or they shall be permitted to proceed without the payment of any further tax; and it shall be the duty of the sheriff of each county into which any negro slave shall be taken by any person or persons whatsoever, to seize such negro slave until the tax hereby imposed be paid, or until he or they shall produce to the sheriff an affidavit, subscribed by him or them before some justice of the peace within this State, duly authenticated by the certificate of the clerk and seal of the court of the county; setting forth that the slave or slaves so seized were not by him or them, or any other person, with his or their privity and consent, brought in evasion or illusion of the revenue laws of this State; and any person guilty of making any false affidavit for such person, shall, on conviction, be deemed guilty of wilful and corrupt perjury; and the owners and possessors of all such slaves so seized shall pay to the sheriff all expense that may accrue in consequence of seizing, keeping and feeding such slaves; and the slaves so seized may be detained by the sheriff until such payment; and in default thereof, the said sheriff may sell the same at public auction, at the court house of the county, upon twenty days' previous notice; which sale shall convey an absolute title to the purchaser.

CHAP. LX.
1836-1837. An Act to incorporate the town of Rolesville. (Pages 322-323).
Sec. 10. That no person shall be qualified to vote at the election of commissioners, who is not a white man of the full age of twenty one years, and a resident of said town at and for three months immediately preceding the election.

CHAP. LXIV. EMANCIPATION.
1836-1837. An Act to emancipate Henry, Fanny and John, the slaves and children of Miles Howard. (Page 327).

Be it enacted by the General Assembly of the State of North Carolina, and it is hereby enacted by the authority of the same, That Henry Howard, Fanny Howard and John Howard, children and slaves of Miles Howard, of Halifax county, at the special request of said Miles, be, and they are hereby emancipated and set free, and shall hereafter enjoy all the privileges of free persons of color.
[Ratified 10th December, 1836.].

CHAP. LXV.
1836-1837. An Act to emancipate Issac, a slave. (Page 328).

Be it enacted by the General Assembly of the State of North Carolina, and it is hereby enacted by the authority of the same, That Isaac, a slave, the property of Robert Belden, of the county of Cumberland, be, and he is hereby, with the consent and at the request of his said owner, emancipated and set free; and, by the name of Isaac Belden, shall hereafter possess and exercise all the rights and privileges which are enjoyed by other free persons of color in this State: Provided nevertheless, that before said slave shall be emancipated, his said master shall give bond and good security, to the Governor and his successors in office, in the county court of New Hanover county, that the said slave shall honestly and correctly demean himself as long as he shall remain in the State, and shall not become a parish charge; which bond may be sued upon, in the name of the Governor for the time being, to the use of the parish and of any person injured by the mal conduct of said slave.
(Ratified 14th December, 1836.)

CHAP. LXXIII.
1836-1837. An Act for the relief of John Timson, a native Cherokee Indian, and his family. (Page 333).

Be it enacted by the General Assembly of the State of North Carolina, and it is hereby enacted by the authority of the same, That John Timson, a native Cherokee Indian, now residing in the county of Macon, his wife Lucy, their children, John C. Timson, Henry C. Timson, Sarah Ann Eliza Timson, Margaret Jane Timson, and such other children as may hereafter be born to the said John Timson, of the body of his present wife Lucy, be, and are hereby invested with full power and authority to enter, purchase and hold land and personal property in this State, and to take the same by gift, devise or descent: Provided, that before any of the aforesaid Indians shall be allowed to acquire lands, or shall be considered and recognized as freeholders, he or she shall first take the oaths of allegiance to the State of North Carolina and the United States of America, in open court, before the Court of Pleas and Quarter Sessions of Macon County.

Sec. 2. Be it further enacted, That the said John Timson and his family aforesaid, shall be, and they are hereby allowed to prosecute and defend suits, and to give evidence, in any court of justice in this State, in all causes, whether civil or criminal, which may be pending therein, under the same rules, regulations and restrictions which now apply to white persons; any law, usage or custom to the contrary notwithstanding.
[Ratified 30th December, 1836.].

****

REVISED STATUTES OF NORTH CAROLINA
PASSED BY THE GENERAL ASSEMBLY AT THE SESSION OF 1836-7
REVISED UNDER AN ACT OF THE GENERAL ASSEMBLY, PASSED
AT THE SESSION OF 1833-4, VOLUME I.
RALEIGH: PUBLISHED BY TURNER AND HUGHES, 1837

CHAPTER XXXIV. CRIMES AND PUNISHMENT. (Pages 192-194).

9. The offence of killing a slave shall be denominated and considered homicide, and shall partake of the same degree of guilt, when accompanied with the like circumstances, that homicide now does at common law. **(1791, c. 335, s. 3. -1801, c. 585. -1817, c. 949.).**

10. Any person or persons, who shall steal or shall by violence, seduction or any other means, take or convey away any slave or slaves, the property of another, with an intention to sell or dispose of to another, or appropriate to their own use such slave or slaves, and be thereof legally convicted, shall be adjudged guilty of felony, and shall suffer death without benefit of clergy. **(1779, c. 142., s. 2.).**

11. If any person or persons shall wickedly, willingly or feloniously carry, convey or conceal any slave or slaves, the property of any citizen or citizens of this State, without the consent, in writing of the owner or owners, his, her or their guardian or guardians of such slave or slaves, previously obtained, or shall feloniously, wickedly, and willingly take, conceal, or permit or suffer the same to be done, with the intent and for the purpose of carrying and conveying such slave or slaves out of the limits of this State, or with the intent and for the purpose of enabling such slave or slaves to effect an escape out of this State, every such person or persons, so carrying, conveying and concealing, or so taking, concealing, or causing or permitting the same to be done, with the intent as aforesaid, shall be taken and deemed to be guilty of felony, and shall suffer death, without benefit of clergy. **(1832, c. 9. -1825, c.1289, s. 1. -1833, c. 18., s.1.).**

12. Any person or persons, who shall, by violence or any other means, take or convey any free negro or free negroes or persons of mixed blood, out of this State to another, with an intention to sell or dispose of such free negro, or free negroes, or persons of mixed blood, and be thereof legally convicted, shall be adjudged guilty of felony, and shall suffer death, without benefit of clergy. **(1779, c. 142, s. 2.).**

17. If any person shall knowingly bring into this State, with an intent to circulate, or knowingly circulate or publish within this State, or shall aid or abet the bringing into this State or the circulation or publication within the State, any written or printed pamphlet or paper, whether written or printed in or out of the State, the evident tendency whereof would be to excite insurrection, conspiracy or resistance in the slaves or free negroes and persons of color within the State, or which shall advise or persuade slaves or free persons of color to insurrection, conspiracy or resistance, such person so offending shall be deemed guilty of felony, and, on conviction thereof in any court having jurisdiction thereof, shall for the first offence be imprisoned not less than one year and be put in the pillory and whipped, at the discretion of the court, and for the second offence shall suffer death without benefit of clergy. **(1830, c. 5, s. 1.).**

18. If any person shall, by words, endeavor to excite in any slave or slaves, or free negro or person of color, a spirit of insurrection, conspiracy or rebellion, such person shall be deemed guilty of felony, and, on conviction thereof in any court having cognizance thereof, shall be sentenced to receive thirty nine lashes on his or her bare back and be imprisoned for one year, and for the second offence shall suffer death without benefit of clergy. (1830, c. 5., s. 2.).

CHAPTER XXXIV. CRIMES AND PUNISHMENT. (Pages 208-211).

71. Any person or persons, who shall steal or sell any free negro or free negroes or persons of mixed blood, knowing the same to be free or stolen, or shall by violence, seduction or any other means, take or convey away any free negro or free negroes or persons of mixed blood from one part of this State to another, with an intention to sell or dispose of such free negro or free negroes or persons of mixed blood, or appropriate the same to his, her or their own use, and be thereof legally convicted, shall, for every such offence, be fined not less than one hundred dollars nor more than one thousand dollars, and imprisoned not less than three months and not more than eighteen months. (1800, c. 562.).

72. If any clerk of the court of pleas and quarter sessions shall knowingly issue any license for marriage between any free negro or any free person of color and a white person, he shall be guilty of a misdemeanor, and, upon conviction before any court having jurisdiction, shall be fined and imprisoned at the discretion of the court; and any clergyman, minister of the gospel or justice of the peace, who shall knowingly marry any free negro or free person of color to a white person, shall be guilty of a misdemeanor, and, upon conviction in any court having jurisdiction, shall be fined and imprisoned at the discretion of the court. (1830, c. 4, s. 2.).

73. Any person who shall entice or persuade any slave to absent him or herself from his or her owner's service, or who shall harbor or maintain, under any pretence whatever, any runaway slave, shall, for every such offence, forfeit and pay to the owner of such slave the sum of one hundred dollars, to be recovered by action of debt, before any jurisdiction having cognizance thereof, and be further liable to the said owner in an action for damages; and such person shall also be subject to a penalty of one hundred dollars, to be recovered before any justice of the peace, by any person suing for the same, the one half to the use of the informer, the other half to the use of the wardens of the poor of the county where suit is brought. And the person committing such offence shall, moreover, be subject to indictment therefor, and, upon conviction, shall be fined at the discretion of the court not exceeding one hundred dollars, and imprisoned not exceeding six months. (1741, c. 35, s. 23. -1791, c. 335, s. 4. -1821, c. 1120. -1830, c. 8.).

74. Any free person who shall hereafter teach, or attempt to teach, any slave within this State to read or write, the use of figures excepted, or shall give or sell to such slave or slaves any books or pamphlets, shall be liable to indictment in any court of record in this State having jurisdiction thereof, and, upon conviction, shall at the discretion of the court, if a white man or woman, be fined not less than one hundred dollars nor more than two hundred dollars, or imprisoned, and if a free person of color, shall be fined, imprisoned or whipped, at the discretion of the court, not exceeding thirty nine lashes, nor less than twenty lashes. (1830, c. 6, s. 1).

75. If any person or persons shall buy of, traffic with, or receive from, any slave or slaves any cotton, tobacco, wheat, rice, oats, corn, rye, pork, bacon, beef, leather, raw hides, iron castings, farming utensils, nails, meal, flour, spirituous liquors or wine, peas, salt fish, flax, flax seed, hogs, cattle, sheep, wool, lumber, staves, tar, pitch, turpentine, fodder, shingles, hoops, white oak heading, potatoes, mutton, cotton or woolen cloth, yarn, wearing apparel, or gold or silver bullion; or if any person or persons shall sell, barter with or deliver to any slave or slaves, any goods, wares and merchandise, or other article of personal property, every person, so offending, shall, for each offence, forfeit and pay the sum of one hundred dollars, to be recovered by warrant before any justice of the peace, and applied, one half to the use of the party suing for the same, the other half to the wardens of the poor of the county: Provided, however, that it shall and may be lawful for any person or persons in the day time only, Sundays excepted, viz: between the rising of the sun and the setting thereof, to buy of, traffic with, or receive from any slave or slaves, any such article or articles, as aforesaid, for which he, she or they may have a permission in writing from his, her or their owner or manager, to dispose of the same: and further, it shall and may be lawful for any person or persons in the day time as aforesaid, to sell and deliver to any slave or slaves, any goods, wares or merchandise, or other thing, (always excepting spirituous liquors, fire arms, powder or shot, or lead, unless these articles be for the owner or employers of such slave or slaves, or by the order of the owner or person having the management of the same,) in exchange for, or payment of the money, or article or articles which the said slave or slaves may have been, by the written permission aforesaid, authorized to sell. (1826, c. 13, s. 1.- 1828, c. 32, s. 1. -1830, c. 15. -1833, c. 19.).

76. It shall not be permitted for the master or commander of any vessel to entertain any slave, negro, or mulatto on board such vessel, at any time between sunset and sunrise, nor during the Sabbath day, unless such slave, negro or mulatto as shall belong to the vessel, or shall have a pass from his, her or their master or mistress, or from some justice of the peace, expressing the time when and the business for which they go on board; and if any slave, negro or mulatto, who has not such pass, or is not stately employed on board the vessel as one of the hands, shall be found on board any vessel in any bay, harbor, creek or river within this State on the Sabbath day or in the night, between sunset and sunrise, he shall be presumed to have been disposing of stolen goods; and the master or commander of such vessel, on complaint and conviction before any two justices of the peace, shall be subjected to a fine for entertainment of such slave, negro or mulatto, of ten dollars for the first offence, and twenty dollars for every succeeding offence, to be applied to the use of the poor of the county in which conviction shall be had; but any person, dissatisfied with the judgment of the said two justices, shall have the right of appealing to the court of the county, the determination whereof shall be final, the person appealing to be subject to the same regulations as in cases of other persons appealing from the judgment of a justice. **(1787, c. 267.).**

77. The offences, mentioned in the seventy fifth section, shall moreover be indictable in the county or superior courts of law, and the defendant, on conviction, shall be fined or imprisoned at the discretion of the court; the fine however not to exceed fifty dollars, or the imprisonment three months; and if it shall appear on the trial that the defendant is a licensed retailer of spirituous liquors by the small measure, he or she shall also forfeit his or her retailing license, and shall be incapable of taking a new license for the space of two years from and after the date of his or her conviction. **(1826, c. 13, s. 2.)**

78. If any slave or slaves shall be found in any storehouse, warehouse, tippling shop, or other place fitted up for trading, unless sent by his, her or their owner, overseer or employer, after the hour of nine o'clock at night, or before daybreak in the morning, or on the Sabbath day; or if any slave or slaves shall be found at any time in any of the aforementioned places, unless sent as aforesaid, where he, she or they shall have been permitted to remain for the space of fifteen minutes, with the door of the aforementioned place closed; or if any slave or slaves shall be seen to carry into the aforementioned places any article or articles supposed for sale, and not bring the same out; or if he, she or they shall bring out of the said

places any article or articles which may have been purchased therein, this shall be taken and received as presumptive evidence against the person or persons owning or keeping the storehouse, warehouse, tippling shop, or other place fitted up for trading, of an unlawful trading with such slave or slaves; to be rebutted, however, like other presumptions, by other circumstances in favor of the accused. **(1826, c. 13, s. 6.).**

79. If any person shall fraudulently give, or cause to be given, to any slave, the property of another, a permission in writing to sell, trade or traffic in any article of personal property, without the consent or authority of the master, owner, or the person having the management of such slave, he, she or they, so offending, shall, upon conviction before any justice of the peace in the county where such offence is committed, forfeit and pay the sum of one hundred dollars, one half to the use of the person suing for the same, and the other half to the use of the wardens of the poor of said county. **(1826, c. 13, s. 3.).**

80. Either of the parties, or master of the slave, being dissatisfied with the judgment of the justice or the verdict of the jury, may pray an appeal therefrom, as in other cases: Provided, that no suit or indictment shall be prosecuted for any violation of the seventy fifth and seventy ninth sections of this act, unless such suit or indictment be commenced within twelve months after such violation. **(1826, c. 13, s. 7.).**

Chapter XXXVII. DEEDS AND CONVEYANCES. (Pages 230-231).

17. No gift hereafter to be made of any slave shall be good or available either in law or equity, unless the same shall be made in writing, signed by the donor and attested by at least one credible witness subscribing; neither shall such gift be valid unless the writing by which the title, by which any slave is transferred, shall be proved or acknowledged, as conveyances of land, and registered in the office of the public register of the county where the donee resides, within one year after the execution thereof, if the donee be in actual possession of the slave so given and transferred; but if, under any special agreement made at the time of the gift, the donor shall remain in possession of the slave so given, then the writing transferring or conveying the same slave shall be proved or acknowledged as aforesaid, and registered within the same time, in the county where the donor resides: Provided, that when any person shall have put into the actual possession of his or her child or children any slave, and the said slave shall remain in the possession of such child or children at the time of

the death of such person, he or she dying intestate, such slave shall be considered as an advancement to such child or children, and be regulated by the laws now in force relating to advancements made to children by a parent in his life time. **(1806, c. 701, s. 1 and 3.).**

18. All deeds of gift of any estate of whatever nature shall, within twelve months after the making thereof, be proved in due form and recorded, or otherwise shall be void and of no force whatever. **(1789, c. 315, s. 2).**

19. All sales of slaves shall be in writing, attested by at least one credible witness, or otherwise shall not be deemed valid; and all bills of sale of slaves shall, within twelve months after the making thereof, be proved in due form and recorded, and all bills of sale and deeds of gift not authenticated and perpetuated in manner by this act directed, shall be void and of no force whatever: Provided, that all sales of slaves, bona fide made and accompanied with the actual delivery of the slave or slaves to the purchaser, and which would be held good but for the provisions contained in this section, shall be and the same are hereby declared good and valid without any bill of sale. **(1784, c. 225, s. 7. -1789, c. 315, s. 2. -1792, c. 363, s. 1.).**

20. When any transfer or conveyance of any slave or slaves shall be in writing, such writing, after being legally proved, shall be registered in the county where the purchaser (he being in actual possession of the slave or slaves so transferred or conveyed) shall reside; but if, under any special agreement at the time of the sale, the seller shall remain in possession of the slave or slaves sold, then in writing, transferring or conveying the said slave or slaves, shall be registered in the county where the vendor lives. **(1792, c. 363, s. 2.).**

21. On all trials at law where a written transfer or conveyance of a slave or slaves, by way of gift, sale or otherwise, shall be introduced to support the title of either party, the due and fair execution of such writing shall be proved by a witness, subscribing and attesting the execution of such writing, but if such witness shall be dead or removed out of the State, then the probate and registration of such writing may be given in evidence. **(1792, c. 363, s. 3. -1806, c. 701, s. 2.).**

22. Every limitation by deed or writing of a slave or slaves, which limitation, if contained in a last will and testament, would be good and effectual as an executory devise or bequest, shall be and is hereby declared to be a good and effectual limitation in remainder of such slave or slaves, and any limitation made or reserved to the grantor, vendor or donor, in any such deed or writing of a slave or slaves, shall be good and effectual in law: Provided such limitation, had it been made to another person, would be good and effectual according to the preceding clause: Provided, also, that all such deeds or writing shall be proved, witnessed and registered as other written conveyances of slaves are or may be by law required to be witnessed, proved and registered. **(1823, c. 1211.).**

CHAPTER XLV. EXECUTIONS. (Page 267).

10. All sales of land or slaves made by any sheriff, coroner, or constable or by any clerk and master in equity, under any execution or decree, shall be made at the courthouse of their respective counties, and such sales shall be made on the same Monday in each and every month on which the several courts of pleas and quarter sessions are generally held for their respective counties, always making the Monday of each county court the only sale day in that month, and if on any sale day as aforesaid, the whole of the property taken by virtue of an execution, or if any property levied on under other executions cannot be offered, by reason that the sale first commenced is not completed for want of time, or cannot be sold on the same day, the sheriff, constable, or other public officer shall be authorized to postpone the same from day to day until the whole shall be sold, on giving public notice at the court house that such sale will be continued on the ensuing day, and all such sales shall commence between the hours of eleven and four o'clock on such sale day: Provided, nevertheless, that nothing herein contained shall be construed to alter in any manner the rules and restrictions, under which sales are by law directed to be conducted and executions required to be returned: And provided further, that nothing in this section shall be construed to alter the days of sale in particular counties as now established by law. **(1822, c. 1153, s. 1. - 1820, c. 1066. - 1821, c. 1096, s. 1.).**

12. No sheriff, constable, or other officer, shall sell any real estate, equity of redemption or legal right of redemption of any real estate, until he shall have advertised the same at least forty days previous thereto, in three public places in his county, nor shall said sheriff or other officer sell any slave, until he
shall have made like advertisement for at least twenty days previous thereto, nor shall said sheriff or other officer sell other personal property, until he shall have made like advertisement for at least ten days previous thereto. And in addition to the three public places above specified, every

sale under an execution issuing from a court of record shall be advertised, by the officer making the same, at the court house of his county. **(1820, c. 1066, s. 1. - 1808, c. 753, s. 2.).**

CHAPTER XLVIII. FENCES. (Page 284).
6. If any slave shall kill any cattle, hog, or horse, not belonging to his master, in any cultivated field, which is not fenced at all, or which is not under sufficient and lawful fence, he or she shall at any time within six months after, be liable to be apprehended on a warrant from any justice of the peace of the county, and on conviction before any two of the neighboring justices shall be subject to and receive thirty nine lashes on his or her bare back, and the owner or overseer of such slave, so offending as aforesaid, shall on proof of the offence committed by such slave, pay such damages as shall be adjudged to have been sustained by the owner of the hog, horse, or cattle, so killed as aforesaid, under the same rules and restrictions as are prescribed in the preceding parts of this act. **(1791, c. 354, s. 2.).**

CHAPTER L. FRAUDS. (Pages 290-291).
8. All contracts to convey or sell land, tenements, or hereditaments, or any interest in or concerning them, or any slave or slaves, shall be void and of no effect, unless such contract, or some memorandum or note thereof, shall be put in writing, signed by the party to be charged therewith, or by some other person, by him thereto lawfully authorized, except nevertheless contracts for leases not exceeding in duration the term of three years. **(1819, c. 1016.).**

11. All contracts and agreements of every description, made after the eighteenth day of May one thousand eight hundred and thirty eight, with any Cherokee Indian, or any person of Cherokee Indian blood, within the second degree, for an amount equal to ten dollars or more, shall be null and void, unless some note or memorandum thereof be made in writing and signed by such Indian or person of Indian blood, or some other person by him authorized, in the presence of two credible witnesses, who shall also subscribe the same. **(1836, c. 8.).**

CHAPTER LXV. LIMITATIONS. (Page 376).

18. Whenever any person or persons shall remain in the possession of a slave or slaves, until such possession is protected by the statute of limitations, the person or persons, so in possession, and those claiming under them, shall be deemed and held to have a good and absolute title to such slave or slaves, against all persons whose claim is barred by the said statute: Provided, that nothing herein contained shall in any way affect the law now in force, that requires all gifts of slaves to be by deed of gift. (1820, c. 38.).

CHAPTER 71. MARRIAGE.
An Act Concerning Marriage. (Pages 386-387).

Section V. If any white man or woman, being free, shall intermarry with an Indian, negro, mustee, or mulatto man or woman, or any person of mixed blood to the third generation, bond or free, he shall, by judgement of the county court, forfeit and pay the sum of one hundred dollars to the use of the county.

Section VI. No minister of the gospel, or justice of the peace within this State, shall presume to marry a white man or woman with an Indian, negro, mustee, or mulatto woman or man, or any person of mixed blood, as in the preceeding section, knowing them to be so, upon pain of forfeiting and paying for every such offence, the sum of one hundred dollars, to be recovered and applied as in the preceding section.

CHAPTER 73. MILITIA.
An Act Concerning the Militia of this State. (Page 395).

Section V. It shall not be lawful for any captain or other militia officer in this State to enroll any free persons of color, except for musicians. (1823, c. 1219).

CHAPTER LXXXVIII. PILOTS. (Page 470).

44. If any slave or slaves shall, with the consent of his or their owner, and not accompanied by a pilot, go off any ship or vessel for the purpose of bringing such ship or vessel over any bar or inlet of this State, or shall pilot any such ship or vessel out and over any bar or inlet, the owner of such slave or slaves shall forfeit the value of such slave or slaves, to be recovered in any court having cognizance thereof, one half to the person suing for the same, the other half to the use of the county where the owner resides. (1812, c. 839.).

CHAPTER LXXXIX. POOR. (Pages 475-476).

19. The owner of every slave, who shall be rendered incapable of service from advancement in years or other disability, shall provide and furnish such slave with the usual allowance of food, raiment and lodging, furnished to slaves in the neighborhood where such slave may be, and if any such slave shall be unprovided for by his or her owner as aforesaid, it shall and may be lawful for the wardens of the poor of the county, where such slave may be, (if the owner of such slave lives in such county) and they are hereby required to furnish such slave with food, raiment and lodging aforesaid, and make a charge of the same to the owner of such slave, which sum so expended the said wardens shall and may recover by warrant against such owner before any justice of the peace, if the sum so expended exceeds not the sum cognizable before a justice by law; if so, then before any jurisdiction having cognizance of the same. Provided always, that the said wardens shall not, at the expense of the owner, provide such slave aforesaid, until they or one of them shall first have given the owner of such slave notice to provide for and furnish such slave, as is herein required, which notice shall be served upon such owner ten days previous to the wardens providing for such slave, and shall and may be issued by any one of said wardens, upon information being given to him, and by him directed to the sheriff or a constable of the county, who is hereby required forthwith to execute the same, and make return of the same to the warden who issued such notice, or to any one of them. (1795, c. 498, s. 1.).

20. If the owner of such slave shall be dead, the executors or administrators of such deceased owner shall provide for such slave, in the manner aforesaid, out of the estate of such deceased owner, and upon failure so to do, the wardens aforesaid shall provide for such slave aforesaid, and proceed against such executors or administrators in every respect, as herein directed against the owner, or if any such slave shall be liable to the direction of any guardian, such guardian shall make the provision aforesaid for such slave out of the estate of his ward, and upon failure, the wardens aforesaid shall provide for such slave as aforesaid, and such executors, administrators and guardians shall be allowed the expense of making such provision for such slave, in their settlements. **(1798, c. 498, s. 2.).**

21. When any such slave shall be in a county other than the county where the owner of such slave, or the executors or administrators of a deceased owner, or guardian reside, the wardens aforesaid may remove such slave to the owner, or to the executors or administrators of the deceased owner, or to the guardian, at the expense of such owners, and at the expense of the executors, administrators and guardian in such cases. **(1798, c. 498, s. 3.).**

22. Any two of the wardens of the poor shall have power and authority to carry the forgoing provisions, relative to disabled slaves, into effect. **(1798, c. 498, s. 4.).**

23. The wardens of the poor in the several counties, or any one of them, shall have power and authority, on information to him or them made, that any person is about to remove out of the county, and has any slave or slaves that are likely to become a county charge, to issue their or his warrant to bring such person before him or them, and take such security by bond, as may deemed sufficient to indemnify the county, which bond may be made payable to the State of North Carolina. And in case such person shall refuse to give bond, as is herein directed, he or they shall have power and authority to commit the said person, and keep him committed until he shall enter into such bonds, or remove the slave or slaves, so about to be left, without the limits of the county. **(1801, c. 584, s. 2.).**

24. All horses, cattle, hogs, or sheep, that shall belong to any slave, or be of any slave's mark in this State, shall be seized and sold by the county wardens, and by them applied, the one half to the support of the poor of the county, and the other half to the informer. **(1779, c. 152, s. 1.).**

25. The several forfeitures and penalties by this act inflicted, for which no method of recovery or application is herein before directed, shall and may be recovered with costs, before any jurisdiction, having cognizance thereof, one half to the use of the informer, the other half to the county wardens, for the use of the poor of the county, wherein such penalties shall be incurred. **(1777, c. 117, s. 13.).**

CHAPTER CII. REVENUE. (Page 515).

All persons, who shall bring negro slaves from another state into this State for sale, shall pay to the sheriff of some one county the sum of ten dollars upon each negro slave brought, and it shall be the duty of the

North Carolina Law

respective sheriffs in this State to collect the tax hereby imposed: But if the said person or persons shall produce to the sheriff of any one county, the certificate of the sheriff of any other county, duly authenticated under the seal of the clerk of the county, in which such sheriff resides, that he has paid the tax hereby imposed, he or they shall be permitted to proceed without the payment of any further tax: and it shall be the duty of the sheriff of each county, into which any negro slave shall be taken by any person or persons whatsoever, to seize such negro slave, until the tax hereby imposed be paid, or until he or they shall produce to the sheriff an affidavit, subscribed by him or them, before some justice of the peace within this State, duly authenticated by the certificate of the clerk and seal of the court of the county, setting forth that the slave or slaves so seized were not, by him or them or any other person with his or their privity and consent, brought in evasion or elusion of the revenue laws of this State: and any person, guilty of making any false affidavit for such person, shall on conviction be deemed guilty of wilful and corrupt perjury, and owners or possessors of all such slaves, so seized, shall pay to the sheriff all expense, that may accrue in consequence of seizing, keeping and feeding such slaves; and the slaves, so seized, may be detained by the sheriff until such payment; and in default thereof, the said sheriff may sell the same at public auction, at the court house of the county, upon twenty days previous notice, which sale shall convey an absolute title to the purchaser. **(1822, c. 1129, s. 8.).**

CHAPTER 111. SLAVES AND FREE PERSONS OF COLOR.
An Act Concerning Slaves And Free Persons Of Color. (Pages 571-593).

    1. Be it enacted by the General Assembly of the State of North Carolina, and it is hereby enacted by the authority of the same, That each and every negro, mulatto or person of color, imported into this State from any foreign port or place, for a slave, or to be held to service or labor, since the first day of January in the year one thousand eight hundred and eight, contrary to the provisions of an act of congress, entitled "An act to prohibit the importation of slaves into any port or place within the jurisdiction of the United States, from and after the first day of January, in the year of our Lord one thousand eight hundred and eight," approved the second day of March, one thousand eight hundred and seven, (except as hereinafter provided,) shall be sold and disposed of for the use of the State. **(Reference: 1816, c. 910, s. 1.).**

2. The sheriff of each county of this State shall, and he is hereby authorized and required to seize and take into his possession every negro, mulatto, and person of color, of the description aforesaid, as well as those which have been, as those which shall be imported as aforesaid, found, or which shall be found in the county of which he is sheriff; and such negro, mulatto, or person of color, so taken in his possession, to sell and dispose of at public sale, (giving previous notice of fifteen days notice of the time of such sale, by advertisement in one of the newspapers published in this State,) to the highest and best bidder, at a credit of six months, the purchaser entering into bond with security, to be approved by said sheriff, for the payment of the purchase money, which money, when received, the sheriff so receiving shall account for and pay to the treasurer of this State, after deducting from the gross amount thereof the several sums hereinafter authorized by him to be retained: the moneys collected by virtue of this act shall be paid and accounted for at the treasury, by the several sheriffs, at the same time and under the same regulations and penalties, as prescribed in accounting for and paying the public taxes. **(Reference: 1816, c. 910, s. 2.).**

3. Where any such negro, mulatto or person of color, as is above mentioned, shall abscond, or so conceal him or herself that he or she cannot be taken by the sheriff, said sheriff may offer a reward, not exceeding one fifth part of the value of such negro, mulatto or person of color, to any person or persons, who shall apprehend and deliver him or her to the sheriff or his deputy, and shall then sell said negro, mulatto or person of color as above directed; or such sheriff may in his discretion proceed to advertise and sell such negro, mulatto or person of color, as directed in the forgoing section, without offering a reward, although such negro, mulatto or person of color may not be in the custody or possession of said sheriff at the time of said sale.**(Reference: 1816, c. 910, s. 3.).**

4. Whenever any person shall discover any negro of the description aforesaid in any county of this State, and give such notice thereof to the sheriff of the county, that he shall, in consequence of such information, obtain the said negro, mulatto or person of color, the person or persons, giving such information, shall be entitled to receive from the said sheriff one fifth part of the sum, for which said negro, mulatto or person of color shall afterwards sell, to be retained, as well as the reward offered, as directed in the preceding section, out of the proceeds of the sale, and paid

North Carolina Law

to the person entitled to the same by the sheriff. **(Reference: 1816, c. 910, s. 4.).**

5. All sales by virtue of this act shall be made at the court house of each respective county; and the sheriff selling, or his successor, in case of his death, resignation or removal from office, , shall execute and deliver to the purchaser, his executors, administrators or assigns, a bill of sale for such negro, mulatto or person of color so sold, which shall vest in the purchaser the absolute property in the same, and the title so acquired shall not be affected by the want of advertisement or by any other irregularity in such sale or proceedings on the part of the sheriff. **(Reference: 1816, c. 910, s. 5.).**

6. Every sheriff, selling as aforesaid, may retain out of the purchase money of such negro, mulatto or person of color, so sold, beside the rewards above directed to be paid, and beside the reasonable charges, at which the said sheriff shall be, in keeping such negro, mulatto or person of color till the day of sale, and in advertising as aforesaid, the further sum of six per centum on the gross proceeds of such sale, which shall be in full compensation for his services. **(References: 1816, c. 910, s. 6.).**

7. Where any person or persons shall have purchased, before the eighteenth of November, one thousand eight hundred and sixteen, for a fair and valuable consideration, any such negro, mulatto or person of color, so imported into this State, contrary to the provisions of the said act of congress, of or from any person or persons originally importing such negro, mulatto or person of color, or the master, agent or attorney of such importer or importers, and such sale or purchase shall not be merely colorable to defeat or evade the provisions of this act, in that case the sheriff, in whose county, such negro, mulatto or person of color is found, and the sheriff of the county where such purchaser resides, shall not proceed to sell such negro, mulatto or person of color: but upon due proof being made of such sale and purchase before the chief justice, or other justice of the supreme or superior courts, such chief or other justice shall give to such purchaser a certificate under his hand, directed to the sheriff of the county where such negro, mulatto or person of color is, or the purchaser resides, specifying the negro, mulatto or person of color, with respect to which such proof shall have been exhibited; and on receipt of such certificate, such sheriff shall execute and deliver to such purchaser or his representative, a bill of sale for such negro, mulatto or person of color; and the benefit of this section shall extend to the assignee or assignees of such purchaser, as well as to such purchaser and his representatives. **(Reference: 1816, c. 910, s. 7.).**

8. The forgoing provisions of this act shall extend and apply to every negro, mulatto or person of color, the issue of any negro, mulatto or person of color, so imported, as aforesaid.(Reference: 1816, c. 910, s. 8.).

9. Every person who shall introduce into this State any slave, from any of the United States, which have passed laws for the liberation of slaves, shall, on complaint thereof before any justice of the peace, , be compelled by such justice to enter into bond with sufficient surety, in the sum of one hundred dollars current money for each slave, for the removing of such slave to the State from whence such slave was brought within three months thereafter, the penalty to be recovered, one half for the use of the State, the other half for the use of the prosecutor, on failure of a compliance therewith; and the person introducing such slaves, shall also, in case of such failure, forfeit and pay the sum of two hundred dollars, to be recovered by any person suing for the same, and applied to his own use. (Reference: 1786, c. 249).

10. All persons who may apprehend and confine in jail or deliver to the owner, any runaway slave, for whom a greater reward shall not have been offered, shall be entitled to recover and receive from the owner of such slave the sum of three dollars, where the owner resides in the county in which such slave may be apprehended, and five dollars, if he reside beyond the limits of such county; and where the runaway slave thus apprehended shall be lodged in jail, it shall be the duty of the jailer to tax the said reward on each slave against such owner, and collect the same with his prison fees. (Reference: 1819, c. 1014, - 1820, c. 1227).

11. If any negro, who shall be taken up as a runaway, and brought before any justice of the peace, will not declare the name of his or her owner, such justice shall in such case, and he is hereby required, by a warrant under his hand, to commit the said negro slave to the jail of the county wherein he or she shall be taken up; and the sheriff or under sheriff of the county, into whose custody the said runaway shall be committed, shall forthwith cause notice in writing of such committment to be set up on the court house door of the said county, and there continued for the space of two months; in which notice a full description of the said runaway and his clothing shall be particularly set down. And every sheriff, failing to give such notice as herein is directed, shall forfeit and pay ten dollars; which said forfeiture shall and may be recovered with costs before any justice of the peace in the county, in which such slave is committed; the one moiety whereof shall be to the county, and the other moiety to the person who shall sue for the same. (Reference: 1741, c. 35, s. 25)

North Carolina Law

12. Where any runaway slave shall be brought before a justice of the peace, said justice shall commit the said runaway to the constable of his district, by his warrant, and therein order such constable to convey the said runaway to his home or the public jail, and may also, if he think proper, order the said constable to give such runaway as many lashes, not exceeding thirty nine, as the said justice may in discretion direct. Every constable, on the receipt of such runaway shall give a receipt for him or her, and, upon failure to execute such warrant or give such receipt, shall forfeit and pay two dollars for the use of the county, to be recovered before any justice of the county where such constable shall reside. **(Reference: 1741, c. 35, s. 30 & 31).**

13. If any sheriff, under sheriff or constable, shall set to work, employ or let out to hire any runaway slave, committed to the custody of any of them, or shall detain such runaway longer in his or their custody than by this act directed, he or they so offending shall forfeit and pay ten dollars, to be recovered before any justice of the peace having jurisdiction thereof: one moiety whereof to be paid to the county, where the offence shall be committed, and the other to him or them, who shall sue for the same; and if any sheriff or his under sheriff, or any constable, into whose hands any runaway shall be committed, by virtue of this act, shall negligently or wilfully suffer such runaway to escape, the said sheriff, under sheriff or constable shall be liable to the action of the party grieved, for recovery of his damages at the common law with costs. **(Reference: 1741, c. 35, s. 32.).**

14. The keepers of the ferries within this State shall give immediate passage to all constables and their assistants, charged with conducting any runaway or runaways, either to the public jail or to such runaway or runaways' master or owner, without charging such constable or their assistants for their ferriage, either going or returning; but all such ferriages of constables and their assistants shall be paid by the county, where such ferry keepers respectively live, and levied, as aforesaid, upon the respective masters or owners of such runaways. **(Reference: 1741, c. 35, s. 33).**

15. When any runaway, whose owner is supposed to be a resident in any other state, shall be committed to any public jail in this State, the keeper of the said jail shall, by the first opportunity after such commitment, send a description of such negro or runaway, together with the account of the time of commitment, and the county where such runaway is committed, to the press, to be advertised in the State Gazette, for which

he shall be reimbursed by the owner of the said slave or runaway. **(Reference: 1741, c. 35, s. 34).**

16. Whenever any negro slave shall be taken up in this State as a runaway, and confined in any jail for the space of twelve months, and the apprehension and confinement of said slave have been advertised in the State Gazette at least six months, and the owner does not apply to prove property in said time, then it shall be lawful for the court of pleas and quarter sessions of the county, in which said runaway is confined, to command their sheriff to expose said negro slave to public sale for ready money, giving three months notice in some public newspaper in this State, at the court house door, and at two other public places in the said county, of the time and place of sale, and of the circumstances under which the said slave is to be sold. **(Reference: 1818, c. 981, s. 1).**

17. The said sheriff shall be allowed two and a half per centum on the amount of sales made under the preceding section. **(Reference: 1818, c. 981, s. 2).**

18. The bill of sale of the sheriff shall vest in the purchaser an absolute right to the said slave; and the sheriff is hereby directed to pay over the residue of the amount of sales, after deducting his commissions and prison charges, to the county trustee, to be applied as county taxes for the use of said county. **(Reference: 1818, c. 981, s. 3).**

19. Upon petition of the owner of said slave or slaves to the court of the county, where the proceeds of said sale are deposited, and upon satisfactory evidence of the right of property of said petitioner or petitioners to said slave, the said court shall direct the payment to the said petitioner or petitioners of the sum paid into the county treasury, taking bond and security from such petitioner or petitioners, when they think proper, payable to the State of North Carolina, to refund said money with interest to the real owner of said slave, should it thereafter appear that such petitioner or petitioners were not the real owners of such slave. **(Reference: 1818, c. 981, s. 4).**

20. If any runaway slave, confined in any jail in this State, his or her owner being unknown, should die, or by the regular process of law be removed from said jail, before a sale of such runaway is effected according to the provision of this act, then and in either of these cases, it shall be the duty of the court of pleas and quarter sessions of the county where the said slave was confined, to direct the county trustee to pay all the expenses of his or her imprisonment out of the county funds: Provided, that the jailer shews to the court that he has complied with the directions of this act

North Carolina Law

requiring the advertisement of runaways. And when such expenses have been so paid by the county trustee, if the owner should thereafter become known, it shall be the duty of the said trustee to recover, for the use of the county, from the owner or his representative, the amount he may have paid on account of the said runaway. **(Reference: 1830, c. 17, s. 1 and 2).**

21. If any slave shall be guilty of producing any forged free pass, or certificate, he or she so offending, shall, on conviction before any justice of the peace, be sentenced to receive as many lashes on his bare back, not exceeding thirty nine, as the said justice may in his direction direct. **(Reference: 1791, c. 335, s. 2).**

22. Whereas many times slaves runaway and lie out, hid and lurking in swamps, woods, and other obscure places, killing cattle and hogs, and committing other injuries to the inhabitants of this State; in all such cases, upon intelligence of any slave or slaves lying out as aforesaid, any two justices of the peace for the county wherein such slave or slaves is or are supposed to lurk or do mischief, shall, and they are hereby empowered and required to issue proclamation against such slave or slaves (reciting his or their names, and the name or names of the owner or owners, if known,) thereby requiring him or them, and every of them, forthwith to surrender him or themselves; and also to empower and require the sheriff of the said county to take such power with him, as he shall think fit and necessary, for going in search and pursuit of, and effectually apprehending such out lying slave or slaves, which proclamation shall be published at the door of the court house, and at such other places as said justices shall direct, and if any slave or slaves, against whom proclamation hath been thus issued, stay out and do not immediately return home, it shall be lawful for any person or persons whatsoever to kill and destroy such slave or slaves, by such ways and means as he shall think fit, without accusation or impeachment of any crime for the same. **(Reference: 1741, c.35, s.40).**

23. No slave shall go armed with a gun, sword, club, or other weapon, or shall keep any such weapon, or shall hunt or range with a gun in the woods, upon any pretence whatsoever; and if any slave shall be found offending herein, it shall and may be lawful for any person or persons to seize, and take to his own use such gun, sword or other weapon, and to apprehend and deliver such slave to the next constable, who is enjoined and required, without further order or warrant, to give such slave twenty lashes on his or her bare back, and to send him or her home; and the master or owner of such slave, shall pay the taker up of such armed slave the same

North Carolina Law

reward, as by this act is allowed for taking up runaways. **(Reference: 1741, c. 35, s. 35, 36 and 37. - 1831, c. 44).**

24. No slave shall go from off the plantation or seat of land, where such slave shall be appointed to live, without a certificate of leave in writing for so doing, from his or her master or overseer. **(Reference: 1741, c. 35, s. 38).**

25. No slave shall be permitted, on any pretence whatever, to raise any horses, cattle, hogs or sheep, but all such belonging to any slave or in any slave's mark, shall be seized and sold by the county wardens, as directed in the act, entitled "An act concerning the poor." **(Reference: 1741, c. 35, s. 39. - 1779, c. 152, s. 1).**

26. In case any slave, who shall not appear to have been properly clothed and fed, shall be convicted of stealing any corn, cattle, hogs or other goods whatsoever from any person, not the owner of such slave, such injured person shall and may maintain an action of trespass against the master, owner, or possessor of such slave in the superior or county court, and shall recover his or her damages with costs of suit. **(Reference: 1753, c. 53, s. 6.).**

27. If any slave shall teach, or attempt to teach any other slave to read or write, the use of figures excepted, he or she may be carried before any justice of the peace, and, on conviction thereof, shall be sentenced to receive thirty nine lashes on his or her bare back. **(Reference: 1830, c. 6, s. 2.).**

28. If any negro slave shall presume to sell any spiritous liquors, by the retail or otherwise, such slave so offending, shall be taken before a magistrate of the county, where he may have committed such offence, and if found guilty, shall receive not exceeding thirty nine lashes on his or her bare back. **(Reference: 1818, c. 974.).**

29. It shall not be lawful for any slave or slaves to play at any game of cards, dice, nine-pins, or any game of hazard or chance, for any money, liquor, or any kind of property, whether the same be staked or not; and any slave, so offending, shall, upon conviction before a justice of the peace, receive a whipping on his or her bare back, not exceeding thirty nine lashes. **(Reference: 1830, c. 10, s. 1.).**

30. Any slave, convicted of setting fire to any woods, under circumstances, which, if the offence were committed by a free person, would subject such free person to a penalty, shall be ordered to receive on his bare back thirty nine lashes. **(Reference: 1777, c. 123, s. 3.).**

31. It shall not be lawful, under any pretence whatever, for any person or persons to allow his, her or their slave, or any slave under his, her or their command or direction, to hire his, her or their time, under the penalty of forfeiting the sum of forty dollars for each and every offence, to be recovered before any justice of the peace, to the sole benefit of the party prosecuting. And it shall be part of the duty and charge of the grand jury, both in the county and superior courts, to make presentment of any slave, who shall be permitted by his or her master or mistress to go at large, having hired his or her time, and on such presentment being made, the court shall issue an order to the sheriff of the county, where such negro may be, to take up such negro, and him or her safely secure so that he can have such negro before the next county court, and it shall be the duty of the sheriff to give the owner notice thereof, (if residing within the county) at least ten days before the sitting of the court; and the said court shall empanel a jury to inquire and try the truth of such presentment, on which trial or inquiry the owner may produce evidence as in other cases; and if the jury shall find that the said presentment is true, such negro shall then be hired out by the sheriff of the county, at public vendue, for the space of one year, taking bond with security for the same, payable to State of North Carolina, for the use of the poor of said county, subject to the payment of any charges respecting said negro: Provided always, that when the owner resides out of the county, the sheriff shall give notice by advertisement in the nearest gazette, for at least two weeks, where a gazette shall be published in the county in which the sheriff shall live, but in other cases the sheriff shall advertise the same at the court house of the county, in which the said slave shall be presented or shall be taken up. Provided always, that when any person who shall hire the negro of an orphan, shall hire to such slave his or her time, the slave shall only be hired out under this section for such time, or the remainder of the time, as said slave may have been hired to such person. **(Reference: 1794, c. 406, s. 1.).**

32. It shall not be lawful for any slave to go at large as a free man, exercising his or her own discretion in the employment of his or her time; nor shall it be lawful for any slave to keep house to him or herself as a free person, exercising the like discretion in the employment of his or her time; and in case the owner of any slave consent or connive at the commission of such offence, he or she so offending shall be subject to indictment, and on conviction be fined in the discretion of the court, not exceeding one hundred dollars: Provided, that nothing herein shall be construed to prevent any person permitting his or her slave or slaves to live

or keep house upon his or her land, for the purpose of attending to the business of his or her master or mistress. **(Reference: 1831, c. 4, s. 2.).**

33. No person shall grant permission for any meeting or meetings of the negroes of others, or people of color at his, her or their houses, or on his, her or their plantation for the purposes of drinking or dancing, under the penalty of forfeiting twenty dollars, on conviction of such offence, in any court having jurisdiction thereof, unless such slave shall have a special permit in writing or otherwise from his or her owner for that purpose; the same to be recovered by any person suing for the same in the name of the State. **(Reference: 1794, c. 406, s. 2.).**

34. It shall not be lawful under any pretence, for any slave or free person of color to preach or exhort in public, or in any manner to officiate as a preacher or teacher in any prayer meeting, or other association for worship, where slaves of different families are collected together; and if any free person of color shall be thereof duly convicted on indictment, before any court having jurisdiction thereof, he shall for each offence receive not exceeding thirty nine lashes on his bare back; and where any slave shall be guilty of a violation of this section, he shall, on conviction, before a single magistrate, receive not exceeding thirty nine lashes on his bare back. **(Reference: 1831, c. 4, s. 1.).**

35. If any number of slaves shall, at any time hereafter, consult, advise or conspire to rebel or make insurrection, or shall plot or conspire the murder of any person or persons whatsoever, every such consulting, plotting or conspiring, shall be adjudged and deemed felony, and the slave or slaves, convicted thereof in the manner prescribed by law, shall suffer death, or be transported as hereinafter provided. **(Reference: 1802, c. 618, s. 1.).**

36. If any slave be found in a state of rebellion or insurrection, or shall agree to join any conspiracy or insurrection, or shall procure or persuade others to join or enlist for that purpose, or shall knowingly or wilfully aid or assist any slave or slaves in a state of rebellion, or engaged in a conspiracy to make insurrection, as by furnishing or agreeing or promising to furnish such persons with arms, ammunition or any other article for their aid and support, every slave, so offending and being thereof legally convicted, shall be adjudged guilty of felony, and shall suffer death or be transported as hereinafter provided. **(Reference: 1802, c. 618, s. 2.).**

37. If any free person shall join in any conspiracy, rebellion or insurrection of the slaves, or shall agree to join any such conspiracy, rebellion or insurrection, or shall procure or persuade others to join or

North Carolina Law

enlist for that purpose, or shall knowingly or wilfully aid or assist any slave or slaves in a state of rebellion, or engage in a conspiracy to make insurrection, as by furnishing, or agreeing or promising to furnish such slave with arms, ammunition or any other article for their aid and support, every free person so offending and being thereof legally convicted, shall be adjudged guilty of felony, and shall suffer death without benefit of clergy. **(Reference: 1802, c. 618, s. 3.).**

38. In all cases, wherein a slave shall be prosecuted for the offences described in the thirty fifth and thirty sixth sections of this act, the court may take for evidence the oath of one or more credible witnesses, the confession of the offender, freely given, without any undue influence either by terror or persuasion, or the testimony of a negro or other person of color, bond or free; but in all cases, where the testimony of one negro or person of color shall be admitted, the same shall not be deemed conclusive and sufficient to convict the person charged, unless the same shall be supported by such pregnant circumstances, as to the jury on such trial shall appear convincing proof, when taken together with the testimony of such negro or person of color. **(Reference: 1802, c. 618, s. 4.).**

39. When any slave shall be convicted of either of the felonies, created by the thirty fifth and thirty sixth sections of this act, he or she shall suffer death, without benefit of clergy, or at the discretion of the court, shall be sentenced to be transported out of this State, and beyond the limits of the United States, under such restrictions and upon such conditions, as good policy and the public safety at the time shall require. **(Reference: 1802, c. 618, s. 5. - 1819, c. 1009.).**

40. Whenever a slave shall be transported, in consequence of the provisions of this act, either by the owner or the State, and such slave shall ever thereafter voluntarily return to and be found in the State, such slave shall suffer death without benefit of clergy, upon due conviction thereof; and if any slave, so transported, shall be brought into any county in this State by his or her master or mistress, or by any other person, such slave shall be forfeited (on proof thereof) to the county into which the same may be brought, and the said slave shall be again transported by order of the county court, and sold for the use of the county. **(Reference: 1802, c. 618, s. 6.).**

41. When any slave shall commit any misdemeanor or offence, which is not by law declared capital, and which, in the opinion of the justice or justices, before whom such offending slave may be carried for examination, shall appear to be of so trivial a nature, as not to deserve a

greater punishment than a single justice of the peace is empowered to inflict, such justice shall, and he is hereby authorized and empowered forthwith to issue subpoenas, if necessary, to compel the attendance of witnesses, and proceed immediately upon the trial of such slave in a summary way, and to pass sentence and award execution: Provided, the punishment extends no further than by ordering the offender to be publicly whipped, not exceeding forty lashes; and where the offence, for which any slave shall be apprehended, shall appear to the justice or justices to be of such a nature, as to deserve any other or greater punishment, such offending slave shall be committed to jail, and stand his or her trial by the proper court having jurisdiction of such offence: Provided, that upon all trials of slaves, before any justice of the peace, for any misdemeanor under this act, any other of the justices of the county, where such slave may be upon trial, may, if they think proper, sit upon and assist in the examination and trial. **(Reference: 1783, c. 190, s. 2 and 3.).**

42. In all cases of offences committed by slaves, of a higher degree than such as are cognizable by a justice of the peace, the courts of pleas and quarter sessions, in their respective counties, shall have original exclusive jurisdiction, except in cases in which the punishment may extend to life, and except also in cases of felonies within the benefit of clergy; and trials of slaves, in the county courts, shall be conducted under the same rules, regulations and restrictions as the trials of freemen. **(Reference: 1793, c. 381, s. 1. - 1816, c. 912, s. 1. - 1825, c. 1291. - 1794, c. 412.).**

43. In all cases, unless otherwise expressly provided, in which a slave shall be charged with the commission of an offence, the punishment whereof may extend to life, or with the commission of a felony within the benefit of clergy, the superior courts of law shall have exclusive jurisdiction within their respective counties; and the trial shall be conducted under the same rules, regulations and restrictions, as trials of freemen for a like offence are now conducted, except as may be herein otherwise provided. **(Reference: 1816, c. 912, s. 1. - 1825, c. 1291.).**

44. Such cases may be removed for trial to adjoining county, upon affidavit of the owner, or in his absence, of the counsel of such slave or slaves, in the same manner as causes may now be removed by freemen; and if it shall appear to the presiding judge, by affidavit of the master, the counsel of the slave, or otherwise, that such slave or slaves cannot have a fair trial in the county wherein the offence is charged to have been committed, it shall and may be lawful for such judge to order the removal of such cause to an adjacent court for trial, notwithstanding the master of

owner of such slave or slaves may neglect or refuse to make an application to the court for that purpose. **(Reference: 1816, c. 912, s. 2. - 1822, c. 1130, s. 2.).**

45. In all cases, where the county or superior courts shall have jurisdiction of offences committed by slaves, the slave charged shall be entitled to a trial by a jury of good and lawful men, owners of slaves. **(Reference: 1793, c. 381, s. 1. - 1831, c. 30, s. 5.).**

46. A slave shall not be tried for a capital offence, but on presentment or indictment of the grand jury; and on his trial for such capital offence, shall, by himself, his master or counsel, have the same right to challenge jurors, that a freemen is now entitled to by law. **(Reference: 1816, c. 912, s. 3. - 1818, c. 972.).**

47. A slave, convicted of a clergiable offence, shall be entitled to the benefit of clergy, in like manner with a free man, and, when he shall pray for the same, the court shall have power to direct and adjudge such corporal punishment, short of death or dismemberment, as to the court shall seem right under all the circumstances of the case; and the entry of such judgment shall have the same legal effects and consequences, as if the slave or slaves were burned in the hand, as in the case of a freeman convicted of a similar offence. **(Reference: 1816, c. 912, s. 4. - 1825, c. 1291.).**

48. When a slave shall be apprehended for any offence, the punishment whereof may affect life, member or limb, it shall be the duty of the sheriff, and he is hereby required to serve the owner of such slave, if known, with notice of trial ten days previous thereto, (which notice shall be proved to the court,) in order that the owner may have an opportunity of defending the said slave; and the costs of said notice, and all other costs attending the trial of any slave, so apprehended, where the owner or owners shall be known, shall be paid by the owner or owners: Provided, the said slave, if a freeman would be liable to the payment thereof. And in case of refusal to pay the same, process may issue from the clerk of the court to compel payment in the same manner as for other costs. **(Reference: 1793, c. 381, s. 2.).**

49. When the owner of any slave, to be tried by virtue of this act, shall not be known, or cannot be discovered or ascertained, or shall reside out of this State, it shall and may be lawful for the court, and they are hereby authorized and required, to appoint counsel to appear for and in behalf of the prisoner, who shall be allowed the same fees as the attorney for the State is allowed for criminal prosecutions, After which, they may proceed to trial in the same manner as if the owner had been notified

agreeable to the directions of this act; in which case the fees for the counsel, clerk and sheriff shall be paid by the county, in which the court is held, in the same manner as other county charges. **(Reference: 1793, c. 381, s. 3.).**

50. All negroes, Indians, mulattoes, and all persons of mixed blood, descended from negro and Indian ancestors, to the fourth generation inclusive, (though one ancestor of each generation may have been a white person) whether bond or free, shall be deemed and taken to be incapable in law to be witnesses in any case whatsoever, except against each other. In all pleas of the State, where the defendant may be a negro, Indian or mulatto, or person of mixed blood, descended from negro or Indian ancestors, to the fourth generation inclusive, (though one ancestor of each generation may have been a white person,) whether such defendant be bond or free, the evidence of a negro or negroes, Indian or Indians, mulatto or mulattoes, and of all persons of mixed blood, descended from negro or Indian ancestors to the fourth generation inclusive, (though one ancestor of each generation may have been a white person,) whether the persons or persons, whose evidence if offered, be bond or free, shall be admissible and the witnesses competent, subject nevertheless to be excluded upon any other grounds of incompentency which may exist. **(Reference: 1777, c. 115, s. 42, - 1821, c. 1123.).**

51. On the trial of any slave charged with committing capital or other offences, the judge or presiding magistrate sitting on such trial shall, before the examination of any negro, mulatto or Indian, charge such to declare the truth. **(Reference: 1741, c. 34, s. 42.).**

52. If any negro, mulatto or Indian, bond or free, shall, upon any trial where he may be examined as a witness, commit wilful and corrupt perjury, he or she shall, upon conviction thereof, be sentenced to receive the same punishment, as is imposed upon a free man for the commission of the same offence. **(Reference: 1741, c. 35, s. 41. - 1831, c. 12.).**

53. In all cases of insurrection or rebellion, or of conspiracy to make insurrection, or to murder or rebel, or any such contemplated conspiracy, insurrection or rebellion, of any slave or slaves, upon the information and at the request of any five justices of the peace of the county in which such conspiracy, insurrection or rebellion shall happen or may be contemplated, the governor for the time being shall be authorized and have power to issue a commission of oyer and terminer, to any one the the judges of the superior courts of law; and in case the said judges are necessarily engaged on their circuits, the governor shall be authorized and

have power to issue a commission to one of the judges of the supreme court, whose duty it shall be to hold said court forthwith, and who shall be clothed with all the powers necessary for the trial of all such slave or slaves, as may be charged with any of the before mentioned offences. (Reference: 1831, c. 30, s. 1.).

54. The prosecuting officer in behalf of the State, attending the said court, shall be entitled to receive the same compensation, as may be allowed by law generally for attending a term of a superior court. (Reference: 1831, c. 30, s. 2.).

55. The prisoner or prisoners, who shall be tried before any court of oyer and terminer, shall have the right of appeal to the supreme court, under the rules and regulations now prescribed by law for appeals. (Reference: 1831, c. 30, s. 3.).

56. When the person, who shall be indicted before a court of oyer and terminer, shall upon affidavit of himself or any other person, shew such circumstances and facts to the court, as would induce the judge, in the regular courts of this State, to remove the trial of said indictment out of the county, the judge holding such court of oyer and terminer may, in his discretion, continue the said indictment, commit or bind over the prisoner, as the case may require, for trial at the next superior court for said county, when the same shall be diposed of, according to the rules and regulations in force for the trial of such offences. (Reference: 1831, c. 30, s. 4.).

57. Any inhabitant of this State, desirous to emancipate any slave or slaves, shall file a petition in writing in some one of the superior courts of this State, setting forth, as near as may be, the name, sex and age of such slave intended to be emancipated, and praying permission to emancipate the same; and the court, before whom such petition shall be filed, shall grant the prayer thereof on the following conditions and not otherwise, viz: That the petitioner shall shew that he has given public notice of his intention to file such petition, as the court house of the county, and in the State Gazette, for at least six weeks before the hearing of such petition, and that the petitioner shall enter into bond with two securities, each to be good and sufficient, payable to the State of North Carolina, in the sum of one thousand dollars for each slave named in the petition, conditioned that the said slave or slaves shall honestly and correctly demean him, her or themselves, while he, she or they shall remain within the State of North Carolina, and that he, she or they will, within ninety days after granting the prayer of the petitioner to emancipate him, her or them, leave the State of North Carolina, and never afterwards come within the same: Provided

nevertheless, that no such emancipation shall, in any manner whatever, invalidate or affect the rights of claims of any creditor of such petitioner. **(Reference: 1830, c. 9, s. 1.).**

58. Any emancipation granted to any slave or slaves, as herein directed, shall be upon the express condition, that he, she or they will leave the State, within ninety days from the granting thereof, and never will return within the State afterwards. **(Reference: 1830, c. 9, s. 2.).**

59. It shall be lawful for any person, by his or her last will and testament, to direct and authorize his or her executor or executors, to cause to be emancipated any slave or slaves pursuant to this act; and such bequest or authority shall be good and available in law and equity, and shall justify said executor or executors in emancipating such slave or slaves at any time thereafter: Provided, he, she or they file his, her or their petition, and pursue the directions of this act, in the same manner as if he, she or they were the absolute owners of such slave or slaves: And provided further, that nothing herein contained shall be taken or held to interfere with the claims of creditors, or exempt any slave, directed to be emancipated, from liability to the claims of creditors: And provided further, that any slave emancipated by an executor, pursuant to the directions of the testator, shall be emancipated on the same conditions and under the same liabilities as herein before set forth: Provided further, that no permission shall be granted to any executor or executors to emancipate any slave or slaves, under the directions of the last will and testament of his or their testator, before the expiration of two years from and after the probate of said last will and testament, unless the said executor or executors shall enter into bond, with approved security, to the State of North Carolina, in double the value of the slave or slaves, proposed to be emancipated, conditioned to be answerable to the creditors of his, her or their testator for the value of the said slave or slaves. **(Reference: 1830, c. 9, s. 3.).**

60. It may be lawful to emancipate, upon the petition filed and under the order of any superior court of law in this State, any slave over the age of fifty years. Provided, his or her owner shall prove, by his own oath or otherwise, to the satisfaction of the court and jury, that said slave has performed meritorious services (which meritorious services must consist in more than mere general performance of duty:) Provided nevertheless, that the petitioner shall swear that he or she has not received, in money or otherwise, the price or value, or any part thereof, of said slave, or been induced to petition for his or her emancipation in consideration of any price paid therefor or to be paid: And provided further, that before such slave

shall be emancipated, the petitioner shall give bond and good security, in the sum of five hundred dollars, payable to the State of North Carolina, that said slave shall honestly and correctly demean him or herself, so long as he or she shall remain in the State, and shall not become a parish charge; which bond may be sued upon, in the name of the State, to the use of the poor, or of any person injured by the malconduct of such slave. **(Reference: 1830, c. 9, s. 4.).**

61. If any slave, other than such as may be emancipated under the sixtieth section of the act, shall refuse or neglect to leave the State, within ninety days after permission to emancipate him or her has been granted, as aforesaid, by any superior court, or shall ever come within the State after having left it, it shall be the duty of any justice of the peace of any county, wherein said slave may be found, to issue a warrant to arrest said slave; and he shall, upon proper proof being made of his or her having violated the provisions of this act, commit him or her to the jail of the county, there to remain until the next ensuing term of the court of pleas and quarter sessions, where an issue shall be made up and immediately tried, whether the accused has violated the provisions of this act; and upon the finding of the jury that the accused has so done, he, she or they shall, by the said court of pleas and quarter sessions, be ordered to be sold, which sale shall vest an absolute right of property in the purchaser in and to the accused, and the proceeds thereof be equally divided between the informer and the wardens of the poor of the county. **(Reference: 1830, c. 9, s. 5.).**

62. If any slave shall refuse or neglect to leave the State as aforesaid, or shall ever come within the same after having left it, it shall and may be lawful for any person to bring suit, in the name of the State, for the joint use of himself and the wardens of the poor of the county, and to be applied by them to the support of the poor of the county, upon the bond which may have been given, in pursuance of the provisions of this act. **(Reference: 1830, c. 9, s. 6.).**

63. It shall be the duty of all grand juries within this State to make presentment of all slaves, who may hereafter be emancipated, who may violate the provisions of this act; and upon such presentment, it shall be the duty of the prosecuting officer of the county, wherein the presentment may be made, to prosecute such slave as herein before provided. **(Reference: 1830, c. 9, s. 7.).**

64. No slave shall be set free but according to the provisions of this act. **(Reference: 1830, c. 9, s. 8.).**

65. It shall not be lawful for any free negro, or mulatto to migrate into this State: and if he or she shall do so, contrary to the provisions of this act, and, being thereof informed, shall not, within twenty days thereafter, remove out of the State, he or she, being thereof convicted in manner hereinafter directed, shall be liable to a penalty of five hundred dollars; and, upon failure to pay the same, within the time prescribed in the judgment awarded against such person or persons, he or she shall be liable to be held in servitude and at labor, for a term of time not exceeding ten years, in such manner and upon such terms as may be prescribed by the court awarding such sentence, and the proceeds arising therefrom shall be paid over to the county trustee for county purposes: Provided, that in case any free negro or mulatto shall pay the penalty of five hundred dollars, according to the provisions of this act, it shall be the duty of such free negro or mulatto to remove him or herself out of this State, within twenty days thereafter, and, for every such failure, he or she shall be subject to the like penalty, as is presscribed for a failure to remove in the first instance. **(Reference: 1826, c. 21, s. 1.).**

66. If any free negro or mulatto shall come into this State as aforesaid, he or she may be arrested upon a warrant from any justice of the peace, and carried before any justice of the peace of the county, in which he or she may be arrested, who is hereby authorized and required to examine into the case; and if, upon such examination, it shall appear to him that the said free negro or mulatto has come into this State, contrary to the provisions of this act, he shall bind him or her over to the next county court of said county, which shall happen thereafter, taking such security for his or her appearance as may be reasonable; and upon neglecting or refusing to give such security, the said justice shall commit such free negro or mulatto to the jail of the county, there to be confined until the next county court, unless, in the mean time, he or she shall give security as aforesaid; and at the said court it shall be the duty of the said court, to inquire into the case, and if it shall appear to them that the said free negro or mulatto has migrated into this State, contrary to the provisions of this act, they shall enter judgment against him or her for the aforesaid penalty, and may award execution thereon; and, if he or she shall have no property or not sufficient to satisfy the said debt, the said court shall adjudge that the said free negro or mulatto shall be hired out for a term of time, not exceeding that prescribed in the sixty fifth section of this act, in such manner and upon such terms as may seem expedient to said court. **(Reference: 1826, c. 21, s. 2.).**

North Carolina Law

67. If after the expiration of the term of service, for which such free negro or mulatto shall have been held in servitude, he or she shall remain in this State for thirty days, such free negro or mulatto, shall be liable to the same penalties and punishments, as are prescribed in the sixty fifth and sixty sixth sections of this act. **(Reference: 1826, c. 21, s. 3.).**

68. Any person, who shall bring into this State, by water or land, any free negro or mulatto, shall forfeit and pay for every such person so brought into this State, the sum of five hundred dollars, to be recovered by action of debt, in the name of the State, for the use of the county, where the offence shall be committed: Provided, that this section shall not extend to masters of vessels, bringing into this State any free negro or mulatto, employed on board and belonging to said vessel, and who shall therewith depart, nor to any person, travelling in or through this State, having any free negro or mulatto as a servant, and who shall with such person depart out of the State. **(Reference: 1826, c. 21, s. 4.).**

69. If any free negro or mulatto in any county of this State, who is able to labor, shall be found spending his or her time in idleness and dissipation, or having no regular or honest employment or occupation, which he or she is accustomed to follow, it shall and may be lawful for any citizen to apply to a justice of the peace of said county, and upon affidavit to obtain a warrant to arrest such person and bring him or her before some justice of said county; and if, upon examination of the cause, it shall appear to said justice that the said free negro or mulatto comes within the provisions of this section, the said justice shall bind him or her, with reasonable security, to appear at the next county court of said county; and in case he or she shall fail to give security, such free negro or mulatto shall be committed to the jail of the county, until the next county court thereafter, and it shall be the duty of the said court, if, upon examination of the case, he or she shall come within the meaning of this section to require such free negro or mulatto to enter into bond, with sufficient security in such sum as may be considered by the court reasonable, payable to the State of North Carolina, conditioned for his or her good behaviour and industrious, peaceable deportment for one year; and in case he or she shall fail to give such security, or shall not pay the costs and charges of the prosecution, it shall be lawful for the said court and they are hereby required to hire out such free negro or mulatto, for a term of time, to service and labor, which to them may seem reasonable and just and calculated to reform him or her to habits of industry and morality, not exceeding three years for any one offence. **(Reference: 1826, c. 21, s. 5.).**

70. All sums of money which may arise under the provisions of the last section from the hire of free negroes or mulattoes, shall be paid to the county trustee for county uses. **(Reference: 1826, c. 21, s. 6.).**

71. The justices of the courts of pleas and quarter sessions, in each of the counties of this State, shall have power, in cases where it may appear expedient, to bind out the children of free negroes or mulattoes, where the parent, with whom such children may live, does or shall not habitually employ his or her time in some honest, industrious occupation. **(Reference: 1826, c. 21, s. 7.).**

72. All persons, with whom any free negro or mulatto may be held to service under this act, shall, and they are hereby required to provide him or her with good and sufficient clothing and food, treat him or her with humanity, and teach him or her some mechanical trade, or some useful and industrious employment, during the term for which such free negro or mulatto may be compelled to serve; he or she shall not be removed from the county by such master or any other person, and shall be produced to the county court at the expiration of the term of service as aforesaid, or whenever thereto required by them; and if any such master or mistress shall violate this section, he or she may be indicted for such offence, in any court of the county, where such offence may be committed, and, on conviction thereof, may be fined or imprisoned at the discretion of the court; and in case such free negro or mulatto shall run away, before the expiration of his or her term of service, he or she shall be compelled to serve, after the said expiration, such a length of time as he or she shall have absented him or herself. **(Reference: 1826, c. 21, s. 7.).**

73. In all cases, arising under the sixty fifth, sixty sixth, sixty seventh and sixty ninth sections of this act, the free negro or mulatto, who is charged with an offence, upon application to the court for that purpose, shall have a right to have the facts of his or her case tried by a jury upon an issue or issues, made up under the direction of the court for that purpose. **(Reference: 1826, c. 21, s. 9.).**

74. All free mulattoes, descended from negro ancestors to the fourth generation inclusive, though one ancestor of each generation may have been a white person, shall come within the provisions of this act. **(Reference: 1826, c. 21, s. 10.).**

75. It shall be the duty of the several county attorneys in this State, to give in charge the sixty fifth, sixty sixth, sixty seventh and sixty ninth sections of this act to the grand jurors, and it is hereby made their duty to present all cases in their county, arising under the said sections,

North Carolina Law

within the knowledge of either of them; and the said attorneys are hereby required, in all cases arising under the provisions of the said sections, to prosecute for, and on behalf of the State; and it shall be the duty of the several courts of this State, before whom any proceedings may be had under the said sections, so to construe the same as to prohibit the evils intended to be remedied; and they are hereby authorized and required to make all necessary rules and regulations, according to the usual course of justice, which may be required for the purposes and objects of the said sections of this act. **(Reference: 1826, c. 21, s. 11.).**

76. If any free negro or person of color, who may be a resident of this State, shall migrate from this State, and go into any other state, and shall be absent for the space of ninety days or more, it shall not be lawful for such free negro or person of color to return to this State; and if any free negro or person of color shall violate this section, he shall be liable to the same penalties as are prescribed for the punishment of free negroes and persons of color who migrate to this State: Provided, that no persons shall incur the penalties or disabilities prescribed in this section, if he or she shall have been prevented from so returning to this State by sickness, or other unavoidable occurrence. **(Reference: 1830, c. 14.).**

77. It shall not be lawful for any free negro or free person of color to intermarry, or cohabit and live together as man and wife, with any slave; and any free negro or person of color, so intermarrying, or cohabiting and living as man and wife with a slave, shall be liable to indictment, and, upon conviction, shall be fined and imprisoned, or whipped at the discretion of the court; the whipping not to exceed thirty nine lashes: Provided, that this section shall not extend to any case, where an intermarriage, or cohabiting, or living together took place, before the first day of March, A. D. one thousand eight hundred and thirty one. **(Reference: 1830, c. 4, s. 3.).**

78. Any person of color, convicted by due course of law of an assault with intent to commit a rape upon the body of a white female, shall suffer death without benefit of clergy. **(Reference: 1823, c. 1229.).**

79. It shall not be lawful for any free negro, mulatto or person of mixed blood, descended from negro ancestors to the fourth generation inclusive, (though one ancestor of each generation may have been a white person,) to play at any game of cards, dice, ninepins, or any game of chance or hazard, whether for money, liquor or any kind of property, or not, with any slave or slaves; and any free negro, mulatto or person of mixed blood as aforesaid, so offending, shall, upon conviction before any court having

jurisdiction, receive a whipping, not exceeding thirty nine lashes, on his or her bare back. **(Reference: 1830, c. 20, s. 2.).**

80. If any free negro, mulatto, or person of mixed blood as aforesaid, shall knowingly suffer any slave or slaves to play at any game of cards, dice, nine-pins or any game of chance or hazard, whether for money, liquor or any kind of property, or not, in his of her house, or in the yard, field or garden attached or belonging to his or her house, he or she shall be liable to indictment in any court having jurisdiction; and, upon conviction, the free negro, mulatto or person of mixed blood as aforesaid, shall receive a whipping on his or her bare back, not exceeding thirty nine lashes. **(Reference: 1830, c. 10, s. 3.).**

81. If any free negro or mulatto shall entertain any slave in his or her house, during the sabbath, or in the night, between sunset and sunrise, he or she shall, for entertaining such slave, be subject to a fine of two dollars for the first offence, and four dollars for every subsequent offence, to be recovered on conviction before any one justice of the peace, and applied to the use of the poor of the county, in which the offence shall be committed, saving to the party the right of appealing. **(Reference: 1787, c. 267, s. 2.).**

82. If any slave shall buy or receive from any slave or slaves, or shall sell or deliver to any slave or slaves, any of the property prohibited to be bought by or received from, or to be sold or delivered to any slave by any free white person, by the laws of this State, he or she, on conviction thereof before any justice of the peace, shall receive on his or her back, not exceeding thirty nine lashes, well laid on by any constable of said county, or other person appointed for that purpose. **(Reference: 1826, c. 13, s. 4.).**

83. If any free negro or mulatto shall trade with any slave, either by buying from or selling to him or her, any article of property, prohibited to be sold or bought from a slave by any white free person by the laws of this State, he or she may be presented by indictment in the county or superior courts; and, on conviction, shall receive not less than thirty nine lashes on his or her bare back. **(Reference: 1826, c. 13, s. 5. - 1828, c. 32, s. 2.).**

84. Either of the parties or master of the slave, convicted under either of the two preceding sections, shall be entitled to an appeal from the judgment of the justice or of the county court; and no indictments shall be prosecuted for so trading with a slave, unless the indictment be commenced

North Carolina Law

within twelve months from the time of the offence committed. **(Reference: 1826, c. 13, s. 7. - 1828, c. 32, s. 3.).**

85. It shall not be lawful for any free negro, mulatto or free person of color, to hawk or peddle, within the limits of any county in this State, without first obtaining a license from the court of pleas and quarter sessions of the county, in which they propose to hawk or peddle, which license shall be granted for one year only, and only when seven or more justices are present, and upon satisfactory evidence of the good character of the applicant, to be approved by said court; and for issuing such license, the clerk shall be entitled to demand and receive from such applicant the sum of eighty cents: Provided nevertheless, that nothing in this act shall be construed, so as to allow such person, coming from another state, to peddle in this State; and if any free negro, or free person of color, shall offend against this section of this act, he or she shall be subject to indictment. **(Reference: 1831, c. 28. - 1830, c. 7.).**

86. When any free person of color shall be convicted of any offence against the criminal laws of the State, and sentenced to pay a fine, and it shall appear to the satisfaction of the court, that the free person of color, so convicted, is unable to pay the fine imposed, the court shall direct the sheriff of the county, where such fine is imposed, to hire out the free person of color, so convicted, to any person, who will pay the fine for his services for the shortest space of time. **(Reference: 1831, c. 13, s. 1.).**

87. It shall be the duty of the sheriff, during the week of court, or as soon thereafter as convenient, publicly at the door of the court house, to hire out such free person of color to any person, who will pay the fine, so imposed, for his services for the shortest space of time, and to take from the person so hiring, bond and security, in double the amount of the fine so paid, payable in the same manner and with the same conditions for the proper treatment of the free person of color, during the time for which he is so hired, as are now contained in apprentice bonds. **(Reference: 1831, c. 13, s. 2.).**

88. The person, to whom the sheriff shall so hire any free person of color, shall, during the time for which the hiring is so made, have the same authority over, and the same right to control and require the services of such free person of color, and shall be liable in all respects to the same obligations and duties as masters now have, and are liable to in cases of apprentices. **(Reference: 1831, c. 13, s. 3.).**

89. If no person can be found who will pay the fine so imposed, for the services of the free person of color so fined, for a space of time not

exceeding five years, then it shall be the duty of the sheriff to hire the free person of color to any person, who will pay the highest sum for his services, for five years, which sum shall discharge the fine; and it shall be the duty of the sheriff, after deducting five per cent commissions, to account for the pay over the money collected by virtue of this act, as other fines: Provided always, that if any free person of color, hired out under the provisions of this act, shall abscond or leave the service of his master before the expiration of his or her time, he or she shall be liable and bound to make up such time, so elapsed, by serving double the time thereof: And provided further, that the fine imposed, shall in all cases be at least equal to the amount of the costs of such prosecution. (References: 1831, c. 13, s. 4.).

****

LAWS OF THE STATE OF NORTH CAROLINA PASSED BY THE GENERAL ASSEMBLY AT THE SESSION OF 1838-1839 RALEIGH: PRINTED BY J. GALES AND SON OFFICE OF THE RALEIGH REGISTER, 1839

CHAPTER X. COUNTIES.
1839. An Act to erect that Territory of this State lately acquired by Treaty from the Cherokee Indians, into a separate and distinct County, by the name of Cherokee. (Page 18).

Be it enacted by the General Assembly of the State of North Carolina, and it is hereby enacted by the authority of the same, That all that part of Macon County bounded as follows, viz: beginning at the junction of the Tennessee and Tuckaseegee Rivers; thence down the main channel of the Tennessee River to the State line of Tennessee; thence with the said Tennessee line, to where it intersects the Georgia line; thence with the dividing line this State from Georgia, Eastwardly, to the Mountain dividing the waters of Hiwassee and Valley Rivers, from those of the Nantahala River; thence along with the highest summit, and the various courses of the said Mountain, to the point of beginning, be, and the same is hereby erected into a separate and distinct County, by the name of Cherokee, with all the rights, privileges, and immunities of the other Counties of this State. **[Ratified 4th January, 1839].**

North Carolina Law

CHAPTER XXII. GAMING WITH SLAVES.
1839. AN ACT to prevent free persons from gambling with Slaves. (Page 32).
   Be it enacted by the General Assembly of the State of North Carolina, and it is hereby enacted by the authority of the same, That it shall not be lawful for any white person to play with any Slave or Slaves at any game of Cards, or at any game of hazard or chance, for any money, liquor, or any kind of property, whether the same be staked or not; and any white person, so offending, shall be subject to indictment, and, on conviction, shall be fined or imprisoned, at the discretion of the Court: Provided, such imprisonment shall not exceed six months. **[Ratified 7th January, 1839.].**

CHAPTER XXIV. MARRIAGES.
1839. AN ACT prohibiting Marriages between free persons of color and white persons. (Page 33).
   Be it enacted by the General Assembly of the State of North Carolina, and it is hereby enacted by the authority of the same, That it shall not be lawful for any free negro or free person of color to marry a white person; and any marriage, hereafter solemnized or contracted between any free negro or free person of color and a white person, shall be null and void. **[Ratified 8th January, 1839].**

CHAPTER XLVIII. MISCELLANEOUS.
1839. AN ACT to emancipate Caroline Cook and her four children, viz: Pamelia, Archibald T., James Ellis, and Martha Jane. (Page 157).
   Be it enacted by the General Assembly of the State of North Carolina, and it is hereby enacted by the authority of the same, That Caroline Cook, wife of Joshua Cook, and her four children, viz: Pamelia, Archibald T., James Ellis, and Martha Jane, slaves the property of Archibald Lovelace, of the county of Wilkes, be, and they are hereby, with the consent and request of their said owner, emancipated and set free, and by their names of Caroline Cook, Pamelia Cook, Archibald T. Cook, James Ellis Cook, and Martha Jane Cook, shall hereafter possess and exercise all the rights and privileges which are enjoyed by other free persons of colour in this State: Provided, nevertheless, that before said slaves shall be emancipated, the said Joshua Cook, or their said Master, shall give bond

and good security in the County Court of Wilkes County, that said slaves shall honestly demean themselves as long as they shall remain in the State, and shall not become a county charge, which said bond shall be made payable to the State of North Carolina, and may be sued upon in the name of the State, to the use of the county, and of any person injured by the malconduct of said slaves. [Ratified 22d December, 1838].

RESOLUTION directing the Secretary of State to issue Grants for Lands sold at the late sale of the Cherokee Lands, in certain cases. (Pages 184-185).

Whereas, by the twelfth section of the Act of Assembly, passed at the last session, authorizing the sale of the Cherokee Lands, the Commissioners who superintended the same were authorized to receive payments in advance, either in whole or in part; and whereas, in several instances, the purchasers of said lands paid in full for them at the time of purchase, and obtained the Commissioners' receipt; and whereas, by the ninth section of the Act aforesaid, the Secretary of State is authorized to issue grants for said lands, only upon proof made to him of payment therefor, by the production of the Treasurer's receipt; and whereas, in the cases referred to, the Treasurer can give no receipt: For remedy whereof, be it

Resolved, That the Secretary of State shall be authorized to issue grants in the cases above referred to, for the lands sold at the late sale of the Cherokee lands, upon the production of the purchaser of a certificate from the Public Treasurer, certifying that it appears from the returns made to him by the Commissioners of sale, that any particular tract of land was paid for in full, to the said Commissioners, at the time of the sale - which certificate the Public Treasurer is hereby empowered to make.
[Ratified 28th December, 1838].

****

LAWS OF THE STATE OF NORTH CAROLINA
PASSED BY THE GENERAL ASSEMBLY
AT THE SESSION OF 1840-41
RALEIGH: PRINTED BY W.R. GALES
OFFICE OF THE RALEIGH REGISTER, 1841

North Carolina Law

CHAPTER IV. CHEROKEE AGENCY.
1840-41. An Act authorising the Governor to appoint an Agent in the County of Macon or Cherokee. (Pages 7-9).

I. Be it enacted by the General Assembly of the State of North Carolina, and it is hereby enacted by the authority of the same, That the Governor of this State be, and he is hereby authorised, after the first day of March, one thousand eight hundred and forty one, to appoint an Agent, who shall, after his appointment, reside in the County of Macon or Cherokee, whose duty it shall be to receive payment, from time to time, of all purchasers of Cherokee Lands, of all or any part of the money due on their several bonds; to ascertain and report to the Treasury Department, once every three months, the condition of the debtors, as solvent, whether sold or unsold.

II. Be it further enacted, That the Agent so appointed shall be authorised to receive from the Public Treasurer, such of the bonds given for Cherokee Lands as the Public Treasurer, with the advice of the Governor, shall deem proper, for which said Agent shall execute to the Treasurer his receipt. Provided, that at no time shall the said Agent hold in his hands bonds and monies received thereupon, to an amount beyond the penalty of his bond; he shall take the bonds to the County of his residence, and there receive all such payments as may be voluntarily made, and institute suits in all cases, when he shall be directed to do so by the Public Treasurer, or when the interest of the State shall in the least seem to require it.

III. Be it further enacted, That the Agent thus appointed, shall receive in payment gold and silver coin, and the notes of all specie paying Banks in this State and South Carolina, and in addition to which the Agent may, and he is hereby required to receive from all debtors of Cherokee Lands, whose permanent residence may be West of the Blue Ridge, the notes of the specie paying Banks of Georgia, payable at Augusta and Savannah; he shall on the first Monday in every month, transmit to the Public Treasurer an accurate statement of his receipts during the month; and he shall be required to pay over to the Public Treasurer, or deposite to the credit of the Treasurer in such Bank as the Public Treasurer may designate, on the first Monday of the months of June, September, December and March, in each and every year, all monies by him received during the three preceding months.

IV. Be it further enacted, That the Agent thus appointed, shall, before entering on the duties of his office, take before the Governor, an oath for the faithful performance of all the duties enjoined by this Act, and shall enter into bond, with sufficient securities, in the sum of one hundred thousand dollars, to secure the honest and faithful discharge of the several requisitions of this Act; which bond shall be made payable to the State of North Carolina, and upon breach of the conditions thereof, or any of them, the Treasurer shall cause the bond to be put in suit in the Superior Court of Wake County, and such bond shall not become void upon the first recovery, or if judgment shall be given for the Defendant, but may be put in suit, and prosecuted from time to time until the whole penalty shall be recovered.

V. And be it further enacted, That the Agent aforesaid shall receive, as a fair compensation for all the services required of him, three per centum on the amount of all sums received and collected; and he may be dismissed from office and a successor appointed at any time that the Governor may believe that his duties are not honestly and correctly discharged, and upon his dismissal from office, it shall be his duty to deliver over to the Treasurer, or to such person as the Governor shall appoint to succeed him, such bonds as may be in his hands and remain uncollected, and shall immediately account with the Public Treasurer for all monies by him received upon said bonds. [Ratified the 30th day of December, A.D. 1840.]

CHAPTER V. CHEROKEE AGENCY.
1840-41. An Act supplemental to an Act passed at the present Session of the General Assembly, authorising the Governor to appoint an Agent to collect the Cherokee Bonds. (Pages 9-10).

Be it enacted by the General Assembly of the State of North Carolina, and it is hereby enacted by the authority of the same, That it shall be the duty of the Treasurer whenever he shall deliver to the Agent appointed by the Act to which this is a supplement, any Cherokee Bonds, to take from the said Agent a memorandum or receipt, specifying the names of the obligors in said Bonds; the amount for which they were given, and the time when they become due, and also the payments made on them severally, and in the event of any of said bonds being lost or destroyed before they may be collected, a copy of the said memorandum or receipt, certified to be accurate by the Treasurer, whose hand writing may be proven by the oath of any person knowing it, shall be received as evidence in the same manner as the original bonds, and a recovery shall be had on them, without the production of the said bonds, any law, usage or custom to the contrary notwithstanding; Provided, however, as preparatory to the introduction of such receipts as evidence in the cases above specified, the loss of the bonds shall be proved in the manner usual in other cases when secondary evidences is offered in lieu of evidence of the first degree. **[Ratified the 11th day of January, 1841.]**

CHAPTER XXIX. FREE PERSONS OF COLOUR.
1840-41. An Act concerning the collection of fines and costs from Free Negroes and Free Persons of Colour. (Page 61).
    Be it enacted by the General Assembly of the State of North Carolina, and it is hereby enacted by the authority of the same, That the Act, entitled "An Act to amend the fifty eighth Chapter of the Revised Statutes," entitled "Insolvent Debtors," passed at the Session of the General Assembly, in the years one thousand eight hundred and thirty eight, and one thousand eight hundred and thirty nine, shall be, and the same is hereby repealed, so far as it extends, or may be construed to extend, to free Negroes and free Persons of Colour. **[Ratified, the 11th day of January, 1841.]**

CHAPTER XXX. FREE PERSONS OF COLOUR.
1840-41. An Act to prevent Free Persons of Colour from carrying Fire arms. (Pages 61-62).
    Be it enacted by the General Assembly of the State of North Carolina, and it is hereby enacted by the authority of the same, That if any free Negro, Mulatto, or free Person of Colour, shall wear or carry about his or her person, or keep in his or her house, any Shot gun, Musket, Rifle, Pistol, Sword, Dagger or Bowie knife, unless he or she shall have obtained a license therefore from the Court of Pleas and Quarter Sessions of his or her County, within one year preceding the wearing, keeping or carrying thereof, he or she shall be guilty of a misdemeanor, and may be indicted therefor. **[Ratified, the 11th day of January, 1841.]**

CHAPTER LVIII. SLAVES.
1840-41. An Act to prevent the transportation of Slaves upon Rail Roads, Steam Boats or Stage Coaches, without written permission from their owners. (Pages 99-100).

Be it enacted by the General Assembly of the State of North Carolina, and it is hereby enacted by the authority of the same, That it shall not be lawful for any Slave or Slaves to be transported on any Rail Road, Steam Boat, or other Vessel navigating the waters of this State, or any Stage Coach, without a permission in writing from the owner or owners of such Slave or Slaves, under the penalty of five hundred dollars for every violation of this Act; to be recovered in the name of the State, from the President, Directors, and Company of said Rail Road, or the owners or Captains of said Steam Boat or Vessel, or the owners of said Stage Coach, as the case may be, by action of debt in any of the Courts of Law in this State, one half whereof shall be for the use of the former, and the other half for the use of the State.

II. Be it further enacted, That if any Slave or Slaves shall escape from his or their owner or owners, by being transported on said Rail Road, Steam Boat or other Vessel, or by means of Stage Coach, the master or mistress or other owner or owners thereof, shall and may recover the value of such Slave or Slaves from the President, Directors and Company of said Rail Road, or the owners and Captains of said Steam Boat or other Vessel, or the owner of said Stage Coach, as the case may be, by an action on the case, in any of the Courts of Law in this State.

III. And be it further enacted, That the provisions of this Act shall not be construed to extend to any Slave traveling in company with his or her master or mistress, his, her, or their agent, or as the servant or attendant of any white person or persons, bona fide employed for that purpose. [Ratified, the 12th day of January, 1841.]

1840-41. RESOLUTION IN FAVOUR OF ISAAC HUNTER. (Page 207).

Resolved by the General Assembly of the State of North Carolina, That Isaac Hunter, representing himself a free man of color, now of the City of Raleigh, who has emigrated into this State from the State of New York, be, and he is hereby licensed and allowed to remain and reside in this State for twenty days, any provision in the law of this State to the contrary notwithstanding; and that each and every the provisions of any penal Statute prohibiting his residence be, so far as he is concerned, suspended; and any penalty, forfeiture or punishment by him already incurred, be, and the same is hereby remitted: Provided, nevertheless, that after the expiration of the said twenty days, the said Isaac Hunter, if he shall not be removed from this State, shall be subject to all the pains and penalties prescribed for free persons of color migrating into this State, by the provisions of an Act, entitled "An Act concerning Slaves and free persons of color." Provided, nevertheless, that if the said Isaac Hunter shall, at any time during the twenty days he is allowed by these Resolutions to remain within the State, visit any non slaveholding State, he shall, on his return, be deemed, held and considered as having thereby forfeited all and every benefit secured to him by these Resolutions.

Resolved, That these Resolutions shall take effect from and after their Ratification. **[Ratified, the 30th day of December, 1840.]**

****

LAWS OF THE STATE OF NORTH CAROLINA PASSED BY THE GENERAL ASSEMBLY AT THE SESSION OF 1842-43 RALEIGH: THOMAS J. LEMAY, PRINTER, 1843

CHAPTER LVIII. MISCELLANEOUS.
1842-43. An Act to amend an act entitled "an act for the establishment and better regulation of Common Schools," passed in the year 1841. (Page 92).

Sec. 6. Be it further enacted, That it shall not be lawful for any County Court in this State, to tax any free person of color, for the support and maintenance of any Common School or Schools in this State. **[Ratified the 25th day of January, 1843.]**

CHAPTER LXI. MISCELLANEOUS.
1842-43. An Act to alter the time of selling Lands and Negroes in Montgomery County. (Page 184).

Sec. 1. Be it enacted by the General Assembly of the State of North Carolina, and it is hereby enacted by the authority of the same, That the time of selling lands and negroes in the counties of Montgomery and Stanly, be changed to the months in which the Superior Courts for the said counties happen, to the Mondays of said Superior Courts.

Sec. 2. Be it further enacted, That this act be in force from and after its ratification.
[Ratified the 25th day of January, A.D. 1843.]

North Carolina Law

****

LAWS OF THE STATE OF NORTH CAROLINA PASSED BY THE GENERAL ASSEMBLY AT THE SESSION OF 1844-45
RALEIGH: THOMAS J. LEMAY, PRINTER, 1845

CHAPTER XXXVI. EDUCATION.
1844-45. An Act to consolidate and amend the acts heretofore passed on the subject of Common Schools. (Page 55).
XXIII. Be it further enacted, That it shall not be lawful for any county court in this State, to tax any free person of colour, for the support and maintenance of any common school or schools.
[Ratified the 8th day of January, 1845.]

CHAPTER XLVI. MISCELLANEOUS.
1844-45. An Act to encourage the culture and manufacture of silk and sugar among the Cherokee Indians in this State. (Pages 71-72).
Whereas a small portion of the Cherokee tribe of Indians are remaining in this State, who are represented by their white neighbors as conducting themselves in a peaceable and orderly manner, and who, under the influence of temperance and religious societies, are fast improving in the knowledge of the mechanic arts, agriculture and civilization; and whereas the Cherokees referred to, who belong to the towns of Qualla and Yuansan, Cheoih, have already commenced the culture and manufacture of silk; and for the encouragement thereof,

Be it enacted by the General Assembly of the State of North Carolina, and it is hereby enacted by the authority of the same, That the provisions of the act, entitled an act to encourage the culture and manufacture of silk and sugar in this State, passed in the year 1836, be, and the same are hereby extended to the said Cherokee Indians now belonging to said towns: Provided, that the provisions of this act not extend to any Indians who are not remaining in said towns by the permission of the Government of the United States, under treaty stipulations.
[Ratified the 10th day of January, 1845.]

North Carolina Law

CHAPTER LXXXV. SLAVES AND FREE NEGROES.
1844-45. An Act to amend the Revised Statutes, entitled "an act concerning slaves and free persons of color." (Page 123).
   Be it enacted by the General Assembly of the State of North Carolina, and it is hereby enacted by the authority of the same, That the seventy seventh section of the said Revised Statutes shall not be so construed as to extend to cases of intermarriage between slaves and free persons of color by and with the consent of the master or mistress of the slaves, had before the passage of this act.
[Ratified the 9th of January, 1845.]

CHAPTER LXXXVI. SLAVES AND FREE NEGROES.
1844-45. An Act to prevent free negroes and mulattoes from trafficing in ardent spirits. (Pages 123-124).
   Be it enacted by the General Assembly of the State of North Carolina, and it is hereby enacted by the authority of the same, That hereafter it shall not be lawful for any free negro or mullato, in this State, to sell, either directly or indirectly, any ardent spirits to any person whatever: Provided that any free negro or mulatto shall be permitted to sell any ardent spirits that may have been made by him or her.
   Sec. II. Be it further enacted, That for any violation of this act, the person so offending shall, for the first offence forfeit and pay the sum of ten dollars, to be recovered before any Justice of the Peace having jurisdiction of the same, to be paid to the wardens of the poor, for the maintenance of the poor in the county in which the offence is committed, and for the second offence, shall be subject to indictment in the Superior Court, and fined or imprisoned at the discretion of the Court.
[Ratified the 8th day of January, 1845.]

CHAPTER LXXXVII. SLAVES AND FREE NEGROES.
1844-45. An Act more effectually to suppress the offence of trading with slaves. (Page 124).
   Be it enacted by the General Assembly of the State of North Carolina, and it is hereby enacted by the authority of the same, That hereafter it shall be lawful, in the same bill of indictment, in different counts, to charge any defendant with trading with slaves, receiving stolen

goods knowing them to be stolen, and petit larceny; any law, usage or custom to the contrary notwithstanding.
[Ratified this 1st day of January, 1845.]

CHAPTER XXIV. CREEKS.
1844-45. An Act to prevent the obstruction of fish passing up the creek called Six Runs, in the county of Sampson. (Pages 169-170).

Be it enacted by the General Assembly of the State of North Carolina, and it is hereby enacted by the authority of the same, That after the passage of this act, it shall not be lawful for any person to obstruct or cause to be obstructed, by any means whatever, the creek called Six Runs, in the county of Sampson, so as to prevent the passage of fish up the said creek, under the penalty of fifty dollars, to be recovered by warrant before any justice of the peace of said county, one half to the use of the informer, and the other half to the use of the wardens of the poor of said county; and any slave so offending, and being thereof convicted before any Justice of the Peace of said county, shall receive not more than thirty nine and not less than ten lashes, on his or her bare back: Provided, that nothing herein contained shall prevent or be construed to prevent any person or persons from working and hauling their seins across the said creek, in the same manner as heretofore in use.
[Ratified the 1st day ofJanuary, 1845.]

CHAPTER XXVI. CREEKS.
1844-45. An Act to prevent the felling of timber in the water courses of the county of Guilford. (Page 171).

Be it enacted by the General Assembly of the State of North Carolina, and it is hereby enacted by the authority of the same, That every person who shall obstruct any of the water courses of the county of Guilford, by felling timber or throwing logs or brush therein, and permit the same to remain in said streams or water courses for the space of twenty days, shall forfeit and pay the sum of ten dollars for each and every offence, to be recovered before a Justice of the Peace, in the name, and for the use of the wardens of the poor of said county.

Sec. II. Be it further enacted, That if the offence described in the forgoing section be committed by a slave, such slave so offending, shall, on conviction, before any Justice of the Peace, receive fifteen lashes.

[Ratified the 2nd day of January, 1845.]

****

LAWS OF THE STATE OF NORTH CAROLINA
PASSED BY THE GENERAL ASSEMBLY
AT THE SESSION OF 1846-1847
RALEIGH: THOMAS J. LEMAY, PRINTER, 1847

Published agreeably to the ninety-fifth Chapter of the Revised Statutes.

Chapter V., Bonds, Cherokee.
1846-47. An Act to amend an act, passed at the last Session of the General Assembly, entitled "an act more effectually to secure debts due for the Cherokee lands, and to facilitate the collection of the same." (Page 19).
 Sec. 1. Be it enacted by the General Assembly of the State of North Carolina, and it is hereby enacted by the authority of the same, That the provisions of the said act be extended to the securities of insolvent purchasers, whenever it is ascertained to the Governor by the agent of the State, the principals are so insolvent and have removed beyond the limits of the State, so that releases from them cannot be had, then and in that case, whenever the said securities, as aforesaid, shall release in manner prescribed, for the principals in said act, the Governor shall be, and he is hereby authorized to deliver up such bonds, to be cancelled in the same manner as if such releases were made by the principals; any thing in that law, to which this is an amendment, to the contrary notwithstanding.
[Ratified 18th January, 1847.]

Chapter VIII. Bonds, &c Transfer of.
1846-1847. An Act to provide for the Transfer of certain funds from the Internal Improvement Fund to the Public Treasury, and for other purposes. (Pages 25-26).
 Sec. 1. Be it enacted by the General Assembly of the State of North Carolina, and it is hereby enacted by the authority of the same, That all the bonds due to the board of Internal Improvement, and secured in whole or in part by mortgage to the amount of fifteen thousand six hundred

and thirteen dollars, as appears from the report of said Board of Internal Improvement, made to this General Assembly, be, and the same are hereby transferred to the Public Treasury.

Sec. 2. Be it further enacted, That the Public Treasurer, upon the receipt of the bonds as aforesaid, shall proceed to collect the same, as speedily as may be; and when so collected, or any part thereof, he shall deposit the same in the Public Treasury, to be used as other public funds.

Sec. 3. Be it further enacted, That the dividends of profits arising on one hundred and twelve shares of stock owned by the internal improvement fund, in the Bank of Cape Fear, be, and the same are hereby transferred to the public fund, until otherwise ordered by the General Assembly.

Sec. 4. Be it further enacted, That all monies received on account of Cherokee bonds, whether principal or interest, for lands heretofore sold, which shall be received at the Public Treasury until the first day of January, 1849, be, and the same are hereby directed to be placed in the Public Treasury, and used as other public funds; and that the Public Treasurer be, and he is hereby directed to carry to the credit of the internal improvement fund, on the books of the Treasury, from time to time, all such sums as may be received under his section; and that he also credit the same fund, for all such amounts as he may receive under the first and third sections of this act, so as to shew at all times the true amount which the public fund is indebted to internal improvement fund.
[Ratified 18th day of January 1847.]

Chapter XII. Cherokee Lands.
1846-47. An Act to amend an act, entitled "an act for the relief of purchasers of the Cherokee lands, passed 1830, chapter 34." (Pages 30-31).

Whereas, it appears that some tracts of land were materially intefered with by Indian Reservations, for which payments have been made into the Public Treasury, and to which the provisions of the present law do not extend, according to the opinion of the Attorney General, under said act: for remedy whereof,

Be it enacted by the General Assembly of the State of North Carolina, and it is hereby enacted by the authority of the same, That the provisions of said act shall extend to all cases where the purchase money has been paid into the Public Treasury, as well as where the bonds are held

by the Public Treasurer; and in case the interest or any portion of the principal should under the provisions of said act be remitted, then and in that case the Public Treasurer is hereby authorized to refund to the person or persons paying the same, such sum as may be adjudged to them under the provisions of said statute.
[Ratified 18th January, 1847.]

Chapter XIII. Cherokee Lands.
1846-47. An Act concerning the duties of the Cherokee Land Agent. (Page 31).
Be it enacted by the General Assembly of the State of North Carolina, and it is hereby enacted by the authority of the same, That it shall be the duty of the agent appointed to receive payment for Cherokee lands, to attend at the town of Murphy, in the county of Cherokee, on the first three days of each Superior Court for said county, for the purpose of receiving payments upon all bonds entrusted to his care by virtue of such agency.
[Ratified 18th January, 1847.]

Chapter XIV. Cherokee Lands.
1846-47. An Act to provide for the sale of certain lands, in Cherokee and Macon counties, which have been surrendered to the State. (Pages 31-36).
Whereas, under the Act of the last General Assembly, entitled "an act more effectually to secure the debts due for Cherokee lands, and to facilitate the collection of the same," several tracts of land, commonly known as the Cherokee lands, were surrendered to the State, and ought to be again sold, as well as to secure homes to the first purchasers, as for the benefit of the State, no revenue whatever being derived by the State from said lands at present: for remedy whereof,
Be it enacted by the General Assembly of the State of North Carolina, and it is hereby enacted by the authority of the same, That all the lands surrendered by insolvents, under the provisions of said act, shall be again sold, under the following rules and restrictions, that is to say, the county court of Cherokee, (a majority of the Justices of said county being present) shall appoint one discreet person, residing in Cherokee county, and the Governor shall appoint two others, not residents of Cherokee county,

who shall constitute a board of valuation, whose duty it shall be to value the lands so surrendered to the State, at a fair cash valuation, in the following manner: 1st, at their present worth, including the improvements placed upon them, by the former purchasers, or their assigns: 2nd, the worth of said lands when sold by the State in September, 1838, including such improvements as were on them at that time; taking into consideration in both cases the locality of said lands, and the facilities the purchasers may have in the transportation of their produce to market; and the said board of valuation shall make out duplicate lists of each class of valuation, as soon as may be, one copy of each class of such lists to be filed in the clerk's office of the county court of Cherokee, and the other they shall transmit to the Governor; and such copy filed in the clerk's office, as by this act directed, shall be kept by the clerk among the records of said court: Provided, that in no case shall the board of valuation hereby authorised place a less valuation upon the aforesaid land, than the rate fixed by the Act of Assembly of 1836, for the respective classes.

Sec. 2. Be it further enacted, That the first purchasers who have surrendered said lands, their heirs, devisees, or assignees, respectively, shall have a pre-emption right to purchase the lands they, or either of them, have so surrendered, at the second valuation by said board: Provided, the right of pre-emption aforesaid, shall extend to no assignee, who may have become such since the surrender aforesaid; the said purchasers first paying one fourth of the purchase money, and giving bond with two or more approved securities, (each of whom shall be considered good in his individual capacity for the whole debt,) to the agent of the State heretofore appointed under the act passed at the session of the General Assembly, held on the 3rd Monday of November, A.D. 1840, entitled "an act authorising the Governor to appoint an agent, in the county of Macon or Cherokee;" and such bonds, for the residue of the payment of the purchaser money, shall be made payable, in four equal annual instalments, bearing interest from date; and upon such bonds, when due and unpaid, suit shall be brought as upon the other bonds given for Cherokee lands, under the laws now in force concerning Cherokee bonds: Provided, nevertheless, that no suit shall be instituted in any Court of the State, when the amount due is within the jurisdiction of a Justice of the Peace; and in all such cases, the agent is hereby required to warrant for the same before some Justice of the Peace: And provided further, that in all cases where it may be necessary to bring a suit in Court, on any of the Cherokee bonds, the amount due and owing by the same parties, (although the same may be on several bonds) shall be consolidated in one action.

Sec. 3. Be it further enacted, That if the person or persons, who surrendered said lands, his, her, or their heirs, devisees, or assigns, should fail to comply with the requisitions of the second section of this act within three months after the valuations by the said board, then and in that case, the said agent for the State is hereby authorised and required to sell and dispose of any tract or tracts so surrendered, to any other person or persons desirous of purchasing the same, at the price of improved lands, upon such purchaser or purchasers first paying one fourth of the purchase money and giving the necessary bonds as required in said second section: Provided however, that if the agent of the State shall not be able to sell or dispose of the said lands at the price of improved lands, as herein provided, within six months from the expiration of the three months mentioned in this section, then, and in that case it shall be his duty to report that fact forthwith to the Governor of the State, accompanied by a list of all such lands, so remaining unsold; and the Governor, if he shall deem the same expedient, shall appoint one or two commissioners, as in his judjment may be deemed necessary, to superintend the sale of the said lands, at public auction, who, before entering on the discharge of their duty, shall execute to the Governor, for the use of the State, bond with approved security, in the sum of ten thousand dollars each, conditioned for the faithful performance of their duty, and accounting for all monies coming into their hands by virtue of their appointment as commissioners aforesaid.

Sec. 4. Be it further enacted, That in the event of a public sale being directed by the Governor, as aforesaid, it shall be his duty to advertise the same, for at least six weeks in not than less three newspapers of this State, setting forth the time and place of sale, which shall be held at the town of Murphy, in the county of Cherokee, and at such time as the Governor may appoint; and he shall also set forth, in the said advertisement, the terms and conditions of the said sale, which shall be the same as those mentioned in the second section of this act; and the Commissioners appointed as aforesaid, shall make a full report of their proceedings, together with an account of the cash by them received, to the Governor, within two months from the close of the said sales, and shall pay over, at the same time, to the Public Treasurer, all sums of money by them received on account of said sales; for which services they shall be allowed such sum as the Governor may deem just and reasonable, not exceeding three dollars per day, for every day that they may be engaged in travelling to the place and superintending the said sales, and making the necessary returns to the seat of Government: Provided however, that the public sale hereby authorised, shall not continue for a longer time than two weeks.

Sec. 5. Be it further enacted, That whenever it shall appear to said agent, that a part of any tract of land surrendered under the act of 1844, had been previously sold by the purchaser from the State to any other person or persons, then and in that case, it shall be the duty of the agent to have due regard to the interests of such subpurchaser at the time of surrender, and to resell to each, under the provisions of this act, according to the interest he or she may have had at the time of such surrender.

Sec. 6. Be it further enacted, That the pre-emption right, granted by the second section of this act, shall not extend to any person or persons who are not actual settlers on the lands, or who do not desire to become permanent residents in said counties of Cherokee and Macon: Provided, that nothing in this act contained, shall interfere with any right which any person or persons may have acquired under any existing law of the State.

Sec. 7. Be it further enacted, That each and every purchaser of any section or sections of said land, having obtained a certificate from the board constituted by this act, shall have full power and authority to institute an action of ejectment in the name of the State of North Carolina, against any person or persons, who may be in possession of such section of land, and shall, on application, refuse to deliver up quiet and peaceable possession thereof, or who shall intrude upon said purchasers, after they enter into possession, or who may hold over after their tenancy shall have expired. And the certificate of the board, to such purchaser, or his assignee, shall be in evidence of title and right to sustain said action: Provided nevertheless, the said purchaser shall give bond and security for the payment of all costs accruing in said action, in case of his failure to recover.

Sec. 8. Be it further enacted, That as a full compensation for the performance by them of the duties herein required, the said board shall be allowed the sum of three dollars, each, for every day they may be necessarily engaged in the discharge of the duties herein imposed, to be paid by the agent of the Cherokee lands, out [of] monies in his hand, upon the affidavits of each of [the] members of said board, setting forth the number of days each may have so served; the receipt of the members of which board shall be received by the Public Treasurer, from the said Cherokee agent as cash, in any future settlement with him; and the said agent shall be allowed such compensation for the services required of him

by this act, as the Governor, Treasurer and Comptroller may allow, upon satisfactory proof made to them, of the number of days which the said agent may have served, or such other evidence of the amount of service performed by him under this act; which compensation shall in no case amount to more than two dollars per day, for each whole day, the said agent may have been so employed.
[Ratified 18th of January, 1847.]

CHAPTER XLLII. Miscellaneous.
1846-47. An Act to amend the 75th section, chapter 34, of the Revised Statutes, entitled "Crimes and Punishments." (Page 107).
    Be it enacted by the General Assembly of the State of North Carolina, and it is hereby enacted by the authority of the same, That it shall not be lawful for any person or persons to sell or barter and deliver, to any slave, or slaves, any gun cotton, fire arms, swords, dirks or other side arms, unless those articles be for the owner or employer, and by the written order of the owner or employer of such slave or slaves, under the penalty of one hundred dollars for each offense, to be recovered, by warrant, before any justice of the peace, and applied, one half to the use of the party suing for the same, and the other half to the wardens of the poor of the county; and, moreover, may be indicted in the county or superior courts of law; and the defendant, on conviction, shall be fined or imprisoned at the discretion of the court; the fine, however, not to exceed fifty dollars, or the imprisonment three months.
[Ratified 18th January, 1847.]

CHAPTER XLVI. Miscellaneous.
1846-47. An Act to provide for the apprehension of runaway slaves in the great Dismal Swamp and for other purposes. (Pages 109-113).
    Whereas, many slaves belonging to persons residing or having plantations in the neighborhood of the great dismall swamp, have left the services of their masters and taken refuge in the said swamp, and by the aid of free persons of color and of white men, have been and are enabled to elude all attempts to secure their persons and induce them again under the just authority of their masters, and their consorting with such white men and free persons of color, they remain setting at defiance the power of their masters, corrupting and seducing other slaves, and by their evil example

and evil practices, lessening the due subordination, and greatly impairing the value of slaves in the district of country bordering on the said great dismall swamp: for remedy whereof,

Sec. 1. Be it enacted by the General Assembly of the State of North Carolina, and it is hereby enacted by the authority of the same, That each and every person, who shall design to employ, or permit to be employed, in the said dismal swamp, any slaves, of which he or she shall be the owner, or shall have the care, use or management, shall before so employing or permitting such slave to be so employed, produce or cause to be so produced, the said slave before the clerk of the court of pleas and quarter sessions of the county in which such slave is so to be employed, and the clerk shall, upon his personal examination of such slave, prepare an exact description of the said slave, specifying therein the name and residence of the owner, manager, hirer or person having the care or superintendence of such slave, the name of the slave, his or her height, complexion, and every peculiar mark or description by which such slave may be most effectually known and identified; and such written description shall be entered upon a book by him to be kept for that purpose, and shall forthwith make out and deliver to the owner, manager, hirer or person having such care and superintendence a fair and true copy thereof, without any interlineation or erasure, certified under his hand and the seal of the court, and the owner, manager, hirer or other person aforesaid, shall before employing such slave, or permitting such slave to be employed in the said dismal swamp deliver such copy to him or her to be kept about his or her person; and if any owner, manager, hirer or person having the care and superintendence of any slave, shall employ, or permit, or suffer such slave to be employed in the said swamp without procuring and delivering to such slave such copy as aforesaid, or shall otherwise offend against the provisions in this section contained, he or she shall be deemed guilty of a misdemeanor, and upon conviction thereof, shall be fined or imprisoned at the discretion of the court having cognizance thereof.

Sec. 2. Be it further enacted, That no free person of color shall work, or employ himself in the said swamp, without having gone before the clerk of the proper court, and caused a description of himself to be taken and registered in the manner prescribed by the forgoing section, and keeping and having ready to produce the copy of such description certified by the clerk as above directed; and any free person of color found employed in working in the said swamp without such copy, shall be deemed guilty of a misdemeanor, may be arrested and committed, or bound over to the next court of the county in which he may be so found, and on conviction thereof, may be punished by fine, imprisonment and whipping, all or any of them, at the discretion of the court.

Sec. 3. Be it further enacted, That if any slave shall be found employed or working in the said swamp without such copy as is prescribed in the first section of this act, such slave may be arrested by the person or persons finding him or her, and upon being taken before a justice of the peace, shall be sentenced to receive thirty nine lashes on his or her bare back; and the person or persons arresting such slave shall be entitled to demand and have of and from the owner, hirer, manager, superintendent or person having the use of such slave, the sum of twenty five dollars, and may recover the same by warrant before any justice of the peace, or may proceed against such slave as a runaway, according to the laws directing the disposition of runaway slaves, and cause such slave to be detained in custody until the said sum of twenty five dollars and all other charges shall have been paid.

Sec. 4. Be it further enacted, That if any slave or any free person of color having obtained or having in his possession any such certified copy as above mentioned, shall in said swamp consort with, or work, or be employed in company with any runaway slave, or any slave not having such copy, such slave or free person of color, shall be deemed guilty of a misdemeanor and shall be punished therefor, the slave by order of any justice of the peace by thirty nine lashes on his or her bare back, and the free person of color, upon conviction in any court having jurisdiction thereof, by fine, imprisonment and whipping, all or any of them at the discretion of the court.

Sec. 5. Be it further enacted, That if any white person shall, in the said swamp, consort or work with, or employ, or engage to work in said swamp any runaway slave, or any slave who shall not have received such certified copy as aforesaid, he or she shall forfeit the sum of one hundred dollars, to be recovered in an action of debt, by any person who will sue for the same, and shall be moreover indictable as for a misdemeanor, and on conviction shall be punished by imprisonment, for not less than three months, or fined, at the discretion of the court.

Sec. 6. Be it further enacted, That if any free negro, who shall be convicted of any offence under this act, and sentenced by the court to pay a fine, shall be unable to pay or procure the same to be paid, it shall be the duty of the court to order him or her to be sold for the said fine, according to the directions of the Statute providing for the sale of free negoes for fines in other cases.

Sec. 7. Be it further enacted, That any person or persons who shall apprehend any runaway slave in the said dismal swamp and deliver such slave to his or her master or owner, or shall deliver such slave into the jail of the county in which such apprehension shall take place, shall be entitled (besides any reward which may have been offered for the apprehension of such slave,) to demand and receive of and from such master or owner, the sum of twenty five dollars, and if not paid on demand, to recover the same, by warrant, before any justice of the peace.

Sec. 8. Be it further enacted, That if any person shall falsely make, forge, or counterfeit, or cause, or procure to be falsely made, forged, or counterfeited, or aid, or assist, in the false making, forging, or counterfeiting of any writing, purporting to be a copy of the registration of the description of any slave or free person of color in this act mentioned, he or she shall be deemed guilty of a misdemeanor, and on conviction in any court having cognizance thereof, shall be punished by standing in the pillory for one hour, by whipping, imprisonment for six months, and fine: all, or any of them, at the discretion of the court, due regard being had to the nature and circumstances of the offence.

Sec. 9. Be it further enacted, That it shall be the duty of the several clerks of the counties of Gates, Chowan, Perquimans, Pasquotank, Camden, and Currituck, to procure from the Secretary of State, whose duty it shall be to furnish them with the same, printed copies of this act, which they shall have put up at the court house doors of their respective counties by the first day of March next: that the expenses of the same, if any, be defrayed from the treasuries of the several counties, and that for a failure to comply with the requisitions of this act, the clerks of the said counties shall be liable to indictment in the county or superior courts, and on conviction shall be fined at the discretion of the court.

Sec. 10. Be it further enacted, That none of the provisions of this act shall be construed to extend to any swamp in the county of Currituck, lying below Indian Town creek bridge, nor to any swamp lands which have been reclaimed and are now or may hereafter be used for agricultural purposes, or to any slave or slaves employed in cultivating the same, nor to any slave or slaves, their owners, employers, or managers, that may be temporarily engaged in such swamp or swamps, in cutting timber for ordinary plantation purposes.

North Carolina Law

Sec. 11. Be it further enacted, That this act shall be in force and take effect, from and after the first day of March next.
[Ratified on the 18th day of January, 1847.]

CHAPTER L. Miscellaneous.
1846-47. An Act to repeal in part an act, passed in 1844 and 1845, entitled "an act to prevent frauds in levying executions issued by a single magistrate and to encourage and facilitate the practice of taking security for the forthcoming of property seized under execution, and to amend the same." (Page 117).

Be it enacted by the General Assembly of the State of North Carolina, and it is hereby enacted by the authority of the same, That so much of the above recited act as provides that all sales of personal chattels shall be made within thirty days after the levy, be, and the same is hereby repealed, so far as relates to slaves which may be so levied upon; and that hereafter, when any execution issued by a justice of the peace shall be levied on any slave or slaves, the sale thereof shall take place within sixty days after the said levy, under the same rules, regulations and restrictions as are provided in said act.
[Ratified 18th of January, 1847.]

CHAPTER LIX. Miscellaneous.
1846-47. An Act in favor of the Cherokee Chief, Junoluskee. (Page 128).

Whereas the Cherokee Chief Junoluskee, who distinguished himself in the service of the United States at the battle of the "Horses-Shoe," as commander of a body of Cherokees, as well as on divers other occasions during the last war with Great Britain, has, since his removal west of the Mississippi, returned to this State, and expressed a wish to remain and become a citizen thereof:

Sec. 1. Be it enacted by the General assembly of the State of North Carolina, and it is hereby enacted by the authority of the same, That the said Junoluskee be, and he is hereby declared a citizen of the State of North Carolina, and entitled to all the rights, priveleges and immunities consequent thereon.

Sec. 2. Be it further enacted, That the Secretary of State be, and he is hereby authorised and directed to convey unto the said Junoluskee, in fee simple, the tract of land in Cherokee county, in district 9, tract No. 19, containing three hundred and thirty seven acres; which said land the said Junoluskee shall be empowered to hold and enjoy, without the power to see or convey the same, except for the term of two years from time to time: Provided nevertheless, that he shall have full power to dispose of the same by devise only.

 Sec. 3. Be it further enacted, That the Public Treasurer be directed to pay unto the said Junoluskee the sum of one hundred dollars, out of any monies in the treasury not otherwise appropriated.

 Sec. 4. Be it further enacted, That this act shall be in force from and after its passage.

[Ratified the 2nd day of January, 1847.]

CHAPTER LXXV. Revenue.
1846-47. An Act to provide for a re-assessment of the lands of this State, and a more accurate enlistment of the taxable polls. (Page 145).

 Sec. 6. Be it further enacted, That in all cases the owner or owners of taxable slaves of this State, and not the hirer, shall enlist them for taxation, whether they be in the possession of the owner on the first day of April or not: Provided, that in all cases where the owner or owners of any such slaves reside out of the State, and the slaves are hired to persons within the State, the hirer or other person having them in possession at the time the list is taken, shall give them in and pay the tax; and on failure thereof, the said hirer or other person having any such slave in possession, shall forfeit and pay a double tax on all such slaves, to be collected and accounted for as other taxes.

RESOLUTIONS.
1846-47. Resolution in relation to the bonds given for rent of Cherokee lands, surrendered to the State. (Page 250).

 Resolved, That the obligors, their heirs, Executors and Administrators, in the bonds, heretofore given to the State, for rents of Cherokee lands surrendered to the State, under the act passed at the last session of the General Assembly, be, and they are hereby absolved and discharged from the payment of one half of the monies mentioned in said bonds: Provided, that this resolution shall in no wise affect the covenants

contained in said bonds relative to the preservation and subsequent surrender of said lands, as therein stipulated.
[Ratified 16th of January, 1847.]

RESOLUTIONS.
1846-47. Resolution in relation to the accounts of the purchasers of the Cherokee lands. (Page 251).

Resolved, That the Comptroller of public accounts be required, from the returns made by the agent for the collection of the Cherokee bonds, to the Treasury Department, to make the necessary and proper entries, on the accounts of the purchasers of Cherokee lands, on the books of his office, so that the said accounts shall show all payments made thereon, whether of principal or interest; and that the said Comptroller be required to continue to make similar entries on said accounts from the returns made by the said agent to the Comptroller's office, from time to time, so that the books and accounts of the said office shall at all times show the actual condition of the accounts of the purchasers of Cherokee Lands.

Resolved further, That the Comptroller shall be allowed for bringing up the aforesaid accounts, to the period when the Cherokee agent is directed to make a duplicate of his returns to the Comptroller's office, the sum of three hundred dollars, to be paid by the Public Treasurer, whenever the said accounts on the Comptroller's books are brought up to the period aforesaid.
[Ratified 18th of January, 1847.]

CHAPTER CXXXI. County Regulations.
1846-47. An Act to alter the times of selling lands and negroes in Richmond county. (Page 277).

Be it enacted by the General Assembly of the State of North Carolina, and it is hereby enacted by the authority of the same, That the time of selling land and negroes in the county of Richmond, be changed in the month in which the superior court for said county happens to the Monday of said superior court.

Sec. 2. Be it further enacted, That this act be in force from and after its ratification.
[Ratified 18th of January, 1847.]

CHAPTER CXCIX. Towns.
1846-47. An Act for the incorporation of the town of Washington. (Pages 328-332).

Sec. 5. That no person shall be eligible to the office of intendant of police or commissioner of the town of Washington except a white male citizen of the full age of twenty one years, who shall have resided in said town six months ....

Sec. 9. It shall be the duty of the intendant of police to see that the laws of the State and the ordinances of said commissioners are obeyed and executed within said town. ...The said intendant shall further have summary jurisdiction to hear and determine all breaches of the peace occurring within the limits of said town, not above the grade of misdemeanors, and to punish all offenders, if free white persons by a fine not exceeding twenty dollars, or by imprisonment not exceeding twenty days; if free persons, but not white, then by fine or imprisonment as above or by whipping not exceeding thirty nine lashes; if slaves, by a whipping not exceeding thirty nine lashes; and the owner or managers of said slaves shall receive reasonable notice of the time of trial and a copy of the warrant for the arrest of said slaves, and in case of their conviction shall be liable for the costs thereof: Provided nevertheless, that it shall and may be lawful in all cases for the person (or persons or in case of slaves their owners or managers) against whom the said intendant of police shall give judgment or pass sentence by virtue of the summary jurisdiction hereby given, or for breach of law or laws relating to said town, or of any ordinances of said commissioners, or for any penalty or penalties given by said law or ordinances, to appeal from said judgment or sentence to the superior court of law for the county of Beaufort, first entering into recognizance with good security before the said intendant for the appearance of said appellant or appellants before the judge of the said superior court at the next term thereof, and for his or their performing and abiding the judgment of the said superior court. And the said person or persons praying said appeal shall be allowed ten days to obtain the said surety: Provided, that execution may nevertheless issue on said judgment or sentence forthwith; and nothing herein contained shall be so construed to stay the same. The said intendant of police is further hereafter vested with the same jurisdiction and powers over all other offences committed by slaves as is now by law given to a justice or justices of the peace out of court, under the same rules, regulations and restrictions as are provided in those cases. ....

Sec. 25. That the said board of commissioners shall have power to cause to be executed the laws of this State on the subject of quarantine and health. They shall have further power, by ordinances, to prohibit all persons recently from any place or places where an infectious or contagious disease is believed to exist or recently have existed, from entering and all goods and chattels from being brought from said place or places, within said town; and by ordinances to fix a penalty for the breach of any of the rules established by them on this subject, which penalty shall be recovered from any and all persons who are liable thereto, by action of debt, in the name of the commissioners of the town of Washington, in any court having competent jurisdiction. The said commissioners shall also have power to take such other precautionary measures to prevent the introduction of infectious or contagious diseases in the said town, as they may deem expedient: said commissioners, upon the certificate of a physician, that a dangerous and infectious or contagious disease is existing in any house within said town, or in case the occupier of any house suspected to contain such disease, shall forbid or prevent the visit of a physician sent by said commissioners for the purpose of examination, shall also have power to forbid and prevent all persons from leaving said house and its enclosures, and take such other steps to prevent communication with the persons so infected, and to arrest the spread of the diseases, as they may deem expedient, and to impose such penalty or penalties for the breach of their ordinance or ordinances made for that purpose, as they shall think proper. At any time, upon the certificate of a physician that any slave or free negro is sick with a dangerous and infectious disease within said town and that he can be removed without endangering his life, the said commissioners shall have power to cause said slave or free negro to be removed and confined to some convenient and proper place without said town, and shall cause him to be there attended to as befits his situation; and it shall be lawful for them to sue for and recover from any free negro or from the owner of any slave so removed, the expense of his or her removal, support, nursing and medical attendance during the time of his or her sickness; and also, in case of his or her death, the expenses of burial, by writ, in the name of the commissioners of the town of Washington, in any court having competent jurisdiction. And any and all persons attempting to prevent or resisting the removal of said slaves or free persons from said town, shall be liable to indictment in the superior court of law for the county of Beaufort, and, on conviction, punished for a misdemeanor. The said commissioners shall have further power to impose such punishments on all slaves or free negroes violating this section or any of the ordinances of said commissioners made by virtue thereof, or on a like subject matter, as they may think expedient, not exceeding one months imprisonment, or thirty nine lashes.

RESOLUTIONS
1846-47. Resolution in favor of James Wiggins and Alexander Nichols. (Page 378).
Resolved, That the Governor of the State be, and he is hereby authorized and directed to accept a deed of release from James H. Wiggins, for Tract No. 1, Panther's Reservation, Macon County, and also a deed of release from Alexander Nichols, for Tract No. 75, District 8, Macon County, and to cancel the bonds of the said Wiggins and Nichols, given for the land aforesaid, in pursuance of an act passed by the General Assembly, at the session of 1844-45, entitled "an act more effectually to secure the debts due for Cherokee Lands, and to facilitate the collection of the same."
[Ratified the 2nd day of January, 1847.]

RESOLUTIONS
1846-47. Resolution in favor of William Morrison and Samuel Bryson. (Page 380).
Resolved, That the Secretary of State be authorized and directed to issue a grant or grants to William Morrison and Samuel Bryson, for Tracts No. 31 and 32, in District No. 9, in the county of Macon, purchased by James Truitt, at the Cherokee land sales of 1836.
[Ratified 18th of January, 1847.]

RESOLUTIONS
1846-47. Resolution in favor of Ezekiel Dowdle and West Truitt. (Page 380).
Resolved, That the Governor of the State be, and he is hereby authorized and directed to accept a deed of release from Samuel Bryson and William Morrison, assignees of James Truitt, for Tract No. 29, in District No. 9, purchased at Cherokee land sale of 1836, in Macon County,

and that he cancel the bonds given for said land by said James Truitt, with Ezekiel Dowdle and West Truitt, his securities, in pursuance of an act passed by the General Assembly, at the session of 1844-45, entitled "an act more effectually to secure the debts due for Cherokee lands, and to facilitate the collection of the same."
[Ratified 12th day of January, 1847.]

RESOLUTIONS
1846-47. Resolution in favor of William Alexander. (Page 381).
Resolved, That the Secretary of State be, and he is hereby authorized to issue a grant to William Alexander for a tract of land in District third, Tract No. 118, Cherokee land sale of 1838.
[Ratified the 5th day of January, 1847.]

RESOLUTION
1846-47. Resolution in favor of Jacob Siler and Joseph Cathey. (Page 382).
Resolved, That the Public Treasurer be authorized and directed to pay to Jacob Siler ninety dollars for time and expenses of himself and Clerk in renting out Cherokee lands surrendered to the State, under an act of the last General Assembly, for expenses in travelling to and from Beattie's Ford, in the county of Lincoln, at the request of the late Treasurer of the State; and for time occupied in travelling to and from Raleigh, to cancel bonds for Cherokee lands surrendered to the State: also that the Treasurer be directed to pay Joseph Cathey the sum of ($16,) sixteen dollars, under the act of 1844-45, entitled "an act more effectually to secure debts due for Cherokee lands, and to facilitate the collection of the same."
[Ratified 8th day of January, 1847,]

RESOLUTION
1846-47. Resolution in favor of Thomas M. Angel. (Page 386).
Resolved, That the Secretary of State be authorized and directed to issue a grant or grants to Thomas M. Angel, of the County of Macon, for Tracts Nos. 92, 93, 94, 95, 101, 102, 103, in District No. 11, in said county, purchased by Henry Hogen, at the Cherokee land sales of 1836:

Provided that said grant or grants shall not issue until the whole of the purchase money has been paid.
[Ratified the 5th day of January, 1847,]

RESOLUTION
1846-47. Resolution for the relief of Mary D. Moore. (Page 388).
Resolved, That the Governor be authorized to direct the agent of the State for the collection of bonds for purchase of Cherokee lands, to sell to Mary D. Moore, of Macon county, Tract No. 94, in District No. 16; and that he be directed to take her bond, with good security, for the amount due for said land at the time of the surrender of the same to the State by the said Mary D. Moore; and that the said Mary D. Moore shall have all the benefits of the act of 1844-45, entitled "an act more effectually to secure the debts due for Cherokee lands, and to facilitate the collections of the same.
[Ratified 12th day of January, 1847.]

REPORT OF THE PUBLIC TREASURER
1846-47. Cherokee Bonds.

Received of Jacob Siler, agent,	16,357.25
Thomas L. Clingman, atto.	220.00
Edmond Jones,	874.67
N.S. Jarret,	24.36
James W. Guinn,	43.00
J.L. Dillard & others,	1,496.96
John Sudderth,	350.00
James Calloway,	50.00
M. Francis, atto. for A. Enloe,	125.00
S. Enloe, and others,	<u>36.85</u>
	19,578.09

****

LAWS OF THE STATE OF NORTH CAROLINA
PASSED BY THE GENERAL ASSEMBLY,
AT THE SESSION OF 1848-49
PUBLISHED AGREEABLY TO THE NINETY FIFTH CHAPTER

North Carolina Law

OF THE REVISED STATUTES
RALEIGH: THOMAS J. LEMAY, PRINTER, 1849.

CHAPTER XXXVI. Crimes and Punishment.
1848-49. An Act more effectually to suppress the traffic with slaves, and amendatory of the 75th section of the 34th chapter of the Revised Statutes, entitled "Crimes and Punishments." (Pages 81-82.).
Section
1. Prohibits buying from slaves iron or steel, whether manufactured or not.
2. Repeals provision as to time of bringing suit.
3. Time of bringing suit limited to two years.

Sec. 1. Be it enacted by the General Assembly of the State of North Carolina, and it is hereby enacted by the authority of the same, That in addition to the articles enumerated and specified in the 75th section of the 34th chapter of the Revised Statutes, entitled "Crimes and Punishments," it shall not be lawful for any person or persons to buy of, traffic with, or receive from, any slave or slaves, any iron or steel, whether manufactured or not, unless the same be with written consent of the owner or manager of such slave or slaves, or for the use of such owner or manager; and any person or persons offending against the provisions of this act, shall be liable to indictment, and on conviction, shall be fined or imprisoned at the discretion of the court, and shall moreover be liable to the same forfeiture or penalty prescribed and to be recovered in like manner as is allowed in the said 75th section of the 34th chapter of the Revised Statutes, for trading with slaves, for any of the prohibited articles enumerated in said section.

Sec. 2 And be it further enacted, That so much of the 80th section of the 34th chapter of the Revised Statutes, as provides that no indictment shall be prosecuted for any violation of the seventy fifth and seventy ninth sections of said chapter, unless such indictment be commenced within twelve months after such violation, be and the same is hereby repealed.

Sec. 3. And be it further enacted, That no bill of indictment shall be found, or presentment made, by the grand jury of any county in this State, for any violation of said seventy fifth and seventy ninth sections, unless such indictment be commenced within two years after such violation.

[Ratified 27th day of January, 1849.]

CHAPTER XLVII. Lands---Cherokee.
1848-49. An Act to facilitate the collection of certain debts given for Cherokee lands, and for other purposes. (Pages 95-97).

Whereas at the different sales of the Cherokee lands, several tracts or parcels of land were sold separately to the same purchaser, and a bond for the whole amount of the purchase money, instead of separate bonds for each tract, was given; and whereas the original purchasers of such lands have, in many cases, sold and assigned the said lands to different persons; and whereas said assignees cannot pay for the tract or tracts so assigned to them and procure grants for the same, without first paying off the whole bond of the original purchaser, and therefore will not, and, in many cases, cannot, pay off said bonds; and whereas the original purchasers have, in many cases, become insolvent, and the amount of their bonds cannot be collected; and whereas in some instances the sureties to the bonds of the original purchasers have satisfied said bonds, and have the agent's receipt in full for the same: Therefore,

Sec. 1. Be it enacted by the General Assembly of the State of North Carolina, and it is hereby enacted by the authority of the same, That in all cases where the original purchasers or their surety or sureties, of Cherokee lands, have failed to pay for the same, it should be the duty of the agent of the State for the collection of debts due for said Cherokee lands, to receive payment from any assignee of said original purchaser or purchasers, his heir, devisee or assignee, for any tract so assigned, and to give said assignee, his heir, devisee or assignee a receipt for the same, particularly specifying and describing the tract or parcel so assigned and paid for. And it shall be the duty of the Secretary of State, upon presentation of said Agent's receipt, to issue a grant for the tract or tracts of land, specified in said receipt, to the person or persons so paying for the same.

Sec. 2. Be it further enacted, That whenever in any case, the purchase money for Cherokee lands has been paid by or collected from the sureties to the original purchaser to the full amount of the bond or bonds given by them, it shall be the duty of the Secretary of State, whenever the fact of such payment has been satisfactorily certified to him by the said agent of the State, to issue a grant or grants for the lands so paid for to the person or persons paying for the same.

Sec. 3. Be it further enacted, That nothing in this act contained shall authorize the agent to receipt for, or the Secretary of State to issue grants for any tract of land to the original purchasers or their sureties, unless the whole amount of the bond in which the price of said tract is included shall have been fully satisfied and paid off.

Sec. 4. Be it further enacted, That this act shall be in force from and after its ratification.

[Ratified 29th day of January, 1849.]

CHAPTER XLIX. Lands---Cherokee.
1848-49. An Act to amend an act, passed at the last session, entitled "An Act to provide for the sale of certain lands in Cherokee and Macon Counties, which have been surrendered to the State." (Pages 97-98).
Whereas no provision was made by the above recited act to require the agent of the State to return to the Comptroller's office an account of the lands resold under the provisions of said act: For remedy whereof,

Sec. 1. Be it enacted by the General Assembly of the State of North Carolina, and it is hereby enacted by the authority of the same, That the Cherokee land agent shall, on or before the first day of May next, return to the Comptroller's office a full and complete statement of all the surrendered lands, valued and resold under the above recited act, setting forth the names of the purchasers, the amount of each purchase, the amount paid, and the amount due, and when due. And in all cases where the bonds of the original purchasers have been cancelled, he shall return a statement thereof to the Comptroller, who shall credit the respective accounts of said purchasers, with the amount of said bonds.

Sec. 2. Be it further enacted, That upon the return of the statement of the agent to the Comptroller's office, shewing the account of sales as aforesaid, the Comptroller shall charge the obligors respectively in his books with amount of each bond; and when payments are made thereon, either to the Public Treasurer or the agent aforesaid, the Comptroller, on being furnished with the evidence of such payment, shall enter the proper credit for the same.

[Ratified 29th day of January, 1849.]

CHAPTER L. Lands---Cherokee.

1848-49. An Act for the relief of James Stewart of Cherokee County. (Pages 98-99).
Whereas Andrew J. Russell became the purchaser of two lots of Cherokee lands, at the land sale in 1838, number (112) one hundred and twelve, and (113) one hundred and thirteen, in district number six, lying in Cherokee county; and whereas the said Andrew J. Russell sold and assigned his interest in said lots to E.R. Scott, and the said E.R. Scott sold and assigned his interest in said lots to James Stewart, of Cherokee county; and whereas the said James Stewart has paid the purchase money for said lots into the Treasury of North Carolina, and the Secretary of State has issued grants for said lots in the name of the said E.R. Scott, and the said Scott has removed from the county, and resides in parts unknown: Therefore,
Sec. 1. Be it enacted by the General Assembly of the State of North Carolina, and it is hereby enacted by the authority of the same, That the Secretary of State be, and he is hereby directed to cancel the grants issued in the name of E.R. Scott for lots numbered 112 and 113, in district number (6) six, of Cherokee lands, lying in Cherokee county, and issue grants to, and in the name of James Stewart for said lots of lands, any law to the contrary notwithstanding; and that this act shall take effect from and after the ratification thereof.
[Ratified 27th day of January, 1849.]

CHAPTER LXXVII. Revenue.
1848-49. An Act to increase the Revenue of the State. (Pages 129-130).
Whereas, There are many wealthy citizens of this State, who derive very considerable revenues from moneys which produce interest, dividends and profits, and who do not contribute a due proportion to the public exigencies of the same:
Sec. 2. Be it further enacted, That hereafter there shall be levied the sum of three cents upon every dollar of profit or dividend safely secured, and actually due or received; upon all sums of money vested in trading in slaves, or vested in sailing or steam vessels.

CHAPTER XCIII. Runaways.
1848-49. An Act to amend an Act, passed at the last session of the General Assembly, entitled "An Act to provide for the apprehension of

runaway Slaves in the Great Dismal Swamp, and for other purposes," and to extend the provisions thereof. (Pages 213-215).

Sec. 1. Be it enacted by the General Assembly of the State of North Carolina, and it is hereby enacted by the authority of the same, That the regulations, requirements, proceedings and other enactments prescribed and enjoined in the first eight sections of an act, passed at the last session of the General Assembly, entitled "an act to provide for the apprehension of runaway slaves in the Great Dismal Swamp, and for other purposes," in regard to slaves and free persons of color employed or at work in the said swamp, and also such persons as employ them, be, and they are hereby extended to, and prescribed for, the like persons employed or at work, or who may employ others in the swamp which lies between Lee's mill, in the county of Washington, and Pamlico river, in the county of Beaufort; and also to such as may be employed or at work, or who may employ others in the swamp which lies between Juniper creek and the lands of Charles Pettigrew, in the county of Tyrrell; and also to such as may be employed or at work, or who may employ others in the swamp lying at the head of Sonto creek, between Durham's creek and Goose creek, in Beaufort county; and that the same penalties and proceedings authorised and prescribed in the aforesaid sections be, and the same are hereby prescribed and authorised against similar persons in like cases offending against any of the provisions of said act as extended and applied to the aforesaid swamps by this act.

Sec. 2. Be it further enacted, That it shall be the duty of the Clerks of the counties of Tyrrell, Washington, Beaufort and Hyde, to obtain from the Secretary of State copies of this act, which, with copies of that to which it is an amendment, shall be posted up at the court house door of their respective counties, by or before the first day of March next; and for failing to comply with the requirements of this section, the said clerks shall be liable to indictment, and, on conviction, shall be fined at the discretion of the court.

Sec. 3. Be it further enacted, That none of the provisions of this act shall be so construed as to extend to any swamp lands which have been reclaimed, and are now, or may hereafter be used for agricultural purposes, or to any slave or slaves employed in cultivating the same, their owners, employers or managers, that may be temporarily engaged in said swamps in cutting timber for ordinary plantation purposes.

Sec. 4. Be it further enacted, That the said Clerks of the County Courts of Gates, Chowan, Perquimons, Pasquotank, Camden, Currituck, Beaufort, Hyde, Washington, and Tyrrell, for preparing and furnishing a copy of the description of said slaves and free persons of color, shall be entitled to receive and demand the sum of fifty cents and no more.

Sec. 5. Be it further enacted, That this act shall be in force and take effect from and after the first day of March next.
[Read three times and ratified in General Assembly this 29th day of January, 1849.]

RESOLUTIONS

1848-49. Resolution concerning the improvement of the Indian Tribes. (Pages 227-228).

Whereas the condition of the various Indian tribes upon the Western frontiers of the United States, appeals to the humanity and justice of the General Government, to devise some plan by which a permanent home may be secured to them, by which their existence as a people may be secured and perpetuated; by which their moral, intellectual and social condition may be improved, and the blessings of civilization and civil liberty at length secured to them:

1. Be it therefore resolved, &c., That we recommend this to the serious consideration of the Congress of the United States, that, in the exercise of their wisdom, they may mature a plan by which the Indian tribes inhabiting our Western Territories may be placed more directly under the paternal care of the General Government; by which a specific region of country may be set apart for their permanent abode, secured to them forever against further encroachment, and undisturbed by the great current of Western emigration; by which their moral, intellectual and social condition may be improved and elevated; by which the blessings of education, civilization and Christianity may be imparted to them; by which they may all be brought together and united in one grand confederation, and thus prepared for the enjoyment of civil and religious liberty; and if found practicable, they may be ultimately admitted into our Federal Union.

2. Resolved, That his Excellency the Governor of the State be requested to transmit a copy of these resolutions to each one of our Senators and Representatives in the Congress of the United States, that the same may be laid before their respective Houses.
[Ratified 29th day of January, 1849.]

RESOLUTIONS

North Carolina Law

1848-49. A Resolution to suspend the collection of Cherokee bonds, until the laying off the Turnpike road from the Georgia line to Salisbury. (Page 229).

Resolved by the General Assembly of the State of North Carolina, That Jacob Siler, the agent of the State for the collection of Cherokee bonds, be instructed, and he is hereby instructed, to suspend the further collection of debts due on Cherokee bonds, until the Turnpike road authorized by the present General Assembly, to be laid out and constructed from Salisbury, West, to the Georgia line, is laid off and the contracts let out; provided the same be properly secured.
[Ratified 29th day of January, 1849.]

RESOLUTIONS
1848-49. Resolutions respecting Slavery in the Territories. (Pages 237-239).

1st. Resolved, That the States came into the Union as equals, and that the citizens of each State are entitled to equal rights, privileges and immunities under the constitution of the United States.

2nd. Resolved, That the proceedings of the Convention by which the Federal Constitution was framed, clearly demonstrate that the institution of slavery was maturely considered, and that the Union of States was finally secured by incorporating into that instrument distinct and ample guarantees of the rights of the slaveholder.

3rd. Resolved, That we view with deep concern and alarm the constant aggressions on the rights of the slaveholder by certain reckless politicians of the North, and that the recent proceedings of Congress, on the subject of slavery, are fraught with mischief well calculated to disturb the peace of our country, and should call forth the earnest and prompt disapprobation of every friend of the Union.

4th. Resolved, That the exactment of any law by Congress which shall abolish slavery or the trade[?] in the District of Columbia, or shall directly or indirectly deprive the citizens of any of the States of the right of emigrating with their slave property into any of the Territories of the United States, and of exercising ownership over the same while in said Territories, will be an act not only of gross injustice and wrong, but the exercise of power contrary to the true meaning and spirit of the constitution, and never contemplated by the framers thereof.

5th. Resolved, That while we do not intend hereby to be understood as conceding that Congress has the power, under the Constitution, to enact a law prohibiting slavery in any portion of the Territories of the United States; yet, for the sake of preserving the peace and promoting the perpetuity of the Union, we are willing that the basis of the Missouri compromise should be adopted in reference to the recently acquired Territories of New Mexico and California, by extending the line then agreed upon to the Pacific Ocean.

6th. Resolved, That we believe the people of North Carolina of all parties, are devotedly attached to the Union of the States; that they regard it as a main pillar in the edifice of real independence, the support of tranquility at home, of peace abroad, of safety, of prosperity, and of that very liberty they so highly prize; that they cherish a cordial, habitual, immoveable attachment to it; and that they watch for its preservation with jealous anxiety; that they believe it is the duty of their public servants to discountenance whatever may suggest even a suspicion that it can in any event be abandoned, and to repel indignantly every attempt to alienate any portion of our country from the rest, or to enfeeble the sacred ties which now link together the various parts.

7th. Resolved, That a copy of the forgoing resolutions be signed by the speakers of the Senate and House of Commons, and forwarded to our Senators and Representatives in Congress with a request that they be laid before their respective Houses.

[Ratified 27th day of January, 1849.]

CHAPTER CXLVI. FISH.
1848-49. An Act to amend and consolidate the several acts now in force, relating to fishing with seines and nets in Tar and Pamlico Rivers. (Pages 294-295).

Sec. 1. Be it enacted by the General Assembly of the State of North Carolina, and it is hereby enacted by the authority of the same, That it shall not be lawful for any person or persons to work any seine in Tar river from the fifteenth day of February and until the twenty fifth day of April, between sun rise on Saturday morning, and sun rise on Monday morning.

Sec. 2. That it shall not be lawful for any person or persons to work any seine or drag net or to set any hedge in Pamlico river, from the fifteenth of February until the twenty fifth of April, between sun set on Friday evening, and sun rise on Monday morning.

Sec. 3. That any person or persons who shall offend against any of the provisions of this act by working a seine, shall forfeit and pay for each and every offence, the sum of fifty dollars, and for working any drag net or hedge, contrary to the provisions of this act, he or they so offending, shall forfeit and pay the sum of five dollars for each and every offence; the above forfeitures to be recovered before any competent jurisdiction, and applied to the sole use of the person who will prosecute for the same.

Sec. 4. If any slave shall offend against the provisions of this act, he or they so offending shall, upon conviction before any justice of the peace, be whipped, on his or their backs, not exceeding thirty nine lashes.

Sec. 5. Be it further enacted, that any person or persons who shall offend against any of the provisions of this act, shall be subject to indictment in the county or superior court, and, upon conviction, shall be fined by said court not exceeding fifty dollars, or imprisoned not exceeding twenty days, at the discretion of the court.

Sec. 6. Be it further enacted, that all laws and clauses of laws coming in conflict with the provisions of this act, be, and the same are hereby repealed.

[Ratified 27th day of January, 1849.]

CHAPTER CCXLVI. TOWNS.
1848-49. An Act for the incorporation of the town of Salisbury. (Pages 456-460).

Sec. 23. That the said board of commissioners shall have power by ordinance to prohibit all persons recently from any place or places where and infectious or contagious disease is believed to exist or recently to have existed, from entering; and all goods and chattles from being brought from said place or places within said town; and by ordinances to fix a penalty for the breach of any of the rules established by them upon this subject, which penalty shall be recovered from any and all persons, who are liable thereto, by action of debt, in the name of the commissioners for the town of Salisbury, in any court having competent jurisdiction. The said commissioners shall also have power to take such other precautionary measures, to prevent the introduction of infectious or contagious diseases in the said town, as they may deem expedient: Said commissioners, upon the certificate of a physician that a dangerous and infectious or contagious disease is existing in any house within said town, or in case the occupier of any house suspected to contain such disease shall forbid or prevent the visit of a physician sent by said commissioners for the purpose of examination, shall also have power to forbid and prevent all persons from leaving said house and its enclosures, and take such other steps to prevent communication with the person so infected and to arrest the spread of the disease, as they may deem expedient, and to impose such penalty or penalties for the breach of their ordinance or ordinances made for that purpose, as they shall think proper. At any time, upon the certificate of a physician that any slave or free negro is sick with a dangerous and infectious or contagious disease within said town, and that he can be removed without endangering his life, the said commissioners shall have the power to cause said slave or free negro to be removed and confined to some convenient and proper place without said town; and shall cause him to be there attended to as befits his situation; and it shall be lawful for them to sue for and recover from any free negro or the owner of any slave so removed, the expenses of his or her removal, support, nursing and medical attendance during the time of his or her sickness, and also in case of his or her death, the expenses of burial, by writ, in the name of the commissioners for the town of Salisbury, in any court having competent jurisdiction. And any and all persons attempting to prevent, or resisting the removal of said slaves or free persons from said Town, shall be liable to indictment in the superior court of law for the county of Rowan, and on conviction, punished for a misdemeanor. The said commissioner shall have other power to impose such punishments on all slaves or free negroes violating this section or any of the ordinances of said commissioners, made by virtue thereof, or on a like subject matter as they may deem expedient, not exceeding one month's imprisonment or thirty nine lashes.

Sec. 29. That the said board of commissioners shall have power to make rules and regulations for enforcing the orderly conduct of slaves and free negroes within said town, and to impose punishments for the breach thereof.

RESOLUTIONS
Resolutions of A Private Nature.
1848-49. Resolution in favor of William Angel. (Page 465).
Resolved, That William Angel, purchaser of section No. 163, in district No. 15, Cherokee land sales of 1836, be released from the payment

of the sum of thirty dollars, with interest from the date of his bonds given for the same: and that the Treasurer be allowed the same in the settlement of his accounts.
[Ratified 27th day of January, 1849.]

RESOLUTIONS
Resolutions of A Private Nature.
1848-49. Resolution in favor of Isaiah Cook and others. (Pages 468-469).
    Resolved, That the Secretary of State be, and he is hereby requested to issue a grant to Isaiah Cook of Macon county, for section No. 3, in district No. 11, purchased by John Poteat at the Cherokee land sales of 1836; also to Nancy Fulton for section No. 18, in district No. 12, purchased by Robert and Jesse Fulton, at Cherokee land sales of 1820; also to David Guyer, for section No. 60, in district No. 17, purchased by David Ballew, at Cherokee land sales of 1838; also Ezekiel Dowdle, for section No. 49, in district No. 13, purchased by James Rodgers, at Cherokee land sales of 1836.
[Ratified 29th day of January, 1849.]

REPORT OF THE PUBLIC TREASURER
1848-49. Cherokee Bonds.

July 1847 Cash received of Jacob Siler, agent, am't collected of Cherokee bonds	2,000.00
Oct 1847 Jacob Siler, agent amount Collected on Cherokee bonds	3,958.00
Dec 1847 Jacob Siler, agent, money collected on Cherokee bonds	1,205.89
Apl. 1848 J. Siler, agent amount collected on Cherokee bonds	3,513.61
June 1848 J. Siler, agent, money on Cherokee Bonds	3,821.00

Oct. 1848 Jacob Siler, agent, amount
collected on Cherokee Bonds   638.85

Oct. 1848 Cash received Jacob Siler, as
advanced payment on lands sold by
Act of Legislature   602.15

Jan. 1847 By Cash paid Jacob Siler for
travelling to and from Raleigh to make returns   53.00

****

LAWS OF THE STATE OF NORTH CAROLINA PASSED BY THE GENERAL ASSEMBLY AT THE SESSION OF 1850-51. RALEIGH: T.J. LEMAY, STATE PRINTER, 1851.

CHAPTER XXII. CHEROKEE LANDS.
1850-51. An Act to provide that copies of certain papers on file in the office of Secretary of State, relating to Cherokee lands, shall be evidence in certain cases. (Pages 60-61).

Sec. 1. Be it enacted by the General Assembly of the State of North Carolina, and it is hereby enacted by the authority of the same, That the list made and transmitted to the Governor, in pursuance of the first section of an act, ratified on the 7th day of January, A.D., 1845, entitled " An Act more effectually to secure the debts due for Cherokee lands, and to facilitate the collection of the same, by the commissioners appointed under the provisions of said act," and all the reports and certificates made to the Governor, by Jacob Siler, the agent for the State, in pursuance of any statute relating to his office or prescribing the duties thereof; and all deeds or written evidences of the surrender of Cherokee lands, by the purchasers thereof, their heirs, devisees, assignees or securities, executed in pursuance of the act aforesaid, or an act entitled an act to amend an act, passed at the last session of the General Assembly, entitled an act more effectually to secure the debts due for Cherokee lands and to facilitate the collection of the same, shall deemed and held to be records; and any part of the list aforesaid, certified to be such by the Secretary of State, and countersigned by the Governor, or copy of any such deed or written evidence of surrender, report or certificate certified by the Secretary of State and countersigned by the Governor in like manner, shall be received in evidence by all courts in this State without further proof.

Sec. 2. Be it further enacted, That this act shall take effect from and after its ratification.

[Ratified 29th January, 1851.]

CHAPTER XXIII. CHEROKEE LANDS.
1850-51. An Act authorizing the transfer of books, bonds, &c., from the Treasurer's office to the Agent of the State, for the collection of Cherokee Land Bonds. (Pages 61-62).

Sec. 1. Be it enacted by the General Assembly of the State of North Carolina, and it is hereby enacted by the authority of the same, That whenever the agent of the State for the collection of Cherokee Bonds, shall have executed his bond to the State of North Carolina, in the sum of one hundred thousand dollars, with good and sufficient security, to be approved of by the Governor and Public Treasurer, it shall be lawful for the Public Treasurer and Comptroller to transfer such books, papers and bonds in their respective offices, as may be necessary to the settlement of the Cherokee land debts to the office of the said agent.

Sec. 2. Be it further enacted, That the said agent shall, on or before the first day of January, in each and every year, make a statement to the Governor, setting forth the amount he has received for Cherokee lands, and whether the same has been in money or in work on the Western Turnpike Road; and also what amount of money has been paid on orders given by the commissioner to superintend the building of the aforesaid road, together with the amount remaining in his possession.

Sec. 3. Be it further enacted, That, hereafter, the receipts of the aforesaid agent of the State for the collection of Cherokee Bonds, showing that full payment has been made for any tract of land in the county of Haywood, Macon or Cherokee, together with the proper certificate of sale, Transfer, deed or warrant and certificate of survey, shall be sufficient evidence on which the Secretary of State may issue a grant to the purchaser or enterer of said tract of land.

Sec. 4. Be it further enacted, That so much of an act of the General Assembly, passed in 1840-41, as requires the agent of the State, in the collection of Cherokee Bonds, to make remittance of moneys collected by him, and report to the Treasurer's office, together with all laws and

clauses of laws, coming in conflict with this act, be, and they are hereby repealed.
[Ratified 27th January, 1851.]

CHAPTER XXIV. CHEROKEE LANDS.
1850-51. An Act to provide relief for the purchasers of Cherokee Lands, secure debts due to the State, and authorize the sale of lands surrendered to the State under the acts of 1844-5 and 1846-7. (Pages 63-67).

Whereas, by acts of the General Assembly, passed at the sessions of 1844-5 and 1846-7, all persons who purchased lands at the sale of 1838, and who were unable to pay for them, were authorized to surrender said lands to the State; and whereas a large number of tracts were surrendered under the provisions of said act; and whereas, by the subsequent act of 1846-7, those lands were assessed by agents appointed under said act, and the purchasers were, upon giving new bonds with approved security, permitted to take up the lands surrendered at the price fixed upon them by the agents of the State; ; and whereas it is but just and right that all purchasers should have the same measure of relief extended to them:

Sec. 1. Be it therefore enacted by the General Assembly of the State of North Carolina, and it is hereby enacted by the authority of the same, That the Governor of the State shall appoint three persons, not residents of Cherokee county who shall constitute a board of valuation, whose duty it shall be to value all the lands surrendered to the State and have not been taken up, also the lands of insolvent purchasers which have not been surrendered, as well as the lands of solvent purchasers (if desired to do so by such solvent purchasers) at a fair valuation: Provided, that no money shall be paid to any claimant, on account of any loss or damage which he or they may have sustained previous to the passage of this act.

Sec. 2. Be it further enacted, That in order to guard the interest of the State, the said board of commissioners shall have no power to reduce the price of any lands valued by them, below the valuation placed thereon by the Commissioners appointed to superintend their survey under the act of 1836, under which act the first quality was valued at four dollars per acre, the second quality at two dollars per acre, and the third quality at one dollar per acre, the fourth quality at fifty cents per acre, and the fifth quality at twenty cents per acre. Provided further, That the said board of commissioners, in valuing the land of solvent purchasers, under this act, shall have no power to reduce the price of any tract below one half of what it was sold for in 1838. And it shall be the duty of the board of valuation to make out duplicate lists of such valuation as soon as may be. One copy of which shall be filed in the office of the clerk of the county court of Cherokee county, and the other they shall transmit to the Governor of the State, to be filed in his office, and the same shall form a part of the records of said offices.

Sec. 3. Be it further enacted, That the commissioners hereby authorized to be appointed, shall, within sixty days after the acceptance of their appointment, meet at the town of Murphy, in the county of Cherokee, for the purpose of proceeding in the execution of their duties; that the commissioners appointed by the county court of Cherokee county shall advertise for thirty days previously, at the Court House and three other public places in said county, and also in both the newspapers published at Asheville, the time and place of meeting of the said commissioners. And all persons desirous of taking the benefit of this act shall, within ten days next preceding the day appointed for the meeting of the commissioners aforesaid, apply either in person or by agent to the commissioner appointed by the county court of Cherokee county, whose duty it shall be to attend for that purpose, and render unto him a list containing the number of the tracts of land, the district in which they lie, and the number of sections of all the lands they desire to be valued under the provisions of this act. And the said commissioner shall enter the same in regular order, in a book prepared for that purpose, so that the board of valuation may, when met, proceed in the performance of their duty as herein required.

Sec. 4. Be it further enacted, That the commissioners aforesaid shall take and subscribe an oath, before some justice of the peace of Cherokee county, that they will, in accordance with the provisions of this act, and to the best of their judgments, value the land aforesaid fairly and impartially as between the purchasers or those entitled to their privileges and the State, and that they will endeavor to do equal and impartial justice between the purchasers themselves; and the said board shall give to each of the purchasers, or the persons entitled to their privileges, whose lands they may value, a certificate setting forth the district and valuation of each tract valued by them as aforesaid.

Sec. 5. Be it further enacted, That the comptroller of public accounts shall furnish, as soon as may be, after the passage of this act, to the agent of the State, who may be entrusted by law with the collection of Cherokee bonds, a full and complete statement, containing the names of all the purchasers of Cherokee lands at the sale of 1838, who were returned solvent under the act of 1844; also the names of all the purchasers whose lands have been surrendered to the State; which statement shall exhibit the amount of the bonds given for the original purchase of each tract of land, together with the date of the same and the several payments made thereon, together with the date of each payment. And upon the receipt of the said statement, the agent shall proceed upon application of the purchasers aforesaid; and upon their producing the certificate of the board of valuation, showing the amount of the valuation of each tract, to deduct the payments which have been made to the State on each tract, from the valuation thereof, and for the balance due, if any, he shall take from the purchasers, or such other person or persons as may be entitled to the privileges of the original purchaser, bonds with good and sufficient security, payable in four annual instalments.

Sec. 6. Be it further enacted, That upon the settlement provided for in the last preceding section being made, and new bonds with good and sufficient security, to be approved by the agent of the State, being given, the said agent is hereby authorized to cancel and surrender up to said purchasers, their heirs, devisees or assignees all the bonds given to the State for said lands: Provided, nevertheless, that in case more than one tract shall be included in the same bonds and only a part of the tracts valued, then and in that case the agent shall not deliver up the bonds to the purchaser, but credit them for the tracts valued upon new bonds being given for such tracts, as in other cases where separate bonds had been given for each tract.

Sec. 7. Be it further enacted, That as a full compensation for the performance by them of the duties herein required, the said board shall be allowed the sum of three dollars each, for every day they may be necessarily engaged in the discharge of the duties herein required, and three dollars for every thirty miles in travelling to and from Murphy, to be paid by the agent of the Cherokee lands out of any monies in his hands, upon the affidavits of the members of the board, setting forth the number of days each may have served; and their receipts shall be received by the Public Treasurer from the said agent of Cherokee lands as cash, in any future settlement with him; and the said agent shall be allowed such compensation, for the additional services required of him by this act, as the Governor, Treasurer and Comptroller may allow, on satisfactory proof being made to them, of the number of days which the said agent may have served, or such other evidence of the amount of service performed by him under this act.

Sec. 8. Be it further enacted, That none of the commissioners herein allowed and authorized to be appointed shall be purchasers of the Cherokee lands or liable on the Cherokee bonds or in any way interested in either.

[Ratified 27th January, 1851.]

CHAPTER XXV. CHEROKEE LANDS.
1850-51. An Act to authorize the sale of Refused Lands owned by the State in the Counties of Cherokee and Macon. (Pages 67-72).

Whereas, in the 4th section of the act of 1836, which authorized the survey and sale of lands acquired of the Cherokee Indians, it is provided, "and the principal surveyor, under the direction of the commissioners, shall cause to be surveyed as much of the said Cherokee lands as in their" opinion will command the sum of twenty cents per acre, and the residue of said land shall remain subject to the disposition of the Legislature, and when the surveyed lands are exposed to public sale, the land of the first quality shall not be sold for less than four dollars per acre; and land of the second quality, not less than two dollars per acre; and lands of the third quality, not less than one dollar per acre; and lands of the fourth quality, not less than fifty cents per acre; and lands of the fifth quality, not less than twenty five cents per acre; and whereas a small proportion of the tracts which were surveyed and offered for sale under the above recited act, did not command the minimum price, and consequently yet remain unsold, which it is the interest of the State should be disposed of:

Sec. 1. Be it therefore enacted by the General assembly of the State of North Carolina, and it is hereby enacted by the authority of the same, That it shall be the duty of the Board of Commissioners, who may be appointed under an act "for the relief of the purchasers of Cherokee lands and to secure debts due to the State," in addition to valuing the lands, as therein provided for, to value all the lands which surveyed under the act of 1836, and which were not sold by the State in 1838; and in fixing a valuation upon said lands, as well as those aforementioned, it shall be the duty of the said Board of Commissioners to take into consideration the localities of said lands, and the facilities which the purchasers may have in the transportation of their produce to market, and all other circumstances which tend to increase or diminish the value of those lands, except the improvements, which are not to be included in the valuation.

Sec. 2. Be it further enacted, That whereas many poor persons, being destitute of homes, have settled on said lands, who have made improvements thereon, with the intention of becoming purchaser; when they were disposed of, in order to furnish all such persons an opportunity of becoming purchasers, who desire to do so, after said valuation is made, it shall be the duty of said commissioners to furnish each occupant with a certificate, setting forth the district and number of the tract by him or her occupied, and also to furnish the agent of Cherokee bonds with a list of all such tracts valued, setting forth the value of each, and the name of each person entitled, in their opinion, to the pre-emption privilege under this act.

Sec. 3. Be it further enacted, That all persons who reside on any of the tracts of land to be valued under the 2nd section of this act, or have made or own improvements thereon, which add value to the land, shall have a pre-emption right to purchase the lands they or either of them have occupied or improved, at the valuation placed thereon by said board; and upon such person or persons presenting to the agent the certificate of the commissioners, to be issued under the 2nd section of this act, and entering into bonds, with two or more securities, to be approved by the agent, payable to the State in four annual instalments for the said valuation, it shall be the duty of said agent, upon receiving the said certificates and bonds, to issue a certificate to the purchaser, setting forth the tract by him or her purchased.

Sec. 4. Be it further enacted, That the provisions of the 3rd section of this act shall extend to the surveyed tracts, if any, in the county of Macon, and shall entitle the persons who may reside thereon, or own improvements on said tracts of land, to pre-emption rights to purchase said lands at the minimum price thereof; and, upon giving bonds as required in the 3rd section, shall be entitled to receive of the agents certificates of purchase as therein provided for.

Sec. 5. Be it further enacted, That the rights of pre-emption, provided for in the foregoing sections of this act, shall extend to all settlers upon vacant lands, in the county of Macon, which have not been subject to entry under the act of 1836; and upon such person or persons making satisfactory proof to the entry taker, that he or she reside on or have improved any of the vacant lands aforesaid, it shall be his duty to issue a warrant to the surveyor of the county to survey such person one hundred acres, to include his or her improvements; and upon the payment to the

North Carolina Law

State of the sum required to be paid for other vacant lands in said county, the grants shall issue as in other cases of entries upon the land which have been subject to entry; and the same fees shall be paid to the entry taker, surveyor and Secretary of State.

Sec. 6. Be it further enacted, That the persons entitled to pre-emption privilege, under the 5th section of this act, shall make their locations and pay the money to the State therefor against the first day of August next; after which time all of the said lands that shall remain vacant or not paid for, shall be liable to be entered as other vacant lands are now entered in the county of Macon, to be paid for at the same price, within six months from the time the location is made; otherwise the same shall be void.

Sec. 7. And Whereas many poor persons, being destitute of homes, have also settled upon the unsurveyed lands in the County of Cherokee, which lands were not surveyed under the act of 1836, because they were not considered worth twenty cents per acre; Be it therefore further enacted, That all persons who, prior to the first day of January, 1851, resided on any of said lands, or had made any improvements thereon which add value to the land, shall be entitled to a pre-emption privilege to one hundred acres, to include their improvements, at twenty cents per acre; and upon making satisfactory proof to the agent of Cherokee bonds that he or she is entitled to the pre-emption privilege within the meaning of this section of the act, it shall be his duty to issue a certificate to such person claiming the pre-emption privilege, setting forth the location of the hundred acres claimed; and upon such certificate, it shall be competent for the persons entitled to the pre-emption privilege to have the said lands surveyed, at his or her own expense, in a square or oblong square, to include his or her improvements; and duplicate copies of such survey shall be made, one to be forwarded to the Secretary of State, and the other to be presented, with the original certificate of occupancy, to the agent; and upon payment being made to him, one fourth of the price of said land, and upon entering into bonds with two or more securities, to be approved by the agent, payable to the State, in three annual instalments, for the remaining three fourths, to issue to said purchasers certificates of purchase, setting forth the number of the tract, the district in which situated, the number of acres and the price sold for.

Sec. 8. Be it further enacted, That the certificates issued to the purchasers under this act, shall entitle them to all rights and privileges the holders of certificates were entitled to under the said act of 1836.

Sec. 9. Be it further enacted, That all persons who make advance payments under this act, shall be entitled to the same discount as provided for under the 12th section of the act of 1836, prescribing the mode of selling Cherokee lands.

Sec. 10. Be it further enacted, That in all cases where two occupants occupy the same lands, or live near each other, unless otherwise agreed upon between themselves, the line shall be run so as to divide the distance equally between their dwelling houses; and in case two persons claim the same improvements and the occupant right thereto, the person having the prior right, unless he has conveyed his claim to the subsequent settler, shall have the right of pre-emption.

Sec. 11. Be it further enacted, That the rights of pre-emption hereby granted to persons residing on, or who own improvements on the surveyed lands of Macon and Cherokee, and also upon the vacant lands in the last named county, provided for in this act, shall have until the first day of October next to avail themselves of the pre-emption privilege and to give lands [bonds?] as required by this act.

Sec. 12. Be it further enacted, That in case the act for the relief of purchasers of Cherokee lands, and this act granting pre-emption rights, shall pass, all lands held under certificates, in the county of Cherokee, shall be liable to the same taxes, both State and county, as other lands in this State.
[Ratified 28th January, 1851.]

CHAPTER XXVII. COMMISSIONERS.
1850-51. An Act to amend the eighty eighth Chapter of the Revised Statutes. (Page 75).

Sec. 1. Be it enacted by the General Assembly of the State of North Carolina, and it is hereby enacted by the authority aforesaid, That the commissioners of Navigation for the port of Wilmington shall be, and they are hereby authorized and empowered, from time to time, to make and establish all such rules and regulations, and to pass all such orders for the port as they may deem judicious, efficient and necessary, for the detection, apprehension or return of slaves escaping or attempting to escape from said port in vessels; and that such commissioners of navigation be further authorized and empowered to establish, and from time to time to alter and regulate the charges and fees of the pilots or harbor masters (as the case may be) of said port, for any services required of them under any rules, regulations or orders made and established by such commissioners of navigation concerning the detection, apprehension or return of slaves attempting to escape as aforesaid.

CHAPTER XLVII. COUNTIES.
1850-51. An Act to protect the Patrol in the county of Onslow, &c., &c. (Pages 115-116).

Sec. 1. Be it enacted by the General Assembly of the State of North Carolina, and it is hereby enacted by the authority of the same, That it may be lawful, after the passage of this act, for the county of Onslow, a majority of the magistrates being present, to lay or levy a tax of not less than twenty five cents, nor more than fifty cents, on each and every black poll in said county, for the purpose of creating a fund to pay the patrol of said county; and that their pay be regulated by said court as heretofore, and that the sheriff of said county be required to collect and account for said tax, in the same manner as other taxes are collected and accounted for.

Sec. 2. Be it further enacted, That if any person or persons shall wilfully and maliciously molest, disturb, or in any manner impede or resist the patrol in the legal discharge of their duty, the person or persons so offending, upon conviction before any justice of the peace in said county, shall forfeit and pay the sum of fifty dollars, for each and every offence, to be applied to the use of the county as part of the fund created for the payment of the patrol.

Sec. 3. Be it further enacted, That this act shall be in force, from and after its ratification.
[Ratified 29th January, 1851.]

CHAPTER CVIII. MISCELLANEOUS.
1850-51. An Act to amend the seventh section of the fifth chapter of the Revised Statutes in relation to Apprentices. (Pages 176-177).

Sec. 1. Be it enacted by the General Assembly of the State of North Carolina, and it is hereby enacted by the authority of the same, That when a citizen of any county of this State, to whom any colored apprentice shall have been heretofore, or may be hereafter bound, shall or may be desirous of moving from the county in which the indentures of apprenticeship may have been executed, to any other county in this State, and shall or may be desirous of taking said apprentice to the county to

which he may be about to remove, for the purpose of having said apprentice there rebound, it shall and may be lawful for the court of pleas and quarter sessions of the county in which said apprentice was originally bound, upon sufficient cause being shown therefor, to grant to such master license and authority to take said apprentice with him to such county of this State, to which he may be removing, for the purpose aforesaid: Provided, however, that the said court shall, before the granting of said license or authority, require the said master to enter into bond, in the sum of five hundred dollars, with good and sufficient security, payable to the State of North Carolina, and conditioned that he will not take the said apprentice beyond the limits of this State, and will cause the said apprentice to be bound in the county to which he is about to remove: Provided further, that the said court shall not grant any license to remove any colored apprentice farther than to a county adjoining the county from which said removal is made.
[Ratified 28th January, 1851.]

CHAPTER CXXII. REVISAL OF PUBLIC LAWS.
1850-51. An Act for revising and digesting the Public Statute Laws of this State. (Pages 248-250).

Sec. 1. Be it enacted by the General Assembly of the State of North Carolina, and it is hereby enacted by the authority of the same, That three commissioners be appointed by the Governor, to collate, digest and revise, all the public statute laws of this State now in force, and including those which may be enacted during the present session of the General Assembly; that in the performance of this duty, they shall carefully collect and reduce into one act, the different acts, and parts of acts, which from similarity of subjects ought, in their judgment, to be so arranged and consolidated; distributing them under such titles, divisions and sections, as they shall think proper, following and retaining the general arrangement and plan of revision as adopted by the commissioners for revising the statute laws of this State, under the act of the General Assembly, as passed at the session of 1833 and 1834, so as to have the whole included in one volume; and in every other respect, they shall complete the said revision in such manner as to them shall seem most useful and proper to render the said acts more plain and easy to be understood.

Sec. 2. Be it further enacted, That the commissioners shall prepare for submission to the next Legislature, such contradictions, omissions, and imperfections as shall appear in the acts so revised, as also any acts which may have been omitted in the former revisal, with such amendments as they shall deem proper to be made; and shall also designate such acts, or parts of acts, if any, as in their judgment ought to be repealed, changed or modified; and may also suggest the passage of such new acts, or parts of acts, as shall seem to them necessary in order to improve and perfect the whole.

Sec. 3. Be it further enacted, That the commissioners shall prepare the said digest and revisal, so that the same may be submitted to the next Legislature, with such marginal notes and references to such sections of any statute as may have been the subject of judicial decision, fixing the construction of such statutes, with a full index, in order that the same may be in readiness for publication as soon as the Legislature shall order and direct.

Sec. 4. Be it further enacted, That the commissioners be authorized to contract, should they deem it advisable, for Legislation of five thousand copies of said work, with such additional numbers as the Legislature shall direct, either securing the copy right of the work, or by disposing of the same to the contractors, as shall appear most to the interest of the State, subject, however, to the approval of the Legislature.

Sec. 5. Be it further enacted, That the said commissioners be allowed until the meeting of the next General Assembly to complete the duties assigned them in and by this act; and as a compensation for their services, shall receive one thousand dollars each, to be paid by the Public Treasurer, on the warrant of the Governor, at such times as to him shall seem right.

Sec. 6. Be it further enacted, That to enable the commissioners to complete their work, and to have the same transcribed for publication, in time for the meeting of the next Legislature, or so soon thereafter as the same may be ordered, it shall be lawful for them to employ a clerk to said commission, at a compensation not exceeding three hundred dollars, to be paid out of the public treasury, upon the warrant of the Governor.
[Ratified 28th January, 1851.]

CHAPTER CLXXXVI. SLAVES.
1850-51. An Act to prevent more effectually the corruption of the slave population. (Page 498).

Sec. 1. Be it enacted by the General Assembly of the State of North Carolina, and it is hereby authorized by the authority of the same, That hereafter it shall not be lawful for any white person to play with and slave or slaves at any game of cards, or at any game of hazard or chance whatsoever, whether for money, liquor or property or not; and any person so offending shall be subject to indictment, and, on conviction, shall be fined or imprisoned at the discretion of the court: Provided, that such imprisonment shall not exceed six months.
[Ratified 28th January, 1851.]

CHAPTER CLXXXVII. SLAVES.
1850-51. An Act to repeal an act of the General Assembly of 1848-49, Chapter 93, entitled an act to amend an act, passed at the last Session of the General Assembly entitled "An Act to provide for the apprehension of runaway slaves in the Great Dismal Swamp and for other purposes." (Page 499).
Sec. 1. Be it enacted by the General Assembly of the State of North Carolina, and it is hereby enacted by the authority of the same, That the act of the General Assembly of the Session of 1848-49, Chapter 93, entitled an act to amend an act, passed at the last Session of the General Assembly entitled an act to provide for the apprehension of runaway slaves in the Great Dismal Swamp, be, and the same is hereby repealed, so far as the same relates to the citizens and residents of the counties of Beaufort and Hyde.
Sec. 2. Be it further enacted, That this act shall be in force from and after its ratification.
[Ratified 28th January, 1851.]

RESOLUTIONS.
1850-51. Resolution for the relief of certain purchasers of Cherokee lands, residing in Macon county. (Page 508).
Resolved, That the benefits of an act of the present session of the General Assembly, to provide relief for certain purchasers of Cherokee lands, shall be extended as well to those purchasers in Macon county who bought in 1836, as those who bought in 1838.
[Ratified 28th January, 1851.]

RESOLUTIONS.
1850-51. Resolution granting land for a church. (page 508).
   Resolved, that ten acres of the unsurveyed land, in the county of Cherokee, belonging to the State, be, and is hereby given to the Baptist denomination in the vicinity of Fort Hembree, for the purpose of building a church thereon,
   Resolved further, That the Secretary of State be authorized to issue a grant for the same, after it shall have been surveyed and its boundaries described, on condition that ten cents per acre be paid to the agent of the State, and his receipt forwarded to the Secretary.
[Ratified 28th January, 1851.]

RESOLUTIONS.
1850-51. Resolution authorizing Jacob Siler agent of the State to correct a mistake in the sale of a tract of land to Isaac Moody. (Page 514).
   Resolved, That Jacob Siler, agent of the State be, and he is hereby authorized to correct a mistake made in the sale of a tract of land to Isaac Moody, which tract appears on the certificate to be No. 141, which should have been No. 140, and that the money paid to said agent and bonds taken shall be made to apply to the tract No. 140 instead of No. 141.
[Ratified 28th January, 1851.]

RESOLUTIONS.
1850-51. Resolution in favor of Jacob Siler. (Page 822-823).
   Whereas, Jacob Siler, agent of the State for the collection of Cherokee bonds, collected on a bond due to the State from John Painter and his securities, and paid over the same to the Treasurer, five dollars and five cents money that was due the State, after deducting a credit which was not perceived at the time of settlement, and whereas said agent, after discovering the mistake, paid back to the said Painter the sum of five dollars and five cents which he had over-paid:
   Be it therefore resolved, That the Public Treasurer pay to the said Jacob Siler or place to his credit five dollars and five cents, the sum paid into the Treasury by mistake, if on examination he deems him entitled thereto.

North Carolina Law

[Ratified 22nd January, 1851.]

RESOLUTIONS.
1850-51. Resolution in favor of Jason Sherrill. (Page 823).

Whereas, at the sale of Cherokee Lands in 1820, Henry Wikle became the purchaser of a tract of land in the county of Haywood, in District No. 2, Section No. 12, containing one hundred and forty seven and three quarter acres, and subsequently conveyed it to Jesse C. Corkerham, who transferred his interest therein to Jason Sherrill, the present occupant; but in consequence of said deed of conveyance having been lost or mislaid, and the said Jesse Corkerham having removed from the State, said Sherrill is unable to obtain a grant for said land, notwithstanding the State has received payment in full therefor:

Be it therefore resolved, That the Secretary of State be authorized to issue a grant to said Jason Sherrill, his heirs or assigns, for said tract of land, upon satisfactory proof being made that he is the present owner thereof, and that payment has been made in full to the State.
[Ratified 27th January, 1851.]

****

LAWS OF THE STATE OF NORTH CAROLINA
PASSED BY THE GENERAL ASSEMBLY
AT THE SESSION OF 1852
PUBLISHED AGREEABLY TO THE FIFTY-NINTH CHAPTER
OF THE REVISED STATUTES
RALEIGH: WESLEY WHITAKER, JR., PRINTER TO THE STATE

CHAPTER LXXXVII. STEALING NEGROES.
1852. An act to prevent the stealing, taking or conveying away of Slaves. (Pages 160-161).

Sec. 1. Be it enacted by the General Assembly of the State of North Carolina, and it is hereby enacted by the authority of the same, That all and every person or persons who shall steal, or by violence, seduction or any other means, take or convey away any slave or slaves, the property of another, with an intention to sell or dispose of to another, or appropriate to his, her or their own use, such slave or slaves, shall, at the time of such stealing, taking or conveying away, be in the possession actual or constructive of the owner or not, or shall, at such time, be in the possession or under the control or direction, lawful or unlawful of some other person than the owner; and all and every person or persons who shall comfort, aid, abet, assist, counsel, hire or command any person or persons to commit any such offence, shall be deemed guilty of felony, and, upon conviction thereof, shall suffer death without the benefit of clergy.

Sec. 2. Be it further enacted, that in an indictment on this act, it shall not be necessary to set out or over, how or with whom was the possession, direction or control of the slave or slaves at the time of the commission of the offence.

Sec. 3. Be it further enacted, That this act shall take effect and be in force from and after the first day of February, in the year of our Lord one thousand eight hundred and fifty three, and not sooner.

[Read three times and ratified in General Assembly, this 24th day of December, A.D., 1852.]

CHAPTER LXXXIX. OBSTRUCTIONS TO THE PASSAGE OF FISH.

1852. An Act to prevent the obstruction of the passage of fish in the waters of Blount's Creek and its tributary streams. (Pages 164-165).

Sec. 3. Be it further enacted, That every free person offending against any of the provisions of this act, shall forfeit and pay for every such offence the sum of fifty dollars to be recovered before any justice of the peace of the county of Beaufort, to the use of the person suing for the same, and if any slave shall violate any of the provisions of this act, he or they shall, on conviction before a single justice of the peace, receive thirty-nine lashes on his or their bare back.

[Read three times and ratified in General Assembly this 25th day of December, A.D., 1852.]

CHAPTER CLXXXI. EMANCIPATION OF SLAVES.

1852. An Act to amend "An Act to emancipate Lucy, a slave, and her child Laura," passed at the session of 1850-51. (Page 666).

Sec. 1. Be it enacted by the General Assembly of the State of North Carolina, and it is hereby enacted by the authority of the same, That the act aforesaid passed at the last session of the General Assembly be so amended that in every part of said recited act in which the word "John

Selph" occurs, the same to be stricken out and the words "Gurdon Deming" substituted therefor, and that all the provisions and restrictions of said act shall operate and have the same force which the same would have had if the words Gurdon Deming had been used in the said recited act.

Sec. 2. Be it further enacted, That this act shall be in force from and after its passage.

[Read three times and ratified in General Assembly this 27th day of December, A.D., 1852.]

CHAPTER CLXXXII. EMANCIPATION OF SLAVES.
1852. An Act to emancipate James Langford, a Slave. (Page 667).

Be it enacted by the General Assembly of the State of North Carolina, and it is hereby enacted by the authority of the same, That James Langford, the property of Jordan Beal, of the county of Northampton, be, and he is hereby, with the consent of said owner emancipated and set free, by the name of James Langford, shall hereafter possess and exercise all the rights and privileges which are enjoyed by other free persons of color in this State: Provided, nevertheless, That before the said slave shall be emancipated, he shall give bond and good security in the sum of five hundred dollars, payable to the State of North Carolina, conditioned that the said James Langford shall honestly and correctly demean himself, and shall not become a parish charge, which bond shall be approved by the court of pleas and quarter sessions of Northampton county and be deposited in the office of said court, which bond may be sued upon to the use of the parish, or of any person injured by the misconduct of said slave: And provided further, That if the said James Langford shall, at any time hereafter remove from the said county of Northampton, and remain out of said county for the space of thirty days, he shall forfeit his freedom.

[Read three times and ratified in General Assembly, this 22nd day of December, A.D., 1852.]

CHAPTER CCIX. TOWNS.
1852. An Act to provide for the better Government of the Town of Lincolnton, and to amend the existing corporate laws of said town. (Page 764).

Sec. 4. Be it further enacted, That no person shall be elected intendant of police or commissioner for the town of Lincolnton except a white male citizen of the full age of twenty one years, who shall have resided in said town six months next preceding the day of election, and who shall possess and continue to possess a freehold in said town assessed for taxation at a sum not less than five hundred dollars, and the coroner, sheriff or constable, or any deputy of either of those officers shall be eligible as intendant of police.

Sec. 5. Be it further enacted, That every white male inhabitant of the town of Lincolnton, of the age of twenty one years, who shall have resided in said town six months next preceding the day of election, and shall have paid a town tax, and also all white male citizens of the State of North Carolina, of full age, who shall possess in said town real estate assessed for taxation at a sum not less than five hundred dollars, shall be entitled to vote for intendant of police and commissioners of said town.

RESOLUTIONS.
1852. Resolution in favor of George Little. (Page 844).
Resolved by the General Assembly of the State of North Carolina, That the public treasurer be directed to pay to George Little, of Raleigh, the sum of [?] hundred dollars, it being the value in full of all demands against the State, for a negro slave Rufus, the property of said Little, Killed in December, 1848, on the Raleigh and Gaston Railroad, while said road was under the care of the agents of the State.
[Read three times and ratified in General Assembly this 25th day of December, A.D., 1852.]

****

REVISED CODE OF NORTH CAROLINA
ENACTED BY THE
GENERAL ASSEMBLY AT THE SESSION OF 1854
PREPARED UNDER THE ACTS OF THE GENERAL ASSEMBLY
BOSTON: LITTLE, BROWN AND COMPANY, 1855

CHAPTER 5. APPRENTICES
1854 - Section, Pages 77-79.
1. Orphans and certain other children of small estate, to be bound out by county court. Certain children of free negroes to be bound out.
2. To whom, and for what time, children to be bound.

3. Duties of masters. Who to be educated.
4. Binding to be by indenture. Remedy for apprentice thereon.
5. Master of children of color to give bond not to remove them out of the county; and to produce them when required. On failure to produce them to be sued and the whole penalty recovered. When colored mariner apprentice may be carried from the county. What shall excuse non-production of apprentice. Master-ship may be surrendered on terms. In certain cases may be taken to adjoining county and bound.
6. Remedy for master where apprentice absents himself after the age of eighteen years.
7. Penalty for harboring orphans and not having them bound out.

1. It shall be the duty of the several courts of pleas and quarter-sessions to bind out, as apprentices, all orphans whose estates are of so small value that no person will educate and maintain them for the profits thereof; also all children under age whose fathers have deserted their families, and having been absent for the term of one year, leaving them without sufficient support, or where application may be made to the wardens of the poor for relief, and the said wardens shall certify the same to the court of pleas and quarter-sessions; also all children under age, whose mothers have secured to them such property as they may thereafter acquire, provided in this case that the children be not remaining with the father, and the court, in its discretion, thinks it improper to permit such children to remain with the mother; also the children of free negroes, where the parents with whom such children may live, do not habitually employ their time in some honest, industrious occupation; and all free base born children of color.

2. Every male apprentice shall be bound to some tradesman, merchant, mariner, or other person approved by the court, until the age of twenty-one years, and every female to some suitable employment till her age of eighteen years, if white, but if colored, till twenty-one.

3. The master or mistress shall provide for the apprentice, diet, clothes, lodging, and accommodations fit and necessary; and such as are white, shall teach, or cause to be taught to read and write, and the elementary rules of arithmetic; and at the expiration of every apprenticeship, shall pat to each apprentice, six dollars, and furnish him with a new suit of clothes and a new Bible: and if upon complaint made to the court of pleas and quarter-sessions, it shall appear that any apprentice is ill used or not taught the

trade, profession, and employment to which he was bound, or that any white apprentice is not taught reading, writing, and arithmetic, as aforesaid, the court may remove and bind him to some other suitable person.

4. The binding of apprentices shall be by indenture, made in the name of the chairman of the county court of the one part, and of the master or mistress of the other part; which indenture shall be acknowledged or proved before such court and recorded, and a counterpart thereof shall remain and be kept in the clerk's office for the benefit of the apprentice; and any person injured may at his cost prosecute a suit thereon in the name of the chairman, and his successors, and recover all damages which he may have sustained by reason of the breach of the covenants therein contained

5. When the court of pleas and quarter-sessions shall bind any child of color, they shall take bond with sufficient security in the sum of one thousand dollars, payable to the State of North Carolina, from the master or mistress, not to remove such colored child out of the county where he is bound, and to produce him before such court, at any time when the court may require it; and also to produce him at the expiration of the term of service; and on failure in either case to produce him, after two several warnings, the county solicitor is hereby directed to bring suit against such person on his bond, for the use of the apprentice, in which the whole sum shall be recovered, as liquidated damages: Provided, nevertheless, that any person bound to a seafaring employment, may be carried out of the county in the ordinary pursuit of his business; and provided further, that no master or mistress shall be subject to a recovery on said bond, who shall make it appear on the trial, that he or she was unable to produce the apprentice, without any default on the part of the said master or mistress: Provided always, however, that the court may, in its discretion, accept the surrender of the mastership of an apprentice at any time, and on such terms as it shall deem just; all which shall be recorded: and provided, moreover, that if the master or mistress shall remove to an adjoining county, the court may, in its discretion permit the apprentice to be carried to that county, to the intent that he may there be bound to the person so removing, but to none other; and when, but not before, the said master or mistress shall exhibit to the court which first bound the apprentice, a duly certified copy of the second binding, together with the indenture and bond, and the court shall be satisfied therewith, then the said master or mistress shall be deemed and held to be discharged thereafter from the condition of the bond first

executed; all which matters shall be recorded, and the certified copy aforesaid, shall be filed with the indenture in that court.

6. If any apprentice, whether colored or otherwise, who shall be well used by his master, and who, if a white person, shall have received from his said master not less than twelve months schooling, shall absent himself after arriving at the age of eighteen years from his master's service, before the term of his apprenticeship shall have expired, every such apprentice shall be compelled to make satisfaction to the master for the loss of his service: and in case any apprentice shall refuse to make such satisfaction, his master may recover by warrant before any justice of the peace, such satisfaction not exceeding sixty dollars, as the justice may determine ought to be made by such apprentice; or the master may have his action on the case against the apprentice for his default: Provided, that no apprentice shall be compelled to make any satisfaction but within seven years next after the end of the term for which he shall be bound to service.

7. No housekeeper shall harbor and conceal, or hire any orphan child, without first obtaining leave of some justice of the peace, under the penalty of ten dollars, one half to the informer, and the other half to the poor of the county; and such justice, on granting permission, shall bind the person by recognizance to bring the said orphan child to the next county court, which shall bind such orphan agreeable to law.

CHAPTER 14. BOATS AND CANOES.
Page 113

Any person who shall take away from any landing or other place where the same shall be, or shall loose, unmoor, or turn adrift from the same, any boat, canoe, or pettiagua, belonging to or in the lawful custody of any person; or any person who shall direct the same to be done without the consent of the owner, or the person having the custody or possession of such boat, canoe, or pettiagua, shall forfeit and pay to such owner, or person having the custody and possession as aforesaid, the sum of two dollars; and the owner may also have his action for such injury.

If any slave shall offend against the provisions of the above section, and be thereof convicted, he shall be whipped, not exceeding thirty nine lashes.

The penalties aforesaid shall not extend to any person who shall press any boat, canoe, or pettigua by public authority; nor to any slave taking the same by order of his master or overseer.

CHAPTER 16. BURNING WOODS AND HUNTING
Page 115.

If any person shall kill or destroy any deer running wild in the woods or unfenced grounds, unless on his own lands, by gun or otherwise, between the twentieth day of February and the fifteenth day of August next succeeding, he shall forfeit and pay for every offence, four dollars, to any person who will sue for the same; and in case the offender be a slave, his owner shall pay a like penalty.

CHAPTER 17. CATTLE, AND OTHER STOCK
Pages 115-117.

Upon complaint made to a justice of the peace by any person that his sheep have been killed or damaged by a dog, the justice shall issue his warrant directed to any lawful officer, commanding him to bring before said justice, within thirty days from the date of said warrant, the owner of such dog, or the master of any slave, or parent of any minor child, reputed to be the owner; and the justice shall summon to appear, at the same time and place, three freeholders, who, together with himself, shall hear the testimony of both complainant and defendant; and if upon trial, the justice and a majority of the freeholders are satisfied that such damage has been done by the dog of the defendant, or by the dog of the slave or minor child of the defendant, the justice shall render judgment against the defendant, in favor of the complainant, for a sum not exceeding twice the amount of the real damage sustained, and issue execution therefor.

CHAPTER 30. COURT HOUSES, PRISONS, ETC.
Page 145.

There shall be kept and maintained in good and sufficient repair, in every county in the State, a court house, common jail, pillory and stocks, at the expense of the county wherein the same are situated; and the courts of the several counties respectively, a majority of the justices being present, shall lay and collect taxes, from year to year as long as may be necessary, for the purpose of building, repairing, and furnishing their several court houses, jails, pillories and stocks, in such manner as they shall think proper; and from time to time shall order and establish such rules and regulations for the preservation of the court houses, and for the government and management of the prisons, as may be conducive to the interests of the public, and the security and comfort of the persons confined.

The common jails of the several counties shall be provided with at least four separate comfortable apartments, one for the confinement of white male criminals, one for white female criminals, one for debtors, and one other for negroes.

CHAP. 34. CRIMES AND PUNISHMENTS.
Pages 203-226.

The offence of killing a slave shall be homicide, and shall partake of the same degree of guilt, when accompanied with the like circumstances, that homicide does at common law.

Every person who shall steal any slave with the intent that the owner, or any one having any interest in such slave, present or future, vested or contingent, legal or equitable, shall be deprived of the use and benefit of such slave, shall suffer death. And every person who, by violence, seduction, or other means, shall take and carry away any slave with the like intent, shall be deemed and held, for every purpose whatever, to have stolen such slaves; and may be so charged in the bill of indictment preferred for the offence. And every person who, knowing any slave to have been stolen as aforesaid, shall, with like intent, convey away, or aid in conveying away said slave, shall suffer death. And in any indictment under this and the following section of this chapter, the property in the slave shall be well laid, if charged to the property of the owner, or any one or more of the persons having such interest as aforesaid.

If any person shall wilfully carry or convey any slave, the property of another, without consent of the owner, or the guardian of the owner, with the intent and for the purpose of enabling such slave to escape out of this State, from the service of his owner, or any one having an interest in such slave, present or future, vested or contingent, legal or equitable, or if any person shall wilfully conceal any slave, the property of another, with such intent and purpose, the person so offending shall suffer death.

If any person shall unlawfully entice, or carry or convey and free negro or free person of color out of the State, with the intent, such free negro or free person of color to sell or dispose of to another, or appropriate to his own use, as a slave, for life or for less time; or shall, within the limits of the State, unlawfully and wilfully sell or dispose of, or appropriate to his own use, as a slave, for life or for less time, any such free negro or free person of color, the person so offending, notwithstanding such free person of color may consent so as to be carried out of the State with such intent, or to be sold within the State as aforesaid, shall suffer death. And it is hereby enacted, that all free persons of color in a state of apprenticeship, or hired or sold for a term of time, by virtue of the judgment of any court, they and their masters, purchasers, and hirers, shall be deemed to be within the provisions of this section.

If any person shall unlawfully entice, or carry, or convey away, from one part of the State to another part of the State, any free negro or free person of color, with the intent such free negro or free person of color, either within or without the State, to sell or dispose of, or to appropriate to his own use, as a slave, for life or for any less time, the person so offending, notwithstanding such free negro or free person of color may consent so to be carried or conveyed with such intent, shall be deemed guilty of a misdemeanor, and on conviction in the superior court of law, shall be fined not less than one hundred dollars, nor more than one thousand dollars, and shall be imprisoned not less than three nor more than eighteen months. And it is hereby enacted, that all free persons of color in a state of apprenticeship, or hired or sold for a term of time by virtue of the judgment of any court, they and their masters, purchasers and hirers, shall be deemed to be within the provisions of this section.

If any person shall wilfully bring into the State, with an intent to circulate, or shall wilfully circulate or publish within the State, or shall aid or abet the bringing into, or the circulation or publications of, within the State, any written or printed pamphlet or paper, whether written or printed in or out of the State, the evident tendency whereof is to cause slaves to become discontented with the bondage in which they are held by their masters and the laws regulating the same, and free negroes to be dissatisfied with their social condition and the denial to them of political privileges, and thereby to excite among the said slaves and free negroes a disposition to make conspiracies, insurrections, or resistance against the peace and quiet of the public, such person so offending shall be deemed guilty of felony, and on conviction thereof shall, for the first offence, be imprisoned not less than one year, and be put in the pillory and whipped, at the discretion of the court; and for the second offence shall suffer death.

North Carolina Law

If any person, by words, shall endeavor to excite in any slave or free negro or person of color, a spirit of insurrection, conspiracy, or rebellion, he shall receive thirty nine lashes on his bare back, and be imprisoned for one year; and for the second offence shall suffer death.

If any clerk of the court of pleas and quarter-sessions shall knowingly issue any license for marriage between any free person of color and a white person; or if any clergyman, minister of the gospel, or justice of the peace shall knowingly marry any such free person of color to a white person, the person so offending shall be guilty of a misdemeanor.

Any person who shall entice, persuade, or tempt any slave to absent himself from his owner's service, or who shall harbor or maintain, under any pretence whatever, any runaway slave, shall forfeit and pay to the owner of such slave one hundred dollars, and be further liable to the owner in an action for damages; and such person shall also pay a penalty of one hundred dollars to any person suing for the same, one half for his use, and the other for the use of the wardens of the poor of the county where suit is brought. And the offender shall moreover be deemed guilty of a misdemeanor, and fined at the discretion of the court, no exceeding one hundred dollars, and imprisoned not exceeding six months.

Any free person who shall teach, or attempt to teach any slave to read or write, the use of figures excepted, or shall give or sell to such slave any book or pamphlet, shall be deemed guilty of a misdemeanor, and upon conviction thereof, if a white man or woman, shall be fined not less than one hundred, nor more than two hundred dollars or imprisoned; and if a free person of color, shall be fined, imprisoned, or whipped not exceeding thirty nine, nor less than twenty lashes.

No person shall sell, deliver, or give to any slave, for his own use, or for the use of any other person, any sword, dirk, bowie knife, gun, musket, or fire arms of any description whatsoever, or any other deadly weapons of offence, or any lead, leaden balls, shot, powder, gun cotton, gun flints, gun caps, or other material used for shooting. Provided, however, that any person may sell and deliver to a slave for the use of the person then having his management, any of the articles above mentioned, he being thereunto authorized by a written permission from such manager, specifying the articles and the amount and quantity so allowed to be purchased for him by such slave. And provided further, that nothing in this section contained shall be construed to prohibit the delivery to slaves, by their managers, of any of the aforesaid articles to be carried from one place to another, or to be carried in the presence of such manager.

North Carolina Law

No person shall trade with a slave on Sundays, or in the night between the hours of sunset and sunrise; either in the buying of, or selling to the slave any article of property whatsoever.

Nor shall any person, at any other time, buy of or receive from any slave, without a written permission for that purpose from the person then having the management of such slave, specifying the articles to be sold, and the probable amount or quantity thereof, any of the following articles of property, to wit: tallow, lard, mutton, suet, oil, grease, soap, cotton, cotton-seed, corn, wheat, rice, barley, oats, or grain of any kind, pork, bacon, beef, flesh of goats, leather, raw-hides, iron, iron castings, steel, farming utensils, nails, meal, flour, wine, spirituous liquor, peas, salt fish, flax-seed, hogs, cattle, sheep, sheep-skin, flesh of sheep, wool, lumber, staves, tar, pitch, turpentine, fodder, hay, shingles, hoops, oak-heading, potatoes, silk, linen, cotton or woolen cloth, or cloth of any kind, yarn, wearing apparel, gold bullion, silver bullion, tobacco, guano, lime, mechanic's tools of every kind, crockery, stone, or wood ware.

Nor shall any person sell to a slave any article which slaves may lawfully buy, unless by written permission of the person then having the management of such slave; or unless the article be sold to such slave in exchange and payment for articles, which may then have been lawfully bought of said slaves.

No person shall sell or deliver to any slave, for cash, or in exchange for articles delivered, or upon any consideration whatever, or as a gift, any spirituous liquor may be a chief ingredient, without permission in writing from the person having the management of such slave, specifying the quantity of liquor allowed to be bought.

If any slave shall be found in any shop, storehouse, warehouse, tippling-shop, or other place fitted up for trading; in the night after dark and before daybreak, or on Sunday; or if any slave shall be found, at any other time, in any of the aforementioned places, and therein shall have been permitted to remain for the space of ten minutes with the door of the said place closed; or if any slave shall convey into the aforementioned places any article of traffic, and not bring the same out; or if any slave shall bring out of any of the said places any article of traffic not carried in by him, the person using such shop, storehouse, warehouse, tippling-shop, or other place fitted up for trading, shall, in each case, be deemed to have unlawfully traded with such slave, and be deemed guilty of a misdemeanor, and may be convicted thereof, unless he be acquitted of the same by proof to the contrary; and in the prosecution for such offence, or for the penalty imposed by the following section, it shall not be necessary to name the article of trade, or whether the offence was in buying or selling.

Any person offending against any of the provisions of section eighty-three, eighty-four, eighty-five, eighty-six, eighty-seven, and eighty-eight of this chapter, shall be deemed to be guilty of a misdemeanor, and on conviction thereof, shall be punished accordingly. Provided, however, that, if the defendant shall have been, at the time of committing the offence, a retailer of spirituous liquors by the small measure, he shall on conviction, moreover, forfeit his license to retail, or any license which he may have taken since the commission of the offence, and shall incapable of taking license again for that purpose, for the space of two years from the date of his conviction. And provided also, that the defendant shall not be imprisoned for a longer period than three months, nor fined more than one hundred dollars. Provided further, that, if the offender be a free person of color, the court may, in the place of imprisonment, sentence him to be whipped not exceeding thirty-nine lashes.

Every species of unlawful trading with a slave, which is forbidden by this chapter, shall, when done by the agent or manager of another, in the course of the business in which he is employed, be deemed to have been done by the consent and command of his principal or employer, unless the contrary be proved; and such agent or manager shall be compelled to testify as a witness concerning the said offence, but his evidence shall in no case be used against himself in any suit or prosecution under this chapter.

If any person shall fraudulently give, or cause to be given, to any slave, a permission in writing to sell, trade, or traffic in any article of personal property, without the authority of the owner or manager of such slave, the person so offending shall be deemed guilty of a misdemeanor.

If any person shall offend against any of the provisions of any of the sections eighty-three, eighty-four, eighty-five, eighty-six, eighty-seven, eighty-eight, and ninety-one of this chapter, he shall forfeit and pay to any one who shall sue for the same sum of one hundred dollars.

It shall not be lawful for the master or commander of any vessel to entertain, or permit to be entertained, any slave or free negro, on board such vessel, at any time between sunset and sunrise, nor on Sunday, unless such slave or free negro shall belong to the vessel, or such slave shall have a pass from his master, and the free negro a pass from some justice of the peace, expressing the time when, and the business for which they go on board; and if any slave or free negro who has not such pass, or is not employed on board the vessel as one of the hands, shall be found on board of any vessel in any bay, harbor, creek, or river within the State on Sunday, or in the night between sunset and sunrise, he shall be deemed guilty of a misdemeanor, and shall receive a whipping not exceeding forty lashes; and the master or commander of such vessel so entertaining , or permitting entertainment as aforesaid, shall be deemed guilty of a misdemeanor; and it shall be the duty every justice of the peace of the county where the offence is committed, to whom knowledge thereof shall come, to issue his warrant to arrest such captain or commander, and recognize him in sufficient bail for his appearance at the next term of the county or superior court, to answer the charge aforesaid.

If any white female shall be convicted of any offence, the punishment or any part whereof shall be branding or whipping, the same shall not be inflicted, but the court, instead thereof, may sentence such female to imprisonment for any length of time in its discretion.

If any white person shall play with any slave or free person of color, at any game of cards, or at any game of hazard, chance, or skill whatsoever, either with or without betting on the said game, he shall be deemed guilty of a misdemeanor.

CHAP. 35. CRIMINAL PROCEEDINGS.
Page 232.

The defendant may be charged in the same indictment, in several counts, with the separate offences of unlawfully trading with slaves, receiving stolen goods knowing them to be stolen, and larceny.

CHAP. 37. DEEDS AND CONVEYANCES.
Pages 244-245

No gift of any slave shall be valid, unless the writing by which the title to such slave is transferred, shall be proved or acknowledged, as conveyances of land, and registered in the county where the donee resides, within two years after execution thereof, if the donee be in actual possession of the slave; but if, under any special agreement made at the time of the gift, the donor shall remain in possession of the slave, then writing shall be proved or acknowledged as aforesaid, and registered within the same time, in the county where the donor resides.

All written sales and conveyances of slaves shall, within two years after the making thereof, be proved in due form and registered, or otherwise shall be void.

When the transfer or conveyance of any slave shall be in writing, such writing, after being duly acknowledged, or proved, shall be registered in the county where the purchaser (he being in actual possession of the slave) shall reside; but if, under any special agreement at the time of the sale, the vendor shall remain in possession of the slave, then the writing shall be registered in the county where the vendor may reside.

CHAP. 45. EXECUTIONS.
Page 277.

All sales of land or slaves, by the sheriff, coroner, constable, or by the clerk and master in equity, under any execution or decree, shall be made at the court house of the county on the first day of the term of the superior court, or on the same Monday in every month on which the courts of pleas and quarter-sessions are generally held for their respective counties; always making the Monday of each county court and the first day of the term of the superior court, the only sale days in that month; and if, on any sale day, the whole of the property taken in execution cannot be sold, or if property, levied on under other executions, cannot be offered for want of time, or cannot be sold, on the same day, the sheriff or other officer may postpone or continue the sale from day to day, until the whole shall be sold, on giving public notice at the court house, that such sale will be continued on the ensuing day. Provided, that nothing herein contained, shall be construed to alter the rules and restrictions under which sales are directed to be conducted, and executions required to be returned; or to alter the days of sale in particular counties, as now established by law. And provided further, that the courts of equity may, in any decree of sale made by said courts, appoint the time and place of sale.

If any sheriff or other officer, who may have levied an execution or other process upon personal property, shall permit the same to remain with the possessor, such officer may take a bond for the forthcoming thereof to answer the said execution or process, which bond shall be attested by a creditable witness; but the officer shall nevertheless, in all respects, remain liable as heretofore, to the plaintiff's claim.

When such a bond shall be taken, the officer shall specify therein the property levied upon, and shall furnish to the surety list of the property in writing under his hand, attested by at least one credible, and stating therein the day of the sale; and the property so levied upon shall be deemed in the custody of the surety, as the bailee of the officer: and all other executions thereafter levied on said property, shall create a lien on the same from and after the respective levies, and shall be satisfied accordingly out of the proceeds of the sale of said property; but the officer thereafter levying shall not take the property out of the custody of the surety. Provided, that in all such cases, sales of slaves shall take place within sixty days, and of chattels within thirty days, after the first levy; and if the sale shall not be made within the time aforesaid, any other officer who may have levied upon the property, may seize and sell the same.

CHAP. 48. FENCES.
Page 295.

If any person, or the slave or servant of any person, shall, with gun, dog, or otherwise, unreasonably chase, worry, maim, or kill any horse, or other stock, or cause the same to be done, when trespassing upon his inclosed grounds, where his fence shall be adjudged insufficient, the occupant of the premises, on complaint being made to any justice of the peace as aforesaid, shall make full satisfaction for all such damages to the party injured, to be ascertained and recovered as provided in the preceding section.

If any slave, without the order of his manager, shall chase, worry, maim, or kill, any horse or other stock, trespassing upon the inclosed grounds cultivated by or under the direction of such manager, he may be apprehended on a warrant from any justice of the peace, and whipped for his offence, not exceeding thirty-nine lashes.

CHAP. 50. FRAUDS AND FRAUDULENT CONVEYANCES.
Pages 300-301.

All contracts to sell or convey any lands, tenements, or hereditaments, or any interest in or concerning them, or any slave; and all leases and contracts for leasing of land, for the purpose of digging for gold or other minerals, or for the purpose of mining generally, shall be void and of no effect, unless such contract or lease, or some memorandum or note thereof, shall be put in writing, signed by the party to be charged therewith, or by some other person by him thereto lawfully authorized, except, nevertheless, leases and contracts for leases (other than those above named) not exceeding in duration the term of three years.

No gift of any slave shall be good or available in law, unless the same shall be made in writing, signed by the donor and attested by a credible witness subscribing thereto. Provided, however, that when any person dying intestate shall have put into the actual possession of his child any slave, who shall remain shall remain in possession of the child at the time of the death of such person, such slave shall be considered as an advancement to the child, and be regulated by the law relating to advancements made to children by a parent in his lifetime.

All sales and conveyances of slaves shall be in writing, attested by a credible witness subscribing thereto, or otherwise shall be void. Provided, however, that all sales of slaves, bona fide made and accompanied with the actual delivery of the slave to the purchaser, and which would be held good but for the provisions contained in this section, shall be good and valid without any bill of sale.

All contracts and agreements of every description made after the eighteenth day of May, one thousand eight hundred and thirty-eight, with any Cherokee Indian, or any person of Cherokee Indian blood, within the second degree, for an amount equal to ten dollars or more, shall be void, unless some note or memorandum thereof be made in writing, and signed by such Indian, or person of Indian blood, or some other person by him authorized, in the presence of two witnesses, who shall also subscribe the same.

CHAP. 54. GUARDIAN AND WARD.
Pages 321-322.

Where any ward shall have lands, and a sufficient number of slaves to cultivate and improve the same, the slaves, (unless otherwise ordered by the court,) shall be employed on the lands and farm of such ward; and all necessary horses, cattle, sheep, and hogs shall be kept upon such lands and farm until the ward shall come of age. Provided, nevertheless, that if the stock grow too numerous, or it shall be to the advantage of the ward, his guardian, by order of the court, shall sell such part of the stock as the court shall think fit; and all plate shall be preserved and delivered to the ward at age, in kind, according to weight and quantity.

Every guardian, where it is not deemed to be the interest of the ward to employ his slaves upon his lands and farm, shall hire out the slaves and rent out the lands. Provided always, that no guardian shall let any land belonging to his ward, for a longer term than the ward be of age, or in other manner than by lease in writing; and that special care be had that the tenant shall improve the farm, and keep the houses, orchards, and fences thereon, or that shall be put on the same, in good and sufficient repair, and leave the same so at the expiration of the lease; and that provision be made in such lease for preventing all kind of waste, and the using of any timber other than for the repairing and keeping up the farm.

CHAP. 65. LIMITATIONS
Page 375.

Whenever any person shall remain in possession of a slave or other personal property, until such possession is protected by the statute of limitations, he and those claiming under him, shall be deemed and held to have a good and absolute title to such slave or other personal property, against all persons whose claim is barred by the said statute. Provided that nothing herein contained shall in any way affect the law that require gifts of slaves to be in writing.

CHAP. 68. MARRIAGE.
Pages 391-392.

All marriages, since the eighth day of January, eighteen hundred and thirty-nine, and all marriages in future, between a white person and a free negro, or free person of color, to the third generation, shall be void.

No minister of the gospel or justice of the peace shall marry a white person with an Indian, negro, or free person of color, to the third generation, knowing them to be so, upon pain of forfeiting and paying for every such offence one hundred dollars.

CHAP. 70. MILITIA
Pages 399, 422- 423.

No captain or other militia officer shall enroll any free persons of color, except for musicians.

In all cases of insurrection among slaves or free persons of color either in any county of this State, or in an adjoining State, or in case of invasion, seven justices of the peace, deeming the emergency to require it, may at their discretion require in writing of the commanding officer of their county to call out the militia under his command, and any volunteer company or companies in said county, in the absence of the officer who is entitled to the command, to suppress or repel such insurrection or invasion, or to protect the inhabitants of their county from the danger to be apprehended; and may again require of the said officer to dismiss his men when they think the danger is over, and the commanding officer may dismiss in like manner.

When there may be outlawed or runaway negroes, committing depredations, or in any way alarming the citizen of any county, or where the guarding of a jail is necessary, three justices of the peace, certifying the same in writing and requesting the officer in command of their county, such officer shall effect the object set forth in said request of the justices, and the expenses of the militia so called out, shall be paid by the court of the county, who may lay a sufficient tax to pay said militia, at the same rates as the regular troops of the United States are by law entitled to, when in actual service.

CHAP. 79. ORDINARIES AND INNS.
Page 448.

If any keeper of an inn, tavern, or ordinary, or vendor or retailer of spirituous or other liquors, shall entertain slaves against the will of their owners, or common sailors against the direction of the masters of vessels to which they belong, he shall forfeit and pay one hundred dollars to the use of the owner of the slave, or master of the vessel.

CHAP. 83. PATROL.
Pages 458-459.

The county court of each county, if the court deem it necessary, shall, at the first court that may be held after the first of January, in every year, or any subsequent court, appoint a patrol committee of three persons, in each captain's district in said county, who shall employ a patrol of such number of persons as they may think necessary to patrol their district. Provided, that nothing herein contained shall be construed to prevent the county courts from appointing such patrol as they may deem proper.

Any person, appointed one of the patrol committee, who shall neglect to discharge his duties, shall pay a penalty of twenty-five dollars, to be recovered on motion to the court by the county solicitor and paid to the county trustee, in aid of the tax in support of the patrol.

The patrol shall visit the negro houses in their respective districts, as often as may be necessary, and may inflict punishment, not exceeding fifteen lashes, on all slaves they may find off their owner's plantations, without proper permit or pass, designating the place or places, to which the slaves have leave to go. The patrol shall also visit all suspected places, and suppress all unlawful collections of slaves; shall be diligent in apprehending all runaway negroes in their respective districts; shall be vigilant and endeavor to detect all thefts, and bring the perpetrators to justice, and also all persons guilty of trading with slaves. The patrol thus employed, or appointed by the county court, or any two of them, shall have such powers as may be necessary to a proper discharge of the duties herein enjoined; and if, upon taking up a slave and chastising him, as herein directed, he shall behave insolently, they may inflict further punishment for his misconduct, not exceeding thirty-nine lashes.

The county courts shall prescribe all necessary rules for the government of the patrol of the respective counties, and the patrol shall be subject thereto, under such fines and penalties as the court shall fix and direct.

The patrol committee shall have full power to discharge any one or more of the patrol, and employ others, at any time when they may think it expedient.

Any person, appointed by the committee one of the patrol, who shall neglect to serve, shall be subject to a penalty of twenty dollars, to be sued for by the patrol committee of his particular district, and paid by them to the county trustee.

The patrol shall receive such compensation for their services as may be allowed them by the county court; and the court, a majority of the justices being present, may lay a tax not exceeding twenty-five cents on each taxable slave, to defray the expenses of the patrol.

CHAP. 85. PILOTS
Page 469.

If any slave shall, with the consent of his owner, and not accompanied by a pilot, go off to any ship or vessel, for the purpose of bringing such ship or vessel over any bar or inlet of the State, or shall pilot any such ship or vessel out of and over any bar or inlet, the owner shall forfeit the value of such slave, to be recovered in the name of the State; one half to the use of the person suing for the same, the other half to the use of the county where the owner resides.

CHAP. 86. POOR.
Pages 473-474.

The owner of any slave, incapable of service from age or other disability, shall provide him with proper food, raiment, and lodging; and if any such slave shall be unprovided as aforesaid, the wardens of the county, where the slave may be, shall furnish him with food, raiment, and lodging, and charge the owner therewith, and may recover against him the price, before any tribunal having jurisdiction of the amount of the demand. Provided however, that the wardens shall inform the owner of their proceedings, as soon as practicable, by notice directed to the sheriff or constable of his county, who shall execute the same forthwith, and make return thereof to the wardens by whom it was issued.

If the owner of such slave be dead, his executors or administrators shall provide for him out of the estate of the deceased; and upon failure so to do, the wardens shall provide for him, and proceed against such executors or administrators in every respect, as against the owner; or if such slave shall be under the control of a guardian, he shall provide for the slave out of the estate of his ward; and upon failure, the wardens shall provide for the slave, and proceed against the guardian in manner aforesaid; and such executors or administrators, and guardians shall be allowed the expense of making such provision, in their settlements.

When such slave shall be in a county other than the county where the owner, or the executors or administrators of a deceased owner or guardian reside, the wardens may remove him to the owner, or to the guardian, at the expense of such owner, executors, administrators, or guardian.

Any two of the wardens shall have authority to execute the foregoing provisions, relative to disabled slaves.

The wardens, or any one of them, on information, that any person is about to remove out of the county, and has a slave likely to become a county charge, may issue a warrant to bring such person before him or them, and shall take such security by bond, payable to the State of North Carolina, as may be sufficient to indemnify the county: And in case such person refuse to give bond, he or they shall have power to commit him, until he shall enter into such bond, or remove the slave without the limits of the county.

All horses, cattle, hogs, sheep, or other stock, that shall belong to any slave, or be of any slave's mark, shall be seized and sold by the wardens, and the proceeds by them applied, the one half to the support of the poor, and the other half to the informer.

CHAP. 98. REPLEVIN.
Pages 501-502.

Writs of replevin for slaves and other personal chattels may be maintained against persons in possession thereof, in all cases in which actions of detinue or trover will lie, except against persons holding the same in custody of the law, under the following rules and regulations:

The plaintiff, or his agent shall make oath before the clerk at the issuing of the writ, that within three years next preceding that time, he hath been in the lawful possession of the property detained, that he has been deprived of the possession thereof without his permission or consent, or unjustly and by fraud, and shall state the value and description of each slave and article of other property, as nearly as he can.

The clerk shall describe in the writ each slave and article of property demanded, and shall annex to each slave and article so described double the sworn value thereof, and shall take of the plaintiff a bond with good security, in double the alleged value of the property demanded, payable to the defendant and conditioned to perform the final judgment on the writ.

CHAP. 99. REVENUE.
Page 506, 509, 510 & 515.

Upon every free male, between the ages of twenty-one and forty-five years, a tax of forty cents; and for every slave of either sex, between the ages of twelve and fifty years, the like sum shall be paid by the owner, and not the hirer; unless when the owner may be a non-resident and his slave be hired, and then the hirer shall list the slave and pay the tax. Provided, however, that the county court may exempt from a poll tax such poor and infirm persons, and disabled and insane slaves, as they may declare and record to be fit objects for exemption.

North Carolina Law

Upon every hundred dollars employed in buying and selling slaves, whether the said capital shall be borrowed or shall be the individual property of the person or company investing the same, during the year ending on the said first day of April, twenty-five cents; upon every hundred dollars employed within the same time in any other species of trade, not in this chapter specially taxed, ten cents.

All free persons, living with, and constituting a part of the family, and all colored persons living by consent on the lands of another, shall be listed by the head of the family, or owner of the land, as the case may be

---

CHAP. 101. ROADS, FERRIES, AND BRIDGES.
Pages 534-535.

It shall be the duty of the overseer of public roads, three days before the day of working, to summon all white males, between the ages of eighteen and forty-five, and free males of color and male slaves, between the ages of sixteen and fifty years, within the district, to meet at such times and places, as to the overseer shall deem convenient, for the repairing or making such roads as may be necessary; and the overseer shall, at the same time, give notice to each free person, or the master or mistress, or overseer of slaves, what kind of tools they shall bring and work with on the road. And whosoever shall, upon such summons, neglect the duty, or any part thereof, required of him, shall forfeit and pay one dollar, per day, for each person or hand so neglecting or failing therein; which may be recovered of the father, or guardian having funds if the person failing be a minor; or, if a slave, of the master.

When an overseer shall not be able to personally notify the persons aforesaid, three days before the day appointed for working the road, he shall leave at the house of such free person, or the master, mistress, or overseer of slaves, and in case there be resident no free white person superintending the slaves residing on any plantation who are bound to work the road, then at the house of any slave, a written summons, specifying the day on which they are required to attend, the place of the road to be worked, and the kind of tools to be brought or used: and the said written summons, left as aforesaid, shall be deemed sufficient notice to the persons required to be notified, to every intent and purpose: and all penalties recovered by an overseer, for default of working on the road, shall be applied by him to the repair of the road of which he is, or may have been, overseer.

No persons, between the ages prescribed for free white men, and slaves and free persons of color, respectively, shall be exempted from working upon the public roads, except such as shall be exempted by the General Assembly, or by the county court on account of personal infirmity; of which the said court, seven justices being present, shall be the sole judge, and except also such as shall send three slaves, or other three sufficient hands to work on the roads: and nothing herein shall be construed to excuse overseers of slaves from working on roads.

CHAP. 107. SLAVES AND FREE NEGROES.
Pages 564-580.

Every negro, or person of color, being a slave, imported into this State from any foreign port or place, for a slave, or to be held to service or labor, since the first day of January, one thousand eight hundred and eight, contrary to the provisions of an act of Congress entitled, "An Act to prohibit the importation of slaves into any port or place within the jurisdiction of the United States, from and after the first day of January, in the year of our Lord, one thousand eight hundred and eight," approved the second day of March, one thousand eight hundred and seven, (except as hereinafter provided,) shall be sold for the use of the State.

The sheriff of each county in this State is hereby authorized and required to seize and take into his possession, every such negro or person of color, who has been or shall be imported as aforesaid, and shall be found in the county of which he is sheriff; and such negro or person of color, so taken, to sell and dispose of at public sale, at the court house door, (giving previous notice of twenty days, of the time of sale, by advertisement in the nearest newspaper published in the State,) to the highest bidder, at a credit of six months, the purchaser entering into bond with security, to be approved by the sheriff, for the payment of the price; which, when received by the sheriff, he shall account for and pay to the public treasurer after deducting from the gross amount the several sums hereinafter authorized to be retained, at the same time, and under the same regulations and penalties, as are prescribed for paying the public taxes.

Where any such negro shall abscond, or so conceal himself that he cannot be taken, the sheriff may offer a reward, not exceeding one fifth part of his value, to any person who will apprehend and deliver him to the sheriff; or the sheriff may, in his discretion, advertise and sell him as directed in the preceding section, without offering a reward, although he may not be in his possession at the time of the sale.

Any person who shall discover any such negro, and give such notice to the sheriff that he shall, in consequence thereof, obtain the negro, shall be entitled to one fifth part of the sum for which the negro shall be sold, to be retained, that and the reward, out of the proceeds of sale, and paid by the sheriff; and the sheriff, or his successor, shall execute and deliver to the purchaser, his executors, administrators, or assigns, a bill of sale for such negro; and the title so acquired shall not be affected by the want of advertisement, or other irregularity, in the sale, or proceedings on the part of the sheriff.

The sheriff may retain out of the price, besides the reasonable charges for keeping such negro till the day of sale, and advertising, the further sum of six per centum on the gross proceeds of sale, in full for his services.

The foregoing provisions of this chapter shall extend and apply to every negro and person of color, and to the issue of every negro and person of color, imported as aforesaid.

Every person who shall introduce into the State any slave, from any of the United States which have passed laws for the liberation of slaves, shall, on complaint thereof before any justice of the peace, be compelled by such justice, to enter into bond with sufficient security, in the sum of one thousand dollars for each slave, for the removing of such slave to the State whence he was brought, within three months thereafter, under the penalty of five hundred dollars for every month's delay; one half to the use of the State, and the other half to the use of the prosecutor.

All persons who may apprehend and confine in jail, or deliver to the owner, any runaway slave, for whom a greater reward shall not have been offered, shall be entitled to recover and receive from the owner a reward of five dollars, when the owner resides in the county in which the slave may be apprehended, and ten dollars, if he reside beyond the limits of such county; and if the runaway shall have been apprehended in any part of the swamps mentioned in section ten of this chapter, not lying in Beaufort or Hyde counties, the apprehender shall, besides any reward offered, be entitled to twenty-five dollars from the owner; and when the runaway slave thus apprehended shall be lodged in jail, the jailer shall tax the reward herein allowed on each slave, against the owner, and collect the same with his prison fees, and all other charges allowed by this chapter.

North Carolina Law

Any slave, taken up as a runaway, may be delivered immediately to the owner, and if not so delivered, shall be brought before a justice of the peace of the county wherein he is apprehended; and if the owner be known, and a resident of that county, the justice, by warrant, shall commit the runaway to some constable of the county, to be by him conveyed to his home, and the constable shall give receipt for the runaway; but if the owner be unknown, or reside out of the county, the justice shall, by warrant, commit the runaway to the jail of his county; and the sheriff shall forthwith cause notice of such commitment to be set up at the court house door of the county, and there continued during two months, in which notice, a full description of the runaway, and his clothing, shall be particularly set forth; and whenever the owner is supposed to be a resident of another State, or to reside as many as fifty miles from where the jail where the runaway is confined, the sheriff or jailer shall also cause said notice to be immediately published in some newspaper published at the seat of government, for six months, unless the runaway is sooner delivered to the owner.

Every person being the owner, or having the use, care, or management of slaves, and employing them in the Great Dismal Swamp, or in the swamp which lies between Lees' Mill in the county of Washington, and Pamlico River in the county of Beaufort, or in the swamp which lies between Juniper Creek, and the lands of Charles Pettigrew, in the county of Tyrrell, shall, before said slaves are put to work in any of the places aforesaid, bring each one before the clerk of the court of pleas and quarter-sessions of the county in which he is to be employed, who shall, upon his personal examination take an exact description of the slave, specifying the name and residence of the person intending so to employ the slave, the height, complexion, and every peculiar mark of description, by which the slave may be most effectually known and identified; and such written description shall be entered by the clerk on a book kept for that purpose, and he shall forthwith make out and deliver to the owner, or to the person having the use, care, management of the slave, a fair and true copy thereof, without any interlineation or erasure, certified under his hand and seal of the court: and the owner or person aforesaid, shall, before putting the slave to work in any of the said swamps, deliver such copy to him, to be kept about his person. And if any owner, or person having the use, care, or management of any slave, shall employ him in any of the said swamps, without procuring and delivering to the slave such copy as aforesaid, or shall otherwise offend against the provisions of this section, the person so offending, shall be deemed guilty of a misdemeanor.

Free negroes working in any of the said swamps, shall procure from the clerks of the proper counties, a similar description of themselves, certified as above directed, and keep it ready at all times when so engaged to be exhibited. And if any free person of color shall wilfully work in any of said swamps without without such copy, he shall be deemed guilty of a misdemeanor; and, on conviction, may be punished at the discretion of the court, by fine, whipping, and imprisonment, or any of them.

If any slave shall wilfully work in any of said swamps, without such copy as is prescribed in section ten of this chapter, he may be arrested by any person; and, on being tried and convicted before a justice of the peace, shall receive thirty-nine lashes on his bare back; and the person arresting such slave, shall be entitled to demand and have from the owner or person having the use, care, or management of the slave, twenty-five dollars; or may proceed against the slave, as a runaway, according to the law directing the disposition of runaway slaves, and cause him to be kept in custody, until the said sum of twenty-five dollars, and all other charges shall have been paid.

If any slave or free person of color, having obtained such certified copy, shall, in any of the said swamps, consort with, or work, or be employed in company with any runaway slaves, or any slave or free negro not having such copy, the slave or free person so offending, shall be deemed guilty of a misdemeanor.

If any white person shall, in any of said swamps, consort or work with, or employ, or engage to work therein, any runaway slave, or any slave who shall not have such certified copy as aforesaid, he shall forfeit the sum of one hundred dollars, to any person who will sue for the same, and shall be deemed guilty of a misdemeanor; and on conviction, may be imprisoned not more than six months; or fined at the discretion of the court.

If any person shall falsely make, forge, or counterfeit, or cause the same to be done, or willingly aid or assist therein, any writing, purporting to be the original, or a copy of a description of any slave or free person of color, employed or about to be employed in any of said swamps, with intent to evade any of the provisions of this chapter, which relate to such persons, the person so offending shall be guilty of a misdemeanor, and on conviction, shall be punished by standing in the pillory for one hour, by whipping, imprisonment for six months, and fine; by all or any of them, at the discretion of the court.

None of the provisions of this chapter respecting working in swamps, shall be construed to extend to any swamp in the county of

North Carolina Law

Currituck, lying below Indian Town creek bridge; nor to any part of the swamps herein referred to, which lie in Beaufort or Hyde counties; nor to any swamp lands which shall have been reclaimed, and may be used for agricultural purposes; nor to any slave employed in cultivating the same; nor to any slave, his owner, employer, or manager that may be temporarily engaged in said swamp, in cutting timber for ordinary plantation purposes.

If any sheriff, jailer, or constable, shall set to work, employ, or let out to hire, any runaway slave committed to his custody, or shall detain such runaway longer than by this chapter is directed, he shall forfeit the jail fees; and if any sheriff, jailer, or constable, to whom any runaway is committed by virtue of this chapter, shall negligently or wilfully suffer such runaway to escape, he shall be liable on his official bond, to the action of the party grieved, for the recovery of his damages.

The expense of carrying a runaway to jail, incurred by any officer, shall be paid by the county, and repaid to the county by the owner; and the same shall be a lien on the runaway in behalf of the county.

Whenever any slave shall be taken up as a runaway, and confined in jail for twelve months, and his apprehension and confinement have been advertised in a newspaper as aforesaid, for six months, and the owner does not apply to prove property in that time, then the court of pleas and quarter-sessions of the county in which the runaway is confined, shall command the sheriff of the county to expose the slave to public sale, for cash, giving two months' notice in some newspaper published in this State, at the court house door, and at two other public places in the county, of the time and place of sale, and of the circumstances under which the slave is to be sold.

The sheriff shall be allowed two and a half per centum on the amount of sales made under the preceding section.

The bill of sale of the sheriff shall vest in the purchaser an absolute right to the slave; and the sheriff shall pay over the residue of the amount of sales, after deducting his commissions and prison charges, to the county trustee for the use of the county.

Upon the petition of the owner of such slave, to the court of the county where the proceeds of sale are deposited, and upon satisfactory proof of the right of property of the petitioner, the court shall direct payment to him of the sum paid into the county treasury, taking bond and security from the petitioner, when they think proper, payable to the State of North Carolina, to refund the money with interest to the true owner of the slave, should it thereafter appear that the petitioner was not such.

North Carolina Law

If any runaway slave confined in jail (his owner being unknown,) should die, or, by the regular process of law be removed from jail before a sale is made, according to the provisions of this chapter, court of pleas and quarter-sessions of the county where the slave was confined, shall direct the expenses of his imprisonment to be paid out of the county funds. Provided that the sheriff or jailer shows to the court, that he has complied with the directions requiring the advertisement of runaways.

Whenever such expenses shall have been paid by the county, the county trustee by warrant shall recover back the same of the owner, or his representatives, when he shall become known, for the use of the county.

Whereas, many times slaves do run away and lie out, hid and lurking in swamps, woods, and other obscure places, killing cattle and hogs, and committing other injuries to the inhabitants of the State; in all such cases, upon intelligence that any slave is lying out as aforesaid, any two justices of the peace for the county wherein he is supposed to lurk or do mischief, are hereby empowered and required to issue proclamation against him, (reciting his name and the name of the owner if known,) thereby requiring him forthwith to surrender himself; and also to empower and require the sheriff of the county to take such power with him, as he shall think fit and necessary, for going in search and pursuit of, and effectually apprehending such outlying slave; which proclamation shall be published at the door of the court house, and at such other places as the justices shall direct. And if any slave against whom proclamation hath been thus issued, stay out, and do not immediately return home, any person may capture him; and in case of flight or resistance, may slay him without accusation or impeachment of any crime.

No slave shall go armed with gun, sword, or other weapon, or shall keep any such weapon, or shall hunt or range with a gun in the woods, upon any pretence whatsoever; and if a slave shall be found offending herein, any person may seize and take to his own use such gun or other weapon, and may apprehend and bring such slave before a justice for trial and punishment, and send him home; and the master or owner shall pay the taker up of such armed slave; the same reward as is allowed for taking up runaways.

In case any slave who shall appear not to have been properly clothed and fed, shall be convicted of stealing any corn, cattle, hogs, or other goods whatsoever, from any person not the owner of such slave, such injured person may maintain an action on the case, against the possessor of such slave, for his damages.

North Carolina Law

No person under any pretence whatever, shall hire to his slave, or to a slave under his control, his time, on pain of forfeiting forty dollars for every offence. And it shall be the duty of all grand-juries to make presentment of any slave, who shall be permitted by his master to go at large, having hired his time; and, on indictment being found for the offence, a capias shall issue to take such slave and secure him in custody, or on sufficient recognizance of his master or others, so that he be before the next court to answer to the indictment. The master shall have notice of the trial, as in other cases is provided, and the court, at the return of the capias, shall impanel a jury to inquire and try the truth of the charge against the slave; and if he be found guilty, he shall be publicly hired out by the sheriff for one year, who shall take bond with security from the hirer for the price, and for furnishing all necessaries, and taking proper care of the slave; and the bond with security shall be for the use of the poor of the county. Provided always, that if such slave be the property of a ward, he shall be hired out for the remainder only of the time for which he may belong to the person from whom he hired his time.

No slave shall go at large as a free man, exercising his own discretion in the employment of his time; nor shall any slave keep house to him or herself as a free person, exercising the like discretion in the employment of his or her time: and in case the owner of slave consent to the same, or connive thereat, he shall be deemed guilty of a misdemeanor, and on conviction be fined not exceeding one hundred dollars. Provided, however, that any person may permit his slave to live or keep house upon his land, for the purpose of attending to the business of his master.

No person shall grant permission for any meeting of the slaves of others, at his house, or on his plantation, for the purpose of dancing, under the penalty of forfeiting twenty dollars, to any who will sue therefor, unless such slaves shall have a special permit in writing from their owners for that purpose; and the person so offending shall be deemed guilty of a misdemeanor.

It shall not be lawful for any slave to be insolent to a free white person; nor to utter mischievous and slanderous reports about any free white person; nor to wilfully trespass on his property or person; nor to intermarry or cohabit with any free person of color; nor for any male slave to have sexual intercourse, or indulge in any grossly indecent familiarities with a white female; nor to produce any forged free pass or certificate of freedom; nor to go from off the plantation or seat of land, where such slave may be appointed to live, without a certificate of leave in writing from his master, or manager; nor to raise any horses, cattle, hogs, or sheep; nor to teach, or attempt to teach, any other slave or free negro to read or write, the use of figures excepted; nor to sell any spirituous liquor or wine; nor to play at any game of cards, dice, or nine pins; nor to play at any game of chance, hazard, or skill, for any money, liquor, or any kind of property, whether the same be staked or not; ; nor to set fire to any woods, except in such manner as is allowed by statute; nor to preach or exhort in any prayer-meeting or other association for worship, where slaves of different families are collected together; nor to traffic with another slave, by buying of, or selling to him, any articles of property, forbidden absolutely, or forbidden, except by written permission, to be the subject of traffic between white persons and slaves; nor to traffic with any other person, by buying of, or selling to him, any article of property, unless such other person may lawfully buy of, or sell the same to, said slave.

All offences mentioned in the foregoing section, and all other misdemeanors done by slaves, mentioned in this chapter, the prescribed punishment whereof is whipping; and all crimes by them committed, whereunto, if done by a free person, extends the jurisdiction of the county court; and all petty offences forbidden by them to be done, shall be cognizable before a single justice of the peace of the county wherein the offence is committed, who shall have full power to issue summons for witnesses, and compel their attendance; and on conviction, the offending slave shall receive not exceeding thirty-nine lashes on his bare back: and in all such trials, as many justices as think proper may sit in judgment.

Whenever any slave shall be convicted before a justice of the peace, of any offence, the master, on behalf of the slave, may appeal to the next county or superior court, on entering into sufficient recognizance for the slave, and giving good security, as in other cases of appeal.

The superior court shall have exclusive original jurisdiction of all felonies and other offences committed by slaves, which, by section thirty-two, are not assigned for trial before a justice of the peace; and the trial shall be conducted in like manner as the trials of freemen for the same offence; and moreover, the jurors shall be slave-owners.

If any number of slaves shall, at any time, consult, advise, or conspire to rebel or make insurrection, or shall plot, or conspire to murder any person, every consulting, plotting, or conspiring, shall be adjudged and deemed felony; and any slave convicted thereof, in the manner prescribed by law, shall suffer death, or transported as hereinafter provided.

North Carolina Law

If any slave be found in a state of rebellion or insurrection, or agree to join any conspiracy or insurrection, or shall procure or persuade others to join or enlist for that purpose, or shall knowlingly and wilfully aid, assist, or encourage any slave in a state of rebellion, or engaged in a conspiracy to make insurrection, every slave, so offending and being thereof convicted, shall suffer death, or be transported as hereinafter provided.

If a free person shall join, or agree to join, in any conspiracy, rebellion, or insurrection of slaves, or shall procure or persuade others to join or enlist for that purpose, or shall knowingly and wilfully aid, assist, or encourage any slave in a state of rebellion, or engage in a conspiracy to make insurrection, every free person so offending, and thereof convicted, shall suffer death.

In all cases, wherein a slave shall be prosecuted for the offences described in sections thirty-five and thirty-six of this chapter, the court may take evidence the oath of one or more witnesses, the confession of the offender freely given without any undue influence by terror or persuasion, or the testimony of a negro or other person of color, bond or free; but in all cases, where the testimony of one negro or person of color only, shall be admitted, the same shall not be deemed sufficient to convict the person charged; unless it shall be supported by such pregnant circumstances in the trial, as to the jury shall appear convincing proof, when taken with such testimony.

When any slave shall be convicted of either of the felonies created by the thirty-fifth and thirty sixth sections of this chapter, he shall suffer death; or at the discretion of the court, shall be sentenced to be transported beyond the limits of the United States, under such restrictions and upon such conditions, as good policy and the public safety at the time shall require.

Whenever a slave shall be transported, in pursuance of the provisions of this chapter, by the owner, or by the State, and such slave shall ever thereafter voluntarily return t, and be found in the State, he shall suffer death, upon due conviction thereof. And if any slave so transported, shall be brought into any county in this State by his master, or, against his will, by any other person, such slave shall be forfeited (on proof thereof) to the county into which he may be brought; and the slave shall be again transported by order of the county court, and sold for the use of the county.

In all cases of insurrection, or of conspiracy to make insurrection, or to murder, or to rebel, or any such contemplated conspiracy, insurrection, or rebellion, of any slave or slaves, upon the information and at the request of any five justices of the peace of the county in which such offences shall happen or may be contemplated, the governor may issue a commission of oyer and terminer, to any one of the judges of the superior courts of law; who shall hold said court forthwith and be clothed with all the powers necessary for the trial of such slaves.

The officer prosecuting in behalf of the State, attending such court, shall be entitled to receive the same compensation, as for attending a term of a superior court.

When any person, indicted before a court of oyer and terminer, shall, upon affidavit of himself or any other, show such circumstances and facts to the court, as would induce the judge, in the regular courts, to remove the trial out of the county, the judge may, in his discretion, continue the indictment, and commit or bind over the prisoner, as the case may require, for trial at the next superior court for the county; when the same shall be disposed of, according to the course of the court.

Any slave, or free negro, or free person of color, convicted by due course of law, of an assault with intent to commit a rape, upon the body of a white female, shall suffer death.

Any inhabitant of this State, desirous to emancipate any slave, may file a petition in writing, in any of the superior courts, setting forth, as near as may be, the name, sex, and age of the slave, and praying permission to emancipate the same, and the court shall grant the prayer, on the following conditions, and not otherwise, namely: (1.) The petitioner shall show that he has given public notice of his intention to file the petition, at the court house of the county; and in the nearest gazette, for at least six weeks before the hearing of the petition; and (2) shall enter into bond, with two able sureties, payable to the State of North Carolina, in the sum of one thousand dollars for each slave named in the petition, conditioned that he shall honestly and correctly demean himself, while he shall remain within the State; and that he will, within ninety days after granting the prayer for emancipation, leave the State, and never afterwards come within the same. Provided, nevertheless, that no such emancipation shall in any manner invalidate or affect the rights of the creditors of such petitioner.

Any person may, by last will and testament, direct and authorize his executors to cause to be emancipated any of his slaves, which shall justify the executor in doing the same; who, to that end, is hereby directed to file a petition according to the preceding section, in the same manner as

North Carolina Law

if he were absolute owner of the slaves; and such slaves shall be emancipated on the same terms and conditions, and under the same liabilities, as are prescribed in the said section. Provided always, that no such emancipation shall, in any manner, exempt the slaves from the claims of creditors. And provided further, that permission to emancipate any slave, under the directions of any last will and testament, shall not be granted within two years after probate of the same, unless the executor will enter into bond with good security, payable to the State of North Carolina, in double the value of each slave emancipated, conditioned to be responsible to the creditors of his testator for the value of said slaves.

Whenever it may be directed by a testator, that any of his slaves shall be emancipated and carried to any State, territory, or country, and it may not be convenient to carry them to the place specially appointed, the court shall designate and prescribe to what other place the slaves shall be carried after, or for emancipation.

Whenever a female slave shall by will be directed to be emancipated , all her issue, born after the date of the will, shall be deemed to have been likewise intended by the testator to be emancipated; and the court shall so declare, unless a contrary intent appear by the will, or by some disposition of the slave so born, inconsistent with such presumed intent.

It may be lawful to emancipate, upon petition, and under the order of any superior court of law, any slave over the age of fifty years, if his owner shall prove, by his own oath, or otherwise, that said slave has performed meritorious services, (which shall be more than mere general duties); and the petitioner will swear that he has not received in money or otherwise, the price or value, or any part thereof, of said slave; or been induced to petition for his emancipation in consideration of any price paid, or to be paid therefor. Provided that, before such slave shall be emancipated, the petitioner shall give bond and good security, in the sum of five hundred dollars, payable to the State of North Carolina, that said slave shall honestly and correctly demean himself, so long as he shall remain in the State, and shall not become a county charge: which bond may be sued upon, in the name of the State, to the use of the poor, or of any person injured by the malconduct of such slave, as often as it may be broken.

Every emancipation granted to any slave, in pursuance of, and according to, the directions prescribed in this chapter, other than emancipation for meritorious services, shall be upon the express condition that such slave, within ninety days from the time of granting the same, shall

North Carolina Law

leave the State, and never thereafter return into it. And, if any such slave shall refuse or neglect to leave the State, within that time, or shall ever come within the State, after having left it, any justice of the peace of the county wherein such emancipated slave may be found, shall issue a warrant to arrest him; and, upon proper proof made of his having violated the provisions of this chapter, the justice shall commit him to the jail of the county, there to remain until the next ensuing term of the county court, where, on indictment found against him for the causes aforesaid, or any of them, the trial shall be by jury; and if found guilty, the offender shall be sentenced to be publicly sold, and the purchaser shall hold him forever thereafter as a slave, and the proceeds of sale be divided equally between the informer, and the poor of the county. Provided, however, that the accused may appeal from the judgment of the court to the superior court of the county.

If any emancipated slave refuse or neglect to leave the State, as is required of him, or shall ever come within the same after having left it, any person may bring suit in the name of the State, for the joint use of himself and the wardens of the poor, of the county, upon the bond given pursuant to the provisions of this chapter.

All grand-juries shall present every emancipated slave, who may violate the provisions of this chapter; and the prosecuting officer shall prosecute such slave as hereinbefore provided.

No slave shall be set free, but according to the provisions of this chapter.

It shall not be lawful for any free negro to migrate into this State; and if one shall do so, he shall be deemed guilty of a misdemeanor during all the time of his stay, and may be indicted from time to time, until he removes out of the State; and on every conviction shall be fined five hundred dollars, for the payment of which he may be hired out as hereinafter directed. Provided, however, that such free negro shall not be indicted within thirty days after payment of the fine, or the expiration of the time of service, adjudged and suffered on a previous conviction.

Any person who shall bring into this State, by water or land, any free negro, shall forfeit and pay, for every person so brought in, five hundred dollars, to be recovered in the name of the State, for the use of the county wherein the offence shall be committed. Provided, that this section shall not extend to masters of vessels, bringing into this State any free negro, employed on board and belonging to such vessels, and who shall therewith depart; nor to any person, travelling in or through this State, having any free negro as a servant, who shall, with such person, depart out of the State.

Free negroes, not now lawful residents and inhabitants of the State, shall never hereafter become so by any length of time, neither they nor their issue; and in all cases where such free negroes are under the age of sixteen, it shall be the duty of the county court of the county in which they reside, to remove them at the expense of the county; and all such as remain to that age, shall be deemed guilty of a misdemeanor, and on conviction, shall be fined five hundred dollars.

If any free negro, who may be resident of this State, shall migrate and go into any other State, and shall be absent for the space of ninety days or more, he shall cease to be a resident and an inhabitant of this State, and it shall not be lawful for him to return to the State; and if any free negro shall return, he shall be deemed and held to have migrated to the State. Provided, that no persons shall incur the penalties or disabilities prescribed in this section, if he shall have been prevented from returning to this State by sickness, or other unavoidable occurrence.

It shall be the duty of the county solicitors to give in charge to the grand-jury, the law relating to the migration of free negroes into the State: and it is hereby made the duty of the grand-jury to present all cases of that kind in their county, arising under this chapter, within the knowledge of any of them; and the said solicitors shall, in all such cases, prosecute for, and in behalf of the State.

If any free person of color shall preach or exhort in public, or in any manner officiate as a preacher or teacher in any prayer-meeting, or other association for worship, where slaves of different families are collected together, he shall be deemed guilty of a misdemeanor; and on conviction, shall, for each offence, receive not exceeding thirty-nine lashes on his bare back.

If a free negro who is able to labor, shall be found in any county spending his time in idleness and dissipation, or having no regular or honest employment or occupation, which he is accustomed to follow, any citizen may apply to a justice of the peace of said county, and upon affidavit, obtain a warrant to arrest such person and bring him before some Justice of the county; and if, upon examination of the case, it shall appear that the free negro comes within the provisions of this section, the justice shall bind him with reasonable security, to appear at the next county court of the county; and in case he shall fail to give security, he shall be committed to the jail of the county, until the next county court thereafter:

North Carolina Law

and it shall be the duty of the court, if, upon examination of the case, it shall come within the meaning of this section, to require such free negro to enter into bond, with sufficient security in a reasonable sum, payable to the State of North Carolina, conditioned for his good behavior, and industrious, peaceable deportment, for one year. And in case he shall fail to give such security, or shall not pay the costs and charges of the prosecution, the court shall hire out such free negro to service and labor, for a term of time which to them may seem reasonable and just, an calculated to reform him to habits of industry and morality, nor exceeding three years for any one offence. And all sums of money which may arise under the provisions of this section, shall be paid to the county trustee.

It shall not be lawful for a free negro to intermarry, or cohabit and live together as man and wife, with any slave; and any free negro offending herein, shall be liable to indictment, and, upon conviction, shall be fined and imprisoned, or whipped ate the discretion of the court; the whipping not to exceed thirty-nine lashes. Provided, that this section shall not extend to any case where an intermarriage, or cohabiting, or living together took place, by and with the consent of the master or mistress, before the first day of November, A.D. one thousand eight hundred and forty-four.

No free negro shall play at all with any slave at any game of cards, dice, or nine pins; nor shall he play with any slave at any game of chance, hazard, or skill, for money, liquor, or any thing of value; and any free negro offending herein shall be deemed guilty of a misdemeanor, and, on conviction, shall receive a whipping, not exceeding thirty-nine lashes, on his bare back.

If any free negro, or person of mixed blood, shall knowingly suffer any slave to play at any game of cards, dice, nine pins, or any game of chance, hazard, or skill, whether for money, liquor, or any kind of property, or not, in his house, or in the yard, field, or garden attached or belonging to his house, he shall be deemed guilty of a misdemeanor; and, on conviction, shall receive not exceeding thirty-nine lashes on his bare back.

If a free negro shall entertain any slave in his house, during Sunday, or in the night between sunset and sunrise, he shall forfeit and pay two dollars for every offence, for the use of the county in which the offence shall be committed.

No free negro shall hawk or peddle in any county, without first obtaining a license from the court of pleas and quarter-sessions of that county; which license shall be granted for but one year, and only when seven or more justices are present, and upon satisfactory evidence of the

North Carolina Law

good character of the applicant. And if any free negro shall offend against this section, he shall be deemed guilty of a misdemeanor.

If any free negro shall wear or carry about his person, or keep in his house, any shot-gun, musket, rifle, pistol, sword, dagger, or bowie-knife, unless he shall have obtained a license therefor from the court of pleas and quarter-sessions of his county, within one year next preceding the time of the wearing, keeping, or carrying thereof, he shall be guilty of a misdemeanor.

If any negro shall, directly or indirectly, sell or give to any person, bond or free, any spirituous liquor, he shall be deemed guilty of a misdemeanor.

Every slave or free person of color, who shall hereafter be convicted of any felony, for which no specific punishment is prescribed by statute, and which is now allowed the benefit of clergy, shall be imprisoned at the discretion of the court, not exceeding two years; and, in addition to such imprisonment, the court may sentence the convict to receive one or more public whippings, or to stand in the pillory, or (if a free negro) to pay a fine, regard being had to the circumstances of each case.

When a slave shall be apprehended or indicted for any offence, whereof the superior court has original jurisdiction, his owner, if known, shall have ten days' notice of the trial, in order that he may have an opportunity of defending his slave; the cost of which notice, and all other costs, attending the trial of the slave, shall be paid by the owner, if such slave, being a free man, would be liable to the payment thereof. And if the owner refuse to pay the same, execution in the name of the State may issue against such owner.

When the owner of any slave who may be tried in virtue of this chapter, shall not be known, or cannot be ascertained, or shall reside out of the State, the court shall appoint counsel to appear for the prisoner, who shall be allowed the same fees as the attorney for the State is allowed for such criminal prosecutions; after which, the trial may proceed in the same manner, as if the owner had been notified agreeable to the directions of this chapter; and the fees for the counsel, clerk, and sheriff, shall be paid by the county having cognizance of the offence, as other county charges.

Negroes, Indians, and persons of mixed blood, descended from negro and Indian ancestors, to the fourth generation inclusive, (though one ancestor of each generation may have been a white person,) whether bond or free, shall be deemed and taken in law to be incapable to be witnesses in any case whatever, except against each other. In all pleas of the State, where the defendant may be a negro, Indian, or person of mixed blood, descended from negro or Indian ancestors, to the fourth generation inclusive, (though one ancestor of each generation may have been a white person,) whether such defendant be bond or free, the evidence of a negro, Indian, and of all persons of mixed blood, descended from negro or Indian ancestors to the fourth generation inclusive, (though one ancestor of each generation may have been a white person,) whether the person whose evidence is offered be bond or free, shall be admissable, and the witnesses competent, subject, nevertheless, to be excluded upon any other grounds of incomptency which may exist.

On the trial of any slave, free person of color, or Indian, the judge or presiding magistrate, before the examination of any slave, free negro, or Indian, shall charge such to declare the truth.

If any slave, free negro, or Indian, upon any trial where he may be examined as a witness, shall commit wilful and corrupt perjury, he shall, upon conviction, be punished as a freeman convicted of a like offence.

In every case where the whole, or part of the punishment prescribed by statute for any offence, shall be imprisonment for a time so long as thirty days at least, and there shall be provided by the statute no difference in the punishment between a white person and a free negro, the court may sentence the free negro to be both whipped and imprisoned; but in such case the time of imprisonment, within the limit prescribed, shall be in the discretion of the court.

When a free negro shall be convicted of any offence against the criminal laws of the State, and sentenced to pay a fine, and it shall appear to the satisfaction of the court, that he is unable to pay the fine imposed, (which shall in all cases be equal to the costs,) the court shall direct the sheriff to hire out such free negro publicly at the court house door, during the term of court, to any person who will pay the fine, or the greatest part thereof, for the services of the free negro for the shortest space of time, not exceeding five years; and the hirer shall have all such power and authority over, and the same rights to control the services of, such free negro, as masters have over free negro apprentices.

Whenever a free negro shall be charged with the maintenance of any bastard child, and he shall be unable to give the bond required in such case, the court may order him to be hired out, in the same manner and under the same rules as are prescribed in the preceding section, for such sum as the court shall adjudge to be proper for the maintenance of the child.

North Carolina Law

When any free negro, for any fine imposed on him for an offence, or for a sum of money adjudged against him in case of bastardy, shall be hired out for the space of five years, the whole fine or sum of money shall be discharged; and the sheriff, after deducting five per centum on the sums collected for any hiring, shall account for the residue, as for other fines; and in these cases, the officers shall have full fees. Provided always, that if any free negro, who may be hired out for his fine, or in pursuance of section seventy-five of this chapter shall abscond or leave the service of his hirer, before the expiration of his time of hiring, such free negro shall be bound to serve double the deficient time. And provided, further, that the person hiring such free negro shall, in open court, enter into recognizance to the State, with two able sureties, in such sum as the court shall direct, that the free negro, during the time of service, shall be furnished with good and sufficient lodging, clothing, medicine, and food; shall be treated with humanity, and be employed in some useful and industrious occupation; shall not be removed from the county, during the time of service, and shall be produced to the county court at the expiration thereof, or whenever, and as often as, the court may order. On breach of the recognizance, the prosecuting officer of the court, which may have directed the hiring, shall enforce and collect the recognizance for the benefit of the free negro, who, on such breach thereof being established, shall be discharged of all further service. And if any hirer shall fail to comply with any of the duties hereby imposed on him, he shall be deemed guilty of a misdemeanor, and may be prosecuted therefor in the county where the hiring took place.

It shall not be lawful for any slave to be transported on any railroad, steamboat, or other vessel navigating the waters of the State, or on any stage-coach, without a permission in writing from the owner, under the penalty of five hundred dollars; one half to the informer and one half to the State, to be recovered in the name of the State against such railroad company, the owner or captain of the boat or vessel, or the owner of such coach, as the case may be. And if any slave shall escape from his owner, by means of such transportation, the owner may recover his value from the said company, owner, or captain of the boat, or owner of the coach, so transporting the slave (as the case may be,) by action on the case. Provided, however, that this section shall not extend to the case of any slave travelling with his master, or with the agent of his master, or as the servant or attendant of any white person, bona fide employed for that purpose.

All free persons descended from negro ancestors, to the fourth generation inclusive, though one ancestor of each generation may have been a white person, shall be deemed free negroes and persons of mixed blood.

CHAP. 111. TOWNS.
Pages 589-590.
　　The Mayor shall, by order of the commissioners, take the list of taxables in the town, in such manner and at such time as the commissioners shall prescribe. If the owners of slaves employed in town shall not reside therein, the hirers shall list them for taxation; and if any person fail to list his taxables within the time prescribed by the commissioners, he shall be liable to a double tax. The commissioners may appoint assessors of the real estate within the town, who, before acting, shall take an oath before some justice of the peace to discharge their duties faithfully and impartially; and the mayor and assessors shall make report to the commissioners within the time prescribed by them.

****

PUBLIC LAWS OF THE STATE OF NORTH CAROLINA
PASSED BY THE GENERAL ASSEMBLY
AT ITS SESSION OF 1854 - 55:
TOGETHER WITH THE COMPTROLLER'S STATEMENT
OF PUBLIC REVENUE AND EXPENDITURE
RALEIGH: HOLDEN & WILSON, PRINTERS TO THE STATE,
1855

CHAP. 27. LITERARY FUND AND COMMON SCHOOLS.
1854-55. An Act concerning Literary Fund and Common Schools. (Page 56).
　　Sec. 29. No county court shall tax any free person of color for the support and maintenance of common schools; and no person descended from negro ancestors to the fourth generation inclusive, shall be taught in said schools.

CHAP. 34. PERSONS OF COLOR.

North Carolina Law

1854-55. An Act to provide for the transmission to the Persons of Color, now in the Republic of Liberia, of the funds belonging to them in this State. (Page 66).
   Sec. 1. Be it enacted by the General Assembly of the State of North Carolina, and it is hereby enacted by the authority of the same, That it shall be lawful for the supreme court of the State, upon application of the reverend William McLain, of Washington City, in the District of Columbia, to order, decree and direct, that any funds in the office of the supreme court, or under its control, belonging to the persons of color, now in the republic of Liberia, who, or their ancestors, may have been slaves in North Carolina, be paid to the said William McLain, to be transmitted by him, or through his agency, to the persons entitled thereto.
[Ratified the 16th day of February, 1855.]

CHAP. 37 REVENUE.
1854-55 An Act concerning Revenue. (Pages 81-82).
   Sec. 48. All free persons, living with, and constituting a part of the family, and all colored persons living, by consent, on the lands of another, shall be listed, by the head of the family, or owner of the land, as the case may be.

CHAP. 42. RIVERS AND CREEKS.
1854-55. An Act to prevent the felling of timber in Big Brush Creek in Randolph County. (Page 100).
   Sec. 1. Be it enacted by the General Assembly of the State of North Carolina, and it is hereby enacted by the authority of the same, That hereafter it shall not be lawful for any free person or persons to cut or fell timber in Big Brush creek, between Josiah Cheek's mills, in said county, and the Chatham county line, on said stream, under a penalty of five dollars for each and every offence, to be recovered before any justice of the peace for said county, upon due conviction thereof, unless the same is removed within the space of ten days, to the use of the person suing for the same; and the person or persons so offending, against the provisions of this act, shall be further liable to be indicted, and fined or imprisoned at the discretion of the court.
   Sec. 2. Be it further enacted, That if any slave or slaves shall offend against the provisions of this act, by direction of their master, or

other person having control of them, upon due conviction thereof, the owner or owners for the time being shall forfeit the sum of ten dollars for each and every offence, one half to the benefit of the poor of said county, and the other half to the person suing for the same, to be recovered as in section the first.

Sec. 3. Be it further enacted, That, should any slave or slaves offend against the meaning and intent of this act, of their own free will, upon due conviction thereof, as provided in section first, shall receive not exceeding thirty nine lashes, at the discretion of the court.

Sec. 4. Be it further enacted, That this act shall be in force in ninety days from and after its ratification.

[Ratified the 14th day of February, 1855.]

CHAP. 44. RIVERS AND CREEKS.
1854-55. An Act to prevent the felling of timber in the Northeast River in Duplin County. (Page 101).

Sec. 1. Be it enacted by the General Assembly of the State of North Carolina, and it is hereby enacted by the authority of the same, That if any person or persons shall hereafter fell any timber in the Northeast branch of the Cape Fear river in the county of Duplin, at any point or place on said river from the upper Kornegay's bridge, near the mouth of Rattlesnake creek, down the same to the mouth of Goshen swamp, or otherwise obstruct the same, the person or persons so offending shall be deemed guilty of a misdemeanor, and may be indicted in the county or superior courts of said county, and, upon conviction, shall be fined, at the discretion of the court, a sum not exceeding fifty dollars.

Sec. 2. Be it further enacted, That if any negro slave be convicted of felling timber into, or otherwise obstructing said river in the county aforesaid, before any justice of the peace of said county, provided his master or mistress, overseer or employer shall have had five days' notice in writing of the charge against him, previous to his trial, he shall, for each and every offence, be punished at the discretion of the justice of the peace: Provided, the same shall not exceed thirty nine lashes on his bare back, which punishment shall be inflicted by the sheriff, constable or such other officer of said country as may have arrested said slave.

[Ratified the 15th day of February, 1855.]

CHAP. 46. SALARIES AND FEES.
1854-55. An Act concerning Salaries and Fees. (Pages 106-110).

Sec. 14. The attorney general and solicitors for the State shall, in addition to the general compensation allowed them by the State, receive the following fees, and no other, to wit: for every indictment which they may prosecute for a felony, perjury, forgery, counterfeiting, passing or attempting to pass or sell, any forged or counterfeited paper or evidence of debt; maliciously injuring or attempting to injure any railroad, or railroad car, or any person travelling on such railroad; stealing or obliterating records; stealing, concealing, destroying or obliterating any will; maliciously burning or attempting to burn houses or bridges; misdemeanors of accessories after the fact to felonies; and for circulating seditious writings among slaves and free negroes, and for persuading them to conspiracy and rebellion, each of them shall receive ten dollars upon conviction of the defendant, to be paid by him.

Sec. 17. ...Recording the decree of the court upon a petition filed for the legitimation of a bastard child, one dollar; for each description of a slave or free negro and certificate thereof, fifty cents.

Sec. 21. ...Maintaining any slave or other property, or any criminal seized by virtue of any legal precept, such sum as may be fixed by the court. **[Editor's note: This section refers to Sheriff's fees.]**

CHAP. 50. TRADING WITH SLAVES.
1854-55. An Act to prevent trading with slaves, in the counties of Mecklenburg and Northampton. (Page 117).

Sec. 1. Be it enacted by the General Assembly of the State of North Carolina, and it is hereby enacted by the authority of the same, That any person in the counties of Mecklenburg and Northampton, who shall be guilty of trading with slaves, for any species of domesticated fowls or poultry, without a written permit from his, her or their master, mistress, or person having the management of such slave, shall be deemed guilty of a misdemeanor; and, upon conviction in the various ways provided by law, shall be subject to all the pains and penalties now imposed upon persons for trading with slaves for other articles of goods, wares and merchandize. **[Ratified the 14th day of February, 1855.]**

RESOLUTIONS.

1854-55. Resolution concerning the distribution of the Revised Code. (Page 129).

Resolved, That on or before the first day of July next, the secretary of State be, and he is hereby directed to write a circular letter to the clerks of the county courts, in each and every county in the State, requesting said clerks to inform him, under their seals of office, of the names of the acting justices of the peace in their respective counties; the secretary of State to lay the said information, when obtained, before the governor of the State; and the governor is hereby directed to forward one copy of the Revised Code, when ready for distribution, to each and every justice of the peace, there qualified and acting as such, and to none others. [Ratified the 16th day of February, 1855.]

COMPTROLLER.
Statements of the Comptroller of Public Accounts, for the two Fiscal Years ending October 31st 1853 and 1854. (Page 183).
Comptroller's Statement.
Public Fund-Receipts
Cherokee bonds $1,631.00

****

PRIVATE LAWS OF THE STATE OF NORTH CAROLINA PASSED BY THE GENERAL ASSEMBLY AT ITS SESSION OF 1854-55 RALEIGH, HOLDEN & WILSON, PRINTERS TO THE STATE, 1855

CHAP. 108. EMANCIPATION.
1854-55. An Act to emancipate Betty, a slave. (Page 89).

Sec. 1. Be it enacted by the General Assembly of the State of North Carolina, and it is hereby enacted by the authority of the same, That Betty, a slave, the property of Joshua Carman, of Cumberland county, be and she is hereby emancipated and set free by the consent and at the request of her master, and by the name of Betty Beebee, shall possess and exercise all the rights and privileges of other free persons of color in this State: Provided, nevertheless, that before this act of emancipation shall take effect, the owner of the said slave Betty, or some person for him, shall

North Carolina Law

file in the clerk's office of the court of pleas and quarter sessions of Cumberland county, a bond with good security, in the sum of five hundred dollars, payable to the Governor of the State and his successors in office, that the said Betty shall demean herself correctly while she remains in the State and not become a county charge, which bond may be put in suit in the name of the Governor for the time being, to the use of the county or person injured by a breach of its condition: Provided, That she do not reside out of the county aforesaid, more than thirty days at any one time; also that she give bond in such an amount as will be approved of by the county court, that she will not become a public charge.
[Ratified the 14th day of February, 1855.]

CHAP. 109. EMANCIPATION.
1854-55. An Act to emancipate Jerry, a slave. (Pages 89-90).

Sec. 1. Be it enacted by the General Assembly of the State of North Carolina, and it is hereby enacted by the authority of the same, That Jerry, a slave, the property of H.B. Williams and S.A. Davis, of Mecklenburg county, be, and he is hereby, with the consent, and at the request of the said owners, emancipated and set free, and by the name of Jerry Bethel, shall hereafter possess and exercise all the rights and privileges which are enjoyed by other free persons of color in this State: Provided, nevertheless, That before the said slave is emancipated, the said Williams and Davis, or either of them, shall give bond and approved security, payable to the Governor and his successors in office, in the county court of Mecklenburg county, in the sum of one thousand dollars, that the said Jerry shall honestly and correctly demean himself as long as he shall remain in the State, and shall not become a county charge; which bond may be sued upon in the name of the Governor for the time being, to the use of said county, and of any person injured by the misconduct of the said slave hereby emancipated.
[Ratified the 8th day of January, 1855.]

CHAP. 110. EMANCIPATION.
1854-55. An Act to emancipate John Good. (Page 90).

Be it enacted by the General Assembly of the State of North Carolina, and it is hereby enacted by the authority of the same, That John Good, a slave, the property of George Bishop, of Craven county, be, and he

is hereby, with the consent, and at the request of the said owner, emancipated and set free; and by the name of John Good, shall hereafter possess and exercise all the rights and privileges which are enjoyed by other free persons of color in this State: Provided, nevertheless, That before the said slave is emancipated, a good and sufficient bond, payable to the State of North Carolina, shall be given in the county court of Craven, in the sum of one thousand dollars, that the said John Good shall honestly and correctly demean himself as long as he shall remain in the State, and not become a county charge; which bond may be sued upon in the name of the State to the use of said county, or any other county of the State, and of any person injured by the misconduct of the said slave hereby emancipated.
[Ratified the 20th day of January, 1855.]

CHAP. 111. EMANCIPATION.
1854-55. An Act to emancipate James G. Hostler, a slave. (Pages 90-91).

Sec. 1. Be it enacted by the General assembly of the State of North Carolina, and it is hereby enacted by the authority of the same, That James G. Hostler, the property of James Anderson, William A. Wright, Armand J. DeRossett, Jr., Joshua G. Wright and Thomas C. Miller, of the town of Wilmington, be and he is hereby, with the consent of said owners, emancipated and set free, by the name of James G. Hostler, and shall hereafter possess and exercise all the rights and privileges which are enjoyed by free persons of color in this State: Provided, nevertheless, That before the said slave shall be emancipated, he shall give bond with good security in the sum of five hundred dollars, payable to the State of North Carolina, conditioned that the said James G. Hostler shall honestly and correctly demean himself, and shall not become a parish charge, which bond shall be approved by the court of pleas and quarter sessions of the county of New Hanover, and be deposited in the office of said court, and may be sued on to the use of any parish or person injured by the misconduct of said James G. Hostler.
[Ratified the 16th day of January, 1855.]

CHAP. 112. EMANCIPATION.
1854-55. A Bill to emancipate Albert, a slave, the property of John Hockody. (Page 91).

North Carolina Law

Sec. 1. Be it enacted by the General Assembly of the State of North Carolina, and it is hereby enacted by the authority of the same, That Albert, a slave, the property of John Hockody, be and he is hereby, with the consent and at the request of said owner, emancipated and set free, and by the name of Albert Hockody shall hereafter possess and exercise all the rights and privileges which are enjoyed by other free persons of color in the State: Provided, nevertheless, That before the said slave Albert is emancipated, the said John Hockody shall give bond and approved security, payable to the governor and his successors in office, in the county court of Halifax, in the sum of one thousand dollars, that the said Albert shall honestly and correctly demean himself as long as he shall remain in the State, and shall not become a county charge; which bond may be sued on in the name of the governor for the time being, to the use of the said county, and of any person injured by the misconduct of the said slave hereby emancipated.
[Ratified the 16th day of February, 1855.]

CHAP. 113. EMANCIPATION.
1854-55. An Act to emancipate Louis, a slave, the property of James Dunn. (Pages 91-92).
Sec. 1. Be it enacted by the General Assembly of the State of North Carolina, and it is hereby enacted by the authority of the same, That Louis, a slave, the property of James Dunn, of Cumberland county, be and he is hereby, emancipated and set free, and by the name of Louis Dunn shall hereafter possess and exercise all the rights and privileges which are enjoyed by other free persons of color in this State: Provided, nevertheless, That before said slave shall be emancipated, his said owner shall give bond with good sureties in the sum of five hundred dollars, payable to the Governor of the State and his successors in office, that the said slave shall honestly and correctly demean himself while he remains in this State, and not become a county charge; which bond shall be filed in the office of the clerk of the court of pleas and quarter sessions of Cumberland county, and may be sued upon in the name of the governor for the time being, to the use of the county or persons injured by a breach thereof.
[Ratified the 16th day of February, 1855.]

CHAP. 114. FISH.

1854-55. An Act to prevent the obstruction of the passage of fish in the waters of South River and Adam's Creek. (Page 92).

Sec. 2. Be it further enacted, That any person or persons offending against any of the provisions of this act, shall forfeit and pay for every such offence, the sum of fifty dollars, to be recovered before any justice of the peace of the county of Craven, to the use of the person suing for the same; and if any slave shall violate any of the provisions of this act, he or they shall, on conviction, receive thirty nine lashes on his or their bare back.

[Ratified the 14th day of February, 1855.]

CHAP. 179. PLANKROADS.
1854-55. An Act to Incorporate the Salem and Clemmonsville Plankroad Company. (Page 187).

Sec. 11. Be it further enacted, That if any person or persons shall refuse to pay the toll at the time of offering to pass the points designated for the collection of tolls, and previous to passing the same, the toll collectors respectively may refuse a passage to the person or persons refusing to pay: and if any person or persons shall pass or drive through or around said place any wheeled carriage or animal liable to pay toll, without paying the same, or if any person or persons shall drive on or use any part of said road or its branches, between the point designated for the collection of tolls, without paying the amounts for which he, she or they are liable, it shall be held that he, she or they are fraudulently using said road, and be liable to a fine of five dollars for each offence, if a white person,, and if a slave or a free person of color to be whipped not exceeding fifteen lashes; the fine to be recovered, and the whipping to be inflicted, upon conviction by warrant before any justice of the peace of any county in which such portion of said road may be situated.

CHAP. 242. TOWNS.
1854-55. An Act to provide for the better Government of the Town of Louisburg, in the County of Franklin. (Pages 314-323).

Sec. 7. ...The said magistrate of police shall further have summary jurisdiction to hear and determine all breaches of the peace occurring within the limits of said town, not above the grade of misdemeanor, and to administer summary punishment on all offenders against the peace, quiet,

North Carolina Law

and good order of said town of Louisburg; if free white persons by a fine not exceeding twenty dollars or by imprisonment not exceeding five days; if free persons but not white then by fine and imprisonment as above or by whipping, not exceeding thirty nine lashes, any or all at his discretion; if slaves, by whipping not exceeding thirty nine lashes: Provided, The owners or managers of such slave receive reasonable notice of the time of trial, and a copy of the warrant for the arrest of said slave, and in case of their conviction, said master, owner or manager, shall be liable for the costs thereof: Provided, nevertheless, It shall and may be lawful in all cases for the person or persons, or in case of slaves, their owners or managers against whom the said magistrate of police shall give judgment or pass sentence by virtue of the summary jurisdiction hereby given, or for breach of any law or laws relating to said town, or any of the ordinance of said commissioners, or for any penalty or penalties given by said laws or ordinances, to appeal from said judgment or sentence to the superior court of law for the County of Franklin. ...The said magistrate of police is further vested with the same jurisdiction and powers over all offences committed by slaves as is now by law given to a justice or justices of the peace out of court under the same rules, regulations and restrictions as are provided in these cases.

    Sec. 14. Be it further enacted, That the town clerk shall within the first seven days of April, in each and every year advertise for twenty days, at two or more public places in said town, notifying all persons subject to pay poll tax to the State, who shall have resided within the limits of said town on the first day of March, immediately preceding or who may have been principally employed in any profession or vocation in said town for two months or more, immediately preceding the said first day of March, and all persons who owned or were possessed of taxable property within said town, on the said first day of March, to give into him before the last day in said month of April, a list of their said polls and taxable property, and it shall be the duty of all such persons, to give in said list within the time specified; said list shall state the number and local situation of the lots or parts of lots given in with the value at which they may have been assessed for taxation, as hereinafter provided, the number of white taxable polls, taxable slaves and taxable free negroes residing on the said last day of April, on the lands of persons giving in said lots. **[Editor's note: This Statute refers to town taxes. The Sheriff has authority to collect State taxes.]**

    Sec. 16. Be it further enacted, That said board of commissioners have power, annually, to levy and cause to be collected in the manner above prescribed, the following taxes, that is to say, a tax not exceeding twenty five cents on every hundred dollars worth of real estate situated within the limits of said town, to be valued as hereinafter provided; for a poll tax not exceeding one dollar, on every free taxable poll, who has resided or been principally employed in said town for two months next preceding the first day of March of each and every year; and a tax not exceeding fifty cents on every taxable slave poll, who has resided or been principally employed in said town for two months next preceding the first day of March in each and every year; and all tax on free poll and slave poll shall be in the relative proportion of two to one.

Sec. 21. They shall preserve the peace and good order of the inhabitants of said town, and of others who may be there, and suppress all riotous and disorderly assemblies, especially on the Sabbath day, whether of free persons or slaves, and for the purpose in this last clause, (any one commissioner shall have power); they shall have power to make regulations and ordinances for the enforcing the orderly conduct of slaves and free negroes within said town.

CHAP. 247. TOWNS.
1854-55. An Act to incorporate the town of Newton, in Catawba County. (Page 343).
Sec. 2. Be it further enacted, That no person shall be eligible to the office of commissioner of said town, unless he shall have resided therein twelve months next preceding his election; and no person shall be entitled to vote in any election for commissioners in said town, except free white men of the age of twenty one years, who shall have resided in said town for twelve months preceding the election.

CHAP. 248. TOWNS.
1854-55. An Act to empower the Commissioners of the town of Wilmington to establish streets in said town and for other purposes. (Pages 356-359).
Sec. 13. Be it further enacted, That the commissioners of said town shall have full power and authority by such ordinances as to them shall seem necessary, to prohibit and prevent all persons recently from any place where any contagious or infectious disease exists, or has recently existed, from entering said town, and all goods and chattels from being

brought from such place to said town, and generally by their ordinances or otherwise, to adopt such other precautionary measures, to prevent the introduction of infectious or contagious diseases into said town, as they may deem expedient; they shall also have power to prevent or restrain communication with the inmates of any house in said town, in which any person may be afflicted with any infectious or contagious disease; and at any time upon the certificate of a physician, that any free negro, or slave is sick with a dangerous and infectious or contagious disease in said town, and that he can be removed without endangering his life, the said commissioners shall have power to cause such slave or free negro, to be removed to some convenient place, without the limits of said town, and there to be confined and attended as his situation requires; and it shall be lawful for them to sue for, and recover from any free negro, or the owner of any slave so removed, the expenses of the removal, support, nursing and medical attendance of such free negro or slave, as the case may be, and also in case of his or her death, the expenses of burial by warrant or writ, in any court having competent jurisdiction; and any and all persons attempting to prevent, or resisting the removal of any such free negro or slave, shall be liable to indictment in the superior court of law, for the county of New Hanover, and on conviction, punished by fine or imprisonment, or both, in the discretion of said court; and the said commissioners shall have full power to impose such fines and penalties, in case of white persons, and such fines, penalties and punishment, in cases of free negroes or slaves, for the violation of any ordinance or ordinances made by them, by virtue of this section, as to them shall seem expedient, provided the punishment of any free negro or slave, shall not exceed one months imprisonment, or thirty nine lashes.

 Sec. 21. Be it further enacted, That the commissioners of said town shall be vested with full power to make such ordinances as to them shall seem necessary to restrain, prohibit and prevent any slave or free person of color from loitering in or about any shop or store in said town, or from sitting down or remaining longer in such store or shop than while actually engaged in purchasing such articles as they may be lawfully authorized to procure, or from entering into any inner room connected with such store or shop; and said commissioners by fines and penalties to be imposed on the owners and keepers of such shops or stores, and by fines and corporal punishment, to be imposed or inflicted on slaves or free persons of color, may secure and enforce obedience to such ordinances as shall be made under the provisions of this section.

CHAP. 249. TOWNS.
1854-55. An Act to amend an Act passed in the year 1836, entitled an Act to Incorporate the town of Greensboro, in the County of Guilford. (Page 360).

Sec. 1. Be it enacted by the General Assembly of the State of North Carolina, and it is hereby enacted by the authority of the same, That it shall be lawful for the free white men residing in the town of Greensboro' hereafter mentioned, who have attained the age of twenty one years, to meet on the first Monday in April, A.D., 1855, and on the first Monday in April in each successive year thereafter, at some convenient place in said town, and vote for an intendant of police and four discreet persons to act as commissioners of said town for the term of one year from the day of said election.

Sec. 3. Be it further enacted, That all free white men of the age of twenty one years, who shall have resided in said town for six months immediately preceding the day of any election and shall have paid a town tax, shall be entitled to vote in said election.

CHAP. 318. CHEROKEE LANDS.
1854-55. An Act for the relief of Solomon Newton. (Pages 445-446).

Sec. 1. Be it enacted by the General Assembly of the State of North Carolina, and it is hereby enacted by the authority of the same, That Solomon Newton shall have a right to purchase section No. 2 of Willnotas' reservation in Jackson county, at a price to be fixed by Jacob Siler and Mark Coleman, who are hereby appointed commissioners for that purpose; and on the value of the lands being ascertained as aforesaid, he may file his bonds, payable to the State in one and two years, in legal instalments with good security, to be judged of by the agent of the State for the collection of Cherokee bonds; and when it is certified to the secretary of State by said agent, that said bonds are fully paid, he shall issue a grant to said Newton of all such rights that the State has in said lands.

Sec. 2. Be it further enacted, That this act shall take effect and be in force from and after its ratification.
[Ratified the 15th day of February, 1855.]

****

PUBLIC LAWS OF THE STATE OF NORTH CAROLINA PASSED BY THE GENERAL ASSEMBLY AT ITS SESSION OF 1856-57 RALEIGH: HOLDEN & WILSON, PRINTERS TO THE STATE, 1857

CHAP. 12. CONSTITUTIONAL REFORM.

1856-57. An Act to amend the Constitution of the State of North Carolina. (Pages 12-13).

Whereas, at the session of the last General Assembly, begun and held at Raleigh, on the third Monday of November, in the year of our Lord, one thousand eight hundred and fifty four, a bill entitled "A bill to amend the Constitution of the State of North Carolina," was read three times in each house of the said General Assembly, and agreed to by three fifths of the whole number of members of each house respectively: And whereas, the bill so agreed to, hath been duly published six months previous to the election of the members of this present General Assembly, according to the clause of section one of article four of the amended constitution, and the directions contained in the second section of the said bill; and it is the intention by this bill to agree to the preamble and first section of the bill aforesaid, containing the said alteration of the constitution of this State: and whereas, a large number of the people are disenfranchised by the freehold qualification now required of voters for members of the Senate; therefore,

Sec. 1. Be it enacted by the General Assembly of the State of North Carolina, and it is hereby enacted by the authority of the same, (two thirds of the whole number of members of each house concurring) That the second clause of the third section of the first article of the amended constitution, ratified by the people of North Carolina, on the second Monday of November, in the year of our Lord, eighteen hundred and thirty five, shall be amended to read as follows: "Every free white man of the age of twenty one years, being a native or naturalized citizen of the United States, and who has been an inhabitant of the State for twelve months immediately preceding the day of any election, and shall have paid public taxes, shall be entitled to vote for a member of the Senate for the district in which he resides."

[Ratified the 11th day of December, 1856.]

North Carolina Law

CHAP. 34. REVENUE.
1856-57. An Act entitled "Revenue." (Pages 33 & 42).
Sec. 22. Upon every hundred dollars employed in buying and selling slaves, upon speculation, a tax of thirty three and one third cents: upon all sums of one hundred dollars and upward, employed in any other species of trade, for profit, by buying and selling, not in this chapter specially taxed, a tax of twenty cents; whether these trades be carried on with cash or upon credit.
Sec. 48. All free persons, living with and constituting a part of the family, and all colored persons living by consent on the lands of another, shall be listed by the head of the family, or owner of the land, as the case may be.

COMPTROLLER'S STATEMENT
1856-57. (Page 108).
Jacob Siler, agent for collecting Cherokee bonds,   200.00.

COMPTROLLER'S STATEMENT
1856-57. (Page 155).
Jacob Siler, agent for collection of Cherokee bonds, 640.00.

COMPTROLLER'S STATEMENT
1856-57. (Page 157).
Jacob Siler, agent for collection of Cherokee bonds, 260.00.

****

PRIVATE LAWS OF THE STATE OF NORTH CAROLINA
PASSED BY THE GENERAL ASSEMBLY
AT ITS SESSION OF 1856-57
RALEIGH: HOLDEN & WILSON, PRINTER'S TO THE STATE, 1857

CHAP. 98. TOWNS.
1856-57. An Act to Revise and Consolidate the Charter of the City of Raleigh. (Page 116).

North Carolina Law

Sec. 74. Be it further enacted, That the commissioners may make all needful ordinances respecting the conduct and demeanor of slaves and free negroes in the city, both by day and night, so as to prevent their assemblage and loitering about shops where ardent spirits are sold, and all unlawful traffic between free persons and slaves; they may impose penalties for the use of the city, on the owners or keepers of such shops, who permit slaves to assemble within or about their premises at night, or on Sunday, and pass laws to punish the slaves so offending, and may also prevent slaves residing without the city from visiting the same in the night or on Sunday, except by written permission from their managers, and then only for good and sufficient cause.

CHAP. 121. TOWNS.
1856-57. An Act to amend the Charter of the Town of Plymouth. (Pages 135-136).
Sec. 1. Be it enacted by the General assembly of the State of North Carolina, and it is hereby enacted by the authority of the same, That the charter of the town of Plymouth, in this State, be so amended as to authorise the commissioners of said town to pass and adopt any regulations they may choose by their by-laws, to search such vessels as they choose at any point on the Roanoke river to prevent the escape thereby of slaves from the State.
Sec. 2. Be it further enacted, that this [act] shall be in force from and after its ratification.
[Ratified the 3d day of February, 1857.]

CHAP. 142.
1856-57. An Act to authorize Joshua Small and his wife Polly, Robert and Elizabeth Small, Anthony Copeland and Warren Boon, to reside in the County of Northampton, for the space of eighteen months. (Page 170).
Sec. 1. Be it enacted by the General Assembly of the State of North Carolina, and it is hereby enacted by the authority of the same, That Joshua Small and his wife Polly, Robert and Elizabeth Small, Anthony Copeland and Warren Boon be, and they are hereby authorized to remain in the county of Northampton for the space of eighteen months, and enjoy all

the rights and immunities that other free persons of color now enjoy under the constitution and laws of this State.

Sec. 2. Be it further enacted, That if the said free persons of color do not remove from the State within the above named time, then they shall become subject to all the laws relative to the emancipation of free persons of color into this State. [?]

Sec. 3 Be it further enacted, That this act shall be in force from and after its ratification.

[Ratified the 2d day of February, A.D., 1857.]

****

PUBLIC LAWS OF THE STATE OF NORTH CAROLINA PASSED BY THE GENERAL ASSEMBLY AT ITS SESSION OF 1858-59
RALEIGH: HOLDEN AND WILSON, PRINTERS TO THE STATE,1859

CHAP. 25. REVENUE.
1858-59. An Act entitled Revenue. (Pages 34-35, 38, & 51).Schedule A.

27. (2) Every taxable poll eighty cents; Provided, That the county court may exempt from poll tax such poor and infirm persons, and disabled and insane slaves as they may declare and record fit objects of exemption.

(10) Every person resident in this State, engaged in the business of buying and selling slaves, whether the purchases or sales be made in or out of State, for cash or on a credit, one half of one per cent on the total amount of all his purchases, during the twelve months ending on the first day of July of each year.

(11) Every resident in this State, not a regular trader in slaves, who may buy a slave or slaves to sell again, whether such purchase or sale be made in or out of the State, for cash or on credit, one half of one per cent on the total amount of his purchases during the twelve months ending on the first day of July of each year.

33. Every poll that is, or will be of the required age on the first day of July of any year, shall be listed that year. Every owner, if in the State, shall list his slaves in the county in which he resides; and if the owner be a non-resident of the State, the hirer or person who has the slaves in

possession, shall list the same and pay taxes. Slaves hired out beyond the limits of the State shall be listed by the owners as well as those employed within the State.

34. Such slaves and other taxable personal estate as are employed on the land of the owner, shall be listed in the county in which the land is listed.

35. Every head of a family, or owner of land or town lot, who, on the first day of July shall have a free person of color subject to taxation, as a member of his family, or in his employment, or living on his land, or in his house, shall list such person for taxation, and pay the tax.

??. (14) Every non-resident of the State, who, in person or by agent, shall purchase any slave or slaves in this State, shall, immediately after such purchase, become liable to pay a tax of one half of one per cent on the amount of his purchase, and upon his neglect or failure to pay such tax, he shall forfeit and pay the sum of one hundred dollars, which shall be collected by the sheriff, one half to his own use and the other half to the use of the State. When the purchase was made by an agent, such agent shall be equally liable for the tax and forfeiture with his principal.

(15) Every non-resident of the State, who, either in person or by agent, brings a slave or slave into this State, and sells, shall pay one half of one per cent on the amount of each sale effected. If he fail to pay this tax, the purchaser shall be liable for the same, and the sheriff of the county in which the sale was made, or in which the purchaser reside, shall collect by distress or otherwise out of the seller, if to be found in his county, and if the seller is not to be found, out of the buyer.

CHAP. 30. SLAVES AND FREE NEGROES.
1858-59. An Act providing for the hiring out of free negroes in certain cases. (Page 70).

Section 1. Be it enacted by the General Assembly of the State of North Carolina, and is hereby enacted by the authority of the same, That whenever a free negro shall be convicted of any offence, not capital, hereafter committed, the court before which he may be tried, shall have power to sentence such free negro to pay a fine in addition to, or in place of such other punishment, or some part thereof, as may be prescribed by law for his said offence, at the discretion of the court.

Sec. 2. Be it further enacted, That the proceeds of hire of any free negro who shall have been hired out to pay a fine imposed upon him, or for

such sum as the court may adjudge to be proper for the maintenance of a bastard child with which he is charged, according to the provisions of section seventy five and seventy six of chapter one hundred and seven of Revised Code, entitled "Slaves and Free Negroes," shall be applied in payment of the costs incurred in the prosecution, and shall be a discharge pro tanto therefrom.
[Ratified the 16th day of February, 1859.]

CHAP. 31. SLAVES AND FREE NEGROES.
1858-59. An Act to prevent the sale of spirituous liquors to Free Persons of Color. (Page 71).

Section 1. Be it enacted by the General Assembly of the State of North Carolina, and it is hereby enacted by the authority of the same, That no person shall sell, or deliver to, or buy for, or be instrumental, either directly or indirectly, in procuring for any free person of color, for cash, or in exchange for articles delivered, or upon any consideration whatever, or as a gift, any spirituous liquors, or liquor of which alcohol is an ingredient, except upon the written certificate of some practicing physician or magistrate stating that the same is necessary for medicinal purposes.

Sec. 2. Be it further enacted, That any person who shall offend against the provision of the forgoing section shall be deemed guilty of a misdemeanor, and upon conviction thereof in any court of record, shall be fined, not less than ten, nor more than fifty dollars.

Sec. 3. Be it further enacted, That in the trial of all indictments under this act, the State shall not be required to prove the negative averment, that said purchase was made without certificate of a physician that the same was necessary for medicinal purposes.
[Ratified the 16th day of February, 1859.]

CHAP. 33.
1858-59. An Act to promote and encourage the planting of oysters and clams. (Pages 77-78).

Sec. 4. Be it further enacted, That if any person shall do any injury to such beds, or shall gather, or take away, any oysters or clams within the lines of the stakes aforesaid without permission first had or obtained from the owner or owners thereof, he shall forfeit for each offence the sum of ten dollars; and if any person shall commit any such offence in the night time, he shall forfeit for each offence the sum of twenty five dollars, and the offences herein created may be recovered by warrant before a justice of the peace by anyone who may sue therefor.

Sec. 5. Be it further enacted, That if any slave shall commit any of the offences herein created, he shall, on conviction before any justice of the peace, be punished by whipping, not to exceed thirty nine lashes.
[Ratified on the 4th day of January, 1859.]

RESOLUTIONS.
1858-59. Resolution in favor of certain entries of Cherokee Lands. (Pages 103-104).

Resolved, That whenever any person who has entered Cherokee lands, and given bonds according to the provisions of the act of 1852, shall complain to the agent for the collection of Cherokee bonds, that land which he had entered had been previously entered, or otherwise disposed of by the State, it shall be the duty of said agent to enquire into the facts, and if he shall be satisfied that the person complaining had entered the land in good faith, and without knowing that it had been previously entered or disposed of, the said agent shall surrender to such person the bond so given by said person, if the same are in possession of or under the control of said agent.
[Ratified the 16th day of February, 1859.]

COMPTROLLER'S STATEMENT. PUBLIC FUNDS.
1858-59. (Page 125).
Cherokee Bonds $1,200

COMPTROLLER'S STATEMENT. PUBLIC FUNDS.
1858-59. (Page 128).
Jacob Siler, Agent for collection of Cherokee Bonds $500.00

COMPTROLLER'S STATEMENT. PUBLIC FUNDS.
1858-59. (Page 137).
Cherokee Bonds $90.00

COMPTROLLER'S STATEMENT. PUBLIC FUNDS.
1858-59. (Page 156).

North Carolina Law

Jacob Siler, Agent for collection of Cherokee Bonds $90.00

****

PRIVATE LAWS OF THE STATE OF NORTH CAROLINA PASSED BY THE GENERAL ASSEMBLY AT ITS SESSION OF 1858-59
RALEIGH: HOLDEN AND WILSON, PRINTERS TO THE STATE, 1859

CHAP. 173.
1858-59. An Act to prevent making obstructions in Swift Creek, in the County of Edgecombe. (Pages 226-227).

Section 1. Be it enacted by the General Assembly of the State of North Carolina, and it is hereby enacted by the authority of the same, That any person making obstructions in the run of Swift creek, whether the same be the natural channel or made by the adjacent land owners above Williams' mill, in the county of Edgecombe, by throwing earth or marl therein, or by any other manner whatsoever, shall forfeit and pay the sum of one hundred dollars, and if by felling timber therein or by any other manner whatsoever, shall forfeit and pay the sum of fifty dollars, for the common school fund of said county, to be recovered before any justice of the peace, in the name of the chairman of the board of superintendents of common schools.

Sec. 2. Be it further enacted, That any slave who violates this act, without direction of his owner or hirer, shall receive not less than fifteen nor more than thirty nine lashes; and the owner or hirer of said slave shall remove the obstruction in ten days after notice, and failing to do so, any person owning land on the creek aforesaid may cause the same to be done and recover the cost thereof from the owner or hirer of said slave, and a conviction of said slave shall be sufficient evidence to charge the owner or hirer with the duty of removing the obstructions.

Sec. 3. Be it further enacted, That any person violating this act shall be guilty of a misdemeanor; and the act shall be in force from and after its ratification.
[Ratified the 16th day of February, 1859.]

CHAP. 174.

North Carolina Law

1858-59. An Act to prevent the felling of timber in the waters of Tuckaho and Trent Rivers. (Pages 227-228).
Section 1. Be it enacted by the General Assembly of the State of North Carolina, and it is hereby enacted by the authority of the same, That it shall not be lawful for any person or persons to cut or fell timbers in the above named waters, to wit: Tuckaho and Trent rivers; any where between Tuckaho bridge, in the county of Jones, and where it empties in the Trent, nor in the Trent any where between upper Quaker bridge and the town of Pollocksville; and all persons offending against this act shall be guilty of a misdemeanor, and upon the conviction of the same in any court of record, shall be fined not less than ten nor more than fifty dollars, if a white person, and if a slave or free person of color, shall receive thirty nine lashes at the public whipping post upon his or her bare back.
Sec. 2. Be it further enacted, That all white persons or free negroes offending against the provisions of this act, in addition to the punishment described in the first section of the same, shall be subject to the penalty of twenty five dollars, to be recovered by any person suing for the same, and the other half to the use of the county.
Sec. 3. Be it further enacted, That all laws and clauses of laws coming within the meaning and purview of this act, be and the same are hereby repealed.
[Ratified the 21st day of January, 1859.]

CHAP. 197. TOWNS.
1858-59. An Act to extend the corporate limits of the Town of Newbern, in the County of Craven, and for the better regulation of the same. (Page 261).
Sec. 25. Be it further enacted, That the commissioners of said town shall be vested with full power to make such ordinances as to them shall seem necessary to restrain, prohibit and prevent any slave or free person of color from loitering in or about any shop or store in said town, or from sitting down or remaining longer in such store or shop than while actually engaged in purchasing such articles as they may be lawfully authorized to procure, or from entering into any inner room connected with such store or shop, and said commissioners by fines and penalties to be imposed on the owners or keepers of such shops or stores, and by fines and corporal punishment to be imposed or inflicted on slaves or free persons of

color, may secure and enforce obedience to such ordinances as shall be made under the provisions of this section.

CHAP. 216. TOWNS.
1858-59. An Act to Amend an Act incorporating the Town of Kenansville, and to provide for the better government of said town. (Pages 291-292).
Sec. 15. Be it further enacted, That the mayor and commissioners shall at the first regular meeting after they are duly organized, or failing at their first meeting, at their next regular meeting appoint of the inhabitants of the town a patrol, not exceeding four in number, whose duty it shall be to patrol the limits of the town twice each week, and oftener if the commissioners shall deem it necessary and so direct, and they are hereby authorized to extend their patrol beyond the corporate limits of said town whenever they shall find it necessary to do so in the discharge of their duties. It shall be their duties to disperse all assembles of slaves and free negroes, and to arrest all such offenders against the criminal laws of the State, or laws and ordinances of the corporation, as they may think necessary, and bring them before the mayor, who shall either bind the offenders to court or inflict such punishment as he shall think proper, not exceeding thirty nine lashes, the owner or manager having been duly notified thereof, and the owner or manager may in all such cases appeal from the decision of the mayor in the same manner and under the same rules and regulations as he may now appeal by law. The patrol, when appointed, shall be compelled to serve under such penalties as the mayor and commissioners shall impose, which shall be collected and applied as all other penalties herein set forth, and for their services they shall receive such compensation as the commissioners shall allow.
[Ratified the 31st day of January, 1859.]

CHAP. 272.
1858-59. A Bill for the relief of Emily Hooper of Liberia. (Page 370).
Be it enacted by the General Assembly of the State of North Carolina, and it is hereby enacted by the authority of the same, That Emily Hooper, a negro and a citizen of the Republic of Liberia, be and she is hereby permitted voluntarily to return into a state of slavery as the slave of

North Carolina Law

her former owner, Miss Sallie Mallett, of Chapel Hill; and that this act be in force from and after the ratification thereof.
[Ratified the 2nd day of February, 1859.]

RESOLUTIONS.
1858-59. Resolution in favor of Jacob B. Evans, of Cherokee County. (Page 393).
    Resolved, That the agent for the collection of Cherokee bonds be and he is hereby authorized to pay to Jacob B. Evans, of Cherokee county, twenty dollars in Cherokee bonds, not otherwise appropriated, it being an amount paid to said agent by error for a tract of land in Cherokee county.
    Be it further resolved, That the agent of the State for the collection of Cherokee bonds be and is hereby authorized to pay to Edmund McNabb, of Cherokee county, the sum of sixty dollars in Cherokee bonds, no otherwise appropriated, it being the amount overpaid by him for an entry of land in said county.
[Ratified the 16th day of February, 1859.]

RESOLUTIONS.
1858-59. Resolution in favor of R.L. Jones and others. (Pages 400-401).
    Resolved, That the agent for the collection of Cherokee bonds be and he is hereby authorized to pay R.L. Jones and others, contractors for making the Western turnpike road, the sums due them in Cherokee bonds under the authority of the former agent of that road, on satisfactory evidence that the work has been done agreeably to contract.
[Ratified the 16th day of February, 1859.]

****

PUBLIC LAWS OF THE STATE OF NORTH CAROLINA
PASSED BY THE GENERAL ASSEMBLY
AT IT'S SESSION OF 1860-61
RALEIGH: JOHN SPELMAN, PRINTER TO THE STATE, 1861.

CHAPTER 13.
1860-61. An Act Concerning Courts of Oyer and Terminer. (Pages 24-25).

Sec. 1. Be it enacted by the General Assembly of the State of North Carolina, and it is hereby enacted by the authority of the same, That in all cases where any slave or slaves is or are under arrest or in prison, and not indicted, as well as when he, she or they is or are indicted, for any of the crimes mentioned in the 41st section of the 107th chapter of the Revised Code, courts of oyer and terminer shall have jurisdiction to try such slave or slaves, and the presiding judge may issue an order for a special venire of jurors, out of which a grand jury shall be empannelled, when and if necessary; and the remainder, or those not required as a grand jury, summoned under the special order, shall serve as pettit jurors, unless excused therefrom; to find bills of indictments against all such slaves so under arrest or imprisoned for such crimes, whether then standing indicted or not heretofore indicted; and the presiding judge shall and may proceed to try, continue, or remove such indictments, whether formerly found, or found during the term of such courts; such continuance or removal to be regulated by the same rules as govern continuances and removals had at the general terms of the superior courts of law.

Sec. 2. Be it further enacted, and it is hereby enacted by the authority aforesaid, That for each week in which a judge shall hold such courts, he shall receive the sum of $90, (ninety dollars,) to be paid by the State treasurer, on a proper certificate of the clerk thereto.

Sec. 3. Be it further enacted, and it is hereby enacted by the authority aforesaid, That this act shall not be affected by the 85th section of the Revised Code, chapter 52, but shall take effect as if such section had never existed, or was now repealed.

Sec. 4. Be it further enacted, That this act shall be in force from and after its passage.

[Ratified the 17th day of January, 1861.]

CHAPTER 19.
1860-61. An Act Concerning Common Schools in North Carolina. (Page 32).

Sec. 8. Be it further enacted, That when questions shall arise as to whether children are descended from negro ancestors within the degrees that deprive them of the benefit of the common school fund, the board of county superintendents may and shall make decisions which shall be binding until the questions are decided by the courts having jurisdiction in such cases, either party having the right to appeal to said courts.

North Carolina Law

CHAPTER 23.
1860-61. An Act to Amend the 16th and 17th Sections of the 34th Chapter Revised Code. (Pages 39-40).

Section 1. Be it enacted by the General Assembly of the State of North Carolina, and it is hereby enacted by the authority of the same. That if any person shall willfully bring into the State, with the intent to circulate, or shall willfully circulate or publish within the State, or shall aid or abet the bringing into, or circulation, or publication of, within the State, any written or printed pamphlet or paper, whether written or printed in or out of the State, the evident tendency whereof is to cause slaves to become discontented with the bondage in which they are held by their masters, and the laws regulating the same, and free negroes to be dissatisfied with their social condition, such person so offending shall be deemed guilty of felony, and on conviction thereof shall suffer death.

Sec. 2. Be it further enacted, That if any person, by words, shall endeavour to excite in any slave or free negro or person of color, a spirit of insurrection, conspiracy or rebellion, such person so offending shall be deemed guilty of felony, and on conviction thereof shall suffer death.

Sec. 3. Be it further enacted, That if any person shall use inflammatory language, the tendency of which would be to excite in any slave or free negro a spirit of insurrection, conspiracy or rebellion, he shall be guilty of a misdemeanor, and on conviction thereof shall be fined or imprisoned, at the discretion of the court.
[Ratified the 23d day of February, 1861.]

CHAPTER 34.
1860-61. An Act to Amend Chapter 107, Section 66, of the Revised Code, Relating to Free Negroes Having Arms. (Page 68).

Sec. 1. Be it enacted by the General Assembly of the State of North Carolina, and it is hereby enacted by the authority of the same, That chapter 107, section 66, of the Revised Code, be amended to read as follows: If any free negro shall wear or carry about his person or keep in his house any shot gun, musket, rifle, pistol, sword, sword cane, dagger, bowie knife, powder or shot, he shall be guilty of a misdemeanor, and upon conviction fined not less than fifty dollars.

Sec. 2. Be it further enacted, That all laws empowering the several county courts of the State to grant licenses to free negroes to carry fire arms, be and the same are hereby repealed.
[Ratified the 23d day of February, 1861.]

CHAPTER 35.
1860-61. An Act to Change the Rules of Evidence in Indictments for Trading With Slaves. (Page 68).

Be it enacted by the General Assembly of North Carolina, and it is hereby enacted by the authority of the same, That in all indictments for trading and trafficking with slaves, or for giving or selling liquor to slaves, wherein it is necessary negatively to aver the consent of the owner or manager of the slave to the trading, selling or giving, that the burden of proof shall rest upon the defendant to show that he had a written license or permit, as required by law, to trade, or give, or sell to the slave.
[Ratified the 23d day of February, 1861.]

CHAPTER 36.
1860-61. An Act to Prevent Free Negroes from Hiring or Having the Control of Slaves. (Page 69).

Sec. 1. Be it enacted by the General Assembly of the State of North Carolina, and it is hereby enacted by the authority of the same, That no free negro, or free person of color shall be permitted or allowed to buy, purchase or hire for any length of time, any slave or slaves, or to have any slave or slaves bound as apprentice or apprentices to him, her or them, or in any other wise to have the control, management or services of any slave or slaves, under a penalty of one hundred dollars for each offense, and shall further be guilty of a misdemeanor, and liable to indictment for the same.

Sec. 2. Be it further enacted, That this law does not apply, and shall not affect any free negro or free person of color who is the legal owner of any slave at the time of the passage of this act.

Sec. 3. Be it further enacted, That this law shall take effect from and after its ratification.
[Ratified the 23d day of February, 1861.]

CHAPTER 37.

North Carolina Law

1860-61. An Act to Prohibit the Emancipation of Slaves by Will. (Page 69).
Be it enacted by the General Assembly of the State of North Carolina, and it is hereby enacted by the authority of the same, That no Slave in this State shall hereafter be emancipated by last will and testament, or deed, or other instrument or conveyance to take effect as to said emancipation after the death of the testator or person executing or making such deed, or other instrument or conveyance, but that all such wills, deeds or other instruments or conveyance in so far as they purport to effect such emancipation, shall be null and void; and no slave so attempted to be emancipated, shall pass under any general residuary clause in any last will and testament, but the testator shall be deemed and taken to have died intestate as to such slave.
[Ratified the 31st day of January, 1861.]

****

PUBLIC LAWS OF THE STATE OF NORTH CAROLINA
PASSED BY THE GENERAL ASSEMBLY
AT ITS FIRST EXTRA SESSION OF 1861
RALEIGH: JOHN SPELMAN, PRINTER TO THE STATE, 1861

CHAPTER 77.
1861. An Act to Authorize the Holding of a Court of Oyer and Terminer in Caswell County. (Pages 49-50).
Section 1. Be it enacted by the General Assembly of the State of North Carolina, and it is hereby enacted by the authority of the same, That the governor of this State shall issue a commission of oyer and terminer to one of the judges of the superior court of law, to try all slaves that may be now confined in the jail of Caswell county, charged with rape or any other felony, which said court shall be held forthwith; and the judges shall be clothed with all the powers necessary for the trial.
Sec. 2. Be it further enacted, That the said court shall be at Yanceyville under the same rules, regulations, powers and restrictions as govern the courts of oyer and terminer appointed to try slaves for insurrection, rebellion, or conspiracy.
Sec. 3. Be it further enacted, That the clerk of the county court, and sheriff, assisted by two justices of the peace, shall draw a jury of thirty six persons, who shall be summoned by the sheriff, from which shall be

made the grand jury and petit jury; and the court shall have power to order a special venire, as in other cases of felony.

Sec. 4. Be it further enacted, That this act shall be in force from and after its ratification.

[Ratified the _____ day of January, 1861.]

****

PUBLIC LAWS OF THE STATE OF NORTH CAROLINA
PASSED AT THE GENERAL ASSEMBLY
AT ITS SECOND EXTRA SESSION, 1861.
RALEIGH: JOHN SPELMAN, PRINTER TO THE STATE, 1861.

CHAPTER 15.
1861. An Act to Alter the Rules of Evidence as Applicable to Indians. (Page 16).

Sec. 1. Be it enacted by the General Assembly of the State of North Carolina, and it is hereby enacted by the authority of the same, That the seventy first, seventy second and seventy third sections of the one hundred and seventh chapter of the revised code be and the same are hereby amended by striking out the words Indian or Indians therein.

Sec. 2. Be it further enacted, That in all cases whatever, Indians shall be competent witnesses.

Sec. 3. Be it further enacted, That this act shall be in force from and after its ratification.

[Ratified the 13th day of September, 1861].

CHAPTER 17.
1861. Militia Bill. (Page 24).

Sec. 9. It shall not be lawful for any captain or other militia officer in this State to enroll any free persons of color, except for musicians, and, in time of actual service, four to each company as cooks, who shall be rationed and paid by the State, and four others as washers, to be rationed by the State, and paid by men of the company for whom they wash.

Sec. 90. That it shall be the duty of any one of the field officers of a regiment, or the oldest captain, should there be no field officer, upon complaint on oath made by any responsible person, that there are unlawful

North Carolina Law

assemblies within his command, or danger of insubordination amongst slaves, to detail a military patrol, designating their duties, and requiring the officer commanding the said patrol to report to him how he has discharged his duty; and the said patrol shall deliver all persons detected in the violation of the law to the civil magistrates for the examination of the charges made against them.

CHAPTER 31.
1861. An Act Entitled Revenue. (Pages 62-76).

Sec. 22. The clerk, on or before the 1st day [of] August in each year, shall return to the comptroller an abstract of the same, showing the number of acres of land, and their value, and the value of town lots, and the number of white and free black poles, and the number and value of slaves, separately, and specify every other subject of taxation, and the amount of State tax due on each subject, and the amount of the whole. At the same time the clerk shall return to the comptroller an abstract of the poor, county and school taxes, paid in his county, setting forth, separately, the tax levied on each poll, and on each other subject of taxation, and also the gross amount of taxes imposed for county purposes.

Sec 54. The following subjects shall be annually listed and taxed one fifth of one per cent, on the value thereof, where a higher or different rate is not specified:

(5) Every person resident in this State, engaged in the business of buying and selling slaves, whether the purchasers be made in or out of the State, for cash or on a credit, one half of one per cent, on the total amount of all his purchases during the twelve months preceding the 1st day of April.

(6) Every person resident in this State, not a regular trader in slaves, who may buy a slave or slaves to sell again, whether such purchase be made in or out of the State, for cash or on credit, one half of one per cent, on the total amount of his purchases during the twelve months ending the 31st of March of each year.

Sec. 60. Every poll that is or will be of the required age on the first day of July of any year, shall be listed that year. Every owner, if in the State, shall list his slaves in the county in which he resides; and if the owner be a non resident of the State, the hirer or person who has the slaves in his possession, shall list the same and pay taxes. Slaves hired out beyond the limits of the State shall be listed by the owners as well as those employed within the State.

Sec. 61. Such slaves and other taxable personal estate as are employed on the land of the owner, shall be listed in the county in which the land is listed.

Sec. 62. Every head of family, or owner of land or town lot, who on the first day of April shall have a free person of color subject to taxation as a member of his family, or in his employment, or living on his land, or in his house, shall list such person for taxation, and pay the tax.

Sec. 63. Personal property, and other subjects of taxation, unless otherwise directed in section 61, shall be listed in the district where the owner or lister resides; but if the owner reside out of the State, they shall be listed in the district where his agent, or the person liable for the tax may reside.

Sec. 70. The sheriff shall annually collect the taxes as set forth in this schedule, and grant to each party paying the tax, a license to carry on his business until the first day of July next ensueing, except in cases where the tax is on non resident traders in slaves, or horses and mule drovers, in which cases no license shall be required:

(14) Every non resident of the State, who, in person or by agent, shall purchase any slave or slaves in this State, shall immediately after such purchase, become liable to pay of one half of one per cent, on the amount of his purchase, and upon his neglect or failure to pay such tax, he shall forfeit and pay the sum of one hundred dollars, which shall be collected by the sheriff, one half to his own use and the other half to the use of the State. When the purchase was made by an agent, such agent shall be equally liable for the tax and forfeiture with his principal.

(15) Every non resident of the State, who, either in person or by agent, brings a slave or slaves into the State, and sells, shall pay one half of one per cent, on the amount of each sale effected. If he fail to pay this tax, the purchaser shall be liable for the same, and the sheriff of the county in which the sale was made, or in which the purchaser reside, shall collect by distress or otherwise out of the seller, if to found in his county, and if the seller is not to be found, out of the buyer.

****

PRIVATE LAWS OF THE STATE OF NORTH CAROLINA PASSED BY THE GENERAL ASSEMBLY

North Carolina Law

AT ITS SECOND EXTRA SESSION, 1861
RALEIGH: JOHN SPELMAN, PRINTER TO THE STATE, 1861.

CHAPTER 73.
1861. An Act Concerning Runaway Slaves. (Page 118).
  Sec. 1. Be it enacted by the General Assembly of the State of North Carolina, and it is hereby enacted by the authority of the same, That the 8th section of the 107 chapter of the revised code shall be altered so as to read as follows: in 8th section, line 4th, strike out the word five and insert the word fifteen, so as to read fifteen dollars; in line 6th strike out the word ten and insert the word twenty five, so as to read twenty five dollars.
  Sec. 2. Be it further enacted, That this act shall apply only to the counties of Bertie, Hertford and Tyrell.
  Sec. 3. Be it further enacted, That this act shall be in force from and after its ratification.
[Ratified the 21st day of September, 1861.]

Chronology of Laws

CHRONOLOGY OF LAWS
1669 to 1790
FROM THE PUBLISHED VOLUMES OF
THE STATE RECORDS OF NORTH CAROLINA
VOLUMES XXIII., AND XXV.

1669 An Act Prohibiting Strangers Tradeing With Indians.

1669 The Fundamental Constitution of Carolina.

1698 Copy of the Fundamental Constitutions of Carolina Agreed on by all Ye Lord Proprietors and Sign'd and Seal'd by them (the Original being Sent to Carolina by Major Daniel) April 11th 1698.

1715 An Act prohibiting Trading with the Indians.

1715 An Act Concerning Servants & Slaves.

1715 An Act for Restraining the Indyans from molesting or Injureing the Inhabitants of this Government and for Secureing to the Indyans the right and property of their own lands.

1720 An Act for the Lessening the Pole and Lands Tax and Preventing of Concealments.

1720 An Act in Explanation of an Act Concerning Servants and Slaves.

Chronology of Laws

1723 An Act for an additional Tax on all free Negroes, Mulattoes, Mustees, and such Persons, Male and Female, as now are, or hereafter shall be, intermarried with any such Persons, resident in this Government.

1729 An Act for the More quiet settling the bounds of the Meherrin Indian Lands.

1729 An additional Act to an Act, for appointing Toll Books, and for preventing People from driving Horses, Cattle, or Hogs, to other Persons' Lands.

1741 An Act Concerning Marriages.

1741 An Act to prevent the taking away Boats, Canoes, or Pettiaguas, from Landings, or elsewhere, without Leave.

1741 An Act Concerning Servants and Slaves.

1746 An Act to fix a Place for the Seat of Government, and for the keeping Public Offices; for appointing Circuit Courts and defraying the Expence thereof; and also for establishing the Courts of Justice and regulating the Proceedings therein.

1748 An Act for ascertaining the Bounds of a certain Tract of Land formerly laid out by Treaty to the use of the Tuskerora Indians, so long as they, or any of them, shall occupy and live upon the same;and to prevent any Person or Persons taking up Lands, or settling within the said Bounds, by Pretence of any Purchase or Purchases made, or that shall be made, from the said Indians.

1749 An Act to confirm the several Acts of Assembly of this Province therein mentioned.

1749 An Act for restraining the Indians from molesting or injuring the Inhabitants of this Government: and for securing to the Indians the Right and Property of their own Lands.

Chronology of Laws

1749 An Act for an additional Tax on all free Negroes, Mulattoes, Mustees, and such persons, male and female, as now, or hereafter shall be intermarried with any such Persons resident in this Government.

1749 An Act for ascertaining the Bounds of a certain Tract of Land, formerly laid out by a Treaty, to the Use of the Tuskerora Indians, so long as they, or any of them, shall occupy and live upon the same; and to prevent any Person or Persons taking up Lands or settling within the said Bounds, by Pretence of any Purchase or Purchases made, or that shall be made, from the said Indians.

1749 An additional Act to an Act for obtaining an exact List of Taxables; and for the effectual Collecting as well as all Arrears of Taxes, as all other Taxes, for the future due and payable.

1753 An additional Act to an Act concerning servants and slaves.

1754 An Act, for Establishing the Supreme Courts of Justice, Oyer and Terminer, and General Gaol Delivery of North Carolina.

1754 An Act for securing the payment of Quit Rents due to His Majesty, and Earl Granville, for quieting the Freeholders in the Possession of their lands, and for other Purposes.

1756 An Act for the Regulation of the Town of Wilmington.

1757 An Act for Preserving Peace and continuing a good Correspondence with the Indians in Alliance with his Majesty's Subjects.

1758 An additional Act, intituled, An Act concerning Servants and Slaves.

1759 An Act to Amend and Continue an Act, Intituled, an Act for the better Regulation of the Militia, and for other Purposes.

1759 An Act for Granting an Aid to his Majesty for paying and Subsisting the Forces and Militia now in the pay of this Province, and for other Purposes.

Chronology of Laws

1760 An Act for the better Care of Orphans, and Security and Management of their Estates.

1760 An Act, for establishing Superior Courts of Pleas and Grand Sessions, and Regulating the Proceedings therein.

1760 An Act for granting an aid to his Majesty.

1760 An Act for obtaining an exact List of Taxables, and for the effectual collecting all Taxes for the Future due and payable, and other Purposes therein mentioned.

1764 An Act for appointing a Militia.

1764 An Act concerning Vestries.

1764 An Act to ammend An Act therein mentioned, concerning Servants and Slaves.

1766 An Act to amend an Act intitled, an Act for rendering more effectual the laws making Landsand other real Estates liable to the payment of debts.

1766 An Act for confirming a lease made by the Tuscarora Indians to Robert Jones, jun., William Williams and Thomas Pugh, Esquires.

1771 An Act to amend an Act, entitled, An Act for the Regulation of the Town of Wilmington.

1774 An Act to prevent the wilful and malicious killing of Slaves.

1777 An Act to prevent domestic Insurrections, and for other Purposes.

1777 An Act for the Encouragement of the Militia and Volunteers employed in prosecuting the present Indian War.

1777 An Act to amend an Act, Intituled, An Act to establish a Militia in this State.

Chronology of Laws

1777 An Act to encourage the destroying Vermin in the Several Counties of this State.

1777 An Act to Prevent burning the Woods.

1777 An Act to prevent hunting with a gun, by Fire Light in the Night.

1777 An Act for Establishing Courts of Law, and for Regulating the Proceedings therein.

1778 An Act for quieting and securing the Tuscarora Indians, and other claiming under the Tuscaroras, in the Possession of their Lands.

1778 An Act to prevent trading with the Cherokee Indians without license first had and obtained; and also to prevent Trespasses upon the Indian Hunting Grounds.

1778 An Act for Ascertaining what Property in this State shall be deemed Taxable Property, the Method of Assessing the same, and Collecting the Public Taxes and other purposes.

1778 An Act to Prevent the Stealing of Slaves or by Violation, Seduction or any other Means, taking or conveying away any slave or slaves, the property of another; and for other purposes therein mentioned.

1778 An Act for Apprehending and selling certain Slaves set free contrary to Law and for Confirming the Sales of Others, and for other purposes.

1779 An Act for amending an Act for making provision for the poor, and for other purposes.

1779 An Act to prevent hunting in the night time with gun and fire light, and other purposes therein mentioned.

1779 An Act to amend an Act, entitled, An Additional Act concerning Servants and Slaves, passed at New Bern in the year One Thousand Seven Hundred and fifty three, and other purposes therein mentioned.

Chronology of Laws

1779 An Act to amend an Act, intituled, An Act concerning servants and slaves.

1780 An Act to amend an Act, intituled "An Act for quieting and securing the Tuscarora Indians, and others claiming under the Tuscaroras, in the possession of their lands."

1780 An Act to amend an Act, intituled, "An Act to regulate and establish a Militia in this State."

1780 An Act for securing the quiet and inoffensive inhabitants of this State from being injured, for preventing such property as hath or may be confiscated from being wasted or destroyed, and for other purposes.

1781 An additional Act to an Act, intitled, An Act concerning Servants and Slaves.

1781 An Act for raising Troops out of the Militia of this State for the defence thereof, and for other purposes.

1781 An Act for securing all articles left by the British troops in this State, taken from the citizens as well as others, and for other purposes.

1782 An Act for Raising troops to compleat the Continental Battalions of this State, and other purposes.

1783 An Act to amend an Act passed in the year of our Lord, one thousand seven hundred and forty one, intituled, An Act concerning Servants and Slaves.

1783 An Act for appointing an agent and holding a treaty with the Cherokee Indians, and for other purposes.

1784 An Act for Enfranchising Ned Griffin, Late the Property of William Kitchen.

1784 An Act to ascertain the number of White and Black Inhabitants, and the Citizens of every Age and Condition in the State.

Chronology of Laws

1784 An Act for Clearing and Opening the Navigation of Tar River and Fishing Creek, in the Counties of Pitt, Edgecombe and Halifax.

1785 An Additional Act to Amend the Several Acts for Regulating the town of Wilmington, and to Regulate and Restrain the Conduct of Slaves and Others in the said Town, and in the Towns of Washington, Edenton, and Fayetteville.

1786 An Act to Impose a Duty on all Slaves Brought Into This State by Land or Water.

1786 An Act to Amend an Act, Entitled, "An Act to Amend an Act, Entitled, 'An Act for Ascertaining What Property in This State Shall Be Deemed Taxable Property, The Method of Assessing the Same, and Collecting Public Taxes.' "

1786 An Act to Repeal the Several Acts of Assembly Respecting Slaves Within This State, as far as the Same Relates to Making an Allowance to the Owner or Owners for any Executed or Outlawed Slave or Slaves.

1786 An Act to emancipate Caesar, formerly a Servant of Samuel Yeargen, Deceased.

1786 An Act to Emancipate Hannah Bowers, a Person of Mixed Blood, Belonging to the Estate of the Late Alexander Gaston Deceased.

1787 An Act to Prevent Thefts and Robberies by Slaves, Free Negroes and Mulattoes.

1787 An Act for the Better Regulation of the Town of Edenton.

1787 An Act for the Better Regulation of the Town of Fayetteville.

1787 An Act to Emancipate Certain Persons therein mentioned.

1788 An Act to confirm the Rights and Titles of several Citizens of this State in certain Negroes therein described, and preventing Unjust and Vexatious Law Suits.

Chronology of Laws

1788 An Act to amend the several Acts of Assembly to prevent dealing or Trafficking with Slaves.

1788 An Act to Emancipate a certain Negro Slave named Phillis, late the Property of George Jacobs, of the Town of Wilmington, Deceased.

1788 An Act to Amend an Act Entitled "An Act to Prevent Domestic Insurrections."

1789 An Act to Emancipate Certain Negroes Therein Mentioned.

1789 An Act for the Relief of Such Persons Who May Bee Wounded by the Indians Within the District of Mero, and for Other Purposes.

1789 An Act to Repeal Part of an Act Entitled, "An Act for Appointing an Agent, and Holding a Treaty With the Cherokee Indians, and for Other Purposes."

1789 An Act to Prescribe the Mode of Paying the Militia Officers and Soldiers for Their Services on an Expedition Carried on Against the Chicamoga Indians by Brigadier General Joseph Martin, in the Year One Thousand Seven Hundred and Eighty-Eight.

1790 An Act for Vesting the Property of Certain Negroes in the heirs of Mark Newby.

****

CHRONOLOGY OF LAWS
1791 - 1795
LAWS OF THE STATE OF NORTH CAROLINA
REVISED, UNDER THE AUTHORITY OF THE GENERAL ASSEMBLY
VOLUME I
HENRY POTTER
RALEIGH: PRINTED AND SOLD BY J. GALES, 1821

1791 An Act to amend an act, entitled, "An act to prevent thefts and robberies by slaves, free negroes and mulattoes," passed at Tarborough, in the year one thousand seven hundred and eighty seven; and to amend an act, passed in the year one thousand seven hundred and seventy four, entitled, "An act to prevent the wilful and malicious killing of slaves."

1791 An act for giving a further time for probate and registration of bills of sale for slaves and marriage settlements.

1792 An act to amend an act, entitled, "An act to prevent the stealing of slaves, or by violence, seduction or any other means taking or carrying away any slave or slaves the property of another, and for other purposes therein mentioned."

1792 An act to amend the seventh section of an act, entitled, "An act to explain, amend and supply the deficiencies of an act, passed last Assembly at Hillsborough, entitled, An act to regulate the descent of real estates, to do away with entails, to make provision for widows, to prevent frauds in the execution of last wills and testaments, and for directing how deeds of gifts and bills of sale of slaves shall be executed, authenticated and perpetuated," passed at Newbern, in October, in the year one thousand seven hundred and eighty four.

1793 An act to extend the right of trial by jury to slaves.

1794 An act to prevent the owners of slaves from hiring to them their time, to make compensation to patrols, and to restrain the abuses committed by free negroes and mulattoes.

1795 An act to prevent any person who may emigrate from any of the West India of Bahama Islands, or the French, Dutch, or Spanish settlements on the southern coast of America, from bringing slaves into this state, and also for imposing certain restrictions on free persons of colour who may hereafter come into this state.

****

CHRONOLOGY OF LAWS
1796 - 1816
LAWS OF THE STATE OF NORTH CAROLINA

Chronology of Laws

REVISED UNDER THE AUTHORITY OF THE GENERAL ASSEMBLY
VOLUME II.
HENRY POTTER
RALEIGH: PRINTED AND SOLD BY J. GALES, 1821

1796 An act to amend, strengthen and confirm the several acts of Assembly of this State against the emancipation of slaves.

1796 An act to prevent people from impeding the free passage of fish up the rivers and creeks in this state.

1796 An act making compensation to the owners of outlawed and executed slaves, for the counties of Bladen, Halifax, Granville, Cumberland, Perquimans, Beaufort and Pitt.

1797 An act to amend an act passed in the year one thousand seven hundred and ninety six, entitled, "An act making compensation to the owners of outlawed and executed slaves for the counties of Bladen, Halifax, Granville, Cumberland, Perquimans, Beaufort and Pitt."

1798 An act to amend the fifth section of an act, chapter sixteenth, passed at Raleigh, on the second of November, one thousand seven hundred and ninety five, providing among other things for the suppression of insurrections.

1798 An act to compel the owners of slaves to provide proper maintenance for such of their slaves as may be rendered incapable of service by reason of advancement in years or otherwise.

1799 An act to amend an act, for giving further time for probate and registration of bills of sale for slaves and marriage settlements.

1800 An act to amend an act, entitled, "An act to prevent the stealing of slaves, or by violence, seduction, or any other means, taking or conveying away any slave or slaves, the property of another, and for purposes therein mentioned," passed at Halifax in the year 1779.

Chronology of Laws

1801 An act to amend the nineteenth section of an act, entitled, "An act for the better care of orphans, and security and management of their estates."

1801 An act to compel persons who are permitted to have their slaves liberated, to give bond and security for keeping such slaves from becoming a public or county charge, and other purposes.

1801 An act to amend an act, entitled, "An act to amend an act, entitled, An act to prevent thefts and robberies by slaves, free negroes or mulattoes, and to amend an act, entitled An act to prevent the wilful and malicious killing of slaves."

1802 An act for the relief of the Tuscarora Nation of Indians.

1802 An act to prevent conspiracies among the slaves.

1805 An act to prevent the masters and owners of vessels and boats, and other persons from trading with slaves.

1806 An act declaring what gifts of slaves shall be valid.

1807 An act to amend the penal laws, so far as respects the trial of slaves charged with capital offences.

1809 An act to prevent speculations in obtaining lands which may hereafter accrue to this state, by purchase from the Indians.

1810 An act extending the law respecting insolvent debtors to free persons of colour.

1816 An act to direct the disposal of negroes, mulattoes and persons of colour, imported into this state, contrary to the provisions of an act of the Congress of the United States, entitled, "an act to prohibit the importation of slaves into any port or place, within the jurisdiction of the United States, from and after the first day of January, in the year of our Lord one thousand eight hundred and eight."

1816 An act to amend the laws **(See 1741, c. 35, 1793, c. 381, 1807, c. 719.)** in force respecting the trial of slaves in capital cases.

Chronology of Laws

CHRONOLOGY OF LAWS
1817 - 1835
FROM THE PUBLISHED VOLUMES OF:
THE LAWS OF THE STATE OF NORTH CAROLINA

1817 On Negro Traders of 5$ for each slave

1817 An act to regulate slaves navigating decked boats in Craven county.

1819 Negro traders.

1819 An act to create a fund for Internal Improvements, and to establish a Board for the management thereof.

1819 An act to prevent fraudulent trading with slaves.

1819 An Act to amend an act passed in the year one thousand eight hundred and two, entitled, "An act to prevent conspiracies and insurrections among slaves.

1819 An Act relative to the apprehension of runaway slaves.

1819 An Act to make void parol contracts for the sale of Lands and Slaves.

1819 An Act to prevent obstructions to the passage of fish up Neuse River, Contentnea Creek and Little River.

1819 An act to repeal certain parts of three acts concerning patrollers, one passed in the year 1794, one other in the year 1802 and the other in the year 1816, so far as relates to the county of Edgecombe.

1820 On negro traders.

1820 An Act to quiet the title of persons in possession of Slaves.

Chronology of Laws

1820 An Act directing the manner in which property levied on by Sheriffs and Constables shall be sold hereafter.

1820 An Act to provide for the payment of costs when a Slave is convicted of a Capital Crime.

1820 An act to prevent the fishing with nett, or netts, at the mouth of Great Contentea Creek.

1821 Slaves bro't into this state, for sale, taxed 10 dollars.

1821 An act directing the time and place of sale of lands and slaves under execution.

1821 An act providing further punishment for harboring or maintaining runaways.

1821 An act to amend and explain the forty second section of an act, passed in the year one thousand seven hundred and seventy seven, entitled "an act for establishing Courts of Law, and for regulating the proceedings therein."

1822 Slaves bro't into this state for sale taxed 10 dollars.

1822 An act to amend an act, passed in 1821, entitled "an act to promote the administration of justice."

1822 An Act to repeal the fifth section of an act, passed in the year 1821, entitled "an act directing the time and place of sale of lands and slaves under execution."

1822 An act directing the time and place of selling lands and slaves under execution.

1822 An act to encourage the apprehension of runaway slaves in the Great Dismal Swamp.

1823 An Act authorising certain limitations of Slaves by deed or writing.

Chronology of Laws

1823 An Act to amend an Act, passed in the year one thousand eight hundred and nineteen, entitled "An Act relative to the apprehension of runaway slaves."

1823 An Act to repeal the forty fourth section of an Act passed in the year one thousand seven hundred and forty one, entitled "An Act concerning Servants And Slaves."

1823 An Act declaring the punishment of persons of colour, in certain cases.

1823 An Act to repeal an Act, passed in the year 1822, entitled "An Act to encourage the apprehension of runaway slaves in the Great Dismal Swamp."

1823 An Act to repeal an act passed in the year one thousand eight hundred and twenty two, entitled "An Act directing the time and place of selling lands and slaves under execution," so far as relates to certain counties therein named.

1823 An Act to repeal an act passed in the year one thousand eight hundred and twenty two, entitled "An Act directing the time and place of selling lands and slaves under execution," so far as respects the counties of Washington and New Hanover.

1823 An Act to amend an act, entitled " An Act directing the time and place of sales of land and slaves under execution.

1823 An Act to repeal an act, passed at the last General Assembly, entitled "An act to regulate the patrol of Richmond county," and for other purposes.

1824 An Act concerning the Lands held under leases from the Tuscarora Tribe of Indians.

1824 An Act to repeal in part, the first section of an Act passed in the year 1823, entitled "An Act to regulate the patrol of Richmond County, and for other purposes.

Chronology of Laws

1824 An Act to regulate the patrol of the counties of Ashe and New Hanover.

1825 An act to amend an act, entitled "an act to prevent the stealing of Slaves, or by violence, seduction, or any other means, taking or carrying away any Slave or Slaves, the property of another, and for other purposes therein mentioned," passed in the year one thousand seven hundred and ninety two.

1825 An Act to amend an act, passed in the year one thousand eight hundred and sixteen, entitled "an act to amend the laws in force respecting the trial of Slaves in capital cases," and to extend the provisions thereof to the trial of Slaves in certain other cases.

1825 An act to amend and explain the eighth section of an act, passed in the year one thousand seven hundred and eighty four, entitled "an act to empower the County Courts of Pleas and Quarter Sessions of the several counties within this State to order the laying out of Public Roads.

1825 An act to repeal in part the several acts of the General Assembly, respecting the sales of land and slaves under execution, so far as regards the county of Gates.

1825 An act for the better regulation of the town of Beaufort.

1825 An act to regulate the patrol of Lenoir county.

1825 An act concerning the appointment and power of patrols in the county of Robeson.

1825 An act to amend an act, entitled "an act directing the time and place of sales of land and slaves under execution in Rowan county."

1826 An act to prohibit the trading with Slaves, except in the manner therein prescribed.

1826 An act to prevent free persons of colour from migrating into this State, for the good government of such persons resident in the State, and for other purposes.

Chronology of Laws

1826 An act to amend the laws regulating the sale of lands and slaves, so far as respects the counties of Anson, Onslow, Wake, Craven, Mecklenburg, Orange, Cumberland, Nash, Stokes, Guilford, Rowan, Davidson, Columbus, Beaufort, Person, Caswell, Rutherford, Brunswick, Pitt, Hyde, Halifax, Randolph, Wayne, Green, Robeson, Chatham, Franklin, Warren, Bladen, Duplin and Edgecombe.

1827-28 An act to regulate the sale of lands and slaves so far as respects the county of Northampton.

1828-29 An act concerning the lands formerly occupied by the Tuscarora Tribe of Indians, lying in Bertie county, on the north side of Roanoke river.

1828-29 An act to alter and amend the act of one thousand eifgt hundred and nineteen, entitled an act prescribing the mode of surveying and selling the lands lately acquired by treaty from the Cherokee Indians.

1828-29 An act concerning the action of replevin.

1828-29 An act to amend an act entitled "an act to prohibit trading with slaves, except in the manner therein prescribed,' passed in the year one thousand eight hundred and twenty six.

1828-29 An act to enforce the payment of taxes from free negroes and mulattoes in certain cases.

1829-30 An act directing the removal of certain papers from the office of the Treasurer to that of the Secretary of State.

1829-30 An act concerning the bonds in the office of the Public Treasurer for the purchase of the Cherokee and Tuscarora lands.

1830-31 An act more effectually to prevent intermarriages between free negroes or free persons of colour and white persons and slaves, and for other purposes.

1830-31 An act to prevent from teaching slaves to read or write, the use of figures excepted.

Chronology of Laws

1830-31 An act for providing further punishment for harbouring or maintaining runaway slaves.

1830-31 An act to regulate the emancipation of slaves in this State.

1830-31 An act to prevent the gaming of slaves, and to prevent free persons from gaming with them or suffering them to game in their houses.

1830-31 An act to amend an act, passed in the year one thousand eight hundred and twenty six, entitled "an act to prevent free persons of colour from emigrating into this State, for the good government of such persons resident in the State, and for other purposes.

1830-31 An act to amend an act, passed in the year one thousand eight hundred and twenty six, entitled "an act to prohibit trading with slaves, except in manner therein prescribed."

1830-31 An act for regulation of the patrol.

1830-31 An act to amend an act, entitled an act to authorise the County Courts in this State to direct the sheriff to sell any slave that may be taken up and confined in any jail as a runaway after certain length of imprisonment and public notice, passed in the year one thousand eight hundred and eighteen.

1830-31 An act to amend the several laws now in force in this State regulating quarantine.

1830-31 An act to authorise Aquilla Day, otherwise called Aquilla Wilson, a free person of colour, to reside in this State.

1830-31 An act to compel owners of slaves to keep white persons on their plantations in certain cases, in the counties of Brunswick and New Hanover.

1830-31 An act more effectually to prevent the depredations of runaway slaves, and to promote their apprehension in the counties of Onslow, Jones, Craven, Lenoir, New Hanover, Brunswick and Carteret.

Chronology of Laws

1831-32 An act for the better regulation of the conduct of negroes, slaves and free persons of color.

1831-32 An act to provide for the collection of fines imposed upon free negroes or free persons of color.

1831-32 An act to amend the first section of an act, passed in the tear one thousand eight hundred and thirty, which authorises free persons of colour to hawk and peddle out of the limits of the county in which they reside.

1831-32 An act to amend the fifth section of an act, passed in the year of our Lord one thousand eight hundred and sixteen, chapter nine hundred and twelve, entitled an act for the more speedy trial of slaves in capital cases.

1831-32 An act pointing out the mode whereby the militia of this State shall hereafter be called into service in cases of insurrection or invasion, and outlawed and runaway negroes.

1831-32 An act to appoint days for fishing with seines, nets, &c. at New Inlet, in the counties of Currituck and Hyde.

1831-32 An act to prevent obstructions to the passage of fish up Neuse and Trent rivers.

1831-32 An act to prevent obstructions to the passage of fish up Tar or Pamptico river.

1831-32 Resolutions. Cherokee bonds.

1833-34 An act to prevent the conveying of slaves out of this State and to prevent injuries being done to live stock upon rail roads.

1833-34 An act more effectually to prohibit the trading with slaves.

1833-34 Appendix of 1833-34 laws contains two Pamphlet Acts from 1822 and 1828.

Chronology of Laws

1833-34 An act directing the sale of lands remaining unsold, acquired by treaty from the Cherokee Indians.

1833-34 An Act to prevent the conveying of slaves out of this State and to prevent injuries being done to live stock upon rail roads.

1833-34 An act more effectually to prohibit the trading with slaves.

1833-34 An act for revising and digesting the public statute laws of this State.

1833-34 An act to emancipate Joe, a slave.

1833-34 An act to emancipate Ned Hyman, a slave.

1833-34 An act to prevent the hauling of seines or obstructing passage of fish on certain days in Upper Broad creek, in Craven County.

1834-35 An Act to amend an act, entitled "an act to prevent the felling of timber in the run of Hogan's Creek in Caswell county," passed in the year eighteen hundred and thirty three.

1834-35 An Act to authorize the Commissioners of Wilmington to assess and cause to be collected, a tax on all slaves whose owners reside out of town; but permit the slaves to work in town.

1834-35 An Act to emancipate Daniel, a slave.

1834-35 Resolutions. Resolutions passed concerning slavery.

****

PROCEEDINGS AND DEBATES OF THE CONVENTION OF NORTH CAROLINA CALLED TO AMEND THE CONSTITUTION OF THE STATE WHICH ASSEMBLED AT RALEIGH, JUNE 4, 1835

Chronology of Laws

TO WHICH ARE SUBJOINED THE CONVENTION ACT AND THE AMENDMENTS TO THE CONSTITUTION TOGETHER WITH THE VOTES OF THE PEOPLE RALEIGH: PRINTED BY JOSEPH GALES & SON, 1836 PAGES 403-425

1835 Constitutional Conventions; Proceedings.

1835 An Act Concerning a Convention to Amend the Constitution of the State (Passed in 1834).

1835 An Act Supplemental to an Act, passed at the present Session, entitled "An Act concerning a Convention to Amend the Constitution of the State of North Carolina.

1835 Constitution of North Carolina Adopted December 17, 1776: And the Amendments made thereto by the Convention which assembled at Raleigh, June 4, 1835.

1835 Declaration of Rights made by the Representatives of the Freemen of the State of North Carolina.

1835 Constitution of North Carolina.

1835 Amendments to the Constitution as Ratified by the People.

****

CHRONOLOGY OF LAWS 1836 - 1837
FROM THE PUBLISHED VOLUME OF:
THE LAWS OF THE STATE OF NORTH CAROLINA

Chronology of Laws

1836-37 An Act to amend an Act, entitled "an act authorising the entering of the unsurveyed lands acquired by treaty from the Cherokee Indians, A.D. 1817 and 1819, in the counties of Haywood and Macon.

1836-37 An Act to prevent frauds on Cherokee Indians, residing in this State.

1836-37 An Act to Reduce into one, the several acts concerning Pilots and Commissioners of Navigation.

1836-37 An Act concerning the Militia of this State.

1836-37 An Act to provide for the collection and management of a Revenue for this State.

1836-37 An Act to incorporate the town of Rolesville.

1836-37 An Act to emancipate Henry, Fanny and John, the slaves and children of Miles Howard.

1836-37 An act to emancipate Isaac, a slave.

1836-37 An Act for the relief of John Timson, a native Cherokee Indian, and his family.

****

CHRONOLOGY OF LAWS
REVISED STATUTES OF NORTH CAROLINA
PASSED BY THE GENERAL ASSEMBLY AT THE SESSION OF 1836-7
REVISED UNDER AN ACT OF THE GENERAL ASSEMBLY, PASSED
AT THE SESSION OF 1833-4, VOLUME I
RALEIGH: PUBLISHED BY TURNER AND HUGHES, 1837

1837 Chapter XXXIV., Crimes and punishment.

1837 Chapter XXXVII., Deeds and Conveyances.

Chronology of Laws

1837 **Chapter XLV.**, Executions.

1837 **Chapter XLVIII.**, Fences.

1837 **Chapter L.**, Frauds.

1837 **Chapter LXV.**, Limitations.

1837 **Chapter 71.**, Marriage.

1837 **Chapter 73.**, Militia.

1837 **Chapter LXXXVIII.**, Pilots.

1837 **Chapter LXXXIX.**, Poor.

1837 **Chapter CII.**, Revenue.

1837 **Chapter 111.**, Slaves and Free Persons of Color.

****

CHRONOLOGY OF LAWS 1839-1855
FROM THE PUBLISHED VOLUMES OF:
THE LAWS OF THE STATE OF NORTH CAROLINA

1839 An Act to erect that Territory of this State lately acquired by Treaty from the Cherokee Indians, into a separate and distinct County, by the name of Cherokee.

1839 An Act to prevent free persons from gambling with Slaves.

1839 An Act prohibiting Marriages between free persons of color and white persons.

1839 An Act to emancipate Caroline Cook and her four children, viz: Pamelia, Archibald T., James Ellis, and Martha Jane.

Chronology of Laws

1839 Resolution directing the Secretary of State to issue Grants for Lands sold at the late sale of the Cherokee Lands, in certain cases.

1840-41 An Act authorising the Governor to appoint an Agent in the County of Macon or Cherokee.

1840-41 An Act supplemental to an Act passed at the present Session of the General Assembly, authorising the Governor to appoint an Agent to collect the Cherokee Bonds.

1840-41 An Act concerning the collection of fines and costs from Free Negroes and Free Persons of Colour.

1840-41 An Act to prevent Free Persons of Colour from carrying Fire arms.

1840-41 An Act to prevent the Transportation of Slaves upon Rail Roads, Steam Boats or Stage Coaches, without written permission from their owners.

1840-41 Resolution in favour of Isaac Hunter.

1842-43 An Act to amend an act entitled "an act for the establishment and better regulation of Common Schools," passed in the year 1841.

1842-43 An Act to alter the time of selling Lands and Negroes in Montgomery County.

1844-45 An Act to consolidate and amend the acts heretofore passed on the subject of Common Schools.

1844-45 An Act to encourage the culture and manufacture of silk and sugar among the Cherokee Indians in this State.

1844-45 An Act to amend the Revised Statutes, entitled "an act concerning slaves and free persons of color."

Chronology of Laws

1844-45   An Act to prevent free negroes and mulattoes from trafficking in ardent spirits.

1844-45   An Act more effectually to suppress the offence of trading with slaves.

1844-45   An Act to prevent the obstruction of fish passing up the creek called Six Runs, in the county of Sampson.

1844-45   An Act to prevent the felling of timber in the water courses of the county of Guilford.

1846-47   An Act to amend an act, passed at the last Session of the General Assembly, entitled "an act more effectually to secure debts due for the Cherokee lands, and to facilitate the collection of the same."

1846-47   An Act to provide for the Transfer of certain funds from the Internal Improvement Fund to the Public Treasury, and for other purposes.

1846-47   An Act to amend an act, entitled "an act for the relief of purchasers of the Cherokee lands, passed 1830, Chapter 34."

1846-47   An Act concerning the duties of the Cherokee Land Agent.

1846-47   An Act to provide for the sale of certain lands, in Cherokee and Macon counties, which have been surrendered to the State.

1846-47   An Act to amend the 75th section, chapter 34, of the Revised Statutes, entitled "Crimes and Punishments."

1846-47   An Act to provide for the apprehension of runaway slaves in the Great Dismal Swamp and for other purposes.

1846-47   An Act to repeal in part an act, passed in 1844 and 1845, entitled "an act to prevent frauds in levying executions issued by a single magistrate and to encourage and facilitate the practice of taking security for the forthcoming of property seized under execution, and to amend the same."

1846-47   An Act in favor of the Cherokee Chief, Junoluskee.

Chronology of Laws

1846-47 An Act to provide for a re-assessment of the land in this State, and a more accurate enlistment of the taxable polls.

1846-47 Resolution in relation to the bonds given for rent of Cherokee lands, surrendered to the State.

1846-47 Resolution in relation to the accounts of the purchasers of the Cherokee lands.

1846-47 An Act to alter the times of selling lands and negroes in Richmond county.

1846-47 An Act for the incorporation of the town of Washington.

1846-47 Resolution in favor of James Wiggins and Alexander Nichols.

1846-47 Resolution in favor of William Morrison and Samuel Bryson.

1846-47 Resolution in favor of William Alexander.

1846-47 Resolution in favor of Jacob Siler and Joseph Cathey.

1846-47 Resolution in favor of Thomas M. Angel.

1846-47 Resolution for the relief of Mary D. Moore.

1846-47 Report of the Public Treasurer, Cherokee Bonds.

1848-49 An Act more effectually to suppress the traffic with slaves, and amendatory of the 75th section of the 34th chapter of the Revised Statutes, entitled "Crimes and Punishments."

1848-49 An Act to facilitate the collection of certain debts given for Cherokee lands, and for other purposes.

1848-49 An Act to amend an act, passed at the last session, entitled "An Act to provide for the sale of certain lands in Cherokee and Macon Counties, which have been surrendered to the State."

Chronology of Laws

1848-49   An Act for the relief of James Stewart of Cherokee County.

1848-49   An Act to increase the Revenue of the State.

1848-49   An Act to amend an Act, passed at the last session of the General Assembly, entitled, "An Act to provide for the apprehension of runaway Slaves in the Great Dismal Swamp, and for other purposes," and to extend the provisions thereof.

1848-49   Resolution concerning the improvement of the Indian Tribes.

1848-49   A Resolution to suspend the collection of Cherokee bonds, until the laying off the Turnpike road from the Georgia line to Salisbury.

1848-49   Resolutions respecting Slavery in the Territories.

1848-49   An Act to amend and consolidate the several acts now in force, relating to fishing with seines and nets in Tar and Pamlico Rivers.

1848-49   An Act for the incorporation of the town of Salisbury.

1848-49   Resolution in favor of William Angel.

1848-49   Resolution in favor of Isaiah Cook and others.

1848-49   Report of the Public Treasurer, Cherokee Bonds.

1850-51   An Act to provide that copies of certain papers on file in the office of Secretary of State, relating to Cherokee lands, shall be in evidence in certain cases.

1850-51   An Act authorizing the transfer of books, bonds, &c., from the Treasurer's office to the Agent of the State, for the collection of Cherokee Land Bonds.

1850-51   An Act to provide relief for the purchasers of Cherokee Lands, secure debts to the State, and authorize the sale of lands surrendered to the State under the acts of 1844-5 and 1846-7.

Chronology of Laws

1850-51 An Act to authorize the sale of Refused Lands owned by the State in the Counties of Cherokee and Macon.

1850-51 An Act to amend the eighty eighth Chapter of the Revised Statutes.

1850-51 An Act to protect the Patrol in the county of Onslow, &c., &c.

1850-51 An Act to amend the seventh section of the fifth chapter of the Revised Statutes in relation to Apprentices.

1850-51 An Act for revising and digesting the Public Statute Laws of this State.

1850-51 An Act to prevent more effectually the corruption of the slave population.

1850-51 An Act to repeal an act of the General Assembly of 1848-49, Chapter 93, entitled an act to amend an act, passed at the last Session of the General Assembly entitled "An Act to provide for the apprehension of runaway slaves in the Great Dismal Swamp and for other purposes."

1850-51 Resolution for the relief of certain purchasers of Cherokee lands, residing in Macon county.

1850-51 Resolution granting land for a church.

1850-51 Resolution authorizing Jacob Siler agent of the State to correct a mistake in the sale of a tract of land to Isaac Moody.

1850-51 Resolution in favor of Jacob Siler.

1850-51 Resolution in favor of Jason Sherrill.

1852 An Act to prevent the stealing, taking or conveying away of Slaves.

1852 An Act to prevent the obstruction of the passage of fish in the waters of Blount's Creek and its tributary streams.

Chronology of Laws

1852 An Act to amend "An Act to emancipate Lucy, a slave, and her child Laura," passed at the session of 1850-51.

1852 An Act to emancipate James Langford, a Slave.

1852 An Act to provide for the better Government of the Town of Lincolnton, and to amend the existing corporate laws of said town.

1852 Resolution in favor of George Little.

1854-55 An Act concerning Literary Fund and Common Schools.

1854-55 An Act to provide for the transmission to the Persons of Color, now in the Republic of Liberia, of the funds belonging to them in this State.

1854-55 An Act concerning Revenue.

1854-55 An Act to prevent the felling of timber in Big Brush Creek in Randolph County.

1854-55 An Act to prevent the felling of timber in the Northeast River in Duplin County.

1854-55 An Act concerning Salaries and Fees.

1854-55 An Act to prevent trading with slaves, in the counties of Mecklenburg and Northampton.

1854-55 Resolution concerning the distribution of the Revised Code.

1854-55 Statements of the Comptroller of Public Accounts, for the two Fiscal Years ending October 31st, 1853 and 1854.

1854-55 An Act to emancipate Betty, a slave.

1854-55 An Act to emancipate Jerry, a slave.

1854-55 An Act to emancipate John Good.

Chronology of Laws

1854-55 An Act to emancipate James G. Hostler, a slave.

1854-55 A Bill to emancipate Albert, a slave, the property of John Hockody.

1854-55 An Act to emancipate Louis, a slave, the property of James Dunn.

1854-55 An Act to prevent the obstruction of the passage of fish in the waters of South River and Adam's Creek.

1854-55 An Act to Incorporate the Salem and Clemmonsville Plankroad Company.

1854-55 An Act to provide for the better Government of the Town of Louisburg, in the County of Franklin.

1854-55 An Act to incorporate the town of Newton, in Catawba County.

1854-55 An Act to empower the Commissioners of the town of Wilmington to establish streets in said town and for other purposes.

1854-55 An Act to amend an Act passed in the year 1836, entitled an Act to Incorporate the town of Greensboro, in the County of Guilford.

1854-55 An Act for the relief of Solomon Newton.

****

CHRONOLOGY OF LAWS
1856 - 1868
FROM THE PUBLISHED VOLUMES OF:
THE LAWS OF THE STATE OF NORTH CAROLINA

1856-57 An Act to amend the Constitution of the State of North Carolina.

1856-57 An Act entitled "Revenue."

1856-57 Comptroller's Statement, Cherokee Bonds.

463

Chronology of Laws

1856-57 Comptroller's Statement, Cherokee Bonds.

1856-57 Comptroller's Statement, Cherokee Bonds.

1856-57 An Act to Revise and Consolidate the Charter of the City of Raleigh.

1856-57 An Act to amend the Charter of the Town of Plymouth.

1856-57 An Act to authorize Joshua Small and his wife Polly, Robert and Elizabeth Small, Anthony Copeland and Warren Boon, to reside in the County of Northampton, for the space of eighteen months.

1858-59 An Act entitled Revenue.

1858-59 An Act providing for the hiring out of free negroes in certain cases.

1858-59 An Act to prevent the sale of spirituous liquors to Free Persons of Color.

1858-59 An Act to promote and encourage the planting of oysters and clams.

1858-59 Resolution in favor of certain entries of Cherokee Lands.

1858-59 Comptroller's Statement, Cherokee Bonds.

1858-59 Comptroller's Statement, Cherokee Bonds.

1858-59 Comptroller's Statement, Cherokee Bonds.

1858-59 Comptroller's Statement, Cherokee Bonds.

1858-59 An Act to prevent making obstructions in Swift Creek, in the County of Edgecombe.

Chronology of Laws

1858-59 An Act to prevent the felling of timber in the waters of Tuckaho and Trent Rivers.

1858-59 An Act to extend the corporate limits of the Town of Newbern, in the County of Craven, and for the better regulation of the same.

1858-59 An Act to Amend an Act incorporating the Town of Kenansville, and to provide for the better government of said town.

1858-59 A Bill for the relief of Emily Hooper of Liberia.

1858-59 Resolution in favor of Jacob B. Evans, of Cherokee County.

1858-59 Resolution in favor of R.L. Jones and others.

1861 An Act to Alter the Rules of Evidence as Applicable to Indians.

1861 Militia Bill.

1861 An Act Entitled Revenue.

1861 An Act Concerning Runaway Slaves.

Index

Index

A

Act of Congress, 385
Adams
  Wm., 57
Alderson
  John, 112
Alexander
  William, 335
Allen
  Drury, 128
  Isabella, 162
  James, 139, 162
  James, an Indian, 62, 63
  Jane, 162
  John, Free man of color., 108
  Mark, 139
Alston
  Anne, 101
  William, 101
Amis
  Thomas, 139
Anderson
  Frank, 128
  James, 408
  Milly, free woman of colour, 128
  Willm., 57
Angel
  Thomas M., 335
  William, 346
Arrington
  Ezekiel, 115
Atkins
  Edmund, 46
  Edmund, Esqr., 45
  Edmund, Superintendent of Indian Affairs., 45

B

Bahama Islands, 130
Baird
  James, 159
Baker
  Simmons J., 177, 204
Ballew
  David, 347
Banks of Georgia, 311
Barrs
  Jemima, 121
  Jemima, a free woman, 121
Basket
  Billy, an Indian., 62, 63
  Thomas, an Indian, 63
  Thomas, an Indian., 62
Bass
  Abraham, 161, 162
Beal
  Jordan, 364
Beam
  Michael, 127
Beasely
  Barnet, 155
Beattie's Ford, 335
Beebee
  Betty, 406
Belden
  Robert, 272
Bell
  William, 121
Benbury
  Thomas, SC, 78
Bently
  Hugh, 210
  Mary, 210
Berry

Index

Susanna, 210
Bethel
  Jerry, 407
Bishop
  George, 407
Black
  Betty, 139
  John, 139
Blackwell
  Joseph, 156
Blount
  Billy, an Indian, 62, 63
  George, an Indian, 63
  George, an Indian., 62
  James, Chief of the Tuscarora Nation, 36
  Thomas, an Indian, 62, 63
Bogye
  Dixon, 139
Boon
  Warren, 417
Boude
  Mr. John, Indian Commissioner, 14
Bowie
  Jno., 57
Boyd
  Richard, 153
Brantly
  James, 57
  Jos., 57
Brickell
  Thomas, 177
Bridgers
  Samuel, an Indian, 63
  Samuel, an Indian., 62
Bridges
  Indian Town Creek, 328
  Kornegays, 404
  Quaker, 423
  Tuckaho, 423
Bright
  James, 160
Briols
  Francis of Guadalupe, 153
British American Colonies, 255
British Colonies in North America, 45
British Island of New Providence, 242, 244
British Sloop of War, 242
British West Indies, 244
Brittain
  William, 204
Brown
  James:, 57
Bryant
  Thomas, 15
Bryson
  Samuel, 334
Buffalo Sam, 139
Bullock
  Zack, 57
Buttler
  George, 57

C

Cabarrus
  Angus, 157
  Stephen, 115, 142
Cain
  Billy, an Indian, 62, 63
  John, an Indian, 62, 63
Caldcleugh
  Andrew, 189
Calloway
  James, 336
Captain Joe
  an Indian, 63
  an Indian, 62
Carman
  Joshua, 406
Caswell
  Richard W., 160
Cathey
  Joseph, 335
Chaponel
  Monsieur, 112
Charles
  Wineoak, an Indian, 62, 63
Charleston, 242
Charlton
  James, 160
  Linney, 116
Charter of King of King Charles, 254
Cherokees
  Cherokee Land, 334
Cheves
  John, 57
Chowan
  NC Counties, 157
Church of England, 16
Clear
  Mary, 120
  Rose Mary, 120
Clingman
  Thomas L., Attorney, 336

Index

Coleman
  Mark, 414
Contagious
  Diseases, 413
Cook
  Isaiah, 347
Copeland
  Anthony, 417
Coppock
  Moses, 57
Corkerham
  Jesse C., 362
Cornelius
  Billy, an Indian, 63
  Charles, an Indian, 62, 63
Creek
  Indian, 13
Creeks
  Adam's, 410
  Big Brush, 403
  Blount, 363
  Brices, 230
  Contentnea, 173
  Deep, 36, 62, 74, 204
  Durham's, 341
  Falling Run, 62, 74, 204
  Fishing, 92
  Goose, 341
  Great Contentea, 176
  Hogan's, 240
  Horse Pasture, 13
  Indian Town, 389
  Juniper, 341, 387
  Rattlesnake, 404
  Six Runs, 318
  Sonto, 341
  Swift, 422
  Town Creek, 328
  Upper Broad, 240

Cunningham
  Elizabeth, 142
  James, 129, 141
  John, 129
Curtis
  Austin, 116
  Austin, a mulatto, 116
  Polly, 141
  Sabina, 141

D

Davis
  Elizabeth, 116
  Grace, 116
  Harriot, 116
  John, 116
  Matthew, Senior, 146
  Rebecca, 116
  Richard, 116
  S.A., 407
  Samuel, 116
Day
  Alexander, 112
  Aquilla, 222
  Aquilla, free person of color., 222
  Richard, 112
  Thomas, free man of color., 222
Delisle
  Anthony S., 172
Deming
  Gurdon, 364
Dennis
  Billy, an Indian, 62, 63
DeRossett
  Armand J., 408
Dickson

  Marton, 57
Dillard
  J.L., 336
District of Columbia, 343, 403
District of Mero, 112, 113
District of Washington, 115
Dowdle
  Ezekiel, 335, 347
Dulaney
  Tho., 57
Dunn
  James, 409
  Louis, 409

E

Earl of Granville, 64
Eaton
  Willm., 56
Edwards
  John, 15
Elizabeth Town, 140
Enloe
  A., 336
  S., 336
Evans
  Jacob, 425

F

Falkner
  Amanuel, 57
  William, 57
Fish
  John, 57
Folsom
  Ebenezer, 57
Forts

Index

Fort Hembree, 361
Francis
  M., Attorney, 336
Freeman
  Edmund B., Secretary, 269
French
  Insinuating themselves., 45
French, Dutch, and Spanish Settlement, 130
Fuller
  Ezekiel, 57
Fulton
  Jesse, 347
  Nancy, 347
  Robert, 347
Fundamental Constitutions, 2
Fussel
  Aaron, 57

G

Gaston
  Alexander, 102
Gaston Railroad, 365
Gauntlett
  Edward, 158
Gautier
  Joseph R., 140
Gazette, 185
George
  Billy, an Indian, 62, 63
  Snip Nose, an Indian, 62
  Snip Nose, an Indian., 63

George the Third, 255
Georgia
  Georgia Line, 343
Georgia Towns
  Augusta, 311
  Savannah, 311
German
  Mary, 127
Gibbs
  John, 57
Glasgow
  J., 115
Glover
  Jno., 57
Good
  John, 408
Gould
  George, Esq, 37
Great Britain, 61, 329
Green
  Allen, 139
  Amelia, a free woman of colour, 138
  Breny, 139
  Charity, 139
  Charlotte, 120, 157
  Crease, 139
  Dolly, 116
  James, Junr, Secretary, 254, 261
  Leon, 157
  Nathan, 116
  Princess, 138
  Pris, 139
  Richard, 116
  Tom, 139
  Willie, 139
Griffin

Ned, a man of color., 91
Guinn
  James W., 336
Guyer
  David, 347

H

Hagans
  Elizabeth, 239
Hall
  Jenny, 130
  Lemuel, 130
  Lemuel, a free man, 129
  Milley, 130
  Seth, 130
  Tabitha, 130
Hamilton
  Thomas, 161, 162
Hampton
  Thos., 57
Handcock
  William, 15
Handy
  Peggy, 120
Harris
  Richd., 57
Harry
  an Indian, 63
  an Indian., 62
Hart
  Eliza, 139
  Nancy, 139
Hawkins
  John, 57
  Phil, 57
Henry
  Caesar, free man of color, 102
Hessian, 84
Hill

Index

Benjamin, 15
Boson, 160
Penny, 160
W.M., 176
Wm., 187, 189
Hockody
  John, 409
Hogen
  Henry, 335
Hooper
  Emily, of Liberia, 424
Hostler
  James G., 408
Howard
  Miles, 272
Howe
  Balaam, 163
  Hannah, 163
  John, 163
  Lucy, 163
  Sally, 163
Howit
  Thomas, an Indian, 62, 63
Hunter
  Isaac, 314
  Isaac, a free man of color., 314

I

Indian
  Indian Slaves, 34
  Tuscarora, 37
Indians, 379, 399, 400
  Catawbas, 45
  Cheoih Town, 316
  Cherokee, 69, 235, 270, 378

Cherokee Bonds, 331, 343, 347, 349, 351, 354, 361, 416, 421, 425
Cherokee Lands, 321, 322, 330, 334, 335, 336, 338, 339, 340, 346, 347, 348, 350, 353, 360, 362, 421
Cherokee, Agency of., 312
Cherokee, Reservation, 320
Cherokee, treaty with., 170
Cherokee, Treaty with., 269
Cherokees, 45, 49, 50, 52, 69, 77, 114, 157, 206, 210, 211, 231, 281, 316, 319, 321, 353
Cherokees in alliance with the French, 52
Cherokees, Agent appointed., 311
Cherokees, Chief Junoluskee, 329
Cherokees, land of., 310
Cherokees, Treaty with, 90
Cherokees, Treaty with., 234, 308
Chicamoga, 114
Chickamawga, 90

Chickamawga, Treaty with., 90
Chief Junoluskee, 330
Chief Sacarusa, Tuscarora, 147
Commissioners of Indian Affairs., 7
Defrauding of., 8
Depredation's of., 6
Friendship of., 46
Hunting Grounds of., 254
Illegal purchasing of Indian lands., 7
Indian Slaves, 3, 35
Indian Town, 55
Indian Towns, 1
Indian Trade, 1, 2, 46
Indian Tribes, 342
Indian War, 68
Indian War, 77
Longboard, a Tuscarora, 147, 148
Meherrin Indians, 13
Nations or Tribes of., 45
Over-Hill Cherokees, 90
Qualla Town, 316
Sacarusa, Chief of the Tuscaroras, 148
Samuel Smith, a Tuscarora, 147, 148

Index

Scalping of., 69, 70
Scalps of., 58
Trading with Indians., 1
Treaty with Tuscaroras, 36
Tuscarora, 36, 37, 62
Tuscarora Nation, 62, 147, 177
Tuscarora Tribe, 190
Tuscaroras, 62, 63, 64, 73, 74, 75, 76, 84, 147, 190, 204, 205, 210
Tuscaroras, Treaty with., 73
Yuansan Town, 316
Ingram
  John, 135
Inlets
  New, 229
Insurrection, 149, 151, 228, 274
Insurrections, 67, 110
Irby
  Wm., 57

J

Jack
  Tom, an Indian, 63
  Tom, an Indian., 62
Jacobs
  George, 110

Jamaica
  Kingston, 152
  Slaves, 160
Jarret
  N.S., 336
Jeffries
  Ozborne, 139
Johnson
  Charles, 115
  Samuel, 112
  Wm., 57
Johnston
  Elizabeth alias Charlotte Green, 120
  Gabriel, Esq., 17
  Gabriel, Esqr., 38
  Gustavus Adolphus, 128
Jones
  Abraham, 151
  Allen, 64
  Allen, S.S., 78
  Austin Curtis, 116
  Edmond, 336
  Isaac, 151
  Jacob, 151
  John, 57, 151
  Lewis, 151
  R.L., 425
  Robert, 62, 63, 64, 74, 147, 148
  Robert, Junr., 62, 74, 76
  Sally, 151
  Sukey, 151
  Thomas, 151
  Willie, 64, 76
Jordan
  George, 57
Josiah Cheek's Mills, 403
Joyner

Nathan, 57

K

Kerney
  Thomas, 15
Kilpatrick
  Francis, 160
King
  Fras., 57
King George the Third, 254
Knight
  Ephraim, 112, 141

L

Langford
  James, 364
Lashley
  Patrick, 57
Lattimore
  William, 15
Leahy
  Mr. John, 15
Lees' Mill, 387
Lightwood
  John, an Indian, 62, 63
List of Tithables, 8
Little
  George, 365
  River, 253
Long Island, 90
Lords Proprietors, 1
Lovelace
  Archibald, 309
Lovick
  Thomas, 112
Lowe
  Thos., 57

Index

Lytle
  Catherine, 121
  frank, 121
  Frank, 121
  John, 121
  Thomas, 121

M

M'Alister
  Blackwell, 156
M'Donald
  Peter, 152
M'Keller
  Lauchlin, 152
Macay
  William, 241
Mallett
  Miss Sallie, 425
Marshall
  John, 120
Martin
  Brigadier General Joseph, 114
  John, 57
  Joseph, Indian Agent, 90
McCand
  John, 57
McKinne
  Richd., 57
McLain
  William, 403
  William, Reverend, 403
McNabb
  Edmund, 425
Meherrin
  Landsof., 14
Meigs and Freeman, 158
Merrick
  George, 116

Miller
  Isaac, an Indian, 62, 63
  Thomas C., 408
Missouri
  Compromise, 344
Mitchell
  Billy, an Indian, 63
  Billy, an Indian., 62
  James, an Indian, 63
  James, An Indian, 62
Moody
  Isaac, 361
Moore
  A., SHC, 187, 189
  Andrew, 120
  John, 120
  Juno, 120
  Mary, 336
  Mary D., 336
  Peter, 120
Morgan
  Samuel, 155
Morris
  Richard Prichard, 117
  William Prichard, 117
Morrison
  William, 334

N

Nassau, 242
American Citizens at., 242
NC

Towns
  Tarborough, 117
NC Counties
  Anson, 151, 264
  Ashe, 191, 264
  Bath, 15
  Beaufort, 133, 135, 264, 332, 341, 360, 363, 386, 387, 389
  Bertie, 15, 36, 62, 73, 147, 148, 203, 263, 433
  Bladen, 106, 133, 135, 264
  Brunswick, 156, 163, 187, 222, 223, 264
  Buncombe, 264
  Burke, 209, 264
  Cabarrus, 190, 264
  Cambden, 146
  Camden, 187, 263, 328, 341
  Carteret, 183, 223, 264
  Caswell, 240, 264, 429
  Catawba, 412
  Chatham, 101, 136, 264, 403
  Cherokee, 308, 330, 340, 349, 351, 353, 355, 356, 425
  Chowan, 104, 105, 153, 263, 328, 341
  Columbus, 264
  Craven, 107, 168, 223, 240, 264, 407, 410, 423

473

Index

Cumberland, 106, 133, 135, 238, 239, 264, 406, 407, 409
Currituck, 55, 146, 163, 176, 229, 263, 328, 341, 389
Davidson, 113, 264
Duplin, 264, 404
Edgecomb, 263
Edgecombe, 44, 56, 92, 174, 422
Franklin, 263, 410
Gates, 194, 263, 328, 341
Granville, 44, 56, 133, 135, 264
Greene, 264
Guilford, 264, 318, 414
Halifax, 92, 112, 133, 135, 141, 204, 254, 263, 272, 409
Haywood, 264, 269, 349, 362
Hertford, 151, 263, 433
Hyde, 112, 229, 264, 341, 360, 386, 389
Iredell, 264
Jackson, 414
Johnston, 263
Jones, 223, 264, 423
Lenoir, 160, 195, 223, 264
Lincoln, 159, 264

Macon, 264, 269, 272, 308, 311, 334, 335, 336, 339, 347, 349, 353, 354, 355, 356, 360
Martin, 146, 160, 204, 239, 263
Mecklenburg, 264, 405, 407
Montgomery, 264, 315
Moore, 264
Nash, 161, 263
New Hanover, 162, 172, 188, 190, 191, 222, 223, 241, 264, 272, 408, 413
Northampton, 44, 56, 203, 263, 364, 405, 417
Onslow, 136, 223, 264, 357
Orange, 179, 264
Pasquotank, 80, 146, 187, 263, 328, 341
Perquimans, 80, 115, 133, 135, 146, 328
Perquimons, 187, 263, 341
Person, 264
Pitt, 92, 133, 135, 231, 264
Randolph, 121, 187, 264, 403
Richmond, 158, 188, 190, 264, 331
Robeson, 195, 264
Rockingham, 264

Rowan, 188, 196, 241, 264
Rutherford, 264
Sampson, 187, 264, 318
Stanly, 315
Stokes, 264
Sumner, 113
Surry, 264
Tennessee, 113
Tyrell, 146, 183, 263, 433
Tyrrell, 341, 387
Wake, 263
Warren, 101, 136, 155, 183, 263
Washington, 151, 187, 263, 341, 387
Wayne, 230, 264
Wilkes, 264, 309
Yancy, 264
NC Towns
  Asheville, 351
  Beaufort, 194
  Brunswick, 55
  Chapel Hill, 425
  Edenton, 93, 104, 148, 255
  Fayetteville, 106
  Fayetteville, 93, 112, 115
  Franklin, 235
  Greensboro, 414
  Halifax, 143, 148, 255
  Hillsborough, 123, 255
  Kenansville, 424
  Lincolnton, 364
  Louisburg, 411
  Mocksville, 188, 196

Index

Murphy, 321, 323, 351, 352
New Bern, 102
Newbern, 119, 123, 140, 148, 230, 255, 423
Newton, 412
Plymouth, 417
Pollocksville, 423
Raleigh, 136, 151, 246, 247, 262, 314, 335, 348, 365, 416
Rolesville, 271
Salisbury, 234, 255, 343, 345, 346
Washington, 93, 332
Wilmington, 44, 55, 60, 65, 93, 110, 172, 242, 255, 356, 408, 412
Wilmington, Commissioner's of., 241
Neale
  Thomas, 120
Netop
  Billy, an Indian, 62, 63
Nevill
  Benj., 57
New Orleans, 242, 243
Newby
  Mark, 115, 116
Newman
  Thomas, 112
Newspapers
  Western Carolinian, 234
Newsum

Amus, 57
Newton
  Solomon, 414
Nichols
  Alexander, 334

O

Overton
  Burdock, 139
  John, 139
  Lemuel, 139
  Rose, 139
Owen
  Billy, an Indian, 63
  Billy, an Indian., 62
Owens
  an Indian, 62
  an Indian, 63

P

Pacific Ocean, 344
Painter
  John, 361
Pamilia
  Sally, 129
Panther's
  Reservation, 334
Parker
  Jona., 57
  Moses, 139
Payton
  Benjamin, 15
Pepper
  Ginger, 139
Person
  General Thomas, 139
  William, 129

Peters
  Charles, 146
Pettigrew
  Charles, 387
  Charles:, 341
Peyton
  Robert, 15
Phillips
  Amy, 128
  Elizabeth, 120
  James, 120
Poteat
  John, 347
Power
  Samuel, 13
Prichard
  Thomas, 116
Pryor
  Phil, 57
Pugh
  Thomas, 62, 63, 64, 65, 74, 76
  William, an Indian, 62, 63

Q

Quakers, 35, 43, 51, 67, 73

R

Reed
  Chelsea, 139
Reefs of Abaco, 242
Republic of Liberia, 403, 424
Richerson
  William, 57
River
  Chowan, 13
  Morattock, 36

Index

Tennessee, 308
Rivers
   Roanoke, 203
   Cape Fear, 404
   Hiwassee, 308
   Holston, 90
   Little, 173
   Meherrin, 13
   Meherrin Neck, 13
   Mississippi, 329
   Neuse, 173, 230
   North, 55
   Northeast, 404
   Pamlico, 341, 344, 387
   Pamptico, 231
   Red River, Louisiana, 242
   Roanoke, 62, 74, 204, 210, 417
   South, 410
   Susquehannah, 62
   Tar, 92, 231
   Tennessee, 115
   Trent, 230, 423
   Tuckaho, 423
   Tuckaseegee, 308
   Valley, 308
   Yadkin, 188
Roads
   Turnpike, 343
   Western Turnpike, 349, 425
Roberts
   Billy, an Indian, 62, 63
Robinson
   Sally, 135
Rodgers
   James:, 347
Rogers
   John, an Indian, 63
   John, an Indian., 62
Rose, a free woman of colour, 157
Rowan
   Matthew, Esqr., 40
Rush
   Benjamin, 116
   Sarah, 116
Russell
   Andrew J., 340
Rutherford
   John, 155

S

Salem and Clemmonsville Plankroad Company, 410
Sallis
   Jno., 56
Sanders
   R.M., 176
Sansum
   Mary Ann, 172
Scott
   E.R., 340
Selph
   John, 364
Seneca
   John, an Indian, 62
   John, an Indian., 63
   Thomas, an Indian, 62, 63
Shad
   Daniel, 139, 142
   Winny, 142

Shaw
   Robert, 112
Sheridan
   Louis, 140
   Thomas, 140
Sherrill
   Jason, 362
Sherrod
   Benjn., 57
Ships
   Brig Ecomium, 242
Siler
   Jacob, 335, 336, 343, 347, 348, 361, 414, 416
   Jacob, Agent, 348, 361, 421
Slade
   Jeremiah, 177
Slaves
   Absalom Spicer, 116
   Albert, 409
   Alexander, 112
   Alice, 153
   Allen, 139
   Amelia, 112
   Amy, 128
   Amy Phillips, 128
   Andrew, 120
   Archibald T, 309
   Austin Curtis, 116
   Bagett, 153
   Balaam Howe, 163
   Betsey, 120, 142
   Bett, 139
   Betty, 108, 112, 142, 406
   Betty Beebee, 406
   Boson, 160
   Breny, 139
   Burdock, 139

Index

Caesar, emancipated, 102
Caroline Cook, 309
Charity, 139
Charles, 146, 153
Charlotte, 157
Charlotte Green, 157
Chelsea, 139
Crease, 139
Dada, 153
Daniel, 139, 241
Daniel Macay, 241
Dolly, 116
Eliza, 139
Elizabeth, 116
Fanny Howard, 272
Frank, 121, 128
Freeman Hill, 160
Ginger, 139
Grace, 116, 139
Gustavus Adolphus Johnston, 128
Hannah, 102, 163
Hannah Bowers, 102
Hannah Howe, 163
Harriot, 116
Harry, 139
Hector, 153
Henry Howard, 272
Isaac, 272
Isaac Belden, 272
Isabella, 162
Jack, 120, 121
James, 129, 160, 161
James Ellis, 309
James G. Hostler, 408
James Langford, 364
Jane, 162
Jenny, 129, 130
Jerry, 407
Jerry Bethel, 407
Jim, 120
Joe, 238
John, 139
John Good, 407
John Howard, 272
John Howe, 163
John Marshall, 120
Joseph, 106, 107, 156
Joseph Blackwell, 156
Joseph Hostler, 239
Joseph Willis, 107
Joshua Cook, 309
Juno, 120
Laura, 363
Leon, 157
Linney, 116
Louis, 409
Lubin, 153
Lucy, 112, 363
Martha Jane, 309
Mary, 108, 127
Mary Long, 107
Matthias, 153
Milley, 129, 130
Morris, 153
Moses, 153
Nancy, 139
Nancy Handy, 120
Nathan, 116
Ned Hyman, 239
Ned, man of color., 158
Pamelia, 309
Peggy, 163
Peggy Handy, 120
Penny, 160
Peter, 120
Phillis, 110
Phillis Freeman, 110
Polly, 141
Prince, 159
Princess Green, 138
Pris, 139
Priss, 139
Rachel, 116
Rebecca, 116
Richard, 112, 116
Rose, 120, 139, 159
Rufus, 365
Sabina, 141
Sally, 129, 135, 163, 189
Sally Howe, 163
Sally Zimmerman, 189
Sam, 112, 139
Samuel, 116
Seth, 129, 130
Silvia, 161
Tabitha, 129, 130
Thomas, 112
Tom, 139
Violet, 161, 162
William, 116, 117
Willie, 139
Winny, 142
Small
  Elizabeth, 417
  Jack, 121, 122

Index

Jack, a person of colour, 121
Joshua, 417
Polly, 417
Robert, 417
Smith
  David, 238
  James:, 57
  John, 210
  Joseph, 210
  Sophia L., 238
  William R., 204
  Wm., 57
Socket
  Billy, an Indian, 62, 63
South Carolina Gazette, 30
Spaight
  Richard Dobbs, 107
  Richard Dobbs, Esqr., 107
Spaniards, 55, 84
Spanish Privateer
  Wreck of., 55
Spears
  Silvia, 161
  Violet, 162
Spelman
  Hannah, 163
  Jacob, 163
  Peggy, 163
  Sally, 163
Spencer
  John, 116
Spicer
  Absalom, 116
  Rachel, 116
Stanly
  John Caruthers, 138
States
  California, 344

Georgia, 45, 308
New Mexico, 344
New York, 314
South Carolina, 45, 49, 50, 108, 109, 311
Tennessee, 160
Virginia, 45, 49, 153, 185, 254
Stewart
  Alexander, 138
  James, 340
  James:, 340
  Lydia, 138
Stone
  Zedekiah, 76
Strickland
  Jacob, 57
  Joseph, 57
Sudderth
  John, 336
Sumpter
  Brigadier General, 108
  Brigadier General Thomas, 108
  General, 108
Swamps
  Dismal, 325
  Dismal, 326, 328
  Goshen, 404
  Great, 55
  Great Dismal, 184, 185, 341
  Great Dismal Swamp, 387
  Quitsnoy, 36
  Quoitsney, 204
  Raquis, 36, 204

T

Taylor

William, an Indian, 62, 63
Thomeguex
  Peter, 120
Timson
  Henry C., a Cherokee Indian., 273
  John C., a Cherokee Indian, 273
  John, a Cherokee Indian, 272
  John, a Cherokee Indian., 273
  Lucy, a Cherokee Indian, 273
  Margaret Jane, a Cherokee Indian., 273
  Sarah Ann Eliza, a Cherokee Indian., 273
Tompson
  James, 15
Truitt
  James, 335
  James:, 334
  West, 335
Tuffdick
  Lewis, an Indian, 62
  Whitmell, an Indian Chief, 73
Turks or Moors, in Amity with his Majesty, 23
Turner
  Simon, 76

Index

V

VA Towns
  Norfolk, 185
Vail
  Miss Betsy, 120
  Moseley, JP, 15
Virginia
  Nottoway County, 155
Virginia Gazette, 30

W

Waddell
  John, 243
  John, Esqr., 242
Wade
  John, 57
Wade's Point, 231
Waite
  John, 120
Walker
  John, an Indian, 62, 63
Ward
  Joseph D., 269
Washington City, 403
Washington District, 114
Webb
  Grace, 139
  Harry, 139
West India, 130
Western Territories, 342
White
  Caleb, 120
  John Jasper, 120
  William, 142
Wiggins
  James H., 334
  John, an Indian, 62, 63
Wikle
  Henry, 362
Williams
  H.B., 407
  John, 57
  Samuel, 139
  William, 62, 63, 64, 74, 76, 160
Willis
  Agerton, 106, 107
Willnotas'
  Reservation, 414
Wilmington, 162
Wilson
  Aquilla, 222
  Aquilla, free woman of color., 222
Women Servants
  Begotten with Child by free men., 21
Wood
  Thos., 57
Woodliff
  Thomas, 57
Wright
  Joshua G., 408
  William A., 408

Y

Yancey
  B., 176
Yancy
  B., 189
  B., SS, 187
Yeargen
  Samuel, 101

ABOUT THE AUTHORS

WILLIAM L. BYRD, III has been involved in genealogical and historical research for more than thirty years. His primary areas of interest are Native Americans, African Americans, West Indians, East Indians and Moors in Virginia, North Carolina, and South Carolina.

He has been published by the *North Carolina Genealogical Society Journal*, the *Magazine of Virginia Genealogy*, *The Rowan County Register*, and *The South Carolina Magazine of Ancestral Research*. He has also co-authored articles with Sheila Stover in the *North Carolina Genealogical Society Journal*, *The Augustan Society Omnibus*, the *Pan-American Indian Association News*, and the *Eagle: New England's American Indian Journal*. He has received an "Award of Special Recognition" from The North Carolina Society of Historians in the category of "The History Article Award" for preserving North Carolina history.

He is a U.S. Army Veteran from the Vietnam era, and served with the U.S. Armed Forces overseas. He is currently retired, and resides with his family in Hickory, North Carolina.

ଓ ଯ

Other Heritage Books by William L. Byrd, III:

Against the Peace and Dignity of the State: North Carolina Laws Regarding Slaves, Free Persons of Color, and Indians

Bladen County, North Carolina Tax Lists: 1768 through 1774, Volume I

Bladen County, North Carolina Tax Lists: 1775 through 1789, Volume II

For So Long as the Sun and Moon Endure: Indian Records from the North Carolina General Assembly Sessions, & Other Sources

In Full Force and Virtue: North Carolina Emancipation Records, 1713-1860

North Carolina General Assembly Sessions Records: Slaves and Free Persons of Color, 1709-1789

North Carolina Slaves and Free Persons of Color: Chowan County, Volume One

North Carolina Slaves and Free Persons of Color: Chowan County, Volume Two

North Carolina Slaves and Free Persons of Color: Pasquotank County

North Carolina Slaves and Free Persons of Color: Perquimans County

Villainy Often Goes Unpunished: Indian Records from the North Carolina General Assembly Sessions, 1675-1789

Other Heritage Books by William L. Byrd, III and John H. Smith:

North Carolina Slaves and Free Persons of Color: Burke, Lincoln, and Rowan Counties

North Carolina Slaves and Free Persons of Color: Hyde and Beaufort Counties

North Carolina Slaves and Free Persons of Color: Iredell County

North Carolina Slaves and Free Persons of Color: Mecklenburg, Gaston, and Union Counties

North Carolina Slaves and Free Persons of Color: McDowell County

North Carolina Slaves and Free Persons of Color: Stokes and Yadkin Counties

www.ingramcontent.com/pod-product-compliance
Lightning Source LLC
Chambersburg PA
CBHW050132240426
43673CB00043B/1642